S0-CNF-481

Infant Development

LISA K. BARCLAY
Department of Family Studies
University of Kentucky

HOLT, RINEHART and WINSTON
New York   Chicago   San Francisco   Philadelphia   Montreal   Toronto   London
Sydney   Tokyo   Mexico City   Rio de Janeiro   Madrid

In loving memory of my mother

Library of Congress Cataloging in Publication Data

Barclay, Lisa K.
  Infant development.

  Bibliography: p.
  Includes index.
  1. Infant psychology. I. Title.
BF719.B37   1985   155.4′22   84-25232

ISBN 0-03-063598-5

Copyright © 1985 by CBS College Publishing
Address correspondence to:
383 Madison Avenue
New York, N.Y. 10017
All rights reserved
Printed in the United States of America
Published simultaneously in Canada
5 6 7 8 016 9 8 7 6 5 4 3 2

CBS COLLEGE PUBLISHING
Holt, Rinehart and Winston
The Dryden Press
Saunders College Publishing

Photo Credits

Chapter 1: *page* 2, Peter Menzel; *page* 5, The Bettmann Archive; *page* 6, The Bettmann Archive; *page* 7, Sigmund Freud Copyright; *page* 9, Christopher S. Johnson/Stock, Boston; *page* 13, The Bettmann Archive; *page* 15, Jim Cron/Monkmeyer Press Photo; *page* 17, Jason Laure, 1984/Woodfin Camp & Associates; *page* 23, United Press International; *page* 28, Nina Leen/Life Magazine.

Chapter 2: *page* 37, Douglas M. Jefferson/Photo Researchers, Inc.; *page* 50, Nancy Hays/Monkmeyer Press Photo; *page* 51, Beryl Goldberg; *page* 53, Wide World Photos; *page* 54, Wide World Photos; *page* 56, Sepp Seitz/Woodfin Camp & Associates; *page* 58, Charlotte Brooks/Magnum; *page* 62, Alan Carey/The Image Works; *page* 74, the Bettmann Archive.

Chapter 3: *page* 86, courtesy of W.B. Saunders Company, from *The Biologic Ages of Man*, ed. D.W. Smith, E.L. Bierman and N.M. Robinson; *page* 95, Jean-Claude Lejeune/Stock, Boston, *page* 99, Jean Shapiro; *page* 101, Wide World Photos.

Chapter 4: *page* 112 (left), Tom Ballard/EKM-Nepenthe; *page* 112 (right), The Bettmann Archive; *page* 115, Kenneth Karp, *page* 117, Irene Barki/Woodfin Camp & Associates; *page* 118, Lilo Raymond, 1980/Woodfin Camp & Associates; *page* 122, Inger McCabe/Photo Researchers, Inc.; *page* 134, Jim Harrison/Stock, Boston; *page* 143, © Frostie 1978/Woodfin Camp & Associates; *page* 146 Richard Howard/*Time* magazine.

Chapter 5: *page* 158 (left), Clif Garboden/Stock, Boston; *page* 158 (right), Jean Shapiro; *page* 164, Suzanne Szasz/Photo Researchers, Inc.; *page* 184, courtesy Gesell Institute; *page* 185, Erika Stone © 1976/Photo Researchers, Inc.; *page* 188, Suzanne Szasz/Photo Researchers, Inc.; *page* 189, Alan Carey/The Image Works; *page* 190, © 1981 Suzanne Szasz/Photo Researchers, Inc; *page* 192, Michael Heron/Monkmeyer Press Photo; *page* 193, Suzanne Szasz/Photo Researchers, Inc.

Chapter 6: page 211, Brice Davidson/Magnum; *page* 213,

(continued on page xiv)

Preface

At the beginning and end of a book an author has the opportunity to address readers in a more informal way than in the text. I want to start out by introducing myself and describing my own interest in the subject of this book.

About the Author

My interest in infant development began when I married a child development major and increased with the births of our four children. At the time that my first child was expected, my only previous information about infants had come from sporadic babysitting, an embryology course that dealt mostly with fish, chicks, and pigs, and one very general undergraduate psychology course. But it is amazing how being pregnant and awaiting the birth of a child can spark one's interest in the subject of infancy.

At that time, during the baby boom of the 1950s, even though many people had fairly large families, few except mothers and perhaps pediatricians seemed to be fascinated with infants. Several of my professional colleagues, both male and female, remarked that they were glad when their own children had passed through infancy and into the "interesting" stages of life. But it seemed to me in watching the development of my own children that infancy itself was a most complex and marvelous life stage, during which new and unexpected things seemed to happen almost every day. My husband, who was still taking courses in child development at that time, agreed. Together we observed and recorded behaviors of our children, and even attempted a few rather uncontrolled and unscientific experiments. I remember vividly the day we tried out the tastes of various substances on our daughter Anne! I also tried to make up for the deficits in my own education regarding infancy by reading whatever I could find on the subject. Aside from advice books for parents, which focused on physical care, there was not much information available. And it is interesting to note that much of what was then considered to be accurate about the very limited sensory and intellectual capacities of infants has since been proven utterly false.

And so I learned and marveled, and became absolutely "hooked" on infancy. I kept detailed baby books on all four children, and I still consider those years during which my children were infants the most interesting, though exhausting, ones I have lived through.

Later, when I returned to graduate school, I continued to learn more about infancy, both through formal course work—though such offerings were limited in the 1960s—and through my own readings and observations. When I came to the University of Kentucky in 1969, I was happy to find that the school had a course in infant development. However, it had not been taught in several years since there had been no one with the interest or the training to attempt it. I volunteered, and have now taught annually what is still the only infant development course offered at this institution. I have had students from home economics, psychology, education, social work, and nursing in this class, as well as some students in other fields who wanted to know more about infancy because they were planning for parenthood. For the last ten years, I have also had the part-time use of our early childhood laboratory facility, which has enabled me to offer my students interactive and observational laboratory experience. In this laboratory, infants and toddlers and their parents come for a weekly one-hour play session during which the students are able to observe and record the behaviors of these children of various ages and of the parents in interaction with their children.

I have found great interest in infancy among my students. Many of them come to the class having had no previous experience with infants or toddlers. Others have worked in child-care situations or have children of their own but are interested in learning more about infants. Fortunately, the knowledge base in the study of infancy has expanded rapidly. Indeed, so much research is being done that it is now a challenge to keep up with it.

About this Book

This book is concerned with infant development, not infant psychology. It therefore has a developmental emphasis and also views infant development within the family and the social context. Some topics that are of interest to psychologists are included, such as perception, memory, cognition, and language. Others, such as physical and motor growth and development, infant nutrition, feeding and toileting, parenting and parent training, or the role of group care of infants, are also included. Thus this book is somewhat unique in that it places more emphasis on topics of particular interest to caregivers and parents than do most books in the field.

The first section of *Infant Development* covers the history of the study of infancy, the methods used in infancy studies, and the various theoretical frameworks on which such studies are based. There are two chapters on prenatal development, which discuss genetics, embryological and fetal development, and the various endogenous and exogenous influences that can affect the development of the infant before birth. Birth and the neonatal period then are addressed, including the various stages of labor, the kinds of medication used in childbirth, the appearance of the neonate, and the adjustments the baby must make to life outside the mother. Subsequent chapter treatment is topical rather than chronological, with each major topic discussed over the entire span of infancy, from the neonatal period to age two. These chapters include discussions of physical and motor development, nutrition and feeding, and perception. There are two chapters on infant intelligence, one concentrating on learning and memory, and the other on cognitive development, particularly the theories of Piaget and Bruner. A separate chapter considers the development of language abilities. The book ends with two chapters on social development. The first considers the infant within the family and deals with such topics as the constructs of attachment and fear. The second chapter on social development addresses social change and its effects on infants, peer and sibling relations, infant and toddler day care, and social psychopathology such as child abuse.

Although many research studies are discussed, this is not a book about infant research. Studies are described to illustrate what infants do, and how researchers have come to understand what they do. In discussing research, my emphasis has been on the concepts involved rather than on the details of the various investigations of any particular point at issue.

Special features of this book include the participatory and observational exercises that appear at the end of each chapter. These are designed to reinforce the ideas and concepts learned in each chapter through actual experience with infants and their families or other caregivers in real-life situations. Some of you, like my own students, may be able to engage in such interaction through a daily or weekly laboratory situation. For those of you without such opportunities, the exercises suggest means of observing, questioning, and evaluating what occurs in the lives of infants in the home, the day-care center, the supermarket, or the playground.

Following these exercises in each chapter are several discussion questions, many of which deal with controversial subjects. They should encourage you to think about issues and to discuss your thoughts with your classmates. You may find that responses to the questions vary because many of them concern personal values and thus have no "right" answers.

Specialized or technical terms used in this text appear in boldface type at their first occurrence. Definitions for these terms can be found in the glossary at the end of the book. Though many of the terms are also defined in the text the glossary definition will usually be more detailed and complete.

About You

I suspect that most of you reading this book are college or university students majoring in child development or in some other human services curriculum that is preparing you to work with young children and their parents. You are probably studying nursing, home economics, early childhood education, social work, or a related discipline. Perhaps you are in a technical school or junior college and are preparing for a career as a paraprofessional in child care. You may even be preparing on your own to pass a competency examination in the Child Development Associate Program. And perhaps some of you are reading this book because you have or plan to have a child and want to learn more about this interesting life stage.

Because it is very likely that you will either be working with infants and their families in your career or that you will be a parent yourself, some of the topics addressed in this book will be important to you even though they may be of little interest to some of the researchers studying infancy. For example, infant nutrition is of only passing interest to the psychologist. But some knowledge of it may be vital to the day-care worker, public health nurse, or social worker, and certainly to the parent. Similarly, information about the relative effects of group care and home care for infants will help child-care personnel, parents, and social workers to make informed decisions relating to child-care alternatives. An understanding of the total family system, including the interactions of the parents, the infant, and any other children, may be of importance to the social worker or counselor helping a particular child or family.

Acknowledgments

Even though a sole author's name may appear on the cover and title page of a book, no book is ever written alone. Many other people help in one capacity or another. I would like to mention just a few of the individuals who have helped produce this book.

First of all, I wish to thank my husband, Dr. James R. Barclay. I owe many of my professional attainments to his unfailing faith in my abilities and his support of my efforts. He has also been very helpful in reading and commenting on the manuscript and in providing many useful suggestions. After thirty years of life together he is still both my best friend and my toughest critic.

Secondly, because they helped spark my original interest in infancy and taught me much of what I learned from direct interaction with infants, I wish to thank my children, Anne, Robert, Gregory, and Christopher. Anecdotes about them when they were infants and toddlers appear in various places in the book to illustrate some of the points I want to make. Now as adults they have cheered me on every step of the way in the writing of this book, shared my disappointments, and praised me for my successes.

Numerous undergraduate and graduate students have been of help in reading and discussing drafts of the book, checking on references in the library, assembling material, and in other ways aiding in the development of this book. These include Mary Binger, Karen Early, Bruce Gage, Sandra Hough, Carol Moradshahi, Michal Morford, Camilla Russell, Bettye Stull, and Wendy Wong. A special word of appreciation is reserved for Cheryl Croll who worked on the glossary and index.

Since nutrition is not an area of specialization for me, I received much help from others in the development of the nutrition sections of Chapters 3 and 6. I would like to thank my colleagues in the Nutrition and Food Sciences Department at the University of Kentucky, Dr. Abby Marlatt and Dr. Darlene Forester, as well as my daughter, Dr. Anne B. Filler, for providing information and for their critical reading of these sections.

I also wish to thank my former dean, Dr. Marjorie Stewart, and my colleagues in the Department of Family Studies at the University of Kentucky, who helped me obtain a sabbatical leave in 1982–1983 to complete my work on the manuscript of this book.

A debt of gratitude is owed to tne following extremely competent and helpful reviewers: Donald Bowers, Community College of Philadelphia; Charles Croll, Broome Community College; Andrew Gilpin, University of Northern Iowa; Edward Mosely, Passaic County Community College. They contributed many useful ideas that have greatly improved the format and contents of this book.

Finally, I wish to thank all those at Holt, Rinehart and Winston who were involved in making this book a reality. In particular, I am appreciative of the efforts of Alison Podel, Developmental Editor, and Jeanette Ninas Johnson, Project Editor, who helped guide the manuscript through all stages of editorial development and production.

CHAPTER **6**

Nutrition, Feeding, and Other Infant Routines   197

CHAPTER **7**

Perceptual Development in Infancy   229

CHAPTER **8**

Infant Intelligence I: Definitions, Theories, Learning, and Memory   270

CHAPTER **9**

Infant Intelligence II: Cognition and the Assessment of Intelligence   310

CHAPTER **10**

Language Development   345

CHAPTER **11**

Socioemotional Development   376

CHAPTER **12**

The Infant in the Social Context of Family and Society   420

(continued from pg ii)
Beryl Goldberg; *page* 216, Michael Weisbrot; *page* 220, Erika Stone/Photo Researchers, Inc.; *page* 224, Jean-Claude Lejeune/EKM-Nepenthe; *page* 225, Alan Carey/The Image Works.
Chapter 7: page 239, © Jerry Berndt, 1982/Stock, Boston; *page* 250, William Vandivert; *page* 254, © Jerry Berndt, 1979/Stock, Boston; *page* 265, © Christopher Morrow, 1980/Stock, Boston.
Chapter 8: page 290, Jason Laure, 1980/Woodfin Camp & Associates; *page* 297, Misha Erwitt/Magnum; *page* 304, courtesy Joseph Fagan III.
Chapter 9: page 313, © Bruce Buchenholz/Photo Researchers, Inc.; *page* 319, Clif Garboden/Stock, Boston; *page* 325, Hazel Hankin/Stock, Boston; *page* 334, Alice Kandell/Photo Researchers, Inc.

Chapter 10: page 351, Beryl Goldberg; *page* 358, Paul Fortin/Stock, Boston; *pages* 369, 370, Erika Stone/Photo Researchers, Inc.
Chapter 11: page 390, James Holland/Stock, Boston; *page* 399, courtesy of Alison Podel; *page* 404, Hella Hammid/Photo Researchers, Inc; *page* 405, Jan Lukas/Photo Researchers, Inc.; *page* 409, Ken Karp; *page* 412, Peter Menzel; *page* 414, Mark Antman/The Image Works.
Chapter 12: page 425, Leif Skoogfors/Woodfin Camp & Associates; *page* 427, The Bettmann Archive; *page* 428, Owen Franken/Stock, Boston; *page* 434, Peter Menzel; *page* 435, © Michael Hardy, 1978/Woodfin Camp & Associates; *page* 442, Erika Stone/Photo Researchers, Inc.; *page* 448, © Bruce Roberts/Photo Researchers, Inc.; *page* 462, © Bohdan Hrynewych/Stock, Boston.

Literary Credits

Drawing, page 46, adapted from an original painting by Frank H. Netter, M.D., from *The CIBA Collection of Medical Illustrations,* copyright by CIBA Pharmaceutical Company, Division of CIBA-GEIGY Corporation.
Illustration, page 59, from Friedmann, Theodore, "Prenatal Diagnosis of Genetic Disease", illustration on p. 35. Copyright © November 1971 by Scientific American, Inc. All rights reserved.
Illustration, page 65, from Friedmann, Theodore, "Prenatal Diagnosis of Genetic Disease", illustration on p. 39. Copyright © November 1971 by Scientific American, Inc. All rights reserved.
Figure, page 84, from figure "Human ova and embryos showing growth and body form from 3 to 8 weeks" (p. 37—After Jordan and Kindred, *Textbook of Embryology)* in *From Conception to Birth: The Drama of Life's Beginnings* by Roberts Rugh and Landrum B. Shettles, M.D., with Richard Einhorn. Copyright © 1971 by Roberts Rugh and Landrum B. Shettles. By permission of Appleton-Century-Crofts.
Figure, page 85, from figure "Development of human face at 4½ weeks, Development of human face at 7 weeks, Development of human face at 10 weeks" (pp. 48–49). By permission of Harper & Row. Publishers, Inc.
Figure, page 90, from W. J. Robbins et al. *Growth,* 1928. Used by permission of Yale University Press.
Table 4.1, page 123, adapted from V. Apgar, A proposal for a new method of evaluation of the newborn infant. Published in *Current Researches in Anesthesia and Analgesia* 32:260–267, 1953.
Graph, page 163, from H. P. Roffwarg, Ontogenetic Development of the Human Sleep-Dream Cycle, *Science* 152 9604–619, 29 April 1966, Figure 1. Copyright 1966 by the American Association for the Advancement of Science. Used by permission of the author.
Figure, page 178, from Conel, J. L. (1939, 1955 & 1959) *The Postnatal Development of the Human Cerebral Cortex.* Volumes 1, 5 and 6. Harvard University Press, Cambridge, Mass. Reproduced by permission of the publishers.
Table 5.3, page 187, from R. S. Illingworth, *The Development of the Infant and Young Child,* 7th. ed., 1975.
Drawing, page 189, from H. M. Halverson, "An Experimental Study of Prehension in Infants by means of Systematic Cinema Records," *Genetic Psychology Monographs,* Vol. 10 (1931), pp. 212–215.
Illustration, page 232, from Bower, T. G. R. "The Visual World of Infants," illustration on bottom of page 82. Copyright © December 1966 by Scientific American, Inc. All rights reserved.
Drawing, page 234, from Movement-produced stimulation in the development of visually guided behavior, by R. Held and A. Hein, *Journal of Comparative and Physiological Psychology,* 1963, 56, 872–876. Copyright 1963 by the American Psychological Association. Reprinted by permission of the publisher and author.
Figure, page 246, after *The Perception of the Visual World* by James J. Gibson, Copyright © 1950, renewed 1977, Houghton Mifflin Company. Used by permission of the publishers.
Illustration, page 247, from Bower, T. G. R. "The Visual World of Infants", adaptation of illustration on p. 90. Copyright © December 1966 by Scientific American, Inc. All rights reserved.
Illustration, page 328, from Bower, T. G. R. "The Object in the World of the Infant", illustration on p. 34. Copyright © October 1971 by Scientific American, Inc. All rights reserved.
Illustration, page 330, from Bower, T. G. R. "The Object in the World of the Infant", illustration on p. 36. Copyright © October 1971 by Scientific American, Inc. All rights reserved.
Graphs, page 436, from Eckerman, Whatley, and Kutz, *Developmental Psychology* vol. 11:1, 1976, pp. 42–49. Copyright 1976 by the American Psychological Association. Reprinted by permission of the publisher and author.
Table 12.1, page 447, from "Infant Day Care: Toward a More Human Environment," Table 1. Characteristics of competent infant caregivers, p. 20. By Armita L. Jacobson. Reprinted by permission from *Young Children* 33, no. 5 (July 1978): 14–23. © 1978 by the National Association for the Education of Young Children, 1834 Connecticut Ave., N. W., Washington, DC 20009.

Studying Infants

CHAPTER 1

INTRODUCTION: THE SCOPE OF THIS BOOK

Infant is a Latin word meaning "without speech." Therefore, infancy properly refers to the period from birth to about one year of age, when the child begins to utter words. During the nine-month period from conception to birth, however, many important events occur that will affect the developing individual. Therefore, a consideration of infancy should include this period of **prenatal** development as well. In a similar fashion, the period from age one to age two is a time of transition from infancy to early childhood. More capable than the infant, the child begins to walk and talk during this time. But the child is not yet, either physically or intellectually, markedly different from the infant. This second year is generally referred to as **toddler**hood in recognition of the child's awkward, toddling walk. Although the title of this book refers only to infants, we shall be dealing with prenatal development and both the first and second year of life after birth.

Notice that the term **development** has already been used several times in the above paragraph. Development implies an interaction between the growing infant and the environment. Development is the progressive change over time that is due partly to this interaction, partly to the overall physical growth of the child, and partly to the maturation of particular mental and physical structures. In the study of infant development we must therefore focus not only on the infant but on the context of the interaction between the infant and the people and events that make up the infant's environment.

This is a book, then, that centers on the infant within the family. For it is the family that provides for the infant the major portion of the nurturance, care, social interaction, and mental and physical stimulation needed

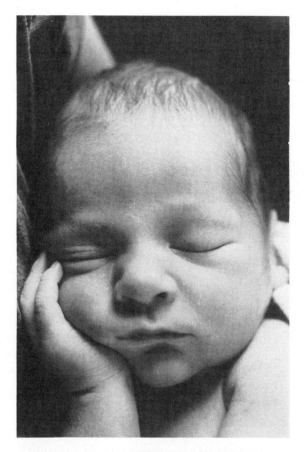

Infancy is the time from birth to age one. This newborn infant or neonate will develop within its family and culture into a unique individual because of the interaction of its particular heredity and the environmental events and people to which it is exposed.

for healthy development. But both the infant and the infant's family are affected by larger social and economic forces such as changing employment patterns, international trade, taxation, economic upheavals such as unemployment and recessions, war and peace in various parts of the world, social mobility, and social changes such as the civil rights movement and the women's movement. Therefore, we must consider these factors and their impact on infants and their families as well.

In this chapter we shall briefly examine the history of the study of infancy, including some of the important theories about infant development, various methods used to study infants, and finally some of the as yet unresolved controversies about the nature of infancy.

A BRIEF HISTORY OF THE STUDY OF INFANCY

Early Lack of Interest

While infancy has been recognized as a distinct life stage from earliest times, it has become a subject of study only fairly recently. Scientific inquiry goes back barely 100 years, and the great current interest in infancy among both parents and developmentalists has arisen only in the last 20 or perhaps 25 years. There are a number of reasons for this late appearance of infancy as a subject of study.

INFANCY VIEWED AS UNIMPORTANT

Although infancy was recognized as different from later aspects of the development of the child, since the infant was helpless and completely dependent upon adults for survival, infancy was viewed for many centuries as a prelude to "real" life rather than as an important stage of life in and of itself (Tucker, 1974). Because of this view and also because the methods of study were not well developed, early scientists such as philosophers, biologists, and educators showed no interest in the study of infants. Very little scientific investigation of infancy was done before the nineteenth century.

INFANTS VIEWED AS AN UNAVOIDABLE BURDEN

Furthermore, since methods of birth control were unreliable and often unsafe, and because little was known about how to regulate fertility, most married adult women spent a large part of their lives either pregnant or caring for a young child. At the same time, very many of these children died in infancy or early childhood. This situation produced two results. First, having a baby was not viewed as the special experience it is by many of today's parents, who expect to have only one or two children. It was often regarded as a fate imposed by nature or the deity upon women, whether they wanted a child or not. Second, because of the high death rate, parents tended to remain somewhat distant from their young children psychologically and often even physically. For example, in some societies babies were often not named until they were six months or more old, when the chances of their surviving had increased. Parents played little with a young child, probably to keep from becoming too attached to a child who would quite likely die.

THE USE OF WET NURSES

The physical distancing sometimes even entailed the use of a **wet nurse,** a hired woman who also had a young child and therefore was producing milk (de Mause, 1974; Illick, 1974). This woman would take care of, and nurse from her own breasts, the other child as well as her own. This practice was well established in ancient Greece and Rome. During the 16th and 17th centuries, the wet nurse often took the child to her home to live, and the parents did not see it again, if it survived, until it was a year or more old. Often the child remained with the wet nurse even after weaning, not returning to live in the parents' home until some time between the ages of two and five (de Mause, 1974). Obviously only the relatively wealthy could afford to hire a wet nurse, but the historical literature suggests that the practice was quite common among those who could afford it and even among many who could not until the 18th century (Aries, 1962).

ABANDONMENT AND INFANTICIDE

Poorer women who produced more children than they could care for or wanted often resorted to more drastic means of solving their problems. Without waiting to see whether the child would live or die, they abandoned it or killed it outright. Such practices were quite common in Europe and America until the last century (de Mause, 1974). Many of the orphanages and foundling homes that were set up by religious institutions, private individuals, and charity groups during the 18th and 19th centuries were intended to rescue abandoned babies and also to provide an alternative to distraught mothers to keep them from killing babies. Because of poor sanitation and nutrition and because foundling babies had little personal attention from adults, the death rate for babies in institutions was even higher than for babies reared at home or by wet nurses.

Changing Attitudes in the 18th and 19th Centuries

It is not surprising that at a time when having babies was often considered a burden, and when so many died that parents avoided becoming too closely attached to their young children, there were not many people interested in studying infants. But in the late 18th and especially the 19th century, principally in Western Europe and North America, economic conditions improved, and knowledge about health and disease increased. Furthermore, children, who had always been useful on the farm, became even more important as an economic asset on the American frontier, where farmland was abundant and cheap, and they gained new economic importance as wage earners in the newly established factories of the Industrial Revolution. For these varying reasons, especially among the expanding European and North American middle class, infancy and early childhood came to be seen as important life stages in and of themselves, not just as preludes to the "real" life of the adult (Aries, 1962). Parents therefore began to invest more emotional capital in their young children, since they were more likely to survive, and to show interest in better ways of raising them. Some parents even decided that infants and young children might be interesting subjects to study.

The forerunners of those who began the scientific study of infancy were philosophers and educators who speculated about this life stage and showed an interest in the care and education of young children. The French philosopher Jean Jacques Rousseau thought that children were born good and that with proper care their inborn virtues would manifest themselves. He therefore described the education of Émile, his ideal child, who was to grow up free of the corruption of society, in the book *Émile* (1762). The Swiss Johann Heinrich Pestalozzi and the German Friedrich W. A. Froebel, the founders of early childhood education, described the growth process of the young child in terms of mental development, which they proposed to foster through specific educational institutions such as the kindergarten. Their writings provoked the imagination of others.

As a result, some scientists undertook the systematic study of infant development through detailed baby biographies, which

Children, and even infants, were in the past often considered to be merely miniature versions of adults, who wore the same kinds of clothes and who took part in the same activities as adults. Notice how the infants and children are pictured in this eighteenth-century painting of the Emperor Francis of Austria and his family. Not only are the youngsters wearing the same types of garments as their parents, but their body proportions are those of miniature adults rather than those of real children.

were day-to-day records of the activities of their infant children. Such records were kept by Charles Darwin in Great Britain and by W. Preyer in Germany. These two eminent biologists were among the first to recognize infancy as an interesting life stage worthy of detailed observation. Their painstaking, detailed notes on the activities of their children were probably unmatched for perceptive detail until the Swiss scientist Jean Piaget produced his observations of infants in the 1920s.

Nineteenth-century biologists and psychologists interested in individual differences between people began detailed statistical studies of height and weight distributions. These studies included infants and young children. They represent the first detailed, scientific studies of large numbers of young children. Developments in the new science of genetics also focused attention on infants, and the studies of scientists such as H. L. F. von Helmholtz of the development of reflexes and of sensory capacities dealt with infants and children as well as adults. A considerable body of information about the physiology of the senses in infants, children, and adults thus began to be developed.

At the same time, because of the growing interest of parents in the healthful and happy development of their children, books and articles in women's magazines, which gave advice on child rearing, became popular during the latter half of the 19th century. An outstanding example was L. E. Holt's *The Care and Feeding of Children*, published in 1894 (Sears, 1975), whose popularity among American parents was probably unmatched until Dr. Benjamin Spock's book on infant care came out in the 1940s (Spock, 1976). This literature for parents dealt mainly with daily routines, discipline, and feeding.

The early scientific studies had emphasized the quantitative differences and simi-

Charles Darwin (1809–1882), the famous biologist who proposed the theory of evolution, also showed great interest in the scientific study of infancy. He kept a detailed record of the activities of his infant son. Although these observations were first recorded in the 1840s, Darwin did not publish them until 1877, long after he had become famous for his work on evolution.

larities between individuals in terms of physical characteristics and sensory capacities. But little study had been done with emotional, social, and intellectual development of infants. It is true that the early baby biographers had been interested in memory development and in the emotions of their infants. For example, Darwin reported some detailed observations of anger in his child. But except for these, little scientific interest was shown in such areas of infancy until very late in the 19th century.

Twentieth-Century Developments

FREUD

Around the turn of the 20th century the Austrian neurologist Sigmund Freud was one of the first to recognize the importance of the early months of infancy. He thought that what happened in the first few months of life had great effect upon the later social and emotional growth of the individual. Freud developed a theory of **psychosexual** development beginning with infancy and emphasizing traumatic episodes as the infant struggled to cope with and master the environment. The origin of the **ego** and **superego**, two psychic forces that helped govern the behavior of the individual, came about by interaction with the environment. And of course Freud saw that this environment included the adults with whom the infant interacted. Such psychic mechanisms of defense as repression, hostility, and denial all were seen by Freud as originating in the controlling or channeling of basic energy drives of the infant through interaction with the family.

Freud believed that sexuality, which to him meant any and all pleasurable bodily sensations, began in infancy. The first such sensation that the infant experienced was sucking. Freud therefore posited the sucking or oral stage, which lasted from birth through the first year. The degree of pleasure or gratification the infant derived from oral experiences Freud thought had a profound effect upon its later development. After about a year, the child passed on into the anal stage, in which the ability to control defecation also resulted in pleasure. Freud thought that children who were too much controlled by parents at this stage would grow up to be stingy, meticulous adults.

Freud based most of his theories, however, on information received from interviews with his adult patients, who recalled for him their earliest memories. Using these impressions and his own childhood memories, Freud built his theories of infant emotional and social development. Although he had children of his own, he was a distant, aloof father, who left child rearing and observations of children to his wife and servants. Thus one can question the data base for his assumptions, since memories are notorious for their selectivity, and since in any event no

Sigmund Freud (1856–1939), who developed psychoanalytic theory and the technique of psychoanalysis, was one of the first to recognize the importance of infancy for later emotional development. He believed that infants and children developed through a series of psychosexual stages and that emotional trauma or deprivation in any one of these stages would result in maladjustment later in life.

one can remember the earliest experiences of infancy. It was left to Freud's disciples and successors, especially his daughter, Anna Freud, and Erik Erikson, to study young children in detail and to refine and correct some of Freud's earlier conclusions.

At first Freud's views were not popular in the United States. They were not fully accepted until the 1930s (Senn, 1975). After this time, Freud's impact on the study of infancy and childhood has been tremendous. For he called attention to the influence of one's perceptions on emerging cognition and emotions. He emphasized the tremendous role that parents and other adults play in the socialization and psychological development of the infant. Thus all later students of infancy are in debt to Freud for his emphasis on the fact that critical important events occur at this early stage of the life of the individual, and that we can only understand what happens later by also studying these early events. Popular literature for parents, such as Spock's *Baby and Child Care* (1976), reflected the influence of Freud's thoughts and helped to spread them (Senn, 1975). In more recent years, Alexander Thomas and Stella Chess (1977) have theorized that Freud's account of early mechanisms of **psychodynamic** development may be related to **temperament**–parental interactions in which children whom they designated "easy" or "difficult" elicit different responses in care giving from different types of parents.

MENTAL-TEST MOVEMENT

The mental-test movement, begun by Alfred Binet and Theophile Simon in France in the early years of the 20th century and carried on by Henry Herbert Goddard, Lewis Madison Terman, and Edward Lee Thorndike in the United States around the time of World War I, also affected the study of infancy. The work done by these scientists in developing tests of mental abilities included studies of older infants and toddlers. They developed a series of tasks such as putting pieces correctly into a form board (a kind of puzzle), stringing beads, and building towers of blocks to measure the developmental rate of young children's intelligence. Thus large amounts of data were accumulated about what was normal intellectual performance for a particular age level and what was either accelerated or retarded. From these individually administered tests, observational scales and group tests were developed to assess these same characteristics. These in turn produced more information.

HALL

Educators and psychologists other than the mental testers also began to be involved in the study of infancy around the turn of the 20th century. G. Stanley Hall started the child-study movement in the 1890s, when he set up the first laboratory for child study at Clark University. Hall's methodology involved interviews with parents and, later, questionnaires, which the parents filled out. These methods probably did not produce very adequate data, as people's memories and interpretations of past events may differ greatly from what actually occurred, and since Hall obtained only the views of the parents and not those of the children. Hall's contributions were valuable, however, because he focused attention on the various stages or aspects of development and because he gathered a great deal of normative information. Furthermore, Hall influenced the direction of study of many of the next generation of researchers, some of whom, such as Terman and Arnold Gesell, had been his students (Sears, 1975). Also, by inviting Freud as a guest lecturer to Clark University in 1909–

1910, his first visit to the United States, Hall helped introduce Freud's theories to American scientists.

SOCIAL MOVEMENTS

During the beginning decades of the 20th century, several social movements in the United States came together in fostering a concern for infant development. One was the increased emphasis on higher education for women. Others were agitation for improved conditions for children and their families and the funding of research on children.

As more women received higher education, more of them became politically conscious and socially enlightened. Some entered professions such as teaching, nursing, and the newly created one of social work. Others were politically and socially active as wives. Both these groups of public-spirited women became concerned with contemporary social problems, including infant health and infant and maternal mortality. They began to educate others through speeches and articles and to lobby with state legislatures, the federal government, and other units of government for improvement and reform. A remarkable woman, Corah B. Hillis, who had lost some of her children to disease while they were very young, campaigned for a long time for the establishment of centers for the scientific study of infancy and infant diseases. At her insistence, the state of Iowa set up the Iowa Child Welfare Research Station at the State University of Iowa in 1917. This unit was the first in the nation devoted to the scientific study of infant nutrition, physical health, and disease control. It later expanded its scope of research to include other aspects of infant and child development.

In addition, concerned women's groups tried to interest mothers in infant health by

In the late nineteenth and early twentieth century, public-spirited men and women worked to improve health, sanitation, nutrition, and the living conditions of young children and their families. They also began to inform the public about healthful ways to raise their children. This well-dressed, healthy, and obviously cherished infant shows the results of such concern.

awarding prizes at state and local fairs to babies who appeared to be the best nourished and most healthy. These women also lobbied for the establishment of specific units of the federal government to deal with the needs of young children and their mothers. Both the Women's Bureau (now in the Labor Department) and the Children's Bureau (now in the Department of Health and Human Services) were established largely because of women's agitation for them. When the Children's Bureau was finally set up in 1912, it was the culmination of more than ten years of hard work by women's groups.

Educated women also were at the forefront in working to alleviate the ills that arose from the migration of rural people to the cities, industrialization, and the immigration of vast numbers of poor and uneducated people from many parts of the world. These efforts included the establishment of settlement houses in slum areas to provide education, child care, and health services to the urban poor. Another remarkable woman, Margaret Sanger, led the effort to inform poor women about family planning and birth control so that they could escape the psychological and financial burdens of having more children than they could manage.

In addition to women, public-spirited men also took steps to improve social conditions. Lawrence K. Frank, an economist, pushed for social causes such as the regulation of child labor and the study of infant and maternal mortality.

Frank continued his activity on behalf of children by campaigning to obtain funds, often from private citizens and private foundations, to establish institutes for research in child development at leading universities. When the Rockefeller family decided to contribute a large sum of money to the study of children in memory of Laura Spelman Rockefeller, Frank was asked to help allocate these funds. The institutes at Teachers College of Columbia University, established in 1924, at the University of California at Berkeley, established in 1927, and at the University of Minnesota, which dates from 1925, are directly traceable to his influence. In addition, he helped to enlarge and strengthen the Iowa Child Welfare Research Station. Although he was not involved in raising funds for them, Frank had a hand in the establishment of three other outstanding centers for the study of child development—the Fels Institute connected to Antioch College in Ohio, established in 1929, the Merrill-Palmer Institute in Detroit, Michigan, which was set up in the early 1920s and is now affiliated with Wayne State University, and that at The University of Michigan, established in 1930.

Thus, because of the efforts of these and many other concerned men and women, there were by the early 1930s several institutes devoted to the scientific study of infants and children that shared their findings with the public. In addition, such units as the Children's Bureau also became active in disseminating information and in sponsoring study about infants and children.

WATSON AND BEHAVIORISM

Meanwhile, the direction of study among American psychologists was shifting away from the types of work done by Freud and Hall. With the introduction of the research on the psychological **conditioning** of animals by Ivan P. Pavlov and his associates in the Soviet Union, there arose in the 1920s among American psychologists an interest in the conditionability of human beings, including infants and young children. Infants were seen as particularly suitable subjects for learning experiments, since they had presumably learned few other behaviors that would compete or interfere with the behavior the experimenter wanted them to learn. In addition, these behavioral scientists were interested in determining the extent to which manipulation of the environment affected learning and hence individual development. The leaders of this movement were John B. Watson and Clark Hull. Watson believed that the environment determined almost all development; he stated that therefore he could take any group of infants, regardless of inborn capacity, and train them to have whatever abilities he chose. He believed and asserted that he could produce physicists or garbage collectors, depending upon the alternative environmental learning opportunities to which they were exposed.

Watson also did some of the important early experiments demonstrating conditioning in young children. His most famous case involved little Albert, who was conditioned to fear furry animals (Watson & Rayner, 1920). Watson would strike a rod that produced a loud noise that scared Albert at the same time as a white rat was brought into the room. Although at first Albert had no particular fear of the rat, after a while he would cry and appear distressed whenever the rat appeared because he had begun to associate it with the frightening noise. He even acted frightened of other furry things such as a white rabbit or the beard on a Santa Claus.

More important than any such experiment itself was Watson's influence upon child-rearing advice that was given to parents of the 1920s. Because he thought that environmental influences were so important, and because he also thought that babies were unable to react to many things happening in the environment at the same time, Watson advised parents to use fixed routines and to avoid overstimulating their infant. Thus babies were to be fed on a rigidly imposed time schedule. Other interactions such as bathing and dressing were to be routine and kept to a minimum. Spontaneous affective interactions such as hugging and holding were discouraged. Watson advised mothers that if they felt they had to kiss their babies, to do so only once a day, and then only lightly on the forehead (Watson & Watson, 1928).

GESELL AND DEVELOPMENTALISM

At the same time as Watson and the behaviorists were doing their research, another group of researchers emphasized the role of an internal timetable that governed individual development. This group of strict internal developmentalists, based on a tradition of biological science, led by Arnold Gesell, began their work in 1911, when the Yale Clinic for Child Development was established with Gesell as director (Senn, 1975). The Gesell Institute at Yale University, as it is now called, is still staffed in part by some of his followers, who are carrying forward the work he began three-quarters of a century ago. The Gesell group posited the idea that unless the environment were extremely deficient or disadvantaged, the individual would develop according to an internal mechanism, much as the developing flower bud unfolds as a result of built-in cues. The emphasis of their studies therefore was on the sequence and the approximate ages at which particular developmental phenomena occurred. They did not intervene actually to change the behaviors of the children they studied. The studies done by Gesell and his associates (Gesell, 1928, 1934; Gesell & Amatruda, 1947; Gesell, Ilg, & Ames, 1974) provide even today the most comprehensive analysis of physical and motor development in infants and young children that is available. Gesell was among the earliest researchers to use the then new technique of motion picture photography to analyze in detail various physical movements. This was done by making a frame-by-frame analysis of the activity or playing the sequence in slow motion. Gesell was also the first child developmentalist to use one-way vision, first using screens and later mirrored glass, to observe child behavior unobtrusively (Senn, 1975).

Other researchers in the Gesell tradition, such as Willard Olson at Minnesota and later at Michigan, studied and quantified other growth data such as maturational ages of children based on bone development in the hand or foot (**carpal** or **tarsal ages**).

One outgrowth of these studies was increased emphasis on studying the same child or group of children over a relatively long time period. This kind of study, called **longitudinal,** was used not only for physical factors, but for intellectual and social ones as well. Terman's study of gifted children, begun at Stanford in the 1920s, the Berkeley Growth Studies begun by Nancy Bayley at the same time at the University of California (and still collecting data at present), T. W. MacFarlane's studies of children born in Oakland in 1928–1929 done through the University of California, and more recent studies done by the Fels Institute are examples of such longitudinal efforts. They enable researchers to relate factors that appear in infancy or early childhood to later ones in the life cycle and to begin to determine what factors may influence succeeding ones.

LATER PSYCHOANALYTIC INFLUENCES

Along with a continued interest in the work of some of the behaviorists of the Watson school, that of the internal developmentalists such as Gesell, and the mental-test movement, the 1930s and 1940s saw in the United States an increasing emphasis on the work of Freud and other psychoanalytic theorists. Freud really became popular in the United States during the period shortly before World War II. His emphasis on early environmental influences upon the developing child led both popular writers of advice books for parents and parents themselves to concentrate upon raising a child in an environment that did not produce frustration. Consequently many people, misinterpreting Freud's theories, encouraged extreme permissiveness in child rearing.

Other theorists in the Freudian tradition, particularly Erikson, became popular in the post-World War II period. Whereas Freud concentrated on psychosexual development, Erikson emphasized **psychosocial** development. He thus viewed the individual's development as taking place within the particular culture and society in which it was raised. He also emphasized the importance of the family. In general, Erikson was more optimistic than Freud, in that he felt that there are self-correcting, self-growth-fostering factors within the individual that can overcome some environmental lapses or negative influences.

PIAGET

Except for the developers of the mental tests, American psychologists had not shown particular interest in intellectual and cognitive development of infants in the early years of this century. This situation began to change in the 1950s as the work of the outstanding Swiss theorist of intellectual development in children, Jean Piaget, began to appear in English translation.

Piaget had begun his work with infants during the 1920s in Switzerland studying his own children. He later studied a variety of other infants and older children as well. Piaget had received his original training in biology. He became interested in intellectual development while serving as a laboratory assistant for Simon, one of the originators of mental tests. Piaget found in testing children that the wrong answers they gave were more interesting and revealing of their thought processes than were the correct ones. He decided to study how thought developed and correctly assumed that in order to do so one had to start at the beginning, with young infants. Conveniently, he and his wife produced three children in the 1920s and early '30s and Papa Piaget therefore had some readily available subjects for study right in his own home.

Jean Piaget (1896–1980) studied how children developed knowledge. Piaget's observations of his own children and others during infancy led him to conclude that by acting upon the objects, people, and events in the environment through the use of sensory and motor capabilities, the infant develops an understanding of self and reality outside self.

Because Piaget wrote in French, and difficult French at that, and since most American researchers did not read French well if at all, his work had little impact in most of North America until translations appeared in the 1950s. Piaget had also not been very popular in America because he did not use measurement techniques and did not report his data in a quantitative manner (Senn, 1975), practices that ran counter to the scientific emphasis of the behaviorist movement of the 1920s and 30s. Since the 1950s, Piaget's work has been increasingly influential in setting the direction of research in the United States and elsewhere.

Piaget believed that intelligence in infancy was qualitatively different from intelligence in later stages of development and that it arose through the interaction of the infant with the people and objects in the environment. The infant learns by physically acting upon these objects and people and through the use of information processed by its senses such as vision and hearing.

Following the leadership of Piaget, many studies continue to be made of the early development of memory, recognition, understanding, interaction with the environment, play, and language. The picture of the infant that is emerging from such studies differs radically from the earlier one held by people such as Watson, or the philosopher William James, who guessed that the world appeared to the infant as a "buzzing, booming confusion." Instead, the infant is now being recognized as a competent, discriminating individual who actively organizes reality, interprets stimuli, and fosters interaction with others. The major limits upon the infant are seen to be physical and motor immaturity and lack of experience against which to judge, limits that prevent the infant from performing some intellectual activities that are within the capability of older children and adults. Important in this altered view of infancy is the emphasis upon the infant as an active inquirer seeking out intellectual stimulation rather than a passive recipient of sensations.

CURRENT TRENDS

Beginning in the 1960s, research into infancy has also begun to focus on the development of infant language. At first, scientists were concerned mainly with what kinds of words and how many were produced at particular age levels. Then they turned to comparing how children in one language community learned their native language as compared to those in another. At present, concern centers on how infants communicate with caregivers, how they interpret the communicative signals given by caregivers, and how this early communication leads to both the understanding of language spoken by adults and the development of a symbolic signaling system known as language in the child.

Social-learning theorists such as J. Dollard and N. E. Miller, who attempted to combine elements of social learning with some psychodynamic principles, and later others, including Albert Bandura (Bandura & Walters, 1963; Bandura, 1969), who focused on a more behavioral approach to roles and models, also studied infants. Whereas the original behaviorists such as Hull and Watson were interested in the conditionability of infant responses, social-learning theorists were more concerned with the effects of adult, child, and peer models upon infant behavior. To what extent does the infant learn by copying and rehearsing behaviors seen in others? Can punishment or reward of the model affect whether and how frequently the infant exhibits the modeled behavior?

In addition, areas of social concern affect the direction of infant research. For example, as more mothers of young children are entering or reentering the labor market, alternative child-care situations are being studied. There is interest and urgency in knowing about the relative effects on the development of an infant of home care by a parent, home care by someone else such as a relative or babysitter, and day care in a center. As more fathers are participating in the raising of their young children, studies to ascertain whether the behaviors of fathers and mothers differ, and whether such differences, if they exist, are important or not, are going on.

Great advances in genetics and medicine in the last few years have helped to save many newborn babies that formerly would have died, but some of these babies have abnormalities that cannot be remedied. Therefore, studies are being done to determine ways to make life most meaningful and productive for such handicapped infants and children. At the same time, studies of prenatal nutrition, genetic engineering such as **gene splicing,** and other new techniques are carried on to determine how abnormalities in infants can be prevented or corrected before birth.

Because more premature and low-birthweight babies survive than in the past, studies of the environment of the high-risk nursery are of importance. The issue here is how to make this very specialized environment needed for physical survival responsive to the intellectual and emotional needs of the infant. If such needs are not met, the baby may survive physically but be less able to learn or to interact with other people because of its early restrictive environment.

Another area of concern is the effect of heredity, one's inborn genetic potential, relative to that of the environment. Studies of early education of infants, toddlers, and preschoolers and of the effects of educating parents to interact with their young children in better ways are trying to determine how much and in what ways society can change the environment to benefit the child. At the same time, studies that try to determine whether temperament is inborn and whether temperament differences can affect learning and interaction with parents and siblings are also being carried on. These obviously concentrate on the genetic aspect of the question. Studies of twins reared separately or together are also carried on, to help determine the relative importance of heredity and environment.

Infant research at present also is concerned with areas in which social development and social interaction between parents and children have not progressed normally or have somehow gone astray. Of concern here are such issues as child abuse, failure to thrive, **infantile autism,** and **childhood schizophrenia.**

As the American family changes, other issues of concern in the study of infants include single-parent families and their effect upon infants raised in them and teen-age mothers and their effects upon the physical, social, and intellectual development of an infant. Also drawing attention is the increase of older women (35 and over) who are having a first child. Many additional areas of study could be cited.

Thus we have come in a little more than a century from a time when the study of infancy was neglected or ignored in favor of other areas that were considered more important or more suitable to a time in which infancy is seen as so fundamental to all other areas of development that older children and adults cannot be rationally studied without considering the events and developments that took place in their infancy.

METHODS OF STUDYING INFANCY

It is important for you to understand some of the ways in which infant research is conducted. Then you will more clearly understand some of the studies that will be described later in this book. You will also be able to make some judgments about how adequate the methods used in some studies were to attain the desired goals. Furthermore, the methods chosen often depend on the theoretical outlook or assumptions of the particular researcher in question. Thus, for

Infants and toddlers can be studied in naturalistic settings, such as the yard in which this child is playing, or in laboratory settings in which conditions can be more accurately controlled. Each of these types of settings offers some advantages and some disadvantages to the researcher.

example, a psychoanalytic theorist would use a different approach, a different number of individuals to be studied, and different means or tools of study from those used by a social-learning theorist. And a follower of Piaget might use different ones from either of the above. Let us briefly examine three different methods of studying infants and then see how these methods relate to the theoretical outlook, the kinds of question asked, the available subjects, and other factors important in designing research studies.

Naturalistic versus Laboratory Studies

Infants can be studied in their own natural environments, such as the home, yard, playground or day-care center. These are the places where they usually spend their time and with which they are familiar. Or else they can be studied in a laboratory setting, which is new and unfamiliar to them.

The laboratory has the advantage of being a uniform setting that can be used with many different infants; such uniformity is, of course, impossible with naturalistic settings, which vary widely from one infant to another. Furthermore, in the laboratory the researcher can control or eliminate interruptions or intrusions. The telephone does not ring; a traveling salesperson or neighbor does not suddenly appear on the doorstep. Other factors such as the amount of space available in which the child can move about, the intensity of lighting, the color of the walls, the number and kind of toys or articles of furniture, or their location can all be precisely controlled. Depending upon what is being investigated, any or all of these factors, or **variables,** can be very important and thus may need to be precisely controlled. Furthermore, in the laboratory setting there may be available devices to monitor and record precisely what the infant or those with whom it interacted did. These devices may include television or motion picture cameras, tape recorders, or devices that monitor such factors as rate of sucking, heartbeat, or respiration of the infant. While all of these devices can also be used in the natural setting, their use there is usually more difficult, and they can be less easily concealed from view. Other advantages of the laboratory include the use of one-way mirrors, which enable a hidden observer to watch what the infant is doing. In the natural setting, the observer would have to be visible to the infant and to those with whom the infant interacts, and the behaviors of both could be significantly altered by the knowledge that such an observer is present.

The natural setting, however, has some advantages. The child is familiar with it and probably behaves in a similar manner on various occasions within this setting. By contrast, in the unfamiliar setting of the laboratory, behavior may be quite different. Therefore, the researcher is more likely to obtain a representative sample of the child's behaviors, in other words a sample that accurately reflects the child's usual behaviors, from observation in a natural setting.

Different kinds of researchers asking different questions tend to use one or the other of these methods. If one is concerned with how a given child usually interacts with the various adults in its daily life, observation in the home and in other day-to-day settings in which the child spends its time are of importance. If, however, one wishes to know how a particular motor behavior comes about, it may be desirable to bring large numbers of infants of varying ages to the laboratory one at a time and make motion pictures or videotapes of each attempting the particular behavior. Then later the researcher can study all these records and draw some conclusions. Similarly, if one wishes to study an infant's reactions to two different pictures by recording traces of its eye movements as it looks from one to the other, it is easier and probably more accurate to do such a study in a laboratory setting.

Because laboratory settings can expose many different infants to the same situation, it is also more usual to use the laboratory setting if large numbers of subjects are being studied. If only one or a handful of children are studied, then uniformity of setting becomes less important, and observations in natural surroundings can be used.

Sometimes, for some kinds of studies, a combination of both methods is useful. For example, a particular behavior may first be noticed to occur in the laboratory. If observation in the home shows that the child also displays this behavior there, it is reasonably certain that the laboratory instance was not an isolated one and the behavior is representative of what the child does. On the other hand the researcher may first notice a behavior in the natural setting and then study its application or its antecedents and consequences more precisely in the laboratory.

Experimental versus Observational Studies

Infants can be studied in either kind of setting detailed above either by observing their ongoing behaviors or by intervening in some way to affect and possibly alter these behaviors in a systematic fashion. **Observational** studies tend to concentrate on what occurs, when, and under what conditions. **Experimental** studies are more concerned with cause and effect relationships and try to determine what alterations in the conditions will alter the type of occurrences that result.

For example, if the researcher wishes to find out how much time a particular child usually spends playing with an older sibling, it may be desirable to observe the child and record how much time he or she spends doing various activities, and with whom. If, however, the researcher is concerned with finding out how crowding in the environment can affect play with a sibling, he or she will want to manipulate the crowding experimentally by introducing various numbers of other people at various times into the same play space. The researcher again records the amount of play with the sibling, only this time for the various levels of crowding. You will notice, by the way, that, in general, experimental studies are more easily done in the laboratory setting, whereas observational studies can be done in either type of setting.

Not surprisingly, the kind of study, observational or experimental, depends in large degree upon one's theoretical outlook. The psychoanalytic and psychosocial theorists, as

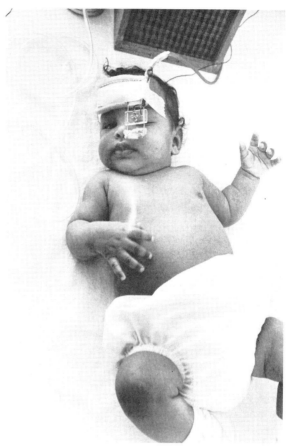

In an experimental study, researchers change one or more of the variables or conditions in the setting in a systematic manner and observe the effects of such a change on behavior. A gentle puff of air, which causes the infant to blink its eyes, is delivered by the mechanism attached to this infant's head. The air puff is paired with a tone. After a number of such pairings, the infant will blink its eyes at the sound of the tone even without the puff of air, which is a behavior it had not exhibited previously.

well as Gesell and his associates and also, to some extent, Piaget, have concentrated upon observational studies. These individuals, however, did some experimental intervention as well. For example, Gesell provided particular precise toys and pieces of equipment for the infants he studied, so that he could compare physical and motor development among differ in many ways from those who remain in the study.

In order to combine the best aspects of both methods of study, studies sometimes combine the techniques of both. For example, one group of infants may be studied in relation to some factor or behavior from ages three to six months. Another group is studied at the same time, while they are progressing in age from five to eight months. A cross-sectional comparison is done for both groups at the five-month and six-month level. If the results show that the groups are very similar on whatever is being compared, the data gathered for the three- to eight-month range can be put together. The researcher has thus made a kind of longitudinal study that covers a range from three to eight months but required only three months instead of the normal five months to complete. Of course, one can never be absolutely sure from a comparison of cross-sectional data that any two groups really are comparable and that the results obtained are similar to those that would have been obtained had one group been studied over the entire five months. But when answers must be sought more quickly than a full longitudinal study would allow, this combined method can be found useful.

Choice of Methods

The method or methods of infant study that are used depend in part on the theoretical frame of reference of the researcher and therefore on the kinds of questions he or she asks. They also depend on the availability of infants to be studied, the kinds of settings that are available, and the time the researcher can devote to the study. Let us consider these briefly.

As already suggested in the preceding sections, certain theoretical outlooks lead one to do research in a particular manner. Social-learning theorists and classical behav-

iorists generally have depended upon experimental studies, usually conducted in the laboratory. Some social-learning studies are done in naturalistic settings, however, and sometimes observation rather than experimental intervention is used. Freudian psychoanalytic theorists generally do their research in natural settings and use observation rather than experimentation. Some of them, however, also use structured laboratory situations such as those allowing a child to play with particular toys while being observed by the researcher.

Some of the studies done by psychosocial theorists such as Erikson have been completed in natural settings and some in laboratories; some were carried on by observation and some used interventions.

Piagetian studies have tended to be observational and in natural settings but some have involved experimental variations and some are done in laboratories. Particularly some of the followers of Piaget have tended to use experimental and laboratory methods in recent studies.

Group size is in part a matter of time and availability and depends in part upon theoretical considerations. Once they have left the hospitals in which they were born, groups of infants rarely can be gathered together easily. Even in day care centers, the number of infants available in any one place generally is quite small. And to persuade large numbers of parents either to bring their infant to a designated place at an appointed hour or to make themselves and the infant available to the researcher in the home at the designated time can be extremely time-consuming and frustrating.

For these reasons, infant studies tend to use smaller numbers of subjects than do studies with older children who are more readily available in group situations such as the school. The one exception to this generalization is the study of newborns in the first few days of life, since large numbers are available in the hospitals in which they were born.

In addition, studies of infants have used smaller numbers because it is difficult to induce any one infant to pay attention very long. Infants tire easily, they are distracted, they take time out to feed, they become bored, they fall asleep. Since obviously most studies depend on the attention of the infant to whatever is going on, the researcher has to wait until the infant is again ready. To wait for the necessary long periods of time with large numbers of infants would be tedious and would also delay completion of a study.

Of course, some infant research is deliberately done with only one or very few infants because the researcher believes that the intensive longitudinal study of one child will reveal more important information than any other method. This type of study can answer some important questions about how a particular mechanism such as speech or memory develops over time in that particular child. It cannot, however, tell if this development is unique in that child or can be generalized to others.

In practice, modern research on infants often uses a combination of all the various methods and sample sizes that have been considered. A study may first be done using only one or a handful of infants, who are observed over a designated time span. Then, as interesting events are observed, the researcher may try doing something to one group of infants and not another and then compare results. Thus some more infants are studied. The intervention can be done in the home or in a laboratory, depending upon what is being studied, the amount and kind of equipment needed, and how results are to be recorded. Some or perhaps all of the infants in the study may be followed along over a set time span and restudied in respect to some or several factors.

Because of the increasing use of computers and the development of better methods of statistical analysis, and because of the invention of improved devices for recording various infant behaviors, more recent studies have generally included somewhat larger numbers of infants. Important studies are still being done, however, particularly in the area of language acquisition, which concentrate intensively on only one child or on a very small number of children.

ISSUES OF CONCERN

Any consideration of the developing infant must include examination of the basic ideas upon which differing people's interpretations of that development are based. For depending upon which of these ideas they believe, different people may reach quite different conclusions about particular trends and behaviors they observe. They may attribute them to different causes, they may see them as having greater or lesser importance for later development, and they may see them as either critical or unimportant for societal concern.

Genetic versus Environmental Variables (Nature versus Nurture)

From at least the time of the ancient Greeks, people have argued about whether we are what we are because of what we have inherited from our parents or because of the influence of other people, the physical setting, and the events to which we are exposed. This is an important question to ask, for if we are only or mainly the result of our **heredity,** our inherited genes, then all is set at the moment of conception. The fate of the person is fixed; his or her potential is quite determined. What happens afterwards is of little consequence in the individual's development. If, on the other hand, we are mainly the products of the influences of the **environment,** the things, events, and people that surround us, then these other factors become of prime importance in determining how we turn out.

For many centuries of human history, these two factors, heredity and environment, were considered an either-or polarity. Some people argued that we were all the result of one, and others argued just as plausibly that we were all the result of the other.

For example, the ancient Greek philosopher Plato thought that the type of education people received determined what kind of work they would do best. Thus in the *Republic* he advocated educating some individuals to be rulers, others to be warriors, and still others to run the daily life and commerce of his ideal state. He believed in the overriding importance of environmental considerations. The 17th-century British philosopher John Locke held a similar view. Locke proposed that at birth the individual was like a "blank slate" upon which environmental factors would write what the person would become. The fact was that very little was known about heredity in those days. And, as we have noted, the American psychologist Watson also said that by manipulating the environment he could determine the eventual outcome for any group of babies, no matter how different they might be at the beginning.

Others, however, have believed that inherited characteristics determine the individual's eventual fate so strongly that the environment can have little or no influence. For example, the French philosopher Rousseau believed that the human individual was born inherently good. In his book *Émile* Rousseau proposed that if left to develop according to his own inborn capacities, the child would turn out to be a near-perfect individual.

Modern scientific studies have attempted to answer the question of the relative importance of genetic and environmental variables. But there appear to be no simple answers. With advances in the science of genetics, particularly with the discovery of the existence and structure of the basic building block of inheritance, the **DNA** molecule, scientists have come to understand better what kinds of factors are inherited and in what way. They also know a great deal more about how things can go wrong, that is, how the substitution of just one component within one of the stairsteps of the DNA molecule can drastically affect the appearance, health, or intellectual development of the person involved. They know somewhat less about how to prevent or remedy such mistakes.

It is known that some characteristics such as racial type, hair color, eye color, sex (barring severe hormonal disruption during early development), and the upper limit of height are genetically fixed at the moment of conception, based upon the genetic material provided by the two parents. Studies appear to indicate that the upper limit of intellectual ability, and certain personality or temperament characteristics, are also largely inherited.

The expression of these characteristics, however, that is, whether the individual exhibits a particular trait, or reaches his or her upper limit in height or intelligence, depends largely upon environmental factors. For example, while height is determined by genetic factors, environmental influences such as disease, nutrition, or the under- or oversecretion of the growth hormone may result in a person being either shorter or taller than genetic predispositions alone would have indicated. Thus, it appears that both the underlying genetic predisposition and the environmental condition that enables that predisposition to be shown are needed in most instances.

And, while there are genetic components to those human functions called behav-

These monozygotic or identical twins, who were separated at four months and raised by two different families, were reunited at age 38 by a TV researcher working on a documentary film about twins. Not only do they look alike, but even after many years in very different environments they show amazing similarities in how they act and in what they like or dislike. A case such as this shows quite clearly the importance of heredity or genetics in the determination of both appearance and behavioral and personality characteristics.

ior, which generally are complex combinations such as thinking, memory, language, and social activity, they are very strongly influenced by environmental considerations.

Of particular importance in trying to determine the relative importance of genetics and environment are studies of twins. Twins can be either **monozygotic** (MZ), that is, deriving from one fertilized egg that later divides into two individuals, or **dizygotic** (DZ),

or coming from two separate fertilized eggs and genetically no more related than any other sibling pair.

Studies comparing the correlations between MZ and DZ twins on various subtests of intelligence tests generally have found that those for MZ twins are significantly higher (Wilson, 1974). This fact argues in favor of the power of genetics. However, the correlations for DZ twins are also higher than those for nontwin siblings or for parent and child pairs. Thus the similarity of environment enjoyed by DZ twins obviously must also play a part.

What about nonintellectual factors? Occasionally, MZ twins are separated shortly after birth and are raised in drastically different environments. When some of them are accidentally reunited many years later, they often show amazing similarities not only in appearance but in overt behaviors, likes and dislikes, career choices, and choice of mates. This kind of similarity again provides some evidence for the force of the genetic component.

On the other hand, DZ twins reared together generally show more similarities to each other than they do to their other siblings (in addition to their performance on intelligence tests). Since they are not genetically more closely related to each other than to their other siblings but share a far more similar environment than they do with the others, these similarities provide evidence for the importance of the environment.

In addition, studies of unrelated children raised together, such as in adoptive or foster homes, have shown a greater similarity between these children and between the children and their adoptive or foster parents, in such aspects as behavior but even in intelligence, than exists between such unrelated children raised in different environments. This fact too shows the importance of environmental factors.

Thus modern science appears to have come closer to solving the problem of nature versus nurture in the sense of admitting that it is not an either-or situation. The individual is a unique outcome or product of his or her genetic blueprint, which from the moment of conception onward is constantly interacting with environmental variables to produce a particular set of outcomes. One important consideration to keep in mind, however, is that this interaction progressses in a forward direction; one cannot go back and repeat an interaction that has already occurred. That is, one can try to remedy or ameliorate a situation that has occurred through this genetic-environmental interaction, but one cannot somehow prevent its occurrence. Thus, for example, doctors can counteract some of the outward physical characteristics resulting from hormonal imbalances or lacks during prenatal development by later administering appropriate hormones or undertaking plastic surgery. But they cannot reverse the development of sex organs inappropriate for the chromosomal sex of the individual, which has already occurred before birth.

Another recently proposed way of looking at this relationship between heredity and environment is to view the infant, and hence the human being in general, as a **psychobiological** organism. That is, the individual is in part determined by biological considerations based largely upon genetics but is also influenced by biological factors in the environment that are not directly related to other human variables. These factors include available food supplies, climate, and disease-causing organisms. Over and above these factors, the individual is influenced by psychological considerations. These include unique capacities that arise from being a human being, such as the ability to use language or manipulate objects. They also may be capacities that arise from interaction with other human beings, such as actually learning a particular language or becoming emotionally attached to a caregiver. From the psychobiological point of view, therefore, all human behavior results from an interaction between both biological and psychological factors, both of which are grounded to some degree in heredity and have environmental determinants as well.

The Infant as an Active or Passive Organism

Related to questions regarding the relative importance of heredity and environment are those concerned with whether the individual is the passive recipient of input from outside or whether it is actively seeking out such input. In general, those theoretical outlooks that have tended to emphasize the importance of environment over heredity have also regarded the individual as more passively subject to environmental stimuli.

Thus operant-conditioning theorists have emphasized the importance of environmental manipulation in order to increase or decrease the frequency of a particular behavior or to enable the individual to learn a new behavior or alter an existing one. The emphasis here is on the environment, not on the individual. The assumption is that, given a change in environmental contingencies, the behavior of the individual will change accordingly.

Social-learning theorists such as Bandura do not view the individual as quite this passive, since they consider such individual variables as previous reinforcement history and personality differences as important determinants of a person's learning.

Maturational theorists such as Gesell and his associates and cognitive theorists such as Piaget and Jerome Bruner view the individual as more actively determining his or her development. Gesell's theory posits that the individual matures in a set manner according to a predetermined sequence that occurs relatively independent of the environment and subject mainly to internal maturational mechanisms. In this view, maturation of the nervous system interacts with new ex-

perience to produce new or altered behaviors. Thus, while Gesell recognizes environmental input, he attributes the major spur to reorganization to active maturational factors within the developing organism.

Piagetian theory holds that the individual from birth on actively seeks out intellectual stimulation from the environment. This interaction with the environment causes the infant to create constantly changing and growing intellectual structures within the mind, which enable the infant to interpret and understand reality. Piaget believed that the infant actively chooses the aspects of the environment, including the human environment, with which to interact and fosters this interaction by actions. Thus he differs somewhat from Gesell in the interpretation of what is an active organism, inasmuch as Gesell emphasized an unfolding from within while Piaget concentrated on seeking stimulation from without. Nevertheless, these two views differ radically from the views of those who perceive the infant to be largely determined by environmental influences without much regard to what the infant brings to the interaction with the environment.

Stages of Development versus Continual Development

A third area of debate centers on whether the developing repertoire of behaviors of the human infant represents a continuum in which there are quantitative changes (changes in the amount of something) or a series of stages that differ qualitatively (differ in kind) from each other. Another possible question is whether some aspects of development represent quantitative change and others represent qualitative differences, or in other words, whether some things develop in stages and others in a continual manner. For example, physical growth can largely be viewed as an instance of quantitative change, since it involves primarily the growth and proliferation of already existing body parts. On the other hand, cognitive growth might be viewed as a qualitative change, if one believes that knowledge of self and of one's surroundings changes not only in amount but in kind as the individual matures.

All of these points of view agree that behaviors change and become more complex with increasing age and maturation. But one sees this change as a continued, fairly smooth progression; the second view sees it as encompassing discrete stages in which behaviors may differ greatly from each other in quality; and the third view holds that one explanation works best for some behaviors and the other for others.

Both the learning theorists and the Yale maturational theorists led by Gesell have interpreted behavioral development as regular and uniform, that is, as largely quantitative. Learning theorists view behavior as resulting from experience. Thus there are changes over time largely as the result of increased experience. All infants do similar things at similar times because they are exposed, to a large degree, to similar experiences. The maturational theorists view change in various behaviors as the result of maturation, which is related to age and is therefore similar in infants of comparable age. If one were to plot out a developmental curve for a variable or set of variables based on either the learning or the developmentalist approach, it would probably be a smooth curve that showed only gradual changes over time. These changes are viewed as characteristic of all human infants. Of course, there is some individual variation, because either the experiences or the maturational timetable are not precisely the same for all. However, the probability that a particular behavior will occur increases as

experience and age increase, regardless of these slight individual differences.

By contrast, both the psychoanalytic and psychosocial theorists such as Freud and Erikson, and the cognitive theorists such as Piaget and Bruner, view development as occurring qualitatively, that is, in successive stages. These stages are believed to differ from one another sufficiently so that no smooth curve of learning can be drawn. According to Freud, each psychosexual stage such as the oral or anal stage has a prominent characteristic. This characteristic may have existed to some degree in an earlier stage and continues to exist in subsequent ones, but it comes to prominence only during the particular stage in question, in which it is all-important. For example, the child's concentration upon the pleasurable sensations of sucking, which is of paramount importance during the oral stage, continues on into subsequent stages of development but is no longer dominant. Thus there appear to be qualitative differences between Freud's stages. These stages appear in a fixed order, which is age-related. With proper environmental input, the individual progresses through all the stages in turn. Only extremely deviant environmental influences may delay the individual's progress to a subsequent stage. According to Freud, some rare individuals may progress to adulthood in some areas but psychosexually may remain stuck in an early stage for life, unless they receive proper therapy such as **psychoanalysis.**

Similarly, Erikson views the psychosocial development of a person as taking place in discrete stages, each of which emphasizes or concentrates on a particular aspect of development in relationship to other people. During early infancy, the individual learns either that other people regularly will provide food and comfort or that the world is a harsh place in which one's needs are met infrequently or incompletely. The person will thus develop either basic trust or mistrust. During later infancy, as the developing child comes to control more bodily functions, the interaction with adults over self-direction will produce either initiative or shame and doubt. Erikson carries the various stages on through the total life cycle of the individual. Each stage is seen as distinct and unique. Erikson does not believe, however, that the stages are so separate that learning missed at one stage cannot be made up later. The individual who had an inadequate or bad experience at one stage is not irretrievably lost but can compensate later for earlier missed opportunities. Thus Erikson's stage theory is not quite as inflexible as that of Freud.

Piaget viewed the various stages of cognitive development as qualitatively different from one another. In other words, not only the amount of thought but also the kind or quality of thinking differs from one stage to the next. The mental structures developed during a particular stage become integrated with and interdependent with the structures of other stages. Each stage thus becomes an integrated whole, a grouping of mental structures that has been built by the individual child in interaction with the environment. However, the mental structures that have been formed during one stage are integrated into mental structures built in later stages. Each stage thus becomes the necessary precursor or antecedent for the next one.

Notice that if one holds to a view of development by stages, and if these stages are indeed qualitatively different from one another, an environmental input that is beneficial for one stage may not be for another. Conversely, one that might be detrimental or harmful in one stage may be neutral or even beneficial in another. Again, many recent students of infant development tend toward an integrated view rather than a stage-based or a smooth-curve view. There is a tendency to see some characteristics as developing incrementally over time and others as being radically different from one period to another. Still other characteristics may develop through an interaction of quantitative and qualitative changes.

Critical Periods

Closely related to theories about stages and the effects of environmental variables upon development in the various stages is the idea of critical periods. This idea was originally derived from studies of animals, in which it was found that there were certain optimal times for particular behaviors to develop. If the opportunity to develop the behavior was thwarted or did not occur, the animal never learned the behavior or learned it in a far more limited manner. For example, baby chicks kept blindfolded so that they cannot see grains of cereal and bits of gravel on the ground before them do not begin to peck at these objects as chicks normally do. If the blindfolds are kept on for several days, the chicks seem unable to learn how to peck even after they are removed.

Similarly, newly hatched goslings tend to follow the first moving object they see. Since that is usually the mother goose, they can follow her to food and water. The scientist Konrad Lorenz, however, made sure that he was the first moving object seen by a group of hatchlings. Sure enough, the group began to follow Lorenz around, just as if he were their mother. When the mother goose was later introduced, these goslings ignored her and kept on following Lorenz; the critical period for learning whom to follow seemed to have passed. Although there have been later methodological critiques of Lorenz's work, it is an intriguing example of the exist-

Konrad Lorenz, a student of animal behavior, has researched the process called imprinting in infant fowl. When these goslings were exposed to him rather than to their mother in the critical period shortly after hatching, they followed Lorenz around just as if he were their mother.

ence of critical periods for certain behaviors in the animal world.

From these animal studies, the question arose whether in the human infant there also were times during which particular experiences would have their most profound and lasting effects. This critical-period hypothesis presupposes that there exist maturational factors that appear or become important at particular ages or at certain developmental milestones, which are also roughly age-related. These maturational factors then would enable the individual to learn a particular response or series of responses best at that time.

For instance, it is known that very young babies tend to look longest at particular kinds of patterns, but slightly older infants appear to prefer different ones, and one-year-olds look at yet different visual effects. Perhaps there are critical periods for learning certain information from what one sees. This visual learning might depend upon exposure to a particulr kind of pattern for young infants, while learning for older ones might be more highly affected by another type of pattern.

There is some evidence for the idea that critical periods in human infancy exist for at least some behaviors. Perhaps "sensitive" is more precise than "critical," since it implies a time of unusual sensitivity to particular environmental inputs but not the one and only time when a behavior can be learned. Such behaviors as early bonding to parents, forming emotional attachments, and learning language all seem to appear best if properly stimulated at the appropriate times. The limits of these sensitive periods for humans, however, are neither as absolute nor as narrow as the critical periods for certain animal behaviors seem to be. Language is learned best if the child is exposed to other people speaking, particularly during the first two years of life. But even children hidden away in closets until much older, such as Genie, about whom we shall learn more in chapter 10, developed relatively good language skills. Infants raised in impersonal institutions, where there is little contact with peers or adults, may lag behind in language, emotional, and social development, as compared to those raised in more typical environments. But if they are removed from the deprived situation, even if they are somewhat older, they improve and begin to catch up.

Thus, while there appear to be optimal or best times for particular human behaviors to be learned or particular developmental milestones to be attained, the human infant is quite malleable and able to attain these to some degree at other, later times.

Indeed, a question is now surfacing that deals with just how important to later development infancy really is. Though most researchers into infancy have stressed the importance of the period as the fundamental basis for all later development, other researchers are so convinced of the self-directing and recuperative powers of the infant that they believe infancy need not be viewed as a special or critical life stage. For example, Jerome Kagan at Harvard cites studies he has done with environmentally and socially deprived and isolated Indian infants in rural Guatemala (Kagan & Klein, 1973). When tested during infancy and up through age ten, these children seemed far behind others on most variables. But by adolescence, their test results were comparable to more advantaged Guatemalan children and to those in a United States sample. Kagan therefore thinks that too much attention is being paid to infancy, in that most infants can later make up for early lacks without apparent harm. Needless to say, his opinion is controversial, and many disagree violently. More studies are needed before definitive answers are available.

Summary

1. Infancy refers to the period from birth to age one. Toddlerhood is the period from age one to two. In this book we deal with the prenatal period, as well as both the first and the second year of postnatal development.

2. Because of the precariousness of life, infancy was not emphasized as an important life stage by either parents or society at large until about 100 years ago. Most research interest has been shown in the last 25 to 30 years.

3. Freud was the first modern scientist to recognize and emphasize the psychological importance of infancy. In the United States, the emphasis during the early 20th century was on infant health and nutrition. Later the influence both of Freud and of Piaget, who studied intellectual development, became important in North America.

4. Infancy can be studied in a laboratory or in a natural setting. Infants can be studied by experimental or observational methods and in cross-sectional or longitudinal designs. The method of study depends in part upon the theoretical orientation of the scientist and in part upon available resources.

5. Current issues in the study of infancy include the relative importance of genetics and environment, whether the infant is an active or a passive organism, whether development is smooth or divided into stages, and whether critical periods analogous to those seen for some animal behaviors exist for behaviors of human infants as well.

Participatory and Observational Exercises

TO THE INSTRUCTOR

The exercises following are designed to help students relate the content of each chapter to actual infants and their families. They are also intended to stimulate class discussion, in addition to or in place of the discussion questions that appear after each of the chapters. In each instance students are asked to interview one or more adults about their behaviors and or perceptions regarding some aspect of infancy, or to observe and record the behaviors of infants or infants and adults in a particular setting. Sometimes specific sites such as day-care centers, social-services agencies, or grocery or department stores are to be visited and products or services available there evaluated. You can be of great help to students if you can suggest sites they can visit, or if you can provide access to parents and others who are willing to be interviewed.

Some of the exercises may be impossible to do because of the unavailability of particular resources in the community in which your college or university is located or because of state or local laws barring the access to certain kinds of information. In addition, some chapters have a large number of exercises, probably more than any one student should have to do. Assigning some to some students and others to other students may be the best method to follow.

TO THE STUDENT

Record your observations on a recording sheet or in a notebook. If you use a recording sheet, be sure to transfer your notes to a notebook later. For each observation, list its date and time, its duration, and its location. Record age, sex, and other pertinent information regarding each person interviewed or observed. For example, in observing two people interacting, you need to specify the relationship between them (such as mother and infant, married couple). Also indicate in what manner you obtained the subjects or the location in which you observed (such as personal acquaintance, volunteer, through your instructor). In order to protect people's privacy, do not use their real name in full but substitute their first name or initials or make up a name.

Indicate how permission to observe or interview was granted. It is usual in many universities and colleges to permit student observations and interviews without going through formal approval channels of the institution, as long as you have obtained the approval of the people you are observing or interviewing (and of parents in the case of children). If you need special permission, be sure to obtain it. Ask your instructor about how to do so.

If observing an ongoing situation, be sure to record carefully what you observe, who participates in what, and for how long. If you are interviewing, be sure to write down the answers to specific questions that you ask. In addition, put down any extra information volunteered by your informant. Remember that the questions given you in these exercises are only a guide for you; you may need to alter or augment them to suit the particular circumstances and respondents in your interview. Some of them are meant only to give you an idea of what areas to ask about, not to be asked word for word as they appear here. Use your judgment about how to phrase them so as neither to offend your source nor lead her or him into a particular way of answering. You may want to ask additional questions or prompt your informant to explain further, by using such prompts as "Tell me what you mean by that" and "Can you explain that further?"

If you have a tape recorder available,

and if your respondent consents, you may tape the interview. It is a good idea, however, to take notes during the interview as well. These can serve as a backup against mechanical failure or background noise that keeps you from hearing what is on the tape. Furthermore, even if your tape is good, you still will need to record whatever nonverbal circumstances you encountered in your interview and a description of the setting, since these will not appear on the tape.

There are different numbers of exercises for each chapter because the content of some chapters is more able to be augmented and explored by observing and interviewing than is that of others. If there are a large number of exercises after a particular chapter, your instructor may want to assign only some and not others or assign different ones to different students.

In some of the chapters, discussion questions appear after the exercises. These questions are designed to stimulate discussion on controversial issues that have been touched upon in the chapter. There are no right or wrong answers to these questions. They serve to probe your feelings and opinions and to enable you to compare them to those of others in your class.

1. People may have quite different perceptions of the nature of infancy. Interview some adults of your acquaintance, young adults, new parents, older adults. In each instance try to find out their perceptions of the following:

a. Are children inherently good? Are they inherently evil and have to be corrected and punished to make sure they will become good? Is the nature of the child neither good nor bad, but subject to the influence of the people and events surrounding it as it grows up?

b. Is the child the kind of person he or she is primarily because of inborn factors? Or is the child's personality and behavior formed more by environmental factors?

c. Does the young infant actively solicit attention and response from caregivers? Or is the infant more passively the recipient of outside stimulation?

d. What are your sources of information about infants? Your parents? Personal experience? Books? Television? Classes? Other? How much have you learned from each of these sources? How much do you trust each source of information?

    e. Do you perceive any portion of infancy to be more important than others? Are there times when infants are particularly sensitive to environmental conditions?

2. Interview some expectant parents or some young couples that plan on having children but are not yet expecting any. What reasons do they express for wanting children? What functions do they think children will fill in their lives? Do you think their expectations are realistic or not?

DISCUSSION QUESTIONS

1. What are the reasons for having children? How realistic are these reasons? Are some reasons better than others? How can the reasons affect the relationship between parents and children? Between spouses?

2. Is parenthood acquired through becoming a biological parent? Just what does parenthood entail?

3. Is infancy a unique life stage? Why or why not?

Egg and Sperm Formation, Genetic Determination, Fertilization, and Related Topics

CHAPTER 2

HISTORICAL PERSPECTIVE ON PRENATAL DEVELOPMENT

Most of what is known about the origin and development of the infant from conception to birth has been learned in comparatively recent times. Theories about the origin of the child and exactly what occurs at conception have abounded since ancient times, but factual knowledge was sparse. Some people argued that the mother was the total source of the infant, others that the father provided the whole baby and the mother merely the place in which it grew. Still others correctly surmised that both mother and father contributed in some manner, but exactly how was not known.

Preformation

One popular theory that was widely held until the 18th century was that of **preformation.** According to this theory, a complete miniature infant was already present within the mother or father before conception. The father's semen (or sperm) either transferred this tiny organism to the mother or served merely to trigger the beginning of its growth. Within the tiny preformed infant were other even tinier ones, that would eventually become its offspring, and within those were still others that would form the subsequent generation. This view is not as absurd as it seems at first, since modern genetic theory seems to show that indeed humans carry within them potential in the form of genes that will affect in some measure all individuals that descend from them for all future generations. Preformation could not explain, however, why an individual in some ways resembled both parents or perhaps some other ancestors. This knowledge had to await the discovery of the laws of genetics by Gregor Johann Mendel in the 19th century.

Long before the invention of the microscope, people had guessed that the sperm of humans and animals must resemble a tadpole with a long tail that enabled it to swim. Followers of the preformation theory who held that the father was the source of the infant even produced pictures purportedly showing the sperm with a tiny, fully formed baby curled up inside its head. Of course no one at that time could guess at the incredibly small size of the sperm, nor how many millions are produced at any one time.

Early Scientific Studies

Anton van Leeuwenhoek, the inventor of the microscope, was the first person to discover what sperm actually looked like. In 1677 he examined both human and animal sperm, but the scientific techniques of that day did not enable him to see the organisms alive, only after they had been stained and mounted on laboratory slides. Still, his work confirmed that the guesses about the shape of the sperm had been essentially correct. He also became aware that the sperm was a much smaller organism than had been supposed.

In the middle of the 18th century, Kaspar Friedrich Wolff studied developing chickens. The chicken is an ideal subject for **prenatal** study, that is, the study of what takes place between conception and birth, or in chickens, between conception and hatching, because the chicken appears only 21 days after the egg is laid. Eggs can easily be opened and their content inspected, so that a scientist can obtain a clear idea of what develops in what time frame by comparing eggs opened on successive days. Furthermore, the living chick can be studied without opening the egg and killing it, by holding the egg up to a bright light or by removing part of the shell but leaving the membrane around

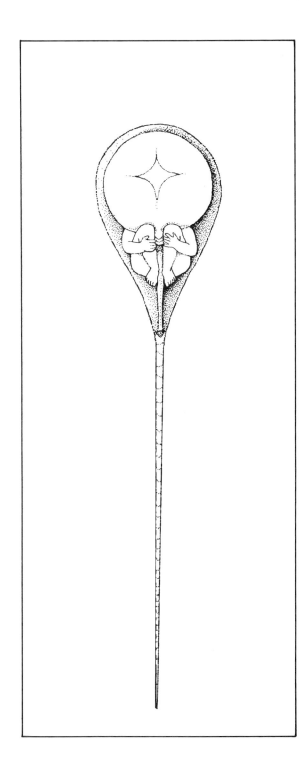

the chick intact. In 1759, Wolff reported his findings that growth of the chick began with a group of what he called globules, which were later renamed **cells.** These globules at first seemed to lack any arrangement related to their future function in the chick. He noticed that they gradually organized into groups, which later formed the various organs and systems. Based upon these studies, Wolff developed the principle of **embryological epigenesis,** the idea that the developing organism, or **embryo,** progresses from a simple to a more complex structure based upon specialized cells that proliferate and differentiate further. Wolff also guessed that both parents contributed equally to the formation of the new individual, but he was unable to explain exactly how this occurred. Lazzaro Spallanzani, an Italian, in 1775 demonstrated that both the sperm and the egg were needed for the formation of a new individual, a discovery that finally ended speculations about preformation.

Nineteenth-Century Studies

In the early 19th century, the German Heinrich Christian von Pander, who also studied the developing chick, first identified the three primary **germ layers,** or primordial layers of cells—the **ectoderm, mesoderm,** and **endoderm**—out of which all parts of the developing body are formed. This discovery supported Wolff's ideas about the grouping of cells and carried them a step further.

Karl Ernst von Baer, an Estonian who is often called the father of modern **embryology,** or the study of development before birth, first identified the egg of a mammal,

Homunculus. A drawing of how people in the past thought the fully-formed tiny baby was passed in the father's sperm to the mother.

that of a dog, in 1827. Previously, scientists had guessed that it was small but did not know how small or what it looked like or where to look for it at what point in time. Von Baer was examining a dog's ovary just before the rupture of the follicle, at which time the egg would be expelled. Thus he was lucky to find an egg in the right place at the right time to be seen relatively easily. When he saw it, he realized what it was. Von Baer also expanded upon von Pander's work in tracing the origins of various organs and tissues from the early cell clusters in the embryo by studying these developments in various mammals, who are, of course, much more similar to humans than are chickens.

Early in the 19th century, two other embryologists, the Frenchmen Jean-Louis Prévost and Jean-Baptiste André Dumas, saw a fertilized egg undergoing **cleavage,** or splitting. They were unable, however, to explain the significance of what they saw. Theodor Schwann, who together with Matthias Schleiden postulated that the cell was the building block of all living organisms, declared in 1839 that both the egg and the sperm were true cells. When they united at conception, another true cell resulted. The cleavage that Prévost and Dumas had observed was thus explained as being the form of cell division undergone by the fertilized egg but similar to the divisions that all other cells undergo as well.

Twentieth-Century Research

Although von Baer had seen a dog's egg a century earlier, the human egg, or **ovum,** was not seen until the 1930s. The ovum is barely visible to the naked eye, since it is about the size of a period made on a typewriter, or 0.135 millimeters (mm) in diameter. By contrast, the sperm is so tiny that it is visible only under great microscopic magnification.

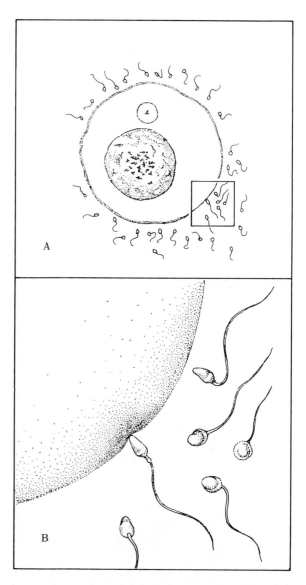

Human egg and sperm. A. The egg and sperm are here magnified about 400 times. Notice how much bigger the egg is. B. The boxed section of Figure A is here shown magnified even further. One of the sperm is shown about to penetrate the membrane of the egg and begin the process of fertilization.

Even though Leeuwenhoek had seen sperm many years earlier under his crude microscope, the living sperm could not be examined until great advances in microscopy had occurred. In fact, live, moving human sperm were not examined under the microscope until the 1950s, and the process of fertilization was not seen until even later. More recent studies of egg and sperm have emphasized the great disparity in size between the two as well as the disparity in number: one egg versus millions of sperm. They have also explained more clearly just what takes place during the process of fertilization and in what sequence.

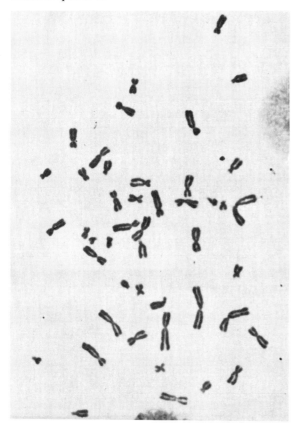

The chromosomes which contain the genes through which all hereditary characteristics are passed on from one generation to the next.

Genetic Studies by Mendel

One cannot leave a discussion of the history of embryology without mention of the father of the science of genetics, the Austrian botanist Gregor Johann Mendel. Although he did his work somewhat earlier, the results of his studies were not published until late in the 19th century. Mendel did not study developing animal organisms directly; his studies were primarily of various plants. The laws of inheritance that he formulated, however, have been necessary to complete the understanding of fertilization and prenatal development. They have been supported by the more recent discoveries of the actual carriers of heredity, the chromosomes, and within them the genes, located on portions of the molecule of *DNA,* or deoxyribonucleic acid.

PRODUCTION OF EGG AND SPERM

Human Genetic Makeup

CHROMOSOMES

The cells of every normal human being contain within their nuclei 46 **chromosomes** arranged in pairs. The word chromosome means "color-bearing body," and these bodies were called thus because they absorbed dyes or stains well in the preparation of cell samples for microscopic study. Other animals have different, species-specific numbers of chromosomes. Each chromosome in turn is made up of many smaller particles called **genes,** which carry within them on the portion of the DNA molecule on which they are located the blueprints for the inherited traits of the individual. A DNA molecule consists of a coiled ladderlike structure, a bit like a spiral staircase. On each rung of the ladder, some of a possible six organic substances are arranged in a particular order. This particular ordered arrangement of chemicals is the basis of how and what each individual inherits and therefore how he or she develops. The structure of the DNA molecule was not discovered until the early 1950s.

Half of an individual's chromosomes, that is, one of each pair, are inherited from the mother and the other half from the father. Thus the chromosomes, and hence the genes and the DNA within them, of both parents participate equally in the determination of inherited traits that a particular individual will possess. Twenty-two of the pairs of chromosomes (or a total of forty-four) are regular chromosomes, also called **autosomes,** which determine a variety of traits. When viewed under very high microscopic magnification, each autosome looks very much like its paired partner.

SEX DETERMINATION

The remaining pair of chromosomes are those that determine the sex of the individual. The sex-determining, or sex, chromosome pattern of the normal female is *XX,* and that of the normal male is *XY.* The sex chromosomes are labeled *X* and *Y* because their shapes appeared to some researchers to resemble the capital versions of these letters of the alphabet. The *X* chromosome is much larger than the *Y* and carries much more genetic material. In humans as well as all other mammals, the father determines the sex of the child, since he can contribute either an *X* or a *Y* chromosome in his sperm. The mother's egg can carry only an *X* chromosome. Thus if the father contributes an *X* chromosome, the individual will be *XX,* or female. If he contributes a *Y* chromosome, the individual will be *XY,* or male. The mother, therefore, has no control over the sex of the child. In the past, particularly in societies in which a male heir was considered of prime importance, women

were often erroneously blamed for producing daughters instead of sons.

It has recently been discovered that the length of time after intercourse before conception actually occurs, as well as the time during a woman's fertile period in which conception takes place, can both affect the sex of the child. There is a greater probability of conceiving a girl if intercourse takes place some time before ovulation and a greater chance of conceiving a boy if it occurs right around the time of ovulation (Rorvik & Shettles, 1976). The reasons appear to be that *Y*-carrying sperm move faster, but *X*-carrying sperm appear to survive longer. The state of the vagina also appears to be a factor, in that *X* sperm can survive in an acid environment, while *Y* sperm can do so only in an alkaline one. Rorvik and Shettles, therefore, also recommend douching with an appropriately acid or alkaline substance before intercourse if a child of a particular sex is desired. The method requires a great degree of agreement and cooperation between both partners to have any chance of success. Furthermore, influencing conception is still not an exact science, and the chances of success even with cooperative efforts are still rather small. Many other researchers have questioned whether it really works at all.

RATIOS OF MALES TO FEMALES CONCEIVED

Given the way the sex of a child is determined, it would appear that the chances of producing an *XX* individual, or girl, would be equal to those of producing an *XY,* or boy. Some researchers hypothesize that equal numbers of both sexes are conceived but that more female than male infants are spontaneously aborted (Carr, 1963), while others think that larger numbers of males are conceived but more males also are aborted.

Some estimate the ratio of conception as high as 150 males to 100 females (Rhodes, 1965). The exact ratio of conceptions is not known because many pregnancies terminate spontaneously so early that a woman is not even aware that she has been pregnant. Thus scientists can only guess at what the sex ratio of these spontaneously aborted embryos might be. It is known that the ratio at birth is 106 males for every 100 females, and that greater numbers of males than females have already been lost through spontaneous abortion (miscarriage) late enough in development that sex determination could be made. Since females tend to have fewer diseases and complications than do males, after birth as well as before, more infant girls than boys survive the first year of life. Around age one, the ratio therefore equals out; at every age thereafter females outnumber males.

One theory for the possible disparity of conceptions favoring males has to do with the relative weight and therefore mobility of X-carrying and Y-carrying sperm. Since the Y chromosome is smaller and carries less genetic material, Y sperm may be able to swim faster and may be more likely to reach the egg first and fertilize it than the slower X sperm. Whatever the reason for the disparity, it is probably helpful that more males than females are conceived and born. For given the relative survival rates of the two sexes, if equal numbers were born, females would begin to outnumber males even earlier in life than they do now.

Mitosis, Meiosis, and Genetic Variability

MITOSIS

During normal cell division, or **mitosis,** which occurs continually in the various body cells throughout life, each chromosome produces an identical copy of itself. One of these two then goes to one of the new cells, or daughter cells, brought about by the splitting of the cell, and the other goes to the other daughter cell. Therefore, during mitosis, the total number of chromosomes in each cell remains the same, 46 in humans, and those in each cell are identical to those in all other cells.

MEIOSIS

Since the new individual will be receiving chromosomes from both mother and father, however, the number received from each must be reduced by half. Thus in the sex cells, also called germ cells, or **gametes,** that is, in the egg and sperm, a special kind of cell division called reduction division, or **meiosis,** takes place during their formation. During the first phase of meiosis, or the first meiotic division, the chromosomes duplicate themselves just as they would during mitosis. The cell within the ovary or testis then divides into two new cells, each having the usual 46 chromosomes. During the second meiotic division, each of the two new cells splits again into two more, but this time without the chromosomes first having duplicated themselves. This time, one chromosome of each of the 23 pairs goes to one of the new cells, and the other member of the pair to the other. At fertilization, as two of these cells each containing 23 chromosomes unite, a total of 46 is once again attained.

GENETIC VARIABILITY

It is a matter of chance which member of a pair of chromosomes goes to which new cell during the process of meiosis. Thus the individual is as likely to inherit from the mother a chromosome that came to the mother from her mother, as one from her father. The same

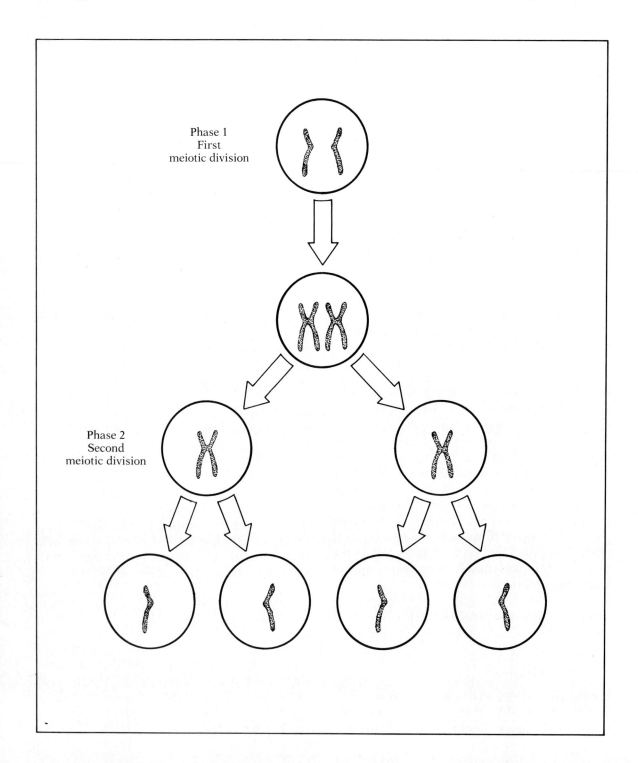

Phase 1
First
meiotic division

Phase 2
Second
meiotic division

holds true of what is inherited from the father and his ancestors. Thus it is mathematically just about impossible for any individual to inherit from a parent the exact set of chromosomes the parent had inherited from one of his or her parents.

In addition, even greater genetic variability, that is, variability of what is inherited, is assured through the process called **crossing over,** which can occur during the first meiotic division before the cell actually divides. In this process the chromosomes of each pair, which lie near each other, may exchange a portion of genetic material with each other. Thus, for example, a group of genes located at one end of a chromosome may switch places with a parallel group located on the same end of the paired chromosome. As a result of this process, neither of the two chromosomes of the pair is now exactly as it was before.

Because of crossing over, the random determination of which of a pair of chromosomes the individual receives from a particular parent, and the fact that the individual receives chromosomes from both parents, billions and billions of genetic combinations within the human species are possible. Indeed, no two individuals, with the exception of identical twins, who come from the same fertilized egg, will ever have the same exact genetic makeup. Of course, the more closely related two individuals are, the more of the same genetic material they are likely to have. Thus siblings, or parents and children, are more alike in both physical traits, behavior, and other factors, than are unrelated individuals. Some of the behavioral similarities may, of course, be attributable to the environment, but obviously the shared genetic inheritance plays a large part.

The tremendous possible genetic variation within any species is important for the survival of that species. For as the environment changes over time, or if events such as a new disease occur, some individuals may be better able to survive and adapt than others because of their unique genetic makeup. Thus particular individuals of a species may survive while others do not, but most importantly the species as a whole goes on.

EXPRESSION OF TRAITS

Not everything on every gene on each chromosome inherited by the individual, however, is expressed, that is, becomes apparent in that person's physical or mental makeup. The reason is that each individual possesses at least two genes, one on each of the pair of chromosomes, for each particular trait. These genes may exist in a variety of relationships to each other that determine how and if a trait is expressed. Some genes exist in a **dominance,** or **dominant-recessive,** relationship in which the effect of one overshadows or cancels out the effect of the other. Other relationships produce a mixed or combined effect, called **mixed dominance.** Both dominance and mixed-dominance effects are visible, or apparent, in the **phenotype,** or physical appearance, of the individual. A **recessive** gene would not have any effect upon phenotype but would appear in the **genotype,** or actual genetic makeup of the individual, and could therefore affect the phenotype as well as genotype of someone in the next generation.

Meiosis. This is the process of reduction division during which the egg or sperm receives only half the number of chromosomes that ordinary cells have. In our example, we are using only one pair of chromosomes for the sake of simplicity. During phase 1 chromosome duplication and cell division similar to that in other cells occurs. But in phase 2, the cells split without further duplication of chromosomes.

Dominant-Recessive Relationship Let us illustrate these concepts by looking at a familiar trait or attribute that occurs in a dominant-recessive relationship, eye color. In humans, the gene for brown eyes is dominant over that for blue eyes. By genetic convention, dominant genes are indicated by capital letters, recessive genes by small letters. Therefore, the gene for brown eyes is designated as *B* and that for blue as *b*. The individual has two genes for eye color, having inherited one from each parent. Thus he or she can have the following possible combinations: *BB*, *Bb*, *bB* or *bb*. Notice that *Bb* and *bB* are really the same, since the order in which the letters standing for genes are written does not matter. Thus three possible combinations or genotypes exist. *B*, however, is dominant over *b*.

A *Bb* individual will have brown eyes, since the gene for brown is dominant over that for blue. Therefore, there are only two phenotypes. *BB* and *Bb* individuals have brown eyes; *bb* individuals have blue eyes.

In order for a recessive trait to be expressed in the phenotype, the individual must be a pure recessive for that trait. That is, he or she must carry it on both genes of a pair and thus have inherited it from both parents. An individual who has two of the same genes (for example, who is *BB* or *bb* for eye color) is called **homozygous** for the particular trait in question. By contrast, a **heterozygous** individual is one who has the two differing genes (such as *Bb*) for the trait. The prefix homo means "same," and the prefix hetero means "different." The fact that the homozygous brown-eyed person (*BB*) and the heterozygous brown-eyed person (*Bb*) look the same or have the same phenotype provides a clue to answer the question why two brown-eyed parents sometimes produce a blue-eyed child. Can you figure it out?

It happens this way. Two brown-eyed individuals, both of whom are heterozygous, or *Bb*, for eye color, have a baby. At conception, the baby has an equal chance of receiving from the egg and sperm any one of four gene combinations: *BB* (homozygous brown-eyed), *Bb* or *bB* (both heterozygous and brown-eyed), or finally *bb* (homozygous blue-eyed). Thus for each child the couple produces, there are three chances out of four that the child will have brown eyes (a child who is *BB*, *Bb*, or *bB*) and one chance out of four that its eyes will be blue (a child who is *bb*).

Be aware that these odds remain the same for each conception. Each is a separate individual act of chance and has no relationship to any previous or subsequent one. Thus if such a couple already has three brown-eyed children, it does not mean the fourth child will have blue eyes. The fourth child still will have only once chance of four to have blue eyes. Indeed, since humans produce relatively few offspring, the odds and ratios based upon the laws of inheritance have been derived from the study of other species which have large numbers of offspring, as, for example, plants such as wheat or corn or animals such as fruit flies. In these studies it has been demonstrated that the phenotypic ratio of 3:1 dominant over recessive holds for offspring of two heterozygous parents.

But what happens if the two human parents in the example are homozygous? If they both are *BB*, they obviously will produce only brown-eyed children. If both are *bb*, all their children must have blue eyes. Now let us look at what happens if one parent is BB and the other is *bb*. All their children would have to be *Bb*, that is, heterozygous for the trait but having brown eyes. Only in the grandchild generation might blue eyes appear again. Finally, let us look at the most complicated situation, in which one parent is homozygous and the other heterozygous for the same trait. Now what happens? That will depend upon whether the homozygous parent has the dominant *(BB)* or the recessive *(bb)* combination. With one *BB* and one *Bb* parent, each child has a 50 percent chance of being *BB* and an equal chance of being *Bb*. In both instances, the child has brown eyes. But if the homozygous parent has the *bb* combination, this together with the *Bb* from the other parent means a 50 percent chance of the offspring being *Bb*, heterozygous, and brown-eyed just like one parent and likewise a 50 percent chance of being *bb*, homozygous, and blue-eyed just like the other parent.

Mixed-Dominance Relationship   As already mentioned, not all traits exist in a dominant-recessive relationship. In a mixed-dominance relationship, the offspring shows traits half-way between those of the two parents. The best example comes from the plant world, in which the offspring of plants with white flowers and those with red flowers often have pink flowers, a cross, or combination, of the white and red of their parents.

Polygenic Traits   Finally, many human traits such as intelligence or height depend not on one pair of genes but on many pairs. Such traits are called **polygenic,** that is, they are based on many genes. It is therefore impossible to ascribe such traits to particular genes or to determine the probability of their occurrence in the same way as can be done for simple traits such as eye color. In addition, many of these polygenic traits are subject to environmental influences, which can alter the way they are expressed. For example, intelligence depends not only upon the combined effects of a number of genes but also upon nutrition both before and after birth, the home environment, and the educational opportunities afforded the individual.

The First and Second Meiotic Division

While the basic process of meiosis, or reduction division, is the same for the production of both the egg and sperm, there are some important differences between the sexes in the timing during which these events occur and in the number of sex cells produced.

OOGENESIS

In the female, **oogenesis,** or the formation of the egg, occurs in two stages widely separated across time. During the **fetal** period, while the woman-to-be is still a tiny developing organism within her mother, a portion of the first meiotic division takes place in the thousands of incipient egg cells already forming in her two developing ovaries. The chromosomes duplicate themselves just as they do during mitosis. Thereafter nothing happens to these incipient eggs until in the course of time one at a time becomes the next one to ripen into a mature egg. A particular egg ripens by chance, that is, any egg could ripen. Ripening occurs at any time from the onset of menstruation, or the **menarche,** at **puberty** till its cessation at the **menopause.** Since puberty occurs around ages 11 to 14, and menopause generally between 45 and 55, the time lapse between the duplication of chromosomes and further events in the life of the egg may be anywhere from about 11 1/2 to 55 1/2 years or more. This time lapse may have important consequences, as we shall discuss later in this chapter.

In addition, although thousands of incipient eggs are located in the ovaries, only a very small number ever develop or ripen beyond this initial stage. For if a woman **ovulates,** or releases an egg, about 12 to 13 times a year for perhaps a maximum of 45 years between menarche and menopause, that yields a total of not more than about 585 eggs. Since a large proportion of women have one or more pregnancies, and ovulation ceases during pregnancy, the number of eggs produced is further reduced. Keep this small number in mind when we discuss the number of sperm a man produces a bit further on.

After the onset of menstruation, an egg each month resumes the process of the first meiotic division begun many years before. This process is triggered by the flow of particular hormones or chemical substances within the body. The egg increases greatly in size, the chromosomes migrate in pairs to opposite sides of the cell, and the cell, or egg, splits unevenly into a large egg and a small **polar body.** Each new cell now has 46 chromosomes in 23 pairs. The polar body is a small, unusable cell that has no further utility and eventually disintegrates. This division occurs during the last few hours before the woman will ovulate, about two weeks after the beginning of her last menstrual period. If the egg is not fertilized by a sperm as it descends from the ovary down a tube to the uterus, no further steps in the process of meiosis occur, and after a while the egg disintegrates. If, however, a sperm penetrates the outer layer of the egg, it triggers the second meiotic division during which the chromosomes become reduced to a single set of 23. The egg divides again into two uneven parts, a small polar body and a large egg, each having 23 chromosomes. The chromosomes in the egg and those in the sperm that has penetrated its outer layer then unite, bringing the total back up to 46 in 23 pairs

and completing fertilization. The polar body may remain attached for a while to the fertilized egg, but it has no further use (Pritchard & MacDonald, 1980).

Thus, in the process of meiosis in the female, only one viable, or functioning, egg results from the two divisions. The polar bodies are merely containers for surplus genetic material, and after they are formed they perform no other function. Therefore, almost all the cellular material, including nutrients, is concentrated in the one relatively large egg cell.

SPERMATOGENESIS

Let us now turn to **spermatogenesis,** or sperm formation in the testes of the male. The testes are analogous structures to the ovaries, but after a time late in the individual's fetal development are located in the scrotal sac, or **scrotum,** rather than in the abdomen. In contrast to the female, in whom the incipient egg cells are present from her own fetal stage onward, the male continually produces new incipient sperm cells during the entire course of life from puberty on into old age.

Beginning at puberty, a large number of these cells at any one time period are at some stage of the process of meiotic division. During the first meiotic division, the chromosomes duplicate themselves, and two cells of equal size, each containing 23 pairs or 46 total chromosomes, are formed. Shortly thereafter, each of these cells undergoes the second meiotic division, each forming two more equal-size cells, each this time with only 23 chromosomes. These four cells then undergo further ripening and assume the typical shape of the sperm, with a head and a long tail. Thus, in contrast to the female, in whom each incipient egg forms only one egg and several polar bodies, in the male all four sperm are truly functional. In addition, while the female produces only one egg each month, the male produces huge numbers of sperm on a continual basis. At any one time, millions of sperm are to be found in the testes, in various stages of the meiotic process. The production of sperm is greatest during adolescence and tapers off slowly with advancing age; even in old age, however, men produce large numbers of sperm. Their capacity to develop and maintain a penile erection, as well as the force of ejaculation of the sperm, both also decrease with age. It is more for these reasons as well as the fact that aged men often have aging partners who are beyond the menopause, that the rate of fatherhood declines in older men.

IMPLICATIONS OF MALE-FEMALE DIFFERENCES

Thus female and male differ during the meiotic process both in numbers of sex cells produced and in the fact that in the female all the eggs that will ever be produced are present from early on while in the male the sperm are continually produced afresh. This disparity may be the reason that older mothers are more likely than younger ones to produce children with genetic and chromosomal abnormalities, while the age of the father, except possibly in instances of **Down's Syndrome,** or Mongolism, does not appear to influence the offspring. The reasoning is that since the eggs are present in the woman for many years before ripening, they are more exposed to possible damage from cosmic rays from outer space, radiation from atomic testing or possible accidents at nuclear power plants, and x-rays from medical diagnostic procedures. In addition, they have been exposed for longer periods to chemical substances such as food additives or pollutants of air or water that also could affect the eggs.

Finally, the aging process of the eggs themselves could lead to their gradual deterioration. The older the woman is at the time of conception, the more likely it is that any or all of these factors play a part. While sperm also can be damaged by radiation or chemicals, they do not run an increasing risk with age, since they are continually produced afresh.

OVULATION AND FERTILIZATION

Ovulation

At a particular point during a woman's monthly cycle, the **pituitary gland** at the base of the brain secretes the hormone **FSH,** or follicle-stimulating hormone (Moore, 1977). This hormone causes the egg cell within the ovary that will become the next one to be released to begin further development. The surrounding cells supply it with extra nourishment. They also produce a fluid-filled blister called the follicle that surrounds the egg as it now lies on the outer surface of the ovary. The two ovaries produce eggs on an approximately alternating basis monthly. However, if one ovary is not functioning or if a woman has one removed surgically, the other one takes over the entire function of egg production and may produce one each month.

RUPTURE OF THE FOLLICLE

The process of ovulation occurs as the follicle ruptures and expels the egg into the abdominal cavity. There is no direct connection between the ovary and the corresponding **fallopian tube** toward which the egg must head. The opening of the tube is funnel-shaped, however, and at that portion of the menstrual cycle projections from it sweep over and partially cover the ovulating portion of

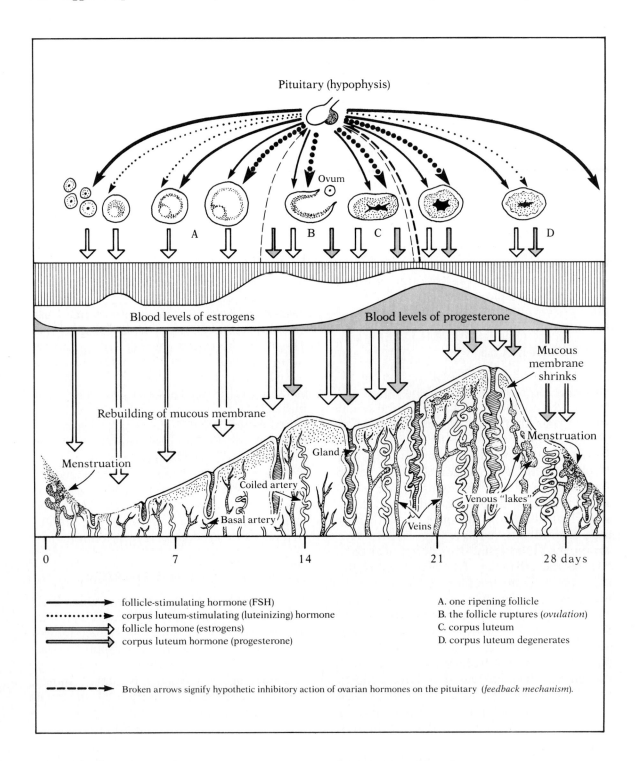

Pituitary (hypophysis)

Ovum

A   B   C   D

Blood levels of estrogens   Blood levels of progesterone

Mucous membrane shrinks

Rebuilding of mucous membrane

Gland

Menstruation

Coiled artery

Menstruation

Basal artery

Venous "lakes"

Veins

0   7   14   21   28 days

follicle-stimulating hormone (FSH)   A. one ripening follicle
corpus luteum-stimulating (luteinizing) hormone   B. the follicle ruptures (*ovulation*)
follicle hormone (estrogens)   C. corpus luteum
corpus luteum hormone (progesterone)   D. corpus luteum degenerates

Broken arrows signify hypothetic inhibitory action of ovarian hormones on the pituitary (*feedback mechanism*).

the ovary (Pritchard & MacDonald, 1980). The tube is also lined with hairlike projections that wave rhythmically and may help to move the egg toward the opening. In addition, the force of the fluid expelled along with the egg as the follicle ruptures may also serve to propel the egg toward the tube. All this activity is important because the egg is not able to move on its own.

ECTOPIC PREGNANCY

Sometimes an egg does not find the opening of the tube but does become fertilized and implants itself elsewhere in the abdominal cavity. On other occasions an egg enters the tube and becomes fertilized there as it should but implants itself in the tube rather than in the uterus. Both of these types of out-of-place pregnancies are called **ectopic.** They occur relatively infrequently, about once in 125 to 300 pregnancies, depending on the institutions reporting the data. About 95 percent of ectopic pregnancies are tubal ones (Niswander, 1981). The rate of ectopic pregancies is rising, however. It increased 136 percent from 1970 to 1978 (Van, 1983). According to the American Medical Association, this increase may be linked to the increase in pelvic inflammatory disease during this same time period, since such disease can cause scarring of the fallopian tubes and slow down or prevent the progress of the fertilized egg to the uterus (Van, 1983).

Since there usually is not an adequate source of nourishment for normal development to occur, ectopic pregnancies generally do not continue for more than a few days or weeks. Occasionally one that occurs in the tube will continue to grow and will eventually rupture the tube. Then surgical intervention becomes necessary, and both the tube and the developing embryo must be removed.

A new test for the possibility of ectopic pregnancy before a woman's tube actually ruptures has been developed. It utilizes the fact that the level of the hormone **gonadotropin** rises greatly over a period of several days in the blood of a woman who is pregnant but is not present at all in that of a nonpregnant woman. Thus blood testing for the hormone over a period of several days in women showing symptoms such as abdominal pain as well as a skipped menstrual period can help to separate those who might be having an ectopic pregnancy from those having other problems. In the case of the former, early surgery before the rupture of the tube can be done (Van, 1983).

CORPUS LUTEUM

The spot on the ovary from which the follicle had ruptured develops a scar called the **corpus luteum,** or yellow body. If conception does not occur, this yellow body reaches its full growth in about ten days from the time the follicle ruptured; it then degenerates just before the onset of the next menstrual period. If the egg has been fertilized, however, this yellow body continues to grow and begins to produce the hormone **progesterone** to prevent further menstruation and to maintain the pregnancy. After a while, other structures formed by the mother and developing baby take over the production of progesterone. The yellow body then stops its work and fades eventually to a small scar on the surface of the ovary.

The relationship of hormones to the building up of uterine tissues, ovulation, and menstruation.

Sperm Production and Ejaculation

Meanwhile, in the male, the sperm that have been developing most recently have ripened and changed their appearance from the relatively rounded one of many other cells to the elongated shape characteristic of mature sperm. The head portion of the sperm contains all the chromosomal material, and the long tail permits rapid movement. The sperm are stored for a short while longer in the testes. There they ripen further, enhancing both their fertility and their ability to move. If they are not discharged soon after this, the sperm decline, die, and are eventually resorbed into the body.

Before actual discharge, the sperm also become mixed with various fluids secreted by the **seminal vesicles** and the **prostate gland.** These fluids provide a vehicle for the transmission of the sperm to the woman's vagina during the ejaculatory phase of intercourse. They also contain a chemical buffer that protects the sperm from the acid environment of the vagina, which could kill many of the unprotected sperm.

The total volume of a typical man's ejaculate is about 3 cubic centimeters, or less than one tablespoon, made up of both sperm and fluid. Yet this amount contains from 300 to 500 million sperm (Moore, 1977). This large number is necessary to ensure that at least one will make it to its ultimate destination, an egg waiting to be fertilized in one of the woman's fallopian tubes.

Route of Sperm

The trip on which the sperm embark at the time of ejaculation is a difficult, long, and hazardous one. Having been deposited near the upper end of the vagina, the sperm must now find the very small opening of the **cervix,** or neck of the **uterus** (womb), enter it, travel the length of the uterus to one of the tubes, and enter the tube. The egg is located somewhere along the upper third of one of the fallopian tubes and is moving down it slowly, propelled by muscular contractions of and fluid pressure in the tube, as well as by the movement of the tube's hairlike projections (Niswander, 1981).

The total distance the sperm must traverse before meeting the egg is about 18 centimeters, or 7 inches. This does not appear very far until one considers the extremely small size of each sperm, and the fact that after the initial force of the ejaculation, each must propel itself largely on its own, though rhythmic contractions of the uterus and tube may help the sperm along as well (Moore, 1977). Furthermore, all along their journey, the sperm are battling downward currents of fluids produced by the woman's body and are thus swimming upstream. Amazingly, it usually takes only a little over an hour for the surviving sperm, usually not more than 300 to 500 in number (Hancock, 1970), to arrive at the egg (Brown, 1955). The optimal time for fertilization to take place is within 24 hours after ovulation; there is a greater chance of abnormality in babies conceived beyond this time (Niswander, 1981). While sperm may live for as long as 48 hours after intercourse, it is thought that fertilization sooner rather than later also improves the chances of having a normal baby since sperm quality appears to deteriorate rapidly.

Fertilization

If intercourse has taken place at the appropriate time, if the ovum is in the appropriate area of the tube, and if no chemical or physical birth control method has been used (and sometimes even if it has been used!), then a number of sperm will reach the ovum as it is slowly moved along the tube. Fertilization generally occurs somewhere along the upper one-third of the tube. It had earlier been believed that only one sperm reached the egg and then immediately fertilized it. Recent studies have yielded photographic evidence, at least from fertilization done in laboratory media, that shows that many sperm reach the egg at just about the same time. They cluster about it on all sides and even manage to spin it around by the combined force of movement of their tails. Eventually one sperm penetrates the tough coating of the egg called the **pellucid zone.** The sperm secretes a special enzyme that dissolves a portion of this coating, enabling it to enter the egg. The material in the sperm's nucleus, particularly the chromosomes, now enters the egg. As mentioned earlier, this process triggers the second meiotic division of the egg, during which an additional polar body is produced and cast off. After that, the nuclear material from the sperm lies side by side with, and eventually mingles with, that of the egg. Thus the fertilized egg again has the full and usual complement of 46 chromosomes, half contributed by the mother in the egg and half by the father in the sperm. The total process of fertilization takes about 24 hours (Moore, 1977).

Although occasionally several sperm may penetrate an egg's pellucid zone, it is usually only the one whose nuclear material first reaches and unites with the nuclear material of the egg that does the actual fertilizing. Any others that may have entered degenerate. Occasionally two sperm may fertilize an ovum; the resultant cell has 69 chromosomes, and the developing embryo usually aborts spontaneously (Carr, 1971). Soon after fertilization is complete, the egg's membrane thickens more and becomes impermeable to any further penetration by other sperm. Now the process of cleavage can begin.

The sperm thus has three important functions to fulfill. It must trigger the second meiotic division of the egg. It must provide its chromosomes to restore the total number of 46 needed. And finally its presence serves to initiate the process of cleavage.

RELATED TOPICS

Multiple Births

FRATERNAL TWINS

Generally only one ovum is released each month by the human female. But if by chance more than one are released and fertilized, fraternal, or dizygotic (DZ) twins, meaning "from two zygotes" (or fertilized eggs), or other multiple births result.

A number of factors appear able to cause dizygotic twinning. First of all, there is a hereditary component. Fraternal twinning tends to run in families. DZ twins have been found to occur several times in each generation, with various sisters and cousins giving birth to them, in families of twins for whom good genealogical records are available. Another indication of the genetic factor in DZ twinning is that if a woman has already had twins, she is five times as likely to produce another multiple birth in her next pregnancy as is a woman who has had only a single birth (Moore, 1977). Not surprisingly, the trait for DZ twinning is carried only by the mother; if twins occur in the father's family, it has no effect on the rate of occurrence (Page, Villee, & Villee, 1976). Another indication of heritability in fraternal twinning is that the rates also vary according to racial groups. For example, fraternal twins are quite rare among the Japanese but occur rather frequently in Nigeria (Nylander, 1969).

Other factors besides an inherited trait

DZ or fraternal twins develop from two separate ova that are fertilized by two different sperm. Thus DZ twins are no more related than any other sibling pair. Although these DZ twins have some family resemblance, they are of the opposite sex and in other ways too certainly are not "carbon copies" of each other.

can also cause fraternal twinning. Older mothers tend to have fraternal twins more frequently than younger ones, with a peak of frequency around the maternal age of 40 (Petterson, Smedby, & Lindmark, 1976; Waterhouse, 1950). Women who have taken oral contraceptives for a long time tend to show a higher rate of fraternal twinning if they become pregnant in the first month after going off the pill (Rothman, 1977). Finally, the fertility drugs such as pergonal that have been used in recent years to trigger ovulation in women who are infertile because they ovulate infrequently or not at all

sometimes will cause more than one egg to ripen and be available to be fertilized (Gemzell, Roos, & Loeffler, 1968). Indeed, the increased frequency of the births of quintuplets and even sextuplets in the last 20 years or so can largely be attributed to the use of these drugs, as such multiple births are otherwise extremely rare.

Since they are the products of two separate eggs, each fertilized by a different sperm, fraternal twins are no more related to each other than any other two siblings. They can be of the same sex or of opposite sex. The reasons that they appear more alike than ordinary siblings are that they are born at the same time and are raised together in the same environmental circumstances. Parents sometimes tend to dress them alike and to treat them as a pair rather than as separate individuals, enhancing the similarity.

IDENTICAL TWINS

By contrast, identical, or monozygotic (MZ), twins or identical multiple births involving more than two individuals come from a single fertilized ovum that at some point early in the process of cleavage splits into two or more distinct and separate cell groups that become separate individuals. Exactly why this occurs is still the subject of speculation.

Since identical, or MZ, twins come from a single fertilized egg, they carry the identical genetic component. They, therefore, are of the same sex and in other respects are very much alike. The differences that occur between MZ twins can be attributed to different environmental influences, which affect development very early. For example, there usually is some difference in birth weight between twins, even MZ ones, because of unequal access to nourishment from the mother. After birth, even though identical twins are

MZ twins develop from one fertilized ovum that early in development splits into two separate groups of cells that develop into two distinct but genetically identical individuals. The physical similarity between monozygotic twins is obvious in this infant pair.

even more likely to be treated as a pair, there are subtle differences in how people and other factors in the environment affect them and act toward them. Thus there are differences of personality and preferences between MZ twins, but they are often quite small. Even when reared apart, MZ twins show amazing similarities, not only in appearance, which is to be expected, but in personality and behavior.

The rate of MZ twinning appears to be the same for all racial groups, about one set of such twins in every 250 live births (Pritchard & MacDonald, 1980). Multiple births in numbers beyond two may be either all MZ

or all DZ or some combination of the two. For example, a set of triplets may be identical, or fraternal, or a combination such as a fraternal twin and two identical ones. The most famous instance of multiple births, since they were the first set of five to survive to adulthood, were the Dionne Quintuplets who were born in Canada in 1934. They appear to have all been identical, an instance of one egg that split several times until five individuals resulted. Some subsequent examples of quintuplets have also been identical, and some seem to be combinations of identical and fraternal twins. Fertility drugs may not only cause multiple ovulation but may also spur the splitting of the already fertilized egg, as some of the multiple births resulting from their use have been combinations of MZ and DZ twinning.

At present, the largest number of multiple births that have been born alive and have survived beyond infancy stands at six, an instance that occurred in South Africa. Although larger numbers have been born, all or some of these babies have not survived.

CONJOINED TWINS

Conjoined, or "Siamese" twins, so called because the first well known set of conjoined twins to survive were Chang and Eng Bunker from Siam (now Thailand), occur when identical twins are formed but during the cleavage process or slightly later the cells forming the two organisms do not completely separate from each other. This condition is very rare, occurring only once in about 400 instances of MZ twinning (Pritchard & MacDonald, 1980). The two individuals are joined to some extent, sometimes just by a flap of skin joining them at the abdomen or head, but sometimes sharing important body parts or systems.

If the connection does not involve too much of critical organs or systems, surgical separation is frequently attempted and often saves both or at least one infant, who can go on to live a normal life. If separation is not possible, the two individuals remain together for life. The original Siamese twins, who lived before surgery for such a condition was developed, survived to adulthood. They both married and spent half the time living with one wife and half with the other. Another famous set of conjoined twins are Masha and Dasha, two women in the Soviet Union. They share many body parts, including a common uterus and a central leg. Extensive scientific studies have been done with these two unusual persons to determine how physiological changes in the body of one might affect not only the physiological but also the mental state of the other as well.

Fertilization outside the Mother

REIMPLANTATION TECHNIQUE

Louise Brown was born in Oldham, England, on July 25, 1978. But she was no ordinary infant. For Louise was the first human baby to be conceived outside her mother's body who, when reimplanted, survived to be born. The technique of mixing sperm with a ripe ovum that had been removed from the mother's ovary, permitting the fertilized egg to multiply until it became a hollow ball of cells, and then implanting it in the mother's uterus, had been used previously with animals. But never before had it succeeded in humans.

Louise's mother had been unable to conceive a baby normally because her fallopian tubes were blocked. Thus, although she ovulated normally, there was no way that ovum and sperm could meet or that the ovum could reach the uterus.

The procedure used in such a situation was developed for use with humans by Dr. Patrick Steptoe, a gynecologist, and Dr. Robert Edwards, a reproductive physiologist. It involves removing, through a small incision in the mother's abdomen, an ovum that is about to rupture from its follicle. The ovum is withdrawn with a needle. It is then placed in a laboratory dish containing appropriate nutrients and blood serum; sperm from the father are added to the dish. After fertilization the egg is allowed to divide in the nutrient medium until it reaches a stage in which it comprises about 200 cells. Meanwhile the mother has been receiving hormone treatments to prepare her uterus for

Louise Brown, the world's first human baby conceived in a laboratory dish who survived to be born, is here shown with her parents as she appeared on the Phil Donahue television show when she was one year old. Mrs. Brown has since given birth to a second daughter through the use of the same technique of reimplanting an externally fertilized ovum into her uterus, so Louise now has a little sister to keep her company.

implantation. At the proper time, the cluster of cells is deposited in the uterus, where, if all goes well, it becomes implanted and grows to term just as any other baby would.

Louise Brown was delivered by cesarean section a few weeks before her due date, because her mother was showing symptoms of **preeclampsia,** consisting of both elevated blood pressure and **edema,** or fluid buildup in body tissues. This condition occurs in some routine pregnancies as well. Louise's progress has been carefully followed by physicians and psychologists, as well as by her parents and the general public. So far she seems to be developing as normally as any other young child.

Some other women on whom the procedure has been tried have not been as fortunate as Louise's mother and either have failed to have the cell cluster implant itself properly or have spontaneously aborted at some time after implantation. A number of women in Great Britain, India, and the United States, however, have also given birth to healthy babies by this method. In the United States, the procedure was pioneered by scientists at the Medical College of Virginia in Norfolk but is now used in many other hospitals as well.

HOST-MOTHER TECHNIQUE

In addition to the reimplantation technique, a procedure of embryo transfer that had been used previously in animals has now been suc-cessfully attempted in humans. In this situation, the fertilized ovum that has undergone the early stages of cleavage is removed from its biological mother and implanted in the uterus of another woman where it may develop until birth. The host mother may have blocked fallopian tubes as well as ovaries that are inaccessible to surgery, thus preventing the use of her own eggs for reimplantation. She may be carrying a genetic defect that she does not wish to pass on, or she may have had her ovaries removed at a prior time because of disease. The first times the host-mother technique was attempted with humans, which occurred in Australia, resulted in miscarriages after several weeks. In February 1984, however, physicians at Harbor-

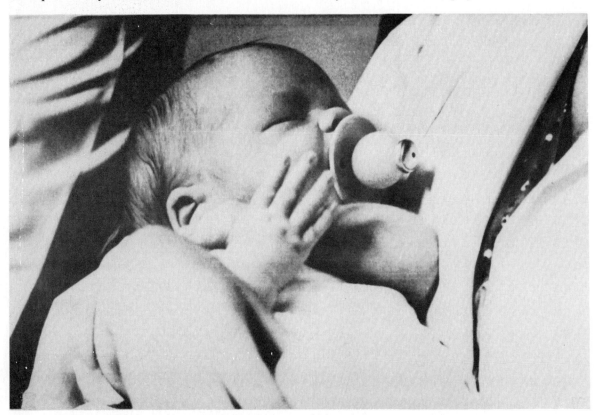

This baby boy, whose name and family have been kept secret, is the first embryo transfer baby ever carried success-fully to term. He was born healthy and perfectly formed in Long Beach, California, in 1984.

UCLA Hospital in California announced that for the first time a woman had safely delivered a baby boy that had been conceived in this manner ("World's First Baby...," 1984).

LEGAL AND MORAL IMPLICATIONS

While both reimplantation and the host-mother procedure can help women who could not otherwise have a baby, they do raise some important legal and moral questions. For example, in animals the host-mother implantation technique is used for a different reason. An ovum from a prize cow can be removed, fertilized with the sperm of a prize bull, and implanted in a genetically inferior cow, who will carry the calf to term. By chemically triggering multiple ovulation in the prize cow and using a number of host mothers, many more offspring of such an animal and a prize bull can be produced in the time it would take the cow to carry just one calf to term.

There is no technical reason that this procedure could not be used in the same way for the same purpose of producing "super-children" in humans. And what if a woman wants a baby that is biologically her and her husband's child but either cannot or does not want to undergo a pregnancy? Can she hire a host mother to carry the baby for her? If she does, who is considered the legal mother of the child, the biological mother or the host mother?

In addition, the host-mother procedure as applied in humans raises ethical questions for some people as well. For one thing, would it be acceptable for a woman to hire a host mother just because she herself did not want to undergo the fuss and bother of pregnancy? And does use of the procedure imply anything about the quality of mothering that a woman who resorts to it might provide?

Both techniques raise a more perplexing moral issue. The method of laboratory fertilization developed by the British scientists generally involves withdrawing a number of ripe ova produced by the mother because of chemical stimulation of the ovaries. Several of these may be fertilized in the dish and may undergo the early stages of cell division. But only the one that appears the most promising is implanted in the mother; the rest are destroyed. Many people belive that the human being exists from the moment of fertilization on. For these people then, the destruction of extra developing eggs is the killing of potential human beings. Artificial insemination is used in the host-mother technique. This procedure also is morally reprehensible to some. Thus even procedures that can help women who otherwise cannot have a baby to produce one have some moral implications that for some people make them wrong and unacceptable.

Genetic Counseling, Prenatal Diagnostic Procedures, and Inherited Abnormalities

Among the characteristics the individual inherits from his or her parents may be undesirable traits leading to illnesses or deficiencies of various kinds. Most of these inherited weaknesses are not life-threatening; indeed most of them go unnoticed. A few, such as color blindness, baldness, or having extra fingers or toes, are obvious, but while they may be annoying they pose no particular threat to the person's health and well-being.

A number of inherited traits, however, can lead to serious illness and even death. In some instances, nothing can be done except to prevent conception lest such an individual be produced. In other instances, environmental interventions after birth can prevent or lessen the severity of the condition.

Some of these conditions have nothing to do with specific genes but occur because the unequal division of chromosomes that sometimes takes place during the meiotic process can lead some individuals to have too many or too few chromosomes. Other conditions are inherited through a dominant trait on a gene and thus will appear even if only one parent carries the trait. This situation is similar to brown eyes in our earlier example of inheritance. Others are recessive genetic traits and thus appear only if inherited from both parents, analogous to our example of blue eyes. Some are carried only on the *X* chromosome and thus affect males and females unequally.

GENETIC COUNSELING

For some prospective parents genetic counseling is a valuable aid in determining their risks of producing a child having an inborn defect. The prime candidates for genetic counseling are people who have a history of heritable disease in either or both of their families, couples who have already produced a child having such a defect, and people of particular racial or ethnic groups in which the incidence of certain heritable diseases is relatively high. For example, parents at risk for producing a child with Down's Syndrome, **sickle-cell anemia,** or **Tay-Sachs disease** can profit from such counseling. Blood tests and other diagnostic procedures given to prospective parents can now determine for at least some inherited diseases whether either or both of the partners may be a carrier of a recessive trait. They can also show if either carries surplus chromosomal material that could affect a child. In such instances, prospective parents can then be apprised of what the probabilities are of producing a normal or an affected child. Couples then can make an informed decision whether to risk a pregnancy or not. If they consider the odds too bad, they may decide on childlessness or adoption.

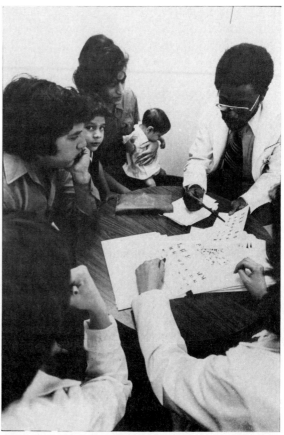

Genetic counselors work with a family to determine whether these parents are at risk for producing a child with a hereditary disease.

In other instances, for which diagnostic techniques applied to prospective parents are not yet available, a genetic counselor may collect a detailed family history to determine who in which family had an inherited disease and what the relationship of that individual to one of the clients was. Although this procedure is not as accurate as direct tests, it does enable the counselor to provide some estimate of the probability of occurrence of a defect when no better technique is available.

Genetic counseling can also be of help to parents who already have a defective child in deciding whether to have additional children. For in many instances it is possible to determine if the error in the child was due to the accidental combination of factors carried on a number of genes, and therefore would be highly unlikely to recur, or whether it was carried on one set of genes and therefore could indeed be transmitted to another child as well.

A number of hospitals, medical schools, and community health centers offer genetic counseling services. In addition, since some inherited diseases primarily affect blacks or Jews, some black and Jewish organizations also offer genetic counseling regarding these specific diseases. Information about the location and services of genetic counseling organizations can be obtained from the National Foundation/March of Dimes, Box 2000, White Plains, NY 10602, and from local chapters of this organization, or from the National Genetics Foundation, 250 West 57 Street, New York, NY 10019.

DIAGNOSTIC PROCEDURES: SONOGRAPHY AND AMNIOCENTESIS

Diagnostic work can also be done during a pregnancy, either to augment genetic counseling by showing whether the baby does indeed have a disorder or to determine the health status of the baby. The primary tools used in such diagnosis are sonography and amniocentesis.

Sonography In the technique of **sonography,** or ultrasound, sound waves are bounced off various portions of the mother's abdomen to produce a picture of the developing baby. The procedure resembles sonar, the type of radar that is used by ships to locate underwater objects. It can only be used to examine the baby after it has grown large

enough to be seen clearly on the picture produced by the sonograph, usually beginning during the second **trimester,** or middle portion, of pregnancy. The procedure can also be used to determine abnormalities of the mother's uterus and other structures at any time. Sonography can give an indication of the size of the baby and its location within the uterus. Relating these facts to how old the baby is can give information on whether development is proceeding normally or not. Abnormalities such as **spina bifida,** in which the spine does not completely fuse and portions of the spinal cord are left exposed, can sometimes be determined through ultrasound. So can **anencephaly,** the condition in which the baby is missing the major portion of the brain. Occasionally, if the baby is lying in an appropriate position, its sex can be determined. This can be important in the event that a sex-linked disease is suspected.

Sonography is a useful technique in that it appears to be relatively safe. It has been used for only a few years, however, and has not yet been proven to be completely without risk for the developing infant (Baker & Dalrymple, 1978; Fanaroff, 1983). Therefore, it should not be used unless there is compelling reason. Sonography can give some of the same diagnostic information that could come from x-rays, which are of established though small risk to both mother and child, as well as information that cannot be obtained in any other way. It can be repeated as often as is considered necessary if a particular developmental sequence in the fetus needs to be followed over time. Furthermore, it can be used in conjunction with amniocentesis, to improve the safety of that procedure.

Amniocentesis In the procedure called **amniocentesis** some of the baby's cells floating in the **amniotic fluid** surrounding the baby are removed, cultured, and then ana-

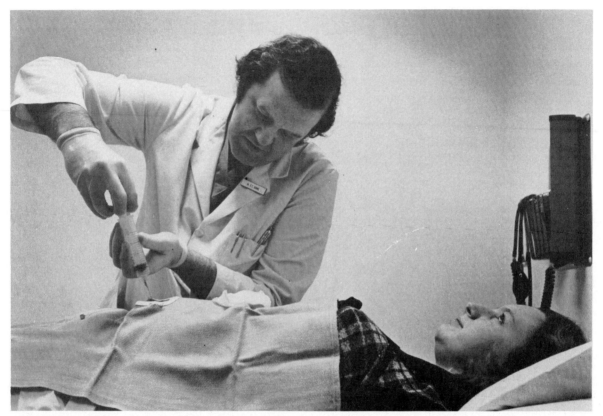

Amniocentesis. After the fetus' location is determined through sonography, the doctor obtains some amniotic fluid through the use of the syringe so that its contents can be studied to find out if the fetus is developing normally and is free of some hereditary diseases or conditions.

lyzed to determine their chromosomal makeup. The procedure cannot be done for chromosomal study before the 14th week of pregnancy; the 16th and 17th weeks are considered the best time (Katz, 1978). Any earlier, too few fetal cells appear in the amniotic fluid, and the quantity of the fluid is too small to permit adequate diagnosis.

To begin amniocentesis, sonography is used to determine the position and location of the baby, to make sure it will not be harmed. A long needle is inserted into the mother's abdomen and through the wall of the uterus into the **amniotic sac** surrounding

the baby, and some of the fluid is drawn off. Floating in the fluid are cells that have been sloughed off by the developing baby. These cells are collected and grown in a nutrient medium. Later they are examined microscopically so that their chromosomal makeup can be determined. The chromosomes in these cells are just like those in all the rest of the baby. Thus the sex of the baby can be precisely determined. If there is too much chromosomal material, this fact too becomes evident.

The cells grown in the medium can also be tested chemically to reveal the presence or

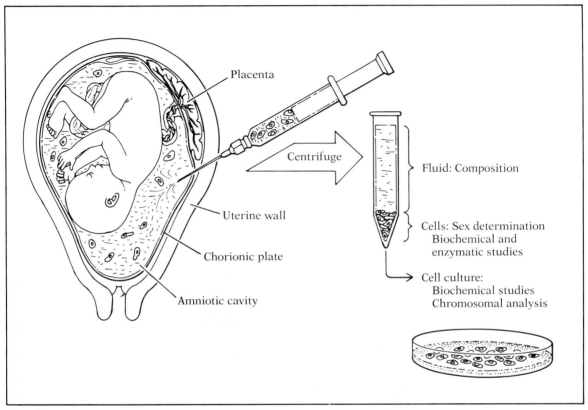

Amniocentesis. During this process, a small amount of amniotic fluid is withdrawn from the amniotic sac via a syringe. Cells sloughed off by the developing fetus are collected through centrifuging, and are then cultured in a nutrient medium. They can later be studied to determine the sex of the baby, as well as the presence or absence of certain diseases.

absence of certain enzymes. This procedure helps to diagnose particular hereditary diseases that manifest themselves through the absence of these enzymes.

In addition to its use in determining possible genetic diseases, amniocentesis is a useful tool in determining the general health status of a developing baby suspected of being at risk. For example, the color of the fluid extracted and whether it contains blood or substances excreted by the baby can tell physicians about the baby's condition. If too

much **bilirubin,** a chemical found in blood, appears in the fluid, blood disease in the developing baby such as **Rh incompatibility** and its consequences are suspected (Pritchard & MacDonald, 1980).

Late in pregnancy, amniocentesis is sometimes used with high-risk diabetic mothers. It can tell doctors whether the baby is still all right or whether the child's condition is deteriorating. In the latter situation, if it appears that the baby might need to be removed early by cesarean section, amniocentesis can also determine the state of maturity of the baby's lungs.

In order to keep the air sacs in the lungs open and functioning properly, a surfactant (a substance with similar properties to a detergent) must be present in the lungs. If the baby is too immature and if not enough of the surfactant is present, respiratory distress can follow and the baby could die. Through amniocentesis, doctors can determine how much of the substance is available (Gluck, Kulovich, Borer, Brenner, Anderson, & Spellacy, 1971). The trick is to keep the mother's diabetes from causing the baby to become too large or from causing other problems and yet have her carry the baby long enough that lung maturity will not be a problem after early cesarean birth.

Amniocentesis carries with it some risks, however, and should not be used unless necessary. Occasionally, in spite of careful positioning through the use of sonography, the needle does penetrate the baby. Instances have also been reported in which the mother goes into premature labor as a result of amniocentesis. And finally, in spite of careful use of sterile instruments, there have been some instances of infection. The spontaneous abortion rate as a result of amniocentesis is about 5 percent at present (Raeburn, 1982).

Finally, when amniocentesis is used to diagnose a genetic disease to which the only solution may be abortion, a drawback of the procedure is the late stage of pregnancy in which it can be done. Since amniocentesis cannot successfully be done before the 14th to 17th week, and culturing the cells takes another two to three weeks, a definite diagnosis cannot be made before about the 17th to 20th week, or about halfway through the pregnancy.

Even if a couple approves of the use of abortion, and many of course do not, abortion that late in pregnancy involves more risks to the mother than one done earlier. A different, more complicated procedure must be used. In addition, even for those who approve of abortion, doing this procedure at a time when the baby is already well formed and may already be felt moving can be more objectionable than one done at an earlier stage. Diagnostic sonography, which also must usually be done fairly late in pregnancy, shares this drawback.

Other Procedures   Researchers are at work on various other procedures to develop better and if possible earlier means of determining genetic and other abnormalities in the developing baby. For example, blood can now be withdrawn from the baby in the latter stages of pregnancy, either for diagnostic purposes or for the exchange of blood if that should prove necessary. Experimental surgery to correct defects in the developing baby has been attempted. A blood test that involves the baby's blood but does not have to draw blood directly from it has also been reported to be in an experimental stage. In 1979 a group of researchers at Stanford University found that cells from the developing baby appear in the mother's bloodstream as early as the 12th week of pregnancy (Altman, 1979). It is not yet known how these cells enter the mother, what possible function they have, or what eventually happens to them. These researchers believe, however, that if these cells could be isolated from those of the mother, cultivated, and examined, they could give earlier and more reliable information about the baby or perhaps provide information about conditions for which there are as yet no other indicators.

CHROMOSOMAL ABNORMALITIES

Occasionally, errors occur during the meiotic division of incipient sperm or eggs. One of the cells receives an extra chromosome, and the other one too few. This happens because the chromosomes in a pair may not separate as they should. After fertilization, the individual in question has either 45 or 47 chromosomes, instead of the usual 46. The extra or missing chromosome can be one of the autosomes, or it can be one of the sex chromosomes.

Abnormalities of Sex Chromosomes
Abnormalities resulting from wrong numbers of sex chromosomes include **Turner's Syndrome,** in which the person has an *XO* chromosomal pattern (one *X* and a missing chromosome indicated by the *O*). Such a person becomes an infertile, underdeveloped female in whom neither breast growth, growth of body hair, nor menstruation begin at puberty. **Klinefelter's Syndrome,** in which an *XXY* pattern is found, comes about because the two *X* chromosomes did not separate and came together with an additional *Y* chromosome provided by the sperm. Individuals with this syndrome look like males but at puberty do not have enlargement of external genitalia and do not produce sperm. The appropriate sex hormone administered at puberty can help both types of individuals by stimulating the growth of sex organs and the development of secondary sex characteristics such as hair or breasts. Thus, although still infertile, the individual appears more normal and may make a better adolescent adjustment. Fortunately both these abnormalities, and some even rarer ones, all occur quite infrequently. Turner's Syndrome occurs about once in 10,000 live female births; Klinefelter's once in 1,000 live male births (Uchida & Summitt, 1979).

An Abnormality of Autosomal Chromosomes: Down's Syndrome The most serious and frequent defect that occurs from an ab-

normal number of chromosomes is Down's Syndrome, which used to be called Mongolism. The overall rate of occurrence of Down's Syndrome is 1 in 660 live births (Smith, 1977), but the heritability of one version, as well as parental age, both affect the incidence. The condition results when an individual has three instead of the normal two chromosomes (called trisomy) at the pair no. 21 position. It is thus an autosomal abnormality. Incidentally, there is some dispute about the numbering of the chromosome. It should really have been called no. 22 rather than no. 21, since it is somewhat larger than the one called no. 22, and chromosomes are numbered according to size within a group. The error occurred because during the 1960s, when chromosomes were first distinguished and grouped, measurements were not yet as precise as at present. Most scientists, however, are following historical tradition and are still calling the chromosomal error resulting in Down's Syndrome trisomy of no. 21 (Falace, 1982).

Down's Syndrome consists of a cluster of abnormalities, most of which generally occur together in the affected individual. They include mental retardation, abnormalities of the heart and other portions of the circulatory system, a tendency toward frequent respiratory diseases, and a relatively large tongue in a smaller than usual mouth, leading to frequent speech problems. The individual usually is of short stature, with short, stubby fingers, and facial features that appear vaguely Oriental. This last abnormality led to the original designation of Mongolism for the syndrome.

In the past, because of their susceptibility to respiratory diseases, few individuals with Down's Syndrome lived beyond childhood. With improved treatment, especially the use of antibiotics, many seem to be approaching a normal lifespan. They generally

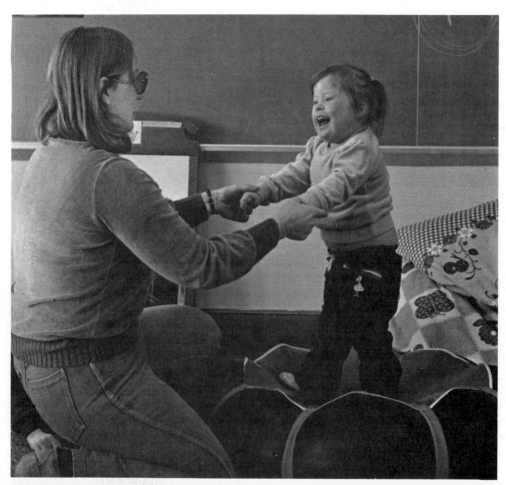

This child exhibits some of the typical physical features of Down's Syndrome or Mongolism. Because she is mentally retarded and also lags behind in motor development, she attends a special school where her teacher is helping her with physical exercises designed to improve her coordination.

are very pleasant, happy, and loving individuals. With new educational techniques, particularly if begun very early in infancy, many people with Down's Syndrome have made more intellectual and educational progress than had been thought possible. Families of such children often indicate that they have brought a special dimension of love and caring to the family. Nevertheless, having to

care for such a child also puts a large measure of responsibility on parents, as well as on siblings, particularly later in life when parents may be dead but the retarded sibling still needs care. In addition, the financial burden of possible corrective surgery, frequent medical attention, special schooling, and, in extreme cases, institutionalization, can be very great. Therefore, prospective par-

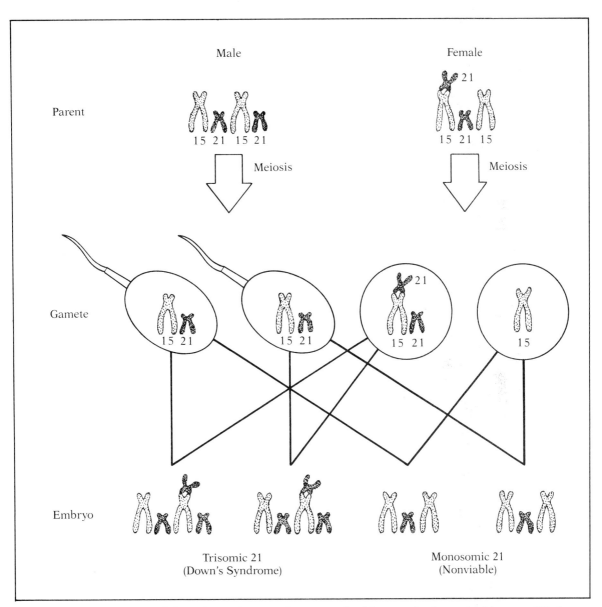

Down's Syndrome transmitted through translocation. One parent (in this example, the mother) has one #21 chromosome attached to a #15. Although the arrangement of her chromosomes is different from the usual, the mother has the appropriate number and is therefore normal. The child, however, receives the extra #21 attached to the #15, as well as two other #21s. He or she therefore has a total of three #21 chromosomes and has Down's Syndrome. If the cell containing no #21 chromosome is destined to become the eventual fertilized egg, it does not survive to develop into an embryo.

ents who appear at risk to produce a child with Down's Syndrome, or those who through amniocentesis have found that they are about to have one, need to evaluate their options and the decisions they will make with great care.

The extra chromosome in Down's Syndrome occurs for either of two reasons, translocation or nondisjunction. About 4 percent of the cases are due to **translocation** (Uchida & Summit, 1979). For translocation to occur, in the formation of one of the parent generation, one no. 21 or a portion of the 21 becomes attached to a no. 15 chromosome. The parent has the entire correct amount of genetic material; it is merely arranged in an unusual manner. He or she is therefore not affected. But if the parent passes on to the baby a normal no. 21 plus the extra no. 21 or the piece of it that is attached to the no. 15, and the other parent also contributes a no. 21, the baby has too much total no. 21 material and will have Down's Syndrome. Translocation can be inherited from either the father's or the mother's family, and the condition can occur because of the error in the chromosomes passed on in either the egg or sperm. Because this condition is heritable, several children in a family can be born with translocation-type Down's Syndrome if one of the parents has such a defective chromosome.

The vast majority of the cases of Down's Syndrome occur because of **nondisjunction** of chromosomes during either the first or second meiotic division. There does not seem to be a hereditary reason for this kind of occurrence. It appears to happen as a result of abnormality of either egg or sperm, though the chance of abnormality of the egg is somewhat higher (Mikkelsen, Hallberg, & Poulsen, 1976). It is thought that about one-third of the cases of nondisjunction are due to the sperm and the other two-thirds to the egg

(Uchida & Summit, 1979). The frequency of nondisjunction rises with increasing maternal age, and paternal age has lately been shown to be a probable factor as well (Stene, Fisher, Stene, Mikkelsen, & Petersen, 1977).

Women under 25 have only 1 chance in 2,000 of producing a baby with the nondisjunction type of trisomy causing the condition. This ratio rises to 1 in 280 for women between 35 and 39. After age 40, the odds become dramatically worse. They are 1 in 80 for women between 40 and 44, 1 in 32 at age 45, and 1 in 12 by age 49 (Hook & Lindsjo, 1980). In addition, paternal age, particularly if over 55, may also affect the incidence of the disease (Stene et al., 1977). It is difficult to separate out the effect of paternal age, since older men tend also to be married to older women. Some scientists studying this problem tend to discount or deny the role of paternal age (Sigler, Lilienfeld, Cohen, & Westlake, 1965; Erickson, 1978); obviously more studies need to be done to determine for sure if and to what extent paternal age may be a factor.

Since the nondisjunction-type of Down's Syndrome occurs because of an error in meiosis, the chance of such an error recurring in a subsequent pregnancy is small, except for the increased risk faced by the much older parent (women over 40 and/or men over 55).

Translocation can be diagnosed in the parent through examination of the parent's chromosomes if there is advance warning that such a condition could be carried, for example if a close relative had produced a child with translocation or if the parent had already produced a child with this condition. In such a case, parents can decide whether to go ahead with a possible pregnancy or not.

Nondisjunction, however, can only be diagnosed after conception has already occurred, although consideration of maternal

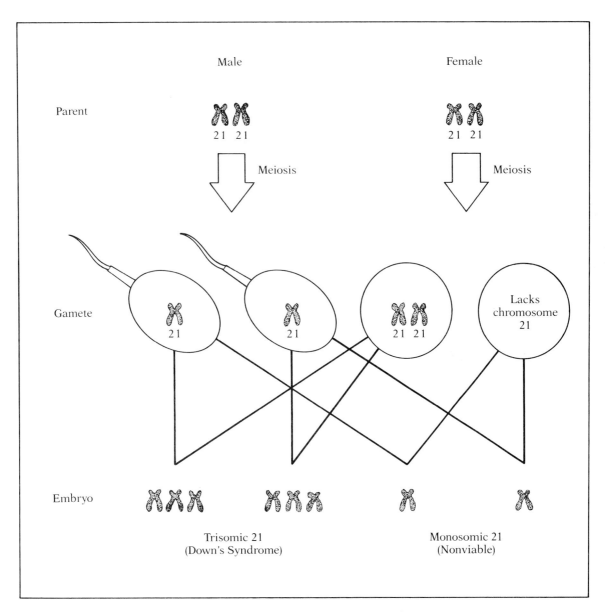

Down's Syndrome transmitted through nondisjunction. During meiosis, the chromosomes of the mother's incipient egg cell did not separate normally. Thus the ovum may have two #21 chromosomes. When the sperm brings its single #21, the fertilized egg has three #21s and develops into a child with Down's Syndrome. If the eventual egg is one containing no #21, it is nonviable and does not develop. Down's Syndrome due to nondisjunction is much more frequent than that due to translocation. Although in both types the father may contribute the two #21s, the mother is much more frequently the one who does.

and paternal age before a pregnancy begins can at least provide some odds for decision making. Both nondisjunction and translocation can be detected through amniocentesis, but of course not until the pregnancy is fairly far along. If the condition is found, parents then can opt for an abortion, if their ethics permit it. For many parents, however, abortion is not an option because their beliefs forbid it. Amniocentesis to determine a possible case of Down's Syndrome is therefore useful and practical only if abortion is a possible option. It is advised mainly in situations where maternal age is over 35 and/or paternal age is over 55, where there is a history of translocation in the family, or where a couple has already had a child with Down's Syndrome.

GENETIC ABNORMALITIES

Defective genes may cause a variety of abnormalities. Some of these abnormalities are relatively unimportant, but some can cause serious or fatal diseases. Table 2.1 lists the most important of these diseases, as well as for each the causes, symptoms, availability of tests of either parents or fetus, possible treatments, and eventual outcomes. Table 2.2 shows the probability of inheriting the trait, depending upon whether the trait is dominant, recessive, or sex-linked, and the status of both parents in relation to it.

The most serious disease involving a dominant gene is **Huntington's disease,** formerly called Huntington's Chorea. It is insidious not only because it is invariably fatal but also because its symptoms generally apppear only after the affected individual has already had children. Thus it can be passed along before a person knows that he or she is affected.

Less serious disorders resulting from a defective dominant gene include certain types of dwarfism, some instances of **glaucoma,** which is an eye disease that can cause blindness if untreated, and **polydactily,** the condition of having extra fingers or toes.

Some hereditary diseases occur through recessive genes. In such instances, both parents may be carriers of the defective gene but are unaffected by the disease because they are protected by a dominant gene. If their child receives the two recessive genes, the child will show the disease.

Some of the more frequent serious disorders involving paired recessive genes are **phenylketonuria** (PKU), Tay-Sachs disease, sickle-cell anemia, **thalassemia,** and **cystic fibrosis.** Please refer to Table 2.1 for details about each.

Finally, a group of genetic defects is caused by the presence of an affected recessive gene on the X chromosome. These diseases therefore affect males and females in different proportions. Since the male has only one X chromosome, the presence of the single recessive gene causes it to affect him as if it were a dominant one; he has the condition or disease. The female, however, since she has two X chromosomes, is affected only if she carries the defective gene on both of them. If it is present on only one, the dominant gene on the other protects her, and she is only a carrier of the disease.

The most serious sex-linked defects are **hemophilia** and **muscular dystrophy,** which are also described in detail in Table 2.1. Other sex-linked conditions that are far less serious include color blindness and baldness. Can you now see why these latter two conditions occur so much more frequently in males than in females?

TABLE 2.1   SOME HEREDITARY DISEASES BASED ON GENE TRANSMISSION

Name of Disease	Usual Age of Onset	Predominant Group Affected (if any)	Rate in Population of Affected Group (for live births)	Diagnostic Test of Prospective Parents	Diagnostic Test of Fetus or Neonate	Symptoms	Treatment and Outlook	Other Information
Autosomal Dominant:								
Huntington's disease (formerly called Huntington's Chorea)	Around age 35	Some possible relation to ethnicity, e.g., higher rate among Appalachian whites	1 in 20,000 live births	None available yet. An experimental blood test usable before possible victims have children was developed in 1983.[1]	None available	Progressive deterioration of nervous system, leading to mental instability and incapacitation	No treatment available. Death follows in middle age.	Since disease does not manifest itself until after most people have had children, it is passed on before victim is aware of having the disease. Therefore, it is difficult to prevent. Work is in progress on a possible diagnostic blood test, which would be used on prospective parents.
Autosomal Recessive:								
1) Tay-Sachs disease	Around six months	Ashkenazi Jews (Jews of Eastern European origin)	1 in 25,000 Ashkenazi Jews in U.S.[2]	Blood test to see if either or both of prospective parents is a carrier	Amniocentesis during pregnancy to determine if necessary enzyme is present or absent	Progressive deterioration of nervous system because enzyme that breaks down fats in nervous system is absent	None available. Death follows inexorably in late infancy or early childhood, usually around ages 2–3.	Since no victim survives to adulthood, disease is passed on by carriers only. However, since Jews tend to marry within their ethnic group, the probability of two carriers marrying is fairly high. A number of Jewish

TABLE 2.1 SOME HEREDITARY DISEASES BASED ON GENE TRANSMISSION (Continued)

Name of Disease	Usual Age of Onset	Predominant Group Affected (If any)	Rate in Population of Affected Group (for live births)	Diagnostic Test of Prospective Parents	Diagnostic Test of Fetus or Neonate	Symptoms	Treatment and Outlook	Other Information
								groups provide genetic counseling and blood testing to determine carriers.
2) Sickle-cell anemia	Can begin at any age with a crisis episode, usually appears in early childhood	Blacks, Caucasians of Mediterranean ancestry	1 in 10 U.S. Blacks is a carrier; 1 in 500 has the disease.	Blood test to see if either or both of prospective parents is a carrier	A recently developed, still experimental test using amniocentesis at weeks 16–18 is now beginning to be used.[3]	Sickling of red blood cells during a crisis because of absence of one protein in hemoglobin. This causes clumping of blood cells in vessels, restricting blood flow, causing clotting and pain. Also rupture of blood cells.	Amelioration of symptoms is only treatment available. Victims have a shorter than normal life span, often dying in early adulthood. Half die by age of 35.	Sickling episodes tend to occur during illnesses that restrict oxygen intake, at times of increased need for oxygen such as during physical exercise, at high altitudes, or at times of psychological stress. Under *very* extreme circumstances, carriers sometimes also have sickling episodes. Anemia results because fragile cells can't be replaced as quickly as they are destroyed.

In the past in Africa and around the Mediterranean, carrier status had some benefit |

Disease	When symptoms appear	Who gets it / frequency	Detection	Symptoms	Treatment & Prognosis
(sickle-cell anemia, continued)					as it provides immunity to malaria. Since this disease is rare in the U.S. at present, the benefit is of little value. In 1983 an experimental treatment including the drug 5-Azacytidine was announced. This drug stimulates the gene producing fetal hemoglobin, which then replaces the abnormal hemoglobin. Fetal hemoglobin does not cause sickling of red blood cells.[4]
3) Thalassemia (2 kinds)					
a) Thalassemia minor: carriers show symptoms of disease		Blacks, and whites of Mediterranean ancestry. 1% of U.S. Blacks are carriers; 16% of Italians are carriers, thus they have Thalassemia minor.	Carrier status can be determined via blood test.	Anemic symptoms	A mild kind of anemia. Like sickle-cell anemia carrier status provides immunity to malaria.
b) Thalassemia major: inherited from both parents, also called Cooley's anemia	During 2nd 6 months of life	Disease rate is 1 in 10,000 U.S. blacks, 1 in 2,500 U.S. whites of Mediterranean ancestry.[2]	A diagnostic test using fetal blood is being worked on. Blood test of infant after about 6 months of age can confirm presence of either kind of Thalassemia.	Weakness, cardiac complications	Blood tranfusions necessary to keep up hemoglobin count in blood. Life expectancy low, as transfusions also cause undesirably high buildup of iron in body, which affects heart. Life expectancy is extended with transfusions. May live to second or third decade with them.

TABLE 2.1   SOME HEREDITARY DISEASES BASED ON GENE TRANSMISSION (Continued)

Name of Disease	Usual Age of Onset	Predominant Group Affected (if any)	Rate in Population of Affected Group (for live births)	Diagnostic Test of Prospective Parents	Diagnostic Test of Fetus or Neonate	Symptoms	Treatment and Outlook	Other Information
4) Cystic fibrosis	Infancy or early childhood	Mainly Caucasians—most common hereditary disease of Caucasians but occurs in other racial groups as well	4% of U.S. Caucasians are carriers.[5] 1 in 3,700 has disease.[2]	Sweat electrolyte testing plus testing of pancreatic function in adults may establish that they have a mild form or are carriers.[6]	None	Mucus build-up in respiratory system leads to problems with breathing. Sweat glands also malfunction. Great susceptibility to pneumonia and other respiratory diseases.	Use of mist-filled tents and physical therapy to remove mucus. Antibiotics and other drugs to combat secondary infections. Death usually occurs in late childhood or adolescence.	With improved treatment, some affected individuals have now survived to early adulthood. It is too soon to know how long they may ultimately survive.
5) Phenylketonuria (PKU)	Early infancy—after protein ingestion begins	Northern Europeans, but exists in other Caucasians as well; very rare in others	1 in 10,000 to 15,000 in Northern Europeans; greatest in Irish—1 in 500 to 800[2]	None	Blood test of infant after beginning of protein ingestion. Best done at 6-14 days of age; should not be done before 72 hours of age, to determine presence of phenylalanine	Progressive mental retardation due to inability to metabolize an amino acid, which causes a toxic substance to build up in the brain and destroy brain cells	A diet very low in the amino acid can prevent mental retardation. Life span is probably normal but it is too early to know, as treatment has only been available for 20-25 years.	With proper diet begun in early infancy and carried on into the teens, normal or almost normal intelligence can be maintained. Since present-day victims have normal or almost normal intelligence, they are more likely to marry and have children than were the severely retarded victims of the past. Therefore, the incidence of the condition may increase.

6) Tyrosinemia (hereditary form)	1–6 months	Swedes and French Canadians[4]	Lower than that of PKU	None	Blood test in neonate for the level of tyrosine and phenylalanine	Failure to thrive, irritation, fever, increase of size of liver, liver and kidney damage	Restriction of tyrosine in diet. Those untreated will die of liver failure in childhood.	
7) Galactosemia			1 in 30,000 to 70,000[7]	None	Blood test of neonate	Jaundice, vomiting, lethargy, feeding difficulties, poor weight gain	Lactose- and galactose-free diet used to prevent liver damage and cataracts of the eyes	
Sex-Linked: (Carried on X-Chromosome)								
1) Hemophilia	Infancy or early childhood	Occurs in any racial group. Because it is sex-linked it occurs much more frequently in males than females. But only females can be carriers.	1 in 8,500 to 10,000	None	Only sex determination of fetus through amniocentesis. Then probabilities can be calculated and parents can decide to abort a male fetus.	Blood from injuries or spontaneous small hemorrhages leaks into joints and organs, causing pain and injury. Blood does not clot because vital blood factors are lacking.	Great care taken to prevent injury. Periodic injection of clotting factor into blood helps (but is extremely expensive). Without injections, death usually occurs in childhood or adolescence. With them, more are living to adulthood.	Hemophilia is often called the "royal disease" because many European royalty of the 19th & 20th centuries were affected. Queen Victoria of England passed the gene on to her children, who then intermarried with most of the other royal families. The most famous hemophiliac was probably Alexis, the son of the last Tsar of Russia and heir to the throne till both were murdered during the Russian revolution. Actually, far

TABLE 2.1   SOME HEREDITARY DISEASES BASED ON GENE TRANSMISSION (Continued)

Name of Disease	Usual Age of Onset	Predominant Group Affected (if any)	Rate in Population of Affected Group (for live births)	Diagnostic Test of Prospective Parents	Diagnostic Test of Fetus or Neonate	Symptoms	Treatment and Outlook	Other Information
								more common than royalty have the disease. As life span increases with injection of clotting factors, more hemophiliacs will marry and perhaps have children. This could cause an increase in the incidence.
2) Muscular dystrophy	Early childhood	Occurs in all racial groups. Victims are almost exclusively males.	1 in 4,500 to 5,000.[2]	None	As in hemophilia, only prenatal sex determination and possible abortion of male fetus; blood test and muscle biopsy in young child	Progressive weakness and muscle wasting	Physical therapy to retard progress of disease. Eventually child is confined to wheelchair; later to bed. Life expectancy is shorter than normal—usually only to early adulthood.	

[1] P. Raeburn (1983, November 9), Genetic Clue Found in Dread Disease, *The Courier-Journal* (Louisville, KY).

[2] K. Benirschke, G. Carpenter, C. Epstein, et al. (1976), in R. L. Brent and M. I. Harris (Eds.), *Prevention of Embryonic, Fetal and Perinatal Disease* (pp. 219–261). (DHEW Publication No. NIH 76-853), Washington, DC.

[3] P. Raeburn (1982, May 10), Simpler, Safer Prenatal Test Developed for Discovering Dread Sickle-Cell Anemia, *The Courier-Journal* (Louisville, KY).

[4] S. Reynolds (1983, January 6), Test Drug for Sickle Cell Anemia Works on Genes, *Lexington (KY) Herald-Leader*.

[5] J. M. Docter (1977), Cystic Fibrosis, in D. W. Smith (Ed.), *Introduction to Clinical Pediatrics* (2nd ed.), (pp. 394–396), Philadelphia: W. B. Saunders.

[6] A. G. F. Davidson, D. A. Applegarth, & L. T. Wong, Diagnosing Cystic Fibrosis in Adults, *New England Journal of Medicine*, 300(20):1164.

[7] R. C. Scott (1977), Inborn Enzymatic Errors, in D. W. Smith (Ed.), *Introduction to Clinical Pediatrics* (2nd ed.), (pp. 386–393), Philadelphia: W. B. Saunders.

TABLE 2.2 PROBABILITIES OF PRODUCING AN AFFECTED CHILD

Type of Inheritance	Parental Genetic Makeup	Probability
1. Autosomal Dominant (e.g. Huntington's disease). Only one gene needed for defect to occur since the conditions are dominant over the normal recessive.	Affected parent + normal parent	50% probability of affected child 50% probability of normal child
	Affected parent + affected parent	75% probability of affected child 25% probability of normal child (provided both parents have only one and not two genes for the condition)
2. Autosomal Recessive (e.g. sickle-cell anemia). For the disease to occur, both paired genes must carry the trait. If only one does, the person is a carrier but does not show the disease since the normal gene is dominant.	Affected parent + normal parent	100% probability of child being a carrier
	Carrier parent + normal parent	50% probability of child being a carrier 50% probability of normal child
	Carrier parent + carrier parent	50% probability of child being a carrier 25% probability of affected child 25% probability of normal child
	Affected parent + affected parent	100% probability of affected child

3. Sex-linked Defects (e.g. hemophilia). Defective gene is on *X* chromosome, therefore in male it acts as if it were dominant. In female, it acts as a recessive gene; thus must be present on both *X* chromosomes for person to be affected. (There are also a few sex-linked dominant traits, but they are very, very rare).	Normal father + carrier mother	daughters:
		  50% probability of normal child
		  50% probability of being carrier
		sons:
		  50% probability of normal child
		  50% probability of affected child

	Affected father + normal mother	daughters:
		  100% probability of being carrier
		sons:
		  100% probability of normal child

	Affected father + carrier mother	daughters:
		  50% probability of affected child
		  50% probability of being carrier
		sons:
		  50% probability of affected child
		  50% probability of normal child

	Affected father + affected mother (a very rare combination, as very few females are affected; thus one mating with an affected male is very unlikely to occur).	100% probability of a child of either sex being affected

The last Russian royal family, which was killed after the 1917 revolution during which the Communists came to power. The Tsarevich (or crown prince) Alexis, shown here in front of his parents and sisters, suffered from hemophilia. In attempting to find a cure for this affliction in their son, the royal couple became friendly with the monk Rasputin, who promised to cure the child through faith but who was hated by the Russian people, and otherwise neglected their governing duties. Some historians believe that their preoccupation with their son's disease and their relationship with Rasputin so alientated the populace that this contributed directly to the success of the revolution. Thus one child's hereditary disease may have profoundly affected world history.

Rh INCOMPATIBILITY

A potentially serious problem that also has a genetic basis but that affects individuals in ways different from the various diseases discussed earlier is **Rh incompatibility** between mother and developing baby. The Rh factor is a blood factor whose presence is deter- mined by a dominant gene. If a person has two recessive genes for this factor, he or she does not produce it. Such a person is labeled Rh negative; the normal individual is Rh positive. The designation Rh came about merely because the factor was first studied in rhesus monkeys and was named after the first two letters of that word. The incidence of Rh negative individuals ranges from 15 percent of Caucasians to 7 percent of blacks and only 1 percent of Chinese (Behrman, 1979).

If an Rh negative woman and an Rh positive man have a child, that child may be Rh positive (depending upon whether the father had two or only one Rh positive gene). But if at some time during this pregnancy some of the baby's Rh positive blood enters the mother's body, it will trigger the mother's immune system to begin the manufacture of antibodies against it. When the woman is pregnant again, if the next baby is Rh positive, that situation will stimulate the production of additional antibodies, which in turn affect the baby by damaging and possibly eventually destroying its own blood. Such a baby is typically born dead or in serious condition. Frequently blood must be completely exchanged shortly after birth to save a baby.

Fortunately, only about 5 percent of Rh negative mothers ever produce a baby with blood damage (Behrman, 1979). In addition, in recent years a special **gamma globulin** compound has been developed, which contains antibodies that will seek out and destroy any fetal blood that has leaked to the mother before her body can begin the manufacture of its own set of antibodies. This compound must be injected into the Rh negative mother within 72 hours after the birth of the first Rh positive child in order to be effective in protecting subsequent children. Furthermore, if she has a miscarriage or an abortion involving a first child, she must receive the injection shortly after that event to protect future children. If she receives a blood transfusion of Rh positive blood, she must receive the gamma globulin also.

If both parents are Rh positive, however, all their children will be Rh positive as well. And if the mother is Rh positive and the father is Rh negative, again there is no problem. The babies will all be Rh positive, as is the mother. The only combination for which a possible threat exists, if treatment is not administered at the proper time, is that of the Rh negative mother with the Rh positive child.

Summary

1. Many unscientific theories about the prenatal origin of the infant existed in the past. Almost all scientific work in embryology has been done during the last two centuries.

2. The human individual inherits various traits carried within the genes, which in turn are located on chromosomes. The human has 46 chromosomes, 23 of which are passed on by each parent in the egg and sperm respectively. The father determines sex by contributing either an X or a Y chromosome.

3. Dominant traits are expressed if present on either of a pair of chromosomes, recessive traits only if present on both chromosomes. Recessive traits carried on the X chromosome affect the male as if they were dominant.

4. The normal complement of 46 chromosomes arranged in 23 pairs is reduced to 23 single chromosomes during the process of meiosis in the formation of egg and sperm. The first portion of meiosis in the female takes place while she herself is still developing within her mother's womb.

5. The male continually produces millions of sperm from puberty onward. The female produces only one ripe ovum per month from some time after the beginning of menstruation at puberty until the onset of the menopause.

6. Twins can be the product of a single fertilized egg that splits (MZ twins) or of two separate eggs that are fertilized separately (DZ twins). The rate of DZ twinning is affected by race, maternal age, and an inherited predisposition to twinning, but the rate of MZ twinning is the same worldwide. Conjoined twins are MZ twins that did not separate completely during development and share some body parts. Multiple births beyond two can be MZ, DZ, or combinations of the two.

7. New techniques such as fertilization outside the mother and reimplantation within her, as well as reimplantation within an unrelated host mother, have been developed in recent years. The legal and moral ramifications of these procedures still need to be explored.

8. Genetic counseling, sonography, and amniocentesis are all helpful in determining possible genetic, chromosomal, and developmental abnormalities in the developing baby.

9. Down's Syndrome, the most frequent chromosomal abnormality, is caused by an extra no. 21 chromosome and results in mental retardation. The most important genetic disorder resulting from a dominant gene is Huntington's disease. Paired defective recessive genes can cause Tay-Sachs disease, sickle-cell anemia, and cystic fibrosis. X-linked diseases include hemophilia and muscular dystrophy.

10. Rh incompatibility can occur if an Rh negative mother carries an Rh positve child. In a pregnancy subsequent to the first, this blood factor incompatibility may lead to serious illness or death of the unborn child. The problem can be prevented by the injection of a special gamma globulin compound soon after the birth of the first child.

Participatory and Observational Exercises

1. Interview several parents about how obvious hereditary traits are passed on. For example, what eye color and hair color does each parent have? What about each child? What hair or eye colors did each of the grandparents have? If you can interview some parents of twins, find out who else in the family has had twins. Is each set of twins identical or fraternal? Are the other instances of twinning in the mother's or the father's family?

2. Talk to several older adults about the reasons for birth defects such as mental retardation. Do they offer myths or "old wives' tales" about the occurrence of such phenomena? What are they?

3. Visit a genetic counseling service, if one exists in your community. Is it a general agency or one that caters to clients showing a specific genetic disease (such as sickle-cell anemia)? What services are provided? Interview one of the counselors and find out the kinds of questions clients are asked and what diagnostic techniques, if any, are used.

DISCUSSION QUESTIONS

1. Is it morally all right to remove a fertilized ovum from one woman and implant it in the uterus of another? Why or why not? What legal problems may parents, donors, and children face in such a situation? Who is the "real" mother of the child? Why?

2. Sometimes ova are removed from a woman, fertilized in a laboratory dish, and then reimplanted in her own body to develop. If more than one such ovum is removed and fertilized outside the mother, what should be done with the others? Are they living beings that are killed if they are disposed of in the laboratory?

Prenatal Development and Environmental Effects on It

CHAPTER **3**

THE TIME FRAME OF PRENATAL DEVELOPMENT

Conceptual and Menstrual Ages

Prenatal development from conception to birth takes about 266 days, or 38 weeks. Calculating time from conception on gives the baby's **conceptual age.** Embryologists generally use conceptual age in describing the sequence of prenatal development. However, since usually it is impossible to know exactly when conception has taken place, obstetricians generally date development of the baby from the date of onset of the mother's last menstrual period. This date usually, but not always, is about two weeks before the actual time of conception. Thus this developmental dating, also referred to as **menstrual age,** begins about two weeks earlier and gives a total of 280 days, or 40 weeks, from last menstruation until birth.

These two ways of dating help account for some of the discrepancies about when events occur that you may find in looking at different books describing the sequence of prenatal development. Unless specified otherwise, conceptual age, that is, the time from conception on, will be used throughout this chapter in describing how and when various body portions develop.

Zygote, Embryo, and Fetus

It is usual to divide the time of prenatal development into three portions. The first, or period of the zygote, lasts for two weeks from fertilization until the completion of implantation in the uterus. The second, or period of the embryo, spans weeks three through eight. The third, or period of the fetus, extends from the beginning of the ninth week of development until birth.

Trimesters

From the point of view of the mother and her obstetrician, the pregnancy is also usually divided into **trimesters,** or three month periods. Thus it is common to speak of the mother's apppearance or feelings during the first, or second, or final trimester. The trimesters, however, do not relate to any particular milestones of development of the baby; they are merely convenient ways of labeling the stages of the mother's pregnancy.

DEVELOPMENT FROM CONCEPTION TO BIRTH

From Zygote to Blastocyst

TRAVEL TO THE UTERUS AND EARLY CELL DIVISION

When we last encountered the fertilized egg, it was beginning its journey down the last two-thirds of the fallopian tube. We should now begin to refer to it by the technical term for a fertilized egg, **zygote.** During this journey down the tube, the zygote is undergoing some remarkable changes. First of all, now that the nuclear material of the egg and sperm have joined, the cell membrane thickens, preventing further sperm from entering. Soon the cell begins the process of cleavage, splitting into two and later into four cells. Since the zygote does not as yet have an outside source of nutrients but is limited to the minute amount of food available in the tiny yolk contributed by the ovum, it does not grow appreciably in size even though the total number of cells increases (Annis, 1978). All the while this small cluster of cells, dividing slowly, continues its journey down to the uterus.

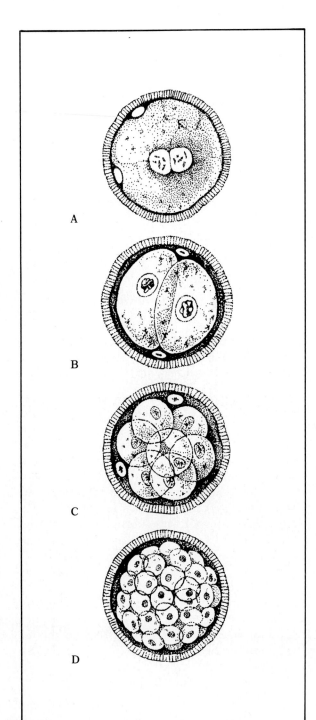

A

B

C

D

After about three days of such division, the zygote has increased to approximately 32 cells, and by the fourth day to about 90 cells. After a while, the rate of cell division becomes irregular, as some divide faster than others. Around this time, the zygote enters the uterus. It now looks like a tight cluster of cells and is therefore called a **morula,** the Latin word for "mulberry." It floats around in the upper portion of the uterus for about two days more, dividing slowly but still not increasing in overall size.

IMPLANTATION OF THE BLASTOCYST

When it has grown to about 200 cells lining a hollow cavity, the **blastocyst,** as it is now called, begins to burrow into the interior wall of the uterus. This action generally occurs between the sixth and seventh day after fertilization, or conception (Moore, 1977). The uterine lining has become soft, spongy, and rich in blood under the influence of hormones during this portion of the woman's menstrual cycle. If fertilization has not occurred or if the blastocyst does not become properly implanted, this spongy, blood-rich layer will be shed at the next menstruation. But if a blastocyst does become implanted, then first the corpus luteum, the small scar on the ovary left by the rupture of the egg, and later the **placenta,** the organ through which the baby will derive oxygen and nourishment from the mother, secrete the hor-

Early cell division. (A) The fertilized egg. The cell nuclei provided by egg and sperm lie next to each other and eventually fuse. The cell membrane thickens to prevent entry of additional sperm. (B) The cell now splits into two, within the thickened membrane. (C) By day 3 after fertilization, the zygote has increased to about 32 cells, but has not grown in total size. (D) By the fourth day, the morula has about 90 cells, and has entered the uterus.

mone **progesterone,** which suppresses further menstruation until after the baby's birth.

As the parasitic blastocyst, which now has lost the pellucid zone that had covered it, burrows into the uterine lining, it ruptures small blood vessels in that lining and begins to absorb nutrients directly from the mother's blood. The blastocyst can do so because it secretes some special enzymes that break down cells in the outer layer of the uterine lining. Now the blastocyst can begin to grow in size as well as in number of cells, and it begins the process of differentiation into different kinds of cells. A group of small interior cells, which will form the baby, become distinct from the larger ones lining the outside of the blastocyst, which will form the placenta, **umbilical cord, amnion, chorion,** and other supportive and protective structures external to the developing baby. The outer cell mass, called the **trophoblast,** divides more quickly than the inner one.

Occasionally, as the blastocyst burrows in, there may be some slight bleeding around this area, which the woman perceives as an unusually early and light menstrual period, occurring around the 24th or 25th day of the menstrual cycle or about 10 to 11 days after conception (Moore, 1977). Because of this "false period," a woman often believes she became pregnant a month after she actually did, and the baby arrives at a time that seems too early. Birth weight and maturity level at birth can serve to indicate whether a baby truly is a month early, or whether the mother was just fooled by this unusual bleeding.

The Embryo

The term **embryo,** which means "swelling" in ancient Greek, is used to refer to the developing baby from the completion of implantation two weeks after conception until the beginning of bone growth at the end of eight weeks. These six weeks encompassing the embryonic period are the most crucial of all periods of development since it is during this time that all body tissues, organs, and systems first develop and proliferate. It is, therefore, during this period that disease organisms, drugs, radiation, or other substances can cause the most harm to the developing baby.

DEVELOPMENT OF BODY PARTS

Two days after the beginning of implantation, the disk of cells that will become the baby has begun to assume the elongated form that will quickly develop into the curved embryo with distinctly forming body parts. By the time two weeks from conception have elapsed, the embryo is safely implanted in the upper portion of the uterus, generally on the back wall. Tufts called **villi** have grown out from the outer layer of the former blastocyst and have burrowed down into the lining of the uterus to obtain nourishment. A layer of maternal scar tissue that will cover the entire embryo has also begun to form.

Cephalo-Caudal Direction of Development The direction of development and growth during the embryonic period is **cephalo-caudal,** that is, from the head downward. The earliest to develop and fastest growing portions of the embryo are the head, brain, and sense organs, followed by what will be the upper regions of the trunk and arms. The last to develop are the areas farthest from the head such as the lower legs and the feet. During this early portion of development, the head takes up as much as half of total body size. By the time of birth, although it still looks disproportionately large, the head will be about a quarter of total body

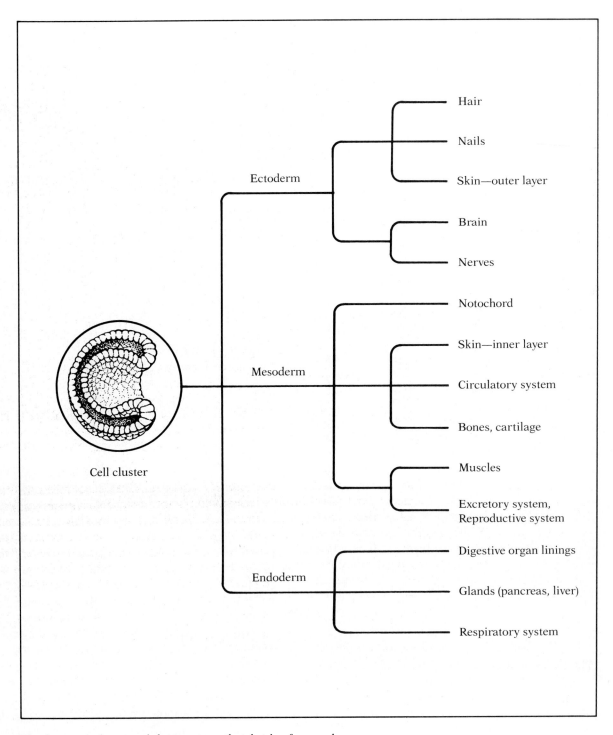

The three germ layers and the structures that develop from each.

length. In adulthood, it comprises only about 10 percent of total height.

Proximo-Distal Direction of Development Growth and development also proceed in a **proximo-distal** direction, that is, from the midline out. Thus those structures located near the midline, or axis, of the body, such as the heart or spinal cord, develop earlier than the more distant parts such as hands or feet. Both the cephalo-caudal and the proximo-distal directions of development continue on into the fetal period and even on into the time after birth. For example, not only is the newborn head quite large as compared to the legs, but the child will develop control over the muscles holding up and moving the head many months before developing the ability to stand or to walk.

Implantation through the 28th Day Once implantation is completed, a period of great growth follows, since the mother's blood now supplies the nourishment needed for growth. The three distinct germ layers out of which all organs and tissues will develop begin to differentiate and assume their distinctive locations in the developing embryo. Ectoderm and endoderm are formed first; mesoderm develops later out of ectoderm. Ectoderm, the outermost layer, will form the outer layer of skin, hair, nails, sense organs, and nervous system. The middle layer, or mesoderm, will develop muscle, bone, inner skin layers, and the reproductive, excretory, and circulatory systems. Finally, out of the innermost layer, or endoderm, will develop the respiratory and digestive systems. By the third week of development from conception all three layers are distinctly present.

The **notochord,** a rigid gelatinous rod that will later be replaced by the bony spine,

forms by the 16th day of development. By the 18th day the embryo has a heart, which begins to beat by the 22nd day (Moore, 1977). On the 18th day a primitive head also appears. On the same day, a neural plate, the beginning of brain and spinal cord, develops. By the next day it has produced neural folds, which fuse by the 20th day in the brain area and by the 22nd day in what will be the spinal cord. The eye and ear both form beginning on the 23rd day. The baby also has the beginnings of a nose. By the 26th day the embryo has buds for the eventual arms and by the next day for the legs as well. On the 28th day there are blood vessels connected to the heart, which pumps blood through them to the rest of the body. The baby is also developing the early stages of what will become kidneys and liver and a primitive gut that will become the digestive system.

Now segments, or **somites,** of mesoderm, which will eventually become muscles begin to form. **Branchial arches** that will develop into jaws, ears, and other facial features begin to form during the fourth week.

By the end of four weeks from fertilization, the embryo is about 10,000 times the size of the fertilized ovum, 4 mm long from crown to rump (Moore, 1977). Since the embryo and later the fetus develop in a curved position, and total height or length would be impossible to determine, prenatal length is generally given as crown to rump, or from the top of the head to the flexure that will become the baby's buttocks area. The developing baby is also infinitely more complex. It has changed from a flat plate to a cylindrical mass attached to an ever narrowing **yolk stalk** and in turn is attached by it to the membranes that envelop it. This rate of growth is the fastest rate that the individual will ever undergo. And it has all occurred at a time in which the mother, except for perhaps wondering why her period is at least two weeks late, may have no inkling that she is already pregnant.

Weeks Five through Eight Between weeks five and eight, the baby's face forms and begins to have some human appearance. At this time the head becomes erect and the trunk straightens out. The external portions of the eyes, ears, and nose form. After the eyelids form, they will close over the eyes during the tenth week and will not reopen till the 26th. By the seventh week, the embryo is recognizable as a human being with typically human features. The tail-like projection at the lower end of the embryo has become relatively smaller and less conspicuous as the rest of the body grows. It will disappear completely by the end of the eighth week. The embryo now has fully formed arms and legs, hands and feet, fingers and toes, though all of these are still extremely small. The arms are bent at the elbows. The baby already has a fully working circulatory system and fully formed, though not yet functioning, digestive and respiratory systems.

During the fifth week, the reproductive system and the kidneys begin to form. The reproductive system at first is made up of the beginnings, or primordia, of both male and female structures, the **Wolffian** and **Mullerian ducts** respectively. Primitive **gonads** that can become either ovaries or testes also begin to develop. The liver begins to produce blood cells. Both the liver and the heart, which at this stage of development are disproportionately large, bulge out in front of the developing baby's body. By the eighth week the kidneys are functioning, concentrating and excreting urine.

The embryo now has a complete skeleton made of cartilage. During the eighth week, external genitalia begin to form, but it is as yet impossible to tell by their appear-

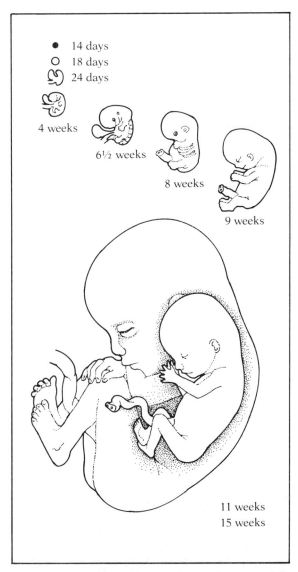

14 days
18 days
24 days

4 weeks

6½ weeks

8 weeks

9 weeks

11 weeks
15 weeks

Development of the embryo. Life-size drawings of the embryo from 14 days to 15 weeks, showing changes in size and complexity of the developing baby.

ance whether they will be male or female. The muscles and nerves begin to work together and are under control of the still rapidly growing brain. But movement at this time is still quite jerky, much like that of a

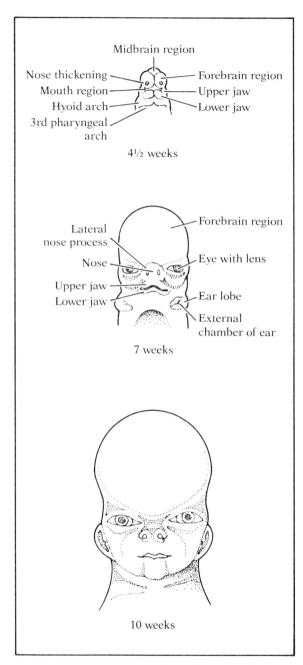

Development of the face of the embryo. This figure details how the branchial arches develop into facial features, and how the eyes and nose assume their location and shape.

string puppet or the people in early movies. Further, the whole body or a large segment of the body reacts in an undifferentiated manner to stimulation. Fine specialization of reactions will not come until much later.

THE PLACENTA

During the embryonic period, a specialized organ, the placenta, has been developed together by embryo and mother. The placenta is the unique organ of mammalian prenatal development, since it permits the baby to develop within the mother until it can fend for itself in the outside world.

Functions The placenta takes care of the exchange of nutrients and oxygen from the mother for waste products and carbon dioxide from the baby. It also manufactures a variety of substances necessary to both the baby and mother for the maintenance of the pregnancy and its eventual termination. The placenta does for the baby the work that will eventually be done by its liver, lungs, kidneys, intestines, and endocrine glands. It prevents any further ovulation or menstruation in the mother and thus maintains the pregnancy by secreting progesterone. It prepares the uterus as well as the bones, muscles, and ligaments of the mother for eventual childbirth and the breasts for **lactation,** or milk production. The placenta also allows protective antibodies from the mother to pass to the baby, thus ensuring that it will be protected against many, but not all, disease organisms both before birth and in the period shortly after birth.

Appearance The placenta itself is a disk of tissue several inches thick and perhaps seven or eight inches (about 18 cm) in diameter. It develops first from the supportive trophoblast tissue surrounding the embryo. Some of the baby's portion of the placenta also develops from the chorion, a sac within which the baby and the amnion containing amniotic fluid grow. The mother's portion of the placenta develops from one of the inner, or **decidual,** layers of the uterus. These are called decidual, which means "shedding," since they are shed, or sloughed off, after birth.

Placental and Umbilical Blood Vessels

The placenta is infused with a tremendous number of branching blood vessels. The placental system resembles a tree, with the umbilical cord and the blood vessels in it forming the trunk, and the proliferating blood vessels of the placenta itself forming the branches and crown of the tree.

The Umbilical Cord

The placenta is connected to the baby via the umbilical cord, which contains two umbilical arteries and the single umbilical vein. According to biological convention that labels as veins those vessels bringing blood toward the heart and as arteries those carrying it from the heart, the umbilical vein brings oxygenated blood to the baby from the placenta, and the umbilical arteries carry deoxygenated blood away.

While blood is flowing in the umbilical vessels, the umbilical cord turns and bends, but the fluid pressure within it prevents it from becoming closed off or unduly twisted. The cord will on occasion become looped around the baby's body and sometimes will even develop loose knots, particularly during birth. For the most part, these are not harmful (Moore, 1977). Only if the cord becomes prematurely pinched off during the birth process will problems with its circulation of blood to the baby result. The cord itself is

about a half inch in diameter. Measurements taken after birth indicate that some babies have much longer cords than others. The average length is about 55–60 cm (24 in) (Pritchard & MacDonald, 1980).

Attachment of the Placenta

The placenta attaches itself closely to the uterine wall, usually in the upper portion of the uterus. Occasionally it attaches itself too far down in the uterus, covering the cervix. Then special provisions must be made for the process of birth, as the placenta may separate too early and endanger the baby during the birth process. This condition is called **placenta previa.** After attachment, the placenta erodes away a further portion of the uterine wall and its underlying blood vessels. The ends of the placental blood vessels now lie in direct contact with the maternal blood supply, separated only by the walls of these placental capillaries. But the two blood supplies do not actually mingle, though blood from the baby may sometimes leak over to the mother, particularly during the birth process. Since the membranous walls of the pla-

The developing baby changes rapidly during the course of embryonic and early fetal development. (A) A 36-day-old embryo. The retina of the eye can be clearly seen as a dark circle. The arrow points to the developing external ear, and H denotes the early stages of the hand. (B) A 41-day-old embryo. Notice how much more developed the head, arm, and leg and external ear (again designated by E) all are. The nose, shown by N, can be seen clearly. (C) A male fetus at ten weeks. Scientists know it is male as the developing male genitals can be seen in this picture. The fingers and toes, elbows, and knees also are all quite clearly visible. (D) A male fetus at 15 weeks. In this picture the external ear, the baby's ribs, and the umbilical cord with its blood vessels can be easily discerned. Although when a fetus is this young his mother probably has not yet felt him move, he is a fully formed, though tiny, baby. (E) A 28-week-old fetus is shown sucking its thumb. The blood vessels of the scalp can be seen through the thin, transparent skin, and the lips, eyelids, external ear and nose are all well formed. If born at this time, the infant would have a chance at survival.

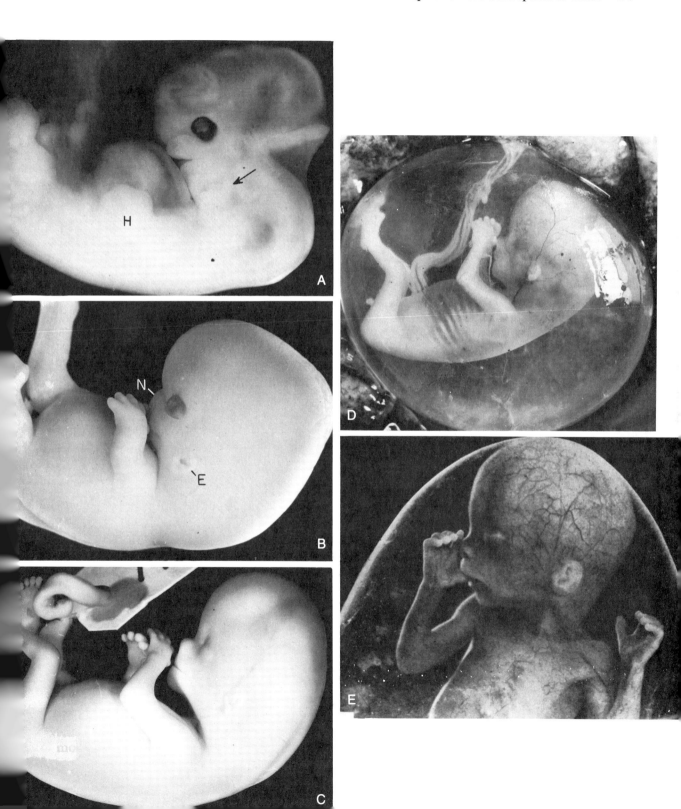

cental blood vessels remain intact, the transfer of nutrients, gases, and wastes takes place through these membranes. Contrary to some popular myths, there is no direct connection between the mother's and baby's nervous system either, though maternal mental states can affect the baby by affecting the mother's circulation of blood and her secretion of hormones.

What the Placenta Does Not Do
According to past folklore, the placenta served to screen out all harmful substances from the baby. Today scientists know that this is not true. The placenta will prevent some substances, particularly those made up of large molecules, from passing to the baby. But alcohol, nicotine, carbon monoxide, other gases or drugs, and viruses will all pass through

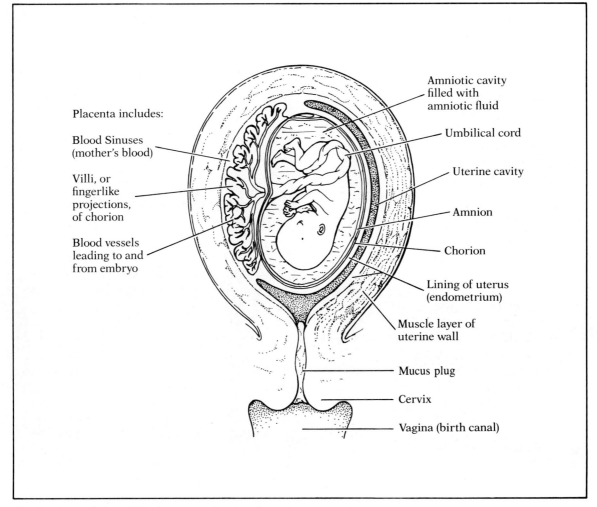

Placenta includes:

Blood Sinuses
(mother's blood)

Villi, or
fingerlike
projections,
of chorion

Blood vessels
leading to and
from embryo

Amniotic cavity
filled with
amniotic fluid

Umbilical cord

Uterine cavity

Amnion

Chorion

Lining of uterus
(endometrium)

Muscle layer of
uterine wall

Mucus plug

Cervix

Vagina (birth canal)

The developing baby within the uterus, showing the various supportive structures.

the placenta to the baby if they are present in the mother.

THE AMNION AND AMNIOTIC FLUID

The developing baby is totally enclosed within a membranous bag, the **amnion** or amniotic sac, which is a supportive and protective structure that has developed out of the trophoblast layer of the blastocyst, beginning on the eighth day after conception (Moore, 1977). Within the amnion the baby floats in a watery substance, the amniotic fluid. Early in pregnancy, most of this fluid seems to be derived from liquid portions of the mother's blood (Gadd, 1970; Seeds, 1968). Later, most of the fluid is probably produced by the baby's own kidneys in the form of urine (Shepard & Smith, 1977). The amnion, cord, and skin may also help secrete some of the fluid. From the time that the digestive and excretory systems are mature enough, the baby continually swallows the fluid and also urinates to form more of it. The fluid's watery environment serves to cushion the baby from environmental harm, such as the mother's movements or if she should fall or be struck. It also maintains the baby at a constant temperature and prevents the baby from adhering to the lining of the amnion itself.

The presence of too much or too little amniotic fluid for a particular stage of development, which can be determined by the use of sonography, can indicate problems in the baby's development. Too little fluid can be caused by a poorly formed placenta or by lack of formation or development of the baby's kidneys. Too much can be caused by malformation of the central nervous system, which prevents the baby from drinking and reabsorbing the fluid (Moore, 1977). The normal maximum is about one liter at the 34th week. After the 35th week, the amount of fluid declines. The decline probably is related to the aging of the placenta toward the end of pregnancy (Dunn, 1977). It also is useful to have less fluid from here on in, as the baby begins to take up almost all the space left within the uterus in the last few weeks before birth.

One important feature of the amniotic fluid is that it enables the baby to float in a state of almost complete weightlessness. Thus it does not have to overcome the force of gravity in order to move about. Particularly during the earlier portions of the fetal period, the baby is extremely active physically. Before this time, there is not enough effective nerve control over movement, and after the sixth to seventh month the environment in the uterus becomes too cramped for easy movement.

The Fetus

GROWTH IN THE EARLY FETAL PERIOD

At the end of eight weeks, when it is about 30 mm long, the baby begins to develop true bone (Moore, 1977). This happens first in the long bones of the upper arms and then of the upper legs. The baby is now referred to as a **fetus,** the Latin word for "offspring."

During the early fetal period, there is continued rapid bone growth, as well as much further differentiation of organ systems. At the beginning of the 9th week, the head is still almost half the body's total size. But now head growth slows down, and the rest of the body grows more. From the beginning of the ninth week to the end of the tenth, the baby doubles its crown to rump length, from 30 to 61 mm.

Nerve-muscle connections now increase and motion becomes more specific, precise,

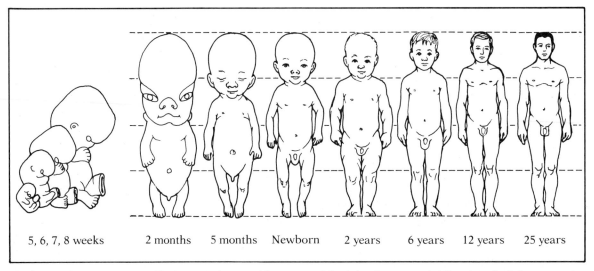

Changes in the relative size of body parts during embryonic and fetal development, childhood, and adolescence.

and fluid, in place of the jerky and total movement that took place earlier. The baby moves around within the amniotic fluid, performing somersaults and other acrobatic feats. It will be a long time after birth before the baby will be able again to move as freely as it does now, for then it will have to overcome gravity to move about.

The thumb moves into opposition with the forefinger on each of the tiny hands. This development prepares the human hand for its characteristic function, that of grasping, which is required for the use of tools.

DIFFERENTIATION OF THE REPRODUCTIVE SYSTEM

The reproductive system, which had begun to form in the fifth week, begins to differentiate late in the embryonic and early in the fetal period. In the male fetus, the primitive gonads now begin to develop into testes, which secrete a hormone, **Mullerian inhibiting substance,** that inhibits further develop-

ment of the primordial female structures (Baker, 1980). At the same time the testes also begin to secrete **testosterone,** the major **androgen,** or male hormone, which promotes the growth and development of the primordial male structures. Thus the Mullerian system (female) is prevented from developing and the Wolffian system (male) proliferates. The various ducts that conduct the sperm and **seminal fluid** will develop out of the Wolffian system.

In the female, no special hormone is needed for the development of female forms. The absence of the Mullerian inhibiting hormone dictates the withering of the Wolffian system and the proliferation of the Mullerian one (Baker, 1980). This system develops into the fallopian tubes, uterus, and a portion of the vagina. The primitive gonads also develop into ovaries, beginning around the twelfth week.

The basic sexual blueprint seems to call for the development of female forms regardless of whether the individual is genetically *XX* or *XY.* If the developing gonads are removed before the seventh week of development, the individual, regardless of genetic sex, develops into a female lacking ovaries but otherwise appearing normal. Additionally, if in the male the hormone inhibiting the Mullerian system is not secreted, the female forms will predominate. But in normal cases, as the male gonads begin to secrete the various male hormones after the seventh week, the two sexes differentiate in their development (Money & Ehrhart, 1972).

Thus the pattern seems to be that development left to itself turns out female, development with the addition of male hormones turns out male. Even after this dividing point is passed during the seventh week, however, male and female organs still look remarkably alike for several weeks. At first, male developments look merely like exaggerations of the female pattern. The **penis** develops out of the same tissues that in the female form the **clitoris** and at first is no larger. The scrotum, in which the testes will later lie, forms out of the same tissues that in the female form the **labia,** or folds surrounding the vaginal opening. Indeed a crease remains in the center of the scrotum, indicating the place at which the two sides fused. External genitalia, however, do show recognizable male or female characteristics by the tenth week (Moore, 1977).

Either the testes or ovaries are located in the lower portion of the abdomen in the younger fetus. But while in the female the ovaries remain there, in the male the testes migrate out of the abdomen and into the scrotum at 28 to 32 weeks of development. Occasionally this move does not happen until after birth and, if too long delayed, must be accomplished surgically. It is important that the testes be located in the scrotum, as the developing sperm from adolescence on will need a slightly lower temperature than body temperature to form properly.

DEVELOPMENT IN THE MIDDLE FETAL PERIOD

The 13th to 16th weeks represent a time of very rapid growth. The legs lengthen and the amount of true bone in the body increases rapidly. By the end of 16 weeks, fetal bone can be seen on x-rays of the mother's abdomen. Digestive secretions from the stomach and liver begin to be produced during this time span. The vocal cords are complete and the baby could cry, except that its mouth and lungs are filled with fluid. Tooth buds of the deciduous, or "baby," teeth form, and sockets for these teeth form in the developing jaws. Tiny nails begin to appear on fingers and toes.

After 16 weeks, the fetus has grown to 140 mm crown to rump length, or about two-fifths the length it will attain by birth. It still weighs only 200 grams (g), however, a small fraction of its eventual birth weight. Growth, particularly in length, begins to slow down in the next few weeks. Also in weeks 17 to 20, the baby begins to produce a special kind of fat called **brown fat** (Reid, 1972). This fat will be needed in the neonatal period to produce heat as it is metabolized. Brown fat forms in the areas around the kidneys and in and below the baby's neck.

Around the 16th to 18th week, an event that is extraordinary for the mother, though it marks nothing special in the baby, occurs. The mother feels the baby move. This development is called **quickening.** Often in the past, the baby was considered a living being only from the time of quickening. It is now known that the baby has already been moving about for quite some time without the mother feeling its movements because it was so tiny. After the quickening, the baby generally becomes very real to the mother. This reality increases as the baby's movements become more powerful and as it grows larger.

The baby develops a downy coat of hair called **lanugo** all over its body. A creamy, white substance, called the **vernix caseosa,** is secreted, which covers the baby's skin and probably helps to protect it from the water of the amniotic fluid. Hair on the head, as well as eyebrows and eyelashes, begins to form. Some babies, however, are born while still nearly bald.

During the 21st to 25th weeks, the fetus grows only a little in length but quite a lot in weight. In addition to the brown fat, regular fat begins to develop and is deposited in a thin layer beneath the skin. As time goes on, more of it develops, until at birth 11 percent of body weight is fat (Moore, 1977). In the 26th to 29th weeks the eyes, over which the eyelids had closed, reopen. Human babies, unlike puppies or kittens, are born with eyes open and able to see.

THE LAST FEW WEEKS BEFORE BIRTH

During the last eight weeks of **gestation,** or prenatal development, the changes in the fetus involve mainly an increase in weight as more fat is formed. Various body structures and systems prepare themselves for the birth process and for life outside the mother. No more new structures develop, however, as all have been formed previously.

The baby's lungs begin to be capable of some limited exchange of gases during the 26th to 29th weeks. If born during this time span, and if weighing at least 1,000 grams, the baby might survive. From 30 to 34 weeks, the **preterm** baby's chances of survival improve greatly, since the lungs are more mature and the baby tends to weigh more. Babies born after 35 weeks may weigh a little less than those born after the full 38 weeks but have almost the same chances of survival, as their lungs and other body systems are almost fully matured.

Occasionally a baby, though carried to term, does not gain the appropriate amount of weight because of insufficiency of the placenta, severe maternal malnutrition, or other factors. Such babies are both smaller and thinner than normal and are called **small-for-date,** or low-birth-weight babies. They share some of the same problems of preterm babies.

During the last few weeks before birth, the fetus generally sheds most of the lanugo, though remnants of it can often be seen in the newborn, particularly on the face and back. During these weeks the baby becomes increasingly inactive. It has become more and more confined and thus unable to move. The mother still feels kicking and other motion, but the time for vigorous acrobatics is past. Toward the end of the gestation period, the baby typically comes to rest head down, with the head pressing upon the lower part of the uterus.

THE ONSET OF LABOR

No one as yet knows exactly what causes labor. It is thought that the birth process may be triggered by the aging of the placenta, the baby's pressure on the uterus as it outgrows its allotted space, the formation of certain hormonelike substances called **prostoglandins** (Karim, 1972), or the secretion of **steroid** hormones by the baby's adrenal glands (Liggins, 1973). Perhaps all of these interact. In any event, the placenta begins to degenerate and ceases to produce progesterone. The steroids may also stimulate the mother to produce **oxytocin,** a hormone that stimulates contractions of the uterus and keeps them going on once begun (Moore, 1977). Approximately 38 weeks after conception, the gestational period is at an end and the baby is ready to be born. But before we consider birth, let us discuss some prenatal environmental factors that can affect the developing baby during the nine-month span from conception to birth.

ENVIRONMENTAL EFFECTS ON THE DEVELOPING INFANT

Maternal Nutrition

Since the nutritional state of the mother both before and during pregnancy is of vital importance to the baby, some consideration must be given to it. All the nourishment that the baby receives, from implantation to birth, comes solely from the mother. And for breast-fed infants, the mother remains the major source of nutrition for some time after birth as well.

Until well into the 20th century, it was believed that the developing baby was a perfect parasite, taking from the mother everything it needed for its own development. If the mother did not have enough for both the baby and herself, the baby had priority. In times of famine, the mother, not the baby, would suffer. A remnant of such beliefs is the still widely held notion that a mother will lose a tooth for each pregnancy in order to supply adequate calcium to the baby.

It is now known that, although the developing infant does receive its nourishment from the mother, it is not a perfect parasite at all. The mother's nutritional state both before and during pregnancy profoundly affects the course and quality of the baby's development. If she suffers, so does the baby. Both animal and human studies have proved that.

ANIMAL STUDIES

In animals, one can make experimental interventions that would be unethical and therefore impossible with humans. In such studies it has been found that if the mother was malnourished during pregnancy, **congenital** (in-born) malformations of the infant occurred far more frequently than for offspring of well-nourished mothers (Warkany, 1944). In addition, a review of many animal studies up to the middle 1970s suggests that nutritional deprivation affects not only the immediate baby the mother is carrying but the baby's descendants as well. Osofsky (1975) looked at the results of these various animal studies and found that they showed rather conclusively that offspring of nutritionally deprived mothers showed abnormalities of size, structure, and function of brain cells. Moreover, these abnormalities were passed on to the next several generations even without further nutritional deprivation. That is, offspring of the abnormal animals themselves were often abnormal also, although these offspring received a normal pre- and post-natal diet.

HUMAN STUDIES

The earliest human studies linking maternal nutrition with infant outcomes were those conducted by Burke (Burke, Beal, Kirkwood, & Stuart, 1943; Burke, Harding, & Stuart, 1949). Notice that in human studies one does not deliberately deprive, one just studies the effects of a deprivation that has already occurred. Burke followed up a large sample of women who gave birth at the Boston Lying-In Hospital. The nutritional status of the mother during pregnancy was classified as excellent, good, fair, poor, or very poor. After birth, infants of these mothers were classified by obstetricians and pediatricians on a four-point scale ranging from excellent to poor on factors of physical health and presence or absence of defects. In comparing the nutritional assessments of the mothers and the health data of the babies, Burke found a high relationship between babies considered in poor physical condition at birth, which included those born with abnormalities, **stillbirths** (birth of a dead fetus), and babies who died shortly after birth, and mothers whose nutritional status had earlier been rated poor or very poor.

WARTIME MALNUTRITION OF MOTHERS

Similar results have been found in two "natural laboratory" situations that occurred during World War II in which maternal food intake was suddenly and severely restricted because of wartime conditions. These are the kinds of situations to which researchers never could or would deliberately expose humans, but when they have already occurred, they provide valuable information that could not be obtained otherwise.

In Leningrad in the Soviet Union there was mass starvation when besieging German forces cut the city off from the rest of the country. People were reduced to eating boiled leather, book bindings, and an occasional rat. Antonov (1947) later reviewed the data on births during and immediately after this period, as compared to earlier and later more normal times. He found that the rates of premature births and miscarriages, as well as of infant deaths in the first few weeks or months after birth, rose markedly during this time. For example, 41.2 percent of the babies born during the siege were preterm and 5.6 percent were stillborn. Furthermore, 30 percent of the preterm and 9 percent of the full-term babies died during the neonatal period. These rates were much higher than those for Leningrad either before or after this period of starvation. Antonov also reported that a very large number of full-term babies suffered from low birth weight.

A similar situation occurred in the Netherlands. Smith (1947) studying these data found that when women who had previously been well nourished suffered from abrupt and severe food shortages, a great increase of preterm and low-birth-weight babies resulted. In addition, half of the nonpregnant women ceased menstruating during this time and for some time thereafter, demonstrating that starvation can have long-term as well as immediate effects upon women of childbearing age and their offspring.

One wartime nutritional study, however, found that some degree of food deprivation might be beneficial (Committee on Maternal Nutrition, 1970). In Great Britain during World War II there were food shortages and food rationing, but not outright starvation. British women who were pregnant thus were deprived of both variety and quantity of food but did not suffer severe deprivation either of calories or of particular nutrients. They did not, however, have much red meat or many refined carbohydrates such as sugars in their diet. It was found that during this period of food rationing, the rate of stillbirths decreased from 38 to 28 per 1,000 live births. Evidently restriction of some of the foods normally found in the maternal diet produced a beneficial result. Of course this occurred at a time when popular mythology still told pregnant women that they ought to eat for two, that is, twice as much as when not pregnant, and many women before the war had done just that. In such instances, wartime rationing may also have resulted in a more sensible and beneficial diet than they would otherwise have had.

RECOMMENDED WEIGHT GAIN

In part because of these British findings, American doctors after World War II began to limit sharply the total amount of weight gain recommended for pregnant women. Many overweight women who became pregnant were told they could gain nothing during pregnancy or were even put on reducing diets, and women of normal weight were re-

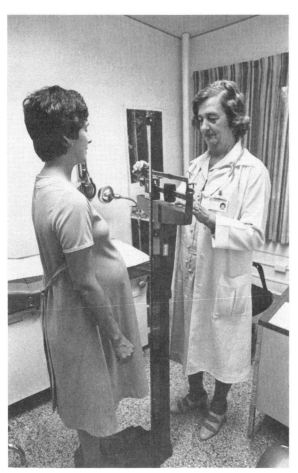

The kinds of foods a pregnant woman eats and the amount of weight she gains during pregnancy directly affect the development of her unborn child. In recent years, doctors have allowed a slightly greater weight gain to make sure that the mother is getting enough of certain vital nutrients needed by her growing baby.

stricted to weight gains of only 15 to 20 pounds overall. These restrictions often had the effect of women virtually starving themselves during pregnancy to forestall the doctor's wrath during monthly weigh-ins. While this practice of restricting weight gain may have prevented some of the complications associated with excessive weight gain during pregnancy, it may also have had a deleteri-

ous effect on many infants who did not receive sufficient amounts of the important nutrients needed for normal development.

For example, a study involving more than 10,000 mothers and their babies found that mothers who had higher weight gains during pregnancy produced babies of higher birthweight and ran a smaller risk of giving birth prematurely. Their infants also grew better and performed better on infant tests during the first year of life (Singer, Westphal, & Niswander, 1968).

Furthermore, it has been shown that mothers who try to lose weight during pregnancy by sharply reducing their intake of calories may harm their babies even if they do not reduce their intake of important nutrients (Churchill & Berendes, 1969). As maternal fat is burned up during severe dieting, the production of substances called **ketones** increases. These ketones may harm the developing fetal brain. Children whose mothers produced large amounts of ketones during pregnancy tended to score lower on intelligence tests at age four than did those whose mothers had produced only normal amounts.

At present, the recommended weight gain for pregnant women is considered to be about 24 pounds spaced out during the course of the pregnancy (American College of Obstetricians and Gynecologists, 1974). The pattern of weight gain is considered as significant as the total amount. Thus the ACOG recommended a 2-to 4-pound weight gain during the whole first trimester (or first three months) and about 0.9 pounds weekly during the course of the second and third trimesters. All except about 3 pounds of this weight gain can be directly related to the developing baby, in that various membranes and fluids, the baby itself, the mother's increased uterine size, and the additional amount of maternal blood needed during pregnancy all total about 21 pounds.

Nutritional authorities recommend for pregnant women the daily addition of about 300 calories to the usual 1800 calories recommended for nonpregnant women. The tricky aspect of this provision is that while this figure generally represents only about a 20 percent increase in calories consumed, the developing baby's needs for protein, vitamins, and minerals far exceed that 20 percent. Therefore, not only must the mother increase her total caloric intake somewhat, but she must change her diet to ensure her baby of the quality of food that it needs to develop optimally. She should eliminate or at least sharply limit those foods that provide most empty calories, such as cake, candy, and most snack foods, and increase her consumption of foods providing protein, vitamins, carbohydrates from whole grains, and minerals. If such consumption is not possible within a total weight gain of about 24 pounds, doctors today often allow a slightly larger weight gain if it will ensure adequate nutrition for the developing infant.

Furthermore, since sufficient amounts of iron and folates, two minerals necessary for the baby's development, are difficult to obtain from a normal pregnancy diet, most doctors today prescribe supplements of these two minerals for the pregnant mother.

Nutritional deprivation at a particular stage of pregnancy is most harmful to the particular structures of the baby that are then being formed. If they do not form properly, later nutritional improvements will not remedy the malformation. Thus a mother with a very erratic weight gain, even though the total is in the approved range, may be depriving her baby of some critical nutrients at some vital developmental stages (Committee on Maternal Nutrition, 1970; Experts assess nutritional disorders. . . . , 1976).

As American women at various socioeconomic levels have been studied in relation to nutritional outcomes for their unborn children, some results similar to those of the wartime deprivation studies have emerged. While not as dramatic as the results of mass starvation, they clearly show that the socioeconomic status of the mother affects her nutrition and therefore the outcomes for her baby. Jeans, Smith, and Stearns (1955) found an increased incidence of premature births as the socioeconomic status of mothers decreased. The Committee on Maternal Nutrition of the National Research Council (1970) found that the lower the maternal socioeconomic status the higher the incidence of low-birth-weight babies. Furthermore, 59 percent of women living in poverty were found to be in serious jeopardy of producing children with underdeveloped brain cells resulting from insufficient nutrition (Livingston, 1976). As family income went up, the degree of jeopardy declined.

Not just maternal nutrition during pregnancy but also the number of years and quality of nutrition before pregnancy appear to be factors. Thus the Committee on Maternal Nutrition (1970) found a relationship between infant mortality and age of mother. For each year under the age of 17 in the mother, infant mortality rates were greater. Thus, the younger such a mother, the greater were the risks for her baby. Both the limited number of years the mother has had available to prepare herself nutritionally for childbearing and the notoriously poor diet of many teen-age girls appear to be responsible for this fact.

Additionally, mothers of any age who have had a poor diet before pregnancy have an increased risk of miscarriage, stillbirth, or premature birth even if their diet improves during pregnancy (Stearns, 1958).

Tobacco

Smoking by the pregnant mother involves risks for her unborn baby, primarily because of the various poisonous substances carried in cigarette smoke. These include, but are not limited to, nicotine, carbon monoxide, and cyanide compounds.

The rate of miscarriage, particularly in the first two months, is higher for smokers than for nonsmokers (Goldstein, 1977; Naeye, 1979; Witter & King, 1980). In one study, it was found that almost twice as many spontaneous abortions occurred among smokers as among nonsmokers (Kline, Stein, Susser, & Warburton, 1977). Most of these aborted fetuses were genetically normal, indicating that environmental rather than genetic events related to smoking were the reasons for the termination of pregnancy (Witter & King, 1980).

Infants born of smokers that survive to term still run a greater risk of death during the **perinatal period,** or the time around birth (Andrews & McGarry, 1972; Bosley, Siebert, & Newcombe, 1981; Crosby, Metcoff, Costiloe, Mameesh, Samstead, Jacob, McClain, Jacobson, Reid, & Burns, 1977). Smoking mothers have a much higher incidence of **abruptio placentae,** the abrupt early separation of the placenta, which results in severe hemorrhage, precipitous labor, and a high probability of a stillborn infant (Mau, 1980). In addition, smokers are more at risk for placenta previa, in which the placenta is implanted below the baby and also separates too early in the birth process, as well as for other kinds of hemorrhage, premature rupture of the membranes, and various infections of the amniotic fluid (Witter & King, 1980).

Both illness and death are more frequent up to the age of five in children whose mothers are smokers. While this frequency may be partly the result of inhalation of smoke during early childhood (passive smoking), it may also partly result directly from prenatal exposure to substances in cigarette smoke. There appears to be some relationship between maternal smoking and sudden infant death syndrome (SIDS), which will be discussed in more detail in chapter 5 (Bergman & Wiesner, 1976; Naeye, Ladis, & Drage, 1976; Peterson, 1981).

Furthermore, babies born to mothers who smoke have lower birth weights. Infants born of smokers typically weigh 150–250 g (up to about 1/2 pound [lb]) less at birth than infants of comparable nonsmokers. Some may weigh as much as 400–500 g (or about 1 lb less than normal), although their gestational period usually is only two or three days shorter (Abel, 1980; Mau, 1980). More than twice as many babies of smokers weigh less than 2,500 g (the cutoff used for prematurity or low birth weight) than do those of nonsmokers (Johnston, 1981). Furthermore, even after birth their growth rate remains retarded as compared to the infants of nonsmokers and in direct relationship to the number of cigarettes smoked per day by their mothers during pregnancy (Naeye, 1981). This effect seems to hold regardless of the weight of the mother before pregnancy or the amount of weight she gained during it. Growth retardation in the children persists till about the age of seven. In addition to lower birth weight, newborns of smoking mothers also tend to be shorter in stature and to have lower skin-fold thicknesses and smaller heads than the babies of nonsmokers (Bosley, Siebert, & Newcombe, 1981).

The retardation of growth of fetuses of mothers who smoke does not seem to be due to decreased food intake by the mothers, although tobacco often has an appetite-suppressing effect. When smokers and nonsmokers matched for total daily dietary intake, as well as for social class and education, were compared, smokers still produced children of lower birth weight even though the total weight gained during pregnancy was the same as for nonsmokers (Haworth, Ellestad-Sayed, King, & Dilling, 1980). Indeed, this study found that many of the smokers ate much more than the nonsmokers during pregnancy and yet produced children of lower birth weight.

The lowered birth weight may in part be due to an interaction between nicotine from tobacco and various nutrients ingested by the mother. This interaction may prevent either the proper absorption of some nutrients or the production within the body of the mother of other substances needed to utilize adequately certain vitamins and nutrients. And of course, if nutrients are not properly absorbed or utilized by the mother, they cannot reach the baby.

In addition, it has been established that nicotine, carbon monoxide, cyanide compounds, and other products contained in cigarette smoke pass from the mother to the baby through the placenta. They prevent the fetus from absorbing sufficient oxygen and thus probably affect the growth of the baby in this manner as well (Bosley et al., 1981). The effect of carbon monoxide, to which the fetus cannot accommodate by increasing its capacity to carry oxygen in the blood, is particularly deleterious to proper growth (Bureau, Shapcott, Berthiaumes, Monette, Blouin, Blanchard, & Begin, 1983). Thus the baby of a heavy smoker lives in a continual state of carbon monoxide poisoning and is unable to obtain sufficient oxygen for normal cellular growth.

Even passive smoking by the mother, that is her exposure to the fumes from the smoking of others in her home or work place, exposes the fetus to the cyanide compounds in cigarette smoke and thus may be harmful to the baby (Bottoms, Kuhnert, Kuhnert, & Reese, 1982).

There is some evidence that the learning ability of the child may be affected through early childhood (Fogelman, 1980). It is only when children reach age ten that no statisti-

cally significant differences can be found between the offspring of smokers and nonsmokers on physical, intellectual, affective, and social variables (Lefkowitz, 1981).

Given these grave consequences of the practice of smoking during pregnancy, many obstetricians as well as public health agencies are now strongly urging women to stop smoking during pregnancy or at least to cut back on smoking as much as possible.

Alcohol

Consumption of alcohol by the mother also can harm the developing baby. Some of the alcohol crosses the placental barrier and is distributed throughout the baby's body and in the amniotic fluid. Since the rate of elimination of alcohol from this fluid is only half that of its elimination from the mother's blood, the amniotic fluid that the baby is constantly swallowing may serve to keep it intoxicated for a long time after the mother has overcome the effect of the alcohol on herself (Brien, Loomis, Tranmer, & McGrath, 1983).

At present no safe level of alcohol consumption during pregnancy has been established. It is known, however, that the consumption of three ounces per day poses a major risk to the unborn child; it is therefore quite probable that lesser amounts may have deleterious results as well. To give you an idea of the amount of alcohol involved, a standard drink at a bar contains about one ounce of alcohol.

Babies born to mothers who consume a large amount of alcohol over a relatively long period of time during pregnancy suffer from a typical cluster of abnormalities that has been labeled **fetal alcohol syndrome,** or FAS (Jones & Smith, 1973). These children may have damage to the central nervous system that results in increased irritability, mental coholic behavior during pregnancy (Hanson, Jones, & Smith, 1976).

Furthermore, the problems of maldevelopment in FAS babies seem to persist beyond the neonatal stage in those that survive. They exhibit markedly retarded development and continue to lag behind their normal peers in weight and height gain, even if removed from their alcoholic mothers and placed in good foster homes (Hanson et al., 1976).

The amount of alcohol in the baby's blood at the time it is born also seems to have a significant effect upon its later development (Sisenwein, Tejani, Boxer, & Di-Giuseppe, 1983). In a follow-up of a group of the children of mothers who were given alcohol in an attempt to arrest preterm labor, it was found that those for whose mothers the therapy failed and who were born within 15 hours of the termination of the therapy still showed developmental and personality abnormalities while four to seven years old. These abnormalities included hyperactivity and lowered performance IQ. Children whose mothers terminated the therapy many hours before birth, and who therefore were born with no alcohol in their blood, were normal in spite of the earlier use of alcohol in therapy. Thus these researchers concluded that binge drinking, if confined to a single or a small number of isolated episodes, would not cause harm to the fetus if done during the later stages of pregnancy unless it occurred just before birth. However, the safest thing to do appears to be to use little or no alcohol at any time during pregnancy.

Narcotics

Babies of mothers addicted to heroin share some of the same problems with babies whose mothers smoke. They also are very likely to be of low birth weight, with more

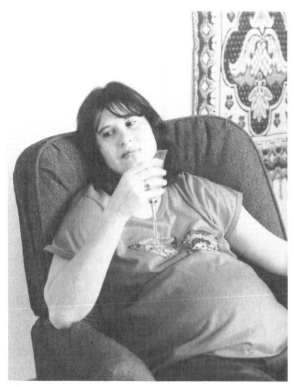

The pregnant woman who consumes alcoholic beverages puts her unborn child at risk. It is not known at present if a safe level of alcohol consumption exists and if so what that might be. Therefore drinking of wine, beer, or liquor during pregnancy is best avoided altogether.

retardation, and problems with physical coordination. They have lower birth weights than normal and are often stunted in height. Many have heart and circulatory defects. Infants with FAS may also show facial abnormalities such as fishlike upper lips, peculiarly shaped eyes, and maldevelopment of the jaws. Many are **microcephalic,** that is, they lack a forebrain or have a very small one and have a correspondingly very small head. These babies are profoundly retarded. The percentage of babies of mothers using alcohol showing such abnormalities is directly related to the amount of alcohol they consumed, as well as to the duration of the al-than half having birth weights under 2,500 g (Householder, Hatcher, Burns, & Chasnoff, 1982). This low birth weight appears unrelated to either maternal nutrition or the amount of prenatal care received. Heroin-addicted mothers may have a much shorter labor than normal. This circumstance subjects the infant to a too rapid passage through the birth canal, which can cause some fetal distress and can also contribute to the fairly high incidence of such babies that are born in a **breech** position, that is, with some body part other than the head presenting.

Of babies born to heroin-addicted mothers, 70 to 90 percent undergo some degree of withdrawal symptoms after birth (Householder et al., 1982). These babies appear normal at birth, but within 24 to 72 hours they develop restlessness, inability to sleep, incessant and shrill crying, tremors or convulsions, vomiting, diarrhea, and extreme hunger but inability to feed well (Kron, Kaplan, Finnegan, Litt, & Phoenix, 1975). Although these symptoms become less severe over time, they may continue for the first two to four months of the infant's life. Because of their restlessness and poor feeding, these infants lag in postnatal weight and height gain. It is usually only in the four-to-six-month period that the general irritability lessens and the babies begin to grow and develop more normally.

The symptoms of irritability not only pose a danger to the physical well-being of the baby but also tend to make the baby unreceptive to visual stimulation and to early attempts by the mother or other adults to establish a relationship. Infants of narcotics-addicted mothers spend less time in a **quiet alert state,** in which they are responsive to visual and tactile stimulation, than do normal infants. Furthermore, because of the irritability, sleeplessness, and crying of the child, mothers and other caregivers tend to

pay it more attention more frequently. Their efforts to soothe such an infant, however, often serve only to heighten these behaviors. And as a result the caregiving adults often report frustration and inability to deal with the infant in a constructive way (Householder et al., 1982).

If the addicted mother goes off the drugs earlier during the course of the pregnancy, the baby after birth is not affected by withdrawal symptoms, although it probably underwent them while *in utero* at the time of the mother's withdrawal. The babies of former addicts, however, often are still more at risk than those of other mothers, since they also are more likely to be of lower birth weight or to be born prematurely (Pelosi, Frattarola, Apuzzio, Langer, Hung, Oleske, Bai, & Harrigan, 1975). Babies of mothers on methadone show similar symptoms and behavioral patterns to those whose mothers are on heroin, but the symptoms are considerably less severe (Householder et al., 1982).

Nonnarcotic Drugs

It is possible that many milder drugs than narcotics can also undesirably affect the developing baby or the events surrounding its birth. For example, in 1983 a group of obstetricians reported two cases of premature separation of the placenta, hemorrhage, and sudden early onset of labor as the result of cocaine use (Acker, Sachs, Tracey, & Wise, 1983). Both women showed these symptoms soon after ingesting cocaine, one by injection and the other by intranasal administration, or "snorting." The first of these delivered a dead infant, and the other delivered a low-birth-weight baby with few vital signs through an emergency cesarean section. Now that obstetricians have been alerted to the possible serious consequences of cocaine use, undoubtedly others will be able to document

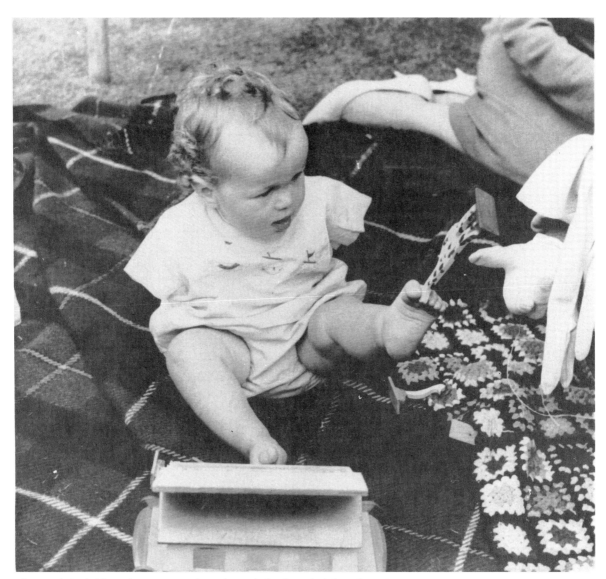

This English child was born to a mother who took the drug thalidomide early in pregnancy. Since he was born without arms, he has learned to use his feet to pick up toys and play with them.

similar cases leading to the implication of cocaine.

The classic case of severe developmental damage from a drug that was at first considered safe and harmless occurred from 1957 to 1962 with **thalidomide.** This drug was developed and widely used, particularly in Europe, as a mild remedy for sleeplessness and pain. Since it was considered safe for pregnant women, it was also used to alleviate the mild nausea often associated with early stages of pregnancy. Several months after it came on the market, doctors began to notice a sudden and mysterious increase of malformed limbs, which hitherto had been very rare, in newborns. These conditions included the absence of arms or legs or both, with often a rudimentary appendage consisting of a few fingers or toes attached directly to the torso. Occasionally a portion of a limb, foreshortened and stunted, was present. Some babies had normal arms but no legs; other had legs but not arms; and some had neither (Lenz & Knapp, 1962).

It was some time after the sudden appearance of numbers of these unfortunate children before the cause-effect relationship between thalidomide ingestion by the mother and the malformation of the children was deduced. Manufacturers of the drug were forced to withdraw it from the market in December 1961.

Luckily for Americans, thalidomide had not yet been cleared for sale in the United States by the Food and Drug Administration. This country therefore was spared the large numbers of affected babies, as only a few babies, whose mothers had obtained the drug while overseas or received it from abroad, were born with the condition. But there were many cases in Britain, Germany, France, and Japan, as well as some in Canada. About 5,000 individuals were affected overall (Pritchard & MacDonald, 1980). Luckily, most of the thalidomide children were born with normal intelligence (Taussig, 1962) and thus have learned to adapt to their disability and have grown to productive adulthood. Many of the countries in which large numbers of these children were born instituted rehabilitation programs to train the children to take care of themselves and developed ingenious **prosthetic devices** (artificial replacement of limbs), special clothing, and tools to help them.

The thalidomide incident showed quite clearly that the portion of the baby that is most vulnerable to damage from chemicals or disease is the portion that is then developing most rapidly. Thus only babies whose mothers took thalidomide during that portion of early pregnancy, days 26 to 50, in which the limbs are formed were affected (Pritchard & MacDonald, 1980). If the mothers took the drug only earlier or later in pregnancy, the children were normal.

This dramatic evidence of the effect of a drug that had been considered harmless on the development of a baby has made medical and pharmaceutical circles more careful about the possible effects of other agents. For one thing, new drugs are now tested on pregnant animals, to make sure that effects that can be found only in unborn babies are not again overlooked. Further, pregnant women are now warned to stay off all drugs, prescription or patent, unless a clear medical need exists, and then to take only what the doctor specifically allows.

Even drugs considered as benign as aspirin are now suspected of possibly causing some malformations or malfunctions if taken in very large doses or at particular stages of pregnancy. For example, it was reported in 1982 that if mothers took aspirin within five days of their child's birth, they subjected themselves and especially their babies to a high risk of abnormality in blood-clotting ability (Stuart, Gross, Elrad, & Graeber, 1982). Thus infants of such mothers need to be watched carefully for signs of possible internal bleeding. If the mother took aspirin after the delivery, the baby was, of course, unaffected, but the mother's risk of blood-clotting abnormality still was increased.

One problem with both prescription and nonprescription drugs is that dosages are usually calculated on the basis of body size. This practice works well for the mother but may result in an overdose for the much smaller body of the baby when the drugs cross the placenta.

No clear causal relationship has been shown for any drug other than thalidomide as far as developmental malformations are concerned. Both LSD and marijuana are suspect, however, as are many patent medicines. In addition, caffeine, which is found in coffee, tea, chocolate, and many soft drinks, has been shown to cause malformations in the prenatal development of laboratory rats (*Caffeine and Pregnancy*, 1980). Although its effect on humans is not yet known, the Food and Drug Administration in 1980 advised obstetricians to counsel pregnant women to avoid or limit their consumption of beverages and foods containing caffeine.

A number of physical and mental abnormalities of development still seem to occur for no explainable reason. Quite possibly some of these may be the effects of drugs sometimes taken by pregnant women that we do not yet know enough about, or they may be the effects of substances in foods or beverages such as caffeine that had been considered safe in the past.

For all these reasons, it is wise for pregnant women to refrain from taking any medication that they have not specifically been told to take during pregnancy. Unfortunately, much of the early critical development of the baby takes place before a woman even knows that she is pregnant. Therefore, caution in using drugs is especially advised for women of child-bearing age who could become pregnant.

Radiation

Occasionally a pregnant woman is exposed to high levels of radiation, generally because she needs radiation therapy for a rapidly growing cancer whose treatment cannot be postponed. The other widespread exposure of pregnant women to excessive radiation occurred when the atomic bombs were exploded at Hiroshima and Nagasaki in Japan during World War II. Indeed, most knowledge of the effects of large amounts of radiation on the developing baby comes from studies that followed up these women and their offspring. The effects of radiation on developing germ cells (the egg and sperm) have already been mentioned. But here we are concerned with the effects upon the baby when exposed to radiation during its development after fertilization.

Those pregnant women that were far enough away from the blast sites to survive but close enough to be exposed to massive amounts of radiation were found to have a much higher than normal number of malformed infants if they were 18 weeks pregnant or less at the time of their exposure (Miller, 1979). The babies' malformations included small heads and mental retardation. If the women had been more than 18 weeks pregnant, the babies did not show these malformations. This finding again demonstrates the heightened vulnerability of those body parts that are in the process of development. Even the children who showed no obvious malformations, however, did show a higher incidence of chromosomal abnormalities than did children not exposed. This fact has led scientists to suspect that genetic **mutations** (changes) may have occurred, whose results may not be apparent for several generations. Children conceived after the bombs were dropped did not show these chromosomal abnormalities (Miller, 1979). The babies exposed to the atomic bomb *in utero* did not seem to have a higher rate of cancers under the age of ten than did children not so exposed. Those already born at the time the bomb was dropped, however, showed a higher rate of leukemia, a cancer of the blood, than did children not exposed to radiation.

In general, the low levels of radiation to which one is exposed in dental x-rays and similar procedures are not enough to cause such damage. A lead apron covering the abdomen should be worn by the mother if dental x-rays must be made. X-rays that are unnecessary or could be postponed until after the pregnancy should not be made, particularly if they involve the mother's abdomen.

Conditions in the Mother

When a pregnant woman contracts a disease, the disease organism can cross the placental barrier and infect the baby, particularly if it is a very small organism such as a virus. For example, rare instances have been reported of babies born with chicken pox or measles, because the mother had contracted the disease late in pregnancy. Some diseases in the mother can, if spread to the baby, produce malformations or handicapping conditions or threaten the survival of the baby.

SYPHILIS

Babies of mothers with the venereal disease of **syphilis** can become infected during gestation. If the baby becomes infected early during the pregnancy, miscarriage may result. Often babies of mothers with syphilis do not contract the disease until about the fourth or fifth month. This means that if the disease is found and treated in the mother early in pregnancy, the baby may not be affected by it. But babies of untreated mothers run a very high risk. About one-quarter of them are stillborn. In addition, the babies that are born alive, although they may not show symptoms of the disease at birth, soon begin to show signs of mental retardation, **hydrocephaly** (excess spinal fluid pressing on the brain), deafness, and wasting of body tissues (Steigman, 1979).

RUBELLA

A disease organism that shows little effect on the mother or on others that may contract the disease but that is especially dangerous for a developing baby is the virus causing **rubella,** or German measles. This mild disease, which generally causes minimal discomfort in children or adults, can cause blindness, deafness, heart defects, and possibly mental retardation in a baby who contracts it early in the process of development. The relationship between the mother having the disease in early pregnancy and the subsequent defects of her baby was first deduced by an Australian doctor after a rubella epidemic in that country during World War II (Gregg, 1942). Since then, a vaccine that prevents rubella has been perfected and is now widely used. This vaccine is administered primarily to preschool children, since they are the most usual hosts of the disease and thus are most likely to spread it to pregnant women. Adult women who have not had rubella in childhood and who show no immunity toward the disease can also be given the vaccine, provided they are not then pregnant and will not become pregnant in the next few months. For even the attenuated or weakened virus used in the vaccine could harm a developing baby.

As was true for drugs and radiation, the rubella virus seems to affect most severely those portions of the baby that are developing at the time of infection. Thus it is most dangerous in the very early stages of pregnancy, often before a woman is aware that she is pregnant. It can cause some damage, however, up to the 12th week of development. Therefore, preventive public health methods, especially vaccination of young children, are vital to protect the unborn. Affected children that are born require much specialized medical care and many years of special education, all of which are far more costly than preventive measures. In addition, the human cost of having a handicapped child as the aftermath of prenatal rubella is great.

TOXOPLASMOSIS

A mother who comes in contact with an infected cat or with soil contaminated by cat feces may contract **toxoplasmosis.** This disease can also be contracted by eating poorly cooked meat that contains the microorganism causing it. While the disease is usually not serious for the mother, it can cause brain and eye damage in the developing baby (White & Sever, 1967). As a precaution, pregnant women should make sure pet cats are disease-free, stay away from strange cats as much as possible, and eat only those meats that are well-cooked.

HERPES AND CYTOMEGALOVIRUS

Two other venereal diseases—Type II herpes and cytomegalovirus—are much less serious to the adult than syphilis but can have devastating results in the baby. Both are present in epidemic proportions in modern America, especially among young adults.

Type II herpes is a genital variation of the virus that causes cold sores. It is spread by sexual contact during active stages of the disease and has no known cure. In the adult it is unpleasant physically and may have serious psychological consequences. But for the baby it is catastrophic.

Herpes rarely spreads to the baby via the placenta. In almost all instances the baby is infected during the birth process by passing through the birth canal of a mother who has an active case of the disease. There is a 60 percent mortality rate among babies born vaginally of mothers with an active infection (Visintine, Nahmias, & Tosey, 1978). Half of the babies who survive develop disorders of the eyes or central nervous system, or both,

which are remarkably unresponsive to treatment.

Thus the only feasible way to prevent herpes from affecting the baby of a mother with an active case is to deliver the baby by cesarean section. A pregnant woman who has genital herpes should have frequent tests throughout pregnancy to determine whether an active stage of the disease is recurring or whether a vaginal delivery can safely be attempted because her case is at that time inactive (Visintine et al., 1978).

Cytomegalovirus is another form of herpes. The baby may be infected via the placenta or during the birth process if the mother has an active case of the disease. In addition, the baby may be infected through the mother's milk after birth if the mother is breast feeding while the disease is in the active stage (Pritchard & MacDonald, 1980). The virus can cause mental retardation, blindness, **microcephaly** (underdevelopment of the brain), or **hydrocephaly** (excessive spinal fluid putting pressure on the brain) in the baby.

DIABETES

Diabetes, a disease resulting from a deficiency of the hormone insulin, can have adverse effects upon the baby also when it occurs in the mother. Diabetic mothers are more likely than others to have a large baby. This condition, known as **macrosomia,** results from the fact that the baby is exposed to extra amounts of blood sugar because of the mother's lack of insulin (White, 1965). At the same time, the baby's body is stimulated to produce extra insulin to make up for that lacking from the mother. The insulin causes the baby's body to convert the extra blood sugars to fats and to store them as layers of fat in the body. Macrosomia may result in difficult labor and, because of the disproportion of size between the baby and the mother's pelvis, can lead to the need for delivery by cesarean section. Although such babies are usually larger than normal, many are born several weeks before term and may have some of the same respiratory difficulties that other preterm babies often develop. Because most babies of diabetic mothers produce too much insulin in reaction to the mother's production of too little, they tend to develop **hypoglycemia,** or low blood sugar, when after their birth they are no longer affected by the mother's high blood-sugar level. This condition also puts them at risk in the neonatal period. In severe cases, convulsions and coma can result (Niswander, 1981).

In addition, diabetic mothers have a higher incidence of preeclampsia and **eclampsia** (a cluster of symptoms including elevated blood pressure and fluid retention), which also make them and their babies more at risk in delivery. Diabetic mothers and their babies are more susceptible than normal ones to infection and are likely to suffer from more severe symptoms from infections. For all these reasons, a diabetic woman should carefully consider the risks of pregnancy with expert medical counsel before becoming pregnant. If she does decide on having a baby she needs to have her pregnancy carefully supervised throughout its entire span.

Summary

1. During the two weeks after conception, the zygote travels down the fallopian tube into the uterus and becomes implanted in the uterine wall. With the rupture of small blood vessels in the uterine lining, it is able to absorb food from the mother's bloodstream and thus can begin to grow and to proliferate various cell layers that will become the baby and surrounding structures.

2. During weeks two to eight the embryo begins to develop all the body tissues, organs, and systems of which the body is composed. The direction of development proceeds cephalo-caudally and proximo-distally.

3. The placenta and umbilical cord, which serve to exchange nutrients and waste products between mother and baby, develop during the embryonic period. The placenta also secretes a variety of hormones and enzymes utilized by mother and baby and screens out some but not all harmful substances from reaching the baby.

4. The fetal period, from the ninth week until birth, is marked by the great physical growth of the developing infant. True bone begins to form, and muscles increase in size and in their connection to nerve endings. The male and female reproductive systems differentiate early in the fetal period, and soon the sex of the baby is evident.

5. The nutritional state of the mother before pregnancy as well as her nutrition throughout it are important for the developing child. A total weight gain of about 24 pounds is recommended for pregnant women at the present time. Gaining too much is better than too little, since maternal undernutrition can lead to the birth of a low-birthweight baby that runs a higher risk of complications.

6. Maternal smoking puts the baby at grave risk for miscarriage or low birth weight. Infants born of smokers have more problems during and after birth, and some of the problems may persist for a number of years after birth.

7. Excessive alcohol consumption by the mother can lead to fetal alcohol syndrome, a cluster of mental and physical abnormalities in the developing baby.

8. Mothers addicted to heroin are at risk to produce a baby of low birth weight. In addition, their babies often suffer from narcotics withdrawal, which can be both physiologically and psychologically dangerous to the child's early development.

9. Substances such as caffeine may interfere with the normal development of the baby. Thalidomide, which was used by some mothers in the 1950s and early 1960s, caused definite developmental defects in babies. Cocaine may cause hemorrhage and the baby's premature birth. Even aspirin, if taken in the last few days before birth, can cause problems with blood clotting in baby and mother. Radiation from x-rays and atomic explosions can also adversely affect the developing baby.

10. Diseases in the mother that have a deleterious effect upon the developing baby or cause it to contract the disease during birth include rubella, syphilis, toxoplasmosis, herpes, and cytomegalovirus. Diabetes in the mother causes the baby to become overly large and may result in high blood pressure and fluid retention in the mother as well as problems relating to the birth process.

Participatory and Observational Exercises

1. Collect a series of myths, beliefs, or "old wives tales" concerning pregnancy from various informants (friends, parents, friends of parents, adults interviewed, etc.). For example, what are some myths regarding sex determination of the child, the best time to become pregnant, problems encountered during pregnancy, remedies for some of the problems, malformations, or odd features of the child? Does any of these myths have any support through scientific evidence?

2. Interview two (or more) pregnant women who are in the last trimester of pregnancy. From each, find out the following information:

How and when did she know she was pregnant? What symptoms did she have? When did she begin to receive medical attention for the pregnancy? When did she feel the baby move? How did this affect her perception of the reality of the baby? How is she preparing for the birth? What kind of birth in what location is she choosing (e.g., medicated, Lamaze, Leboyer, husband present, in hospital, at home, in birthing center, delivery by physician, delivery by midwife, etc.)? Where did she obtain information about pregnancy and labor?

3. Interview a pregnant woman who has been a smoker. Has she stopped smoking? If so, why did she do so? What information about the effects of smoking did she obtain, and from where? If she is still smoking, does she plan to quit further along in pregnancy? Why or why not? Does she perceive any connection between her smoking and the status of her baby?

DISCUSSION QUESTIONS

1. Should the government require labeling of liquor bottles with information about the dangers of liquor consumption for the unborn baby of a pregnant woman? Why or why not? What about cigarette packages—should they carry such an additional warning?

2. Discuss various beliefs about prenatal development that you and your classmates have heard about. How do you think each started? Why do people cling to such myths, many of which have no substantiation in scientific fact?

Birth and the
Neonatal Period

CHAPTER 4

THE TRANSITION TO PARENTHOOD

The decision whether or not to have a child is a profound and difficult one. Indeed, some couples, about 5 percent of the population (Bane, 1976), have always opted for voluntary childlessness, and their number does not appear to be decreasing. But for the vast majority of American couples, the major decision becomes when to have a child and how many children to have. The trend today seems to be toward smaller families than in the past. Many couples want only one child, or perhaps two. Also, with later marriage ages, at least for some groups, and with the increasing employment of women, many families are postponing the time at which they have a first child, often until the woman is in her mid-thirties.

Regardless of the time at which the transition to parenthood occurs, it spells profound changes for both partners. A couple will now become a threesome. For a long time the partners will have the responsibility for the care and nurturance of a child that at first is almost totally helpless. The child represents a great investment of time, effort, emotion, and certainly money. No longer will they be able to plan spur-of-the-moment outings; they will need always to provide for the care of the child. Just when the total cost of the family will increase, the family's income may decline substantially, since many employed women quit their jobs or reduce their workload to half-time when they have their first child.

Becoming a mother is a major transition for many women. During pregnancy a woman may worry about her health and that of her baby, as well as about her appearance. She may be unsure of her capacities to mother and worried about the changes the baby may cause in the relationship with her husband. Her appearance and sexual re-adjustment after giving birth may also be sources of concern. She may miss the stimulation of an outside job and the company of her colleagues.

In American culture until recently, people have given little thought to the role of the father beyond the act of conception. That is not necessarily true in other cultures. For example, in some the father goes through the process of **couvade,** in which he develops symptoms of labor at the same time that his wife does. Modern American men are increasingly asking for a larger participatory role in the preparation for birth, the birth process itself, and the care of their child after birth.

Stresses upon the father include worries about his parental abilities, his ability to support his growing family, and the health of his wife and developing child. He too may be concerned about changes in his partner's appearance and mutual sexual readjustment after the birth, as well as about the influence of the new stranger upon the dyadic relationship between himself and his wife.

Because the period of pregnancy and childbirth is not an easy one for the prospective parents, they need help and support from their families, friends, and health-care professionals. In addition, they must be able to communicate with each other and share their fears and concerns. It is helpful if they can obtain accurate information about the physical and psychological changes that occur during pregnancy and about the process of birth. Childbirth education classes conducted at many hospitals and doctors' offices and by private individuals include such information in their teaching. Fathers are encouraged to attend. In addition, health-care professionals must be interested and willing to answer questions and provide information if a couple request it at any stage of pregnancy or birth.

After the baby is brought home, the parents face additional aspects of this transition. The newborn demands vast amounts of round-the-clock attention. One complaint of many new mothers is the unbelievable fatigue they feel in the first few weeks, when the baby's demands are greatest and they are just recuperating from the birth process. Many fathers are eager to share in caring for their infants, and their participation is especially important at this early time.

In recognition of this need, some countries, such as Sweden, allow a form of paternity leave for men after the birth of a child. This "child leave" system, instituted in Sweden in 1974, allows working parents to take a total of nine months' leave, which they can split between them in any way they wish, while receiving 90 percent of their pay (Levitan & Belous, 1981). Thus, for example, the mother can take 9 months and the father nothing, she can take 5 months and he 4, they can each take 4 1/2 months and so on. In addition, Swedish parents can work a six-hour (rather than the usual eight-hour) day, with proportionally lower pay but the same job security as full-time workers, until their child reaches the age of eight (Bohen & Viveros-Long, 1981).

While some enlightened companies in the United States have also begun to grant paternity leaves, the practice has not really caught on in this country so far. Many men achieve the same end by scheduling vacation leaves for the time the baby is expected. Among younger, better educated parents in particular, the trend today is toward a sharing of the preparation for birth, the birth itself, and the parenting of the child. Mothers still do the larger share of child-care tasks in most families, but many fathers are willing and eager to participte much more than their fathers ever did. In part this trend follows from the increased employment of women, less rigidity in expectations of behaviors appropriate to the two sexes, and the increased mobility of the population, which makes it less likely that other relatives are there to help with the baby. Still, the advent of the child marks a transition in the lives of both parents that is important, often difficult, and, it is hoped, gratifying. It will change them for the rest of their lives.

SOCIETAL ATTITUDES TOWARD CHILDBIRTH

Childbirth in Other Cultures

From earliest times, childbirth in most cultures has been surrounded by a degree of awe, mystery, and ritual. The capacity to nurture and bring forth a fully formed infant has inspired fear, respect, and occasionally even worship. The fertility of women has been viewed as parallel to the fertility of the fields; therefore, many primitive cultures worshiped goddesses of fertility, who were usually portrayed as extremely pregnant women.

Traditionally, in most cultures, males have been excluded from childbirth. A recent cross-cultural study of birthing practices found that only 2 of 186 nonindustrialized cultures allowed men actively to participate in the birthing process; only 27 percent allowed the father to be present at birth (Lozoff, 1982). Close female friends and relatives, including women that specialize in the delivery of infants, congregate around the woman in labor to keep her company and assist with the birth and early care of the infant. Occasionally the woman who gives birth is kept away from her husband and all other men for a period of days, weeks, or months after the event and spends her time in a separate hut in a

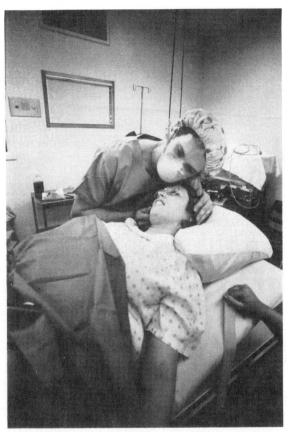

It is now quite customary in many hospitals for the expectant father to be present at his child's birth. After spending the earlier stages of labor together, this couple is now prepared to go to the delivery room together also. The father has been suitably dressed in mask, cap, and scrub suit so that he can watch his daughter or son being born.

and other paraphernalia were used only during this time. Female relatives and friends would gather, and the baby would be delivered by a midwife, a woman trained to deliver babies and care for them and their mothers. Until the late 18th century, childbirth in America was considered a social rather than a medical event and was attended exclusively by females (Dye, 1980; Wertz & Wertz, 1977). Then a transition took place. Some births were still managed by midwives in the presence of female friends and family, but increasingly, doctors came to be involved. Therefore, childbirth came more and more to be viewed as a medical event with female friends and relatives excluded from it (Dye, 1980).

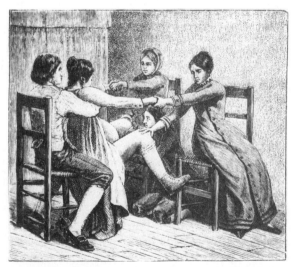

Childbirth in 19th-century America. In the past, births were generally managed entirely by women, such as the midwife and her two assistants in this picture. Male doctors were used only if forceps had to be used or if the mother was given anesthesia. This picture is unusual in that a man, probably the laboring woman's husband, is present at a woman-attended birth. Notice that the birthing woman is sitting up, a position later abandoned for the convenience of doctors, but increasingly used again today to facilitate expulsion of the baby.

separate portion of the village or at a distance from it (Lozoff, 1982).

Childbirth in America in the Past

In early America, people usually followed customs not too different from those just described. Until well into the 19th century, many larger houses had a special bedroom used only for childbirth. Special bed linens

The Shift to Doctors and Hospitals

Childbirth in Europe, as in America, had traditionally been exclusively the province of women, but in the 17th century doctors began to enter the field. Their entrance coincided with the invention of **forceps,** a kind of tongs, which are placed around the baby's head during the birth process and used to pull the baby out if normal means of delivery fail. The two British physicians who invented forceps became enormously sought after for problem deliveries. Other doctors became interested as well. Since a mechanical device was involved, and since such devices were considered the more natural province of men, it now seemed appropriate for men to participate in some childbirth situations.

Another reason for increased involvement of men was the development of **anesthetics** (drugs that produce loss of sensation) and their application in childbirth. During the 19th century Queen Victoria of England popularized anesthetics in childbirth when she used chloroform while her own children were being delivered. Only physicians were trained to use anesthetics, however; thus, if a mother wished such aid, she had to call on a physician rather than a midwife. These European developments spread to America in the mid-to-late 19th century.

Until around the turn of the 20th century, even with the increased use of physicians in childbirth, almost all babies were born at home. But in the period before World War I, well-to-do women, particularly those that wished to use anesthetics, began to have their babies in hospitals. Eventually, most women, except those living in very isolated areas, followed suit. In the period from the 1920s to the 1970s, increasing numbers of babies born in the United States were delivered in hospitals. For example, 55.8 percent of all deliveries in the United States in 1940 were done in hospitals or clinics; by 1970 the figure had risen to 99.4 percent (Landis, 1982). In most of Europe, however, home deliveries and those in nonhome settings other than hospitals such as birthing centers never lost their popularity.

Along with the change in America to hospital delivery and in part resulting from it, other developments affected childbirth. On the one hand, scientific medicine as practiced in modern hospitals has increased the chances for survival and a normal outcome for at-risk mothers and babies. The use of anesthetics, fetal monitors, forceps, cesarean section, infusion of blood and oxygen in emergency situations, and well-equipped, neonatal high-risk nurseries all have contributed to making childbirth a far safer experience for those experiencing complications.

On the other hand, moving childbirth to hospitals mandated the use of physicians rather than midwives, since most hospitals in most states allow only physicians to use their facilities. Because almost all family practitioners and obstetricians, the doctors most likely to be delivering babies, were males, assisting at childbirth became almost exclusively restricted to men. Many women have in recent years come to question how much about childbirth, particularly its psychological aspects, can be understood and appreciated by someone who can never undergo it.

Another far-reaching result of hospital delivery was that since hospitals were the place one went if ill, childbirth came to be regarded as a form of illness rather than as a normal process. Doctors, who spend most of their training learning about illnesses and abnormalities, also came to regard pregnancy and childbirth as types of abnormal conditions, in which the woman was treated as if she were ill. Thus during the 50-year-period from about 1920 to 1970, women were often sedated heavily as soon as they entered the hospital, were often unconscious when their babies were born, and were kept in bed (particularly in the early days) for long time periods (Dye, 1980; Leavitt, 1980). Furthermore, doctors came to regard themselves as, and indeed became, the ones who delivered the child, rather than just assisting the laboring woman and her baby in what was essentially a natural process.

Current Trends

ASSISTANCE BY WOMEN AGAIN

Since the early 1970s, there have been some changes of attitude and practice regarding childbirth. More women are again involved in assisting at childbirth. Some are among the increasing number of women physicians. Many are midwives, who today are registered nurses who have earned a Master's degree in the specialty of midwifery. They are thus highly trained professionals able to assist at normal deliveries, which comprise the vast majority. There are about 2,500 trained nurse-midwives in the United States today (Landis, 1982). Many states allow midwives to assist at normal hospital deliveries if an obstetrician is present in the hospital to take over should a crisis develop. Midwives also are allowed to do independent home deliveries in some states.

ALTERNATIVE LOCATIONS FOR CHILDBIRTH

Increasingly, some women are rebelling against giving birth in a hospital atmosphere that implies illness and abnormality. In response, hospitals often are setting up birthing rooms that have brightly painted walls, instead of hospital white or green, and comfortable, homelike curtains and furnishings. Some hospitals as well as some women's groups have set up birthing centers, which

are located near hospitals but are separate institutions. These too have a homelike atmosphere. Women go to birthing centers only if it appears that they will be able to have a normal delivery. They generally go home the day of the birth. If complications should develop during the birth, the nearness to the hospital means mother or baby or both can be brought there quickly if necessary.

In addition, a few more women are opting to have their babies at home. This practice, which had never completely died out in the more isolated, rural areas of the country, is now reappearing in urban areas. Some physicians and midwives are now consenting to assist at home deliveries, provided there is no indication of any abnormality or problem. Because emergencies can occur even in such situations, most authorities question the safety of home birth for all except those living too far from a hospital to make hospital or birthing center delivery feasible. These changes notwithstanding, the vast majority of American women (99.1 percent in 1979) deliver their babies in hospitals (Landis, 1982).

EASING OF HOSPITAL RULES

In addition to revamping their delivery areas, many hospitals have taken other significant steps in the last 10 to 20 years that have markedly changed the birth experience for mothers and infants. Rules regarding who may be present at birth and afterwards have become considerably relaxed. Most hospitals and doctors today permit the father to be present at the delivery if he wishes, often even at a cesarean delivery. In addition, many hospitals permit the father as well as the mother to hold the baby shortly after birth. Some provide that the threesome can spend several hours together in the recovery room before the baby is taken to the nursery and the mother to her room. The father generally can visit both mother and baby for an extended time each day. These practices are a far cry from the days in which fathers generally saw their baby only briefly at very limited times through the glass of the nursery window and probably did not get to touch the child until it was brought home.

Another increasing trend is that of rooming in. In this situation the baby spends all or most of its time in the mother's room rather than in a nursery. The mother thus participates in giving care and becomes much more acquainted with her child than if it came to her from the nursery only at infre-

quent intervals. Modified rooming in, in which the baby is with the mother all day but is taken to the nursery at night, is sometimes used.

THE LAMAZE METHOD

The greatest recent changes in childbirth involve the delivery itself. Foremost of these probably is the increased popularity of prepared childbirth. The major method taught in the United States today is that pioneered

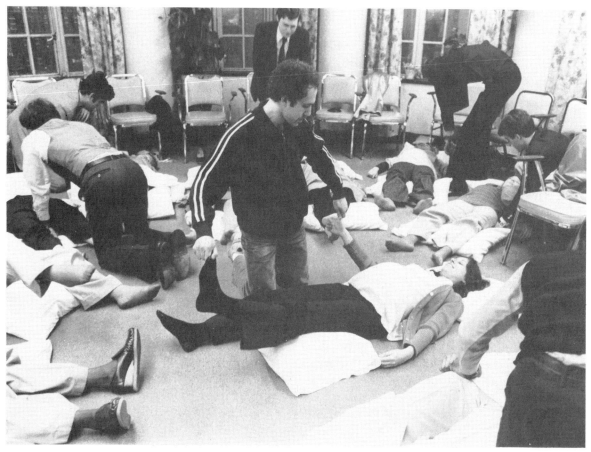

A Lamaze childbirth preparation class. Expectant mothers are learning to relax and to ignore sensations often interpreted as pain, such as being pinched in the thumb and toes, as is the woman in the foreground. This training will be used during labor to block out the pain that sometimes accompanies contractions.

by the French physician Fernand Lamaze (Ewy & Ewy, 1970, 1976).

The **Lamaze method** involves education of both mother and father during the last six weeks of pregnancy in various techniques of breathing and relaxation that will ease the birth process. The father is included since he is expected to be present during labor and delivery and assist the woman. Lamaze instruction also includes detailed information about the various stages of labor and birth and what to expect during each. A visit to the hospital and inspection of labor and delivery rooms is often included. If the woman is a single parent or if the father is unwilling or unable to participate, a close friend of the woman is trained as the labor coach to go through the labor and delivery with her.

Since Lamaze-trained women know what to expect from labor and delivery and have learned relaxation techniques that generally ease the discomfort of labor, many of them use less medication during delivery than do other women. In addition, women who have received such training feel more in control of their labors and deliveries and generally remain calmer and more able to cooperate with physicians or midwives in the birth process. Advocates of the method stress, however that it does not guarantee painless delivery and that if needed, some medication should be given.

CHANGES IN MEDICATIONS

Changes in the use of medication have also occurred. Although the total use of medication in childbirth is on the increase, with about 95 percent of births using some form of it (Brackbill, 1978), the kinds and amounts of drugs are changing. Today there is less dependence on general anesthesics and on more powerful drugs and more likelihood of use of local anesthetics and milder **analgesics** (sub-

stances that deaden response to pain). As a result, more mothers are awake and participating in the baby's birth and can interact with their child shortly after birth. Also, because of the use of milder substances for shorter time periods, babies absorb less of these. These matters will be discussed and terms defined in detail as we consider the birth process a little further on in this chapter.

LEBOYER BIRTHS

Since the early days of the psychoanalytic movement there has been some speculation that the trauma of birth had a lasting effect on the personality development of the child. This theory was a favorite of Otto Rank (1929), one of Freud's early collaborators. No substantive research, however, has documented Rank's ideas.

Dr. Frederick Leboyer (1975), a French obstetrician, has recently advanced similar ideas about the effects of the birth process on the baby and has suggested ways to make this process as easy and nontraumatic for the baby as possible. Leboyer says that the light level, temperature, and noise of the delivery room are so different from what the baby has been used to that birth becomes a frightening and painful experience for this immature organism. He therefore advocates letting the baby emerge slowly, letting it begin breathing on its own, and cutting the cord rather late, after all pulsation in it has ceased. He requires dim lights in the delivery room, a temperature as close to body temperature as is feasible, and a low noise level—people at such deliveries generally speak in whispers. After the baby is born, it is put into a warm water bath reminiscent of the amniotic fluid in which it has been floating. The mother is then allowed to hold her baby.

Leboyer says that babies born by this method are calmer and easier to care for. He

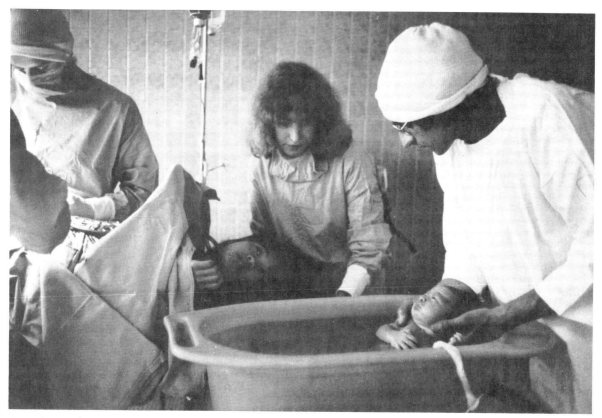

A newborn infant in a Leboyer bath. The warm bath water is supposed to remind the infant of the amniotic fluid in which it has spent its prenatal life. Notice the neonate's alert expression. Although this baby does not appear particularly pleased, other babies have been reported to have smiled when put in such a bath.

reports that babies often smile during the bath. Other researchers have been unable to replicate these results. Therefore the scientific community is still quite skeptical of this method. Some American doctors and some of the educated public, however, are quite vocal about using it, and therefore a number of hospitals now permit this birthing option.

OTHER CHANGES

Some mothers choose birthing while partially submerged in water. They base this option upon the assertion made by some an-

thropologists that the human species spent some time as an aquatic mammal and has only fairly recently (as evolutionary time goes) returned to land. Thus underwater birth is considered by them to be more natural for the baby, as well as providing a continuity from the watery state within the uterus. Unfortunately, since the human baby must breathe soon after birth, some babies delivered underwater have drowned.

Other changes involve options in the position and location used during the birth process. The position of lying flat on the back with the feet upraised in stirrups (the **litho-**

tomy position) has been accepted in America for many years primarily for the convenience of the doctor. It forces the woman to push against gravity, however, making it more difficult for her to participate in the delivery. Many women also complain that it is extremely uncomfortable. Interestingly, no nonindustrial culture uses such a position (Lozoff, 1982). In 70 percent of these cultures, the woman is in a position in which her torso is upright, either sitting, standing, kneeling, or squatting. In some modern delivery rooms, birthing chairs, in which the woman can be upright during delivery, are used. Sometimes

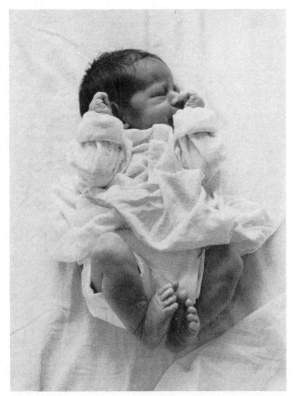

Although the newborn infant looks quite helpless, he or she already has well-functioning sensory capacities that enable him or her to see, hear, and react to various tastes, smells, and to being held or touched. Furthermore, reflex behaviors enable the infant to root, suck, and protect itself from a number of possible dangers.

women are allowed to give birth sitting up in the labor bed rather than lying on a delivery table. There is some indication that delivery in the upright position also helps the baby, since gravity causes most of the blood in the placenta and cord to flow into the baby during such a delivery. This situation may decrease the chance of **anoxia,** or lack of oxygen, for the baby during delivery and immediately thereafter and lessen the chance of brain damage resulting from lack of oxygen. The increased amount of blood may also help prevent **anemia,** though it may elevate the level of bilirubin, a chemical produced by the breaking down of excess red blood cells, in the neonate (Pritchard & MacDonald, 1980).

THE BIRTH PROCESS

The process of giving birth begins with a period of labor. Then comes the delivery of the child, which may be normally through the vagina (birth canal) or surgically. It may or may not be aided by drugs.

Normal Labor and Delivery

EARLY INDICATORS

The first sign that birth may occur soon is often the process of **lightening,** or a downward shifting of the baby's weight within the mother. It usually occurs about two weeks before birth as the baby's head moves down into the pelvic inlet, which is the space between the bones of the pelvis through which the child must pass to be born (Pritchard & MacDonald, 1980). The mother now feels lightened pressure on the upper abdomen but greater pressure upon the bladder. Lightening is more likely to occur before a first birth than before subsequent ones; in many later births the baby's head may not descend to the pelvic inlet until the mother is already in labor.

A woman may also know that the time of birth is only a day or two away when she loses the mucus plug that has closed up the opening of the cervix. Sometimes the mucus will have a little blood in it. Bleeding that involves more than a few drops of blood, however, is a danger sign and needs to be reported immediately to the doctor or midwife. Occasionally the first sign of impending labor is the rupture of the membranes and the gushing or leaking out of amniotic fluid. In most cases, however, the membranes do not rupture until later on in labor.

ONSET OF CONTRACTIONS

The most usual indication that birth is imminent is the beginning of contractions of the uterus. Many women are aware of some contractions for several weeks before birth. These are **Braxton-Hicks contractions,** colloquially called false labor. They prepare the uterus for true labor later, but they remain irregular and do not become stronger. True labor contractions, by contrast, are regular, increase in intensity, become more closely spaced, and generally do not stop once they have begun (Niswander, 1981).

Initial labor contractions may begin as far as 30 minutes or as close as 5 minutes apart. At first they last about 30 seconds, but gradually they become longer. They are mild at first, not much different from Braxton-Hicks contractions in intensity. Some women experience them as similar to menstrual cramps. These contractions signal the beginning of true labor.

Labor and childbirth can be divided into three stages (Friedman, 1978). The first stage involves effacement, or thinning, and then dilation of the cervix of the uterus. The second stage involves the birth of the baby, and the third, the expulsion of the placenta.

The initial stage can be further subdivided into three phases: effacement, dilation, and transition.

EFFACEMENT, DILATION, AND TRANSITION

During the **effacement** phase of the first stage of labor, the tissues of the cervix thin out. As a result, in the next phase the opening of the cervix can expand from a tiny one to one large enough to allow the baby to emerge. Many women have little or no discomfort during effacement. They may feel sociable or talkative between contractions. A few appear apprehensive and "eager to get on with it." Diversionary activities such as conversation, watching television, napping, or a card game are usually helpful in relaxing a woman and reducing apprehension. A back rub often helps to reduce soreness of the lower back, where early labor is often felt the most. For most women, lying down is not required or recommended during this portion of labor, and they feel better if they can remain physically active.

Since the woman has no control over the uterine contractions, she needs to relax and let them run their course. She can neither stop them nor help them along in any way. This phase of labor may take from 1 to 24 hours; the most usual is 8 to 12 hours. Effacement usually takes longer with first babies than with subsequent ones, as does the next phase.

After effacement is well along, the middle portion of the first stage of labor begins. During this phase, effacement is completed, and **dilation** (expansion) of the cervix up to a diameter of about eight cm takes place. This portion of labor takes about five to nine hours for a first baby and about two to five hours for subsequent ones. Contractions now are about three to four minutes apart and last longer, usually about 45 seconds to one

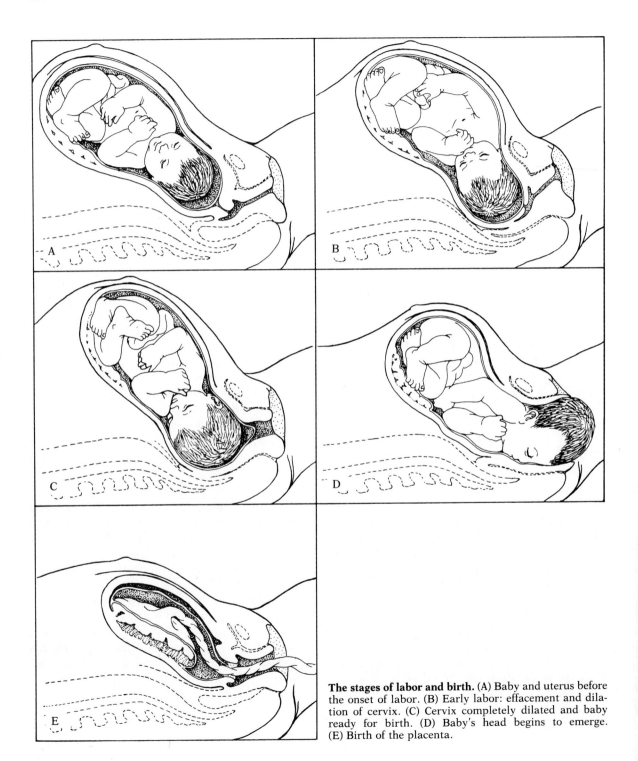

The stages of labor and birth. (A) Baby and uterus before the onset of labor. (B) Early labor: effacement and dilation of cervix. (C) Cervix completely dilated and baby ready for birth. (D) Baby's head begins to emerge. (E) Birth of the placenta.

minute each. They are also more intense than those in the preceding phase and may become increasingly uncomfortable.

During this phase of labor women generally are admitted to the hospital. Of course if there has been some complication or if a problem is suspected, a woman may be admitted much earlier in labor or even before labor has begun.

Upon admission, the woman is prepared for delivery, using various antiseptic measures. The progress of her labor is thoroughly checked. Then she is usually reunited with her husband or partner (or her labor coach) in the labor room. She may now feel the contractions quite strongly and be in little mood for conversation. Companionship and encouragement are still very important to her, however, particularly if this phase of labor has been long and exhausting.

The third, or **transition,** phase of the first stage of labor ensues as the cervix becomes dilated to its maximum diameter of 10 cm, allowing the baby's head to emerge through the cervix and into the vagina. This portion of labor is the most difficult and intense part of the whole sequence. Contractions now come every two to three minutes and last as much as a minute and a half each, so there is little time for rest between them. They are also quite strong and are painful for some women. Luckily the transition phase is short, usually lasting for only five to 20 contractions. Then the second stage of labor, the birth of the baby, begins.

BIRTH OF THE BABY

During the actual birth process, contractions become a bit further apart than they were during transition. The woman now has a great urge to push. Indeed, for the baby to be born without the aid of mechanical means, the woman must actively push, for more pressure is required to expel the baby than the muscles of the uterus alone can supply. Most women find this stage of labor a big relief from what has come immediately before. The pain may be less intense, and pushing feels so much better than just lying there waiting for intense contractions to take their course.

This second, or expulsion, stage of labor may take as long as 2 hours for a first baby, or it may be quite short, 30 minutes or less, with a subsequent one. The average is about 1 1/4 hours (Niswander, 1981). As the birth appears imminent, the woman is moved from the labor room to the delivery room and placed on the delivery table, unless she is to give birth in an alternative setting. She is draped in sterile sheets, and the birth area is again washed with an antiseptic solution.

If a spinal anesthetic or a local one to the area around the vaginal opening is to be used, it is administered at this time. An **episiotomy,** a small cut into the **perineal** area at the base of the vaginal opening, may also be performed. The purpose of the episiotomy is to prevent tearing of the tissues if the birth happens too quickly to allow adequate stretching or if the baby's head is quite large. Tears heal with greater difficulty than a clean cut. There is some controversy about episiotomy, as some midwives and mothers think it is used too often, even if it is not needed. They think that if birth of the head were managed very slowly, tearing would not be a threat and episiotomy not necessary. Many doctors, however, think that the procedure is clearly needed in many instances.

If a woman has had a general anesthetic and is, therefore, not conscious, or if she has insufficient strength to expel the baby, or perhaps if the baby is being born too slowly, forceps may be used to assist in the birth. The forceps are gently positioned, one section at a time, around the baby's head, then are joined and the baby is assisted out of the birth canal. When forceps are used today, they are used only in the low-forceps condition, when the head can be seen clearly enough that forceps can be accurately placed without injuring the head. In the past, high-forceps deliveries, when the baby was still so far up that accurate placement could not be made, were also done. At present, a baby having so much difficulty as to warrant high forceps is instead delivered before this point by **cesarean section,** or surgical removal through the walls of the uterus and abdomen.

In some instances, this second stage of labor is delayed because the baby is not positioned properly to emerge in the usual head-first manner. Sometimes the baby is lying in a **transverse,** or crosswise manner; sometimes it is presenting (coming into view) feet first (modified breech) or buttocks first (frank breech). Although breech babies can sometimes be delivered vaginally, particularly if they can be turned while still *in utero*, or if they are relatively small and the mother's pelvic opening is large, accepted medical practice at present is to deliver breech and transverse babies by cesarean section. That forestalls the stresses of a prolonged vaginal delivery on both baby and mother. About 4 percent of babies present in one of the breech positions and another 1 percent in the transverse position; 95 percent present in the easier head first position (Niswander 1981; Pritchard & MacDonald, 1980).

If the baby is presenting normally, the head can be seen at the vaginal opening as the second stage of labor reaches its climax. This is called **crowning.** With the next contraction, the head usually emerges. This portion of the delivery is done very slowly, to prevent damage to the baby's head or tearing of the mother's perineum. Often a woman is asked to stop pushing partway through the contraction that brings out the baby's head, to help slow down the process. After the head emerges, the baby slowly turns so that one shoulder at a time can emerge. Finally, usually during the next contraction, the rest of the baby is born.

Immediately upon the birth of the baby, or often even when only the head has emerged, delivery room personnel will begin to remove mucus from the baby's mouth and nose with a suction apparatus, so that the baby can begin to breathe without aspirating, or taking up, this mucus into the lungs. Many babies cry spontaneously after birth, and with the

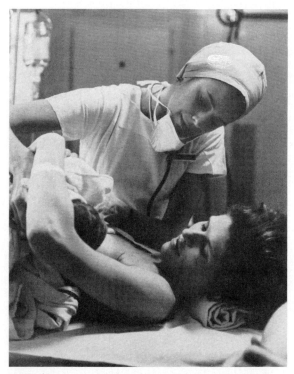

This mother is inspecting her newborn and putting it to her breast just moments after its birth. The baby's sucking helps the mother's uterus to contract and therefore helps prevent hemorrhaging. Since strong anesthetics that render the mother unconscious or groggy are less frequently used today than in the past, most birthing women today are fully awake and can interact with their babies shortly after delivery.

first cry they begin to breathe. Others begin breathing on their own without crying at all. Fewer babies today than in the past are born groggy or sluggish and showing some difficulty breathing on their own because of the effects of anesthesia, since different, less strong anesthetics are now generally used. For those babies that do need help to begin breathing, mechanical respirating devices are available in the delivery room. Slapping the baby on the bottom, the technique so often seen in movies, has been out of favor for a long time.

It is routine practice in many hospital delivery rooms to check the baby's vital signs at 1 minute and 5 minutes after birth (and sometimes at 10 minutes as well) according to the **Apgar Scale.** This scale, devised by the anesthesiologist Dr. Virginia Apgar (1953), assesses the baby's functioning on five factors: heart rate, respiratory effort, muscle tone, reflex irritability, and color. On each item, a score of 2 represents best functioning, a 1 shows marginal functioning, and a 0, a lack of any perceptible functioning. The baby's total score thus may range from a 10 for a "perfect" baby to a 0 for a baby in extreme danger or already dead (see Table 4.1).

At the one-minute evaluation 70 to 90 percent of newborns receive a score of 7 or above, indicating that they are doing all right; at the five-minute evaluation they score as well or better. Few babies receive a perfect 10 on the one-minute evaluation, since good skin color is rare one minute after birth. A baby scoring below 5 is of some concern; one scoring 3 or below is considered in serious jeopardy. Many babies improve markedly from the one-minute to the five-minute evaluation. But almost 97 percent of even those babies scoring below 3 at five minutes develop without noticeable aftereffects. Thus most babies who will have serious consequences also have low Apgar scores, but only few babies with low Apgars actually do show problems (Nelson & Broman, 1977).

TABLE 4.1 APGAR SCALE

Function	0	1	2
Heart rate	No heartbeat seen, heard or felt	Heartbeat less than 100 beats per minute	Heartbeat of 100-140 beats per minute
Respiratory effort	No breathing within 60 seconds of birth	Irregular, slow breathing	Good breathing with lusty crying
Reflex irritability (in response to stimulation: usually to suctioning of mouth and nose)	No response	Moderate or slow response	Facial grimace, sneezing or coughing (or spontaneous voiding of bowel or bladder)
Muscle tone	Completely limp	Moderate muscle tone, limbs moderately flexed	Good muscle tone, flexed limbs
Color	Gray or blue	Pink body but gray or blue hands and feet	Pink all over

Adapted from V. Apgar (1953), A Proposal for a New Method of Evaluation of the Newborn Infant, *Current Researches in Anesthesia and Analgesia, 32*:260–267.

DELIVERY OF THE PLACENTA

The third stage of labor, after the birth of the baby is completed, involves the expulsion of fluid, blood, and the placenta. This stage takes only a few minutes and often is not noticed by the mother because she is so engrossed with her baby. There are further contractions of the uterus, but they are milder than those during the birth of the baby. After the placenta is expelled, an injection of the hormone oxytocin is given to the mother to help contract the uterus further and to prevent excess bleeding. If there has been an episiotomy, it is now repaired with stitches.

THE BABY IMMEDIATELY AFTER BIRTH

Shortly after the birth of the baby and before the placenta is expelled, circulation through the umbilical cord ceases. This occurs because a substance in the cord hardens when exposed to air and constricts the blood vessels in the cord. The baby should be breathing on its own by now. After umbilical circulation has stopped, the cord is clamped off and cut, either before or after the birth of the placenta.

Usually the baby is placed on the mother's abdomen shortly after birth, often before the cord is cut. After the cord is cut, the mother is frequently allowed to hold the baby, unless she is not sufficiently alert because of anesthesia. In most deliveries the baby is soon taken aside to be cleaned up. The stump of the cord attached to the baby is treated with an antibiotic to prevent infection. Vitamin K is injected into the baby to prevent hemorrhaging. Footprints or handprints are made for identification, and the baby has an identification bracelet or necklace bearing the mother's name put on. Either at this time or within a few hours,

penicillin or a silver nitrate solution is put in the baby's eyes. This is done to prevent infection and subsequent blindness, should the mother have gonorrhea that the baby could have picked up in its passage through the vagina. The baby is then warmly wrapped up to prevent heat loss, or else put under a radiant-heat panel, and often taken to the newborn nursery. However, the practice of letting neonates spend the next few hours with the mother or both parents is increasing in modern hospitals. It is done to maximize the alert postnatal period of the baby in facilitating bonding between the parents and the child. Obviously, if the mother's or baby's condition after birth does not warrant it, this period of acquaintance must be postponed.

Birth by Cesarean Section

Cesarean birth is the process whereby the baby is delivered via an incision made in the mother's abdomen and uterus. The term refers to the way that Julius Caesar reputedly was delivered after his mother died while bearing him.

REASON FOR ITS USE

Cesarean delivery is used in cases of **dystocia,** or difficult labor, in which vaginal delivery would be impossible or highly risky for either mother or infant. These situations include those where the placenta is implanted over the cervical opening or where the baby's head is too big in relation to the mother's pelvic bone structure. There are also instances in which contractions of the uterus are not strong enough either to produce effacement and dilation or to push out the baby. Situations in which the baby is presenting in an unusual manner, such as breech, or those in which vaginal delivery has gone on without results too long and the baby is showing signs of distress also may indicate that cesarean section is advisable. Cesarean section may be used to deliver a baby before term if the mother is at risk because of **hypertension** (high blood pressure) or if the baby is in danger of deteriorating because of Rh incompatibility or maternal diabetes.

Since cesarean section involves major surgery, anesthetics must be used. There has been a recent trend toward the use of spinal anesthetics, during the use of which the mother remains conscious, rather than general ancsthetics, unless the procedure has to be done on an emergency basis. If the mother is conscious, she can see and often even hold her baby after birth. Some hospitals allow fathers to be present at cesarean births if they wish to be and if the mother consents.

INCREASE IN USE

The rate of cesarean delivery in the United States has increased fourfold in the last fifteen years (Otten, 1984). Currently, as of 1982, cesareans make up about 18.5 percent of all deliveries (Otten, 1984), and the rate is much higher, as high as 40%, in some hospitals. This increase has caused some physicians as well as women's groups concern that cesareans may be done in some instances in which vaginal birth would have been quite feasible.

The increase in cesarean delivery as a percentage of all deliveries may be related to the drop in **parity,** that is, the fact that mothers today have fewer babies than in the past. Thus in 1964, one-fourth of all deliveries were of first babies; by 1979 this figure had risen to one-half (Pritchard & MacDonald, 1980). Since women who deliver a first baby vaginally will in all likelihood also deliver subsequent ones that way, the decrease in

subsequent babies has decreased the vaginal delivery rate and thus may have indirectly raised the cesarean rate.

Many cesarean deliveries may be done because doctors fear possible complications from vaginal delivery that could subject them to being sued. To play it safe, they choose cesarean.

Modern diagnostic devices such as fetal monitors may also contribute to the increase of cesarean births. They are able to spot, often before any other method, signs of possible distress in the infant that could be indications for surgical intervention. But the use of the monitors may also unwittingly be contributing to an increase of unnecessary cesareans. First, transient aberrations in fetal heartbeat or other measured indices may be diagnosed as major problems requiring massive interventions, where a wait-and-see attitude might have resulted in a normal vaginal delivery of a baby that really did not have problems. Second, the use of a fetal monitor confines the mother to lying on her back in a labor bed. This position often prolongs labor and may result in complications. If the mother could have moved about, even gone walking up and down the corridor, her activity could have reinstated labor that had stopped or hastened a slow one.

ADVANTAGES AND DISADVANTAGES

The facts here present a mixed picture. On the one hand, studies done at medical facilities in Seattle and New York show that the risk of brain damage to breech babies is lower with cesarean than with vaginal birth (Pakter, 1980; Wazach, 1980). Low-birth-weight babies and those of very high birth weight also show fewer complications if delivered by cesarean (Pakter, 1980). And a

1983 study found that among breech babies weighing less than 1500 g, 29 percent of those delivered by cesarean died, while the death rate was 58 percent of those delivered vaginally (Main, Main & Maurer, 1983). Therefore, for this type of baby, even though there is a high mortality rate either way, that for cesarean birth seems to be only half that for vaginal delivery.

But cesarean birth does involve major surgery. It therefore poses a higher risk for both mother and child than does vaginal delivery, unless risks of a vaginal delivery would be even greater, as for breech babies or those with heads too large to be born vaginally. Maternal mortality from cesarean delivery is only 20 to 70 per 100,000 such births, which is lower than that for vaginal births had been not too long ago (Bottoms, Rosen, & Sokol, 1980). However, this does present a death risk that is from two to four times what it is for vaginal births (Otten, 1984). Even for infants, the risk of death after the procedure is less than a third of what it was in 1950, but still presents a greater risk than an uncomplicated vaginal delivery.

In addition to the increased risk involved in surgery, cesarean delivery may have other unfavorable consequences as well. Some scientists speculate that the stimulation of being subject to uterine contractions and passing out through the birth canal may help to activate responses such as breathing in the newborn (Behrman, 1979). The cesarean baby does not receive this kind of stimulation. Although no studies to date have absolutely verified this speculation, it is a fact that some babies delivered by cesarean show some degree of difficulty with early respiration (Barden, 1977). Further, since cesarean section mandates the use of anesthetics, the baby born this way may be drowsy and sluggish at first. This too may result in problems of beginning breathing. Since a surgical procedure is involved, the mother has a longer recuperative period than if she had given birth vaginally. She generally must remain in the hospital a few days longer.

REPEAT CESAREANS

Once a woman has given birth by cesarean, many doctors will deliver subsequent babies only in the same manner, because they fear a rupture of the uterus during labor. This danger was certainly to be considered in the past, when most cesarean incisions were done vertically. At the present time, a low, transverse cut (called the bikini cut because the mother will be able to wear a skimpy bathing suit without showing the scar) is generally used. It is much less likely to rupture.

In 1982, on the basis of studies of more than 2,800 vaginal deliveries by women who had had a previous cesarean, the American College of Obstetricians and Gynecologists (ACOG) approved the use of vaginal delivery in some subsequent deliveries after a first cesarean birth (Young, 1982). A more recent extensive study of women with previous cesareans who wished to deliver a subsequent baby vaginally has also been reported (Martin, Harnis, Huddleston, Morrison, Propst, Wiser, Perlis, & Davidson, 1983). Of these, about 60 percent succeeded in giving vaginal birth; the rest delivered again by cesarean. The rate of complications for these mothers and babies from either procedure was approximately the same. Thus it seems that a majority of women who have had a previous cesarean can safely deliver vaginally with a subsequent pregnancy. It may be some years, however, before young doctors trained since the ACOG announced its new stand will be doing most deliveries. Whether many trained previously will change their methods of delivery after a cesarean is not yet known.

APPEARANCE OF THE CESAREAN BABY

The baby born by cesarean may look somewhat different at first from the baby born vaginally. It does not show any of the molding or distortion of the head that babies normally acquire from traveling through the narrow birth canal. Instead its head is nicely rounded. If cesarean was selected ahead of time as a result of a known complication, the delivery may take place several weeks before the actual due date to make sure the mother is not yet in labor. In such a situation the baby may be somewhat smaller, weigh less, and have less of a fat layer under the skin than the newborn at term.

If delivered more than a few weeks before term because of problems in either mother or baby, the infant may suffer from respiratory distress just as may vaginally delivered preterm babies. Most babies delivered by cesarean, however, function quite well and make up for any early problems very quickly.

Anesthetics and Analgesics in Childbirth

Anesthetics and analgesics are used in childbirth to control or diminish the sensation of pain or both. Anesthetics are pain killers that cause loss of sensation in the nerves. They may be general, resulting in total loss of consciousness, or local, affecting only a particular region of the body. Analgesics deaden response to pain by causing the brain not to interpret pain signals as pain. Generally, analgesics are milder in their effects upon mother and baby than are anesthetics.

THE PERCEPTION OF PAIN

The degree of pain perceived by a woman in labor, and hence the amount and kind of anesthetic or analgesic needed, varies greatly depending upon the length, severity, and possible complications of the labor, as well as the relative size of the baby and the mother's pelvic area. Some individuals seem to have a higher pain threshold, that is, to be more impervious to pain than others. Cultural factors also seem to play a part. In cultures in which childbirth is assumed to be painful, mothers complain of pain; in those in which pain is not expected, mothers seem to feel, or at least report, little or no pain. Finally, in North American culture, the degree of training and knowledge that the mother has received about childbirth seems to make a difference, in part, perhaps, because the informed, prepared mother feels more in control. She may be more relaxed because she knows what to expect. She may also be blocking out sensations that could be interpreted as pain because she has been taught to do so. In general, mothers who have had childbirth preparation, particularly Lamaze training, seem to deliver with the use of less medication, and with less discomfort, than mothers not so prepared. Some require no medication at all.

Childbirth without medication, however, is the exception rather than the rule in current American birthing practices. It has been estimated that 95 percent of the hospital births in the United States as of 1978 used some form of analgesics or anesthetics or both (Brackbill, 1978).

ANALGESICS

Three types of analgesics may be used during the first stage of labor. **Sedatives** are generally given in pill form during the first, or effacement, phase. Their purpose is to help the woman rest before active labor begins. Sometimes sedatives are given in combination with **tranquilizers,** which reduce tension and enable the woman to relax. The combination of the two drugs may have longer effects than would either one separately. Tranquilizers may be administered orally, or they may be given as an injection. True **analgesics** given during the first stage include demerol and norephine. They relieve pain by depressing the central nervous system. Frequently they are administered **intravenously,** but sometimes they are given in an **intramuscular** injection. They are usually used later in labor than sedatives or tranquilizers.

ANESTHETICS

Two types of anesthetics, the epidural block and the caudal block, are used during the first and second stages of labor locally to numb the pelvic area and relieve discomfort during contractions. A caine derivative, similar to the drugs used during dental work, is injected into the epidural or caudal cavities at the base of the spine through a catheter, or tube, in the back. The catheter remains in place from about five cm dilation of the cervix until the end of delivery. Injections may be given through it as needed to reduce pain.

Anesthetics used during the delivery, or second, stage of labor only may be one of four types. The first is either a spinal or a saddle block, in which an injection of a caine derivative is made directly into the spinal fluid between the fourth and fifth lumbar vertebrae in the lower back. The second is a pudendal block, a local injection to the pudendal nerves that bring sensation from the vagina. The third is a local perineal block, which is a local anesthetic, again usually of a caine derivative, applied to the perineal area. It is particularly useful for an episi-

otomy. The fourth type is inhalant gas, usually nitrous oxide, which produces a temporary and light state of sleep.

EFFECTS ON THE INFANT

It has been known for quite some time that almost all drugs used during labor and delivery, except for mild muscle relaxants, are able rapidly to cross the placental barrier and affect the baby (Finster, 1974). Many drugs, though they enter the fetal circulation before birth, affect the baby's brain only after birth. If sufficiently large doses of drugs are used, or if the labor is long and drugs are administered over a long time span, these effects on the baby's brain may depress responses of the newborn such as respiration and sucking. Most **neonatologists,** doctors specializing in the care of newborns, and anesthesiologists believe that these effects are transitory and leave no permanent aftereffects (Finster, 1974). Others, however, are afraid that anesthetics and analgesics used in childbirth may have long-lasting behavioral and intellectual aftereffects extending on into middle childhood (Brackbill, 1978). It is known that in some animal species anesthesia of the mother may lead to permanent damage to the fetal brain and may result in subsequent behavioral alterations as well (Butcher, 1979; Rodier, 1979). The question is whether these kinds of results can be generalized to humans. There seems to be some evidence, such as from the large-scale studies done through the Collaborative Perinatal Project, that suggests that there may be aftereffects of maternal anesthesia in the child up to the age of seven years (Brackbill, 1978). On the other hand, critics of this view think that the data from this study were wrongly interpreted and that aftereffects attributed to anesthesia and analgesia might often be the results of fetal **asphyxia,** or lack of oxygen, that occurred independent of medication but was not diagnosed at birth (Shearer, 1979).

RECENT TRENDS

In any event, particularly since it has not yet been proven absolutely that medication poses no risk for the baby, physicians have in recent years become more conservative in the types and amounts of anesthetics they are using. Milder anesthetics to the spinal area have largely replaced general anesthetics that rendered the mother unconscious over long time periods, except in the cases of some cesarean sections (Shearer, 1979). The amounts used and the total time span over which they are used are carefully monitored to make sure that no more is used than the bare minimum needed.

Some consumer groups and childbirth training organizations have been pressuring the federal Food and Drug Administration (FDA) to provide labeling and package inserts on drugs used in childbirth, informing the consumer of possible risks and effects. The FDA has refused to do so, on the grounds that evidence of risks and effects is as yet insufficient, except for short-term effects on the infant that do not in their view appear to be harmful.

CONTINUING DEBATE OVER MEDICATION

The whole subject of medication in childbirth has aroused strong feelings among both the professional medical community, who generally favor it, and lay consumer groups, who express doubts and sometimes are vociferous in their opposition. Since the evidence for either stand is not yet compelling, expectant mothers are urged to discuss their own attitudes and preferences about anesthesia and analgesia with their doctor or other

health-care professional. Doctors and other professionals in turn should be able to express their attitudes and preferences as well. Then, it is hoped, some agreement about how a particular birth will be handled can be reached, subject of course to possible changes if complications arise. Such discussion should take place early in pregnancy for two reasons. First, if a woman finds she cannot agree with her doctor, she can still change to another whose philosophy is closer to hers. Second, she should have this matter decided well before she goes into labor, for that is a poor time to reach such an important decision.

Certainly there have been cases in which anesthetics and analgesics have been used in amounts or for time periods that are unwarranted. Wise and conservative use of these drugs, however, probably has made the birth process more comfortable for many women. It may even have lowered the risks for some mothers and babies by expanding the options for reaching a successful outcome, such as the use of forceps or cesarean section, which would be impossible without such drugs. But in an uncomplicated delivery, if a mother should want a minimum of drugs or none at all, there is no reason why her wishes should not be followed.

BIRTH ORDER AND SIBLINGS

Possible Effects of Birth Order

Psychologists and lay people have speculated upon the possible effects of birth order upon personality and other characteristics of children. There is relatively little agreement among scientists, however, and few well-controlled studies to shed light on the matter. For example, Alfred Adler (1927) postulated that all later siblings, since they were younger and smaller, would feel inferior to the oldest, and would try to compensate for the disparity. These compensatory techniques and their effects carried over into adult life. More recent studies have shown that the birth order as well as the sex of siblings can indeed relate to personality.

First-borns are more likely to have higher IQ scores (Belmont & Marolla, 1973) and to attend college and graduate school (Poole & Kuhn, 1973). Oldest and only children therefore tend to become high achievers and are over-represented in such achievement-oriented occupations as law and medicine. They also are over-represented in the astronaut corps, the presidency, and membership in Congress, as well as in inclusion in *Who's Who in America* (Bradley, 1982; Campbell, 1971).

In personality, first-borns tend to be more oriented toward adults rather than age-mates. They are more responsible and cooperative in their behavior than are later-borns and more prone to feelings of guilt for transgressions or omissions (Altus, 1967). They are less sociable and less popular with the peer group than are later-born children (Clarke-Stewart, 1977). First-borns show a tendency toward dependency upon adults in childhood and to be more conforming to social expectations throughout life (MacDonald, 1969). Oldest daughters in families with no boys tend to be treated more like oldest sons by their fathers and generally are among the highest-achieving females. Of course these studies are correlational; they show that certain factors are related, but they cannot clearly establish cause.

Furthermore, many of the differences that appear due to birth order may be due to socioeconomic and educational factors. Higher-income families and those having higher levels of education tend to have fewer children; thus later-borns are more likely to be in families of lower social and educational attainment.

An intriguing question is whether the birth experience itself, either upon the mother or the child, may be the cause of some of these differences related to birth order. It is common knowledge that first labors are generally longer and first births more difficult than subsequent ones. Do parents therefore treat first children differently from later ones? Does the longer and more difficult labor in some way, physically or psychologically, affect the child differently? Are later children more social because their birth experiences might have been easier? Or do parents, especially mothers, react to them differently because they arrived more easily? Or are there other, as yet unexplained, causes for the differences that appear to exist between first-born and later-born children?

Of course, parents of subsequent children are also very different from the way they were the first time. They have gained in experience and self-confidence. Any subsequent child is not as intrusive as was the first that changed the couple relationship into a threesome. And finally, there is the whole complex of relations among siblings. Any child beyond the first is born not only to parents but, as it were, to the sibling as well. The older sibling is there, as model or competitor, from earliest awareness on.

Siblings and the Birth Process

Another area of present interest is the effect of the birth on the older sibling. How does the child react to being displaced by the new baby that commands so much parental time and effort? Is there a better time or a worse time for the second child to come; in other words, is there some optimal spacing? Some authorities suggest that if the second child is born before the older child is two years old, the older is relatively unaffected because he or she has not yet formed such a strong sense of self as to feel threatened by the newcomer (Koch, 1956). If the older child is four or older, the new baby also represents less of a threat because by then the older child has a secure niche in the family, and has peer friends. But between ages two and four, a new sibling may adversely affect the emotional attitudes of the older child. The effect of subsequent siblings is less severe than that of the second, as the oldest has already lost the status of only child with the birth of the second, and any other children never were the only one.

And finally, in our discussion of the birth process, we should consider the place of the older sibling. To what extent does and should an older sibling participate in the birth of a younger one? In a cross-cultural study of birthing practices of 186 nonindustrialized cultures performed by Lozoff, she found that in only 11 percent were children specifically allowed to be present. In another 25 percent they were specifically excluded, and no information was available about the rest (Lozoff, 1982). In the past in this country, when deliveries were in the home, siblings generally saw the new baby shortly after birth. Indeed, if they were quite a bit older and female, they might be present at the birth. They helped care for the new infant. As babies came to be delivered in hospitals, siblings were excluded from the birth process. Most of the time they could not even visit the mother and did not see her or the new baby until mother and baby came home.

Some parents are now trying to obtain permission from hospitals and doctors to have older siblings present at birth. They reason that if mother and father can develop a close bond with the baby shortly after birth, older siblings should be able to do the same. This is an interesting idea and deserves to be explored further but with some precautions. Preliminary research with children under age six who witnessed the birth of a sibling suggests that the experience may be disturbing or unsettling to some of the children, even though they were prepared for the birth and had an adult with them to explain things (Leonard, Irving, & Ballard, 1979). If this is so with a normal birth, what might the effect be if an unforeseen complication occurs? At the present time, most hospitals do not allow children to witness the process of birth, though they often may visit their mother and new sibling shortly afterward.

THE NEONATE

Appearance

The newborn baby, or **neonate,** often looks very different from the parents' idealized version of a baby. The baby's skin may be grayish or slightly pink and is wrinkled and wet from its long stay in the amniotic fluid. As the skin dries from its long soaking after birth, it may begin to crack and peel in spots, further detracting from the baby's appearance. The white vernix is usually still evident, particularly in folds and creases. The baby may be born with blood on it if the perineal area tore or was cut during the delivery.

While considering the appearance of the baby's skin, it is important to note that babies of all racial and ethnic groups have relatively light skin at birth. The pigmented layer in the skin that will result in variations of skin color based upon heredity is activated by light, particularly sunlight. Since the baby has developed in a dark, sunless place,

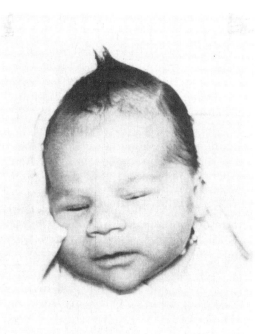

The typical neonate has a somewhat elongated head from the effects of passage through the birth canal. The face occupies only a small portion of the head, and the chin is small and recessed. Many neonates keep their eyes closed even when awake, because the eyes are sore from drops that have been put in the eyes to prevent infection.

its skin at birth shows little of the color it will eventually assume. With continued exposure to light after birth, the baby's skin slowly begins to assume the particular shade that its inheritance dictates.

If the baby has been delivered vaginally, its head may be molded from the birth process, producing an elongated, somewhat oddly shaped appearance. Since the bones of the skull are not yet rigidly joined to each other, this molding does not harm the baby. The head will slowly resume its rounded shape in the first few weeks after birth. In addition, the baby may look battered from a rough passage through the birth canal. That is be-

cause labor is hard work for the baby as well as the mother. Mucus and water may still be present in the mouth, nose, and ears. The baby's skin is puffy because extra fluid has been absorbed in the last few days to prepare for birth. This fluid helps prevent dehydration in the first few days after birth before the mother produces milk and the baby is ready to absorb it. Even so, the baby may look scrawny when compared to pictures of slightly older babies that the parents have seen, especially if the baby is preterm or of low birth weight. For all these reasons, parents are often a bit shocked when they first glimpse their baby in the delivery room.

Adjustments to Life outside the Uterus

RESPIRATION

Very shortly after birth, as the umbilical circulation ceases, the baby must begin to supply its own oxygen by breathing. A very short period without sufficient oxygen can be tolerated by the newborn, but prolonged oxygen deprivation, or **anoxia,** can result in various types of neurological damage, including mental retardation and cerebral palsy. Since at birth the air sacs, or **alveoli,** in the lungs are still collapsed and clogged with fluid, the first breath, which begins to clear and expand them, is the most difficult one of all. Some authorities maintain that the birth cry is not a true cry but is really just the baby's first gasping effort at breathing.

For several days after birth the baby's breathing may remain shallow and irregular. The baby wheezes, coughs, and gags. It may spit up mucus that has been expelled from the lungs. The irregularities of breathing and other events are due in part to the immaturity of the baby's respiratory system and in part to the continued presence of fluid and mucus in the lungs. New parents often worry about the baby's breathing because it sounds so labored and may be irregular, but that is normal for the neonate and improves over time.

Most babies begin to show good skin color shortly after their breathing has become established. It is quite normal, however, for the newborn's fingers and toes to appear slightly bluish for some time after birth, because the baby is still absorbing somewhat insufficient amounts of oxygen. As its respiratory system matures, its breathing becomes deeper and more regular, more oxygen is absorbed, and the extremities assume a healthy pink color.

CIRCULATION

In addition to respiration, and in conjunction with it, the baby's circulatory system must make some immediate adjustments after birth. The heart has, of course, been pumping blood since very early in gestation. But now it must circulate blood to and from the lungs to get rid of carbon dioxide and pick up oxygen, and it must stop circulating blood to and from the placenta via the umbilical vessels.

The umbilical circulation ceases as the vessels constrict, and thereafter the cord is cut. Two shortcuts in circulation that were useful during prenatal development when all oxygen came from the mother but that can be deadly once oxygen comes from the baby's lungs also must stop functioning shortly after birth. The **ductus arteriosus,** a connection between the **aorta** (the major artery leading from the heart) and the veins leading from the lungs to the heart, must close off. This connection had served as a bypass for most of the blood before birth, letting only a small amount reach the lungs, just enough to supply them with needed oxygen. Since after birth all the body's blood must circulate to

the lungs, the ductus constricts, and the new way of circulating blood to the lungs begins.

In addition, an opening between the two sides of the heart, the **foramen ovale,** had also helped provide a shortcut for most of the blood flow away from the lungs in fetal circulation. This opening must close up shortly after birth. As the opening closes, oxygenated blood from the lungs and deoxygenated blood going to the lungs are kept separated, increasing the efficiency of oxygen supply to the body. Occasionally the opening does not begin to close or does not close completely. A surgical technique has been available since the 1960s that permits closure and thus allows the child to lead a normal life thereafter.

The baby also needs to begin controlling three other processes shortly after birth. These are adjustment of temperature, food intake and digestion, and the elimination of waste products. All these processes, while vitally important to maintain the baby's life, are not as immediately critical at birth as are respiration and changes in circulation.

TEMPERATURE CONTROL

Because temperature control in the newborn is inefficient, keeping warm poses a formidable task. The baby has trouble maintaining its temperature because it has less fat, which is an excellent insulator, beneath the skin than it will have later in life. In addition, the brain centers controlling temperature regulation are still immature. Also, the baby is not yet taking in nourishment and thus cannot **metabolize** (break down chemically and utilize) food to produce body heat. And finally, the baby has a much higher ratio of exposed skin surface to total body weight than has an older child or adult and therefore loses heat much more quickly.

The normal neonate has one excellent means of producing heat. During fetal development, a special kind of fat called brown fat because it actually looks brownish is laid down in the area of the neck and around the kidneys. This fat is metabolized during the neonatal period, producing heat to sustain the baby (Reid, 1972). Even so, the baby's body temperature usually drops several degrees after birth, and special steps must be taken to restore and maintain adequate body temperature.

To help in this effort, radiantly heated baby beds or radiant panels suspended above the baby are used in the delivery room. The baby is also warmly wrapped to prevent further heat loss after it is removed from the de-

livery area. For the first few months of life, warm clothing and snug wrapping in a blanket are customary. Some anxious parents and grandparents overdo this and encase the baby in too much clothing. Since the inefficiency of temperature control works the other way as well, that is, the baby is also not very good at cooling off, overdressing can be a cause of distress and discomfort.

Because the temperature-regulating mechanisms in the young baby are not yet working very well, a minor ailment can often trigger a high fever in a very short time. Fortunately, a high fever in a very young baby may not be as damaging to the brain as it is

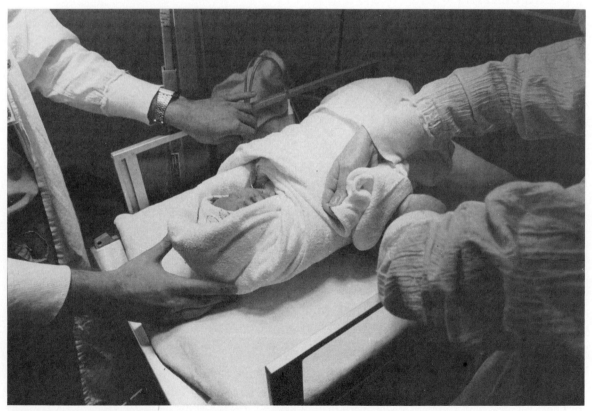

Since the neonate's temperature control mechanisms do not yet function very well, it is important that the baby be kept warm. This two-day-old infant is being readied to go home from the hospital by being warmly dressed and snugly wrapped in a blanket.

in an older infant or child. Nevertheless, prompt medical attention should be paid to a high fever in a child of any age, and, if necessary, steps to reduce it such as a tepid sponge bath should be tried.

Within the first few months, the baby's ability to maintain body temperature improves greatly. During this time, the child will have developed more fat under the skin and will have grown appreciably in size, reducing the ratio of skin surface to body weight. The temperature centers in the brain will have matured further and consequently are working more efficiently. Therefore, after this time, the need for very warm clothing and for wrapping decreases, unless, of course, the baby is outdoors in cold weather or is in a very cool room. In addition, the older baby becomes more active, and since activity generates heat the baby is better able to keep warm.

FOOD INGESTION AND DIGESTION

Ingesting and digesting food is a whole new experience for the baby. Luckily the neonate is born very well equipped by nature for the task of sucking. The newborn has a receding chin and lower lip and fat pads in the cheeks that enable it to come up close to the breast and suck without losing hold and while still able to breathe. Furthermore, both the rooting reflex used to find the nipple and the sucking reflex are fully operational in the normal infant at birth; indeed, the baby may have practiced sucking while still in the uterus. Pictures taken of fetuses that have had to be clinically aborted show some of them sucking their thumbs while still enclosed within the amniotic sac.

The normal newborn is thus able to suck within moments after birth, although the sucking reflex may temporarily be slightly depressed in the infant whose mother has received much medication for the birth. In many instances, after delivery the baby is given to the mother to put to her breast while both are still in the delivery room. Of course, at this time the mother as yet has no milk and the baby could not digest it even if she did, but some important benefits derive from this early sucking. The baby begins to receive **colostrum,** a pale watery fluid secreted by the mother's breasts, which contains some nutrients but more importantly provides antibodies that will protect the baby against disease in the critical first few weeks. The baby has already acquired some temporary immunity against diseases to which the mother is immune by absorbing antibodies from her blood through the placenta before birth. The antibodies in the colostrum enhance this immunity. In response to the baby's sucking, the mother secretes the hormone oxytocin, which stimulates the uterus further to contract in size and helps to prevent hemorrhaging from the uterus. This initial sucking also stimulates the mother's production of the hormone **prolactin,** which helps to produce the flow of milk. We will return to the baby's sucking and mother's milk production in more detail in chapter 6.

EXCRETION AND ELIMINATION

The final neonatal adjustment the baby must make is to the excretion and elimination of the waste products of the body's metabolism. The kidneys have been functional for quite a while before birth, and the baby has been urinating while in the womb. Most of the excretion of waste products, however, has been taken care of by the mother. Now the kidneys must take over almost all of the excretory function, except for the little done by the skin.

The first elimination of the baby's bowels usually occurs in the first few days. It is the **meconium,** a greenish black product made up of sloughed-off intestinal cells, mucus, and materials swallowed by the baby while floating in the amniotic fluid. Occasionally a baby in distress during a complicated labor may void meconium into the amniotic fluid and aspirate some of this into the lungs during birth. This can cause pneumonia in the neonate. The meconium that is present in the baby's first few bowel movements often frightens new parents because of its different appearance if they have not been told what to expect. After the baby has passed the meconium and begins to take in nourishment, it begins slowly to produce true stools. Breast-fed infants produce a soft, yellowish, cheeselike stool that does not smell unpleasant, while the stools of bottle-fed infants are darker, harder, and often have an unpleasant odor. Breast-fed babies almost never suffer from constipation because there are natural laxatives in mother's milk. Even in bottle-fed babies, constipation is rare and can usually be alleviated by adding a little extra sweetening to the milk. On occasion, however, all infants may strain and push and act as though they were in distress during elimination. Unless the bowel movement is indeed abnormally hard or the infant produces nothing after repeated attempts, there is no cause for alarm.

All infants urinate and defecate with great frequency during the first few weeks. Indeed, many new mothers complain that at first they spend most of their time either feeding or diapering the baby. After a time, as the physiological mechanisms controlling these processes mature, their frequency diminishes.

Sensory Capacities

The newborn's senses are functioning at birth. While it is not known how much the baby **perceives,** that is, how much of this sensory input is processed by the brain, it is known that the eyes, ears, and other **sensory end organs** are performing their functions in a remarkably complex and skilled manner. In this chapter we will briefly consider the infant's sensory capacities as evidenced in the first few hours and days after birth. A detailed consideration of the sensory and perceptual capabilities of the infant as they develop from the neonatal period onward will be found in chapter 7.

VISION

There is some debate whether neonates have an inborn ability to perceive forms and to show a preference for particular visual displays or whether they merely have some inborn predispositions to attend to certain kinds of visual stimuli. Marshall Haith (1979), who believes the latter, thinks that neonates react in a systematic fashion to visual displays. He has put these systematic approaches together into a set of "rules" according to which the infant operates. The first rule is: If awake and the light is not too bright, open the eyes. The second is: If awake and having the eyes open and no light is seen, search for it. The third is: If you find a light, look for edges on it. The final rule is: If you find an edge, look back and forth across it.

The neonate, even while still in the delivery room, is able to **track visually,** that is to follow a moving object with the eyes. It can do so provided the object is moving slowly, is moderately bright, and is at the proper distance, about 8 to 10 inches, for the baby to see it fairly clearly. This tracking may be erratic at first, inasmuch as the baby will only develop smooth tracking movements with practice, and will usually only cover a portion of the visual field. This tracking behavior does fit in nicely with Haith's rules.

Newborns fixate on and track shapes resembling human faces more so than different visual displays (Fantz, 1961, 1963). Some people have interpreted this apparent preference to mean that the neonate has an inborn sensitivity to human features, but according to Haith's formulations, the infant may merely be looking at a display that has a high amount of edge or contour and then be scanning across these edges (Sherrod, 1979). It so happens that the human face is the most likely such display the infant will see.

Newborns also show a preference for a pattern of black and white stripes over an equivalently bright area that is uniformly gray (Fantz, 1958, 1961, 1963). They are able to tell the difference between these two when the stripes are only 1/8 to 1/16 of an inch wide. The preference for stripes again fits in well with Haith's rules, inasmuch as a striped pattern shows a lot of edge while a uniform gray pattern has none.

In any event, whether because of the "faceness" of human faces or because they happen to have a high degree of edge or contour, neonates tend to look at the faces of caregivers. This tendency is helped along by the fact that while feeding or otherwise attending to the infant, caregivers tend to hold their faces at the 8—10-inch distance at which the neonate can see most clearly.

HEARING

Although at birth the neonate may still have water in the ears, and the ear canals may be swollen, it is able to hear. The infant will blink its eyes at a sudden loud noise or will move as if startled and show a change in heart rate (Illingworth, 1975). Even in the delivery room, the baby will turn the head in the direction from which a sound comes at a rate much better than chance (Wertheimer,

1961); this behavior can be elicited with a good deal of success in the first few days after birth (Muir & Field, 1979).

The newborn appears to be most responsive to sounds that are within the range of the human voice, particularly the female voice which is of higher pitch than that of the male (Wolff, 1963). Neonates also are calmed by repeated rhythmic sounds, perhaps because they have been exposed to such sounds, particularly to the beat of the mother's heart, before birth. After birth, however, recorded heartbeat sounds do not appear superior to other rhythmic sounds that are new to the baby, such as music or the ticking of a clock (Brackbill, 1971).

Neonates also move their bodies in rhythm with human speech, which adults do also, as early as 12 hours after birth (Condon & Sander 1974). This process is called **interactional synchrony** by Condon and Sander. They found that American neonates whose parents spoke English would react this way to speech in either English or Chinese but would not move in rhythm to tapping sounds or to repetitive vowel sounds that do not resemble human speech. They suggest that this indicates that the human infant is born receptive to the sounds of human language, so that it can begin at birth to lay down the form and structure of the language that it will hear for many months before speech begins.

OTHER SENSES

As early as 1932, Jensen was able to demonstrate that newborn infants react in different ways to different taste and temperature stimuli. They seem to prefer some tastes over others and to prefer warm objects to cold ones (Jensen, 1932). Newborn babies prefer sweet things and will suck more on a nipple delivering water sweetened with glucose than on one delivering plain water (Crook & Lipsitt, 1976). When given a salty solution, they will reduce sucking (Crook, 1976).

Beginning on the first day after birth, babies can turn their heads away from unpleasant odors, showing that they can to some extent localize the source of an odor as well as interpret it as unpleasant (Engen, Lipsitt, & Kaye, 1963). Neonates can also distinguish between different odors, such as those of anise, vinegar, alcohol, and asafetida (Engen, Lipsitt, & Kaye, 1963). In addition, newborn babies in the first few days seem to be able to recognize the smell of their own mothers. MacFarlane (1977) tested this ability by exposing neonates to the breast pads their nursing mother had been wearing and to those of another nursing mother. The babies turned significantly more in the direction of their own mother's pad, indicating to MacFarlane that they already recognized its distinctive smell.

Thus it appears that the neonate comes into the world equipped with adequate sensory capacities to begin to interact with sensory stimuli provided by the environment. As the infant's brain begins to organize these sensory inputs, perception will be added to this early sensory responsivity. This ability will be discussed in chapter 7.

PRETERM, LOW-BIRTH-WEIGHT, AND POSTMATURE BABIES

While the overwhelming majority of babies are born within plus or minus ten days of the 266-day gestation time (or 280 days from the onset of the mother's last menstrual period), some babies are born before or after this allotted time span. And some babies, though born at the appropriate time, weigh less than the 2500 grams, or about 5 1/2 pounds, considered the minimum for survival without special help.

Preterm and Low-Birth-Weight Babies

Since preterm and low-birth-weight babies share some problems, we will consider them together. Babies born earlier than 35 weeks conceptual age are considered preterm. Babies weighing less than 2500 grams who are born later than 35 weeks are considered low-birth-weight or small for date babies. At present, the prematurity rate in the United States is 7.1 percent of white and 17.9 percent of nonwhite live births; that of low-birth-weight babies is 7.1 percent of white and 13.4 percent of nonwhite live births (Glasgow & Overall, 1979). The differences between racial groups are most probably due to socioeconomic circumstances relating to nutrition, family size, and the availability of adequate prenatal and perinatal care. Preterm and low-birth-weight babies account for 50 percent of all deaths that occur in the newborn period, and those that survive beyond this time have a death rate in the first two years that is still three time that of normal-term babies. In addition, there is a higher incidence of sudden infant death syndrome, of child abuse, and of inadequate bonding between parent and infant in preterm and low-birth-weight babies (Glasgow & Overall, 1979).

Low birth weight is usually due to an insufficiency of the placenta, which has retarded the nutrition and therefore the growth of the baby, or to deficiencies in the nutrition or general health of the mother. Such babies usually lack **subcutaneous** (under the skin) fat. They often have a wrinkled appearance, possibly because they may have earlier developed some fat and then absorbed it as development without sufficient nourishment continued. Low-birth-weight babies often are shorter than expected for conceptual age and have a head disproportionately large for body size.

Preterm birth occurs because of various

conditions that cause the uterus to be unable to retain the baby to term. Such babies tend to be thinner than normal babies, since they have not had the extra time in the uterus to build as much of a fat layer. Hence they generally do not look wrinkled. Often preterm babies are not only thinner, but smaller in size as well, particularly babies born much earlier than 35 weeks. Some babies born very early may weigh as little as 900 grams, or 2 lb, and be as small as a doll. They may almost fit into an adult's cupped hand. Obviously, the smaller and earlier born the baby is, the more likely it is not to survive or at least to have severe problems with survival.

Sometimes it is difficult to determine whether a baby is preterm or of low birth weight. The time of conception may have been difficult to pinpoint, and gross appearance characteristics at birth may not be so clear that a determination can be made. An instrument often used to determine gestational age and hence which type of baby one is dealing with is the *Dubowitz Scale* (Dubowitz, Dubowitz, & Goldberg, 1970). It consists of checking certain indicators, such as how the baby lies on the back and abdomen, how far the arms can be moved, and the positions in which the legs and arms are maintained at rest. As these indicators change somewhat with increasing gestational age, an inference can be made as to the true age of the baby and therefore if it is preterm or of low birth weight. Since both kinds of babies share many problems, however, many of the methods of dealing with them are similar.

Problems common to both preterm and low-birth-weight babies include those involving temperature maintenance and nutrition. In addition, preterm babies frequently have problems with respiration and excess bilirubin (a substance in the blood). While both low-birth-weight and normal babies sometimes have problems in these latter two areas as well, the probability is considerably higher

for preterm infants. Low-birth-weight babies have a higher incidence of congenital malformations than do normal or preterm babies, including a ductus arteriosus that fails to close at birth. They are also much more likely to develop hypoglycemia, or low blood sugar, which can be dangerous in the neonate (Glasgow & Overall, 1979).

TEMPERATURE CONTROL

The problem of temperature control for the preterm and low-birth-weight infant is much greater than for the normal baby because they both have less fat to act as an insulator and because their proportion of exposed skin to body size is even greater than for the normal baby. In addition, the preterm baby has an even less mature brain, which has more difficulty monitoring temperature changes. The heated incubator, or isolette, which can be maintained at body temperature and can prevent the cooling off of the infant without having to encase it in layers of clothing, has been of great help in maintaining a constant and sufficiently high temperature for the infant. In recent years, radiantly heated open beds have also come into use. In addition to maintaining temperature, these have the added advantage of affording easier access to the baby by hospital personnel. They also enable the baby to obtain some environmental stimulation that is difficult to come by when in an isolette. It includes being able to see and hear people and events around them or being touched by nurses, doctors, or their own parents.

NUTRITION

Nutritional problems may involve immaturity of the digestive system, lack of coordination between sucking and swallowing, or feebleness of sucking. In the former situation, the type and composition of milk or other nutrients given to the baby must be carefully adjusted. If the baby cannot absorb any or absorbs only insufficient amounts of nutrients by mouth, intravenous feeding (by a syringe delivering nutrients directly into a vein) is used. Sucking and rooting develop by the 32nd week after conception, but the baby is unable to coordinate sucking and swallowing until the 34th week (Niswander, 1981). Therefore, feeding through tubes leading directly to the stomach, a technique known as **gavaging,** is often used until the baby has coordinated sucking and swallowing or until the baby is physically strong enough to suck with enough vigor to maintain its nutrition.

Mothers of such babies who wish to breast feed but whose babies cannot yet suck at the breast are taught to stimulate their breasts and to express milk manually or with the use of a breast pump. This milk can often be fed to the baby via gavage. Then when the baby is strong enough to commence sucking, the mother's milk supply will still be available. Since breast milk is least likely to cause nutritional problems for preterm infants, many hospitals have set up milk banks to provide breast milk from mothers having an excess. This milk is then fed to those babies whose mothers do not produce sufficient milk, who cannot breast feed, or who have already left the hospital and are too far away to provide their own breast milk to the still-hospitalized baby.

RESPIRATION

Respiration is a particularly severe problem for the preterm infant. The lungs are often too immature to be able to handle the exchange between oxygen and carbon dioxide efficiently enough to maintain life. In addition, many preterm babies are too weak to exert the effort involved in breathing. For these babies, an airway delivering oxygen or air under pressure to the lungs with mechanical support of the breathing process is used. A far more serious problem present in babies that are extremely preterm is **hyaline membrane disease.** In this condition, a glassy-looking membrane forms over the immature lung tissue and prevents the exchange of gases in the air sacs or alveoli. It has been found that the injection of a steroid compound to the mother 24 hours before delivery can help prevent the development of this condition in the infant who is less than 30 weeks conceptual age (Liggins & Howie, 1972, 1974). However, many others who deliver prematurely go into labor unexpectedly, and their labors are often quite rapid. And since the steroids do not help if used later in labor, or if the baby is beyond 30 weeks gestational age, hyaline membrane disease still occurs with some frequency in preterm infants.

A variety of methods is used to treat the condition. Most involve the introduction of moist oxygen under some pressure into the baby's lungs. This procedure must be executed carefully, since too much oxygen can cause blindness in the baby. Others have tried hyperbaric chambers, similar to the decompression chambers used by deep-sea divers, with the idea that if external pressure is increased, the baby's blood may absorb more oxygen.

EXCESS BILIRUBIN

Bilirubin is a chemical produced during the breakdown of red blood cells. A particular enzyme in the liver processes the bilirubin and reduces it to harmless substances in the normal individual. Newborn babies, including preterm ones, are born with an excess of red blood cells, since more are needed for fetal circulation than for circulation after birth. This excess must be disposed of after the baby is born. Even in the normal newborn, however, the liver falls a bit behind in converting the bilirubin, resulting in the slightly tanned appearance, often referred to as a pumpkin color, of the newborn during the first few days after birth.

In the normal baby, this excess bilirubin is promptly processed after the first few days, the tanning fades, and the baby is all right. In some preterm infants, however, the bilirubin level becomes too high, and the body alone cannot rid itself of the substance. It has been found that special lights can be used to help the baby's body hasten the breakdown of bilirubin. Its eyes carefully shielded, the baby is placed under the bilirubin lights for a portion of each day. The condition of excess bilirubin, to the degree that the lights must be used, is occasionally present in full-term babies as well. But it is far more common in preterm ones. Fortunately, it can now be corrected without lasting problems for most babies.

Causes and Prevention of Preterm Birth

The best way to treat preterm birth is to prevent it. That is more difficult than it sounds, for some of the factors that can cause prematurity can be long-standing conditions or habits that cannot easily be changed or whose effects can only be somewhat ameliorated later.

One major cause of both preterm birth and of low birth weight is inadequate maternal nutrition. The role that inadequate nutrition during pregnancy plays in increasing the rate of miscarriage, prematurity, and death of babies during the perinatal period has been documented in studies of starvation in wartime. These studies have been discussed more extensively in chapter 3. More difficult to document, but highly suspect, is poor nu-

trition during a woman's formative years, while she herself is still a child and adolescent. The use of convenience foods and fast-food restaurants, as well as our social emphasis on slimness, all may have a detrimental effect upon the American diet, especially that of young women. Although we see few instances of nutritional deficiency diseases such as rickets or pellagra, or of outright starvation, in the United States today, the diets of growing girls are often high in fats, sugars, and salts, and low in nutrients important to the eventual growth of a baby. Thus, while an adequate diet during pregnancy is also of importance in preventing preterm birth and producing a health baby, a woman with a long history of inadequate diet can do little to ameliorate the situation imposed by the past.

In addition, smoking, alcohol, and narcotics all appear to play a part in the incidence of preterm and low-birth-weight babies, as has been discussed in chapter 3. Since the use of these substances often involves long-standing habits, many women find it difficult to stop using them during pregnancy, and the baby eventually suffers the consequences.

Another factor in preterm birth as well as low birth weight is lack of prenatal care or inadequate prenatal care. For many women, the idea of seeing a doctor or nurse before the actual onset of labor (or even then) is an unknown concept because of lack of money, lack of knowledge, or the unavailability of health-care professionals in a particular area. Thus conditions that could threaten the pregnancy or cause its premature termination are not discovered and therefore cannot be corrected. Not surprisingly, the prematurity rate is highest among those groups least likely to obtain prenatal care: the poor, rural people, and nonwhites.

Multiple babies often are related to both

low birth weight and preterm birth. When a woman is carrying two or more babies, the food supply to each may be smaller than that to just one baby. In addition, the multiple babies fill the uterus to capacity earlier during the gestational period than does a single baby, which can result in earlier labor. For both these reasons, twins, triplets, and other multiple births tend to be born prematurely more often than are single births, and each baby tends to weigh less than a single, full-term baby. The larger the number of babies, the more likely that they will be born earlier and that each will weigh less.

Too many pregnancies spaced too closely together seem to be another factor leading to prematurity. The depleted uterus may not have had time to recover adequately from a previous pregnancy before the next one commences. Then it may not be able to support the next baby all the way through the normal gestational period.

As more very young girls have babies, it has been found that the rate of preterm and low-birth-weight deliveries in this group is much higher than in mothers between the ages of 20 and 35 (Babson & Clarke, 1983). Therefore, there is a much higher incidence of death among these babies than in those born to mothers over the age of 20. Since the uterus and its supporting structures are not fully mature till about 18 to 20 years of age, but many girls are capable of becoming pregnant at 13 or 14 or sometimes younger, it is easy to see that problems can come about in such a pregnancy. In addition to prematurity or low birth weight, the psychological problems of a child having to care for another child are profound.

At the other end of the childbearing age scale, similar results are also seen. Preterm birth is also higher than average among older mothers, above the age of 35. Here too, other problems, such as the higher incidence

of genetic and chromosomal disorders, add to the risks incurred by the mother and baby.

The major factors that correlate with preterm birth as well as with low birth weight are lack of prenatal care, short space of time since last pregnancy, and mother younger than 18 or older than 35, as well as previous problems with pregnancy and birth, being nonwhite, and the unmarried status of the mother (Eisner, Brazie, Pratt, & Hexter, 1979). The last two factors probably relate to socioeconomic circumstances and hence to nutrition and lack of prenatal care. These data came from a study that used all live birth statistics for the United States in 1974. While causation can only be inferred and not postulated from a correlational study, this one had such a large data base that it can safely be inferred that the relationship could well be causal.

Other Problems

While medicine has come a long way toward solving the physical problems precipitated by preterm birth, scientists are only beginning to comprehend that there might be some neurological and psychological problems as well. It has been known for some time that even when offered the best of physical care, preterm babies, when they reach the equivalent of term, or 38 weeks gestation age, still lag behind full-term newborns in some respects. Recent work has begun to show what the causes of some of this lag might be.

While the baby in the uterus is exposed to much kinesthetic, auditory, and **vestibular** (inner ear, relating to balance) stimulation from the watery environment of the uterus, the sounds made by the mother, particularly her heart beat, and the constant motion and change of position as the mother goes about her daily tasks, the newborn preterm baby is often in a world of very low stimulation (Newman, 1981). There is little sound in an isolette, except the hum of the instruments regulating temperature and air inputs. While loud, this hum is quite monotonous. There is little motion of the environment and certainly no sustained rhythmic motion. Except for occasional examinations or diapering, usually done through ports in the isolette, the baby gets very little kinesthetic stimulation. Even feeding involves little handling. True, the baby is able to look around (unless the eyes are shielded from bilirubin lights), while the baby in the uterus cannot look at anything, but there is usually little to see. Of course, there is some question about how much the preterm newborn is able to see anyway. Thus, the preterm infant is in a state of stimulus deprivation as compared not only to the full-term infant but even to the baby of comparable gestation age who is still being carried in the mother's womb (Newman, 1981).

Some work done at the University of Washington, which uses a specialized rocking isolette with heart-beat noises piped in via a tape recorder, appears able to alleviate some of this deficit (Barnard, 1972; 1975). A similar approach, using an oscillating waterbed, has been tried by researchers at Stan-

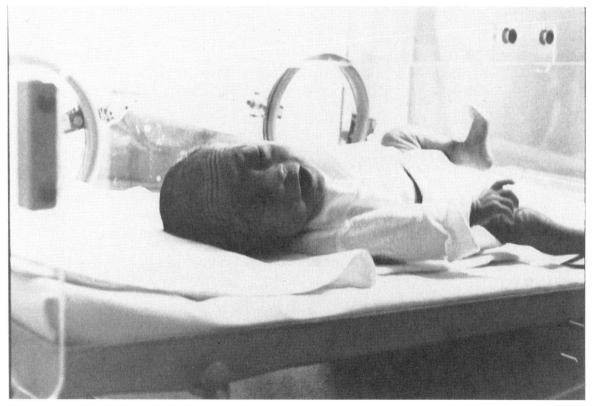

The preterm or low-birth-weight baby in an isolette receives the benefit of a warm, relatively germ-free environment in which the oxygen and humidity levels can be precisely controlled. However, such a baby is exposed to little sensory or social stimulation.

ford University with encouraging results (Korner, Kraemer, Haffner, & Cosper, 1975). And, as already mentioned, many hospitals are switching from the use of isolettes to radiantly heated open beds, in which the baby is less isolated. A recent review of the tactile and vestibular stimulation projects used during the late 1960s and the 1970s concluded that they resulted in improved weight gain, motor development, and respiratory functioning for babies exposed to such stimulation while in the high-risk nursery (Schaefer, Hatcher, & Barglow, 1980).

Another factor important in ensuring good psychological development of the preterm baby is the early establishment of the mother-infant bond and the maintenance of maternal feelings of affection and competence in spite of formidable physical problems and barriers and the length of time that will elapse before the mother can take her baby home.

Many mothers show extreme anxiety about their babies not only because they worry about the infant's precarious hold on life but also because they are afraid to do anything for or with the baby lest they cause harm. While many mothers of full-term, robust babies are also afraid to handle them at first, mothers of tiny, fragile-looking, preterm babies are even more apprehensive. Furthermore, they are often physically separated from their babies by the infants' confinement in the isolette and by other mechanical contrivances. The only reality of their babies may be an occasional glimpse through the nursery window. When the mother goes home after a few days, leaving the baby behind in the hospital for what may be weeks or even months, with only a brief daily visit, this sense of separation may be heightened. All during the baby's stay in the hospital the mother may handle the child little or not at all. And after the baby goes home the mother

may continue to treat the preterm infant more as a fragile toy than a real baby that needs holding and cuddling.

The preterm baby thus receives much less not only of kinesthetic stimulation but also of the psychological stimulation inherent in being picked up, held, rocked, and played with, even after the child has developed physically beyond the premature stage. Furthermore, because the baby has been kept distant from the mother during a prolonged hospital stay, the mother has had less opportunity to be reinforced by the reactions, eye contact, and smiles of her child that usually serve to keep maternal nurturant behavior going in mothers of full-term babies.

Studies have shown that mothers of preterm babies who are separated from them by hospital routine and because of the babies' condition show delayed bonding and report negative perceptions of their babies (Jeffcoate, 1979). At a time when the baby was long out of danger, such a mother would still show high levels of anxiety about the child and persist in believing that it was in danger. Even a low-risk preterm birth can cause a crisis in the relationship between mother and father (Trause & Kramer, 1983). This distress decreased after the baby joined the family at home. Eventually, after several months had elapsed, such parents of low-risk preterm babies reported becoming more attuned to each other's feelings than did those of a comparison group whose babies were born at term.

Many hospitals are now attempting to alleviate the early lack of interaction. Mothers are allowed to help care for their babies in the high-risk nursery as soon as possible. Babies who are strong enough are removed from the isolette at intervals and given to the mothers to hold and cuddle and often to feed. When mothers go home from the hospital they are encouraged to return for as long as possible each day, not just as casual observers but as active caregivers. It is being recognized that the psychological well-being of these babies is as important as their physical care and that the ideal physical environment of the isolette or even the open bed may not be ideal on a 24-hour basis for the baby, the mother, and particularly for the establishment of interaction patterns between them.

Some scientific evidence is beginning to lend support to such procedures. For example, Barnett conducted a study in which some mothers of preterm and other high-risk infants were allowed to participate in the early routine care of their babies while in the hospital (Barnett, Leiderman, Srobstein, & Klaus, 1970). A control group was not able to do so. The experimental mothers showed affective interaction such as cuddling and smiling. They began to participate in baby care and eventually assumed the major responsibility for such care without feelings of inadequacy or undue worries. When these mothers were compared to the controls after they took their babies home, Barnett found that they expressed greater confidence in their ability to care for the babies, demonstrated greater skill in infant care, and showed a higher level of attachment than did control mothers.

There is some evidence that lack of adequate bonding with infants separated from their mothers because of prematurity or other risk factors that require special care may result in failure to thrive or in child abuse by the parent. Preterm and low-birth-weight babies have three times greater risk than term babies of being abused by parents or other caregivers during infancy or early childhood (Schmitt & Kempe, 1979). This relationship holds even when socioeconomic status is held constant (Klein & Stern, 1971). Failure to thrive in children under the age of two usually results from the deliberate withholding of food from the child, which is also

a form of child abuse (Klein & Stern, 1971). In addition, there is evidence that the sensory and affective deprivation experienced by some of these babies may have long-term effects upon their perceptual and intellectual development (Drillien, 1961; Drillien, Thomson, & Bargoyne, 1980). Again, most of these indicators are correlational, meaning that causation cannot be posited but only inferred.

Postmature Babies

Babies born more than two weeks beyond the due date, or more than 40 weeks conceptual age, are **postmature.** In the past, some postmature babies have been born a month or more beyond the expected time. At present, postmature babies are rarely allowed to continue their gestation more than 20 days beyond term. Either labor is induced through the use of an oxytocin-related drug, or the baby is delivered by cesarean section.

Postmature babies usually have drylooking skin that feels quite hard to the touch. They have little or no fat. It is presumed that they look this way because they have been using up their fat as the placenta has become far less efficient in supplying nutrients to the baby. Vernix and lanugo are usually absent, and the baby may have long fingernails and long, well-developed scalp hair. Postmaturity up to three weeks beyond term is far less of a risk to the baby than prematurity, since its body systems are usually fully developed. Thus, except for the lack of fat and possible problems associated with the induction of labor or cesarean delivery, postmature babies who are not allowed to go more than three weeks beyond due date generally do well. After three weeks beyond term their mortality rate rises significantly.

In addition, the parents of a postmature baby are psychologically ready for the birth, whereas those of a preterm baby have to adjust quickly to the arrival of their child somewhat earlier than expected. Therefore the adjustment process is usually easier for the former, even though the baby may have some complications or the birth was a cesarean delivery.

ASSESSMENT OF THE NEONATE

In addition to the immediate assessment of the state of the neonate by the Apgar Scale and the determination of whether an infant is preterm or small for date via the Dubowitz Scale, other instruments may be used somewhat later during the neonatal period, when the infant is out of immediate danger. Their purpose is to determine the neurological intactness of the infant in cases where brain or spinal cord damage is suspected, such as those of some preterm infants or those having undergone a delivery involving problems such as anoxia, an exceedingly long labor, or fetal distress.

The earliest of the neurological examinations designed systematically to assess neonates was the *Prechtl Neonatal Neurological Exam* (Prechtl & Beintema 1964). This

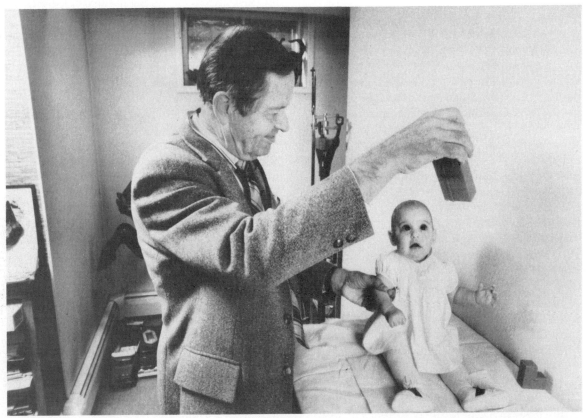

Dr. T. Berry Brazelton, who developed the Neonatal Behavioral Assessment Scale or NBAS, is here shown testing a somewhat older infant. The Brazelton NBAS is the most frequently used screening device to test for neurological integration of the newborn infant.

system used the infant's ability to **habituate** (decrease in responsiveness) to a stimulus to test for neurological intactness, since neurologically impaired infants generally lack the capacity to habituate and instead continue to respond to stimulation (see chapter 5 for a detailed discussion of habituation). The drawback of the Prechtl system, however, was that it measured only the infant's reactions to noxious or unpleasant stimulation and not to the more usual kinds of nonsocial and social stimulation the infant encountered in everyday life.

Because of this drawback, the Prechtl Exam has been superseded by the *Brazelton Neonatal Behavioral Assessment Scale*, or NBAS (Brazelton, 1973). This instrument tests the infant's reactions to both social and nonsocial stimuli, as well as to both pleasant and disturbing ones, in order to determine its level of neurological integration. The examination includes 26 categories of behavioral items and 20 reflexes that are assessed over a 20-to-30-minute time period. The examination should be given after the child is at least three days old.

The reflex testing is designed to determine whether gross neurological abnormalities are present. The behavioral items are based on environmental stimuli, including social interpersonal ones likely to be used by caregivers in interaction with the infant. The items include response decrement to various social and nonsocial stimuli, **orienting** to social and nonsocial stimuli, motor responses, cuddliness, consolability, self-quieting activity, and irritability.

The examiner manipulates the **state** of the infant (such as being alert or drowsy, crying or sleeping) and tries to elicit its best performance. Only best performance is scored, since Brazelton believes that the ability to recover from a disorganized state and to function adequately thereafter is more predictive of the infant's later functioning than is the presence of a disorganized state at some point during the examination.

Because the NBAS uses typical stimuli and is scored on the basis of optimum performance, it is helpful in predicting later normal functioning of those infants who show some neurological involvement at birth but recover from it later.

Brazelton recommends that the infant be tested with the parent or parents present and that the examiner explain and comment on specific infant reactions. Parents can learn much, he believes, from seeing how their child reacts to particular kinds of stimulation and by understanding the techniques the infant uses to maintain or resume control of, to defend, and to console, itself.

Summary

1. Becoming parents is a physically and psychologically stressful experience for many people. The vast majority of married people, however, wish to become parents, although they want fewer children than in the recent past.

2. Childbirth changed during the 19th and 20th centuries from a social event, managed by women, that took place in the home, to a medical event, managed by men, that took place in a hospital. In the last two decades, however, the birth process has become more humanized and individualized through such changes as the increase of Lamaze births, the use of birthing rooms and birthing centers, the increasing entry of women into obstetrics, and the reappearance of midwives.

3. Normal vaginal birth proceeds through three stages: effacement and dilation, the birth of the baby, and the delivery of the placenta. During the first stage, which readies the uterus for delivery of the baby, contractions increase in strength, length, and proximity to each other. During the second stage, the mother must actively cooperate to expel the baby, or else mechanical means such as forceps must be used. The expulsion of the placenta is easier and often is unnoticed by the mother, who is busy attending to her newborn.

4. Cesarean delivery involves removal of the baby through an incision in the mother's abdomen. It is used if there is a complication such as disproportion in the size of the baby's head and the mother's pelvis, breech or transverse presentation of the baby, or poor progress of labor. The rate of cesarean delivery has increased greatly in recent years, but overall the procedure also is safer for mother and baby than in the past.

5. Anesthetics and analgesics are used in childbirth to control or diminish the mother's sensation of pain. Although most women in labor receive some type of pain relief, the kinds and amounts of anesthetics used have changed, and most mothers are awake during the birth of their baby. The drugs in anesthetics and analgesics enter the baby's bloodstream before birth through the placenta and can temporarily depress the baby's responses such as breathing and sucking after birth.

6. The neonate must immediately upon birth begin to adjust to changes in respiration and blood circulation that involve the use of its lungs to obtain oxygen. Because temperature control is inefficient at first, the baby must be kept warm. Soon the baby begins to take in nourishment through sucking and excretes and eliminates the waste products of its body.

7. The newborn baby can see, hear, taste, and smell far more effectively than had been thought in the past. Neonates seem to prefer visual displays that resemble human faces, and sounds that resemble either the rhythmic beat of the heart or the human, especially the female, voice. They prefer sweet substances over salty or bitter ones, and they move their bodies in synchrony with adult speech.

8. Preterm babies are those born more than three weeks before they are due; low-birth-weight babies are those born at or near term but weighing less than 2500 g. Both share problems relating to temperature control and the efforts involved in breathing and sucking. In addition, preterm babies may have immature lungs and excess bilirubin in the blood. Babies kept in low-stimulus environments such as isolettes because of these conditions may be exposed to less environmental stimulation than are normal infants. Parents may have problems with establishing an early close relationship with their child because of these mechanical barriers. Recent attempts to overcome these problems have shown some success.

9. Assessment of the neonate includes the Apgar Scale, used to determine immediate vital signs at birth, and the Dubowitz Scale, used to decide whether a baby is preterm or of low birth weight. Neurological scales include the Prechtl and the Brazelton. Because the Brazelton measures the infant's reactions to social and nonsocial, pleasant and unpleasant stimulation, it is considered the best predictor of later neurological functioning.

Participatory and Observational Exercises

1. Visit a prepared-childbirth (Lamaze) class. What kinds of couples are participating? Factors to observe or inquire about might be ages, races, socioeconomic standing, educational level, whether a couple is expecting a first or subsequent child. How typical of the child-bearing population do you think these couples are? In what ways, if any, do you think they are unusual? What are they doing in the class? How does each activity relate to what will happen during birth? Interview one couple about their training in the class, as well as about their expectations regarding the birth experience.

2. Visit the labor and delivery areas of a local hospital. Describe the physical setting. Does it appear homelike, warm and supportive, or institutional, cold, and "scary"? What do you think your reaction to it might be if you were the woman in labor admitted there? Interview some of the nurses and other staff if possible. From their descriptions of what they do, does it seem as though they regard childbirth as a natural experience or a disease? What attitudes do they express toward their patients?

3. Interview an obstetrician and/or a nurse-midwife. Obtain their perceptions of the nature of the birth process. How much time during labor does each spend with a particular patient? How frequently does he or she check on the patient while in the hospital during labor? How dangerous is birth perceived to be by this health-care professional? Would the individual consent to do a delivery in a birthing center? At home? Why or why not? If the person would, under what conditions or restrictions? Does he or she favor the use of anesthetics in uncomplicated births? Why or why not? What is the person's attitude about the bonding process between infant and parent(s) after birth? How does he or she support the attitude in actual practice? After the interview, decide what may be the advantages and disadvantages of having labor attended by an obstetrician vs. a nurse-midwife.

4. Visit a local department store or a discount merchandiser such as K-Mart and find out what kinds of baby equipment, furniture, toys, and clothing for infants it carries. Check prices and variety available. How much does it cost to set up a minimally but adequately equipped nursery for a newborn? How much does it cost to dress a new baby? Project the costs over the first year, remembering that babies outgrow clothes and that their needs for toys and equipment change over time. How much can be spent if money is no object? How sturdy are the various articles of furniture, equipment, clothing, and toys? Which of them are necessities, and which are optional?

5. Interview a couple as soon after birth as possible (within the first week if you can). Be sure to obtain the father's, as well as the mother's, opinions and descriptions. Ask about the following from each:

   a. What was the labor like? How did they know it was the real thing? When did they go to the hospital, birthing center, or clinic? What happened after that? How prepared were they for the various events that occur during labor? How unexpected were some of these events? How did they cope with them?

   b. Have them describe the moment of birth. What did the baby look like to each? What was their first reaction to the event of birth? When did each get to first hold the baby? How much time could they spend with the baby and with each other after the birth?

c. What were the biggest adjustments to becoming parents? In the hospital? When at home? How have they handled these adjustments?

6. Interview the parents of a preterm infant or one born by cesarean section. Ask them as many of the questions in number 5 above as appear appropriate. In addition, inquire about the following:

a. If the baby was born quite a while before the due date, what special problems did they face in the sudden adjustment to parenthood?

b. In the case of the cesarean baby, how soon did the mother feel her physical strength and stamina returning? To what extent has it returned at the time of the interview? Has the slower recovery process hindered adjustment to the baby and the resumption of household routines?

c. If the baby was in a high-risk nursery, were parents able to visit there? When and for how long? Beginning how soon after birth? Were they allowed to hold the baby? Was the mother allowed to breast feed it?

d. What special problems do they feel they have encountered because of the baby's (or mother's) condition? How have they tried to cope with them?

7. If you can, observe newborns in a hospital nursery. (Note: If the hospital(s) in your community has rooming in only, and no nursery for newborns, you may not be able to do this. Try to visit a friend who is in the hospital to have a baby and observe her rooming-in baby, and that of her roommate if she is in a semiprivate room. This will provide you with fewer babies to observe, but it is better than no observation at all.) What is the appearance of a normal neonate? Are there differences in appearance between babies? Describe them. Can you see individual differences in activity level? What are they? Are there discernible differences between babies in the length and intensity of the various sleeping and waking states? In the amount and kind of crying? Observe breathing in neonates. How does it differ from that of a somewhat older child?

8. If possible, observe babies in a high-risk nursery also. Some hospitals allow students to do this, but others do not. How does the physical environment of a high-risk nursery differ from that of the normal newborn nursery? Why? What about the level of staffing? What implications might this have for the sensory and emotional development of the babies? How does the appearance of these babies differ from that of other neonates? Are parents participating in caregiving? What do they do? How does hospital staff try to maximize their own and the parents' interactions with the infants?

DISCUSSION QUESTIONS

1. Keeping a critically-ill preterm, low-birth-weight or severely handicapped baby alive costs thousands of dollars, much or most of it from public funds. Should doctors and other health-care professionals take heroic measures to keep such children alive, or should they provide only routine care? Why do you hold the position you do?

2. In a normal, uncomplicated birth, should the emphasis be more on the psychological well-being of the laboring woman, or on the prevention of possible complications through the use of devices like fetal monitors? Support your argument with information.

3. What preparations should a couple make to ease the adjustment process of going from being a dyad to a triad with the birth of a baby? Discuss with your classmates what personality factors in prospective parents may ease the adjustment process.

Growth of Basic Functions: Physical and Motor Development

INTRODUCTION

When Jill and David had their first baby, they worried when the baby lost weight after birth while still in the hospital. In their minds, this loss meant that something must be wrong with the baby, or else that either Jill or the hospital nurses were not caring for it properly. For a while they suffered and worried in silence. Finally, they asked their doctor and found out that such weight loss is perfectly normal for all newborns. Thus reassured, they were able to stop worrying and concentrate upon getting to know their child.

Another couple, Sam and Lu, had a very small baby called Joey. But Joey was not small for date. It was simply that both parents were very small people, and their son inherited this trait. Joey began life at the 10th percentile in the growth charts and remained at the same relative place all during infancy. When he began walking, at the unusually early age of nine months, his head barely reached the top of the coffee table. By the time he was seven, Joey had turned into a crack pool player. His head, however, barely reached the pool table top, and he had to boost himself up on the edge of the table to make his shots. This is an example of a normal child whose growth pattern remained at the lower end of the physical growth norms all during childhood. Since he never deviated by much in his growth patterns but remained at the same level in relationship to other normal children, there was no cause for worry. Both of these examples illustrate why knowledge of what is normal in physical and motor growth and development can be helpful to parents and others dealing with infants.

CAPACITIES AND ADJUSTMENTS OF THE NEONATE

The neonatal, or newborn, period extends from birth to four weeks of age. Although the human neonate is more helpless and dependent than the neonate of any other mammalian species, he or she is far more capable than had previously been suspected. The infant is born with certain reflex mechanisms as well as some relatively well-developed sensory and motor capacities. These aid the infant in protecting itself and obtaining food, as well as signaling for the attention of caregivers.

Early Appearance

The normal infant loses 5 to 7 percent of body weight in the first few days of life. This loss occurs as some of the excess water in the tissues is excreted and as the baby uses up some stored fats to maintain body temperature and other body mechanisms. As the mother's milk comes in during the days after birth and the baby begins to nurse, this weight loss is reversed, and most babies are up to their birth weight again by the 10th day of postnatal life.

As the baby regains the lost birth weight and shows further weight gain, it loses some of the wizened appearance that may have been there at birth and begins to assume the typical rounded appearance of babies. The skin, which may have peeled at first, begins to clear and becomes smoother and less transparent. Small white bumps resembling pimples that may have been visible on the face and elsewhere clear up during this time. The baby's skin color, which may have been somewhat mottled at first, becomes a more even and healthy pink. In black babies, the skin slowly begins to darken toward its eventual shade as the baby is increasingly exposed to sunlight.

The newborn's head at first seems disproportionately large, up to 25 percent of total body length. In the adult it is about 10 percent of the total. The circumference of the head is the widest portion of the newborn, exceeding that of the chest. The bones of the head slowly return to their proper place and shape after the molding they received passing through the birth canal, and during the first month the baby's head becomes more rounded. The two **fontanels,** or soft spots, one at the top and the other at the back of the head, are still quite pronounced. The **mandible,** or lower jaw, is quite small in the neonate, causing the baby to have a receding chin.

The neonate has a relatively small chest and a rather large, protruding abdomen. The limbs are quite short and are held in a partially flexed position even when the infant is awake. The fists are tightly closed, and both arms and legs tend to be in a flexed position while the baby is asleep.

The normal term baby's weight averages 3.4 kg (7 1/2 lb), with boys slightly heavier, on the average, than girls. Ninety-five percent of babies weigh between 2.5 kg (5 1/2 lb) and 4.6 kg (10 lb). The length of the neonate averages 50 cm (20 in) with boys again showing a slightly greater average length than girls. Ninety-five percent of newborns are between 45 and 55 cm (18–22 in) in length. The average circumference of the head is 35 cm (14 in) (Guthrie, Prueitt, Murphy, Hodson, Wennberg, & Woodrum, 1977).

The newborn's body has a higher concentration of water than does the body at any subsequent age. Of neonatal body weight, 75 percent is made up of water, 11 percent of fat, and 11 percent of protein, or muscle, and of bone. (Eichorn, 1979). In adult females the comparable proportions are 52 percent water, 31 percent fat, and 16 percent muscle; for adult males they are 52 percent, 14 percent, and 33 percent, respectively. The muscles of the newborn are small and not firm in consistency. After the baby begins to exercise them, and as the muscle cells develop more nuclei and the number of nerve-muscle connections

increase, the muscles become firmer and more powerful.

The umbilical stump, left after the cord has been tied and cut, shrivels up and generally falls off after about six to ten days. During the first few days of postnatal life the stump should be cleaned with alcohol daily, and the baby should be given sponge baths only, to minimize the risk of infection. After the stump falls off, the baby may be bathed by immersion in water.

The neonate has limited ability to concentrate urine in the kidneys. It therefore voids frequently, often more than eighteen times a day. Because of this loss, the baby needs to ingest large amounts of fluid. After the initial postnatal period during which extra fluids present at birth are utilized, the baby can dehydrate very quickly if it does not ingest sufficient amounts of fluids. If an infant cannot take any or enough fluids by mouth because of illness or other complications, intravenous fluid therapy may be used.

Generally the newborn easily adjusts to respiration and maintenance of body temperature, as well as to food absorption and elimination, during the early portions of this period. It makes other adjustments, such as control over enzyme secretion and utilization, the development of an immune system, and the development of blood clotting mechanisms, more slowly and may be at some risk until these are adequately established.

Sensory and Motor Capacities

ORIENTING

The neonate exhibits an orienting response. **Orienting** is a response to change in the environment evidenced by attention to such change. The neonate orients to visual displays, sounds, touch, and other sensory stimuli. Besides being visible to the observer, orienting can also be inferred from measurement of heart rate. A sustained deceleration of heart rate in the newborn is interpreted as showing that the infant is orienting to a particular stimulus. Rapid acceleration of heart rate after an initial brief deceleration, on the other hand, is interpreted as a sign of a defensive reaction (Lipsitt & Jacklin, 1971).

HABITUATION

The neonate also has the capacity to habituate to stimulation. **Habituation** is a decreased response that occurs to continued presentation of a stimulus. It is mediated by the central nervous system and is specific to that particular stimulus (Berg & Berg, 1979). Habituation is sometimes confused with fatigue or adaptation in the sense organ itself. If the baby's response decreases because of fatigue, there should be a lowered response rate to any stimuli that are directed to a particular sense organ. Therefore, if after this decrement the response rate increases when a stimulus is changed or when one is substituted for another, it can be inferred that habituation and not fatigue was the cause of the original decrement. When researchers substitute one stimulus for another to check on the rate of change of response, the procedure is called **dishabituation.**

Habituation is a central nervous system function that involves a primitive kind of learning and memory. It thus represents a more advanced adaptation than does sensory adaptation or fatigue of end organs (McCall, 1971).

Habituation is an important mechanism in that it enables the developing infant to shut out or stop attending to stimuli that have become familiar and instead to focus upon new or changing ones. Just think of what would happen if people had to attend to all stimulation coming to their bodies from external and internal receptors! They would be so bombarded with stimulation that they could hardly make sense of any aspect of life. It is fortunate that right from birth the baby can attend to some stimuli and "tune out" others to which it has become habituated.

In addition, the neonate can react to annoying stimuli in a defensive manner such as turning the head away, closing the eyes, squinting, squirming, and using its hands protectively.

PHYSICAL STRENGTH

Newborns are surprisingly strong physically and can make a number of postural adjustments. When placed on the back (supine) or on the abdomen (prone) the neonate can turn the head from side to side. In the prone position, it can very briefly raise its head from a flat surface. Because the baby can actively move its head and when supine can flail with its arms and hands, it is almost impossible for a newborn to smother under blankets or other covers in the crib.

The normal baby can maintain a clear airway for breathing by coughing, sneezing, and crying, all of which help to clear the throat and nose of mucus from the lungs. Very young babies breathe only through the nose; it is only after the age of four to five months that the baby opens its mouth and breathes through it if the nasal passages are clogged (Illingworth, 1975).

Sudden-Infant-Death Syndrome

In the past, **sudden-infant-death syndrome,** or SIDS, was often wrongly attributed to smothering under blankets or to the child's inability to clear its throat of mucus or other obstructions. Parents also often blamed themselves for neglecting to do something and thus causing the baby's death. The affected baby appears healthy and unperturbed when put to bed but in the morning is found dead without apparent cause, without any sign of struggle, and having made no noise. While the exact cause or set of causes is not yet known, it is known that the condition does not result from parental negligence or from smothering.

SIDS rarely occurs in neonates and shows the greatest incidence in the two-to-three-month period (Davis, 1977). There are 6,000 to 7,000 reported cases annually in the United States (Valdes-Dapena, 1979), which makes it the greatest cause of death in American babies in the one-to-six-month age range (Hoppenbrouwers & Hodgman, 1982). It occurs worldwide about once in 350 live births.

The syndrome is more frequent in male than female infants, in second-born babies, and in those whose older sibling has died, or nearly died, of the condition (Hoppenbrouwers & Hodgman, 1982). It occurs most often in preterm infants, babies of low birth weight, and those of lower socioeconomic standing. Infants whose mothers are under 20 years of age are five times more likely to die of SIDS than those whose mothers are between 20 and 30 (Babson & Clarke, 1983). And, as already mentioned in chapter 3, mothers who smoke are much more at risk for producing a SIDS baby than are nonsmokers. Of course some of these factors interact. For example, young mothers are more likely to be of lower socioeconomic status and to have given birth to a low-birth-weight or premature infant. And babies of smokers are also more likely to be of lower birth weight.

Since SIDS occurs more often in fall or winter, when upper respiratory infections are more usual than at other times of the year, some authorities have suspected that such infections are the cause. Pathological examination after death, however, usually fails to show the presence of organisms causing such infections. Others think that the brain centers governing respiration cease to function and the baby thus "forgets" to breathe (Naeye, 1980). Still others hypothesize that the organs that tell the brain about too high a concentration of carbon dioxide in the body malfunction, breathing therefore stops, and the baby dies.

Recently, it has been hypothesized that SIDS occurs as a result of the interaction of several of these factors at a particular time in the early life of the infant (Hoppenbrouwers & Hodgman, 1982). Any of these factors occurring in isolation, or their occurrence sequentially rather than at once presumably would not result in SIDS. The first of these factors seems to be mild **hypoxia,** or insufficient absorption of oxygen, both before birth and in the first few months after birth (Naeye, 1973). Most babies in whom this condition appears seem to adapt to it successfully by such strategies as increasing their rate of breathing. But the SIDS baby does not seem to adapt, and other factors interact with the hypoxia to make it more serious. These factors include the change in sleep states that occurs during the first few months of postnatal life, with a reduction of **active sleep** and an increase of **quiet sleep.** We will consider these various sleep states a bit farther on in this chapter. These changes appear related to changes in the brain's regulation of both heartbeat and respiration, and seem to proceed somewhat differently in infants who will die of SIDS than in normal infants (Harpet, Leake, Hoffman, Walter, Hoppenbrouwers, Hodgman, & Sterman, 1981). Sleep **apnea,** the temporary cessation of breathing during sleep, usually during active sleep, occurs in all young infants, possibly in relationship to these changes of regulation, but it usually decreases in frequency over time (Booth, Leonard, & Thoman 1983). Normal babies begin to breathe again after such episodes, and SIDS babies do after most of them. But then, some interaction between the chronic hypoxia, sleep apnea, and the changes in brain control over heartbeat and respiration, plus possible environmental factors such as the amount of various gases and pollutants in the air, takes place such that the SIDS baby does not resume breathing after an apneic episode and therefore dies (Hoppenbrouwers & Hodgman, 1982).

In an effort to forestall such an event, some families are now using home monitors on their babies (Southall, 1983). These devices are designed to detect the apneic episode after which the baby does not resume breathing and then to sound an alarm. Parents can attempt to resuscitate the baby. This device, however, presents many problems of its own. First of all, it is expensive. Second, the problem remains that unless a previous child in a family has died of SIDS, or the child in question has had a near miss that was noticed, it is difficult to know which babies might be at risk. For even in the higher-risk groups, the actual incidence is only a fraction of the total number of such babies. Finally, parents using such a monitor for their infant show great anxiety about whether the device is working properly, whether they will hear it and respond in time, and whether they will be able to save the baby even if all else goes well.

Even though there has been a concentrated effort for more than 10 years to determine the cause or causes of SIDS so that it can be prevented, there still are no definitive answers. Much more is known than before about what factors may intersect in a vulnerable child, but a lot of this knowledge is explanatory after the fact, rather than preventive. Thus SIDS remains a puzzling condition.

Temperament Differences

The word **temperament** refers to a set of inborn predispositions, which interact differ-

ently with environmental circumstances in different individuals and which produce differences in individual self-regulation as well. It is thus a person's distinctive style of behavior, a regular way of acting and reacting toward particular events or people.

Temperament differences between infants can be observed from the time of birth onward. In any newborn nursery one can see babies that seem peaceful, quiet, and unaffected by what is going on around them and others who appear on edge, fussy, and reactive to every bit of stimulation. Still others are somewhere between these two extremes. Because of the early appearance of such differences between babies, it is quite probable that temperament has a genetic base, that is, that it is largely due to heredity. Studies of twins have tended to support the genetic hypothesis (Buss & Plomin, 1975; Matheny, Wilson, Dolan, & Kranz, 1981; Torgerson & Kringlen, 1978), showing that temperaments of monozygotic, or identical, twins were more alike than those of dizygotic, or fraternal, twins.

Furthermore, temperament differences can be reliably observed and rated in neonates (Thomas & Chess, 1977). Particular temperament characteristics remain stable from very early, such as days two to four, to somewhat later in neonatal life such as after the second week (Sostek & Anders, 1977). Further stability of temperament beyond the neonatal period will be discussed later in chapter 11.

These temperament differences have implications both for individual development and for the interactions between infant and adults that influence this development. Thus the high-strung, fidgety baby that is constantly into everything may develop some motor skills more quickly than the baby who is content to sit and watch the world go by, placidly observing but interacting very little. The quiet baby may need to be drawn out,

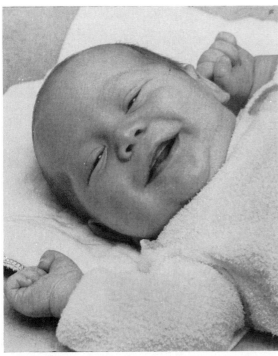 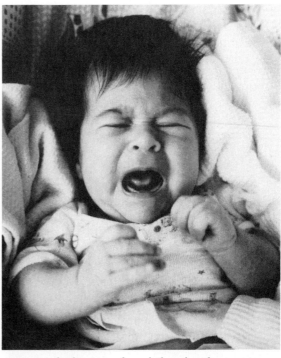

Temperament differences in infants, which can be observed from birth on, affect the reactions of parents and other caregivers toward the child. A placid, easygoing infant (left) is much easier and gratifying to care for. By contrast, a high-strung, fussy baby who often reacts negatively to adult efforts at social interaction or caregiving may be much more difficult to deal with.

forced to respond and interact with things and people by caregivers, while the overly active baby may need to be steered toward an environment and activities that are less stimulating. Furthermore, the baby that is fussy, active, and demanding may be much more difficult for the caregiver to cope with than the placid baby, who reacts slowly and favorably to most environmental events, and these differences can affect the interactional patterns that develop between child and caregiver (Brazelton, 1969).

There is some evidence that parents adapt their caregiving styles to their infant's particular temperament characteristics. Schaffer and Emerson (1964) in a study of mothers and babies in Scotland found that these babies could be divided into "cuddlers," who allowed themselves to be held closely, and "noncuddlers," who resisted such efforts. Some mothers also showed preferences of style, some being more interested in physically handling their babies while others preferred to interact with them more at a distance. Mothers tended to adjust to infant styles and to respond by holding, hugging, and carrying the cuddlers but by exposing the noncuddlers to more distant kinds of stimulation such as showing them things to look at or talking to them. In some instances, however, parental and infant styles were so much at odds that each individual had trouble adjusting to the other's preferred patterns of behavior.

Adjustment to Family Routines

Because of physical differences such as gestational age, weight at birth, health status, the effects of anesthesia, and other factors, and because of differences of temperament between infants, each neonate behaves according to a particular rhythm of its own in matters such as sleeping, feeding, excreting, and eliminating waste. There are, of course, similarities between babies of the same age; young babies all sleep relatively more than older babies, and young babies tend to be hungry and nurse more frequently than older ones. An intriguing question for researchers is how the neonate adjusts its rhythms to those of the family with whom it lives. How does the infant adjust to spending more of the day awake and more of the night sleeping? How does the infant's early preference for 6 to 10 feedings at irregular times come closer to the mother's preferred schedule of feedings every 3 1/2 to 4 hours?

Rhythms exist in the infant even before birth. Mothers report that fetuses have active periods interspersed with quieter ones, and that these periods alternate in a patterned, regular way. After birth, infants show rhythm in sleep-wake cycles, excretion, elimination, and feeding. To some extent these rhythms are **endogenous,** that is, governed by internal mechanisms; but to some degree they are also under **exogenous,** or environmental, control (Thomas & Chess, 1977). These early rhythms at first develop separately from each other and do not mesh or coordinate well with each other. They also do not mesh well with established family routines. Thus many babies spend more time awake at night than in the daytime, demand to be fed just as the rest of the family sits down to a meal, or wet or soil the diaper just after it has been changed. Over time, parents and others try to modify these patterns or exert some control

over them. This process whereby endogenous processes become coordinated with the timing of exogenous environmental events such as caregiving is called **entrainment.** For example, parents may try to keep a baby awake and alert as long as possible in the evening to ensure that when it goes to sleep it will sleep through most of the night. Or they may try to awaken and feed the baby just before an adult mealtime. These efforts help to modify the baby's rhythmic behaviors. Indeed, most babies appear to be highly receptive to environmental cues and adapt by regulating their endogenous processes to conform to them (Sander, 1977). The baby's own temperament and state of maturation, however, also play a large share in determining how quickly and smoothly entrainment takes place.

Another influence on the baby's rhythms is the **circadian,** or 24-hour, cycle. To some extent this cycle influences the baby even before birth, since the mother eats, sleeps, and works according to this cycle. The disruption of this cycle when people travel accounts for the phenomenon of jet lag, in which their bodies want to keep on eating, sleeping, excreting, and performing other functions according to the times of the cycle appropriate to where they came from rather than where they arrived. Over a period of several days, body rhythms adjust to the hours of day and night at the new location. Precisely how that occurs is not yet known. In the same way, the baby in the first few weeks and months of life also begins to adjust to the day-night cycle of the environment, so that over time it sleeps more and longer during the night hours but is awake, plays, and feeds more during the day.

In addition, babies show a fine-tuned adjustment to specific rhythms of their own families over and above the adjustment to circadian rhythms. This adjustment is best demonstrated with babies who are moved from one foster home to another. The tempo of a new family is a bit different from that of one a baby has become accustomed to, and the moved baby will react by irritability and fussiness for a time until the adjustment is made.

STATE IN INFANCY

Definition and Importance of State

The concept of **state** is an important one in a consideration of infancy. State can be defined as a group of variables at a given point in development that determine the organism's readiness to act or react (Emde, Gaensbauer, & Harman, 1976). State can also be defined in terms of the actions or reactions that ensue as a result of the readiness of the brain. Approached in this way, state can be called a group of patterns of relatively stable behaviors that tend to repeat themselves (Prechtl, Akiyama, Zinkin, & Grant, 1968). States beyond the age of one year are relatively well organized, but those in the infant are not yet as fully developed (Berg & Berg, 1979) and are subject to some degree to manipulation by caregivers (Packer & Rosenblatt, 1979). Thus, changing an infant's position, exposing it to particular visual or auditory stimuli, or satisfying basic physiological needs such as hunger can all serve to modify or change the infant's state.

State is important in a consideration of infancy, since the infant's ability to control alertness and wakefulness in response to environmental circumstances, particularly to caregiver circumstances, plays an important role in establishing and maintaining interactions between infant and caregiver. Thus, the degree to which an infant can be alert and respond to cues from the caregiver is important in establishing social, cognitive, and later, language interactions.

In research on infancy, state needs to be carefully considered as well, since the kind and quality of infant response is related to the state of the infant at that time. For example, in studying learning, it has been found that conditioning cannot take place when the baby is asleep and is probably inhibited if the baby is in a drowsy state (Berg & Berg, 1979). Furthermore, it is more difficult to determine if learning has really taken place when the baby is in a state of high activity such as when hungry. For at such times a large number of random behaviors, possibly including those the experimenter has tried to teach the baby, are likely to be emitted. It is easy to confuse some of these random behaviors with true learned behaviors.

States in Early Infancy

Six states can be discerned in the neonate.

1. active, or **REM (rapid eye movement)** sleep
2. quiet, or **non-REM** sleep
3. drowsy awakeness
4. alert awakeness
5. fussing and high activity
6. crying
(Packer & Rosenblatt, 1979; Wolff, 1959)

During active, or REM, sleep, the neonate makes gross limb movements and some fine muscle movements, flutters its eyelids, and shows rapid movement of the eyeballs. The baby also makes facial grimaces, stretches its torso, and may make some sounds. Older children and adults do not move, except for the rapid movement of the eyeballs, during REM sleep. It is during this phase of sleep that older children and adults dream. Whether the young baby experiences phenomena similar to dreams is not yet known.

In the phase of quiet, or non-REM, sleep, the baby makes few movements, generally only some jerks and twitches resembling the Moro reflex, a response similar to startling produced by a loud noise or a change in position. Conversely, it is during non-REM sleep that a lot of muscular activity occurs in those older than infants.

The drowsy state comes either just before falling asleep or upon awakening. During the drowsy state, the eyes have a dull, glazed appearance, and if sleep is to follow, the lids slowly close.

The awakening baby will change from a drowsy to a quiet alert state, in which it is fully awake but remains physically relatively inactive. The infant orients to sound and focuses the eyes on visual objects. There is heightened responsiveness to social cues such as the face or voice of the parent. This is an important state both for early bonding between neonate and parents and because later in infancy it becomes the optimal time for learning and social interaction.

After a period in the quiet alert state, the baby will change to a state of being actively awake. Now there is a lot of arm and leg movement and possibly vocalization that is not crying. The eyes are still wide open but are not fixating on a particular object. Although the baby is still fully awake, learning and social interaction do not take place as easily as during the quiet alert state.

The crying state may follow any other state but usually comes after a period of being either actively awake or asleep. The baby kicks its arms and legs vigorously as if in distress and cries loudly. Often a baby in either the actively awake or the crying state can be returned to the quiet alert state by being picked up and held upright.

In addition, studies by Prechtl (1965) and Korner and Thoman (1970) suggest that no baby may be fully awake when lying supine or flat on the back, even though the eyes are open and the child appears to be quietly alert. They argue that the young baby is only fully awake and receptive to learning or social interaction if put in an upright position such as sitting in an infant seat or being held upright by an adult. These researchers attribute the apparent failure of many earlier experiments involving infant learning to the postural situation of the infant, that is, that in most experiments the infant was kept lying flat on its back. Replications of some of these earlier experiments with infants sitting up have yielded somewhat different and more encouraging results. An even more recent study (Gregg, Haffner, & Korner, 1976), however, suggests that the difference is due not to upright position per se, but to a change of position. Evidently sensations to the inner ear, caused by the change of position of the baby, tend to return it to a quiet alert state and increase its susceptibility to learning.

Individual rhythmicity can be seen in how much time a particular baby spends in the various portions of this cycle as compared to other portions. Some babies spend more time awake than the average right from birth on, some are sleepers that spend more time than usual in sleep, some have long quiet alert phases, and others have shorter ones. Some babies spend a lot of time actively awake or crying or both, others spend relatively little time in this manner.

Changes in Sleep-Wake States as the Infant Matures

In the period immediately following birth, the infant undergoes rapid state changes, about once every 90 seconds (Packer & Rosenblatt, 1979). When the immediate postnatal handling of the infant by delivery room personnel is over, the baby is apt to remain in a quiet alert state for quite a long time. As much as seven hours of the first day may be spent awake, even though birth has been an exhausting experience. This is considered by many to be an extremely important time for the initial social interaction between parents and the newborn to take place (Hales, Lozoff, Sousa, & Kimball, 1977; Klaus & Kennell, 1976). After this, the infant spends much of the remainder of the first 24 hours in sleep.

Beginning with the second day, infants spend even more time asleep and also begin to use a good deal of their awake time in sucking and feeding. Only by the seventh day postnatally does quiet alert time again reach the level it was at on the first day (Packer & Rosenblatt, 1979).

After the first week, the neonate sleeps about 16 to 17 hours of every 24. Sleep records kept by parents show that in the first four weeks babies have alternating periods of sleep and wakefulness about evenly distributed between the day and night hours (Parmelee, Wenner, & Schulz, 1964).

At the time of birth, term babies spend about equal amounts of time in both kinds of sleep, active and quiet. Active, or REM, sleep appears to be the more primitive. Very young preterm babies show the highest proportion of active sleep and the least of quiet sleep. Preterm babies born somewhat closer to term, however, are in some respects more mature than term babies of the same post-38 week conceptual age in that they have longer periods of quiet sleep (Booth, Leonard, & Thoman, 1980). It is thought that the high amount of active sleep in the young infant may be important in that it may provide the **afferent** stimulation, that is, stimulation coming from other parts of the body to the central nervous system, which is needed for its optimal development. The baby is still too immature to provide such stimulation for it-

self in any other way (Roffwarg, Muzio, & Dement, 1966).

In the newborn, sleep is controlled by the brain stem. As the **forebrain** matures and begins to assume control over quiet sleep in the period of from one to three months after birth, the amount of active sleep decreases (Parmelee, Wenner, Akiyama, Schulz, & Stern, 1967). Active sleep continues to decrease and quiet sleep to increase, until by age one only 30 percent of sleep is active (Roffwarg et al. 1966).

Sleep cycles in infancy begin with active or REM sleep, followed by quiet or non-REM sleep. In older children and adults, the pattern is just the opposite: sleep begins with non-REM sleep and then is followed by REM sleep. Infants change to the adult pattern at some time during the first six months, generally in the latter portion of that time period (Berg & Berg, 1979). Since a disruption of the sleep cycle, such as through forced wakefulness or jet travel across numerous time zones, can cause adults to start temporarily with REM sleep, Berg and Berg hypothesize that the infant's change to the adult pattern may reflect maturation of adaptation to the diurnal, or circadian 24-hour cycle. Each sleep cycle in the infant lasts from 50 to 60 minutes; then another cycle begins, or else the infant awakens (Roffwarg et al., 1964). This pattern continues from about two weeks preterm (as observed in prematurely born infants) to about the age of eight months in premature as well as term infants (Stern, Parmelee, & Harris, 1973). The kind of sleep within cycles changes, however, even though the length of each cycle does not. By three months the baby sleeps twice as long in quiet as in active sleep during each cycle, and as it grows older, the ratio of quiet to active sleep increases.

Rapid eye movements can also be found

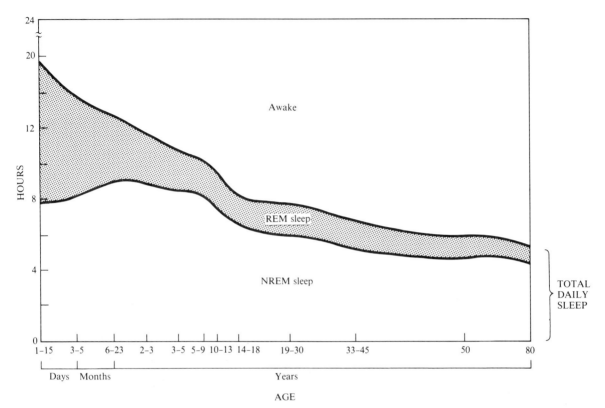

Changes in the total amounts of sleep and the relative percentage of sleep that is REM sleep with increasing age. Notice how large a percentage of the sleep of the neonate is REM sleep and how greatly this declines as the child becomes older.

in the very young baby during nonsleep states in which the baby's eyes are wide open and during crying. In the drowsy state just before sleep, rapid eye movements, sucking, fussing, and crying can all be observed (Emde et al. 1976).

Some changes of the organization of behaviors including sleep seem to occur at definite developmental points. In the preterm infant, one such shift, governing sleep behavior, occurs at around 32 weeks true conceptual age, or around six weeks before term, when active sleep, which has up to then been increasing in amount, begins to decline (Par-

melee et al. 1967). Around the same time, both active sleep and quiet sleep assume their typical form and can be reliably identified (Dreyfus-Brisac, 1970).

There appears to be another basic shift of behavioral organization between one and three months of age (Emde et al. 1976). This shift includes changes in sleep patterns. Thus, after two to three months, the boundaries between sleep and wakefulness become more distinct. Rapid eye movement states during wakefulness become less frequent (Emde et al. 1976). This shift also includes changes in the ratio of quiet and active sleep, as already

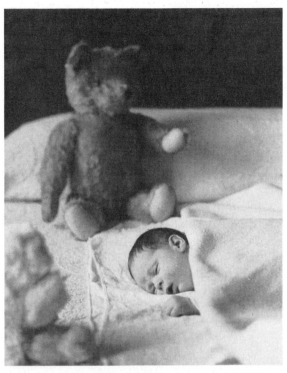

The young infant spends a large portion of each 24-hour period in sleep. At other times the child may be in a quiet alert state, during which learning occurs most easily, actively awake and moving arms and legs, fussy, or crying.

indicated. In addition, there are changes in **EEG (electroencephalograph,** or brain wave) patterns, responsiveness of the autonomic nervous system, and activity during awake time. Some changes also involve perception, **affect** (or emotions) and learning.

On the EEG, more mature patterns typical of older children and adults appear during this time. **Sleep spindles,** which typically appear on the EEG patterns of sleeping adults during non-REM sleep, begin to appear around two months during the infant's periods of quiet sleep (Berg & Berg, 1979). At three months, precursors of **alpha waves** appear in the baby's EEG patterns while awake. Alpha waves are typical of the adult awake pattern.

There are also quantitative changes in sleep, that is, the child sleeps less as it matures. Two rapid decreases in sleep occur, one around age one month and the other in the five to seven month range (Emde et al., 1976). At other times the decrease is slower and more gradual.

About 5 to 6 weeks after birth, babies begin to sleep more during the night and to show greater wakefulness during the day. Although the total amount of time spent asleep does not change appreciably at this time, having done so a week or two earlier, the baby begins to spend longer periods of time in sleep and longer ones awake. By 16 weeks, each sleep period may last twice as long as it did at birth (Parmelee et al., 1964). By this time, a day-night pattern usually has become established, with longer periods of sleep at night, much to the relief of parents and other adults. The daytime periods of sleep are now clearly naps. And the baby may even sleep all through the night or awaken only once.

Major changes in sleep-wake patterns beyond very early infancy are less related to state and are more subject to entrainment. They also relate to individual temperament and activity level. Many infants carry the pattern of a morning and an afternoon nap on into the second year, but others drop the morning nap quite early and rely only on a long afternoon nap to carry them through the day. Bedtimes vary considerably, based primarily upon family convenience but to some degree on individual rhythms. In addition, the total amount of sleep required, which has varied among individual babies from birth on, remains somewhat different as babies grow older: some require more than others on into toddlerhood and perhaps beyond.

STATE-RELATED EMOTIONAL DEVELOPMENT

Although emotional expressions such as smiling and crying are primarily social activities and have profound effects upon caregivers and upon the caregiver-infant interaction, early aspects of these behaviors appear to be more closely related to infant states than to true emotions mediated by social situations (Emde et al., 1976). Caregivers, especially parents, however, generally perceive and interpret these early emotions as voluntary social behaviors and are therefore pleased by the infant's smile or upset by its crying. Thus these state-related emotional behaviors of early infancy are important not only as precursors of deliberate social ones but because they help to form the early attachment of adult to infant.

Smiling

Early infant smiling can be categorized into two types: endogenous, due to internal stimulation only, and exogenous, due to external stimulation (Emde et al., 1976).

Only endogenous smiling is present at birth. It occurs in the neonate during REM sleep and during those waking states in which rapid eye movements can also be discerned. Preterm infants produce more REM smiles than do term babies. This fact and the fact that endogenous smiling declines during the first few months are indications that endogenous smiling is probably based on brain stem activity. As the cortex of the brain matures, it inhibits this activity. By three to four months, endogenous smiling occurs only rarely, and it usually disappears almost completely by six months (Emde et al., 1976).

Exogenous smiling develops in the first and second month after birth. At first, it is more likely to occur while the baby is asleep or drowsy, in response to sounds such as a bell or rattle (Sroufe, 1979). Soon it is more likely to occur while the baby is awake. In this early period from 1 1/2 to 2 1/2 months, exogenous smiling is nonspecific, that is it may occur as the baby sees a stimulus that is social or nonsocial, familiar or unfamiliar. Even at this time, however, babies are a bit more likely to smile at a familiar than an unfamiliar stimulus. This would tend to show that such early smiling already has a cognitive component involving memory (Sroufe, 1979).

Social smiling, a form of exogenous smiling which is elicited especially by the human face, begins around 2 1/2 to 3 months (Emde et al., 1976). Familiar faces are more likely to elicit social smiling than unfamiliar ones, though the young baby will still readily smile at strangers.

Nonsocial but clearly exogenous smiling occurs as the baby learns to control a contingency and then smiles as it becomes aware of this control. For example, moving a mobile by vigorously kicking its legs elicits smiling in the three-to-five-month-old infant (Watson, 1982).

After three months, smiling becomes more specific, that is, it occurs primarily in a social situation or where the baby is controlling a contingency (Emde et al., 1976). Since social smiling to the caregiver is generally reinforced by reciprocal smiling, talking, and other kinds of attention from the adult, it tends to become more frequent when adult attention is available. Smiling at controlling the contingency shows that the baby has learned that it is in control and that smiling is deliberate. Thus smiling has been affected by both learning and motivational factors (Emde et al. 1976). It is no longer just a state-related expression.

Furthermore, smiling at a familiar stimulus, besides implying the working of memory, also suggests that pleasure as a motivational factor is present. This smiling may turn to outright laughter by four months (Sroufe, 1979), indicating great pleaure or joy. At first, laughter occurs mainly as a result of physical stimulation such as tickling, but by the second half of the first year the baby laughs in response to interesting or incongruous events. By the end of the first year and during the second, sustained joy or elation can be discerned in the toddler, particularly in anticipating events that will occur and in planning such events (Sroufe, 1979).

Crying

Crying is an important early behavior since it is the infant's first means of attracting adult attention and help. It appears to be a physiological mechanism that is present from birth and that declines as other means of communication such as social smiling arise. That it can function even earlier than the usual time of birth is shown by the fact that preterm babies cry also. The cry of the young preterm baby is, however, much more shrill than that of the term neonate.

It is uncertain whether the amount of infant crying is subject to learning. On the one hand, Etzel and Gewirtz (1967) report a study in which mothers decreased the crying of their infants by ignoring it but responding with attention to the infant's smiling and eye contact. On the other, Bell and Ainsworth (1972) demonstrated that attention to the crying child did not increase crying and ignoring the crying did not extinguish it. Mothers who responded promptly to the cries of their young infants did not end up with "spoiled" one-year olds; in fact Bell and Ain-

sworth asserted that these children cried less than those whose mothers had ignored their crying. More recently researchers have debated the adequacy of statistical methods involved in the latter study and hence the validity of its conclusion (Gewirtz & Boyd, 1977; Ainsworth & Bell, 1977). It may be that parental response to crying resulting from physical distress does not foster increased crying, whereas response to "bored" crying might increase its frequency.

Peter H. Wolff, who has studied crying in young infants in great detail, has found that three distinctive types of cries already occur in the neonate (Wolff, 1959). Interestingly, mothers in the first few days after birth can distinguish between the types of cries and react appropriately to them.

The first of these is the "hungry" cry. Wolff cautions, however, that this cry is not always related to hunger. It is a basic cry that is used not only to signal hunger but also in other situations if the other types of crying do not bring rapid results. This cry begins with soft moaning and then changes to a sequence of cry-inspire-pause-cry-inspire, and so on. Mothers respond to this cry promptly but do not sense it as an emergency.

A second cry is the "mad," or angry, cry. It is similar to the hunger cry, but mothers take more time in responding, as if they sense that it is a cry of boredom rather than a request for help.

The third distinctive cry is the "pain" cry. It begins quite suddenly without the soft moaning of the early stages of the hunger cry. The baby will cry out loudly, then hold its breath and cease crying for a moment, then expire, inspire, and cry again. This cry leads the caregiver to drop everything and rush to the baby, sensing the emergency.

Around the age of three weeks, the baby develops a fourth distinctive cry. Wolff has called it a "fake" cry because he believes it does not signal any particular event but is used merely as a demand for attention (Wolff, 1959). This perhaps is ascribing too much motivation to a behavior that may be primarily physiologically programmed.

An indication of this physiological base can be found in the research done by Emde (Emde et al., 1976). In recording the day-to-day behavior of a group of young infants, Emde found that all of them showed significant periods of unexplained crying, which he labeled fussiness. He says that this unexplained crying, when severe, is what has usually been called colic by parents and doctors. Though he does not relate this fussiness to any of the specific kinds of crying described by Wolff, it is probably an instance of either a fake cry or perhaps a mad cry.

Nonhungry fussiness is found especially in the first three months after birth. It does not appear to be related to parenting variables, such as how quickly parents respond to the child, the manner of feeding used, or parental personality styles. Emde, therefore, thinks that fussiness must be a behavior that is caused internally, that it exists as a biologically programmed means of communicating distress to caregivers, and that it declines with age as the central nervous system matures and the baby develops other ways of communicating. Thus, as social smiling begins, fussiness begins to drop out of the baby's repertoire. Also, around the time that fussiness declines, after two or three months, the baby begins to use its awake time differently. It begins to interact with its environment, with caregivers and inanimate objects. The baby smiles, coos, shows interest in novelty, and begins actively to explore objects (Emde et al., 1976). All of these actions indicate a more mature brain controlling behaviors, and with this increased maturity, fussi-

ness declines. It is usually completely gone by the age of six months.

The quality of infant crying appears to be related to temperament. When the cries of infants rated by their mothers as easy, average, and difficult were played for other, nonrelated mothers, these women rated the cries of the difficult and average as more irritating and "spoiled-sounding" than the cries of easy babies (Lounsbury & Bates, 1982). Furthermore, sound spectrograph analysis of the cries supported the maternal ratings, indicating that the cries of the former two groups did indeed sound more demanding.

REFLEXES IN THE INFANT

Reflexes are involuntary activities controlled by lower brain centers, primarily the **brain stem** and the **spinal cord.** These activities occur automatically and mechanically when the appropriate stimulation of a body area takes place. As the **cortex** of the brain matures, it can inhibit or override many of these arousal mechanisms. Then the corresponding reflex will diminish or disappear, or else the activity, while it persists, becomes less stereotypic as it comes under cortical control. Some reflexes are present at birth, and others cannot be found until at some specific time after birth. Many reflexes either disappear completely or the activity involved comes under cortical control during infancy, but some, such as the knee jerk or eye blink, persist and yet remain under **subcortical** control. These reflexes can be elicited involuntarily all during life.

There exist several views about the relationship of reflexes to later voluntary behaviors (Zelazo, 1976). Some researchers believe that reflexes must disappear completely and reflex control of an activity must be totally gone in order for the behavior to be replaced by similar but voluntary actions controlled by higher brain centers (di Leo, 1967). In this view, one behavior must be actively inhibited before the other begins. If that does not happen, a problem in brain development or function may be indicated (Gotts, 1972).

Others think that reflexes do not actually disappear but become less stereotypic and more adapted as cortical control develops. These activities then also can be initiated or inhibited voluntarily. Thus the reflexes develop into voluntary activities, which sometimes will retain some reflexive components but become primarily cortically activated. The outstanding exponent of this view is Jean Piaget (1952), who thought that reflex activity in early infancy was the basis of all knowledge. As the infant practiced reflex behavior, adjustments in the reflex came to be made in response to environmental stimuli. Piaget called these adjustments **accommodation.** As the infant accommodates reflex behavior to environmental contingencies, this behavior changes. For instance, Piaget said that the sucking reflex, which exists at birth, becomes modified as the baby adjusts to sucking from the particular breast or bottle that is offered. Because of such adjustments and increased practice, sucking becomes more efficient and better coordinated over time and becomes more of a voluntary rather than reflexive activity.

Finally, some researchers believe that the relationship between the reflex activity and the later voluntary behavior is so close that exercising the reflex will actually hasten and enhance the development of the voluntary behavior. Thus Zelazo, Zelazo, and Kolb (1972) demonstrated that if allowed to practice the stepping reflex, in which the infant makes steplike movements if held upright with the feet on a flat surface, he or she will increase the number of steps taken. Similarly, others have found that true walking oc-

curred earlier in babies allowed to practice this reflexive stepping than in those who were not encouraged to do so (André-Thomas & Ste. Anne-Dargassies, 1952). Some of the proponents of this last view offer as an explanation that this occurs because practice of the activity leads to reinforcing, or rewarding, consequences, such as seeing more of the environment than one could while lying down. The baby, therefore, repeats the activity on a voluntary basis in order to receive the reinforcement and incidentally develops the skill involved. The decline in stepping seen in most infants over time may also be related to arousal state and to body weight (Thelen, Fisher, Ridley-Johnson, & Griffin, 1982). Babies in a high state of arousal made more stepping movements than those not in such a state, and lighter-weight babies did so more than heavier ones. Thus the decline of stepping after early infancy may be a function of the baby's muscles being too immature to effect movement of its increasingly heavy legs.

While it therefore appears that reflexes and later voluntary behavior are not completely different behaviors, the extent to which the one influences the development of the other has not been established with complete certitude even for walking.

Reflexes are useful in a diagnostic assessment of the neonate and young infant. The possibility of central nervous system damage or dysfunction can be inferred if a reflex develops very much later than it should, is absent altogether, or persists long beyond the time at which it should fade. If a reflex disappears and then reappears later, or if one that should be **symmetrical** (involving both sides of the body in the same manner) is instead **asymmetrical,** (one-sided), then too there is the suspicion of damage to the brain or spinal cord or possibly to a peripheral nerve.

Reflexes cannot always be elicited, however. They can be inhibited or suppressed by particular events such as the state in which the infant is found. That is, if the infant is asleep, tired, hungry, or else has just been fed, a reflex may not be produced even though the infant is appropriately stimulated. Therefore, several tests to determine the presence or absence of a particular reflex, administered at varying times and while the infant is in various states, should be used.

In addition to their diagnostic value, some reflexes perform useful functions that help the infant to maintain important processes until cortical control of such processes can be established. For example, the rooting and sucking reflexes enable the baby to locate the nipple and to nurse.

Some transitory reflexes that can be found early in infancy and then disappear may have had an earlier evolutionary function (di Leo, 1967). These include the plantar grasp reflex, the tonic neck reflex, the Babkin reflex, and the Moro reflex. Some reflexes appear to develop into later voluntary activities, either directly or with a pause between the involuntary and the voluntary behavior. These include stepping and palmar grasping. For details about the reflexes of early infancy, please consult Table 5-1.

Other reflexes appear later than the neonatal period and seem to have a facilitating relationship to motor developments such as sitting and creeping, which occur when the reflexes appear. These include the various righting reflexes and the Landau reflex. They are shown in Table 5-2.

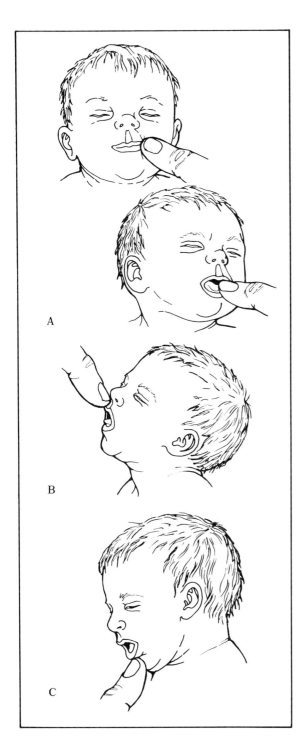

Rooting Reflex. (A) As the corner of the mouth is stroked, the head, mouth and tongue move toward that side. (B) If the middle of the upper lip is touched, the upper lip and tongue move up and the head lifts. (C) If the lower lip is stroked downward toward the chin, the lower lip and tongue move downward and the head is lowered.

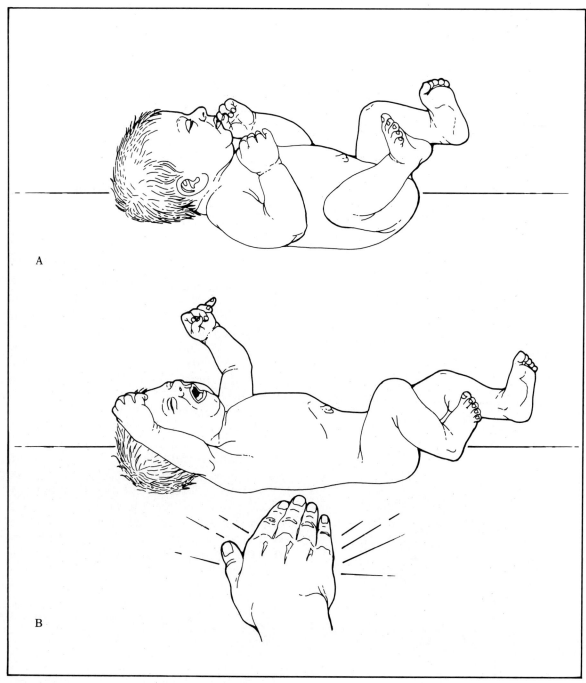

Moro Reflex. (A) Baby at rest. (B) In response to a sudden loud noise, the baby flings out its arms and legs and opens its hands, keeping tips of thumb and forefinger togther.

TABLE 5.1 SOME NEONATAL REFLEXES

Name of Reflex	Description	Usual Age of Onset	Usual Age of Disappearance	Significance of Absence or Persistence; Other Information
A. Reflexes of mouth area				
1. Rooting	When corner of mouth is stroked, infant turns head, tongue, and mouth in that direction. When middle of upper lip is touched, upper lip and tongue are raised and head extends. When lower lip is touched and finger moves toward chin, infant moves lower lip and tongue downward and flexes head downward.	2–3-month fetus	Diminishes by 12 weeks as conscious seeking for nipple takes over. Can be seen in sleep till 7 months postnatally.	Easier to elicit when infant is hungry than at other times. Absence indicates neurological defect. May be depressed in neonate because of anesthesia, anoxia, or infection. Persistence may indicate problems with neurological organization.
2. Sucking	When finger or nipple is placed in infant's mouth, infant sucks. If finger or nipple is withdrawn, head flexes.	2–3-month fetus	Changes from a reflex to a voluntary behavior over time. Can be seen in sleep till 7 months postnatally.	Easier to elicit when infant is hungry than at other times. May be depressed or absent in neonate if anesthetized in birth process, anoxic, or suffering from infection. Usually recovers as such a condition clears up. Absence indicates neurological defect.
B. Hand reflexes				
1. Palmar grasp	Pressure on the palm results in flexion of fingers and grasping of the object.	4–6-month fetus, but is weaker. 8-month fetus has firm grasp. Reflex is strongest at term.	Weakens considerably by 8 weeks. Is usually gone by 2–3 months, sometimes as late as 5–6 months. Is superseded by voluntary grasp.	Weaker in infant with central nervous system depression. Is stronger than normal and persists in infants with cerebral palsy. Absent in cases of lesions of the spinal cord. May have had a purpose earlier in evolution.

TABLE 5.1 (*Cont.*)

Name of Reflex	Description	Usual Age of Onset	Usual Age of Disappearance	Significance of Absence or Persistence; Other Information
2. Babkin (Hand-Mouth)	Pressure on both palms causes infant to close the eyes and open the mouth. Usually the head is turned to one side.	Can be elicited in neonate	Diminishes in intensity in the first month; is gone by 3–4 months	Weak response indicates central nervous system depression. Return of reflex after disappearance indicates dysfunction of central nervous system. Persistence of reflex may indicate mental retardation.
C. Foot reflexes				
1. Plantar grasp	Similar to palmar grasp, but involving sole and toes. Weaker than palmar grasp.	4–6-month fetus; strongest at term	8–12 months, but weakens considerably before this	Very strong and persistent in infants with cerebral palsy. As with palmar grasp, may have had a purpose earlier in evolution.
2. Withdrawal	Pinprick on the sole of foot causes withdrawal of foot, with flexion of foot, knee and hip.	Present in neonate		May be weak or absent in baby that has presented breech with legs extended for birth. Absent on one side if sciatic nerve on that side has been damaged.
3. Crossed extensor	When leg is extended, knee is held and sole of foot is pricked with a pin. The other leg flexes, then adducts (moves toward midline), and extends.	Portions of reflex are present in 6–7-month fetus. Adduction is not present till 37th week. Full response present in normal neonate.	1–2 months	Absence indicates spinal cord defect or injury of nerves involved in reflex. Persistence indicates lesions of pyramidal tract of nervous system. Reappearance of reflex after disappearance suggests damage has occurred to spinal cord. This reflex is interpreted by lay observer as the infant's attempt to push away or protect against injuring agent to other foot.
4. Babinski	When side of sole is scratched from heel to toe there is dorsal flexion (i.e., toward the sole) of the big toe, and fanning out of the other toes.	Portions of reflex are present in 4–6-month fetus. Premature infants flex all the toes. Fanning out develops later.	Persists to various degrees until 12–18 months	Absence indicates dysfunction of the lower spinal cord. Persistence may indicate spastic conditions in the legs. Persistence on one side may mean paralysis due to blood vessel blockage on that side.

		Whole reflex is present in term babies.		Reappearance after disappearance occurs with meningitis, spinal cord injury, or other disorders of the central nervous system.
D. Reflexes relating to position changes made by examiner to infant				
1. Doll's Eye	As infant's body is held stationary, turning the infant's head from side to side causes the eyes to stay fixed and not move with head. As head is moved up and down, eyes also remain fixed.	6–7-month fetus; fully present in preterm neonates	Between 10 days and 1 month as visual fixation matures	Persistence or return after disappearance indicates abnormality of brain development.
2. Tonic Neck Reflexes a. Asymmetrical	As infant lies on back, if examiner turns the infant's head, the arm and leg on the side to which it is turned extend while those on the other side flex (called fencing position).	6–7-month fetus; present in preterm infants; hard to elicit in term neonates; most easily elicited at 2–3 months	Usually gone by 6–7 months	Abnormality indicated if it occurs only on one side but not the other, as head is turned. Delay in disappearance may indicate motor immaturity or deficit, cerebral palsy, or other spastic disease.
b. Symmetrical	When head is flexed and then extended, flexion of legs and extending of arms results.		Disappears as infant learns to creep and crawl, as limbs must begin to move independent of head movement	Helps normal infant to get onto its hands and knees. Overactiveness of reflex in child with cerebral palsy prevents extension of legs in any situation in which head is raised.
3. Moro	As baby lies on back, head support is removed, and head is allowed to drop 1 inch (2½ cm). Then follows abduction and extension of arms, followed by adduction as if in embrace. The hands are open but the fingers are held curled. Then arms return to sides. The reflex can be elicited less reliably by banging on the table next to the infant, causing head to move.	Present in preterm babies after fetal age of 7 months, but muscles not strong enough to bring arms up in the embrace movement	Disappears in term infants by 3–4 months, in preterm infants by 4–6 months	Absence indicates depression of central nervous system. Persistence indicates possible mental retardation and brain damage. Asymmetry of reflex may be result of palsy of one arm or injury to collarbone or the bone of the upper arm during the birth process. Sometimes if infant is holding an object in one hand, the reflex is also asymmetrical.

173

TABLE 5.1 (Cont.)

Name of Reflex	Description	Usual Age of Onset	Usual Age of Disappearance	Significance of Absence or Persistence; Other Information
4. Startle (often confused with Moro, but not the same)	A sudden noise or touching the infant on the chest causes flexion of the elbow and the hand to remain closed as the baby startles.	Early infancy, but later than the Moro reflex; is never present in the first few weeks	Merges with the adult startle pattern, which persists throughout life	
5. Placing	If the front of lower leg or the arm is brought against the edge of a table, the infant raises the leg to place the foot on the table or the arm to place the hand on the table.	8–9 month fetus. Is present at birth in term babies except those extremely small; is present in most preterms after 24 hours.	About age 1 year	
6. Positive support (standing)	If soles of infant's feet are allowed to touch a solid surface, the hips and knees extend and infant supports weight on rigid legs.	8–9-month fetus; present at birth	Disappears in many at 2–3 months. Some infants may still have reflex in 3–7 month period till replaced by voluntary standing at 7 months.	
7. Stepping (walking)	When infant is held upright with soles on a solid surface and is moved forward with slight tilt to one side and then the other, infant takes steps with alternate feet, after positive support reflex takes place.	8–9-month fetus. Preterm babies walk on toes; term babies on soles.	Between 5–8 weeks. With practice may continue till voluntary walking begins. If neck is extended, may show reflex after it disappears under other conditions.	

Based on R. S. Illingsworth (1975), *The Development of the Infant and Young Child* (6th ed.), Edinburgh: Churchill Livingston.

TABLE 5.2 LATER INFANT REFLEXES RELATING TO MOTOR DEVELOPMENT

Name	Description	Usual Age of Onset	Usual Age of Disappearance	Significance of Absence or Persistence; Other Information
A. Righting Reflexes—Relate to basic motor activities and develop at ages most useful in supporting these activities				Righting reflexes absent in severe cerebral palsy
1. Neck Righting	If the head is turned, infant turns body in that direction while lying on the back.	Slightly present at 7 months fetal age and at birth; strongest at 3 months	9–12 months	Helps infant to begin rolling over
2. Labyrinthine Righting of Head	Infant can lift head reflexively from surface, first prone (on belly) and later supine (on back).	2 months prone; strongest at 10 months; 6 months supine	Persists	
3. Body Righting		7–12 months		Modifies neck righting and helps infant to sit and later to stand
4. Landau	If infant is held under abdomen and head is pressed downwards toward trunk, legs flex and are drawn up against trunk.	3 months	Usually 1 year, but may persist till two years	Helps infant to get into position for crawling and later creeping. May grow out of Labyrinthine Righting Reflex.
5. Tilt	If body is tilted, head is moved so it is held upright.	6 months	Persists	Helps neck righting reflex and helps child to sit and stand. Absence suggests dysfunction of central nervous system.

TABLE 5.2 *(Cont.)*

Name	*Description*	*Usual Age of Onset*	*Usual Age of Disappearance*	*Significance of Absence or Persistence; Other Information*
B. Others				
1. Parachute	If infant is held belly down and is suddenly lowered toward a surface, arms are extended downward as if to protect from impact.	6–9 months	Persists through life	Absent or very weak in infants with cerebral palsy. Asymmetric indicates injury on one side. May have had evolutionary purpose. Occurs even in blindfolded baby, therefore is not a visual but a vestibular (inner ear) reaction.
2. Support Reactions a. Lateral Propping	When sitting, if body tilts to one side, hand on that side props body so infant does not fall over.	5–7 months	Persists	Abnormal or absent propping responses probably indicate abnormality.
b. Posterior Propping	If sitting infant is pushed backward, both arms extend out to keep from falling.	9–10 months	Persists	

PHYSICAL GROWTH

Weight and Length

As previously stated, the average baby weighs 3.4 kg (7 1/2 lb) at birth and is 50 cm (20 in) in length, with males slightly exceeding females in both dimensions. After the initial weight loss in the first days after birth, the baby gains at the rate of about 20 g a day for the first five months and about 15 g a day for the remainder of the first year. This gain results in a doubling of birth weight by about five months and a tripling by the first birthday. During the second year, the rate drops appreciably, to only about 2.5 kg (5–6 lb) for the entire year.

The average baby grows in length about 25 to 30 cm (10–12 in) during the first year. That is, the baby increases half again its birth length during the year. During the second year, the toddler grows another 12 cm (5 in). It is usual to speak of the length of the child lying down during the first year to 18 months and of its height while standing thereafter.

Head and Brain

The baby's head, which appears overly large at birth, continues to grow quite rapidly during the first year. Head circumference increases from 35 cm (14 in) at birth to 44 cm (17 in) at six months and 47 cm (about 19 in) at one year. This rapid growth is primarily due to the rapid increase in brain size. The brain undergoes great growth from about the 30th week of fetal development until age one postnatally. At birth the brain weighs about 335 g, or 12 oz. It thus represents about 10 percent of total body weight. By contrast, the adult brain, which weighs about four times as much as it did at birth, represents only 2 percent of total adult weight (Walk, 1981).

The brain and sensory systems are relatively well developed at birth, and the infant brain looks pretty much like a smaller version of that of the adult, with all the different lobes and other areas already clearly demarcated. Brain growth that occurs in the postnatal period involves mainly the proliferation of **glial cells,** which provide support and structure within the brain, and the **myelination** of existing brain cells (as they become covered by a fatty sheath that enables impulses to travel more rapidly). In addition, some of the branching portions of brain cells called **dendrites** and **axons** increase in size and number of branches and in how intertwined and connected they become with others. There probably is no increase in the number of **neurons,** the nerve cells that actually transmit impulses, after birth. The brain reaches two-thirds of its adult size by one year and four-fifths of adult size by two years of age (Vaughan, 1979).

During the second year, as brain growth proceeds more slowly than in the first, the head circumference increase also slows to one-fifth of what it had been in the first year, or a little over 2 cm. As the brain and the bones of the head approach their adult size, the head bones begin to fuse, and the fontanels close. The posterior fontanel appears closed to the touch by about four months postnatally; the anterior one diminishes in size after about 6 months and generally closes during the period of 9 to 18 months (Smith & Owens, 1977).

Growth Charts

Norms for physical growth are provided in growth charts produced by the National Center for Health Statistics (NCHS). These norms are derived from the Health and Nutrition Examination Survey made in 1971 and 1972 for children 18 months to 36 months and

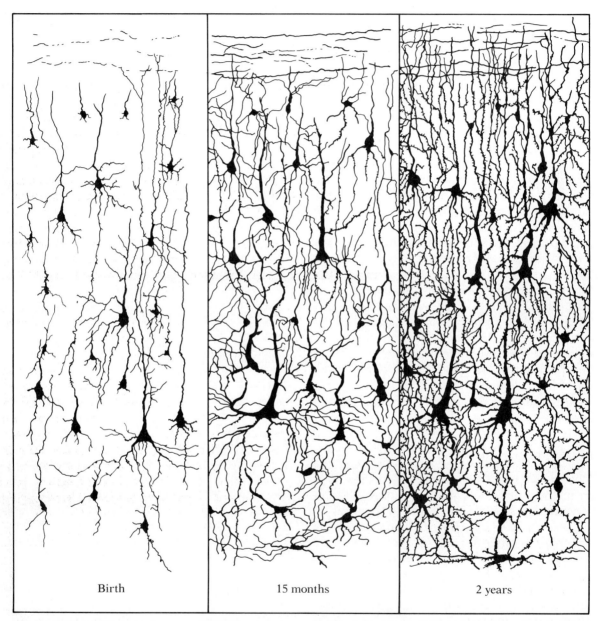

Birth	15 months	2 years

The human brain from birth to age 2. The increasing complexity of the infant's brain. These three drawings show similar areas of the cortex in the newborn, at 15 months, and at 24 months. Notice that although the total number of nerve cells is about the same at each age, there is increasing development of connections between these cells as the infant's brain matures.

from the longitudinal studies made at the Fels Institute in Ohio for children under 18 months (Eichorn, 1979). Unfortunately, the latter included only white, middle-class children in one section of the country. Therefore, the applicability of the birth-to-18-month norms to other racial, ethnic, geographic, and socioeconomic groups can be questioned.

These norms are available in four charts for each sex for the birth-to-36-month period: length for age, weight for age, weight for length, and head circumference. On each chart, percentile levels from the 5th to the 95th are indicated for the 0-to-36-month span, enabling pediatricians and others to record and plot a particular baby's growth pattern according to where it fits with data collected from the samples of children in the two studies used to establish the norms.

These growth charts are useful in helping spot deviations that may indicate abnormalities in the growth process. For example, using the weight-for-length chart, a baby that continues to gain weight but does not grow appreciably in length, or one that grows in length but shows little weight gain, can easily be spotted. Abnormal head growth, either too great or too little, can be found and assessed by plotting the chart for head circumference. On the other hand, the charts also help to indicate normal development. Thus a baby that is at the 5th percentile for weight at birth and makes regular weight gains but remains at the 5th percentile during all of the first year can be assessed as having a sufficient and proper weight gain for its own individual growth pattern. Thus rate of growth is seen as more important than absolute magnitude of growth. Individual babies vary widely from one another, based on genetic and prenatal factors; and comparisons between babies, made by parents and others along the line of "How much did your baby gain in the last month as com-pared to my baby?" are not helpful in assessing a baby's status.

Preschool Nutrition Survey

The Preschool Nutrition Survey (Owen, Kram, Garry, Lower, & Lubin, 1974), another study that collected data on large numbers of infants and children, found that even in infancy, height, weight, and head circumference increased systematically with an increase in socioeconomic level. Of these three, the factor least affected by socioeconomic class was weight, because there tends to be less obesity in the higher socioeconomic levels. That is, some poor children were obese, probably because they received excesive calories from fats and carbohydrates but were still malnourished, while others were underweight, but the averaging of data concealed the underweight ones. Most middle- and upper-class children weighed more than the underweight poor children but less than the obese ones. Black children were taller and heavier than white children of comparable ages but had less fat in their tissues as measured by skin-fold tests. Black children were also more advanced maturationally and showed greater **ossification** of bone, that is the formation of true bone from earlier cartilagenous bone structures (Eichorn, 1979).

Tooth Development

At birth the deciduous teeth, so called because they will be shed, are present beneath the gums, and the buds of the permanent teeth have begun to form. An occasional baby is born with one or more of the deciduous teeth already erupted. During the first few weeks after birth, the gums often grow and re-cover such teeth. If they do not, the teeth are sometimes removed to facilitate nursing.

The first tooth, usually a lower central

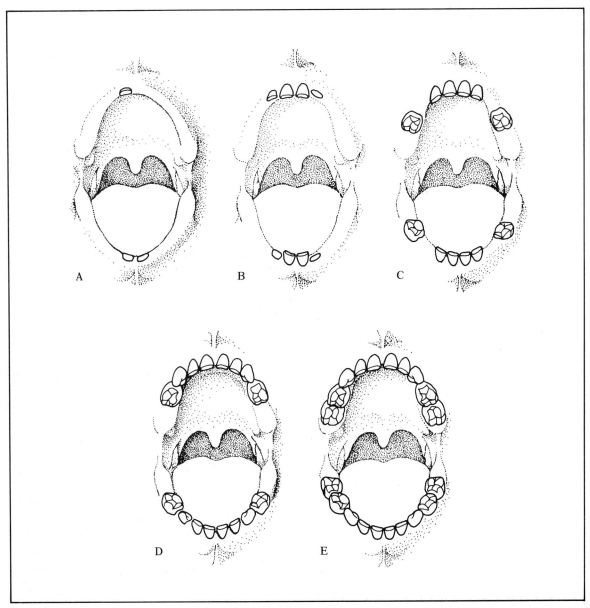

Eruption of the deciduous teeth. (A) In the 6–8 month period, the two lower central incisors and then one or both upper central incisors usually appear. (B) By age one year, the lateral incisors have also erupted. (C) During the second year, the first molars appear. (D) Then the cuspids erupt, usually before the second birthday. (E) Finally, between ages 2 and 3, the second molars appear and the child has a complete set of 20 deciduous teeth.

incisor, appears most commonly between the ages of six and eight months, though some babies acquire it earlier and some still do not have a tooth visible at their first birthday. The first tooth is shortly followed by the other lower central incisor. Next to come are the two upper incisors, followed by the upper and lower lateral incisors. Most one-year olds have six to eight teeth. In the second year, eight more teeth appear—the first molars and cuspids. The final deciduous teeth, the second molars, usually appear sometime late in the third year (Schour & Massler, 1940). There seems to be little or no relationship between the timing of tooth appearance and skeletal development or other physical growth (Cohen & Hooley, 1977).

MOTOR DEVELOPMENT

Basic Studies

Many of the important studies of motor development were done during the 1920s and 1930s; more recent investigators have added relatively little information. The outstanding investigators into infant motor development were Arnold Gesell and Mary Shirley. Gesell and his various associates at Yale University performed enormously detailed studies of motor development from early infancy on. They used motion pictures, a new research tool at that time, to analyze the components of motor acts in children. By photographing behaviors at high speed and then playing them at normal speed, they were able to see these behaviors in slow motion. They also were able to do frame-by-frame analyses of particular movements and thus were able to detect small variations and developments that occurred over time. *An Atlas of Infant Behavior* (Gesell, 1934), for example, contains

more than 3,000 photographs taken from these analyses, which show infant motor activities in great detail. The Institute of Child Development was established to house the research efforts of Gesell and his associates. Although he is no longer living, research is still being done there by some of the people he trained.

Shirley (1933) followed the motor development of a group of 25 babies over the first two years of life. She was primarily interested in determining whether motor skills develop in an invariant order, with some being necessary precursors to later ones. The studies of both Gesell and Shirley found that motor skills in the first year develop in a relatively invariant order, following the cephalo-caudal and proximo-distal pattern that has also been found for the physical development of the baby before birth.

Gesell (1928) divided infant motor development into four periods, each spanning about a quarter of the first year. During the first quarter year, the infant develops control over the muscles of eye movement, allowing visual tracking of objects. During the second quarter, the infant develops control over the muscles governing the head and arms. It can now hold up its head and grasp objects in the environment. In the third quarter of the first year, the baby gains control over its trunk and hands, enabling it to sit, begin crawling, and manipulate objects and transfer them from hand to hand. Finally, during the last quarter of the year, it learns to control its legs and feet, as well as to grasp objects between the thumb and forefinger. Now the child can creep, then stand, then cruise, and perhaps even begin walking, and it can grasp objects in the characteristically human pincer grasp. Gesell emphasized that each of these developmental milestones was necessary for the next level of development to oc-

Newborn
Fetal posture

1 month
Chin up

2 months
Chest up

3 months
Reach and miss

4 months
Sit with support

5 months
Sit on lap;
grasp object

6 months
Sit on highchair;
grasp dangling object

7 months
Sit alone

8 months
Stand with help

9 months
Stand holding furniture

10 months
Creep

11 months
Walk when led

12 months
Pull to stand
by furniture

13 months
Climb stair steps

14 months
Stand alone

15 months
Walk alone

cur. Each one successively served to widen the child's horizons and to enable it to explore the environment to a greater degree.

Shirley's major interest lay in finding whether the sequence of stages of motor development could be divided into discrete orders or groups, with possible variation within each group but no variation in the sequence of the orders or groups. She was able to find from her analysis of the data on the 25 babies in her longitudinal study that there existed five separate orders of development including an intermediate one between the second and and fourth that could overlap slightly with either of them or could be a separate stage in its own right.

The first order, which developed in her babies by a median age of 20 weeks, involved passive postural control such as lifting up the head when lying down, sitting on an adult's lap, straightening the knees while being lifted upright, and making stepping movements while held upright. Shirley labeled these movements as passive, since they occurred in response to things done to the baby by other people rather than being initiated by the baby.

The second order, developing at a median age of between 25 and 31 weeks, involved assuming postural control of the trunk, including such skills as sitting alone briefly, rolling, standing well with support, and pushing upright by straightening the knees.

The intermediate, or third, group of skills involved efforts at locomotion such as scooting forward or back while lying on the abdomen. Sometimes these skills overlapped with others; some of Shirley's babies developed these skills along with those of the second order, while some did not develop them

until they developed those of the fourth order. Some babies developed them as a discrete separate stage. Because of its tendency to overlap with other orders, Shirley did not assign a median age of development to this order.

Late in the first year, at a median age of 40 to 50 weeks, Shirley found that her babies had entered a fourth order, involving leg control. They could now move about on all fours, stand while holding onto furniture, and finally pull themselves up into a standing position.

Ultimately, after a long time gap, and already into the second year, at a median age of 60 weeks, toddlers reached the fifth and final order, which involved independent standing and then walking.

Because she found the sequence of orders invariant across her 25 babies, except for some individual differences between babies within each order and the occasional overlap of the third order with others, Shirley thought that motor development must be primarily the result of the unfolding of predetermined abilities. She, therefore, leaned in the direction of nature in the nature-nurture dichotomy and thought that motor development could be ascribed primarily to built-in maturational factors in the child rather than to environmental influences.

The related question of whether practice at a particular motor skill could affect the rate at which such a skill developed has also intrigued researchers. Outstanding in trying to answer this question were various studies of motor development by Wayne Dennis (1941) and Myrtle McGraw (1940, 1943). These studies showed that both practice and maturation play a part in skill development.

The sequence of motor development as investigated by Mary Shirley. The ages represent times the average baby achieved a developmental milestone. Modern babies tend to reach these a few days or weeks earlier than did those studied by Shirley. Better nutrition or changing child-rearing practices may be a factor in this change.

Arnold Gesell (1880–1961) was one of the outstanding researchers who studied the physical and motor development of young children. Here he is shown testing one of his infant subjects in his laboratory at Yale University.

Dennis studied infants who deliberately had been kept lying on their backs with no chance to move about until the age of nine months. Having had no chance to practice sitting or standing, these babies were unable to do either when given the opportunity at a time at which children raised normally could have done so quite easily. Once the opportunity for practice became available, however, Dennis' infants began to develop these skills.

During the period from six to nine months during Gesell's third period, the infant acquires control over the trunk and hands. He or she can now sit without support and can manipulate toys and other objects.

Eventually they mastered them but later than did children exposed to normal environmental circumstances.

On the other hand, the need for physical maturation before a skill can be mastered is evident from McGraw's study of bladder control in twins. She began training one twin very early in infancy and delayed training the other until the first had achieved about 90 percent success. While it was a long, hard process to train the first twin to this level, the second could be trained almost immediately and reached the same level as the first

very quickly. McGraw saw this difference as an indication that practice was of little consequence until the child was sufficiently mature to acquire the particular skill.

In summary, we may conclude from these studies that motor development depends largely upon the maturation of the higher brain areas that control muscular activity and upon the maturation and growth of the muscles and other supportive structures themselves. However, the opportunity to practice motor skills at the maturationally appropriate times, or even a bit later, makes the individual more skillful and coordinated than without practice and can make up for earlier lack of practice.

Individual Differences

Even though the studies of Gesell, Shirley, and others have demonstrated that motor skills develop in a relatively constant sequential order, individual differences in the rate of development as well as occasional deviations from the sequence occur. These variations may be due to temperament differences between children, leading more active babies to develop some skills earlier than more sedentary, placid ones. They may be due to inborn differences in the rate of maturation that are related to sex or race or to particular genes inherited from the parents. The child's maturity at birth also is a factor. For babies at birth may be of different conceptual ages, depending upon whether they are born preterm, at term, or postmature.

Not only are preterm babies behind term babies in the development of motor skills, but at the time when they should be of the equivalent conceptual age, they may still lag behind the normal newborn in that they possess a less mature reflex pattern and poorer muscle tone and move more frequently during periods of active sleep (Illingworth, 1975; Booth et al., 1980). Interestingly, preterm babies may be ahead of term babies in other factors such as heightened activity level or longer periods of quiet sleep. When it comes to physical and motor abilities, the preterm infant may not catch up totally with the term baby until about two years of age, even if the preterm infant suffers from no other complications beyond prematurity itself (Vaughan, 1979).

A baby born at term but of low birth weight may also lag behind a term baby of normal weight. Such a baby may have an even longer catch-up time than a preterm baby of the same birth weight, since low birth weight may be caused by more serious problems during prenatal development than prematurity is. Finally, a baby handicapped in one or more motor or sensory areas may lag behind in development relating to that area but may develop in the unaffected areas within the appropriate age range.

Any or all of these factors can account for the fact that even perfectly healthy babies may deviate by several months from the average in achieving various developmental milestones. This deviation can be in either direction, that is, the baby may be either ahead of or behind the average. Furthermore, except for preterm and low-birth-weight babies, who may narrow the developmental gap between themselves and term babies as time goes on, differences in the rate of development between babies usually become more pronounced as babies grow older. For example, in the first month there may be a difference of only a few days between the time a placid and an active baby acquires a particular skill. But by the time these same babies reach the age of one year, they may be several months apart in some aspects of motor development.

Thus researchers, parents, and others should focus concern not on how closely the child adheres to a timetable based on averages of many babies but on whether the child is making progress over time and is developing particular skills in approximately the usual sequence.

Detailed Description

As we consider the sequence of motor development in infancy and toddlerhood, the most precise descriptions of the time that particular developmental milestones are achieved are still those of Gesell (1928). Most of the more recent studies still cite the norms de-

TABLE 5.3 THE PRINCIPLES OF DEVELOPMENT

These may be summarised as follows:

1. Development is a continuous process from conception to maturity. This means that development occurs in utero, and birth is merely an event in the course of development, though it signals the beginning of extraneous environmental factors.

2. The sequence of development is the same in all children, but the rate of development varies from child to child. For example, a child has to learn to sit before he can learn to walk, but the age at which children learn to sit and to walk varies considerably.

There is a sequence of development within each developmental field, but the development in one field does not necessarily run parallel with that in another. For instance, though the stages in the development in grasping and in locomotion (sitting and walking) are clearly delineated, development in one field may be more rapid than in another. A child with cerebral palsy involving the lower limbs only will be late in learning to walk, but if his intelligence is normal the development of manipulation will be average. I have termed this lack of parallelism between different fields of development 'Dissociation'.

3. Development is intimately related to the maturation of the nervous system. For instance, no amount of practice can cause a child to walk until his nervous system is ready for it.

4. Generalised mass activity is replaced by specific individual responses. For instance, whereas the young infant wildly moves his trunk, arms and legs, and pants with excitement when he sees something interesting which he wants, the older infant merely smiles and reaches for it.

5. Development is in the cephalocaudal direction. The first step towards walking is the development of head control—of strength in the neck muscles. The infant can do much with his hands before he can walk. He can crawl, pulling himself forward with his hands, before he can creep, using hands and knees.

From R. S. Illingworth, *The Development of the Infant and Young Child* (Edinburgh: Churchill Livingston, 1975), 131.

veloped by Gesell and have made few changes in the times or the sequence he spelled out with such clarity more than 50 years ago (Illingworth, 1975; Vaughan, 1979). The few changes that have been made reflect changes in child-rearing practices that either enable children to practice skills they are ready for somewhat earlier than in the past or else put less emphasis on early acquisition of skills, such as toilet training, than in the past. Improved child health and nutrition have also enhanced both physical growth and motor development for many young children and have changed some of the norms slightly.

In spite of individual differences, certain principles of development apply to all children. and are useful to consider in the study of motor development. A summary of these principles is found in Table 5.3.

BIRTH TO THREE MONTHS

The neonate can turn its head from side to side while lying on its abdomen, or prone. The baby lies with its knees drawn up under the abdomen and its arms flexed. In this position, the baby can very briefly lift its head from the surface. The infant has very little head control otherwise, however; the head bobs and sags when the infant is held belly down supported on the adult's hand or when pulled to a sitting position (Vaughan, 1979). By the fourth week, the baby can begin to lift the head off the bed for a longer time. By 6 weeks the head is held at body level when the baby is held belly down. And by about 8 weeks, although the head lags behind as the baby is pulled up into a sitting position, the child begins to show some control of it. By 12 weeks, control is much better, though the head still bobs a little (Vaughan, 1979). By three months the prone baby can lift not only its head but also its chest off the bed.

During the first few months, the baby on its back, or supine, will flail out with arms and legs and roll the body a bit from side to side. These movements develop from both the Moro and the tonic neck reflexes. The baby also spends much of the time lying in the typical "fencing" position as a result of the tonic neck reflex, looking at its extended hand as its head is turned toward it. Because

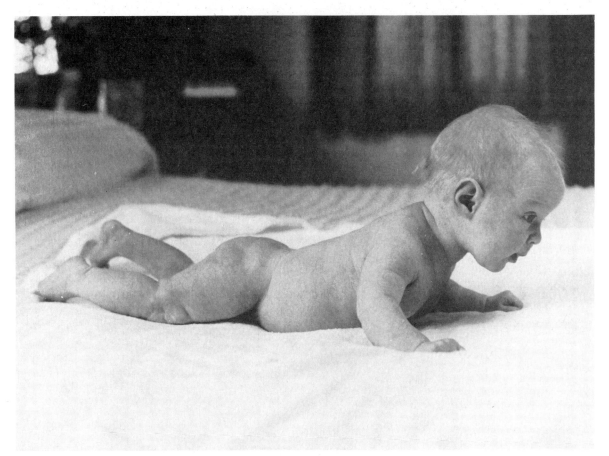

The newborn infant can barely raise the head from the surface, but within the first few months, control of the muscles of the head, neck, and arms develops. Now the infant can view what goes on quite easily. But he or she cannot yet get up on hands and knees to crawl or creep.

the young baby keeps its head turned to the side, crib toys and other interesting things to look at should be suspended at the sides of the baby's bed rather than overhead.

The newborn baby holds its hands tightly fisted. If something is put in them, the grasp reflex causes the baby to hold onto it. In the second month, as the reflex weakens, the baby may grasp an object only briefly before letting go. This reflex weakens greatly and is almost gone by about eight weeks, when active grasping under the control of the central nervous system can begin. Active grasping also develops out of early coordinated movements of the arms and hands that are symmetrical (Vaughan, 1979) and begins with the arms flung out to the sides and then bringing them to the midline to grasp. These movements may be remains of a portion of the Moro reflex. Even later, as the baby reaches out to the adult, the movement may still start with the arms flung out to the sides before coming toward the midline. The baby may also begin to swipe with the hands at objects before its eyes. Swiping involves batting with the whole hand, without attempt-

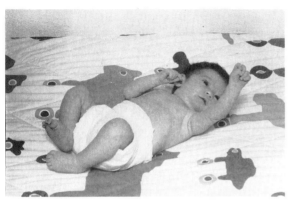

A one-month-old lying in the tonic neck reflex position or fencing position, with the arm and leg on the side toward which he or she is facing flung out, and the other arm and leg flexed. He or she also is holding both hands tightly fisted, showing that the grasp reflex has not yet weakened appreciably.

objects suspended overhead, crib toys can be moved from the sides to the overhead position.

Babies suck on a hand or finger from birth or even earlier. This activity is probably reflexive at first. After the first month, the baby seems to bring its hand to its mouth deliberately to suck, no longer merely reflexively.

By the third month, new and skillful uses of the hand begin to develop. One use is reaching with one hand for the other and holding the two hands together while bringing them toward the face. A second use is trying to bring an object held in one hand to the mouth and then mouthing it. At first the infant does not succeed; nevertheless it opens its mouth at the appropriate time and then closes it. After some practice, the baby perfects this activity, generally during the fourth or fifth month. The third use is intently gazing at the hands while holding or waving them before its face. The infant spends much time wiggling its fingers, moving its hands slowly and then quickly in the line of sight

ing to grasp. As the tonic neck reflex weakens after the third month, the baby begins to hold its head at the midline when lying supine. Now that the baby can see and swipe at

Swiping with no contact of object	Swiping with some contact	Palm grasp	Mitten grasp
8 weeks	3 months	4 months	6 months
Raking with middle finger to grasp object in palm	Beginning thumb–forefinger grasp	Dropping an object voluntarily (release of grasp)	Advanced thumb–forefinger grasp
7 months	8 months	9 months	1 year

The development of hand use during the first year.

(Gesell, 1928). As the baby lies supine, it also begins to look at its kicking. By three months this looking is helped by the fact that the baby can raise its head up to have a better look.

FOUR TO SIX MONTHS

In the 4-month-old the head lags only a bit at the beginning when the infant is pulled to a sitting position, and wobbles slightly while the infant is sitting. Four weeks later the head does not lag or wobble, and the back is held straight (Illingworth, 1975). Just before

6 months, the baby can begin to sit up with support in the high chair and enjoys sitting up for some length of time (Vaughan, 1979). By 6 to 6 1/2 months, the baby can sit alone without back support. When pulled from a sitting to a standing position at 5 to 6 months, the infant supports its own weight but, of course, needs to be held by the adult to prevent falling over. During the 6th month, the infant may flex and then straighten its knees while standing with adult help.

Most babies begin to roll over while lying during the five-to-six-month period. Generally, rolling from the abdomen to the

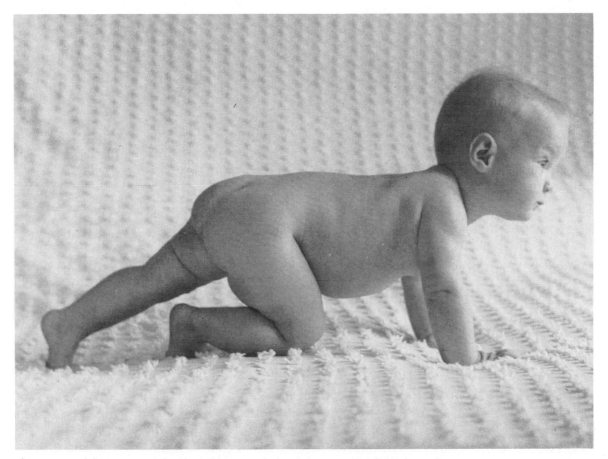

The creeping infant moves on hands and knees with the abdomen raised from the surface.

back comes before the back to abdomen roll (Vaughan, 1979). At this time caregivers must be especially careful not to leave the infant lying where it could roll off and fall.

At four months the baby can grasp a cube in the palm of its hand. If offered another, the infant drops the first to grasp the second (Illingworth, 1975). By six months, such an object is transferred to the other hand so the second object can be grasped. Now the baby uses a mitten grasp, with the thumb in opposition to all the other fingers together, as if wearing a mitten (Vaughan, 1979). While grasping an object, the baby likes to shake it. Rattles and other noise-producing objects delight the baby at this age.

Some infants begin to move across the floor, playpen, or crib shortly before six months by vigorously flailing with the arms and legs while lying supine. A little later they rear up on their hands and knees from a prone position and then flop frontward or backward across the floor.

SIX TO TWELVE MONTHS

Around six months the baby usually learns to sit up from a lying position by bending its legs away from its body and bending its waist while rolling. Objects can be reached while supine by pivoting on the buttocks. Soon, generally between seven and nine months, crawling and then creeping commence. **Crawling** involves propelling oneself forward or backward with the abdmen still touching the floor; **creeping** begins when the abdomen is off the floor and the baby moves on hands and knees. Many children begin both crawling and creeping in a backward direction.

Many creeping infants begin to pull themselves into a standing position as they encounter objects such as chairs or playpen rails to hold onto. The eight-month-old can

A creeping baby may pull itself into a standing position by grasping the rails of the crib, a chair or table, and pulling itself up. The child may then cruise, which is walking sideways while holding on to objects such as crib rails or furniture. The parents of this infant need to be alert to the child's newly-learned skill, and make sure the crib side is put up when they are not there to keep an eye on him.

stand quite steadily for a short while if there is a person or object to hold onto. Unfortunately, the child stands with its knees locked and does not know how to release and fall, something the child could do earlier when stood up by an adult. This is a nice example of a behavior that is first reflexive, disappears, and then reappears as a voluntary one

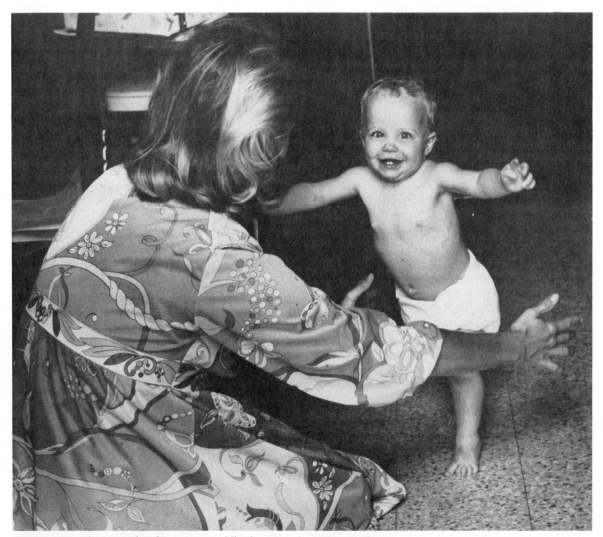

Between 13 and 15 months, the average toddler begins independent walking.

later. Several weeks later, the child finally masters how to reach the floor again, either by letting go and stiffly falling back or by bending at the waist or hips, putting the hand or hands on the floor, and then letting the rear down. By nine months, the child will take steps if its hands are held. This stepping appears to be quite different from the reflexive stepping seen in the neonatal period, although in some children it develops from it.

Allied to this development is **cruising**, the process of walking sideways while holding onto objects. It generally occurs around nine to ten months of age but only in those babies living in environments affording them objects such as furniture to hold onto.

Grasping also improves during this time span. The seven-month-old can rake at small objects with its fingers but cannot yet manage to pick them up (Vaughan, 1979). Then it uses the middle finger to push objects toward the thumb and forefinger for them to grasp. Soon the true thumb-forefinger grasp develops, and by eight months the baby can successfully pick up tiny objects. Babies at this time also turn and squeeze objects, and by nine months they use the forefinger to poke at various objects (Vaughan, 1979). In the nine-to-twelve-month period, coordinated but now asymmetrical use of the two hands develops. One hand is used to hold an object, while the other does something (poking, probing, squeezing) to it. This behavior is the basis of all later use of tools, a uniquely human, or at least primate, attribute.

By nine months, the baby begins voluntarily to let go of objects. He or she will drop toys, food, and other things. When the adult reaches for an object held by the child and grasps it, the child will release it. If the adult asks for the object, the child holds it out but will not release it. Between 11 and 12 months, the child will release an object in response to the adult's requests in words or pantomime (Vaughan, 1979). At about one year the child begins throwing objects rather than just dropping them.

The one-year-old generally can walk if someone holds one hand. Some children begin walking independently by one year or even earlier, but most do not begin until early in the second year.

THE SECOND YEAR

Between 13 and 15 months, if not earlier, independent walking begins (Illingworth, 1975). The child is now referred to as a toddler. For the first few weeks after beginning to walk, the toddler will lock its knees and walk stiffly, swinging each leg from the hip to make sure the knees will not buckle and cause the child to fall. The toddler also tends to stand on the inner rims of the feet, with the ankles practically touching the floor and

with the feet planted wide apart. This stance is probably an unconscious attempt to lower the center of gravity and hence to prevent falling. As the child becomes more confident with added practice, walking becomes more normal; the legs bend at the knees and are less stiff, and the child stands squarely on the soles of the feet.

By 15 months, the child creeps upstairs and soon thereafter begins to climb the stairs in a walking position if an adult holds one hand (Vaughan, 1979). By 18 months the child can get up and down the stairs alone through a combination of creeping and stepping, and by two years he or she can get up and down by stepping alone but using both feet per step (Illingworth, 1975). An 18-month-

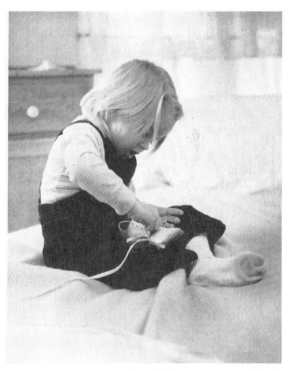

During the second year, the child begins to use self-help skills such as undressing. She or he also may attempt such activities as lacing shoes. However these dressing skills, which are more difficult than undressing, are usually not mastered until much later.

old child enjoys pulling a wheeled toy. At this age the toddler can also run but does so rather stiffly. The two-year old runs easily (Vaughan, 1979) without falling. By age two the child can also kick a ball without losing balance (Illingworth, 1975).

The child becomes much more skilled in using its hands. The 15-month old can put a pellet into a bottle and try to retrieve it, though unsuccessfully (Vaughan, 1979). Such a child can also build a two-to-three-block tower and can hold two cubes in one hand at once (Illingworth, 1975). By 18 months the child can dump pellets back out of the bottle and can build a tower of three to four cubes (Vaughan, 1979).

With this increased control of the small muscles in the hands, the child also may begin showing some self-help skills. Shoes and socks are pulled off. The child may also unbutton or unzip articles of clothing and begin to take them off. Putting on, zipping, and buttoning clothes are more difficult skills, so they will not appear till much later. The child does, however, begin to cooperate in the dressing process by holding out the appropriate foot and putting the arms up over the head as the caregiver dresses the child. The toddler also can turn the pages of a book one at a time and scribble with a pencil or crayon. She or he begins to play with blocks and beads, becoming engrossed for rather lengthy time periods.

Summary

1. The neonatal period extends from birth through the first four weeks of life. The newborn loses some weight but regains it by the 10th day. At birth the head is disproportionately large, and the baby's muscles are weak and contain a high proportion of water.

2. The neonate is able to orient to changes in the environment and to habituate to stimulation that continues. Both these behaviors are important in enabling the baby to adjust to environmental input.

3. Sudden Infant Death Syndrome, the greatest killer of young infants today, seems to have multiple, interacting causes that includes mild hypoxia, temporary cessation of breathing during sleep, changes in brain regulation of breathing, and possible environmental pollutants in the air. But no definite cause or prevention has as yet been found.

4. Temperament differences are apparent even in neonates; some infants are more active, others, more placid. Infants and caregivers must adjust to each other's temperament characteristics in order to interact successfully. In addition, infants must adjust their rhythms to the 24-hour day and to family routines.

5. Physical growth in the infant proceeds in a lawful fashion that can be charted according to growth charts based on studies of large numbers of infants. Wide individual differences exist, but as long as growth proceeds in a regular fashion there is no cause for alarm.

6. The young infant goes through a variety of sleep-wake states. Their duration and relationship to each other change as the infant's brain matures.

7. Early emotional indicators such as smiling and crying may at first be related more to infant state than to social factors. Smiling at first is caused by biological factors within the baby and only later comes in response to social stimulation. The baby produces several distinct types of cries that are distinguished by and reacted to differently by caregivers.

8. Reflexes are involuntary activities controlled by lower brain centers that can be reliably elicited. Early reflex behavior can perform useful functions for the neonate until voluntary control can begin. Reflexes also serve a diagnostic purpose, since their absence, irregularity, or persistence help in assessing possible brain damage.

9. The basic studies of infant motor development were done many years ago by Gesell and Shirley. Their work still is the most comprehensive study of the sequential development of motor skills during the first two years of life.

10. Babies appear to go through sequential, usually nonoverlapping, stages of development that are roughly age-related. Development of motor skills proceeds in the same cephalo-caudal and proximo-distal directions as did early physical development.

11. Early motor development involves head control. Then hand usage becomes more skilled. With increased development of the muscles of the trunk, arms, and legs, the baby begins to sit, turn, crawl, and creep. Finally the baby can stand alone and begins independent walking. During the second year, additional motor skills such as running and walking up and down stairs develop.

Participatory and Observational Exercises

1. Observe a young infant or infants in a home or day care situation. Can you spot examples of the tonic neck reflex, the rooting and sucking reflexes, reflexive stepping, and the Moro reflex? Under what circumstances is each produced? How old is the infant in question? Should this reflex be apparent under the circumstances and in an infant of this age?

2. Observe an infant at home or in an infant day care center for an hour a week for a three-to-four-week period. Try to be there while the infant is awake, and try to schedule each visit at about the same time of day. Observe physical and motor activity. Does the child appear to be on schedule, ahead of, or behind the norms for its age in motor development? Is there any activity that the infant perfects or improves in over the time period of your observations? Describe the changes over the time span of your observations.

3. Visit a group setting in which you can observe several infants and toddlers of differing ages. A day care center or church nursery would be ideal. Or try a park or playground frequented by caregivers with infants and toddlers. Observe younger and older infants and toddlers, and compare the sizes and configurations of their bodies. How does head size as a portion of total body size compare in younger and older infants? What about the length and shape of arms and legs? What about motion of arms and legs? How does muscle tone compare? How coordinated are movements of younger infants as compared to older ones? When does coordination seem to improve? What physical capabilities, such as hand use, are much more skilled in older children? What means of locomotion are used? Compare a toddler just beginning to walk with one who has been walking for a while. What differences do you observe in the way they walk?

4. Interview parents of a baby that is about one to two months old. Do they perceive the establishment of a mutual rhythm between themselves and the baby in such matters as eating and sleeping? Who has had to adjust the most? How was it done? What adjustments must still be perfected? Have they experienced any disruptions of rhythm, such as through illness of the infant or use of a stranger as a caregiver, etc.? How was this disruption handled?

5. Ask the same parents as in no. 4 about their infant's crying. How frequently does the infant cry? Do they recognize what the infant wants from the kind of cry? How many different kinds of cries can they distinguish?

What does each mean to them? How can the crying infant best be consoled?

6. Observe older infants and toddlers at play with several kinds of play equipment. What kinds of body activities does each piece of equipment encourage? How important is each for the child's motor development? If possible, do some of this observation in a play area for toddlers or in a day care center that has equipment for using large muscles as well as small ones.

DISCUSSION QUESTIONS

1. Should parents be encouraged to practice reflexive activities such as stepping with their infants in order to have infants produce voluntary motor activities earlier?

2. Are the swimming classes offered in many communities for young babies and their mothers useful in promoting motor development in the infants?

Nutrition, Feeding, and Other Infant Routines

INTRODUCTION

Food is the basic necessity, along with oxygen, for the infant's survival and development. The amounts and kinds of food given to the infant are vital for healthy growth. In addition, feeding has interpersonal and social components. The close relationship developed by mother and baby during feeding situations is important in maintaining the mother's milk flow and in sustaining her solicitude and attention. These latter two qualities are also usually developed in the mother or any other feeding caregiver with a bottle. The relationship also is of importance beyond nutrition for the infant, who needs the warmth, attention, and **cutaneous** (affecting the skin) stimulation from being held and cuddled, as well as the visual experience of the adult's face close by for optimal emotional and sensory development. As the baby becomes older and can participate in family mealtimes by sitting at table in a high chair and eating a modified form of what the rest of the family eats, the social aspects of eating become increasingly important.

Parents and other caregivers generally show concern about the achievement of reliable bowel and bladder control. Although most children complete such training beyond toddlerhood and thus beyond the scope of this book, earlier stages of such training begin in late infancy and in toddlerhood and thus will be discussed briefly.

NUTRITIONAL REQUIREMENTS IN INFANCY

Calories

The Nutritional Research Council of the National Academy of Sciences, a panel of experts in the field of nutrition, recommends that the daily **caloric** intake in infancy be 55 **calories** (amounts of food producing energy equivalent to a calorie of heat) per pound of body weight from birth to 3 months, 52 calories per pound from 3 to 6 months, 50 from 6 to 9 months, and 47 from 9 to 12 months. Thus, for example, a two-month-old baby weighing 10 lb needs 55×10, or a total of 550, calories per day.

Milk alone will meet these caloric requirements for the first three months of life. After about three to four months, the baby has a higher caloric requirement than milk alone can supply, and supplemental foods, usually beginning with cereals, are added to the diet (Smith, 1977).

Nutrients

The human diet, including that of infants, needs six major classes of nutrients for proper nutrition (Barness, 1979; Goodhart & Shils, 1973; Latham, McGandy, McCann, & Stave, 1970). These are as follows: (1) **proteins,** (2) **carbohydrates,** (3) **fats,** (4) water, (5) **minerals,** and (6) **vitamins.** The diet must supply all of these nutrients in adequate amounts, neither too small nor too large, or complications can arise. The total amounts, as well as the relative proportions, of particular nutrients needed in the diet vary during the individual's life cycle. Thus the requirements for infants are somewhat different from those for older children and adults. In addition, there are individual variations based upon sex, body build, hormone secretions, and the presence or absence of certain enzymes resulting from genetic factors that affect the requirements for certain nutrients.

It is usual to express the amounts of particular nutrients recommended in the diet in terms of **Recommended Daily Allowances,** or RDAs. These RDAs have been developed by the Nutritional Research Council. RDAs, while adjusted for sex and age levels, cannot, of course, be tailored to consider a particular individual's specific needs. They, therefore, serve as guides, but modifications based upon a particular child's needs may need to be made upon the advice of a pediatrician or nutritionist.

PROTEINS

Amino Acids Proteins are composed of chemical substances known as **amino acids,** which serve as the building blocks from which the various organs and systems of the body are made and replenish themselves. The human body can manufacture a few amino acids for itself out of other substances, but most can only be obtained through the ingestion of protein food. Eight amino acids are essential throughout life. Two additional amino acids that are of lesser importance in later life are, however, essential in infancy. Animal proteins tend to contain more and better proportions of the essential amino acids than do vegetable proteins. Thus milk plays a most important role in infant nutrition in supplying all of the essential amino acids that the body cannot make for itself. Later in the course of infancy, other protein-rich foods such as meats, eggs, legumes (vegetables of the pea and bean family), and cereals are added to the diet and supplement the proteins found in milk. The RDA for protein is 2.2 g per kg of body weight up to 6 months, 2 g per kg from 6 to 12 months, and 23 g daily totally for ages one to three years.

Kwashiorkor If there is severe protein deficiency in infancy or early childhood, a disease called **kwashiorkor** results. Sometimes a child ingests a sufficient amount of total calories to sustain life but is on a diet lacking protein. Often the child with kwashiorkor is suffering not only from protein deficiency but from total calorie deficiency as well. This condition involving protein plus calorie malnutrition is known as **marasmus.** Children with kwashiorkor develop **edema,** or swelling, and show a loss of pigmentation of the hair, which usually becomes reddish. They fail to grow properly and exhibit a generalized apathy and lack of well-being. Perhaps most serious, brain growth slows appreciably. Thus kwashiorkor has the most devastating effect upon children during the times that brain growth should be most rapid, particularly in the first year and to some extent in the second; this effect is irreversible even should nutrition improve later. If the brain cells do not develop branches and interconnections as they should during this sensitive period, they cannot make up for this lack of growth in the future.

Kwashiorkor is most likely to occur in societies in which no adequate alternative protein sources are available or acceptable for young children after the baby is weaned from breast milk. It also occurs at times of natural or man-made disasters such as famine or war. It has recently been found with increasing frequency in developing countries in which mothers have been persuaded that the modern way is to bottle feed but cannot afford to buy adequate amounts of cow's-milk formula and often feed babies only a little milk diluted with much sweetened water. It is occasionally found even in North America among infants and children of the very poor, who also find it difficult to purchase adequate amounts of protein foods.

CARBOHYDRATES

Carbohydrates are the sugars and starches. Their major function is to provide energy for body maintenance. The major source of carbohydrates for infants is milk. Human milk contains large amounts of **lactose,** a form of sugar. Since cow's milk contains less lactose, other sweeteners are added to cow's-milk formulas. Later, cereals and fruits begin to supply some of the carbohydrates needed by the baby.

There is no specific RDA for carbohydrates in infancy. Instead, the amount needed is calculated on the basis of total calories consumed. Every 100 calories ingested by the infant should include 12 g of carbohydrates.

FATS

Fats are important in the human diet because they represent the greatest long-term energy supply of all foods. They provide twice as many calories per unit of weight as do either proteins or carbohydrates. They are also necessary to the body in becoming part of the structure of body membranes, and they help to store energy in body tissues.

Fats are absorbed into the body in the form of **fatty acids**. Three fatty acids are considered essential in human nutrition. One of these, linoleic acid, is especially important for the infant. It is found in plentiful amounts in human breast milk.

Infants under the age of one year have less efficient means of absorbing fats than do older children. Thus the amounts and types of fats consumed by infants over and above those in milk must be carefully regulated. Meats and eggs, both of which contain some fats, should be introduced gradually and in small amounts later in the first year, as milk consumption levels off. Foods of high fat content such as bacon, cold cuts, cheeses, butter, and margarine should be avoided in infancy and used only very sparingly if at all in the second year.

A basic amount of fat in the infant diet is a necessity, however, though no specific RDAs are provided. Therefore, skim milk, which contains very little fat, should not be used in infant feeding to control excessive weight gain, as the lack of fats could lead to inadequate brain cell development (Smith, 1977). Instead, other nutrients such as carbohydrates can be somewhat restricted.

WATER

Some nutritional experts include water as a basic nutrient; others consider it in a class by itself. We shall include it under our discussion of nutrients here. Water is important in nutrition because it is the major component of the human body. It is found in all body tissues and structures. Water also functions as a solvent for various salts, chemical compounds, and dissolved gases in the body. It plays a role in the control of body temperature through evaporation; acts as a lubricant in blood, saliva, and other fluids; helps in the excretion of waste products in sweat and urine; and is very important in the maintenance of the balance of chemicals and **electrolytes** (sodium, magnesium and potassium) in the body's fluids.

When body size is taken into account, infants have a relatively higher water requirement than do adults (Barness, 1979). This is partly due to the fact that a higher proportion of the infant's body than the adult's is made up of water. It is also caused by the faster metabolism of the infant, which results in greater water loss through excretion and elimination. Finally, the higher ratio of exposed body surface to total body size in the infant as compared to the adult results in faster dehydration by water loss through the skin in the form of perspiration.

The amount of water needed by a baby is usually adequately supplied by the milk the baby is drinking. This is especially true for breast-fed infants, since human milk is quite dilute and the baby ingests a lot of water in breast milk (Barness, 1979). In case of severe and prolonged vomiting or diarrhea or both, however, a baby may be losing water faster than it can be replenished by drinking milk alone, or the child may not even be able to keep down the milk. Since severe dehydration is dangerous for the baby, fluids other than milk or in addition to milk must be given. Water or a gelatin dessert dissolved in water can sometimes be tolerated even if milk is not. A sick toddler can be given a carbonated soft drink that both helps to settle the stomach and provides needed water. If no fluids can be ingested via the mouth, a dehydrated baby must be hospitalized and be given fluids intravenously.

The infant loses a lot of fluids through sweating in very hot weather. This loss may not be evident to the parent or other caregiver, since when there is little humidity, sweat evaporates as soon as it reaches the skin. Therefore, in hot and particularly hot and dry weather, all infants, but especially bottle-fed ones, must be offered water so that they may assuage thirst. The breast-fed baby who resists a bottle or whom parents do not want to learn to drink from the bottle can be given water in a teaspoon or an eyedropper and later from a small cup. All water fed to young infants should be boiled and then cooled to room temperature.

MINERALS

Minerals are inorganic substances required for body function. They are essential ingredients of body structures and are also needed in the body fluid. Unlike proteins, carbohydrates, and fats, minerals do not provide energy for body functions, but they are essential in order for these functions to occur properly.

Minerals are made up of two groups, the macrominerals, of which sizeable amounts are widely distributed throughout the body, and the microminerals, which are present in much smaller amounts. The macrominerals include calcium, phosphorus, sodium, chlorine, potassium, and magnesium. The most important microminerals are iron, iodine, fluorine, and zinc. Details about the dietary sources, functions, and conditions caused by insufficiencies or excesses of the minerals are presented in Table 6.1.

The normal infant whose mother has been adequately nourished during pregnancy and who receives adequate amounts of breast milk or formula during the first few months after birth should have stored or receives adequate amounts of all the minerals needed for healthful development except possibly iron and fluorine.

If the mother has had an iron-rich diet in pregnancy, the baby should have enough iron stored in its body to last for the first five or six months. Thereafter, additional iron either through iron-rich foods or through commercial iron supplements may be needed. Premixed infant formulas also generally contain supplemental iron. It is primarily because of this added iron that pediatricians at present recommend the use of formula rather than whole or diluted cow's milk up to one year of age in the bottle-fed baby or the baby that has been weaned from the breast before age one (Smith, 1977).

The preterm baby or one of low birth weight may not have stored up adequate iron to last through the initial five to six months. Neither will the baby whose mother has had a poor diet during pregnancy. Because of this lack and because many normal babies do not receive adequate iron in their diet after they have exhausted their inborn supply, iron deficiency remains a serious health problem for infants in the United States. The Preschool Nutrition Study found that iron deficiency occurred frequently in children from all so-

TABLE 6.1 MINERALS IN INFANT NUTRITION

Name	Source	Need	Body Parts Where Found; Functions	Problems and/or Diseases Associated with Deficiency or Overconsumption
1. Macrominerals				
Calcium	Milk; later other milk products, leafy vegetables, oranges, bread made with milk solids	Higher in infants and toddlers than in older children and adults due to fast bone growth and the fact that calcium is absorbed poorly	Mostly found in skeleton, with some in other tissues. Calcium is the major structural component of bones and teeth. It helps regulate blood clotting and contractions of the heart muscle and plays a part in conduction of nerve impulses.	Deficiency occurs at times of mass starvation, when nursing mothers cease adequate milk production and no substitutes are available. It can also occur if babies are fed formula extremely diluted with water and sweeteners.
Phosphorus	Milk, lean meats, whole-grain cereals	Somewhat less than the need for calcium, as phosphorous absorption is more efficient	Also found in the skeleton in combination with calcium and in other body tissues. Important in bone development. Phosphorus also helps to control cell division, reproduction, transmission of genetic material, transport of proteins, absorption of carbohydrates, and in the buffering system.	Feeding of *undiluted* cow's milk to neonates causes its high phosphorus level to lower blood calcium level, and tetany (convulsions) can result. Therefore, cow's milk formulas must be diluted with water for young infants.
Sodium	Common table salt, which occurs naturally in many foods including cow's and human milk	There is no specific minimum, but need is small. Adequate amounts occur naturally in milk and other foods, with no additional salt needed.	Found in extracellular body fluid and skeleton. Sodium controls body water concentration and maintains balance of fluids within and outside body cells. It plays a part in conducting of nerve impulses and in muscle contractions.	Most Americans, including infants, get about five times as much sodium as necessary. There may possibly be a link between high salt intake in infancy and hypertension in adulthood. The habit of eating too salty food may begin in infancy and thus contribute to later

				hypertension. In recent years, baby food manufacturers have stopped salting baby foods, to discourage formation of the habit of oversalting.
Potassium	White potatoes, bananas, oranges, grapefruit, tomatoes; a little in milk	Very small; generally met through a normal diet. Infant receives enough in milk, and later in fruit juice as well.	Almost all (97%) is in body tissue cells, the rest in extracellular fluid. Along with sodium, potassium helps maintain fluid balance, muscle contraction, and conduction of nerve impulses.	There rarely is potassium deficiency in infancy, unless there is extreme fluid loss through vomiting or diarrhea.
Magnesium	Milk, whole-grain cereals, green vegetables, potatoes	Much lower for infants than for older children and adults. Milk and later cereals and vegetables provide all that is necessary.	Stored in bones similarly to calcium. Magnesium is important in maintaining fluid balance (along with sodium and potassium) and for neuromuscular activity. It activates certain body enzymes needed for metabolism of proteins, carbohydrates, and fats.	Deficiency is rare in infants. Occasionally deficiency can occur in older infants in conjunction with kwashiorkor or marasmus.
2. Microminerals				
Iron	Normal neonate has enough stored to last 5–6 months. Later sources are whole-grain and iron-fortified cereals and breads, leafy vegetables, peas, beans, egg yolk, and meats, especially liver. Most commercial formulas contain iron.	About ten times what is needed should be ingested, as human iron absorption is poor.	Found mainly in the blood, needed for oxygen transfer in the hemoglobin molecule of red blood cells	Iron deficiency anemia can occur if prenatal supply of iron is not sufficient, or if diet of older infant does not include enough iron-rich food. Iron deficiency is the most common deficiency among American infants and children.

TABLE 6.1   MINERALS IN INFANT NUTRITION (Continued)

Name	Source	Need	Body Parts Where Found; Functions	Problems and/or Diseases Associated with Deficiency or Overconsumption
Iodine	Seafoods, dairy products, some vegetables. Added to iodized table salt. If mother's diet contains adequate iodine, infant should get adequate amounts in breast milk.	Only a small amount is needed, but iodine is very important.	About half is found in the thyroid gland; the rest is distributed throughout body tissues. Needed to produce thyroid hormones governing energy metabolism.	Hypothyroidism results from lack of iodine. An extreme form of childhood hypothyroidism, cretinism, results in mental retardation.
Fluorine	Drinking water, either occurring naturally or added. Also in meats, fruits, vegetables, and cereals. Breast-fed babies not yet eating other foods probably don't get enough from breast milk; supplemental fluorine should be given them. Most formulas have added fluorine.	Only a very small amount is needed, but it is very important in infancy as this is a time of very rapid bone and tooth development.	Mostly found in bones and teeth. Fluorine is necessary for proper formation and mineralization of bones and teeth. It helps prevent tooth decay.	Lack of fluorine can cause improper bone and tooth formation. Tooth decay is more prevalent in those lacking adequate fluorine. Topical fluoride application to the teeth is helpful. Massive oversupply in diet or water can cause discoloration of teeth.

cioeconomic levels and was the greatest nutritional deficiency in infants (Owen, Kram, Garry, Lower, & Lubin, 1974).

Fluorine, which is necessary for the proper development of bones and teeth, is most usually found in drinking water. The water either absorbs it from rocks and minerals through which it flows, or has fluorine added to it at filtration plants. Commercial formulas may contain some fluorine, and homemade formulas, since they use water, may also contain some. It is doubtful whether enough of the fluorine that the nursing mother may ingest in her drinking water can reach the baby in breast milk. Therefore, pediatricians often recommend supplemental fluorine, especially for breast-fed babies (Smith, 1977). It is usually in liquid form and is added to any supplemental drinking fluids such as fruit juice, or it may be mixed with vitamin D and perhaps vitamin C and is given in drop form as a vitamin-mineral supplement. In addition, as soon as the child has teeth, it is wise to use topical fluoride applications to the teeth during regular dental checkups and to brush with a fluoridated toothpaste.

VITAMINS

Grouping The vitamins are a class of nutrients that are essential in small quantities for the maintenance of normal cell structure and body metabolism. They are chemical compounds that were not isolated and recognized until the 20th century. The diseases associated with the deficiency of particular vitamins have been known, however, though not understood, since earliest times.

It is usual to divide the vitamins into two groups, those that are water-soluble and those that are fat-soluble. The water-soluble vitamins are the various B vitamins and vitamin C; the fat-soluble ones are vitamins A, D, E, and K.

The water-soluble vitamins cannot be stored for any length of time in the human body; therefore, some amount of each one is needed daily. By contrast, the fat-soluble vitamins are stored in body tissues for varying time periods, and daily intake is not as important as that over a span of weeks or months. Table 6.2 lists the important vitamins, their dietary sources, functions, and deficiency diseases.

Deficiencies Vitamin deficiencies severe enough to cause diseases occur rarely in modern American infants. The reasons are that well-nourished mothers can supply sufficient amounts of many vitamins to their babies through breast milk, and commercial formulas usually contain added vitamins, as well as minerals. In addition, many pediatricians recommend the use of supplemental vitamin drops for infants. Vitamin D in drop form may be particularly important for babies in cold climates during the winter, when they may not be exposed to much sunlight. Infants also ingest various vitamins in the foods they add to their milk diet. For example, fruit juices provide vitamin C, cereals provide various of the B vitamins, and many fruits and vegetables contain vitamins A, C, K, and some of the B vitamins as well.

Problems relating to vitamin deficiency can occur, however, if a nursing mother is severely malnourished, if the baby is preterm or for other reasons has not stored up before birth some of those vitamins that can be stored, or if the nursing mother is on a fad diet that severely restricts some basic nutrients and therefore deprives her baby of them. For example, a recent newspaper article reported the case of a baby with such severe vitamin B_{12} deficiency that the infant was comatose when brought to the hospital. The breast-feeding mother was on such a

TABLE 6.2   VITAMINS

Name	Function	Source	Deficiency Disease and Symptoms
Water-Soluble The B Vitamins 1) Thiamin (B₁)	Carbohydrate metabolism; transmission of nerve impulses	Lean meats, liver, legumes, whole-grain cereals and breads	Beri-beri (rarely found in infants; found in toddlers only in cultures eating mostly polished rice, or among extreme food faddists)
2) Riboflavin (B₂)	Production of energy from utilization of carbohydrates and proteins	Milk, organ meats, lean meats, cheese, eggs, leafy green vegetables	Very rarely occurs
3) Niacin (nicotinic acid)	Carbohydrate and fat metabolism, chemical reactions important in the body	Poultry, meats, fish, peanuts, enriched breads, and cereals	Pellagra (found in cultures depending on corn as main source of food). Symptoms are rough, red, sore skin; diarrhea; lethargy; neurological symptoms if prolonged and severe.
4) Pyridoxine (B₆)	Carbohydrate, protein, and fat matabolism	Liver, lean meats, legumes, bananas, potatoes, whole wheat	Rarely occurs in young infants. It can occur in older infants if no supplemental foods are given, as milk is low in pyridoxine.
5) Pantothenic acid	Carbohydrate and fat metabolism, manufacture of cholesterol and some hormones	Liver, meat, eggs, whole-grain cereals	Very little needed by infants. Milk supplies all that is needed by young infants. Deficiency is rare.
6) Biotin	Protein metabolism; aids production of fatty acids	Organ meats, legumes, egg yolks; is also produced by bacteria in human intestines	Deficiency rare unless massive amounts of egg whites are eaten raw (which prevent absorption of biotin)
7) Cyanoco-balamin (B₁₂)	Helps form red blood cells, helps body form various proteins	Milk, meats, other food of animal origin	Pernicious anemia occurs if the intrinsic factor—a substance secreted by stomach necessary for Vitamin B₁₂ to be absorbed—fails to be secreted. Intramuscular injection of B₁₂ is needed to counteract this lack.
8) Folic acid (folacin)	Helps produce nucleic acid for cells, helps produce red blood cells in bone marrow, helps hemoglobin formation	Meats, yeast, leafy green vegetables, whole grains. Some may be produced by intestinal bacteria.	Folate deficiency occurs in baby if mother does not get enough during pregnancy and lactation.
Vitamin C (ascorbic acid)	Protects vitamins A and E so they can be used; aids formation and maintenance of connective tissue, aids in healing of wounds, helps iron absorption	Citrus fruits and juices, tomatoes and tomato juice, cabbage, sweet potatoes, green, leafy vegetables. Human breast milk may contain some also.	Scurvy is the deficiency disease.Rarely seen in infants and toddlers. Symptoms include painful joints and swollen, bleeding gums.

TABLE 6.2   VITAMINS *(Continued)*

Name	Function	Source	Deficiency Disease and Symptoms
Fat-Soluble Vitamin A	Helps maintain skin, surface of eye, and surface of gastrointestinal and genitourinary tracts. Vitamin A helps maintain adequate growth and prevents night blindness.	Milk, liver, egg yolks, salt-water fish, vegetables containing carotenes (yellow and red vegetables)	Deficiency is rare as liver can store up to a one-year's supply. Overdose of Vitamin A can result in a toxic condition.
Vitamin D	Aids absorption of calcium and phosphorus to build and maintain bones and teeth	Sunlight, fish liver oils, fortified milk, cereals, liver, salt-water fish	Rickets. Symptoms include bone abnormalities: bowed legs, curvature of spine, protrusion of breastbone, collapse of ribs.
Vitamin E	Prevents formation of toxic products in body tissues as a result of metabolism	Vegetable oils, whole-grain cereals, leafy green vegetables, legumes	Vitamin E deficiency rarely occurs in humans, except in some premature babies who have stored up little vitamin E before birth. Symptoms include swelling, skin lesions, and changes in blood chemistry.
Vitamin K	Produces clotting factors in blood needed to stop bleeding	Leafy green vegetables, egg yolks, soybean oil, liver; is also synthesized by bacteria in human intestine	Intestinal bacteria probably supply all vitamin K needed. However newborns do not yet have these bacteria. Therefore, an injection of vitamin K is given shortly after birth, to prevent hemorrhaging. Sometimes intensive antibiotic therapy kills bacteria and results in vitamin deficiency.

strict vegetarian diet that she ate no animal proteins at all. Consequently she was ingesting no B_{12}, which is derived from animal sources only, and was passing none on to the baby. The baby recovered from this crisis after therapeutic administration of vitamin B_{12}. Since this episode, doctors have been alerted to recommend supplemental B_{12} in tablet form for nursing mothers on strict vegetarian diets.

Vitamin Fortification Various foods usual in the diet of toddlers and older children are fortified with vitamins and thus should provide them additional amounts of these substances. For example, oleomargarine is fortified with vitamin A, pasteurized milk with vitamin D, corn meal with vitamin C, and various breads and other baked products with several B vitamins, as well as the mineral iron.

Junk Food and Vitamin Deficiencies

In spite of fortified foods, however, some toddlers run the risk of vitamin deficiency after weaning because of poor diet. In part it is a matter of economics: fresh fruits and vegetables, meats, and dairy products are expensive foods that many poor people cannot afford. Therefore, instead of these more expensive foods, toddlers from poor families may eat large amounts of rice, bread, corn meal products, or beans, which contain some but not all necessary vitamins. Furthermore, many young children of all socioeconomic groups today eat large amounts of junk food in place of food that is good for them. In addition to being low in vitamins, junk foods generally are high in fats, sodium, and refined sugars, all of which make them especially poor choices for toddlers. Yet many toddlers subsist on a diet made up primarily of potato chips, cupcakes, candy, and soft drinks, with an occasional meal from a fast-food outlet. It is very important that adults who work with infants and toddlers, such as day-care staff, nurses, and pediatricians, be alert to signs of vitamin deficiency in these children. They should counsel parents about the importance of adequate diet for their children. Infant and toddler day-care centers and other agencies that provide meals in group settings should make sure that the meals they serve children are nutritionally adequate, are pleasing in taste and appearance, and introduce the children to a variety of different foods.

METABOLIC DISORDERS REQUIRING NUTRITIONAL MANAGEMENT

Some specific disorders can occur in infancy as a result of inborn errors in how various food substances are metabolized, or broken down and assimilated by the body. The traits for these disorders are carried on recessive genes. Thus a child will have a metabolic disease if he or she inherits the trait from both parents, both of whom are carriers. Some of these diseases have already been mentioned in the consideration of hereditary diseases in chapter 2. Here we shall emphasize the nutritional management necessary to prevent or at least minimize the effects of the particular disorder.

Disorders of Protein Metabolism

A number of metabolic disorders involve errors in the breaking down of various proteins. In these instances, a faulty gene prevents the functioning of a particular enzyme that breaks down a certain amino acid. The amino acid consequently builds up beyond the safe level and begins to damage particular portions of the body. The three most important disorders involving protein metabolism are phenylketonuria, tyrosinemia, and maple-syrup urine disease.

PHENYLKETONURIA

Phenylketonuria is caused by the absence of an enzyme in the liver that breaks down **phenylalanine**. This substance accumulates in the body and disrupts brain function, leading to mental retardation. Phenylketonuria, or PKU, ocurs most frequently in individuals of Northern European ancestry. The incidence is 1 in 10,000 to 15,000 live births.

The condition can be diagnosed through the use of a blood screening test administered at least 72 hours after birth and preferably somewhat later (Scott, 1977). Since many babies are discharged from the hospital before this time and reaching them to administer a blood test after discharge is difficult, some medical authorities are now advocating testing within the first 24 hours

(Schoen, Cunningham, & Koch, 1983). Treatment consists of controlling, though not completely eliminating, dietary phenylalanine, through the use of a special infant formula in which the phenylalanine level is precisely fixed. As the child becomes older, other foods added to the diet must be strictly controlled for acceptable levels of phenylalanine. The special diet is usually continued up to adolescence, at which time the excess phenylalanine no longer can damage brain cells. Children in whom this regimen was instituted early in infancy appear to have normal or almost normal intelligence, although they have a higher incidence of emotional problems than normal children. Whether these are due to the metabolic condition, to family tension over the condition and its management, or to some other factor is not yet known.

TYROSINEMIA

Tyrosinemia is a disease involving two distinct conditions, both of which can be controlled through dietary management. Hereditary tyrosinemia occurs because of the decrease of activity of an enzyme that in turn causes an increase of the amino acid **tyrosine** in the blood. The condition causes mental retardation as well as damage to the kidneys and the liver. Neonatal tyrosinemia is a transient condition caused by a temporary deficiency of the same enzyme. When the enzyme begins to be secreted in sufficient amounts, usually after several weeks beyond birth, neonatal tyrosinemia disappears.

Hereditary tyrosinemia occurs less frequently than PKU. It is most prevalent among Swedes and French Canadians. The neonatal form occurs more frequently than the hereditary form and is not confined to any particular ethnic group.

Both forms of tyrosinemia can be detected through blood screening in the neonatal period, and both can be controlled through dietary management. Hereditary tyrosinemia is treated through the restriction of two amino acids, tyrosine and phenylalanine, to very low levels, again through the use of a special formula fed to the baby. Neonatal tyrosinemia is treated by the daily administration of 100 milligrams (mg) of vitamin C (Scott, 1977). Restriction of the two amino acids in the diet is not necessary in the neonatal form of the condition.

MAPLE SYRUP URINE DISEASE

Maple syrup urine disease, which occurs quite rarely, also leads to mental retardation. It is caused by the body's inability to break down three amino acids. The presence of these substances in the baby's urine causes a maple syrup-like odor of the urine, which is the reason for the name. The lack of appropriate enzymes can be diagnosed in the newborn by a blood test. Appropriate dietary management, using a formula very low in the three amino acids, helps to control the disease.

Disorder of Carbohydrate Metabolism

There is one major disorder of carbohydrate metabolism affecting infants, **galactosemia**. Fortunately the condition is very rare, occurring only once in 30,000 to 70,000 live births (Scott, 1977). This hereditary disorder causes the infant to lack a particular enzyme needed to break down the sugar **galactose** into glucose. At birth the baby appears normal, but after it begins to ingest milk, symptoms including vomiting, lethargy, lack of weight gain, and enlargement of the liver appear. If left untreated, the condition leads to liver damage, brain damage, and the development of **cataracts** in the eyes. Treatment involves the restriction of both the sugars galactose and lactose in the infant's diet.

OTHER NUTRITION-RELATED DISORDERS

Two other conditions related to nutrition that can adversely affect infants and toddlers are obesity and lead poisoning.

Obesity

There is some evidence that if obesity begins in infancy, not only the size but also the number of fat cells found in the body increase (Brook, Lloyd, & Wolff, 1972). Later weight loss can reduce the size but not the number of fat cells. This could help to explain why individuals who suffer from obesity have so much trouble losing weight even if they diet rigorously, and why lost weight has a tendency to be regained shortly. At present, reliable longitudinal studies linking obesity in infancy to that in adulthood are still lacking. Most of the data available are based either on retrospective accounts or on cross-sectional studies, so that one cannot with absolute certainty link childhood and adult obesity.

Should this preliminary evidence prove correct, however, it could have vast implications, inasmuch as obesity is a major health problem among children and adults in the United States at present. If the number of fat cells developed in infancy does indeed relate to later weight problems, then careful management of infant weight gain, especially in the period of from two to six months postnatally when much fat tissue develops (Eichorn, 1979) appears to be important for ensuring later health. The appealing roly-poly infant in whom parents and others have delighted for so long may be more at risk for future health problems than the thin one about whom parents have tended to worry and fuss.

Lead Poisoning

In sufficient amounts, which for toddlers and young children can be quite small, lead can damage the nervous system. Its effect is cumulative, inasmuch as lead that has been incorporated into the body remains there and is not removed over time. A significant amount of lead is inhaled by all individuals living in our automotive society from the fumes of leaded gasoline released by automobiles. In addition, young children in the one-to-six age range often ingest lead through eating chips of leaded paint (Chisolm, 1979).

The eating of nonnutritive substances is called **pica.** It tends to occur more frequently in certain cultural groups and at certain life stages than in others. Pregnant women, especially in the rural South, for example, sometimes eat soil or laundry starch. Pica in young children often involves eating flaking paint chips. Since older, deteriorating buildings often were painted with lead-based paints in the past, and since such paint is apt to be in poor repair and flaking off walls and radiators, children living in such buildings run a high risk of developing lead poisoning. Even if they do not eat the paint, they may still be exposed to higher than safe levels of lead since this substance can also get into house dust and be inhaled.

Early symptoms of lead poisoning include increased irritability, loss of appetite, and decreased play. Vomiting, constipation, and abdominal pain usually follow. If nothing is done about the condition at this time, more severe symptoms occur about four to six weeks later. These include persistent vomiting, seizures, loss of consciousness, and **ataxia,** or loss of coordination.

More than half of the children brought to medical attention after the onset of symptoms show permanent and severe brain dam-

Infants and toddlers living in older, deteriorating dwellings in which lead paint chips may be flaking off walls and radiators are at risk for lead poisoning. They may either eat the chips, a condition known as pica, or they may inhale lead particles in household dust. The lead thus accumulated in the body leads to nervous system damage.

age in spite of treatment (Chisolm, 1979). Treatment consists primarily of using chemicals to leach out the excess lead from the child's body. But prevention is really the only treatment that has a reasonable outlook. Therefore, if parents want to prevent lead poisoning in their children, they must be careful to keep them away from walls, radiators, and other objects that could have lead-

based paint on them. It has also recently been found that frequent washing of walls and floors in older dwellings will significantly reduce the amount of house dust and hence the amount of lead inhaled by children in such dust and therefore prevent some of the buildup of lead in their bodies.

If possible, a move to a dwelling in better condition would be the best preventive for lead poisoning; but for many families that is economically impossible. In addition, children as well as adults should as much as possible stay away from heavily traveled streets where lead from automobile exhausts is highly concentrated.

BREAST MILK IN THE INFANT DIET

Advantages of Breast Milk

Infants fed breast milk for the first months of postnatal life derive from it all the nutrients, vitamins, and minerals needed for survival and development, with the possible exception of iron and fluoride (Gartner, 1978; Scott, 1977).

Careful comparison studies of human and cow's milk show that human milk contains 50 percent more lactose and 20 percent more fat than does cow's milk (Gartner, 1978). The fat in human milk, much of it in the form of **linoleic acid,** is also more **unsaturated** than that found in cow's milk. Whether these facts have any effect on the later prevention or amelioration of **atherosclerosis,** the deposit of fat in the walls of the blood vessels and heart, in breast-fed babies is not yet known. Saturated fats such as those found in cow's milk do contribute to atherosclerosis in adults.

Human milk contains less total protein than does cow's milk, probably because the calf grows faster than the human baby and therefore needs more daily protein. The relative amounts of the various protein substances also differ. Thus human milk contains **taurine,** a **bile** acid, while cow's milk does not. Since human babies require a lot of taurine for the optimal development of brain cells, and since no one is yet sure how much of it the baby stores up before birth for later

use, taurine may be a more important ingredient of human milk than has been realized.

Cow's milk has a greater concentration of **casein,** a protein substance that is difficult for the human baby to digest. By contrast, human milk has high concentrations of two other more digestible proteins, **lactoalbumin** and **lactoglobulin**. Human milk also contains less sodium and phosphorus but more iodine and vitamin B$_6$ than does cow's milk. All these differences are probably significant for optimal development of the human baby. For example, too much phosphorus can cause convulsions in the young baby. Thus, while much work has been done to improve artificial formulas based upon cow's milk or other sources such as soybeans, in order to make them as close to human milk as possible, a really good imitation is difficult to achieve.

Even if cow's milk or vegetable-based milk substitutes could be made nutritionally perfect, they would still lack another important characteristic of human milk, the protection from disease organisms provided through antibodies in the milk (Barness, 1979; Gartner, 1978).

Mother and child share a common bacterial environment. That is, because of their close contact, they become hosts to the same microorganisms. If a new disease factor such as a different strain of bacteria should invade the baby, it will invade the mother also. Her body immediately begins to manufacture antibodies to combat the foreign substance, and some of these antibodies are quickly transmitted to the baby in the mother's milk. Thus at a time when the baby's body is still too immature to produce antibodies for itself, the mother provides these important substances to her child.

In addition to this protection via antibodies, breast milk also appears to foster the growth of benign intestinal bacteria and to

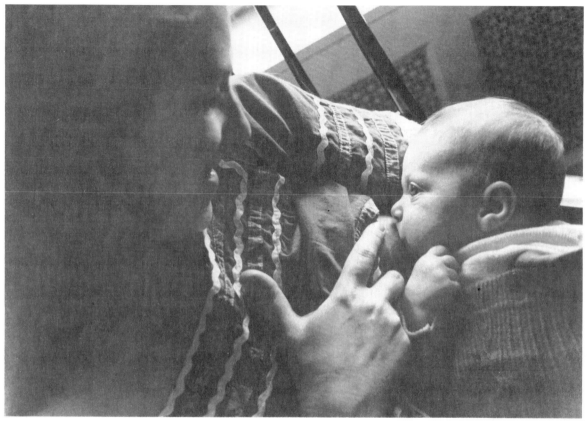

Breast milk provides the optimal mixture of nutrients needed by the human infant for proper development and also supplies antibodies that provide protection from many diseases. Furthermore, the breast-fed baby is held just at the distance at which he or she can best see the mother's face, and the mother in turn usually looks at the baby while feeding.

hinder the growth of those causing diarrhea and other intestinal complications. The incidence of such problems is much lower in breast-fed than in bottle-fed infants. This difference is, of course, also due in part to the fact that breast milk is less easily contaminated than bottled milk.

Finally, allergic reactions to breast milk are virtually unknown. By contrast, many babies develop allergies to other animal proteins such as those found in cow's milk. Preterm babies are preferentially given mother's milk, usually expressed by the mother and fed to the baby by tube and later in a bottle, because they are more likely to tolerate it than any other kind of milk. Milk banks have been set up at many hospitals from which preterm babies whose mothers are not available, and other babies whose mothers may not produce sufficient milk but who are allergic to various cow's milk formulas, can acquire surplus milk donated by nursing mothers who produce an oversupply.

This type of allergy should not be confused with **lactose intolerance,** which is an inability to digest the lactose found in any milk. This condition is virtually unknown in people of Northern European ancestry but is present in about 7 of 10 American blacks and also occurs in American Indians and Orientals (Ament, 1979; Smith, 1977). The incidence of lactose intolerance in the first two years of life has been estimated to be only 0.4 percent to 7.5 percent in American infants (Woodruff, 1976). Therefore, it only rarely presents a problem in infant feeding.

Contraindications to Breast-Feeding

There are, however, contraindications to breast-feeding for some mothers and their infants. First of all, infants with the metabolic disorders described earlier cannot be fed either human or cow's milk but must have specially constituted formulas designed to be very low in the substances the body is unable to metabolize.

Second, since breast milk can transmit drugs as well as antibodies, mothers who are taking drugs that could harm the baby should not breast-feed (Committee on Drugs, 1983). It is wise for any nursing mother who is prescribed a drug to inform her physician that she is breast-feeding. Then if the drug may be harmful to the baby, another could be substituted, or if there is no substitute, the baby should be put on formula instead. Since 1980, United States government regulations require that all prescription drugs that could be transmitted in breast milk include a package insert that details possible effects of the drug on the baby.

One important group of drugs that should not be taken while breast-feeding are the various birth control pills, since they contain powerful hormones (Cohen & Strebel, 1979). Instead, another method of contraception should be used during this period. Inci-

dentally, breast-feeding itself, often reputed to be nature's own contraceptive, is a far from perfect one among well-fed modern women who feed their babies on a schedule of from 6 to 8 or 10 feedings a day. It should not be relied on for protection against a too early subsequent pregnancy.

Other drugs taken by the mother that appear in breast milk and that can adversely affect the baby include all **narcotics** with the exception of morphine, as well as **anticoagulants,** thyroid and antithyroid preparations, many tranquilizers and sedatives, and some cough medicines (Cohen & Strebel, 1979; Committee on Drugs, 1983). In addition, if the nursing mother smokes, some of the compounds released in smoking also find their way to the baby via the milk. Many doctors recommend that nursing mothers temporarily give up smoking.

Third, substances other than drugs can also be passed on to the baby in breast milk. These include various disease organisms. Therefore, mothers with certain diseases, such as tuberculosis, should not breast-feed either. Again, medical guidance is needed to determine whether a mother having a disease should or should not breast-feed her infant.

Some substances that the mother eats can also enter breast milk and affect the baby. Most of them do not have serious consequences, and in most instances it is better for the mother to stop eating them than to discontinue breast-feeding. These foods include highly spiced dishes and those that cause the formation of gas in the intestine, such as cabbage or radishes. Some babies develop allergic reactions to tomatoes or chocolate eaten by the mother. Some even show allergic reactions to cow's milk proteins ingested by their mothers by developing **colic** (Jakobsson & Lindberg, 1983). When the mothers were taken off cow's milk proteins, the infants' symptoms disappeared. Nursing mothers, therefore, need to be aware that babies can be affected by these foods, and if necessary they should experiment and eliminate those that appear to cause trouble.

Finally, some women are unable to breast-feed. Some do not produce adequate amounts of milk. Others have problems with the size or shape of their nipples, and some develop such sore nipples that breast-feeding must be discontinued. These problems can often be prevented by prenatal massaging and other preparation of the breasts. Nipple shields worn for nursing can also be helpful in some instances. But in spite of such aids, many women find that they simply cannot breast-feed.

Cultural Reasons for Breast-Feeding or Bottle-Feeding

LACK OF OPTIONS IN THE PAST

In part, the decision of how to feed a baby is affected by sociocultural circumstances. Before modern sanitation and advances in the science of nutrition made cow's milk and other formulas safe and relatively good substitutes for human milk, mothers who could not or would not breast-feed had few alternatives. Wet nurses were sometimes employed by upper-class women. Milk from cows, goats, donkeys, and other animals was used if a family could not afford a wet nurse or if none was available. A variety of devices used to feed infants have been preserved from ancient and medieval times. They include various funnels, bottles, and other containers from which the baby could suck or which served to pour or dribble milk or gruel into its mouth. Because of poor sanitation and because the various kinds of animal milk differed greatly from human milk, the sur-

vival rate for babies fed these substances was not very high until the recent past.

THE SITUATION IN DEVELOPED COUNTRIES

In modern, developed countries, various commercially prepared formulas and home-prepared ones, such as those made with evaporated milk, water, and a sweetener, can be made safe from contamination and to approximate reasonably, though not completely, human milk. Mothers, therefore, have more options. Which option they choose depends to a large degree on what their peers do as well as on the mother's own employment status.

Shifting Trends   Thus, bottle-feeding became fashionable among educated, middle-class women in the 1940s, while most poorer women were still breast-feeding. By the 1960s, the poor and the less well-educated had begun to imitate the middle class and were largely using bottle-feeding, just as the middle class was beginning to swing back toward breast-feeding. The low point for breast-feeding was 1968, when only 27 percent of American infants were fed that way (Lozoff, 1979). Since then, breast-feeding has increased, primarily at first among middle-class women, especially those with some college education who were not working outside the home. As of 1981, a little over 55 percent of newborns were breast-fed, and at five to six months, almost 25 percent still were (Update, 1981/1982). The percentage of American babies being breast-fed is rising annually. For example, a large survey of mothers conducted by Ross Laboratories, the manufacturer of a number of infant formulas, revealed that in 1981 more than twice as many American infants began life being breast-fed than in 1971 (Martinez & Dodd, 1983). In addition, babies were kept on breast milk longer; the biggest gains in the rate of breast-feeding from 1971 to 1981 were among babies in the five-and-six month age groups. While the highest incidence of breast-feeding occurred among middle-class mothers, the greatest rate of increase was among less educated and less well-off women (Martinez & Dodd, 1983). The proportion of working-class women that now breast-feed is higher than at any time in the last few decades (Lyon, Chilver, White, & Wollett, 1981).

A number of parent-sponsored groups such as the **La Leche League,** which has chapters throughout the country, offer information and support to expectant mothers who want to breast-feed. Doctors and hospital personnel are also more supportive and better trained in helping an inexperienced woman initiate breast-feeding than they were in the recent past.

Working Mothers   A number of American mothers are choosing to feed their babies formula at present because they, like many

Breast-feeding is often difficult for mothers who work, since most American employers do not provide either the time or location to perform this activity. Although this mother appears to have an employer who permits her to feed her baby at work, the setting is certainly not conducive to an unhurried, pleasant feeding interaction between mother and infant.

other women, have remained in, or returned to, the labor force. Indeed, the lowest rates of breast-feeding in the Ross survey were for babies older than two months whose mothers were employed full-time (Martinez & Dodd, 1983). These mothers have little choice about how to feed their infants during working hours, because most American industrial and business concerns do not make provision for child care on the premises. Mothers, therefore, usually cannot reach their children to breast-feed during breaks or lunch hours. Some exceptionally motivated mothers breast-feed while home and express and save the milk for feedings while they are away. Some use a combination of breast- and formula-feeding. This combination works all right for some babies, but others may refuse the bottle or refuse the breast.

Some countries, including France, China, and those in Scandinavia, provide for working nursing mothers and their babies. In some instances, day-care centers are offered at places of work and time off to nurse the baby is granted. In other instances, lengthy maternity leaves, or initial return to part-time work, or some combination of these, are provided. We have already mentioned in chapter 4 the Swedish practice of granting leaves or a reduced workday for either or both parents after the birth of the child. In China, mothers are allowed 56 days of maternity leave, and after they return to work are given two breaks daily to breast-feed their infants (Butterfield, 1982).

THE SITUATION IN DEVELOPING COUNTRIES

Paradoxically, as interest in breast-feeding is increasing in the United States and other developed countries, bottle-feeding has become more fashionable in many of the developing countries. There it is often viewed as being modern and up-to-date. In many countries in Asia and Africa, most infants are breast-fed early in infancy, but the practice is ending earlier and bottle-feeding is substituted long before the baby's need for milk as the major source of food is over (Popkin, Bilsborrow, & Akin, 1982). For the poorer people in these countries, this trend has had disastrous consequences. Because sanitation practices in less developed areas of the world are often minimal, water as well as cow's milk may be contaminated with disease organisms. Little or nothing is known about sterilizing water, milk, and baby bottles to kill microorganisms. Refrigeration is usually unavailable, so that even if formula is prepared free of disease organisms, it probably cannot stay that way for very long. For these reasons, illness and death among infants from diarrhea and other intestinal problems is on the rise in many parts of the world, in spite of the introduction of vaccines, antibiotics, and other measures designed to decrease infant mortality.

Furthermore, cash income in many such countries is extremely low, and the cost of baby formula or cow's milk is high. It has been estimated that in developing countries the purchase of baby formula in adequate amounts properly to nourish an infant may take up to half of a family's cash income (Jelliffe & Jelliffe, 1977). Therefore, babies are often fed either formula or cow's milk diluted with large amounts of water and sugar to make them go farther and cost less. This diet can result in severe protein-calorie malnutrition, retarding brain growth as well as general physical growth and development. Citizen groups in the developed countries have been agitating to force manufacturers of infant formulas to stop advertising their products in less developed countries in an effort to increase breast-feeding and lessen the problems caused by indiscriminate bottle feeding. Some major manufacturers of infant formulas have agreed to stop such advertising as of 1984.

A FINAL WORD ON FEEDING

In the final analysis, a mother needs to choose that method of feeding with which she feels most comfortable and secure and that is best suited to the particular situation in which she and her infant find themselves. For though breast milk clearly is more advantageous for most babies, a mother who breast-feeds unwillingly and resentfully may do more harm than good. Similarly, a mother who cannot breast-feed because of physiological or work-related constraints, or one who chooses not to, should not feel inferior or guilty.

FEEDING PATTERNS IN INFANCY

The First Few Days

The normal infant is born with enough extra fat accumulated in the last few weeks of gestation that feeding is not needed in the first few days until the mother's milk comes in. Babies are also born with slight edema resulting from extra water present in body tissues. This water helps to prevent dehydration in the period before milk drinking commences. The baby is born ready to suck, however, since both the rooting and sucking reflexes are functional.

The baby's sucking is necessary in initiating and continuing the mother's production of milk. Prolactin, the hormone necessary for milk production, is secreted by the mother in response to the stimulation to the breasts provided by the infant. The **ejection reflex,** or **let-down reflex,** which allows the milk to flow, also depends upon the infant.

Oxytocin, the hormone responsible for this reflex, is secreted by the mother when she hears the baby's cry or touches, smells, or puts the baby to the breast (Pritchard & MacDonald, 1980).

Additionally, sucking during the neonatal period enables the infant to absorb colostrum, a watery fluid secreted by the breasts in the first few days before the onset of milk production. Colostrum contains more protein and minerals but less sugar and fat than the milk that is to follow (Pritchard & MacDonald, 1980). It thus may provide a little nourishment to the baby, though rather small amounts of it are secreted and ingested. The most important function of colostrum appears to be its ability to transfer antibodies against various diseases to the baby. Thus the colostrum provides temporary immunity against a number of diseases until the mother's milk can begin to provide antibodies also, and until the baby's own body can begin to manufacture its own.

Milk Production and Early Feeding

True milk begins to come in late in the first week after birth, generally by the sixth to seventh day (Pritchard & MacDonald, 1980). The quantity at first is small, but the increasingly vigorous sucking of the baby causes milk production to increase as the baby's daily requirements become greater.

The neonate will require being put to the breast about 6 to 10 times during a 24-hour period in the first week. Bottle-fed infants also need relatively frequent feeding. Hospitals generally start bottle-fed babies on sweetened water but begin formula feeding by the third day or sometimes earlier. This practice is probably not necessary for the baby's nutrition, but may relieve the anxiety of some mothers who are afraid their babies are not getting sufficient nourishment.

During the second week, and for most of the rest of the first month, the breast-fed or bottle-fed infant will nurse up to six to eight times daily, at fairly irregular intervals that average about 3 1/2 to 4 hours apart. The infant will ingest about 12 fluid oz of milk daily during this second week of postnatal life. This amount rises gradually to about 24 oz at the end of the month. During this month the baby develops much better control over the muscles involved in sucking. Sucking therefore becomes more efficient, and the baby can ingest more milk in a shorter time period. Sucking and swallowing have also become much better coordinated, and so the baby gags and spits up less than earlier. Since the baby can begin to recognize the breast or bottle and responds to their sight by grasping the nipple and sucking, the rooting reflex is no longer necessary and begins to disappear.

Between one and three months, milk consumption increases to about 30 to 35 oz daily, equivalent to about one liter, or one quart. The baby now takes more at each feeding, and the number of feedings usually drops to about five or six. One night feeding has usually been eliminated. Some babies have also begun to skip the second night feeding and are sleeping through the night.

Introduction of Solids and Juices

In the two-to-four-month period, the baby's swallowing mechanism matures sufficiently so that it can now begin to handle solid foods. However, because of the possibility of allergic reactions and because the baby does not yet need the additional food, most pediatricians at present advise postponing solid foods until at least the three-to-four-month period and preferably even later (Smith & Owens, 1977). Many advise waiting until the second half of the first year, or adding only cereal or fruit during the four-to-six-month period (Committee on Nutrition, 1983).

After about four months, when many babies have a higher caloric requirement than milk alone can supply, cereal is often added to the diet of many of them. At first it is diluted greatly with milk, and only a small spoonful is offered. Usually, the baby pushes it all out. Having a solid put on the tongue is a new sensation, which the baby is not quite able to cope with at first. Over time, it learns to swallow more and push out less, unless, of course, the food is disliked.

Because of the possibility of allergies to a particular grain, pediatricians generally advise starting the baby on only one single-grain cereal. If there is an adverse reaction, that grain is no longer fed. If there is not, another grain can be added a bit later. For if the baby is started on a multigrain cereal, or if several different cereals are tried on successive days and the baby shows intolerance, the detective work involved in finding out which grain is at fault becomes complicated. Later on, as other foods are added, the same technique is followed. Only one new food is added at a time, and no other new one is introduced for several days thereafter.

Most babies adjust to the taste and texture of cereal and to swallowing food put on the tongue with a spoon within a few days. If a baby continues to resist cereal and is old enough for solid food, a pureed fruit may be substituted. Even if a baby tolerates cereal well, fruits are usually added to the diet a few weeks after cereal. Some pediatricians now advise adding fruit first, and cereal only later, since the possibility of allergic reactions to cereals is greater. Around the age of five months, vegetables may be added, and a month or so later meats and egg yolk as well.

Fruit juices are often begun after the first few months so that the baby will receive additional vitamin C. Orange juice is usually the first juice given, but tomato, apple, or grapefruit juice can be tried as well. Some babies have allergic reactions to juices; then vitamin C in drop form should suffice, and juices can be postponed until later when the baby is more likely to tolerate them.

Later Consumption of Milk

As the baby begins to eat significant amounts of solid foods, milk consumption begins to level off. Eventually, the amount of milk drunk daily will even decline. Some babies become so entranced over eating solids that they consume too little milk. If that happens, parents are usually advised to feed some milk first, then to follow with the solids, and then to offer as much more milk as the baby desires. The Committee on Nutrition of the American Academy of Pediatrics (1983) has recommended that infants be fed either breast milk or formula until at least the age of six months and preferably for the whole first year of life. Whole cow's milk should not be introduced until after six months, and then only if the infant is already consuming a balanced diet of cereals, vegetables, fruits, and other foods that will supply essential nutrients such as iron that are lacking in cow's milk.

The Three-Meal Schedule

As the baby begins solid foods, the number of feedings again declines. Most babies in the 3- to-7-month range will want four to five feedings daily; some begin to adjust to three to four during this time. By 8 to 12 months, almost all babies have adjusted to a three-meal schedule similar to that of older children, with perhaps some small snacks between meals.

When the teeth begin erupting, chewable finger foods can be given to the baby.

Zwieback, crackers, pieces of banana, or small, peeled pieces of pear are suitable. After this time, many babies want to begin feeding themselves other foods, although it will be a long time before they can handle a spoon. Therefore, parents often must endure the spectacle of the baby insisting on eating cereal or vegetables with its fingers. After the baby has some teeth, foods with more texture such as chopped foods are added to the

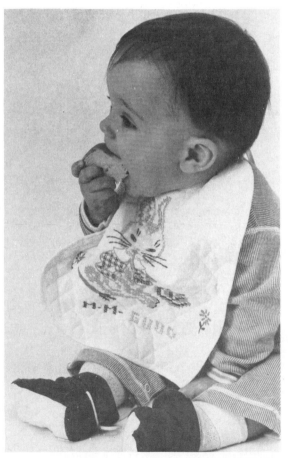

The baby who has begun to eat solid foods and who has some teeth with which to bite and chew delights in feeding itself. Although self-feeding at first may be messy and time-consuming, it is important in helping the child learn to master self-help skills.

baby's diet in place of the pureed fruits, meats, and vegetables. The baby also can begin to handle bits of hamburger, meat loaf, scrambled eggs, or potato that have been prepared for the family. Finally, usually around one year of age or a bit later, most toddlers are entirely on table food, with supplemental milk. Some foods that the family may eat, of course, are unsuitable for a child of this age. They include highly spiced foods, fried foods, and highly salted foods. If such foods are prepared for the family, another should be substituted for the toddler.

Chewing Food and Using a Cup

During this first half of the second year, as cuspid and molar teeth erupt, the child becomes more adept at chewing and can handle larger pieces of table food more easily. Usually the toddler also begins to handle a spoon. At first the spoon is as likely to be held upside down as right side up, but over time the child manages to get more and more food to the mouth using the spoon.

Around this time, the child also becomes quite adept at handling a cup. Drinking from a cup, but with an adult holding it, has generally begun somewhat sooner, but now the toddler begins to control the cup and bring it to his or her lips to drink without adult aid. Special cups with handles and snap-on lids that allow liquid to come out only slowly are helpful at this stage.

WEANING

The process whereby the baby gives up sucking milk from breast or bottle and changes entirely to drinking from a cup is called **weaning**. The subject can arouse strong feelings, often conflicting ones, in mothers and other caregivers. Many mothers look forward eagerly to a time when they need not be constantly available for breast-feeding or have the daily chore of preparing bottled feedings. Others are reluctant to end the close, special relationship that breast-feeding especially, but also well-handled bottle-feeding, promotes. Some mothers alternate between these two ways of feeling and have trouble resolving them.

Some babies are weaned easily, indeed almost wean themselves. Others are so strongly attached to breast or bottle that they resist mightily any change in feeding patterns. Children seem to differ greatly in their readiness for weaning. Some babies tire early of the whole business of sucking, whether from breast or bottle, and happily switch to a cup. Others will take orange juice or water from a cup but will refuse milk from any source except breast or bottle. Breast-fed babies sometimes are weaned first to a bottle, as mothers tire of breast feeding or return to work, and only later are entirely weaned to a cup. This process is easier if the breast-fed baby has earlier received some supplementary bottle feeding, either some of the mother's expressed milk, or juice, or water. Some breast-fed babies who have had no experience with a bottle show complete disinterest or revulsion when confronted with one later in infancy. Such babies are often weaned straight from the breast to the cup.

Psychoanalytic Interpretations

Psychoanalytic theorists argued in the past that weaning before the child was ready, that is, before the child was out of the oral stage of psychosexual development, would lead to undesirable personality development. They suggested that early weaning would lead the individual to seek for other means of oral gratification such as thumb sucking or compulsive eating and, later in adolescence or adulthood, smoking (Hall & Lindzey, 1957). Phenomena of oral aggression, such as biting, name-calling, or using foul language, were also regarded as possible consequences of abrupt or early weaning. Research done in the 1950s and 1960s did not support these theories. Weaning, therefore, is no longer seen as a very critical event, provided the child had a good feeding relationship with the caregiver before weaning, and that adequate alternative sources of protein such as meats and cow's milk are available after weaning.

Weaning in Protein-Poor Cultures

In cultures in which no adequate alternative protein sources exist in sufficient quantities for young children, and in which bottle-feeding has not yet become fashionable, babies are generally kept on breast milk until the mother's next pregnancy suppresses the production of milk, which may be as late as age two or three. Some cultures even regulate how soon a nursing mother can resume sexual relations with her husband, to ensure that the baby will not be deprived of milk too early. If there are no other protein sources available after weaning, or if cultural strictures dictate that toddlers not be fed meats, eggs, or other available protein-rich foods, conditions such as kwashiorkor can result. Indeed, the word kwashiorkor means "the sickness the child gets after the birth of the new baby" in a West African language, showing that these people had figured out the connection between the cessation of breast-feeding and the onset of the disease.

Weaning in the United States

Since in the United States today alternative sources of protein are easily available for all but the very poor, weaning a baby need not be a nutritionally disastrous event. Of course, caregivers must be sure the child is receiving adequate amounts of other foods providing not only the protein but also the minerals and vitamins that had formerly been ingested in milk or formula drunk from breast or bottle. These include milk drunk from the cup, meats, dairy products, and many other foods that should by now already be a part of the child's diet.

Weaning in the United States generally takes place late in the first or early in the second year. Some babies begin to wean themselves as early as six months, when interest in milk as well as milk consumption often declines as new foods are introduced. The breast or bottle at bedtime is generally the last noncup feeding that is given up. Evidently at times when the child is tired it still wants the comfort of a familiar way of feeding. The activity of sucking may also serve to reduce tension at the end of a long and perhaps frustrating day.

Nursing-Bottle Caries

The bedtime feeding, particularly if it is a bottle-feeding of milk or of other liquids high in sugars, can be damaging to the health of the child's teeth. The child often keeps the bottle in the mouth as sleep occurs, and residue of the milk remains on the teeth and in the oral cavity. This residue harbors bacteria that cause decay. Dentists have recently reported severe cases of **caries,** or tooth decay, in young children who have clung to a bedtime bottle for some time after appearance of the deciduous teeth (Shelton, Berkowitz, & Forrester, 1977). If a child insists on a bedtime bottle, dental authorities recommend the use of water, with perhaps a few spoonfuls of a natural, relatively unsugared juice such as apple juice added for flavor. If possible, the child should rinse its mouth and have its teeth brushed before bedtime and eliminate the bedtime bottle completely. It seems that even breast milk may cause such tooth decay if mothers continue to breast-feed older infants and toddlers at frequent intervals during the night (Brams & Maloney, 1983). Thus, even in breast-fed babies, it is wise to eliminate night feedings as soon as the baby is able to manage without them and certainly before the teeth erupt.

DEVELOPMENT OF BOWEL AND BLADDER FUNCTIONS

Early Development

The neonate is unable to concentrate urine as efficiently as the older infant (Guthrie, Pruiett, Murphy, Hodson, Wennberg, & Woodrum, 1977). Therefore, the bladder is frequently voided, usually beginning on the day of birth. The baby's first bowel movements consist of the meconium, discussed in chapter 4. Normal neonates begin to produce transitional stools consisting of the last of the meconium and the waste products of beginning nutrition around days four to five, and as the baby begins to drink milk, it evacuates typical yellowish-brown stools.

In the first month, the baby may have from two to eight bowel movements a day, at irregular times. Three to five is the most usual. By the age of one month, both urination and elimination are a bit less frequent. The baby now most usually has a bowel movement upon awakening. By two or three months, the baby may have only two daily bowel movements, usually shortly after feedings, and may also stay dry for increasingly long periods of time. Around four months, defecation occurs much later than at the end of a meal. Since the baby now begins to

spend some time sitting up, the muscles controlling excretion and elimination must adjust to this postural change and begin to function in a slightly different manner.

Toilet Training

BEHAVIORS INVOLVED

By the time the baby is nine months old, it has some voluntary control of the **anal sphincter**. Good control of the sphincter of the bladder follows later. The child does not yet understand, however, the social imperatives relating to toilet behavior and therefore is still much too young to begin training. Toilet behavior is a complicated sequence. For it entails recognizing the physiological cues, maintaining sphincter control, signaling the caregiver or getting oneself to the bathroom, removing appropriate clothing, taking the correct position, and finally releasing sphincter control. This sequence requires mature muscular control, language or an alternative communication device, and intellectual understanding of what one is expected to do. Most children are well into the second half of the second year before they can master the whole involved sequence, and they are even older before they can do so without occasional accidents.

IN NON-WESTERN CULTURES

In many non-Western cultures, toilet training is likely to be attempted more casually and later than in our own, especially in warmer climates, where toddlers can be outdoors with a minimum of clothing. Since they neither soil indoors nor use diapers that must be washed, their early toilet training is not considered of great importance.

In some non-Western cultures, however,

Toilet training is not much of a problem in cultures that flourish in warmer climates in which children can be left naked and outdoors most of the time. This infant being cared for by two older siblings is therefore under little or no pressure to keep from soiling garments, diapers, or the environment.

mothers condition their babies to urinate upon a signal from them. In parts of Africa, mothers hiss to induce babies to urinate while outdoors and held away from their own bodies; and among the Chinese, mothers often whistle to obtain the same effect (Wolf, 1972). Potty training also begins quite early in China, at least for those children who are in day-care centers (Butterfield, 1982). By the age of one year, they are expected to use the potty when they need to urinate and to sit on it after naps or feedings until they defecate.

IN THE UNITED STATES

Because the baby is dry for long periods and because bowel behavior is fairly regular, some American caregivers attempt to begin training late in the first year by rushing the child to the toilet or potty at the first signs or by leaving the child sitting there for extended periods at the time that such a physiological function usually occurs. Both methods really involve training the adult rather than the child and are therefore not recom-

The older toddler, who has acquired both adequate muscular control and the intellectual understanding of what is expected, can often be toilet trained rather easily. The child's eagerness to acquire mastery and to please parents or other caregivers contributes to successful toilet training.

mended by most modern American child-care experts.

The age at which American toddlers successfully accomplish toilet training seems to be increasing. In a comprehensive study done during the 1950s (Sears, Maccoby, & Levin, 1957), parents reported that toilet training was accomplished at the average age of 18 months, except for occasional accidents during the night. By the 1960s this figure had risen to 22 months according to a California study (Heinstein, 1966). In the last couple of decades, American parents appear to have become even more relaxed about the toilet training of their children. This attitude may reflect more knowledge of children's physical and intellectual development, or it may be because families today are smaller and an untrained child is therefore less burdensome. Perhaps the widespread use of paper diapers, which frees many adults from the onerous job of washing and folding cloth diapers, also plays a part.

In the 12-to-18 month period, usually later rather than sooner within this time span, some training can be attempted. Most pediatricians advise waiting until closer to the 18-month-date to avoid frustration of both parent and child. If the child is provided with a low potty chair, which it can reach without adult help, and if appropriate clothing such as training pants, which the child can remove easily, are worn, this process is helped. Toddlers may need frequent reminders, however, since they can become so engrossed in play that they ignore physiological cues until it is too late.

Most children learn daytime control before control at night, and bowel control is perfected before bladder control is complete. In general, probably reflecting their greater physiological maturity all along, girls train a little earlier than boys. After a little boy has mastered bladder training, he also needs to learn to urinate while standing, usually not until during the third year.

The average toddler is not completely successful in bladder or bowel training until some time between ages two and three. The child is spurred on in this development by the wish to gain mastery over the environment, including doing things alone, without adult aid. Therefore, the child is usually eager to learn the appropriate toilet behavior when he or she is physiologically and intellectually mature enough to be able to do so and understands what is expected. Occasionally an opposite trend occurs. As the child gains mastery, he or she tends to do the opposite of what the adult wants and to disregard appropriate toilet behavior as a means of self-assertion. In general, ignoring and thereby extinguishing this behavior and positively reinforcing appropriate toilet behav-ior usually ends such a problem in a relatively short time.

If parents do not put inordinate emphasis on toilet training, if they wait until a child is physiologically and intellectually ready, and if they treat accidents that inevitably occur casually, the child usually will train herself or himself without too much difficulty.

Summary

1. The developing infant and toddler needs a variety of nutrients to grow and to maintain good health. These include proteins, carbohydrates, fats, water, minerals, and vitamins.

2. Several metabolic disorders that require nutritional management can occur in infants. These are phenylketonuria, tyrosinemia, maple syrup urine disease, and galactosemia. In addition, obesity seems to have its origins in infancy, and lead ingested by the child can produce lead poisoning.

3. Human milk is the best food for the infant in the first few months of life. It differs from cow's milk formulas in the kinds and proportions of nutrients it contains, and it also provides the infant antibodies to resist disease. Only in cases of metabolic disorders, certain diseases in the mother, or her use of particular drugs that enter breast milk and can harm the baby is breast milk not advised.

4. Breast-feeding is on the increase in the United States, and mothers who do so tend to keep the child on breast milk for a longer time period than in the recent past. Return to work outside the home seems to be a major reason for not breast-feeding among American women today. In developing countries, mothers are ending breast-feeding earlier, and the change to either formula or cow's milk poses many health and nutritional problems for their children.

5. Milk, either from the breast or from a commercial formula, provides most of the nutrients needed by the young infant. A few substances, such as some minerals and vitamins, may need to be added to the diet of all babies, and especialy to those of babies born preterm or of low birth weight. Only after four to six months should supplemental feeding, usually of fruit or cereal, begin. Later on, vegetables and meats are added to the infant diet.

6. Feeding is important not only because it provides necessary nutrients but also because it provides a time of important interaction between infant and caregiver, especially the nursing mother. Later, mealtimes become important times of social interaction between the infant and the rest of the family.

7. Young infants urinate and defecate with great frequency. As the older infant or tod-

dler begins to establish some control over these functions, parents and other caregivers begin to train him or her to use socially accepted ways and locations for satisfying these physiological needs. Much of this training, however, is successful only in the third year, beyond infancy and toddlerhood.

Participatory and Observational Exercises

1. Observe a young baby feeding from breast or bottle. Can you see indications of the rooting and sucking reflexes? What kinds of interactions are taking place between infant and caregiver during feeding? After the feeding, interview the parent(s). Discuss the kind of feeding used (breast or bottle). Why was the method used chosen? What advantages does the caregiver perceive for this method over the other? Any disadvantages? What are they? What plans regarding feeding does the caregiver express for the infant as he or she becomes older?

2. Go to a super market and check through the section that stocks baby foods. What different kinds are available? How much variety is there (both within a brand and across brand labels)? To which nutritional group or groups does each food belong? Check the labels of various foods for ingredients listed. Look especially for the following:

    a. Are cereals single-grain or multiple-grain? Are grain contents clearly listed?

    b. Do vegetables contain salt? Sugar? Other additives?

    c. Do fruits contain sugar? Other additives?

    d. Does each food have directions for preparation or storage listed on the label?

    e. Are nutrients, and percentages of RDAs for each, listed? Are calories per total or per serving listed?

    f. Do any of the products contain supplemental vitamins or minerals? For example, are grain products fortified? Is there additional iron in formula mix?

    g. Go to the pet food section and look at some cans or boxes of pet food. What is listed on their labels? How does the kind and amount of information given compare to what is given on baby foods?

3. Observe infants and toddlers of various ages at mealtimes (at home or in day care). Record what each child eats, the amounts, and her or his behaviors during the meal. Check with caregivers what foods the child eats at other meals. Is the child getting a nutritionally appropriate diet? Is each child allowed to self-feed to the degree possible for his or her maturity level and the kind of food being eaten? Is the meal a social as well as a nutritional event? Explain.

4. Discuss with some mothers of infants and toddlers what they think is a proper diet for a child the age of theirs. Where did they obtain their information? How accurate does it appear to be?

5. If possible, talk also with the mother of an infant or toddler who is on a special diet because of an allergy or a hereditary nutritional disease. What does the diet entail?

What modifications has she had to make in the foods she would normally have been feeding her child? How does she obtain the special food (if one is needed) that her baby receives? What problems, if any, has she encountered with the use of the special diet?

6. Interview the parents of an older toddler who has begun or has almost completed toilet training. Find out when they began, what their level of success was, and what the child's reactions were. What frustrations did they and the child encounter? How were they handled? If they had to begin all over with another child, what would they do differently, if anything, about toilet training? If possible, interview a second set of parents of a similarly aged toddler and compare the responses of the two sets of parents. Can you detect differences between the two toddlers in how easily and/or rapidly toilet training has progressed (at least according to parent report)? If there are differences, to what factors might they be attributable?

DISCUSSION QUESTIONS

1. How appropriate is it for baby formula companies to advertise and promote their products in developing countries?

2. Should a mother breast-feed because of the nutritional advantages for the infant even if she has strong feelings of distaste for the procedure?

3. How can we change societal attitudes about chubby babies being most appealing so as to prevent overfeeding that could lead to later problems with obesity?

4. How important is toilet training in our society? Why?

Perceptual Development in Infancy

CHAPTER

7

A

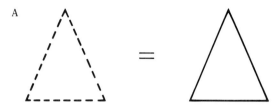

According to Gestalt theorists, even newborn infants can interpret that the dashed lines represent a figure. In this instance, the dashed lines form a triangle, and the infant is believed to perceive the triangle rather than a series of dashes.

B

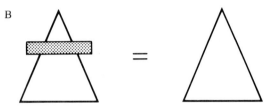

T. G. R. Bower found that infants who saw this figure interpreted it as a complete triangle with a rectangle in front of it. In other words, they interpreted the triangle as a closed figure, even though they did not see the whole figure.

C

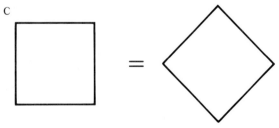

Gestalt theorists believe that infants perceive both of these squares as being the same, with the second merely rotated in space.

demonstrated that they recognized it as the figure seen before. It should be noted, however, that other experimenters have had problems in attempting to replicate Bower's work. The Gestaltists also believe that the infant already understands that an object rotated in space remains the same object although its appearance may be drastically altered. For example, a square that is tilted appears more like a diamond (fig. C). Can the baby account for the tilt and still perceive the object as a square? The Gestaltists would argue that the infant can do so. According to their view, the infant is born with the perceptual ability to discriminate and organize stimuli and lacks only the experience to interpret their meaning, which will be acquired over time.

Other psychologists that tend toward the nativist position include Robert Fantz (1961b, 1965), who believes that form perception is an inborn capacity of the infant.

ETHOLOGICAL VIEW

Somewhat similar is the point of view of Gibson (1969), who believes that particular species, including humans, are sensitized by nature to certain properties of objects they are likely to encounter. This is the ethological viewpoint, based on the study of animal behavior. Thus, such properties as contour, movement, depth, or a tone within a particular range of wavelengths may sensitize infants of a certain species, while different characteristics may sensitize other species. Therefore, Gibson believes that the perceptual characteristics of the human face or the human voice are inherently important to the human infant and are consequently responded to by the infant's perceptual systems. Gibson believes, however, that this sensitivity increases with experience, and therefore, she gives some emphasis to the empiricist position. For example, Gibson did some experiments in depth perception with animals that were prevented from seeing in order that she might demonstrate the role of experience. In summary, she thinks that although the infant is born without very well-developed perceptual capacities it does not need to start from scratch constructing external reality to make sense of sensory stimuli. Instead, the infant is able to transfer perceptions of critical aspects of a stimulus from one situation to another, because he or she already possesses inborn sensitivity to certain stimulus properties of such environmental objects.

THE IMPORTANCE OF LEARNING

Other researchers such as D. O. Hebb (1949, 1958) and Piaget (1952, 1954) think that although perception has both learned and unlearned components, the learned ones predominate. They believe that the infant is born with little perceptual competence beyond rudimentary figure-ground discrimination and that in actively seeking stimulation from the environment the infant gains the experience that enables it to understand the nature of objects including their localization in space, three-dimensionality, and permanence. Early experience and stimulation of sensory end organs is critical for perceptual development to take place. Hebb likens this experience to the critical periods in animal development. He also believes that perception mediates between sensation of a stimulus and the organism's response to the stimulation, that is, perception interprets the stimulus before the individual reacts to it. In infancy, experience is necessary to provide the basis for this mediational capacity.

Thus Hebb and Piaget also lean more in the direction of constructivism than toward innate meaningfulness of stimuli.

EXTREME CONSTRUCTIVISM

Finally, perhaps the most extreme supporter of the importance of experience is Richard Held (Held & Hein, 1963), who believes that activity by the infant is necessary for the development of perception of space. In his view, restriction of activity results in total lack of development of perceptual ability. To demonstrate this theory, Held and A. Hein (1963) built an apparatus they called the kitten carousel, in which one kitten walked in a circle on the carousel for three hours daily. On the other side of the carousel was another kitten, which was moved passively by the walking motions of the first by being placed on a trolley with its paws hidden from its sight. The kittens were thus exposed to the same visual stimuli, but only the walking one had the opportunity to be active. After 10 days, when both kittens were tested for depth perception, the active kitten was able to discriminate depth much better than the passive one, which performed at no better than the chance level.

While all of these theoretical positions have some research evidence in their support, the evidence for any one is not yet compelling. The field of infant perception does not yet have many clear answers to the questions that have been asked. Much work remains to be done to determine the degree to which perceptual capacities are inborn, to what extent they are species-specific, and what the role of activity or experience may be. Further, for perceptual capacities that are apparent later than in the neonate, the relative importance of maturation and experience must be determined more accurately than it has been so far.

PROBLEMS AND FACTORS IN STUDYING INFANT PERCEPTION

Problems

Studies of infant perception are difficult to undertake. It is hard to hold the attention of young infants. They become fatigued, fall asleep, or cry and fuss. They need frequent

The kitten carousel. The active kitten (A) walks around, moving the passive kitten (P) in a circle on its trolley. Kitten (P) neither moves its legs and feet nor is able to see them.

feeding and diapering. It is difficult to persuade parents to bring the infant to a laboratory and next to impossible to do most perception studies in the home. Infant perception can only be determined in indirect ways since babies cannot answer questions and therefore cannot indicate directly what they perceive. Also, no one can be sure that even if infants do perceive some stimulus, their perceptual capacities can be measured in the same way as can those of adults. That is, it is not sure that an infant will react like an adult to a change of tone or to the form of an object, even though the infant may in fact perceive it in the same way as an adult. Thus one cannot generalize from the fact that the infant's response either resembles the adult response or differs from it.

Studies involving vision and hearing are somewhat easier to do than those involving other sense modalities. That is because it is easier to expose infants to visual or auditory stimuli and to observe their reactions than to expose them to other stimuli. For this reason, and also because these two perceptual modalities have been studied more in older children and adults and therefore are more familiar to researchers, studies of visual and auditory perception, especially visual, make up the vast majority of those done with infants. Very few studies involve taste, smell, touch, and vestibular perception, and therefore little is known about how much of these perceptions is present in the newborn and how they develop beyond birth.

Researchers in the field of infant perception have developed some of the most innovative and creative methods of study. They have been quick to use new technological advances such as **holography** (three-dimensional photographic imagery, done with the use of lasers), sensors to detect tiny eye movements, special prismatic goggles, artificially created sounds, and many others to conduct experiments with infants. They have also adapted the results of studies of brain physiology and perceptual experimentation with animals to infant studies. The four major means of studying infant perception involve orienting, preference, habituation, and conditioning.

Orienting

Orienting, as noted previously, is the process of attending to a stimulus on a sensory level. It is similar to reflexive behavior in that the infant does not orient voluntarily but is drawn to the stimulus. The infant turns in the direction of a sound or looks at a light, not because it necessarily wants to but because the brain responds automatically to the stimulation. From orienting it can be inferred that the infant is at least aware of the stimulus, although it cannot be said whether in fact the higher brain centers are in any way processing this information, that is, attaching any meaning to it.

Preference

Preference involves exposing the infant to two stimuli and noticing which one seems to be attended to more. The infant may be given two slightly differing visual displays to look at or two different-flavored liquids to suck,

and the rates of looking or sucking for each stimulus are recorded and compared. The idea is that if the infant prefers one stimulus over another, the experimenter can infer that it can perceive the difference between the two. Preference studies are, therefore, useful in determining what kinds of stimuli or what components of these stimuli attract infants. The major drawback to preference studies is that if the infant does not show a preference for one stimulus over the other, the experimenter cannot know if this failure is because the infant does not perceive a difference or because it perceives but does not prefer one over the other. In such an instance, either of the two remaining methods, habituation or conditioning, can often be used to determine the answer.

Habituation

Habituation is based on the fact that repeated exposure to the same stimulus makes that stimulus "old hat." The infant becomes bored and no longer attends. Habituation is different from fatigue, a state in which the end organs are tired and no longer respond to any stimulation. It has been shown that even in neonates, ceasing to pay attention to a stimulus is due to habituation, not fatigue (Friedman, 1972). If a new, somewhat different stimulus is introduced and the infant dishabituates, that is, begins to attend to the new stimulus, the experimenter can then infer that the infant has perceived the difference between the two stimuli.

Conditioning

Finally, an infant can be conditioned to respond to a particular kind of stimulation. **Operant conditioning** is a form of learning that takes place when the infant receives reinforcement or reward for performing a particular activity in a particular stimulus situation. Eventually the infant will perform the activity in the presence of the appropriate stimulus even if only rewarded once in a while. Operant conditioning can be used creatively in perceptual research with infants. For example, researchers can condition an infant to look to the left every time it hears a particular tone, by reinforcing this looking with an interesting visual display on the left. After conditioning has taken place, the infant will turn to the left every time it hears that tone, even if the researcher shows the reinforcer (the visual display) only once in a while. It can then be determined whether the infant perceives other tones as the same or different from the one it has been conditioned to. If the infant looks to the left when a similar but not exactly the same tone is sounded, the sound must appear the same to the infant. If the child does not turn, it can be assumed that he or she perceives the sound as different.

Since both habituation and conditioning involve memory, they may be better ways of determining perception than are orienting and preference, which may be measures merely of sensory discrimination that do not yet involve higher brain centers (Cohen, De Loach, & Strauss, 1979).

VISUAL PERCEPTION

It used to be thought that the human infant was functionally blind at birth. That is, although the eyes were open and reacted to light and darkness, scientists believed that the infant was incapable of seeing anything. Thus stories by mothers and nurses of babies looking around and following with their eyes, even in the delivery room, were usually discounted as foolish nonsense by the so-called experts. This view has been radically altered

by studies of infant visual competency beginning in the 1960s.

Visual Competency of the Newborn

LIMITATIONS

The visual perception of the newborn is limited partly by the size, shape, and movement of the eyeballs, and partly by its sensory immaturity.

The Eye   The newborn infant's eye is almost as large as it will be at adulthood, but its shape is considerably shorter or flatter. Therefore, the image of what is seen would be focused somewhere behind the back of the eyeball, and what falls on the retina is somewhat fuzzy and out of focus. Furthermore, the muscles controlling the shape of the lens, which also would contribute to sharpening the image, barely function at birth (Haynes, White, & Held, 1965). Thus the newborn's eyes are rather like a camera on which the lens adjustment is stuck. Only pictures of objects at a certain distance appear at all clear; those closer or farther away look blurred. Visual acuity is probably no better than 20/300 to 20/200 (Dobson & Teller, 1978). In other words, the newborn infant is very nearsighted. It sees most clearly objects that are 19 to 22 cm (8 to 10 in) away from the eyes. Anything closer or farther away looks very blurred. Parents and other caregivers need to take this fact into account in holding the infant so it can see their faces and in presenting other objects for the neonate to look at.

The newborn baby's eyes also lack the ability to **converge,** that is to focus both eyes on an object in such a way that only one joint image is interpreted, or "seen," by the brain (Wickelgren, 1967). Scientists know that each eye sees an object in a slightly different manner, since the eyes are some distance apart. But the brain puts together these two images so that the person perceives only one, three-dimensional object. When a young infant looks at a nearby object, however, the left eye tends to look at the left portion of the object, and the right eye at the right portion. Therefore, it is doubtful if the brain can as yet produce a single, integrated image. And finally, coordination of eye movement, so that both eyes move in the same direction, is evident only about 50 percent of the time in the newborn (Wickelgren, 1969). The rest of the time the eyes appear to move independently of each other, which sometimes gives the baby a cross-eyed or wall-eyed appearance. The lack of coordination probably also hinders the infant from seeing only one image of an object.

Sensory Immaturity The **retina**, that portion of the back of the eye on which the sensory receptors for vision, the rods and cones, are located, may still be immature at birth. Furthermore, the **fovea**, the area at the center of the retina in which the largest number of sensory cells involving color vision are located, may change considerably from one month before birth till four months postnatally (Duke-Elder & Cook, 1963; Mann, 1964). It is questionable whether in the human infant the foveal depression already exists at birth, or whether other cells that will later move to the sides of it are still located in front of this area when the baby is born. Also, there may be only a single layer of cone cells, rather than multiple layers as will exist later. Since anatomical studies of the infant eye are only possible with infants that have died, there is some doubt about these findings based on autopsy studies. That is, to what extent are the eyes of a dead infant similar to those of a living one? Studies with monkeys

that are among the closest relatives of humans show that in them the foveal depression is unobstructed at birth (Haith, 1980). That may also be true of human infants. Thus, there is some uncertainty about whether in the newborn the retina is already able to transmit to the brain an accurate version of what is seen, or whether that ability only develops later. There also is some question whether, because of these possible changes in the fovea, the young infant has better vision centrally (Haith, 1978; Lewis, Maurer, & Kay, 1978), that is, using the fovea, or peripherally, using other portions of the eye (Bronson, 1974). In other words, can the newborn infant see better what is straight ahead or what is off to the side in its field of vision? The answer will have implications for adults in how they should hold the infant in relation to their own faces and where they should put toys so that the infant can see them.

The optic nerve, which transmits visual impulses from the eye to the brain, is still incompletely myelinated at birth (Langworthy, 1933). Myelin is the fatty sheath surrounding nerve cells, which increases the efficiency and specificity of the transmission of nerve impulses. Myelination of the optic nerve proceeds more quickly, however, than that of the rest of the nervous system and appears to be complete at some time between three weeks (Last, 1968) and four months of age (Mann, 1964; Nakayama, 1968; Walton, 1970). The visual cortex, the portion of the brain that interprets visual impulses, is also immature and incompletely myelinated at birth (Conel, 1952). The various branching extensions of the nerve cells are as yet sparsely connected to one another. Nevertheless, the visual cortex is functioning to some degree even in the neonate (Karmel & Maisel, 1975). The question is, to what extent can the newborn infant's brain already interpret visual information coming to it?

For all these reasons resulting from limitations of the physical structures and immaturity of the mechanisms, visual acuity, or keenness of vision, in the neonate is poor. The baby sees best only those objects that are a relatively short distance from the eyes, are moderately bright, and are slowly moving.

ABILITIES ALREADY PRESENT

Tracking   The newborn can track a slowly moving stimulus for a while, but its eyes tend to fall behind. The infant will then make a series of rapid eye movements in an attempt to catch up with the moving stimulus. Moving stripes appear to be easier for the newborn to track than is a small object moving against a stationary background (White, Castle, & Held, 1964).

Regulation   The neonate has the ability to regulate looking. It can turn away from a visual display and avoid looking at it as well as fixate on a visual display at will.

Maturation of Abilities

As the fovea and the brain begin to mature, tracking improves in the first few weeks. Coordination of eye movement also appears to improve with practice. As the baby does more tracking of moving stimuli, the two eyes tend to move together in a more coordinated manner. By two months, babies tend to look with both eyes at the same aspect of a visual display.

The muscles controlling the shape of the lens also mature between two and six months after birth, so that the lens of the six-month-old functions as well as that of the young adult. The baby's lens begins to be able to change so as to focus on more distant objects around two months, at which time the baby probably can see clearly objects that are about six to eight feet away. Close vision also improves; with the accommodation of the lens and improvements in convergence, infants of two to two and a half months can clearly see objects about five inches from the eyes and by three months can see those only three inches away (White, Castle, & Held, 1964; Aslin, 1975).

Being able to see close objects more clearly means that after about two months babies can easily begin to observe their own hands as they play with them before their eyes and can also see objects hung at the side of the crib for them to swipe at. Seeing objects farther away allows the baby to recognize familiar objects such as the bottle or familiar people such as parents, as they appear at a distance. With the gradual lessening of the tonic neck reflex after three months, the baby will also be able to see clearly toys hung overhead in the crib.

Perception of Color

BASIC QUESTIONS

Scientists have been interested in knowing if young infants perceive color or if their world appears in black and white, as it does to many animals. If color vision is not there at birth, when does it appear? This ability also has to do with the maturity of the fovea, since that is the area of greatest concentration of cones that govern color vision, and whether the baby has central or peripheral vision in early infancy. For peripheral vision would more likely lack color.

When infants do perceive color, scientists have also wondered whether they do so in a manner similar to or different from that of adults. For example, do young babies per-

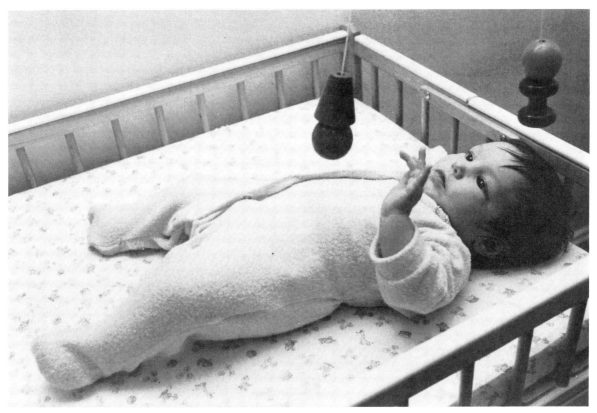

As the infant's visual abilities improve and the tonic neck reflex lessens, he or she can begin to clearly see objects suspended overhead. This infant is not only looking at the toy, but is also swiping at it with the hand to make it move.

ceive that a bluish green object is green and that a greenish blue object is blue, in the same way that adults do? Do colors that seem brighter than others to us, such as yellow, also appear brighter to the infant?

TESTING

In the past it had been difficult to test young infants for color vision, since it is easy to confound color with brightness. For example, showing infants a yellow area and a blue area and trying to assess preference may be telling nothing about the infant's perception of a color difference but only about the rela-

tive brightness of the two areas. That is, if the yellow appears brighter and the infant spends more time looking at it, this may be because the infant perceives a difference in colors and prefers yellow, or it may be that the infant is merely responding to the brighter display in the absence of color vision. Trying to control for brightness also has its drawbacks, since it can be done only using adult standards of brightness, which may differ from those of infants.

A recent solution to the problem has been to test for color perception while systematically varying brightness. That is, the brightness of the blue field is varied while that of the yellow is kept constant; then the yellow is varied while the blue is held constant. As the various preferences are compared, responses to brightness can be separated out from those for color. Then researchers can determine to which dimension the infant is responding.

COLORS SEEN

Using such methods, it has been found that infants as young as two months appear able to discriminate some colors but not others from an undifferentiated white (Teller, Peeples, & Sekel, 1978). Orange, red, pink, reddish purple, blue, and blue-green are perceived by the two-month-old as different from white, but white and yellow still appear the same. Thus, in trying to eliminate sexism from the nursery by using yellow garments and blankets for babies of either sex, rather than the traditional pink or blue, parents may unwittingly be cutting down on color contrasts that their young infants are able to see. For while the baby could distinguish either pink or blue from white, it sees the yellow as the same as white.

Eleven-to-twelve-week-olds can successfully discriminate red from green (Schaller, 1975). And by four months the infant seems to see all the colors that adults see (Fagan, 1974) and now can even distinguish yellowish green from green and yellow from white. Therefore, from this time on, parents can dress the baby in any color they wish and know that the baby perceives it as different from other colors.

CATEGORICAL PERCEPTION OF COLOR

By four months, infants seem to categorize colors, that is, to establish arbitrary boundaries between them, in the same way that adults do. For example, as color changes from blue to green, there is some point at which adults will no longer report the color as blue but will instead perceive it as green. Infants at four months and beyond, though they, of course, don't report this change verbally, seem to make the transitions around the same boundaries as adults (Bornstein, Kessen, & Weiskopf, 1976). Categorical color perception in infants is usually tested using habituation. The infant is habituated to a particular color, and then another that differs slightly is presented. If dishabituation occurs to the new color, the experimenter infers that the infant must have perceived the color as belonging in a different category, that is, as having crossed a categorical boundary. If there is no dishabituation, it is inferred that the infant perceives the new color as within the same category as the preceding one.

Perception of Contour

EARLY SENSITIVITY

Contour, the edge of an object against a more neutral background, seems to attract and hold the visual attention of the young infant. One of the "rules" Haith (1979, 1980) said operated for the young infant was to scan contour. This scanning seems to follow a plan; that is, the infant intentionally moves the eyes to cross the edges between a dark line and the bright background (Haith, 1980). The more contour presented, for example at the corners or apexes of a black triangle against a white background, the more the baby will scan the corners rather than the rest of the figure or the background (Salapatek & Kessen, 1973). Young infants tend to scan horizontally rather than vertically (Salapatek, 1968), partly because horizontal eye movements use fewer eye muscles than do vertical ones and are therefore easier for the young infant. In addition, horizontal movements are probably controlled by only one side of the brain, while vertical ones require coordination of both sides (Haith, 1980). Therefore, vertical movements require more maturation of the brain. Young infants tend to look more at the vertical edges than the horizontal edges of visual displays, since as they scan horizontally their eyes cross more contours in that way (Haith 1968; Kessen, Salapatek, & Haith 1972). In this instance the infant's scanning ability and the physical properties of the stimulus interact.

Infants also tend to look more at striped patterns consisting of narrow black stripes against a white background than at an undifferential gray area that is equally bright, that is, reflects as much light. Babies as young as 2 weeks can distinguish a pattern of stripes 1/8 in. wide from a gray array; by 12 weeks their visual acuity has improved to the point that they can distinguish stripes only 1/64 in. wide (Fantz 1965, 1966). Again, the important factor here seems to be contour, particularly in the first month. When looking at human faces or the pictures of faces, young babies therefore tend to look at the side edges of the faces against the background.

Implications of the infant's early sensitivity to contour should be pretty obvious to those tending it. Designs that have a lot of contour are most likely to be scanned. Therefore, any visual display having a great deal of contrast between black and white, such as a large newspaper headline, is likely to be visually scanned by the young infant if it is properly positioned and at the optimal distance from the baby.

CHANGES IN SCANNING

After the age of two months, babies begin to scan more of the total figure and concentrate less on the edges or corners (Salapatek, 1975). Infants, therefore, begin to scan internal features of faces such as the eyes. At the same time, the kinds of displays the infant prefers also change (as we shall discuss in more detail later). Both of these changes suggest that a developmental process depending upon maturation of the cortex of the brain is involved. This may be an indication that vision has come under control of the cortex, that the "rules" existing for neonate vision no longer operate or at least are not as powerful as before, and that instead the infant now begins to look for meaning in visual displays (Bronson, 1974; Salapatek 1975). Supportive evidence for this maturational explanation comes from the indication that babies born four weeks preterm demonstrated the same changes in what they were looking at but four weeks later than did term infants (Fantz, Fagan, & Miranda, 1975). Yet they would have had the equivalent experience of looking as did term babies at equal times after birth, not four weeks later. Thus a maturational factor, and not just experience, must account for this difference.

Beyond two months, infants are attracted to visual displays by such attributes as complexity, discrepancy, and novelty, and perhaps an inborn sensitivity to certain visual displays such as human faces. We shall consider these here.

Perception of Complexity

Complexity of the total pattern, rather than merely the amount of contour in it, becomes important at this two-month transition stage. Complexity relates to meaning of a pattern. That is, a complex pattern is usually not just a series of lines but consists of some kind of meaningful configuration: a checkerboard, a bullseye, a picture of a person or object. Because of this increase of meaning with increased complexity, more complex patterns that have less contour are looked at more than less complex ones showing greater amounts of contour. For example, two-month olds prefer a bullseye to stripes by about a 2 to 1 margin (Fantz, Fagan & Miranda, 1975).

Contour and complexity, however, often go hand in hand. That is, a more complex pattern usually also has more contour than a simpler one. Numerosity, or the number of units in a figure, also is related to both contour and complexity. For example, a 64-square checkerboard design has more numbers of units, and also more complexity and more contour, than does a 16-square checkerboard. These various aspects of a design are therefore difficult or impossible to separate from each other and to present experimentally to an infant one at a time. As a result it becomes difficult to ascribe an infant's design preference to just one of these factors.

An interesting study seems to have overcome this problem. D. J. Greenberg and S. Z. Blue (1975) designed an experiment using small versus large circles as the stimulus figures. The small circles have as many elements as, and equal complexity to, the large, but because they are smaller, they have less total contour. Separating out these factors in this ingenious manner, Greenberg and Blue found that both an increase in the total number of elements and an increase in contour in a visual display were necessary to induce babies to shift their attention to the new display. That is, there had to be more circles, and the circles had to be larger. Contour alone did not appear to be the deciding factor in attracting attention.

Two-month-olds, however, prefer moderate complexity over extreme complexity of visual displays. If they are shown a checkerboard with a great many squares and one with a moderate number, they prefer to look at the latter. It is only as babies become older than two months that they prefer increasingly complex patterns. This preference is probably also indicative of further cortical maturation. Therefore, parents and other caregivers of babies around the age of two months should present them with toys and visual displays that have meaning and that have some but not too much complexity.

Perception of Discrepancy

Infants seem to have built a mental idea of what something is supposed to look like quite early. When something looks discrepant from this idea and yet is still similar enough to relate to it, infants will gaze at it the longest, more so than they will at something they have seen before (Kagan, 1970). If, however, the display is so discrepant that the infant cannot relate it to the original display, the infant will not look at it for long. Therefore, from five months on, displays showing moderate discrepancy are attended to more than those that are familiar or those that are highly discrepant. The baby evidently perceives the familiar display as one that has been seen before and the highly discrepant one as so different that it cannot be figured out. But the moderately discrepant one is just new enough to be different and just different enough to be challenging and yet decipherable. Thus attention to discrepancy can be plotted on a graph to resemble an inverted U. Infants will pay the most attention to moderately discrepant stimuli and the least to those either the same as previous ones or too discrepant to recognize (McCall, Kennedy, & Appelbaum, 1977).

Discrepancy may entail a change in the shape or size of an object, the addition, deletion, or rearrangement of a particular feature or features, a change of color, or one of spatial orientation. Thus a face with three eyes or with only one eye, a dog twice as big as an automobile, an extremely elongated face, a person with bright blue skin, or an upside-down person might appear as discrepant stimuli to an infant.

Babies as young as four to five months react to discrepancy of orientation, looking longer at a display whose elements are rotated in space, such as the upside-down person. They also recognize discrepancy in the arrangement of elements of the display, such as a face with scrambled features (Cornell, 1975).

Parents and other caregivers have empirically discovered the importance of moderate discrepancy in capturing and holding an infant's attention. For example, they make faces at the baby, show exaggerated facial expressions of joy or horror, pitch their voices high, and exaggerate pronunciation in order to assure the baby's attention (Stern, 1975).

Salience, or meaning, of visual displays is also related to discrepancy. Thus babies up to about two to three months look longer at familiar than unfamiliar displays. But by three to four months, they look at unfamiliar displays and those able to be interpreted, that is, that have meaning to the baby, longer than familiar ones or those consisting of random, nonmeaningful elements, even if the latter have more contour or complexity. A face is looked at longer than a display of equal size with more elements and greater contour that consists of a mere random assortment of meaningless elements.

Perception of Faces

Much research has been done with infants gazing at human faces and representations of faces such as photographs, three-dimensional models, and drawings. Researchers ask whether infants are inherently drawn to look at human faces or do so only because faces

happen to be readily available sources of contour. Researchers also ask what aspects of faces are most salient, or meaningful, to infants at particular ages and whether these aspects change over time. Some questions also deal with whether infants can perceive the differences among schematic drawings, pictures, three-dimensional models of faces, and real faces and which they prefer. Finally, researchers want to know whether realistic faces (those in which elements are in their proper places) are preferred over faces having scrambled features or too many or too few of particular features and whether this preference might also change with age.

REASONS

Researchers that lean toward an ethological and nativist position such as J. Bowlby (1958) and C. Goren (Goren, Sarty, & Wu, 1975) believe that babies prefer to look at faces because they have an inborn sensitivity to faces that facilitates bonding to the mother or other caregivers and thus is important for infant survival. That is, the baby's predisposition to look at faces leads parents and other caregivers to develop positive, nurturant feelings toward the baby and to want to care for and protect it. Thus a study by Goren found that neonates only a few minutes old already preferred facelike features over other visual displays, long before they could have learned anything about the importance of human faces.

Others such as Haith argue that very young infants look at faces not because of any intrinsic meaning in them but because faces happen to have a lot of contour (Haith, 1978). Particularly the contrast between the forehead and hairline and between the chin and the top of the dress or shirt provides contour, as does the side of the face against the wall or other background. Young infants do not fixate on the eyes; if the gazes of adult and infant meet, it is due to adult adjustments, not to the infant (Hittelman & Dickes, 1979). Thus early infant "interest" in faces does not seem to Haith to be due to any attempt at interaction but only to the presence of contour.

BEGINNING OF PREFERENCE

Even if very young infants look at faces not because of any inborn preference but only because of perceptual features of the face, they do begin quite early to build a preference for faces over other visual displays.

Although the Goren study found interest in faces in newborns, L. Hainline (1978) discovered that four-week-olds do not prefer a picture of a face to a nonface object of equal size, brightness, contour, and symmetry. Perhaps the Goren study did not control adequately for these factors. But around seven weeks, infants not only show some preference for the picture of the face but now begin to look especially at the eyes. This change may be because they have associated eyes in real faces with movement, while the eyes in the displays used in testing do not move. That is, discrepancy may be the major factor once again. But perhaps they had learned that eyes belong in faces and therefore are checking for their presence. Ten-week-olds react much like seven-week-olds (Hainline, 1978) but will still look at an equally complex nonface pattern almost as long as at a face (Haaf & Brown, 1976). At some time not long after 10 weeks, this changes to a strong preference for the human face. Babies 12 weeks old look longer at a picture of a real face than at a schematic one, a scrambled schematic one, or a picture of a real face having but one central eye (Lewis, 1969). At 15 weeks, babies show a clear preference for faces over other displays (Haaf & Brown, 1976). Thus, some

beginning perception of faceness seems to begin to override complexity as the condition for looking in the period from about two to four months. This fits in well with the idea that vision comes under cortical control at around two months, and that meaningfulness then becomes of major importance.

PORTIONS OF THE FACE NOTICED

But even though in the period of from seven weeks to four months babies begin to prefer to look at pictures of faces over other displays, the face does not at first have to have all components correctly placed. Infants under three months show little preference among faces missing eyes or having one eye, two, or many eyes (Gibson, 1969). Only by three to four months do they begin to prefer faces with two eyes. Although a four-month-old baby will look almost as long at pictures of one-eyed faces, it will laugh more at the two-eyed version (Lewis, 1969).

Pictures of real faces also are preferred over schematic drawings of faces, and those with features in the correct place over those with scrambled features (Fantz, 1961a; Fantz & Nevis, 1967b).

AGE-RELATED PROGRESSION IN ATTENTION

Older babies scan faces for briefer periods than do younger ones, but they try to maintain eye contact better, and they also smile and vocalize more to faces (Lewis, 1969). Haith and I. Mann (1971) see these developments as a maturational progression. Babies younger than seven weeks attend mainly to the outline of the face since the important aspect still is contour. After seven weeks, babies begin to look more at the face itself, particularly at the eyes, showing their increasing attention to complexity. From the age of three to four months onward, they prefer a face that has features in the appropriate places over one with features in the wrong places, as they begin to see the face as a compound rather than a set of components. But the scrambled features do not appear to "bother" four-month-old infants. By six months the scrambled features seem to make infants uneasy. Haith and Mann (1971) suggest that babies do not perceive facial features such as eyes and mouth as separate entities that together make up the face until after they show interest in faces as such; therefore scrambling does not bother them until they recognize features in and of themselves and can tell that they are out of place. J. F. Fagan (1977) makes a similar point, that younger babies see features as components of the face but only by five months see them as compounds, that is, that the components have to be put together in a particular way. There is some question as to how early the various elements of a face are put together into a compound mental picture by infants rather than being perceived as a series of components. This change may not happen till about five months (Caron, Caron, Caldwell, & Weiss, 1973; Fagan 1977) as infants begin to attend to other features such as the mouth and nose. Thus in the four-to-six-month period babies begin to be drawn to discrepancy in faces by showing greater attention to them than to nondiscrepant ones. And by six months inappropriately placed features disquiet the baby.

Perception of Depth

DEFINITION

An area of considerable interest to researchers has been how early and by what means the baby can perceive depth. Depth percep-

tion entails such things as seeing a three-dimensional object as differing from a flat, two-dimensional picture of the object or from a drawing. It also has to do with perceiving that objects moving toward the infant may either hit or miss the infant. Also the infant has to be aware that objects in the visual field are located at varying distances from the infant. And finally, depth perception entails understanding the possibility of falling from a high place by being aware of the drop-off.

HOW PERCEIVED

Depth can be perceived because of a number of different factors that operate separately or in unison. Some are **monocular** cues, that is they apply whether the individual is looking with one eye or both. Monocular, or one-eyed, visual cues include texture and shading. These two characteristics are present in true three-dimensional objects and in good photographs and well-drawn pictures of these objects but not in schematic drawings. **Pattern density** also provides a cue, regardless of whether one eye or both are used. Pattern density refers to the fact that as one looks at a uniformly patterned surface such as one with dots or checks, individual units appear both smaller and closer to one another as they become more distant from the observer. Another cue that operates even with monocular vision is **motion parallax**. This is the phenomenon that as one moves the head, a stationary object appears to move in the opposite direction from one's head in front of a stationary background. That is, if, for example, I am looking at a house that is in front of a mountain, when I move my head to the left, the house appears to move to the right. The closer to the observer the object is located, the greater this apparent motion becomes. Thus one can ascertain the distance of ob-

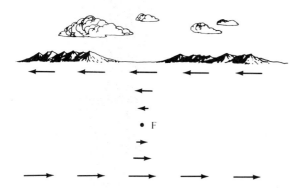

Motion parallax. When an observer fixates the gaze on point F, the fixation point, and moves the head to the left, objects closer than point F appear to move in the opposite direction, to the right. Those farther away, than point F appear to move in the same direction as the observer's head, to the left.

jects by moving the head and watching the apparent motion of the observed objects.

Binocular cues, those that apply only when both eyes are used, are based upon **binocular parallax.** Binocular parallax has two aspects, convergence and binocular disparity. **Convergence** refers to the angle between the two eyes as they focus upon a visual object. When an object is very close, the angle between the eyes is great; as an object moves further away, the angle becomes smaller. Internal mechanisms in the brain enable the individual to calculate the distance of an object from the angle of convergence, based on nerve feedback from the muscles controlling convergence of the two eyes. **Binocular disparity,** or **stereopsis,** refers to the fact that because of the distance between the two eyes, each eye sees a particular object from a slightly different angle. The disparity between the two views is greatest for nearby objects and least for those farthest away. The brain puts together these two views in such a way that the individual sees only one object but is aware of depth in the visual field.

RESEARCH STUDIES

Research into the depth perception of infants tries to answer whether depth perception is inborn or develops later. If it does develop later, is this development a function of maturation or of practice, or is it due to an interaction between both these mechanisms? When does depth perception begin to include fear of falling off heights? What does this awareness tell about the relative importance of maturation and practice? Studies of depth perception in infants have used techniques such as preference, habituation, conditioning, the infant's reaction to looming objects, attempts at grasping, and willingness or unwillingness to cross over an apparent drop-off to determine whether and when infants perceive depth and also when they begin to fear it.

Preference Studies   Some of the earliest studies on depth perception in infants were the preference studies done by Robert Fantz in the 1960s. These were experiments to determine whether infants perceived photographs of three-dimensional figures such as faces to be different from schematic drawings of these faces, according to how long they looked at each display (Fantz, 1966; Fantz & Nevis, 1967a). Presumably, if they looked longer at the photographs than at the drawings, they were perceiving the apparent depth of the former. Fantz also was interested in knowing whether infants relied more on binocular disparity or on texture and shading as cues for three-dimensionality and whether age was a factor in both these processes. In order to control for binocular disparity, half of the infants viewed displays with one eye covered, and the other half of the infants looked with both eyes. Fantz found that infants appeared to use texture and shading cues rather than binocular cues, since there was little difference in looking preference between those using one eye and those using both. Age was a factor in that infants under two months preferred the drawing while those over two months preferred the photograph. Of course this preference does not answer the question of whether the younger infants did not perceive depth, since their preference for the drawing could have been based on the fact that it had more contour. And it should be remembered that contour is especially salient to younger infants. It is fairly certain, however, that by two months, if not earlier, there was perception of depth, based primarily on texture and shading cues.

Conditioning Studies Because of the limitations of preference studies, other paradigms to study depth perception in infants have also been used. Bower (1965a) used a conditioning study to determine whether infants have the notion of size constancy, that is, that an object that moves farther away will appear smaller to the observer but in fact has not shrunk in size. The adult observer can account for the apparent size differential by perceiving that the object is now farther away but is still the same size as before. Can infants do the same and, if so, how early in life? Bower also wanted to discover whether judgment concerning size constancy is inborn or acquired. In addition, he wished to determine whether retinal image size (the size of the image cast on the retina), binocular disparity, or motion parallax was the most important variable in depth perception of infants.

In his ingenious experiment, 70-to-85-day-old infants were first conditioned to turn their heads whenever a 12-in cube appeared at a three-foot (ft) distance. They were rein-

forced for appropriate head turning by the experimenter, who reared up and went "peek-a-boo" to the infant. After the babies reliably turned their heads to the appearance of the appropriate cube, a 36-in cube that appeared at either a three- or a nine-ft distance as well as the original cube at a nine-ft distance were alternately presented, and infant head turning was recorded. Notice that the 36-in cube that was nine ft away would cast a retinal image the same size as that of the training cube, while at three ft its image would be larger. The training cube at the new distance would cast the smallest image of all.

If the infants reacted to retinal image size, they should have turned their heads

Conditioned Stimulus	Test Stimuli		
	A	B	C
True Size			
Distance from Infant	3 feet	9 feet	3 feet	9 feet
Retinal Size			

Bower's experiment to determine infant perception of depth and size constancy. If infants reacted to retinal size, they would look at Stimulus C, which has the same retinal size as the conditional or training stimulus. Instead, Bower found that they looked most often at Stimulus A, which was the same size as the conditional stimulus but was farther away and therefore cast a smaller retinal image. Bower concluded that young infants already had the ability to perceive depth and therefore could compensate for the decreased retinal size of objects that were further away.

most for the 36-in cube at nine ft, since its retinal image was the same as that of the original training cube. Instead, Bower found that infants reacted more to the training cube at the new distance than to the larger cube at either three or nine ft. Indeed, they turned least to the larger cube at nine ft, the one that cast the same size of retinal image that the training cube at the original distance had.

Therefore, Bower concluded that the infants were reacting not to retinal image size but to the real size of the cube. He thought that this indicated that two-and-a-half-month-old infants could already account for apparent disparity in object size by making allowance for distance, therefore showing that they must perceive depth and also have some notion of size constancy. Bower later replicated the experiment, this time using younger infants who were just 40 to 60 days old. He also used a **virtual object,** an apparently three-dimensional image projected by a shadow caster on a screen, with half of his infant subjects and a real object with the other half. This was done to control for motion parallax, since, when the head is moved, virtual objects appear to move in the same direction as the head and thus in a direction opposite to that of real objects. These younger infants behaved similarly to the older ones in that they also turned their heads the most to the cube with which they had been trained, even though it was now farther away. However, because the infants who saw the real object did this task better than those who saw the virtual object formed by the shadow caster, Bower concluded that motion parallax cues were also of help to infants in determining distance.

Unfortunately for Bower, other experimenters have found that while infants do indeed account for distance, this factor is more important than actual size of the object in determining attention. McKenzie and Day (1972) found that if objects were more than one meter (m), or about three ft, away, infants tended to disregard them, while they attended to those closer than one m, irrespective of object size. This finding has left the question of the infant's understanding of size constancy still unanswered.

FURTHER RESEARCH

A more recent experiment done by R. Fox (Fox, Aslin, Shea, & Dumais, 1980) has tried to settle the problem of how soon infants perceive depth in the visual field. Infants of varying ages were shown a projected image of a randomly moving series of dots that produced a slowly moving rectangle visible only if the observer, who wore special goggles, already had depth perception. Fox and his associates reasoned that if an infant wearing the goggles tracked the motion of the rectangle, it must see this object and therefore already have depth perception. Infants younger than three months did not track this stimulus at a rate better than chance, but the performance of 3½-month olds was somewhat better than chance. The 4½-month olds tracked the moving rectangle much more frequently than either of the younger groups. These researchers concluded that depth perception, at least of moving objects, has its beginnings around 3½ months of age and improves as the infant becomes older.

VISUAL LOOMING

Some research into depth perception has used visual looming, the increase of apparent size that occurs as an object moves toward the infant, and the infant's reactions to this phenomenon to determine whether the infant perceives the approach of the object and hence perceives varying degrees of depth.

This kind of study also has to do with meaning, inasmuch as the infant has to interpret that the approaching object will hit it if the object continues on the same trajectory. Early studies had found that infants as young as two months often blink their eyes at the approach of a real object (White, 1971) but not that of a projected image that appears to be approaching (White, 1963). By four months this blink becomes a consistent response. Burton L. White hypothesized that the onrush of air accompanying the approach of the real object gave a cue through pressure changes perceptible on the skin that helped the infant see it coming. Bower (Bower, Broughton, & Moore, 1970a; Dunkeld & Bower, 1976) has maintained that infants as young as two weeks avoid a looming object, widening the eyes, wrenching the head aside, and finally batting at the approaching object with the hands. They appear to avoid both real and virtual objects, though real ones more frequently and intensely. Experience does not seem to play a part as infants avoid even objects with which they have had no previous experience such as the image of a rotating disk (Dunkeld & Bower, 1976). Bower, therefore, believes that, since avoidance exists in very young babies and can be seen in reaction to the approach of objects they have never before encountered, depth perception as well as the avoidance responses must be inborn mechanisms.

As with so many of Bower's studies, this one too has created controversy. For example, A. Yonas questions Bower's interpretation of the infant's hand movements and maintains that in the younger infant the so-called defensive reaction is nothing more than the result of the baby's visual tracking of the upper contour of the moving object. As the object approaches close to the infant, head control is lost, and as the head jerks backward the arms rise up reflexively (Yonas

& Pick, 1975; Yonas, Bechtold, Frankel, Gordon, McRoberts, Norcia, & Sternfels, 1977). According to Yonas, one-to-two-month-olds react in this way both to objects on a collision course and to those on a noncollision course. Since they don't discriminate between them, Yonas concludes that their behavior must be merely reflexive. In studying older infants, Yonas found that four-to-six-month olds begin to try to avoid an imminent collision by making evasive movements. They also blink the eyes to objects appearing on a collision course but not to others. Eight-to-nine-month-olds react even more strongly.

A more recent study by Yonas and his associates with 14- and 20-week-old infants showed that both groups showed visual convergence upon an approaching object but that only the 20-week olds reached toward the object and made defensive reactions to it (Yonas, Oberg, & Norcia, 1978). Thus, while some depth information appears obtainable through convergence to infants as young as 14 weeks, binocular parallax appears to operate only from about 20 weeks on to produce valid cues about depth. Therefore, Yonas believes that true avoidance behavior cannot appear before the establishment of binocular parallax, or at about four and a half to five months. The issue of the age of onset of avoidance behaviors, therefore, is as yet unresolved, and more studies of so-called defensive behavior at the approach of a moving object must be made.

THE VISUAL CLIFF

Parents as well as researchers have observed that young babies do not appear to fear falling from heights, but older babies by the time they crawl and walk certainly do. Since some perception of depth seems present before babies begin active locomotion, researchers have attempted to link the devel-

An infant on the visual cliff. Although the plexiglass is plainly visible and is being touched by this child, he refuses to leave the centerboard and crawl out over the apparent dropoff.

opment of fear to depth perception and to practice in locomotion.

The instrument such researchers usually choose is the visual cliff, an apparatus designed by Eleanor Gibson and Richard Walk (Gibson & Walk, 1960). It consists of a clear sheet of plexiglass on legs. One portion has a checkerboard pattern placed directly under the plexiglass, while the other portion has the pattern several feet below it. Since the size of the checkerboard pattern is the same throughout, that on the deep side appears smaller since it is farther away. It, therefore, gives the appearance of a drop-off or cliff. A centerboard is put across the middle at the point of the apparent drop-off. The infant is placed on the centerboard facing the apparently deep side and the mother or experimenter tries to entice the child to crawl toward her or him across this apparent chasm.

Animal experiments have shown that young animals show fear at going over to the apparent deep part at the time that locomotion begins and their eyes become functional. Thus chickens and goats on the first day of life, and kittens and puppies shortly after their eyes open, refuse to cross the barrier. These experiments tend to indicate that avoidance of heights is an inborn or a maturational phenomenon. Human infants, by the time they can crawl, at about six months or older, avoid crossing to the deep side about 90 percent of the time (Walk, 1966). It is difficult to determine, however, whether this behavior is inborn or learned inasmuch as in humans the ability to locomote comes relatively late, after a lot of learning could already have taken place. Thus, by the time human infants can be tested by letting them crawl on the visual cliff, they may have learned to fear heights from other experiences, such as falling or almost falling from a bed or out of a chair.

Therefore, heart rate when exposed to the deep side of the cliff has been used as an indicator in infants too young to locomote (Campos, Langer, & Krowitz, 1970). It has been shown that infants beyond the neonatal period show a sustained deceleration of heart rate while orienting to a stimulus and a brief deceleration followed by acceleration of heart rate as a result of fear. Thus, monitoring the changes in heart rate can indicate whether the infant is orienting or is afraid. In this study, babies aged 55 and 106 days respectively were placed on the center of the visual cliff apparatus, facing either toward the shallow or the deep end. Both groups showed some deceleration of heart rate when placed facing the shallow side and even more deceleration when placed toward the deep side. The experimenters concluded that babies were visually orienting when placed on either side, since heart rate decelerated, and that they perceived the difference in height between the two sides, since heart rate decreased even more when they were looking over the deep side. The lack of heart rate acceleration appeared to demonstrate, however, that these infants were not yet afraid of falling over the apparent cliff. Therefore, Joseph Campos concluded that fear of heights must be either maturational or learned but is not inborn in the human infant. Later experiments by the same group of researchers have demonstrated that five-month olds show the same pattern of deceleration on the deep side as did the younger infants, while nine-month olds react with heart rate acceleration and thus presumably are indicating fear (Schwartz, Campos, & Baisel, 1973). That this response depends upon practice in locomotion rather than on maturation seems to be shown by a further study, in which infants who had more experience crawling showed greater fear on the visual cliff than those of the same age with less crawling experience (Campos, Hiatt, Ramsey, Henderson, & Svejda, 1978). In addition, those infants who received earlier practice developed fear earlier than those not exposed to such early practice (Campos, Svejda, Bertenthal, Benson, & Schmid, 1981). Thus, it now appears that depth perception develops earlier than fear of depths and that fear of falling is a learned response that develops as a result of both the development of depth perception and especially experience with locomotion.

Visually Directed Reaching

RELATION TO DEPTH PERCEPTION

Visually directed reaching is closely related to depth perception, since presumably infants need some knowledge of depth to reach accurately toward an object before them. In addition to depth perception, reaching also involves a knowledge of the location of the

hand or hands, the length of the arm or arms, whether the object in question can be grasped or not, as well as the motor abilities involved in how to move the hand, when to stop, when to open it, and when to close it around the object. Thus studies of visually directed reaching can also provide information about the infant's developing notion of the reality of visible objects. Unfortunately, the results of these studies are not as yet clear.

STUDIES WITH YOUNG INFANTS

Some studies purport to show visually directed reaching already existing in rudimentary form in neonates (von Hofsten, 1982). When an object appears before a neonate, more hand movements seem to be directed in the general direction of the object than in other directions. Bower claims to have found visually directed reaching in infants as young as seven days (Bower, Broughton, & Moore, 1970b). But others interpret hand activities in these younger babies as being merely crude forms of swiping and maintain that real attempts at reaching do not begin until the age of two months (White, Castle & Held, 1964). Bower also maintained that even the seven-day-olds reacted with surprise when their hands closed around a virtual object and thus came up with empty air, indicating that even this early in life they had a notion of the graspability of objects. An attempted replication of Bower's study showed reaching results in only 5 percent of the cases, however, and found that when infants did seem to reach they did so equally for a real object suspended in front of them and for a picture of the object pasted on a distant background (Dodwell, Muir, & di Franco, 1976). Therefore, it is still a question if young babies do reach for what they perceive to be real objects at graspable distances, if instead they are merely moving their arms, and if they have some notion of what distinguishes a real, graspable object from one that is an illusion or a picture.

STUDIES BY YONAS

In trying to determine when binocular information begins to be used in visually directed reaching, F. R. Gordon and A. Yonas (1976) showed virtual objects at various distances to babies between 20 and 26 weeks of age. The babies reached more frequently for objects that appeared within graspable distance, but their reaching skills were not very accurate. Furthermore, when reaching for a virtual object, babies showed none of the surprise that Bower, Broughton, and Moore had reported when the infants did not come up with something of substance. At the same age, 20 weeks, babies also reach toward a looming object as it approaches (Yonas, Oberg, & Norcia, 1978).

Thus between five and six months, infants use binocular cues and reach more for objects at graspable distances than for those too far away. The motor act of reaching is not yet very coordinated, however, and infants miss more often than not in attempting to grasp an object.

Gordon and Yonas attribute the infant's lack of surprise when grasping a virtual object and finding nothing of substance to this inaccuracy of reaching. In other words, the baby does not expect to be able to grasp the object very often; therefore, when the hands close on nothing, the baby is not upset. It merely thinks it did not reach accurately enough.

RECENT WORK

A more recent study (Rader & Stern, 1982) appears to offer some support for both the positions of Bower and Yonas but still offers no final solution to the debate. Infants 8 to 16 days old made movements that could be interpreted as reaching significantly more toward a ball than toward a blank background. But they also reached for a picture of the ball, although less frequently than for the real object. Thus Rader and Stern concluded that neonates do make arm movements that can be judged to be attempts at reaching and make them more frequently to real objects, less often to two-dimensional representations, and still less often to a blank field. Neonates seem to have some depth perception that directs them to reach more frequently for real objects and pictures of objects that show some cues relating to depth than for a blank background. Since there was some reaching even for the blank background, however, either this perception is not yet very good, or infants do indeed make some random arm movements that some of the time can be wrongly interpreted as attempts at reaching. Thus, for very young infants, both the frequency of reaching and the use of binocular cues for depth as an aid to reaching are still matters of debate.

IMPLICATIONS

Regardless of whether visually directed reaching is an inborn propensity or whether it is a developmental phenomenon, practice appears to be important in the further development of this skill. Therefore, parents and caregivers should make sure that from very early in infancy, the child is exposed to interesting and yet safe objects within graspable distance with which to play. These include the crib gyms suspended overhead from rail to rail, which afford the baby various moving plastic parts that can be swiped at, grasped, or moved. As the child begins to sit up, other toys attached by suction devices to the tray of a high chair or other baby chair are useful. Rattles, blocks, and other objects that can not only be grasped but also brought to the mouth are good. Of course adults must make sure that all such objects are too large to be swallowed or aspirated, have no pieces that can be removed by the baby, and are painted with nontoxic paints.

AUDITORY PERCEPTION

History

Early scientists studying infancy, such as W. Preyer, the author of a famous baby biography, thought that newborn infants could not hear (Preyer, 1882). Even in the 1920s, textbooks were still proclaiming that the neonate was deaf (Stern, 1924). Mothers, on the contrary, often reported that their babies reacted with kicking and other movement to loud and sudden sounds even before birth. Experiments showed that the experts had been wrong and the mothers were right: even fetuses react to some sounds. Peiper (1925) devised a study in which an automobile horn was sounded in front of the mother's abdomen. More than one-third of the fetuses involved in this study reacted at some time, though not always, to the sound, usually by "drawing their bodies together," as the mothers described it. Later L. Sontag (1966) sounded a doorbell clapper on a wooden block placed on the mother's abdomen and also found increased activity such as kicking and body movements by fetuses in response to the sound. Thus babies appear able to hear or at least to respond to sounds several months before birth.

Basic Auditory Abilities of the Newborn

At birth, the myelination of the auditory nerve is already complete (Hecox, 1975). Therefore, sound impulses are probably transmitted to the brain in a more advanced fashion than are those from other sense organs. The portion of the brain that processes hearing is still quite immature, however, and the interpretation of sound is probably quite primitive at first. Furthermore, there is some question whether the two sides of the brain are already working together in the newborn or whether each side is processing sound impulses independently (Conel, 1952). If they do so independently, then the infant probably senses two distinct sounds.

Acuity of hearing also is poor at first. The infant can hear only moderately loud sounds. In part this limitation results from the accumulation of mucus and fluid in the ear canals from the infant's immersion in the amniotic fluid. Even after the canals begin to clear, they may remain swollen for a while. Furthermore, the infant's ear canals are not yet fully developed at birth, and the small bones of the inner ears that transmit sound waves still have connective tissue attached and are not yet able to move freely. For all these reasons, young infants do not hear well. As the canals clear and the structures develop and mature, hearing acuity improves.

In spite of the immaturity of the brain and the lack of acuity, the neonate reacts to sound. A loud sound can trigger a Moro reflex; later on, startling at a sudden unexpected sound will appear as well. Newborns also have some ability to localize the source of sound. Michael Wertheimer (1961) was able to test a baby only 10 minutes old, using a gadget that made clicking sounds. The baby turned its eyes and head toward the direction from which the sound came at a rate somewhat better than chance, leading Wertheimer to conclude that the baby heard the sound.

Heart-rate studies have indicated that the newborn infant can hear and can discriminate between loudness of sounds to some degree. Orienting to sounds tends to make the heart rate of neonates accelerate, and it accelerates more for a very loud sound than for a moderately loud sound.

Studies of auditory perception in infants have been concerned mainly with localization of sound sources and with the infant's ability to distinguish speech from nonspeech sounds and the various sounds in human speech from one another.

Localization of Sound Source

As already indicated, Wertheimer found that newborns turned their eyes in the direction from which a sound came. He concluded not only that the neonate heard but also that it was able to determine where the sound came from. Of course, if the baby was hearing two distinct sounds with the two halves of the brain, then it turned in the right direction only because that was the source of the louder sound; if the baby heard one sound but coming to both ears, then Wertheimer's conclusion about sound localization would be correct. Although some later studies have not shown similar responses in the neonate, even more recent ones have shown that Wertheimer probably inferred correctly that the neonate can localize sound. For example, J. Alegria and E. Noirot (1978) found that infants just one to seven days old turned in the direction from which a male voice came out of a loudspeaker more than they turned in the same direction without such a voice. D. Muir, J. Field, and M. Sinclair (1979) reported that infants as young as four days turned in the direction of the sound of a rattle with 81 percent accuracy.

Adults localize sound by comparing the relative amplitude or loudness of the sound as it comes to the two ears and by mentally noting the disparity between the times at which impulses reach the two ears. That is,

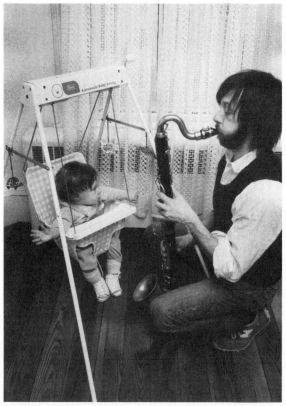

Even very young infants are responsive to sound and will turn in the direction from which a sound comes. This somewhat older infant appears entranced by father's musical performance.

sounds appear louder to the ear closer to the sound source. And, since the ears are separated from each other by the distance of the diameter of the head, sounds reach the ear closer to their source a fraction of a second before they reach the other ear. If a sound comes from a source equidistant from both ears (such as squarely in front of, behind, or above the listener) it will reach both ears at the exact same time.

Since young infants are capable of localizing sounds to some degree, their brains may process this information in ways similar to those of adults. Because the infant head is much smaller than that of the adult, however, the differences in both loudness and arrival time of a sound are smaller than for the adult, and the task of localization, therefore, somewhat more difficult. Furthermore, as the head grows, the infant must account for the increased distance between the ears by adjusting the mental processes involved in localization. Bower (1974) suggests that rather than constantly recalibrate with the progress of head growth, the young infant localizes sound by turning the head until the sound hits both ears simultaneously; only as the head begins to approach adult size is more precise localization learned.

Perception of Differing Sounds

REACTIONS TO VARIOUS SOUNDS

Different kinds of sounds appear to alert, soothe, or distress babies. Sounds in the middle range of frequency, which include human speech, tend to alert babies and draw their attention. Low-frequency sounds serve to soothe them, and those of high frequency cause them to respond with distress. Complex sounds, such as those produced by musical instruments or human speech, attract more attention than do pure tones. Infants are also soothed by rhythmic sounds such as music or the ticking of a clock. They do not appear to like sounds that are just noise (Butterfield & Siperstein, 1972). Very loud sounds produce evidence of distress such as startling, flailing with the arms or legs, and sometimes crying. If a sound has a very short duration, infants may not react to it at all, indicating that perhaps their perceptual equipment cannot yet process such a brief sound.

RESPONSE TO THE HUMAN VOICE

Babies appear especially responsive to the sound of the human voice (Eisenberg, 1965). Indeed, adult singing can be used to reinforce particular infant behaviors, while nonspeech sounds that are acoustically as complex cannot be so used (Butterfield & Siperstein, 1972). From very early in infancy, babies appear to associate the sound of the voice with human beings (Eisenberg, 1965). For example, in an experiment by Alegria and Noirot (1978) very young infants heard a human voice coming from either side. When they turned in the direction of the voice, they saw either a plain white cloth or else the person producing the sounds. These infants, who were less than a week old, reacted with crying and other signs of distress if they saw only the cloth that appeared to produce the voice sounds. They evidently already expected to see a person when they heard the human voice. Early in infancy, babies appear to recognize the sound of their own name if spoken by the mother (André-Thomas & Autgerden, 1961), to distinguish the mother's voice from those of others (Mills & Mellhuisch, 1974; Bower, 1974), and to prefer hearing it over the voices of other people (de Caspar & Fifer, 1980).

If the mother's voice appears to come from the mouth of a stranger or vice versa, three-month-olds appear agitated and upset (Bower, 1974). They evidently have associated the sound of a specific voice with a particular physical appearance. At this age, babies also appear to listen longer to speech sounds than to other sounds. Sucking dishabituates to shifts in speech, such as slight changes in pronunciation as a result of regional accents, but not to shifts of equal magnitude in pure tones produced by various mechanical devices (Trehub, 1973). Four-month-olds will react more to speech in their own language than to that in other languages (Bower, 1974). All this of course helps the infant not only to interpret the speech of others but to learn the skills needed to develop her or his own speech. The development of speech will be dealt with in detail in chapter 10.

PERCEPTION OF SPEECH

Methodology of Study   Studies of the perception of speech generally use a habituation paradigm involving nonnutritive sucking. The infant is allowed to suck on a pacifier, and the sucking activates a mechanism that produces a sound. As the sound continues to be produced, the infant eventually habituates and stops sucking. If a sound that appears new or different to the infant is introduced, the infant dishabituates and resumes or increases sucking in order to keep hearing the new sound. Study of the rate of change of sucking, therefore, can indicate whether infants perceive two sounds as being the same or different. If the infant neither resumes sucking nor increases the rate of sucking, one can assume that it does not perceive the new sound as different from the old one. But if sucking either resumes or increases, then one can assume that the infant perceived the new sound as different.

Discrimination among Similar Sounds
Such studies have shown that within the first 48 hours, neonates already can discriminate between some sounds (Butterfield & Cairns, 1974) and that one-month-old infants are beginning to be able to distinguish between two quite similar voiced and unvoiced consonants such as "puh" and "buh" (Eimas, Siqueland, Juscyk, & Vigorito, 1971). Similarly, two-month-olds distinguished between "da" and "ta" (Eimas, 1975b). Four-month-

olds did even better than the one-month-olds on the "puh"—"buh" distinction.

Categorical Perception   In both these instances, infants not only discriminated sounds but seemed to perceive the sounds categorically, that is by arbitrarily setting a boundary between two close sounds and assigning them to the two different categories. This ability is similar to the categorical perception of color found by Bornstein that we discussed earlier. As noted, there was a point in looking at stimuli changing from blue to green at which the infant no longer perceived the stimulus as greenish blue but perceived it instead as green. Auditory categorical perception works in much the same way: sounds that are quite similar to each other but have been labeled as different in speech are perceived as two different sounds, using an arbitrary boundary that is the same for people speaking one language but may differ from that used by those speaking another. For example, English-speakers distinguish categorically between the sounds of l and r; Chinese and Japanese do not. It is for this reason that when these latter speakers produce a sound that is on the border between categories, English-speakers interpret it as being in the erroneous one. I have a Chinese friend who appears to me to be pronouncing Cleveland as "Crevar" and Columbus as "Crumbus." He is really not doing so, but his pronunciation of the l sounds to me like an r.

On the other hand, sounds quite different from each other but labeled as coming from the same category are not discriminated from each other. Thus, while people from different regions may pronounce a particular sound quite differently from what most people are accustomed to hear, most Americans have no trouble understanding the word they are pronouncing. So when the

New Englander says that he went to a concert in the "pahk" and heard someone playing the "tuber," people from other parts of the country may laugh at his pronounciation, but they know what he is talking about.

Categorizing sounds into distinct groupings is probably useful to the infant in that it limits the total number of sounds the child must learn. It does not appear, however, to be a uniquely human attribute, since some other animals that do not learn language also perceive sounds categorically. Therefore, its possible relationship to language learning in human infants is still in doubt.

"Puh" and "buh," the sounds used by P. Eimas and his colleagues in their study, differ from each other only in **voice onset time** (VOT), which refers to whether low- or high-frequency components of the sound are heard first by the listener. When these sounds were produced in the laboratory by a voice synthesizer on which VOT could be precisely varied, it was found that infants did not distinguish at better than chance between two sounds within the same adult category that differed widely in their VOT. But they discriminated accurately between those with relatively similar VOT that crossed the adult sound category borders.

Two-month-olds also distinguish categorically between sounds that differ from each other only by the place in the mouth in which they are articulated. P. A. Morse (1972) and Eimas (1974) found that two-month-olds successfully distinguished between the sounds of b, g, and d. Similarly, they can differentiate between vowels and between sequences of vowels and consonants that differ from each other just a little (Trehub, 1973).

Eimas believes that these studies show that infants have available to them some inborn **phonetic** code, or a code regarding language sounds that enables them to judge whether two speech sounds are the same or different. At first, infants seem to divide sounds into more categories than do adults, and babies raised in different cultures, in which the categories may be different, still all categorize originally in the same way. For example, as we have already discussed, Japanese and Chinese speakers do not distinguish between the sounds of l and r in the same way that English-speakers do. And Thai speakers divide the p and b sounds somewhat differently from English-speakers (Abramson & Lisker, 1970). Yet infants in all these language groups discriminate between sound categories similarly to one another, regardless of whether adults do or not (Eimas, 1975a). Therefore, Eimas believes that this early categorical perception is inborn; only later does experience with a particular language alter and reduce in number the categories according to which sounds are perceived as different in that language.

Auditory Stimulation

All the research on auditory perception discussed here obviously has implications for infant caregiving. First of all, the facts that newborns are already sensitive to sounds, prefer rhythmic sounds, and seem distressed by loud ones can help parents in structuring the environment. Music that is not too loud but has a definite rhythmic beat can be used to calm a fretting baby. Depending on the family's preference, such music can be anything from Bach to the Beatles to the Beach Boys; the baby does not care. Since babies seem to like both rhythm and the sound of the human voice, rhythmic singing, such as the lullabies that have been used from time immemorial, also has a calming effect.

Second, since babies are so attuned to the sounds of human speech, and since eventually they will need to concentrate particularly upon the sounds that exist in their own language, they should be exposed to much human speech from the beginning. Parents sometimes have the mistaken notion that there is no point talking to a baby until the child is old enough to produce language. That is emphatically not so. In order to develop the sensitivity to the sound categories used in the particular language children are to learn, they must be exposed to speech in that language long before they begin to produce their own words. Since speech and language perception are so closely tied to the learning of language, we shall discuss this subject in greater detail in chapter 10.

OTHER PERCEPTUAL MODALITIES

Taste and Smell

Taste and smell are closely linked, inasmuch as taste tells one only if a substance is sweet, sour, salty, or bitter. All else that is called taste is really a function of smell, which enables one to tell the difference between roast beef and fish or to distinguish between eating a piece of apple and a strawberry. Consider how badly everything "tastes" when your nose is stopped up from a bad cold and you cannot smell the food you are eating. Feeling texture as well as seeing what one is eating obviously provide some clues as well, but smell seems to be the most important factor in identification and appreciation of various foods.

Few studies of the perception of taste and smell have been done with infants, probably because methodological problems are great. It is known, as has already been indicated in chapter 4, that neonates can differentiate some smells and some tastes from one another, and that they seem to prefer some tastes and odors over others.

The preference for sweet tastes seems to be inborn and exists across cultures (Mayer, 1976). Even neonates will suck longer and more vigorously on a nipple containing a sweetened solution than on a neutral one and will stop sucking if it turns salty (Jensen, 1932). Of course, the frequent use of sweet substances such as candy or ice cream as special treats or as reinforcers with young children in American culture and many others may enhance this inborn proclivity for sweetness. Beyond this preference, many taste preferences appear learned. Families that salt or spice foods heavily will have children who prefer salty or hot foods, while those who eat a more bland diet will probably have children who turn up their noses at chili or pickled herring. Most people can remember that their first taste of quinine water or beer made them wonder how anyone voluntarily drank either; many people as adults enjoy these beverages.

Newborn infants seem to find some odors, such as those of acetic acid (vinegar) or ammonia, unpleasant and will turn away from them, while they turn toward or persist in smelling the odors of vanilla or anise (Lipsitt, Engen, & Kaye, 1963). Therefore, it can be inferred that they can differentiate between these odors. To some extent, cultural learning plays a part in later smell preference, as some smells that are considered acceptable and pleasant in some cultures are regarded as offensive and bad in others. For example, the Chinese love a particular form of bean curd, whose smell is extremely offensive to most Westerners. Occasionally young children will express pleasure at smells that most adults consider aversive, such as those of mothballs, cleaning fluid, gasoline, or paint. Since these substances are poisonous or otherwise dangerous, young children obviously should not be given the chance to explore them by smell or in other ways.

Touch

Touch involves both the perception of the touch of other people and objects upon the infant's skin and the infant's ability to distinguish objects after having touched them with the fingers.

Cutaneous sensation is present at birth. Neonates will react to swaddling, or being wrapped up in a tight blanket, by becoming quiet. The same reaction occurs if they are folded or put back into the fetal position, with the adult hand held firmly on the baby's abdomen.

Most infants react positively to being held and cuddled, although some seem to prefer less of this kind of contact. There is also some question about the extent to which skin-to-skin contact between mother and neonate is important in the establishment of bonding between the two. Contrary to folklore, there is little skin-to-skin contact between infant and mother shortly after birth in most primitive cultures (Lozoff, 1982), since either the mother or the infant is bathed or rubbed after delivery. Even if the baby is placed with the mother after this process is completed, either or both are usually wrapped or dressed. In most of these cultures, however, the infant later has much bodily contact with the mother since it is usually breast-fed on demand, and often sleeps in the mother's bed at night. The results of studies on the efficacy of early skin contact for American neonates, who may receive less of this later physical contact, are ambivalent. Some seem to show increased bonding and lower rates of failure to thrive and of child abuse, while others have found few if any differences. We shall discuss this early contact in the context of bonding in chapter 11.

The role of touch in learning about the nature of objects will be discussed a little later in the consideration of cross-modal perception, since studies of touch are usually combined with studies of visual perception to see whether the one enhances the other.

Vestibular Perception

The mode of vestibular perception deals with the perception of a change of position or orientation that occurs in the brain because of a change of pressure of the fluid in the semicircular canals of the inner ear. The reflex activities of babies in response to sudden position changes, such as the Moro reflex, show that there must be some sensory capacity for detecting position change even in the neonate. Furthermore, studies that show that infants will return to a quiet alert state if picked up and held vertically, and that change in vestibular sensation through position change is necessary to make sure the infant is awake and attending (Gregg, Haffner, & Korner, 1976), tend to indicate that vestibular perception is important in maintaining or restoring various states in infancy.

Perception of Pain

Not much study of the perception of pain has been done. It is thought that the neonate perceives less pain than the older infant but that sensitivity to pain increases rapidly in the first few days after birth (Lipsitt & Levy, 1959). The withdrawal reflex apparent in the baby when the heel is pricked indicates that some sensation of pain is present even in the neonate, but it may be only at the level of the spinal cord or lower brain centers.

If male babies are circumcised, this procedure is usually done within the first day or two after birth and without the use of anesthetics, on the assumption that pain perception is still rather immature. Of course, anyone who has watched the obvious distress and discomfort of babies being circumcised recognizes that they certainly feel pain. It is not known, however, to what extent, if at all, the cortex of the neonate's brain receives and processes such information.

The sexes seem to differ in the perception of pain. Infant girls are more sensitive than boys to an air jet to the abdomen (Bell & Costello, 1964) and seem to perceive more pain when mild electric shock is used (Lipsitt & Levy, 1959). At least infant girls show a stronger reaction to pain than do infant boys (Notermans & Tophoff, 1967). All these results, however, come from studies using extremely small numbers of subjects and thus should be accepted only with some caution.

CROSS-MODAL PERCEPTION AND THE INTEGRATION OF PERCEPTUAL SYSTEMS

Have you ever stepped on a tack while walking barefoot? All your previous experience with tacks probably consisted of seeing them holding up posters on walls or bulletin boards or else using them to put up such posters with your fingers. Yet you knew exactly what this sharp object under your foot was, with no prior experience.

Cross-modal perception refers to this fact that an individual may recognize an object in a modality in which it has not been experienced because he or she has learned about it in another modality and is able to transfer this information from one to the other. For example, you may be able to identify by touch an object hidden in a grab-bag with which you have been familiar only by sight. Or you may recognize visually an object or event that you had previously only heard but not seen.

It is known from this kind of experiences that cross-modal perception occurs in older children and adults. But what about infants? Do they have such abilities, and if so, are these inborn or learned? Are the senses integrated with one another at birth, or does the infant need to learn how to put together the information received from the various perceptual modalities? Are some senses dominant over others, and does this dominance change over time?

Early infant behavior appears more dependent upon touch and vestibular perception. The neonate is more responsive to being wrapped and held and to position changes than to other kinds of perceptual stimulation. Later the infant depends more upon visual and auditory perception (Birch & Lefford, 1963, 1967).

Some perceptual researchers such as Bower (1974, 1982) and Gibson (1969) suggest that the infant is born with integration of sense modalities. Bower believes that the infant has an inborn unity of senses and in fact only later begins to differentiate among them. Gibson believes that common features of objects in the perceptual world can be perceived in the same way across sense modalities. There is some support for these views, since some integration of senses appears to be present at birth. For example, the neonate will turn its head in the direction of a sound and will visually scan that area of space (Wertheimer, 1961). Sounds also seem to affect visual preference in neonates, indicating the possibility of some integration of the two senses. Thus newborn infants who were exposed to auditory stimulation while looking at displays of various light intensities looked more at those of low intensity, while infants not exposed to the sound looked more at those of moderate light intensity (Lawson & Turkewitz, 1980; Lewkowicz & Turkewitz, 1981).

Some cross-modal transfer certainly does exist by four months (Mendelson & Ferland, 1982). Infants of this age were presented with a recorded syllable repeated in either a regular or irregular rhythm. When subsequently shown a silent film of a puppet moving its mouth in either the regular or irregular rhythm, infants tended to look longer at the puppet producing the novel rhythm, that is, the one they had not heard. Thus they were able to transfer the perceptual property of regularity or irregularity of an auditory stimulus to a visual one and to react to the novelty of the visual stimulus that matched the unfamiliar auditory one. Seven-month-olds are able to transfer complex patterns from one sense modality to another (Allen, Walker, Symonds, & Marcell, 1977). When these infants were habituated to either a visual or an auditory sequence of patterns and then exposed to the patterns in an altered sequence in either the same or the different modality, they were able to recognize the difference in patterns both within the same modality and across modalities. In other words, babies who learned the sequence visually were able to tell that the sequence was out of order when they either saw or heard it. And those who learned it by hearing were able to hear the discrepancy or to spot it visually.

Other researchers such as Piaget (1952, 1954) believe that perceptual integration is not inborn but the result of experience over time, as the infant acts upon the perceptual world. For instance, H. G. Birch and A. Lefford (1963, 1967) believe that cross-modal integration occurs quite late, after the period of infancy, perhaps only in middle childhood for some modalities. But as systems become integrated, responsiveness via any sense modality also becomes more selective, that is, the child responds to some aspects of a visual or auditory stimulus but not to others. As

with so many other areas of interest about infancy, much work remains to be done.

PERCEPTION IN HANDICAPPED INFANTS

Parents of handicapped infants worry about their baby's development. How will she know me if she is unable to see? How can I communicate with a child who is hard of hearing? What about my child who has cerebral palsy and cannot crawl or walk or may do so much later than the normal child? Will he learn to fear heights and avoid them the way a normal baby does? There is as yet not a great deal of information available on perceptual development in handicapped infants. Thus little is known that can be useful to parents and other adults in planning the environment of the handicapped infant so as to substitute experience in one perceptual modality for that in another.

Blind Infants

Most of the little that is known about perception in the handicapped comes from the area of visual perception and deals primarily with babies that are totally blind or have some perception of light only. The person who did the most work with blind babies and their parents was Selma Fraiberg (1970, 1975) at the University of Michigan. She developed many techniques for parents to use in enhancing their baby's normal development of social and motor abilities in spite of the visual handicap.

RECOGNIZING PARENTS BY SOUND

Fraiberg found that if parents talk to the infant frequently, the infant will begin to recognize them and distinguish them from strangers by the sounds of their voices. Social smiling, which in the sighted baby occurs most often at the sight of the familiar adult, will occur at about the same time in the blind infant in response to the familiar voice. By about five months, the baby will react selectively to parents and strangers, smiling more and making vocal responses to parents but not strangers. In the six-to-nine-month period, the blind infant will show the same wariness toward strangers that can be observed in the seeing child, reacting quizzically or sometimes with fear. If held by the stranger, the child may stiffen and act as if uncomfortable; when the mother takes the child, it relaxes and snuggles up.

MOTOR DEVELOPMENT

Blind children are affected in their motor development. Postural abilities such as turning, sitting up, and getting on all fours develop normally, but those involving what Fraiberg called self-initiated mobility, such as creeping, pulling self to a standing position, cruising, and walking may be delayed or absent unless adults intervene. Fraiberg explained that what impels the child to creep, and later to walk, is the interesting object the child sees that is just out of reach. Since the blind baby cannot see such an object, this motivation is missing.

KNOWLEDGE OF OBJECTS

The blind child, therefore, must learn about the existence of objects "out there" using touch and hearing, in other words, using its hands in response to sounds. In observing blind infants and children, Fraiberg noticed that many were unable to use their hands effectively and just held them limply against the torso with the arms bent in fetal position.

She, therefore, reasoned that since reaching, coordinated hand use, and grasping depend so much upon seeing both objects and the hands themselves, these skills had to be especially taught to the blind child by means of games involving both hands, special noise-producing toys, and lots of reward for hand use. Such games include various versions of "pat-a-cake." She also suggests fostering coordinated hand use by letting the bottle-fed baby grasp the bottle with both hands and at first putting the child's hands on the bottle to begin this activity. With the use of various sound-producing objects, the baby gradually learns that the sound-producing toy in the hand and the sound out there are the same object. Then it begins to reach toward the sound. This action usually happens at around 10 months, much later than visually directed reaching occurs in the sighted child. The blind child now also begins to track moving objects by sound and gradually perfects grasping them.

LATER MOTOR DEVELOPMENT

Fraiberg believed that not until the baby reaches toward an object on a sound cue will it attempt to crawl and creep. Now the parent must present the object at a distance, and eventually the baby who can support itself on hands and knees will creep toward the object. Pulling to standing position, cruising, and walking follow, but later than in the sighted child. Fraiberg found that most of her blind babies walked at around the age of 17 months if they were given practice in moving toward the sound of an object they desired.

OTHER CONSIDERATIONS

A lot of parental interaction with the baby and the use of toys producing sounds are necessary for normal development of the blind baby in other perceptual, motor, and social areas. Toys have been modified for use with the blind. For example, balls have bells put inside them, so that they jingle as they roll.

Some postural positions that interest the sighted baby are boring to the blind. The prone position, in which a baby typically raises its head and looks around, is of little use to the blind child. Such a child prefers to lie on its back or to sit. Graspable toys suspended at the side or above the crib are therefore even more important for the blind infant than for the sighted one. Since hand use and manipulation of toys is facilitated by being in a sitting position, blind babies should be allowed to sit with a table or tray containing objects for manipulation as soon as they are able to sit up with some support.

Hearing-Impaired Infants

Most hearing-impaired individuals have some residual hearing, that is, they are able to hear some kinds of sounds to some extent and are not totally deaf. Thus, while the major strategies for the blind child revolve around the substitution of other senses for sight, the strategy for the hard-of-hearing child is to save and use as much hearing as still remains and make sure it is not overwhelmed by the use of other sensory areas. It is vitally important that hearing-impaired infants learn to use whatever residual hearing they possess. Otherwise, they are likely to depend on other sensory and perceptual modalities and never develop the listening skills that would help to assure as normal development as possible.

Thus the major responsibility of both professionals and parents is first to identify a possible hearing problem as early as possible and second to begin to teach listening skills to the infant as soon as the handicap is realized.

IDENTIFICATION OF HEARING LOSS

A number of indications appear in the behavior of the infant that could be symptomatic of hearing loss (Northern & Downs, 1978). These indications usually consist of the lack of response to particular stimuli or the lack of development of age-appropriate pre-language and language behaviors. A hearing loss should be suspected, however, only if the infant lacks such responses on a consistent basis. An occasional failure to respond in an appropriate manner to a particular stimulus situation could be due to fatigue, inattention, habituation, or the competition for attention from a more interesting stimulus. Therefore, parents should not leap to conclusions based upon a single instance of the lack of such a response.

According to J. L. Northern and M. P. Downs (1978), hearing loss can be suspected in the period from birth to four months if the child does not either startle at a loud sound, sometimes awaken from sleep if a loud sound is produced, or sometimes cry when a sudden loud sound is produced. In the period from four to seven months, a hearing loss may be indicated if the baby does not begin early in this period to turn toward a sound source that is out of sight and begin to search for it visually. By seven months, the normally hearing infant should be able to turn directly toward a sound source that is out of sight. In addition, babbling, which usually begins in this period in both normal and hearing-impaired children, should continue and increase in the normal child. If it diminishes or ceases altogether, a hearing loss can be suspected. The normal infant will coo and gurgle in response to unseen sounds, such as the mother talking from out of sight or the sound of music or the doorbell. It will turn easily to find a sound source located to one side and after nine months to a sound source located all the way behind the child.

The normal infant will begin to imitate sounds during the last three months of the first year, but the hard-of-hearing infant will not. While the normal infant produces a wide variety of sounds with a wide range of pitches, the infant with limited hearing will produce few sounds and only within a limited range of pitch or else will gradually stop making sounds at all. The normal child will make some consonant sounds as well as those of vowels; the hard-of-hearing child may produce only vowel sounds. Finally, on into the second year, while the normally hearing child will begin to produce words that can be understood by others, the hard-of-hearing child will either produce none or some with such distortions of sound that they cannot be understood.

AUDIOMETRIC EVALUATION

Once a hearing loss is suspected, the infant needs to be evaluated by professionals such as physicians and audiologists. Some testing for hearing loss can be done with even very young infants, using sounds coming from different directions and rewarding the child for head turning in the appropriate direction by presenting a lighted doll or figure to look at in the appropriate place. By controlling the volume of the sound once the child has learned the appropriate head-turning response, some estimate of the degree of hearing loss can be made. As the infant becomes older and has a greater repertoire of behaviors, more precise methods of testing using a variety of infant responses to sound can be used.

Once a hearing loss has been determined, a hearing aid can be fitted and can be worn by the child. In the past, the degree of amplification of sound needed for the child with a profound hearing loss required the wearing of a bulky apparatus on the chest and thus was not practical for very young infants. The advent of sophisticated, small, and lightweight microchip circuitry in the last few years has altered this. Lightweight behind-the-ear aids can now be successfully fitted for babies as young as a few weeks. Thus, as soon as a hearing loss can be determined, the infant who needs amplification of sound in order to hear can begin to use a hearing aid.

TRAINING IN LISTENING SKILLS

The hard-of-hearing child must be given a reason to listen and to indicate to others that he or she has heard a sound (McArthur, 1982). Otherwise the child will seek comfort only from sight and touch of the caregiver alone and will "tune out," or stop using what residual sound can be heard. Therefore, the first job of parents or teachers after a hearing loss is suspected, even before it is definitely diagnosed, is to begin to teach the infant to listen for sounds and to make this listening a gratifying experience.

The child must be alerted to the existence of sound. You can begin by trying to attract the child's attention by calling her or his name when the child is looking at you. Turn on the radio or the television, perhaps even louder than normal (until the child has a hearing aid) and try to induce the child to react to the sound. Act happy and pleased if he or she does. Talk to the child while feeding and dressing him or her just as you would to a hearing child, so that the child will come to associate what can be heard of the adult's voice with comfort and attention. Since the hard of hearing often can best hear sounds of lower frequency, the father's voice may be even more important to such a child than the mother's.

As the infant becomes older, sounds in the environment should be pointed out, and the relationship between the object and the sound it produces should be stressed. When

If a hearing loss is suspected, a child should be evaluated as soon as possible by a professional audiologist to determine the extent of the handicap and to plan remedial strategies. Although the child in this picture is of preschool age, audiometric testing can be done with young infants using techniques such as reinforcement for head turning to hearing a sound.

possible, the sound should be related to the sight or touch of the object producing it. A slamming door, a drum that is banged on, the telephone, or the vacuum cleaner are good objects for such teaching. Outdoors the rumble of trucks or trains going by, the sounds of thunder when it storms, or the wail of sirens of emergency vehicles should be pointed out to the child and listened to. The older infant or toddler can have a hand held to the radio, television, or vacuum cleaner and can feel the vibrations that produce the sound, as well as listen to them.

In addition, parents and teachers can use toys that make sounds to focus the child's listening (Mavilya & Mignone, 1977). Shake a rattle and move it in a circular pattern before the eyes of a young infant to induce it to track the sound-making object visually. As the infant can begin to grasp and shake toys, use those that will produce a noise when shaken. As the infant begins to sit and later to crawl and creep, toys that make noise when moved are useful. The infant is thus motivated to move them to produce the sound. As the child begins to walk, push toys and later pull toys that make noise can be used. Dolls and stuffed toys that produce sounds are also helpful.

LANGUAGE DEVELOPMENT

Language development in the hard-of-hearing child may be quite retarded or may never occur if the child is not given special training in listening or if the hearing loss is not remediated through the use of a hearing aid. Even with such help, language development poses some special problems for individuals with hearing loss. A more detailed discussion of language development in the hard-of-hearing child will be found in chapter 10.

Summary

1. Perception is that portion of cognition through which sensory information is processed and organized. The various aspects of perception include visual, auditory, gustatory and olfactory, tactual, pain, and vestibular. The bulk of scientific studies of perception, in infants as well as in older children and adults, have been conducted with either visual or auditory perception.

2. Infant perception is difficult to study both because infants go through rapid state changes and because they are nonverbal and hence their perception of various stimuli must be assessed by indirect means. These means include the use of the infant's orienting responses, preference for certain stimuli, habituation to stimuli, and conditioning.

3. Newborn infants are able to see, but because of immaturity of the various muscles of the eye, they see best objects that are about 8 to 10 in away. Their eyes also lack the ability to converge and to coordinate movement. In addition, the retina is immature at birth and the fovea does not seem to have attained its later appearance or functioning. The optic nerve is not yet fully myelinated. For all these reasons, visual acuity in the neonate is limited.

4. As both nerves and muscles mature, the infant is better able to focus on visual displays and to track moving objects. Color vi-

sion is present for at least some colors by two months and perhaps sooner. Four-month olds seem to see all the colors that older children do. Color perception in infants is categorical, just as it is in older children and adults.

5. Young infants are visually sensitive to contour and will scan areas of a display having high degrees of contour in preference over areas of low contour. They prefer stripes to undifferentiated displays of equal brightness.

6. With increasing age, complexity and later meaning of a patterned display become more important than contour. Later yet, a moderately discrepant display will attract the infant's greatest attention.

7. Infants seem to be drawn especially to displays of the human face. At first this attraction may be due to the great amount of contour a face presents. Young infants look most at the edges of the face. Later they look at interior features and seem to prefer faces whose features are placed correctly. Three-dimensional faces are preferred over schematic drawings. Older infants attend to faces with scrambled features but appear uneasy about them.

8. Since young infants prefer three-dimensional displays over flat ones, it has been assumed that they perceive depth in the visual field. Research into depth perception has produced contradictory results. The best evidence indicates that depth perception is attained around the age of 3 ½ months and improves with increasing age.

9. Infants seem to respond defensively, however, to objects that appear to be approaching them on a collision course. Whether this reaction is a reflexive one based on visual tracking of the moving object or is based on some understanding of the possibility of being hit is still being debated.

10. Fear of falling, as tested on the visual cliff, seems to develop as infants have the opportunity to locomote. Before this time, infants express interest and surprise, but not fear, upon exposure to the apparent dropoff.

11. Although the auditory nerve is well myelinated at birth, the hearing areas of the brain are immature, and the ear canal as well as the bones of the inner ear are not yet fully functional. It is known that the neonate hears but not how well such hearing is interpreted.

12. The newborn can localize sound at better than a chance level. It is soothed by rhythmic sounds and reacts defensively to loud sounds. Young infants are especially responsive to the sound of the human voice.

13. From the age of one month, infants seem able to discriminate between sounds made in speaking that are very similar to each other but that are heard as categorically different by some adult speakers. At first all infants, regardless of their language group, divide sounds categorically in the same manner. Over time, each infant becomes most sensitive to categorical distinctions that exist in its native language.

14. Neonates can distinguish smells from one another and turn away from some that they seem to perceive as unpleasant. Some perception of taste also appears inborn, as newborns will suck longer on a sweet than a neutral solution and will stop sucking if it turns salty.

15. Tactual and pain perception have been studied only a little. Infants seem to react positively to being held and stroked and to being swaddled. Pain perception seems to increase greatly in the first few days after birth. Girls appear more sensitive to pain than boys or at least react more strongly to it.

16. An area of current interest is whether the various perceptual systems are integrated at birth or whether this integration and the ability to interpret what has been learned in one modality in another is a learned response. Some evidence seems to support either position.

17. Blind and hearing-impaired infants must be exposed to special activities and have their environments, including toys, modified to make up for the deprivation of perception in a particular modality. If they are given such special remediation from early in infancy on, their development in other perceptual areas, as well as motor and speech functioning, can proceed in a relatively normal manner.

Participatory and Observational Exercises

1. In order to do the following exercises, you will need access to both younger and older infants. It would be helpful to visit a day-care center or church nursery in which a number of infants of varying ages are available. If this is impossible, try to make several

home visits to some infants of different ages and try out some of the exercises with each. Then compare your observations for infants and toddlers of the different ages.

a. What do young infants look at? Try slowly moving a bright large toy before a very young infant who seems wide awake. Remember to hold it at the distance that the young baby can focus on. Does the infant track visually? How smooth or jerky is the tracking? What happens if you move the object beyond the midline? Try the same with a slightly older infant, one who is two to three months old. What differences, if any, do you notice in tracking? What happens when you hold the object farther away? Does the infant still seem to see it and track it? Does either the older or younger infant appear to be reaching for the object? Does he or she reach for it when it is closer or farther away? Or not at all?

b. With the same infants as in a. above, shake a rattle or ring a small bell to one side of each infant while it cannot see the noise-producing object. How does the infant respond? Now make the noise on the other side of the infant. What happens? How do very young and somewhat older infants differ in their response to sound?

c. Now concentrate on visually directed reaching in somewhat older infants. Use infants from about three months old onward. Hold out an appealing toy at a distance at which the infant can reach it and also farther away. What happens? Can you see differences in reaching behavior in younger, middle, and older infants? How does the ability to gauge accurately the location of objects improve with increasing age and experience?

2. Observe a parent or other caregiver trying to calm a fussy, crying younger infant. What techniques does she or he use? How does each technique affect a particular perceptual modality? What seems to work in calming the infant? Why do you think it does?

3. How do adults use the voice to soothe a baby? Observe some parents or caregivers interacting with infants and record the songs, chants, and nonsense words they use with each one. If you can, observe parents and infants from another culture, if any are available in your community. How do the songs and chants differ from those used by "average" American caregivers? In what ways are they similar? Do there appear to be cross-cultural "universals" in soothing babies?

4. Talk to parents about their infants' taste and smell preferences. What tastes does each baby like? Dislike? What smells does the baby like or dislike? How similar are babies to one another in taste and smell preferences? Are there some tastes and smells that seem universally liked? Disliked?

5. If there is a preschool for handicapped children in your community that provides a perceptual stimulation program for infants, arrange a visit to it. You may be able to find out from your local United Way or from the public schools if such an agency exists in your community. A program for visually or hearing-handicapped children would be especially interesting. Observe the teacher and the parent working with a child or children. What kinds of activities do they do? How do the activities serve to help the child use what residual vision or hearing he or she has? How do they help the child to substitute other sense modalities for one that is lacking or too deficient for practical use? What specialized toys and other equipment are used? Are suggestions or assignments given to parents to do with the children at home between teaching sessions?

6. Observe infants interacting with various

toys and play equipment. What sensory and perceptual skills does each help to teach the infants?

DISCUSSION QUESTIONS

1. Do you think it is better for the young infant to be exposed to too much or to too little perceptual stimulation? What can be the results of each?

2. Can you think of ways that moderate discrepancy is used in advertising on television or in magazines to draw the observer's or reader's attention? What are some recent examples you and your classmates can recall? How effective is the technique?

3. Parents in the 1920s were told that young infants could not see or hear much of anything and that they should be kept in situations of low stimulation. Do you think this practice has affected people who were infants at this time? If so, in what ways might it have? Think about your own grandparents, or perhaps your parents, who were raised at this time, in your considerations of this question in class discussion.

4. Have you heard any myths or old wives' tales about infant perception? Compare those you have heard with any that your classmates have heard.

Infant Intelligence I: Definitions, Theories, Learning, and Memory

CHAPTER **8**

INTRODUCTION

As a newborn, Baby Anne reflexively sucked on anything that was brought to her mouth. At one month, she would spit out the pacifier if offered when she was hungry, but she eagerly sucked on the nipple of her bottle of formula. She had learned what provided food, and what did not, from her interaction with the various items to suck on. That is, she had learned to **discriminate**.

Six-month-old Robert shook his rattle to hear the sound it made. He also banged it on the high-chair tray, hit his older sister with it when she came too close, dipped it into his cereal, and dropped it on the floor. He was figuring out a variety of ways to use the rattle. But when his mother took the rattle and hid it under a diaper on the high-chair tray, Robert was dumfounded. Where had it gone? He had not yet learned that things keep on existing even if they are not visible. When his mother did the same thing two months later, Robert lifted the diaper off immediately and laughingly held out the rattle. He had figured out that hidden objects still existed and could be retrieved.

In later infancy, Anne had to go to the doctor's office for a series of shots. Each time, a nurse in a white uniform talked to her in a friendly manner and then gave her the injection, which hurt. A few weeks later, Anne's family took her with them to a restaurant for Sunday dinner. As soon as she saw the waitresses in their white uniforms, she began to cry. To quiet her, some waitresses came over and began to talk to her in a friendly fashion, but in response she cried more loudly. Finally, her parents had to take her home. Obviously, Anne had learned to associate women in white with shots that hurt.

When Greg was 15 months old, he toddled into his parents' bedroom and discovered that his father had left some of his things lying around. Soon Greg emerged, wearing his father's shoes, with a necktie clumsily twisted around his neck, and with a big pipe hanging down from his mouth.

Chris was a year and a half when Grandma came to visit, and he was taken to the station to meet her train. The next time he saw the train going by down in the valley, he cheerfully announced, "Grandma coming." Memory was obviously involved. But he was also symbolizing, connecting Grandma's arrival to the appearance of the train. All these mental activities—learning through association and **discrimination,** problem solving, modeling, and generalizing, as well as the use of memory and symboling shown by the children—are aspects of cognition, or knowledge. Cognition in turn affects and relates to intelligence.

DEFINITIONS

At this point we must consider just what intelligence is, how it relates to cognition, and how cognition in turn relates to the other mental activities that have been illustrated. For only by understanding these concepts and how they operate in the infant can one begin to appreciate the changes that occur in the thinking and behavior of children from birth to the end of toddlerhood, as exemplified by the children just described. In this chapter we will consider some differing outlooks on intelligence, some ways of studying it in infants, and the processes of learning and memory. In the following chapter, we will deal with the development of cognition, especially as formulated by Piaget, and finally consider the various ways of assessing intelligence in infancy.

Structure and Function

Important concepts in an understanding of intelligence are those of structure and function. **Structure** refers to what something is composed of or made up of. For example, a house is a structure made up of wood, and perhaps brick, of sheetrock, wires, pipes, windows, doors, and the like. **Function** refers to use or activity and is what a structure is used for or does. In general, functions are by-products of structures and cannot occur without the existence of the appropriate structures. The house in our example functions to provide shelter for its inhabitants. That is, its function is to protect the people in it from extremes of heat or cold, from rain or wind or snow, and to enable them to perform such tasks as cooking, sleeping, or keeping clean within it.

Notice that structure and function interact. If the function of the house changes because more people come to live there, it may need to be increased in size or divided into a duplex, thus altering the structure. Conversely, if the structure is altered, as for example if a room is made into an office, then the function of the house may change, from serving as a residence only to serving as both residence and office.

In the same way as with the house, the human body has various physical structures, which perform a series of physical functions. Many of these bodily structures are called systems. Each system contributes to the total body, which is a mega-system, or all-inclusive system. Thus, there is the structure called the digestive system, which functions to digest food, and the skeletal system, which functions to provide support to the body and to enable movement.

In addition to the physical structures and their functions, the human being also has mental, or psychological, structures with their concomitant functions. The difference is that the physical structures are physically apparent. One knows one has a mouth, a stomach, and an intestinal tract from either seeing them or feeling sensations from them or perhaps from seeing illustrations of such parts. One knows what their functions are and that they are performing them correctly most of the time. Mental or psychological structures, however, cannot be identified as readily because they are not made up of readily observable physical components. They are hypothetical constructs, that is, entities that are inferred to exist because of the way the human mind functions. Thus, such constructs as intelligence, conscience, or the emotions are mental, or psychological, structures that are thought to exist in all individuals. Of course, many of these psychological constructs have a physiological basis in the brain. That is, particular brain areas have been identified as those in which emotion, the contents of memory, or other structural components originate. Again, it probably is useful to distinguish the brain, which is a physical structure of the body, and the mind, which is a construct describing functional properties of the brain.

These psychological structures, in turn, relate to psychological functions such as thinking and feeling, which are processes through which these structures operate to interact with reality outside the individual. And just as physical structures and functions interact, influence, and change one another, so do psychological ones.

Intelligence

The psychological structure that is the capacity of an individual to act purposefully, think rationally, and deal effectively with the environment is **intelligence** (Wechsler in Matarazzo, 1978). Alternatively we could say that intelligence is the capacity of the individual to adapt to the environment (Piaget, 1952, 1954, 1970). Intelligence thus has to do with knowledge and how knowledge originates and develops or becomes structured within the individual.

Many theorists have debated about how intelligence is structured, that is, what its components are. J. P. Guilford (1967) for example, has proposed that human intelligence is composed of 120 separate factors of which more than 90 have been isolated statistically. R. B. Cattell (1971) has proposed that intelligence is composed of two major portions, which he labeled crystallized and fluid. **Fluid intelligence** is one's innate capacity based upon inherited intellectual structure. **Crystallized intelligence** entails mental ability based on stored information that is acquired through learning and exposure to one's culture. Thus fluid intelligence is the basic substrate upon which crystallized intelligence can develop, and it is relatively independent of environmental effects, while crystallized intelligence depends largely upon environmental influences such as education. Fluid intelligence is present to some extent from birth on, whereas crystallized intelligence begins to develop in infancy as the child interacts with environmental events and people, and it continues to change and develop throughout most of life.

Cognition and Its Functions

The act or process of knowing is called **cognition**. Since it is an activity or process, cognition is a function, and it is the major function of intelligence. Cognition is the function through which the intellectual structure is used and modified, that is, through which knowledge is absorbed, adapted, classified, and used. The major hallmark of cognition appears to be organization. Data received

from the senses, from previous experience, from learning and symboling are all categorized, interpreted, and thus organized so that they can be used to guide further actions and thoughts.

Cognition, therefore, involves a variety of separate and subordinate functions, which act upon knowledge in different ways. **Learning** is the function by which knowledge, or information, is acquired. **Memory** is the function through which knowledge is processed and stored for later retrieval. Concept formation and symboling enable the individual to interpret and classify information so that he or she can act on the environment in a purposeful and effective manner. Other functions, such as problem solving and reasoning, are further aspects of learning. Problem solving represents a higher function of cognition.

The use of language is a subset of symboling and therefore also is a functional subdivision of cognition. Because language is such an important and unique aspect of human cognition we shall devote an entire chapter (chapter 10) to a detailed consideration of this psychological function and only mention it in passing here.

Perception is a special form of cognition rather than a subordinate function of it, inasmuch as perception too involves learning, memory, and concept formation. Perception is that form of cognition that deals specifically with the intake, processing, and interpreting of sensory information. We have already discussed perception in chapter 7. For a schematic view of how the various structural and functional aspects of intelligence relate to each other, please see figure on page 274.

Additionally, cognition may involve such relatively nonmental processes as the emotions, personality, and social consciousness (Flavell, 1977). For example, the intensity of emotional arousal affects learning. Temperament characteristics, which are enduring

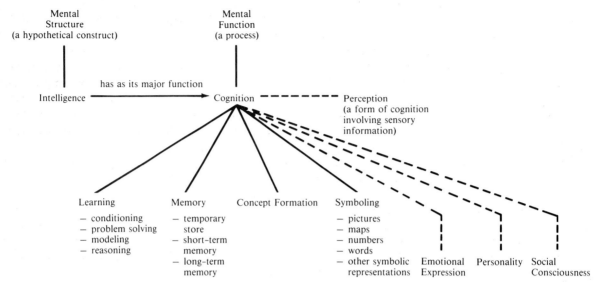

The relationship between structure and function in intelligence.

components of an individual's personality, also enhance or restrict particular cognitive functions. Therefore, these processes, although not cognitive functions per se, affect the way the individual perceives and interprets reality and thus the way he or she organizes cognition. Let us now look at some aspects of cognition in greater detail.

LEARNING

Learning is any relatively permanent change in behavior that is due to practice and not primarily to maturation, fatigue, or the effect of outside agents such as drugs. Learning interacts with maturation, however, in that it does not take place until the individual's maturational level disposes her or him toward it. That is, learning does not occur until a structure is able to be built or modified, and before that time, training does not help in learning. This fact explains why older infants are able to learn behaviors and relationships that younger ones are incapable of

mastering. Thus, learning is an adaptive process resulting from the interaction of environmental experience and the individual's internal organization of his or her intellectual structure.

MEMORY

In the process of memory, information is stored either temporarily or on a long-term basis so that it can be recalled, recognized, or compared to some other piece of information at the required time. Memory is composed of three aspects: recognition, recall, and associative memory. The very young infant appears to be able to use only recognition and some limited associative memory; these functions become more developed later, and the ability to use recall appears. What is remembered may be put into a momentary temporary store, be remembered for a brief period in short-term memory, or remain relatively permanently in long-term memory (Sigel, 1981).

CONCEPT FORMATION

One function of cognition is to form **concepts,** which are a set of attributes, characteristics, or classificatory properties common to a group of actions, objects, symbols, or other mental representations. Concepts, therefore, are ways of organizing information. Such attributes as round or blue, or such classificatory terms as human or mammal, involve concepts.

Researchers have sought to determine how early in infancy conceptual thinking is possible. It now seems that infants may begin to understand concepts based upon visual representations around the age of seven months (Cohen, 1979; Fagan, 1976, 1977, 1978).

SYMBOLING

The function of **symboling** involves the arbitrary representation of an event, object, action, quality, or concept by something else, the symbol, that stands for it. A picture, a written or spoken word, a map or diagram, or a number are all examples of symbols. Language, either spoken or written, probably represents the most important use of symboling. While concepts deal with generalizations or commonalities across individual bits of information, symbols refer to specific entities. Of course, concept information and symboling can interact greatly with each other. For a symbol or group of symbols such as a word or words is often used to describe a concept. The symbol then becomes a specific term used to label a general category or concept.

THEORETICAL ISSUES

While theorists generally agree on what intelligence is and on how the various functions play a part in it, they differ widely in their view of the origins and development of intelligence. These diversities depend on the extent to which intelligence is attributed more to the organism itself and to the particular genetic variables that predispose the organism to particular intellectual development, in which the individual is generally seen as actively involved, or, contrarily, the extent to which intelligence is viewed as due more to influences from the environment, with the individual in the role of a reactive recipient. The earliest disputes about these matters arose from the debate between philosophers about the relative importance of nature and nurture, or heredity and environment. More recently, the argument has involved the **organismic** versus the **mechanistic** view of the developing individual. These two sets of arguments are related, inasmuch as the organismic view in general attributes more to heredity than to environment, while the mechanistic view is more concerned with environmental influences.

Nature versus Nurture

The nature-nurture controversy, to determine whether particular abilities are inborn or due to environmental variables, has been long and particularly fierce in the area of intelligence. The reason, in part, is that the victory of either position could have far-reaching social and political consequences. Today, however, the either-or argument is largely passé; most scientists recognize that intelligence results from an interaction between nature and nature.

It should, nevertheless, be kept in mind that if one adopts the position that genetics are the major determinants, then differences between groups of people based upon racial stock or ethnic group can be posited to exist. It is only a small step from that position to the one in which certain groups are then considered to be inherently superior intellectually to others, and the concept of master races and servant races can begin to emerge.

If environment is the major determinant, on the other hand, then it follows that a particular culture or environment can produce the particular type of individual desired. Indoctrination in a particular ideology and the behaviors that follow from it can presumably thus produce lovers of democracy, loyal communists, servant classes resigned to their fates, or whatever those in control wish. The people in George Orwell's *Nineteen Eighty-four* are good examples of what follows from this kind of indoctrination.

In former years, philosophers and psychologists tended to ascribe intelligence very much to either one or the other of these polarities. Thus, for example, the 17th-century philosopher John Locke thought that the individual's mind at birth was like a blank slate, upon which environmental experience entered all that resulted in intellectual formation. He also believed that the senses were the source through which all knowledge was acquired. This sensory information was used in making associations between what had already been acquired earlier and what was new, and these associations were what was entailed in the process of learning.

The early-20th-century American psychologist John B. Watson (1918) took a similar environmentalist view. In the 1920s he made his famous remark that he could take any infant and with suitable training eventually produce a doctor, lawyer, or chief, or whatever other occupation he had in mind (Elkind & Flavell, 1969). Except for instances of gross defects, the environmental experience regardless of the genetic makeup of the individual would have the most critical effect upon the individual's development. More recent learning theorists such as B. F. Skinner have held much the same position of emphasis on the environment.

The nativist position, on the contrary, was that there were basic inborn dispositions toward knowledge in the human mind and

that these enabled the individual to learn and to solve problems. Philosophers such as G. W. von Leibnitz and Immanuel Kant held such positions. In the modern era, these views stressing inborn potential have led to two widely diverging currents of thought, one stressing the concept of fixed intelligence, emphasizing individual differences between people, and the other viewing human intelligence as a unique, species-specific development that is largely determined by the genes but is relatively similar, particularly early in life, across individuals since they share a common human genetic heritage. We shall look at these modern views in detail a little further on, since they also can be viewed within the context of the controversy over the active versus the passive organism.

Organismic versus Mechanistic

The infant can also be viewed either primarily in an **organismic,** or active and dynamic manner, or else in a more **mechanistic,** passive way. This difference is a modern outgrowth of the old nature-nurture debate. Most modern students of intelligence take an intermediate position, somewhere between the two extremes. Depending upon where on the continuum between the two extremes one believes the truth to lie, one will emphasize particular interventions or experiences or will see them as irrelevant. Thus this debate over the nature of infant intelligence has repercussions on the education of parents, early childhood education programs, the manufacture and use of toys, the media, and politics. For example, if intelligence is subject to change through environmental manipulation, then infant intervention programs and parent education programs designed to promote infant intellectual development make sense. If inherent genetic makeup is the principal determinant, then such programs are a waste of money and effort, for they will do little to alter inborn individual differences.

ORGANISMIC

Proponents of the organismic view, concentrating more on structure of intellect than on its functions, want to know what structures can account for behavioral stability as well as behavioral changes in infancy. They generally perceive the infant as an active seeker for information and stimulation, influenced primarily by maturational factors that are species-specific. Holders of the organismic view see infant intellectual development as a biologically programmed sequence that is, at least at first, relatively unaffected by sociocultural influences. According to this view, there are thus few differences between individual infants at first in rates of development, since these rates are largely determined by biology and maturation. There is also little stability across ages in the same individual because maturational factors may result in very different kinds (as well as degrees) of performance on intellectual tasks. Adherents to this view include cognitive theorists, behavioral geneticists, and those scientists basing their ideas upon evolutionary and ethological studies.

Cognitive Theorists Such theorists as Piaget, Werner, and Bruner have thought that the infant actively constructed its own reality subject to maturational level and the biological constraints imposed by species-specific structures that have evolved over the millenia.

Thus culture and social class are viewed as relatively less important than the interactions between the infant's inborn mental structure and environmental opportunities that are relatively similar for all infants. Cognitive theorists generally stress maturation

as an important variable, for they believe that experience can be used and integrated into intelligence only insofar as the intellectual structures are mature enough to do so. Cognitive theory will be extensively discussed in chapter 9.

Behavioral Geneticists Scientists concerned with **behavioral genetics** study how the genes and the evolution of the human species interact to result in human behaviors. Such scientists see human intelligence and human behavior as subject to continued genetic influences. Although there are obviously individual differences among humans as to the particular combinations of genes each has inherited, the human gene pool shows basic similarities across all individuals, since by the process of natural selection those individuals deviating too far from the basic human blueprint did not survive to transmit their genetic endowment.

Within all human individuals, particular genes and combinations of genes are programmed by nature to begin their activities or to have their influences become manifest at particular periods of development, both prenatally and postnatally (McClearn, 1971). Some genes may make their effects felt in infancy; others may not produce an effect until later on in early childhood or even adulthood. G. E. McClearn uses as an example Huntington's Disease which, although the result of a gene defect, does not manifest itself until middle adulthood (McClearn, 1970). In the same way, particular genes relating to human intelligence may begin to produce effects at various times. Whatever inborn potential an individual or a species may have, this potential does not become activated all at once but only gradually and in interaction with all previous genetic influences and environmental experience.

Thus, the various developmental processes, while subject to some environmental influence, depend largely upon the continuing and new effects of genes. Therefore, species-specific developmental functions appear in all infants at approximately the same time. The beginning of language is an example, since it occurs in the same way at the same time in children differing greatly in ethnic group, culture, and even, to some extent, intellectual capacity.

The relatively invariant effect of the genes is considered to be strongest in early infancy. It becomes somewhat less determining, though still very important, with increasing age, as other factors such as culture and education begin to exert an influence.

This genetic viewpoint has been described in pictorial terms by the embryologist C. H. Waddington (1962). Waddington described the developing human as if it were a ball rolling along the contours of a landscape, which he called the creod. The **genotype,** or genetic blueprint, of the individual determines the contours of the landscape, and the **phenotype,** or physical expression of the genetic blueprint, determines the position of the rolling ball. The contours can also be affected by cultural variables, which channel the movement of the individual into one direction rather than another. In addition, the rolling ball can be displaced from its path by the force of intervening environmental events. If these environmental interferences are changed within a reasonable time, the ball may return to its course and continue on as before, but if they continue to make their influence felt, it may remain permanently on an altered course. For example, if an infant suffers short-term nutritional deprivation, it will recover from or make up for the consequences, but if nutritional deprivation persists, the infant may suffer from permanent lack of adequate brain development, stunted physical growth, and perhaps even death.

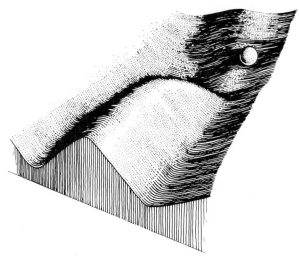

Waddington's epigenetic landscape. The individual is like the rolling ball, whose motion is channeled by the terrain, or heredity. But the motion of the ball can be displaced from its course by outside forces, such as environmental input.

Waddington envisaged the contours of the landscape as a trench. At first, in the period corresponding to early infancy, the creod is narrow with high walls. Later as the child progresses into later infancy and beyond, the valley widens as the walls become lower and slope outward. This schematic presentation tries to demonstrate that behavior in early infancy is highly canalized, or determined, by genetic factors, and it is difficult for the infant to deviate from the course. As environmental events begin to have greater influence upon the child over time, the child's individual variation increases and the course may be altered.

Evolutionists and Ethologists   Students of human evolution and ethologists, who study human culture and compare it to other animal cultures, try to determine how the human brain differs from that of other species and how this difference affects both species-specific, genetically determined and culturally influenced behavior. They reach the same conclusion as behavioral geneticists, namely that early human behavior is highly determined and that later on individual differences and the influence of the sociocultural environment become more pronounced (Scarr-Salapatek, 1976). However, instead of ascribing this change over time to the selective "turning on" of successive gene effects, they find it in the study of which portions of the brain seem to predominate in the determination of behavior at particular times during mammalian and specifically human development. Since the genes ultimately also control the development of the brain, these two points of view really are not very dissimilar.

Evolutionists and ethologists point out that the more primitive lower brain structures of humans, the "old brain," are similar to those found in other species, including far more primitive ones. These structures control many early functions and behaviors of the newborn and young infant. Later on, as the "new brain," or the cortex, assumes control, human behavior deviates more from that of those animals having little or no cortex, although such behavior is still quite similar to that of closely related animals that also show much cortical activity. Eventually, since the human cortex is far more complex and developed than that of any other species, human behavior becomes very species-specific (Flavell in Scarr-Salapatek, 1976). For example, mammalian behavior is very similar at birth: all newborn mammals can suck. Later on, as human development begins to differ from that of many other mammals, primate behavior still remains quite similar across species. In the first few months, the development of humans and great apes does not differ very much, except that apes are a bit more precocious in motor ability. Finally, as conceptual thinking, symboling, and particularly the use of language begin, human

development, while still very much the same within the species, begins to diverge more and more from that of the closely related apes. By late childhood or early adolescence, humans differ greatly from other primates.

The new brain is also much more subject to environmental influence than the old brain, which is more highly programmed. Thus most activities of more primitive animals have a determined quality to them: they must occur when the proper eliciting stimuli occur, and under such conditions they usually cannot be prevented or stopped. Some human activities that remain under the control of lower brain centers also retain this determined quality. For example, activities controlled by the autonomic nervous system such as breathing or digestion occur without conscious thought and indeed are but little influenced by cortical activity. By contrast, voluntary, thinking activity can vary widely, depending upon learning, memory, motivation, emotion, cultural conditions, and other influences that have some environmental basis.

The human infant, therefore, is sensitive to, and prepared for, instruction by adults in the cultural content of a particular group and in the adaptive mechanisms the group has learned for survival in particular environmental circumstances. This ability to profit by instruction, because little beyond the more primitive behaviors has been programmed by nature, has been called the human infant's "tutor-proneness" by Jerome Bruner (1972). The relative lack of brain programming, the openness to instruction, and the long period of immaturity of the human child during which instruction can be given all interact to make human beings intellectually the most flexible, teachable, and culturally influenced of all creatures.

Thus evolutionists and ethologists also view infant behaviors as becoming progressively more individualized and subject to interaction with environmental variables as the infant matures. Furthermore, they see the infant as actively eliciting interaction from environmental events and people. Evolutionists may stress culture a bit more than do the behavioral geneticists, but basically both groups envisage the infant as relatively determined early in life and becoming progressively more flexible and individualized over time because of both internal and environmental variables.

MECHANISTIC

By contrast, proponents of the mechanistic viewpoint stress the role of learning and the development of associations based upon environmental factors almost to the exclusion of internal factors such as genes or brain structures. Therefore, they are more interested in functions of the intellect rather than its structure and usually put the greatest emphasis upon the role of the environment in affecting the individual. In their view, particular individualized experience provides particular information through which the child learns. The behaviors learned by the child are, therefore, the result of environmental action upon the child, rather than the child's actions upon the environment, as cognitive theorists believe.

Thus, the developing infant is seen as a passive reactor to environmental events rather than an active instigator of interactions. Individual differences are recognized as very important and are usually viewed as largely the result of sociocultural differences, that is, as due to differential environmental influences. It is debated, however, whether such individual differences are already discernible in early infancy and remain stable throughout life or whether maturational factors that are similar across all infants are more determinant of early behavior. Some proponents

of the mechanistic view, such as the participants in the mental-test movement in the early 20th century, tended to ascribe individual differences more to inborn, genetic, differences of intellectual capacity. Although they saw the individual as more passive than do the organismic theorists, they ascribed more importance to predetermined influences and less to learning than to most of the more current mechanistic theorists.

The mental-test movement, composed of such scientists as Sir Francis Galton in Great Britain and Lewis Terman in the United States, led to the belief that individual intelligence was fixed by inborn factors. Terman and Galton found that individuals that were intellectually competent in childhood tended to remain so throughout life and that highly intelligent people tended to produce intelligent children. By basing their interpretations of these results on the notion of a fixed intelligence these scientists obviously ignored environmental factors as well as the bias built into their test items. Nevertheless, the idea that certain groups of individuals are inherently intellectually superior and will pass this superiority on to their children has had great appeal to many people and has resulted in such diverse outcomes as the eugenics movement of the early 20th century, the restrictive immigration laws passed by the U.S. Congress in the period after World War I, and the continued debate among some scientists over the possible intellectual superiority of certain racial groups over others.

Most of those holding the mechanistic viewpoint, however, regard behaviors as the most important aspects of human intelligence to study. The major questions asked by these researchers generally focus on what uses particular behaviors have, and how such behaviors relate to one another. In this orientation, early learning that can be demonstrated in infancy is interpreted as being the establishment of a rather linear relationship between antecedents and consequences, that is, the building of associations between them. Only later does the infant begin to test hypotheses and develop strategies leading to problem solving, thus becoming a more active learner.

RESOLUTION

What can be the resolution between these opposing viewpoints stressing nature versus nurture and the organismic versus the mechanistic approaches to the development of human intelligence? It appears useless to concentrate upon either intellectual structures or functions to the exclusion of the other, since the two appear to exist in an interacting relationship. Therefore, many present-day theorists assume an interactionist position between the two extremes. While cognitive theorists, behavioral geneticists, and ethologists concentrate more on structural variables, they recognize the importance of functional ones as well. And learning theorists such as Albert Bandura (1976), although devoting more study to functional processes, acknowledge the important role of structure that cannot be overlooked in determining the working of these processes.

Concerning the relative importance of heredity and environment, an interactionist view has also emerged. That is, most scientists at present believe that hereditary factors provide the upper limits or boundaries to intellectual development but that environmental influences provide the experiences necessary for this intellectual development to take place. Yet, at the same time, there probably are species-specific inborn capacities that enable human infants to learn particular typically human behaviors, which the infants

of other species, even if exposed to the same environmental conditions, do not learn.

LEARNING

All animals, even very simple ones, are capable of some learning. Human learning is probably the most advanced form of learning. The adult human is capable of making more complex associations and solving more difficult problems than can members of any other species. The human infant, however, does not begin postnatal life as a very sophisticated learner. The intellectual structure of the infant must be built through environmental interaction and through the incorporation of such interaction into experience through adaptation.

Interest in the systematic study of infant learning has been shown primarily by those scientists who adhere to a functionalist position and by those who emphasize the role of environmental influences in the development of specific cognitive abilities. Most American studies of infant intelligence and cognition until the 1960s and a large number since then have been studies of infant learning.

Questions and Issues

Researchers have studied infant learning for a variety of reasons. First, they ask if learning can occur more quickly or be more long-lasting in an organism that does not yet possess any or many learned behaviors, such as the newborn infant. If so, what should be learned by the infant at this time, and how can this learning best be assured to take place? The notion of critical periods enters in: is there an optimum time for infants to learn certain things, or is there a broad time frame within which they can learn them with equal facility? If there is a critical period, for what kinds of learning does it hold, and how narrowly defined is it?

Second, researchers question the possible influence of early experience upon later learning. For example, what might be the connection between early reflex behavior, such as stepping, and later walking? What effect may a deprived home environment during infancy have upon later ability to learn in school?

Third, researchers have wanted to know whether practice or maturation is more important in facilitating such learning, as Myrtle McGraw explored in studies of twins.

Finally, researchers want to determine whether incentives or rewards work with infants and young children in the same way that they do with animals and adults, as E. L. Thorndike has explored.

Parents and other adults also have asked questions about infant learning. These include how what parents do or do not do may affect their infant's intelligence. Thus they wish to find out whether they and other care-givers need to do particular activities to foster infant learning and whether particular toys or other items should be used at certain times in the infant's life for learning to proceed most effectively.

Many of these questions as yet have no definitive answers. Often the experimental and observational evidence that would supply answers is still lacking; the research has not yet been done. In other instances, the outcomes of studies are equivocal; some seem to indicate one kind of answer, and others another kind. But some questions have been answered. For example, it is known from McGraw's twin studies that behaviors that are beyond the maturational abilities of the infant cannot be learned or at least take a very long time to learn. It is also known that reinforcement works with infants, but that contrary to many animals, infants be-come bored and cease to work for reinforcement once they have solved the particular problem posed. It is known that while infants can be conditioned, this process generally takes much longer than it does with older children, suggesting that infants learn more slowly. We shall deal with some of these answers in more detail further along in this chapter.

Learning and Conditioning

In order to understand the various ways in which infant learning has been studied, let us briefly turn to a consideration of the relationship between learning and conditioning and the two types of conditioning studies that can be done to see if learning has taken place.

STUDYING LEARNING BY STUDYING CONDITIONING

One cannot know directly that an individual has learned something, since one cannot climb inside the brain and see the altered or enhanced neural connections. Thus it can only indirectly be inferred that learning has taken place if the individual shows a behavior that was not there before (and cannot be attributed to other factors such as maturation), no longer produces a previously used behavior, or shows a change or modification of an existing behavior. Therefore, learning is often studied by means of **conditioning,** the process whereby an association is established between two environmental events or between a behavior and an environmental event. This association results in the behavioral changes just cited. Thus it can be reasoned backward and decided that since the behavior has changed, the association has been made, and therefore learning has taken place. Conditioning is a less general term than learning, since learning can occur in other ways than the establishment of such associations. For example, problem solving is a higher form of learning. It consists of combining several previously learned behaviors in a new and unique manner in order to attain a goal that was unattainable before. Observational learning, which involves observing the behavior of others and then producing that behavior or one similar to it in an appropriate situation is also a form of learning. It is usually not considered a form of conditioning, however, but a form of social learning.

THE TWO TYPES OF CONDITIONING

There are two types of conditioning, classical and operant. **Classical** conditioning involves learning an association between two previously unrelated events, for example, Anne's learning to relate a woman in white to an injection. **Operant conditioning** entails forming such an association between a behavior of the individual and a subsequent environmental event called a reinforcer. Thus infants learn to cry when hungry, since such crying usually brings someone with food, a very powerful reinforcer. We shall consider both kinds of conditioning in greater detail a bit farther on.

STIMULUS GENERALIZATION AND DISCRIMINATION

Stimulus generalization and discrimination among stimuli can occur as part of either classical or operant conditioning. Stimulus generalization refers to the fact that, once a response has been learned to a particular stimulus, it will probably be made to a similar one as well. My daughter Anne's reaction to the waitresses in their white dresses is an example. Having associated the pain of an in-

jection with the white-clad nurse, she generalized her negative reaction to others in similar clothing. Most of the time stimulus generalization is a useful and convenient response, for it enables individuals to react to a somewhat new situation or event in a way they have already learned. Therefore, they do not need to learn a brand-new response for each situation they encounter.

Discrimination is the process by which the individual corrects for overgeneralizing in situations in which stimulus generalization is not useful because the differences between the stimuli are important. For example, the child who has learned to call any large four-legged animal standing in a pasture "cow," if confronted by a horse in a pasture, must learn to discriminate between cows and horses. In the process of doing so, the child learns a new concept or category, as well as the name or label, for the new animal.

Classical Conditioning

EXPLANATION

Classical conditioning began to be studied systematically by the Russian physiologist Ivan Pavlov (1927), who discovered the phenomenon early in this century. It involves pairing an existing environmental event or stimulus (the **unconditional stimulus,** or UCS), which in nature frequently results in a response (the **unconditional response,** or UCR), with a new stimulus (the **conditional stimulus,** or CS), which does not evoke such a response or evokes it only infrequently. Over time, the individual associates the two stimuli. Then when the CS alone is presented he or she responds by emitting the **conditional response,** or CR, which is quite similar to the UCR. In order for classical conditioning to take place, the CS has to be presented just

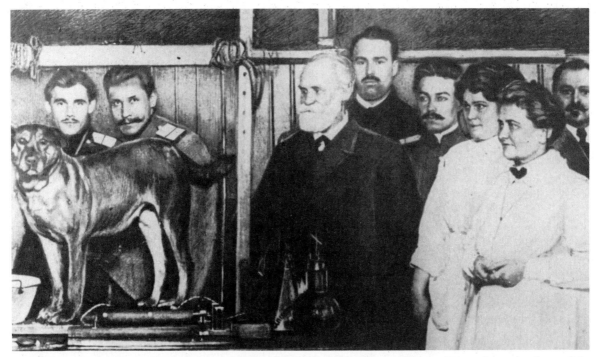

Ivan Pavlov (1849–1936) is shown here in his laboratory in the early 1900s with some of his assistants and one of the dogs used in the experiments that demonstrated classical conditioning.

before the UCS in repeated paired trials. Eventually, the CS alone will evoke the response. Unless the two stimuli are presented together, however, thereafter, at least once in a while, the CR will eventually fade out. It is usual to say that conditioning, or learning, has occurred when the CS results in the CR with greater frequency than before conditioning or training was begun. (For a schematic presentation of classical conditioning, see figure on page 285.)

A good example of a classical conditioning experiment is Pavlov's experiment with a dog. He found that the dog began salivating as soon as food was put in its mouth. Salivation is an UCR, one that occurs naturally in the dog (as well as the human) when food is tasted. Then Pavlov began to ring a bell just prior to putting food in the dog's mouth. Over time, the dog became conditioned to the bell, that is, began to salivate at the sound of the bell, even before the food was introduced. Eventually, the sound of the bell alone produced salivation. Every so often, however, Pavlov still had to pair offering the food with ringing the bell, or salivating to the bell would decline and eventually disappear.

Classical conditioning has limited applicability, since it can only be used in a situation in which a response to a stimulus (i.e. an association) already exists. Classical conditioning is used to induce the individual to produce this response to a new, previously neutral stimulus. The most usual preexisting associations are reflex activities.

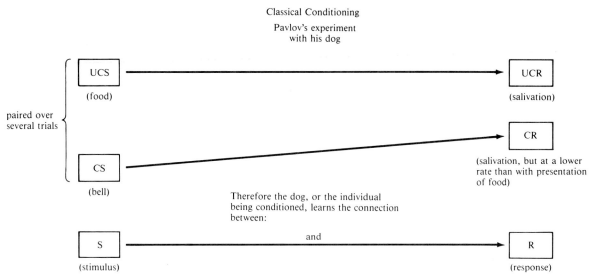

Classical conditioning shown schematically. The example here involves Pavlov's original experiment with a dog and the presentation of food.

STUDIES WITH INFANTS

Scientists have studied classical conditioning in infants because they wished to determine if newborns were already able to make the associations needed to be conditioned to respond to certain stimuli. If newborns could not, then at what ages would infants begin to show such learning? Would infants be conditioned more easily than others, since their minds presumably were not yet filled with previously learned associations? Finally, would certain associations be easier for infants to form than others?

Except for a few early studies in the United States in the 1920s and 1930s, most of the classical conditioning studies with infants up till the 1960s were done in the Soviet Union and elsewhere in Eastern Europe. Since the 1960s more such studies have been done in North America, but the number is still not great; for example, only one was reported for the period 1976 to 1982 (Hirschman, Melamed, & Oliver, 1982).

The Soviet and Eastern European studies generally have concluded that classical conditioning takes place more quickly as infants become older. The North American studies do not seem to agree with this finding, and so the question of whether classical conditionability increases with age is still open. However, as will be discussed later, increasing age does help in these studies, as infant memory improves, as maturation of the nervous system and motor areas enables the child to perform more behaviors, and as state assumes a less important role. An excellent review of classical conditioning theory and the methodology of studies done with infants in the United States and the Soviet Union in the period before 1976 can be found in an article by H. E. Fitzgerald and Y. Brackbill (1976).

PROBLEMS ASSOCIATED WITH STUDYING INFANT CONDITIONING

The Neurological System Fitzgerald and Brackbill (1976) posit that there is an interaction between the CS being used and the portion of the neurological system that governs the modality of the CR to it. Responses governed by the autonomic nervous system appear more easily conditioned to the passage of time. For example, babies used to being fed after three hours will be hungry and cry as the three-hour period comes to an end. Babies who have learned that a puff of air will be blown in their eyes every two seconds learn to blink their eyes a moment before the puff in order to avoid it. But other kinds of responses not governed by the autonomic nervous system such as somatic responses are more susceptible to cutaneous, visual, or auditory stimulation. Thus, there seems to exist some stimulus-response specificity in infancy, outside which it is difficult or impossible to demonstrate conditioning. Therefore experimenters must be careful in using CS appropriate for the CR they are studying.

Memory As we shall discuss in detail subsequently, memory in the young infant is not well developed and prevents the learning of associations if two events occur more than just a moment apart. The CS must precede the UCS, but only by about a second, or the infant will not learn the association. Thus, conditioning in infants is often difficult to demonstrate, not because of inability to learn but because of insufficient memory, which experimenters did not take into account.

Lack of Behaviors Newborn infants have a very limited number of reflex behaviors, and only some of these are amenable to conditioning. Few other behaviors beyond reflexes can be used in classical conditioning with the very young. Before the age of three months, only sucking and head turning can be conditioned with some reliability. Heart rate, which has sometimes been used, yields equivocal results (Hirschman, Melamed, & Oliver, 1982). By contrast, animals that are capable of many voluntary behaviors very early, such as chicks, are much better subjects for classical conditioning.

Orienting If an infant orients to a stimulus, he or she can learn a more complex association and learn it more easily than can an infant who does not orient and hence probably pays less attention to it (Ingram & Fitzgerald, 1974). There is no way, however, to force an infant to orient, and it is often difficult for an experimenter even to know for sure if and when the infant is doing so.

State In addition, infant state is an important variable. Conditioning cannot occur if the infant is asleep, and probably it will not take place if the infant is drowsy or crying (Sameroff & Cavanaugh, 1979). Since state changes, particularly in early infancy, occur so rapidly, classical conditioning of infants is difficult to attempt. By contrast, since operant conditioning relies upon the infant's emission of an initial behavior, the presumption is that the infant will not emit one unless it already is in an appropriate state to do so. Thus state is not quite as crucial a variable in operant as in classical conditioning.

Motivation In both classical and operant conditioning studies, it has often been found that an infant will master a task, that is, learn a particular association or response, and then will stop doing it. This sequence does not appear to be a matter of forgetting but instead seems to be that infants will learn in order to solve a problem (Papoušek & Bernstein, 1969). The infant finds that figuring out the contingencies of a situation provides far more reward than whatever reward is given for performance of the task. Thus building and testing out hypotheses about what is required to do a task are reinforcing, but repetition of the task once mastered is not, even if an external reward is provided, so the infant becomes bored and stops doing it (Bower, 1982).

Effort It may also be that infants do not make some associations simply because they take too much effort, and the young infant has little energy to spare (Rovee-Collier & Lipsitt, 1981). That is, if the effort appears to exceed what is gained from the behavior, the infant does not appear to bother to learn it or at least does not perform it.

Naturalness of a Behavior There seem to be some inherently human behaviors and associations that infants can learn and more unnatural or species-wrong ones that they cannot. For example, smiling in human infants can be used in conditioning, because it is a normally occurring human response. Twisting the buttocks, a response analogous to tail wagging in dogs, cannot be reliably conditioned in the human infant, though tail wagging can in the puppy. It simply is not a usual human behavior.

Crossing Modalities Finally, there is some question whether classical conditioning studies have sometimes been unable to show conditioning not because the infant was unable to learn at all but because the particular learning situation was too difficult. Some studies involved two different sensory modalities, which made the particular task too difficult for the infant (Sameroff, 1971; Sameroff & Cavanaugh, 1979). For example, the UCS may be the taste of a substance, while the CS is a particular tone. Thus the infant has to switch from responding to taste to responding to sound, a change that may be difficult or impossible for a very young infant. Since this type of cross-modal transfer may not be possible for the young infant, experimenters might wrongly conclude that the infant is incapable of learning at all, rather than that learning can occur if the tasks are made less difficult.

For all of these reasons, some researchers doubt whether human infants can be conditioned at all (Millar, 1974) or whether only a small number and kind of behaviors, but not others, are subject to conditioning (Abrahamson, Brackbill, Carpenter, & Fitzgerald, 1970). In addition, some students of behavior change in infants such as A. J. Sameroff (1971, 1972) believe that changes in performance that seem to be the result of conditioning actually are changes resulting from a developmental adaptation of the early reflexes. That is, changes in behavior are more likely to be the result of internal regulation and adaptation of functions rather than of manipulation by the experimenter of external variables.

ISSUES OF DESIGN

A problem that existed with some of the earlier studies of classical conditioning in infancy was the use of very small numbers of infants, often just one. Therefore, the results or lack of them could be due to the idiosyncratic situation of a particular infant and might reveal very little about infants generally.

In addition, control subjects were rarely if ever used in these early studies. This lack made it difficult to say if true conditioning took place, or if pseudoconditioning had produced the behavior.

Pseudoconditioning occurs when an environmental event or stimulus causes a heightened motivational or arousal state in the infant, who then proceeds to emit many behaviors including the one being conditioned. It is difficult to judge whether the infant has learned the required association or is just responding at a heightened level to the situation in general. Pseudoconditioning is usually controlled for in experiments by subjecting control infants to the same environmental events but in random order and determining if they also emit the response.

Therefore, situational circumstances that could have led to misinterpretation of the results of experiments must be carefully considered as the results are evaluated (Wickens & Wickens, 1940). Furthermore, anyone who plans a study of infant conditioning must be careful to control for as many of the problems of infant nature as well as design as is possible.

CLASSICAL CONDITIONING STUDIES

Nevertheless, a number of studies that appear to show classical conditioning in young infants have been reported. The earliest involved the famous case of Albert and the white rat (Watson & Raynor, 1920), in which 11-month-old Albert learned to fear the rat because J. S. Watson sounded a loud noise every time Albert reached for or touched the rat. After a while, Albert cried every time he saw the rat, even after Watson no longer made the noise. He had come to associate the rat with the disagreeable noise. Furthermore, Albert showed stimulus generalization. He seemed afraid and began to cry not only at the appearance of the rat but also when he saw a white rabbit and even a white-bearded Santa Claus.

Mary C. Jones (1924) demonstrated in a study using counterconditioning what could have been done to help Albert overcome his conditioned fear. **Counterconditioning** involves the gradual elimination of a CR by substituting another incompatible CR for it. Peter, a toddler, was brought to her for help because he showed unreasonable fear of a white rabbit. Jones paired the appearance of the rabbit at the far end of a large room with activities that Peter enjoyed, such as playing with a favorite toy or eating ice cream. It is difficult to react with fear and to enjoy ice cream at the same time. Over time Jones was able to bring the rabbit closer, until finally Peter was happily holding a favorite toy in one hand and petting the rabbit with the other. He had learned a new association, that of the rabbit with pleasant activities, to replace the one of rabbit and fear.

Dorothy Marquis (1931) demonstrated that classical conditioning was possible with very young infants, not just with older ones and with toddlers such as Albert and Peter. She conditioned infants who were only two to nine days old to open their mouths at the sound of a buzzer paired with the presentation of the bottle. In her experimental group 8 of the 10 infants learned to open the mouth at the sound of the buzzer alone. Later critics have pointed out that since each infant's bottle contained milk and the baby was allowed to suck after opening the mouth, this was really an operant conditioning experiment with milk as the reinforcer for mouth opening rather than a classical conditioning study pairing the buzzer and mouth opening. Additionally, Marquis did not report what happened with her controls, and therefore the effects of pseudoconditioning cannot be ruled out. That is, the sound of the buzzer could have raised the total activity level of some of the infants, resulting in many behaviors including mouth opening.

In a later study, Marquis (1941) showed

that infants could be conditioned to a particular time interval. She fed one group of infants on a three-hour schedule, and another group on a four-hour schedule. Then she switched each group to the opposite schedule. The former three-hour babies fussed during the last hour before feeding, while the former four-hour babies were difficult to rouse and feed after only three hours. One can speculate that since the passage of time can be used to cue other conditional responses, this may be the manner in which infants learn to adjust to the particular temporal routines of their own families.

L. P. Lipsitt and H. Kaye (1964) also demonstrated classical conditioning with infants less than a week old by pairing a tone with the immediate presentation of a pacifier. A control group also heard the tone and was given a pacifier to suck, but these events occurred in random order rather than as paired occurrences in order to control for pseudoconditioning. Lipsitt and Kaye found that experimental infants began to suck at the tone, while control ones did not.

Lipsitt, Kaye, and T. N. Bosack (1966) then used a narrow tube rather than a pacifier. The tube placed in the mouth of two-to-four-day-olds, delivering a sweet solution for five seconds, served as the UCS, and the tube alone, without the sweet solution, as the CS. A control group again received random presentations of both conditions, to control for pseudoconditioning as well as the reinforcing effect of sucking itself. This study showed that experimental infants increased their sucking to the CS of the tube without sweetener, while the control infants did not. Therefore, the experimental group had evidently learned to associate the tube with the sweet solution.

The experimental evidence seems to indicate that classical conditioning can begin to be used with a limited number of behaviors in infants a few days old. Most other studies of classical conditioning utilizing more complex behaviors cannot be made until both the brain and the physical-motor abilities of the child are sufficiently developed. In addition, experimenters must make sure that they are indeed using classical conditioning and that the CR of the infant is not also being reinforced to yield an operant conditioning situation instead. Furthermore, experimenters need to be absolutely sure that the infant is able to produce the behavior, that it does not involve situations such as cross-modal transfer that may be too complicated, and that the infant's performance will not drop off as a result of boredom. In part because of such problems associated with classical conditioning, recent learning experiments involving infants have been more inclined to use operant conditioning.

Operant Conditioning

EXPLANATION

Many behaviors occur without any stimulus to elicit them. These can be referred to as emitted behaviors since they seem to be produced spontaneously by a particular organism. In the young human infant, such behaviors as waving the arms and kicking the legs seem to be spontaneous.

Operant conditioning has to do with the consequences of an emitted behavior or response, rather than with what may have elicited the response. Contingent upon the emitted behavior of the individual, other stimuli in the environment are made available. How the individual interacts with these stimuli results in changes in the rate of the original response, either raising or lowering its frequency of occurrence. That is, the consequences of a behavior affect its likeli-

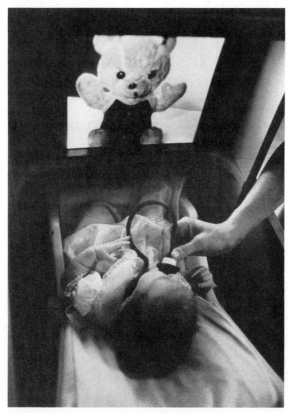

In operant conditioning, the consequences of a behavior determine its rate of repetition. This infant is learning that the rate at which she sucks on the nipple controls the focus of the picture on the screen in front of her. She may be taught that it will appear clearly only if she sucks rapidly, or else that it will do so only if she sucks quite slowly. As experimenters change these conditions or variables, she changes her sucking behavior accordingly.

hood of repetition and hence whether it is learned or not. (See page 291 for a schematic representation of operant conditioning.) This fact was found many years ago by Thorndike (1933), who determined that a behavior was either strengthened or weakened depending upon what effect it produced. That is, incentives or rewards seem to affect learning. Thorndike called this sequence the law of ef-

fect. Skinner (1938) later refined it into the principles of **reinforcement,** which state that any behavior whose consequences are either pleasant (positively reinforcing) or serve to remove pain or discomfort (negatively reinforcing) will most probably be repeated. Conversely, a behavior that results in the removal of pleasure or the imposition of pain will probably not be repeated.

For example, if a person throws a nickel into a Las Vegas slot machine and hits a $25 jackpot, he or she is likely to continue playing the machine. If taking an aspirin reduces the pain of a headache, a person is likely to use aspirin again for the next headache. Conversely, those behaviors resulting in the termination of pleasant conditions or the onset of pain or unpleasant ones (both called punishment) will tend to be repeated less frequently or not at all. If one person's talking results in another's yawning and looking bored, the speaker will stop talking or at least change the subject. If touching a hot stove causes a child pain in its fingers, it will not only jerk its hand away but is unlikely to touch the stove again.

Thus, by selectively reinforcing some behaviors and punishing others, the frequency of the former is increased and that of the latter decreased. In practice, it has been found that with young infants, punishment often does not eliminate a behavior as well as does following it with no consequences at all, a process called extinction. If a behavior is neither rewarded nor punished but instead is ignored, then over time it will cease, or become extinguished. For example, yelling at a child who demands candy may be less effective than ignoring such a demand altogether, since paying attention by yelling may be reinforcing the child while ignoring it gives no reinforcement at all. Furthermore, severe punishment may suppress not only the behavior it is supposed to but also many others,

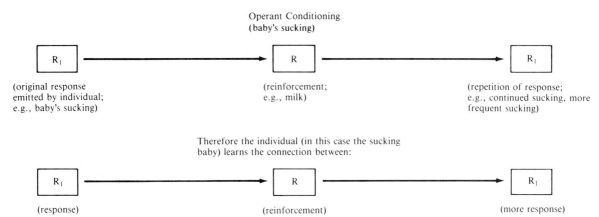

Operant conditioning shown schematically. The example here involves an infant sucking to obtain milk. Reinforcement by the milk results in more sucking.

some of which may be quite useful. Fear of punishment may, however, serve as a basis for the socialization of young children. That is, young children may learn to perform appropriate behaviors partly so as to avoid punishment.

PRIMARY AND SECONDARY REINFORCERS

Students of human learning also distinguish between two types of reinforcers, primary and secondary. Primary reinforcers are rewarding in and of themselves because they satisfy biological needs. Food, water, and the removal of pain are all primary reinforcers. Secondary reinforcers are those whose reinforcing qualities are learned through their being paired with primary reinforcers. For example, since the mother provides food for the baby, that is, is paired with the breast or bottle, she becomes a secondary reinforcer for the baby even when she is not providing food. That is, the presence of the mother becomes reinforcing. Other secondary reinforcers for the infant are adult attention and, later, praise. Money is an important second-

ary reinforcer for most older children and adults, and grades are secondary reinforcers for college students.

Secondary reinforcers in operant conditioning acquire their reinforcing properties from being paired at first with primary reinforcers in a classical conditioning paradigm. However, secondary reinforcers maintain their reinforcing properties even if later they are never paired with the original primary reinforcers. Thus one's mother remains a strong reinforcer even for most adults, many years after she has ceased to be the source of food or reliever of discomfort.

In the 1970s, some students of human learning posited that social reinforcers, such as the adults important in the infant's life, function as primary rather than secondary reinforcers (Yarrow, Rubenstein, & Pederson, 1975). Adult speaking, smiling, and eye contact, therefore, may be reinforcing to the human infant in and of themselves and not just because they are associated with food or the relief of discomfort. This intriguing notion also fits in well with ethological theories about uniquely human behaviors and unique sensitivity to certain species-specific behaviors.

OPERANT CONDITIONING OF INFANTS

Behaviors of the very young infant amenable to operant conditioning include head turning, vocalizing, and sucking. Later, as smiling develops, it too becomes conditionable. Hand movements such as patting, pulling, and grasping, and foot kicking can also be used as the infant matures and demonstrates the ability to perform such behaviors. The frequency, intensity, and pattern of any of these behaviors can be increased or decreased by selective reinforcement. An infant can be taught to turn its head to the sound of a tone, later to smile when a particular display is presented, and perhaps later yet to kick its feet at the sight of a particular toy. The child can learn to discriminate, such as being reinforced for turning its head to the left when seeing a red light and to the right for a green light. The contingencies can be changed, as when the child has been reinforced for turning its head to a bell, but now receives reinforcement only for turning to a buzzer. The ability to make this adjustment demonstrates both stimulus generalization and discrimination. Finally, the amount of reinforcement delivered can be made dependent upon the magnitude or frequency of the child's behavior; for example, more sweet fluid can be delivered for more sucking, or a mobile can be made to move faster, the faster the baby kicks its feet. Experimenters are, of course, less interested in the specific tasks the infant learns than in the infant's ability to learn a new behavior, to adjust to changed contingencies, and to control these contingencies. There is nothing particularly important about actually turning in a particular direction because of a sweet fluid reinforcer or kicking to make a mobile move. What is important is that these reactions provide evidence of the infant's ability to learn.

More recent operant conditioning studies usually have used somewhat larger groups of infants than did the earlier classical conditioning studies. They also have tended either to use control groups or to have the infants act as their own controls by later studying the same infants' performance under conditions in which the contingencies were changed. For example, after the experiment is completed, the reinforcer can be administered noncontingently, that is, unrelated to performance of the behavior, to either the experimental infants at another time, or to a group of controls. This is done to determine if it alone, regardless of when administered, can affect performance of the desired behavior. By such means these studies have more successfully eliminated either heightened arousal level or pseudoconditioning as possible explanations of altered infant behaviors.

SUCKING AND HEAD TURNING

When suitable behaviors are chosen, operant conditioning has been demonstrated in neonates within the first few days. It appears easier for neonates to learn in an operant conditioning situation than in one involving classical conditioning, perhaps because the kinds of memory needed for the two types of conditioning probably differ. This difference will be discussed in more detail in our consideration of memory.

E. R. Siqueland and Lipsitt (1966) used the rooting and sucking reflexes in their study of infant conditioning, since both are present at birth in normal infants. One-day-old babies were touched lightly on one cheek, and when they turned in the direction of the touch, they received sweetened water delivered through a nipple. After the infants had mastered this sequence, the experimenter touched both cheeks in random order, but the reinforcer was given only for turning to the original side. This procedure controlled for mere reflexive head turning at the touch to the cheek. When this behavior was mastered, the experimenters introduced two auditory stimuli, a bell and a buzzer. Now the babies were trained to turn to one side at the sound of the bell, and to the other at the sound of the buzzer; only turns in the appropriate direction for each stimulus received reinforcement. When the babies had learned this behavior, the contingencies were reversed: the bell side now became the buzzer side. Most of the infants were able to master this reversal as well. After 30 trials, the experimental babies did about 2 ½ times as well in appropriate head turning as did a group of controls who had been exposed to all the same stimuli but in a random fashion.

Sucking on a nipple will increase in neonates when a sweetened fluid is delivered through a nipple and decrease when plain water is given (Kobre & Lipsitt, 1972). Sucking itself, even without the reinforcer of a sweet fluid, can be reinforcing. But a rounded nipple is preferred over a blunt one (Lipsitt & Kaye, 1964), and a nipple is preferred over a piece of rubber tubing (Lipsitt & Kaye, 1965). Experience with one, however, will affect behavior toward the other; infants who already had practiced on the nipple sucked more often when switched to the tubing than did those not previously exposed to the nipple.

When a sugared solution is used as the reinforcer, neonates suck more efficiently, having higher overall rates of sucking than for plain water (Bosack, 1973). With the sweet solution, however, there is a lower rate of sucking within bursts, as if the baby were savoring the taste. This lower rate is made up for by sucking longer overall and making fewer pauses. Thus even the young infant already seems well able to control a behavior it can produce in order to maximize the reinforcement delivered.

In neonates the rate of nonnutritive sucking can be altered through operant conditioning to earn reinforcement in another modality. Five three-day-old infants were reinforced for sucking more frequently than their mean sucking behavior at baseline by hearing their own mother's voice, and five others were reinforced in the same manner for sucking less frequently than at baseline (De Caspar & Fifer, 1980). In all instances, those not performing the appropriate behavior heard instead the voice of an unrelated woman. These three-day olds were able to modify their sucking behavior so they would hear their own mother. When the conditions were switched, that is the more frequent suckers now were reinforced for sucking less frequently, 8 of the 10 were successfully able to adapt to the new contingencies. The fact that the infants not only learned the first behavior but were able to make the switch showed that these changes in sucking were really due to conditioning and that slower sucking was not just a generalized reaction to the sound of a voice. Evidently, problems of cross-modal transfer that may exist for the CS and the UCS in classical conditioning do not seem to affect the operant relationship between response and reinforcer produced in different modalities. Parenthetically, it is interesting to note that three-day olds could already distinguish their own mother's voice from that of a stranger. Also, the mother's voice must by the third day already have assumed secondary reinforcing qualities by having been paired with such primary reinforcers as food or the relief of discomfort.

EFFECTS OF INCREASING AGE

In general, it has been shown that while some operant conditioning can occur in infants of all ages, the older an infant is the more easily and quickly does it become conditioned. Maturation obviously seems to play a part in conditionability.

The effect of increased age on performance was demonstrated in a series of studies done by H. Papoušek (1967), a Czech psychologist now working in West Germany. Babies were trained to turn their heads to one side at the sound of a bell. As soon as each baby turned its head, it received milk through a nipple as reinforcement. When babies had mastered this behavior, they were trained to turn to the other side at the sound of a buzzer. Babies were trained during one feeding session a day to perform these activities and were considered adequately trained if they turned their head five successive times without error.

Papoušek found that under these circumstances, all babies, even the youngest, were able to learn the appropriate behaviors, but the time required depended upon the age at which they began training. Babies who began when they were three days old took an average of 18 days to learn the sequence, while babies who began at three months took four days, and five-month-olds mastered it in less than three. Since maturational level obviously seems to affect how quickly infants will learn to perform a rather complex discrimination task, it becomes relevant to determine whether it is more economical for both the infant and researcher (or parent) to begin the learning of tasks somewhat later when learning can occur more efficiently, or whether the mastery of a task is so important that it must be learned early even though that learning takes longer.

Additionally, maturation plays a part in operant conditioning in determining the kinds of behaviors that can be altered. Younger infants are able to engage in fewer activities than older ones. Thus some behaviors that can be successfully conditioned in older infants cannot be in younger ones primarily because the younger ones may not have the necessary physiological maturity.

A good example of how both these factors are involved in everyday life is toilet training. First, there is the question whether early learning to control bowel and bladder function is so important that parents should take an inordinate amount of time to teach it. Many modern parents think not, and therefore postpone toilet training until the child can learn it relatively quickly. Second, there is the question whether the younger infant has the physiological maturity needed to learn this skill. It probably does not, and therefore the parent may be wasting time with early training attempts.

TIMING OF REINFORCEMENT

Studies of older children and adults have shown that reinforcement must occur in some temporal relationship to a response in order for the individual to make the necessary association. That is, a reinforcer must be administered at a time soon after a behavior is emitted to affect the subsequent rate of such a behavior. For example, rewarding a good behavior many weeks after it occurs is unlikely to increase its frequency. However, relatively long delays, as long as 10 seconds (which is a long time in an experimental situation), do not prevent learning in older children and adults; indeed such delay may aid in the retention of the behavior. But infants have trouble learning if reinforcement is even briefly delayed. In infants younger than seven months, a delay of three seconds will prevent learning, while a delay of one to two seconds will result in much slower learning than if reinforcement is immediate (Millar, 1972). Again, this example shows the effects of the interaction of learning and memory in the infant, since the infant does not learn the behavior because it cannot remember rather than because it is incapable of learning.

REINFORCING EFFECTS OF NOVELTY

As infants become a bit older, they also appear to be conditioned more easily to novel or changing stimuli than to familiar or unchanging ones. This fact relates to the idea of moderate discrepancy discussed in the previous chapter as well as to the infant's tendency to become bored once a task has been figured out. When either the mother's face and voice, those of a stranger, or the sight and sound of a new toy were used as the reinforcer for head turning with two-month-old and five-month-old infants, J. Koch (1968) found that either the stranger or the toy worked better as a reinforcer than did the mother. Koch's study also found, in agreement with the results of Papoušek's work, that the older infants were conditioned more rapidly under all three conditions than were the younger ones.

CONTROL OF CONTINGENCIES

Older infants and toddlers are also conditioned more easily if they have some control over the contingencies of reinforcement, that is, if their response leads not only to the appearance of the reinforcer but also if its degree or quality affects the amount or type of reinforcer produced. For example, C. K. Rovee and D. T. Rovee (1969) demonstrated that if the speed of rotation of an overhead mobile depended upon the speed of an infant's kicking, the infant learned to kick quickly or slowly alternatively in order to alter the speed of motion of the mobile. Similarly, when head movement was linked to movement of the mobile, infants who controlled the mobile's movements by moving their heads looked more at the moving mobile than did controls who were exposed to moving mobiles whose motion they could not influence (Watson & Ramey, 1972). When sucking was used to bring a picture into focus and maintain it there, infants quickly figured out the minimum amount of sucking necessary to accomplish this, and would not suck more than the minimum amount (Siqueland & De Lucia, 1969). One-year olds were conditioned easily if their responses brought forth an interesting display (Lipsitt, Pederson, & De Lucia, 1966). Thus the responsiveness of the environment to actions of the infant, rather than the amount or type of reinforcement used, seems to be the more critical variable in infant learning (Watson, 1971). If the infant finds it has no control or if the opportunity to learn such control over the environment is not available, the infant may lose interest in learning. This latter situation probably exists in institutions in which infants receive little adult attention, and it may also obtain in some overcrowded and problem-filled low-income homes.

IMPLICATIONS

The infant learns from operant conditioning situations that there is predictability in its world. Particular actions bring about expected results. The infant learns to relate its own actions to environmental events and learns cause and effect relationships. With developing memory, the infant expects certain events to take place and certain predictable outcomes to follow. For this reason, the infant will learn more easily if it perceives itself as having some control over the situation instead of being exposed to random events. This is an important fact for parents and other adults to recognize. They must make sure that the infant is given the opportunity for control and also that their responses to the infant's behaviors are relatively regular and predictable.

It may be concluded that operant conditioning plays a more important part in infant learning, particularly with younger infants, than does classical conditioning. Since much operant learning takes place in social situations, one of the most important aspects of such learning is that the infant begins to understand that its own behaviors can have some influence not only upon the nonhuman environment but more importantly upon the behaviors of other people. Thus the infant learns about predictable consequences of behavior as well as about the degree of control it can exercise upon the environment.

Social Learning

While traditional learning theory has dealt with externally formed associations and externally administered reinforcers, social-learning theory emphasizes the importance of vicarious, symbolic, and self-regulatory mechanisms in the individual to produce learned behaviors (Bandura, 1977). Recent social-learning theory, especially as propounded by Bandura, represents a rapprochement between mechanistic learning theory and cognitive theories of intellectual development, since it recognizes the importance of internal cognitive and motivational variables in determining behavior. Modern social-learning theorists believe that many human behaviors are learned through vicarious reinforcement, when someone else is seen being reinforced for a particular behavior. Other behaviors are learned through the symbolic internalization of observed behaviors for later adaptive use and through the process of self-reinforcement (Bandura 1971, 1972, 1978).

VICARIOUS REINFORCEMENT

As the infant observes what results from the behavior of others, it learns what to expect from performing itself a similar behavior in a similar situation. This observational learning is especially useful in situations in which the contingencies cannot otherwise be clearly ascertained. That is true in most social situations, which are highly susceptible to cultural determination. In addition, by observing the reactions of others to various kinds of reinforcers, the infant learns what kinds of reinforcers, particularly secondary ones, are to be interpreted as rewards and what kinds as punishments. Finally, the infant can learn about hazards in the environment, such as the consequences of falling from high places or touching hot objects, by observing what happens to other people in those situations without having to try them all out for itself.

MODELING

In addition to learning what kinds of responses will be reinforced in what way in certain social situations, infants can learn to perform skilled acts by watching others perform them through **modeling**. This is especially true of motor behaviors. By observing models the infant receives immediate feedback about what behaviors are appropriate to attain a goal. Learning these behaviors through trial and error would be not only much more laborious but in some instances impossible.

Observational learning from models is also important for learning emotional responses. As the infant observes others express emotion in response to certain regularly occurring stimulus situations, it learns to produce these appropriate emotional responses in similar situations. The infant may learn to express fear when it perceives danger or laughter when it perceives incongruity, by watching adults show these responses in such situations.

Observational learning does not, however, involve merely the mimicking of behav-

Social modeling is a powerful and efficient way of learning. By imitating the skilled motor behaviors of these aspiring dancers, the toddler is able to learn some of their steps much more easily and quickly than if she had to practice all by herself. Whether she will grow up to be a dancer is another matter.

iors observed in others. Instead, elements of the observed behaviors of others are organized and adapted into new, individualized patterns of behaviors. These patterns are based not only on information obtained from the model's behavior but also on the particular situation in which the infant finds itself and the infant's own perceived pattern of self-reinforcement.

In early infancy, as soon as imitation becomes possible, modeled behaviors are imitated immediately if at all, since the infant has little memory capacity. For example, there is some evidence that young infants may mimic adult facial expressions (Meltzoff & Moore, 1977; Field, Woodson, Greenberg, & Cohen, 1982). In later infancy, however, a behavior may not be performed immediately upon being modeled by someone else but instead is stored away in symbolic fashion in memory for later retrieval. This symbolically stored behavior is a situationally adapted pattern, not just an association formed through conditioning. It resembles what Piaget has called deferred imitation. Older infants and toddlers can imitate some quite complex behaviors. For example, complex play sequences were successfully imitated by 19-month olds, while younger children, at 12 and 15 months were able to imitate correctly portions of such modeled play sequences (Fenson & Ramsay, 1981).

SELF-REINFORCEMENT

In addition, the individual regulates her or his own activities to a large degree by specifying the level of performance that is acceptable and then reacting to performance by reinforcing or punishing the self. To use an adult example: If a woman decides to lose two pounds this week, diets conscientiously all week, and finds when she step on the scale that she has indeed lost the two pounds, she has a feeling of satisfaction that is her self-reinforcer for dieting. She may even use a material self-reinforcer such as buying herself a new scarf as a reward. Conversely, if she goes off her diet and gains, she will punish herself by telling herself that she is no good, or ugly, or has no will power. Although very young infants may not yet use self-reward or self-punishment, somewhat older ones soon begin to set standards of performance by which to judge themselves. Just watch a baby's disgusted look as it is unable to manipulate a toy the way it wants to or drops something it had wanted to keep holding. Thus self-reinforcement based upon an evaluation of performance and its consequences probably begins quite early as the infant practices skilled behaviors.

The effects of social learning in infancy have not yet been studied by scientists in any organized manner. Thus, the theory can be presented, but studies to show its application cannot. It is unfortunate, since social-learning theory appears to be able to explain many infant behaviors that are otherwise difficult to explain. Experimental evidence is still needed to support the theoretical formulations.

Critical Periods in Infant Learning

It is much debated whether there are critical stages for the acquisition of particular skills in infancy or whether early intellectual development is fairly plastic and skills can be acquired over a broad range of time. We have already discussed the fact that maturational readiness is needed for learning to occur and that in general older infants learn associations more easily and quickly than younger ones.

The **critical-period** concept implies that particular patterns of behavior or thought are learned most effectively at certain times. One extreme view, based upon animal studies of the first few days of life, holds that if not learned at these times of particular sensitivity, certain behaviors might not be learned at all.

At the other extreme, those who believe in the plasticity of early intellectual development point to the lack of relationship between precocious development of some behaviors and the later development of others. For example, children who crawl, creep, or walk early may or may not talk in complete sentences any earlier than those who learn these motor skills later. Furthermore, children are subject to wide differences of cultural and social circumstances and yet develop in specifically human ways, thus indicating that there must be a good deal of flexibility in the timing for learning many behaviors.

Each point of view has some supporting evidence, but none is compelling. For example, studies done by the Harvard Preschool Project (White & Watts, 1973; White 1975) have shown that critical differences between competent and noncompetent children are apparent before age three. B. L. White therefore believes that a critical time for cognitive development in infancy is between 10 and 18 months. During this time span, in which independent locomotion and language develop, the kind of environmental variables provided by adults become crucial. Less competent children, who are exposed to inferior environmental circumstances, according to White remain handicapped for the rest of their intellectual development.

On the other hand, there is also evidence for flexibility, inasmuch as children who lag behind age norms because of cultural or other environmental conditions at one point in development may catch up at some later point. For example, Jerome Kagan (1972) has studied Indian children in the highlands of Guatemala, who because of very restrictive and isolating child-rearing practices lag behind North American children both motorically and cognitively when tested at age one. They appear to catch up, however, during the toddler and preschool periods and appear entirely normal when observed at the end of this time span.

Thus, while additional work needs to be done, it appears that there is no one, narrow, critical point in human learning, analogous to the short period in which the chick can learn to peck or the duckling or gosling to follow its mother. The human mind seems capable of adapting to a variety of cultural and environmental circumstances for learning. The human infant actively seeks intellectual stimulation and in most environments is able to develop cognitive abilities in similar ways and at relatively comparable times. While infancy itself appears to be an important period in the establishment of human learning, there is no narrow time within it at which particular behaviors must be learned if they are to be learned at all. Within reasonable limits, the human mind is flexible and adaptable to many learning situations.

Implications for Parents

Since babies are conditionable to some degree and for some responses from birth on, it is important for parents to realize that their behaviors toward the infant affect the child's subsequent behaviors toward them. That is, the infant learns from interaction with the parent how to make its needs known, how to suck more efficiently, as well as a variety of other motor and social interactive behaviors. Thus parental consistency is important. If the parents' behaviors toward the infant vary greatly, the infant has more difficulty learning what it is to do. In addition, if there is no contingent relationship between the infant's behaviors and what follows from them, the infant is less likely to learn.

Because of the conditionability of infants, some experimenters as well as parents have attempted to enrich the infant's environment in order to enhance or speed up learning. This practice may be useful for infants who otherwise might spend their time in very unstimulating environments such as foundling homes or other institutions. The average middle-class home probably has a sufficiently rich environment to satisfy the growing curiosity of the infant, and the introduction of too many toys and other stimuli may in fact subject the infant to more stimulation than it can profit from. Furthermore, unscrupulous toy manufacturers as well as book authors sometimes try to convince parents that only if they buy such and such expensive toy or follow such and such book of advice can they hope to raise an infant who learns adequately. In truth, many less expensive toys and even household objects are perfectly adequate, and loving, consistent parental care is much more important than following particular "gimmicky" advice.

MEMORY IN INFANCY

Definition

Memory is that mental process whereby an experience is perceived and then stored in the mind and analyzed for eventual retrieval

conceptual framework for the consideration of this topic. We shall follow this method of organization in our subsequent discussion.

Since we have taken an extensive look at conditioning in human infants in the preceding section, we shall not deal much with the role of memory in conditioning. The exception will be studies showing how temporal or spatial displacements affect memory and therefore learning. The particular aspects of memory related to Piagetian ideas about intellectual development will be discussed within the context of Piagetian theory in general in chapter 9. Here we shall consider merely how some of what Piaget has theorized fits into Watson's scheme of the development of short-term and long-term regenerative (or recall) memory. The major portion of our discussion will, therefore, focus on a consideration of what has been learned through habituation and preference studies about the existence and development of infant recognition memory in its short-term and long-term aspects and on the kinds of information that infants appear to use in activating recognition of stimuli.

STUDIES OF RECOGNITION: HABITUATION AND PREFERENCE

Methodology   The most usual ways of studying infant memory involve either habituation or preference, and they generally use visual displays, although occasionally auditory material is used instead. Occasionally cross-modal studies involving vision and another perceptual modality are used. According to Watson (1979), **habituation** involves short-term recognition (or reactive) memory, while preference deals with long-term recognition memory. You may now wish to use your recall memory to remember some of the discussion in chapter 7 involving habituation

and preference studies of visual and auditory perception. While these reveal some interesting information about perception, they also tell some things about the infant's memory. If your long-term recall memory is not too good, you may want to use recognition memory instead and reread those portions of chapter 7.

Familiarization   Habituation and preference both involve the concept of familiarization (Werner & Perlmutter, 1979). In the habituation paradigm previously described, an infant is exposed to a stimulus until it habituates to it, or ceases to respond to it. Then another stimulus is introduced, and if the infant dishabituates, or responds anew, the researcher infers that it has perceived a difference. Habituation thus involves memory, since the infant must remember the previous stimulus long enough to judge whether the new one is the same or different.

Preference studies to determine the existence of memory involve presenting successive paired stimuli for specified time intervals (Fantz, 1964). One of the stimuli remains the same throughout trials, while the other changes from trial to trial. If the infant remembers a stimulus from a previous trial, it should prefer to look at the new or changed one and thus gaze at it for a longer time interval. Preference can also be ascertained by presenting only one stimulus at a time, alternating between one an infant has already seen and a new one. Presumably, in this situation, the infant will fixate longer on a new stimulus than one seen previously. Interestingly, successive and simultaneous comparisons of stimuli by infants often lead to quite different experimental outcomes (Werner & Perlmutter, 1979). The reason is that simultaneous presentations are more sensitive measures of retention after brief familiarization, while successive presentations more accurately measure forgetting. Thus, in instances of partial forgetting, an infant may be able to distinguish a briefly shown and therefore familiar, though partially forgotten, display from an unfamiliar one during a simultaneous presentation, because it recognizes some features of the familiar display. But when the objects are shown sequentially only, the infant may look at the familiar object as much as at the new object, and thus appear to show total forgetting, while in reality only partial forgetting has occurred.

In addition, experiments with infant memory involving habituation or preference may differ from one another in terms of whether the time span during which the infant gazes at a display is controlled either by the experimenter or by the infant. The former entails exposing the infant to a one-second or five-second or some other timed visual display or to a fixed number of trials. The latter allows the infant to determine the length of time used to familiarize itself by timing only from the moment the infant begins to attend to the stimulus and turning off or removing the display only after the infant stops gazing at it. Here too, there appear to be differences in experimental outcomes depending upon which approach is used. For example, in infant-controlled situations, discrimination of the familiar from the new does not change with increasing age, as even young infants can do this task successfully, while in experimenter-controlled situations there appears to be some developmental change.

Habituation Studies of habituation were used first to study perception and only later were adapted to the study of memory as well. They appear to show that neonates can briefly remember a stimulus to which they have become habituated, by showing dishabituation when a new, different stimulus is presented (Fagan, 1970; Friedman, Carpenter, & Nagy, 1970; Friedman & Carpenter, 1971). Since even neonates have this skill, older infants quite obviously also are subject to habituation (Cohen & Gelber, 1975).

Preference In recent years, studies of recognition memory in infants have tended to concentrate on preference rather than habituation. Joseph Fagan III has done a series of studies of visual preference in infants, dealing with human faces in various positions and involving classes of faces as well as abstract geometric figures. These have shown that five-to-six-month-olds could remember a visual display they had seen even over a span of several hours (Fagan, 1970, 1971). They tended to forget, however, if intervening irrelevant stimuli were shown between the two trials. Faces were recognized as such more easily if presented right side up than upside down, and familiar ones were discriminated more easily in the upright condition (Fagan, 1972) by five- and six-month-olds. Four-month-olds could discriminate between the same face in the two orientations but could not discriminate (or at least did not show preference) between different faces in the same orientation. That is, they knew the same face when seen once right side up and once upside down, but they did not differentiate between two different faces both presented right side up. Cohen (1977) used female faces shown to 18- and 24-week-old infants, and found they could not discriminate between those of similar individuals. Among the older infants, memory for photographs of real faces was better than that for line drawings. Thus the more like a real face the display was, the easier it was for the infant to remember. Interestingly, five-to-six-month-old girls appeared to remember slightly better than did boys.

Later experiments by Fagan have studied the infant's growing capacity to form the

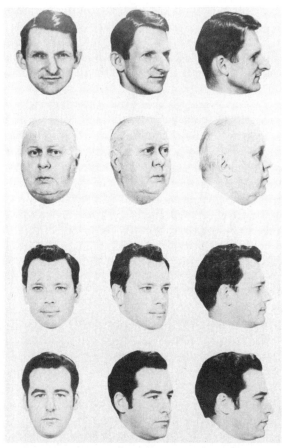

One of the experiments conducted by Joseph Fagan III to test infant memory involved these four series of faces. When familiar or unfamiliar faces in different poses were shown to seven-month-olds, they were usually able to recognize a familiar face, even if they previously had seen it from a different angle. But they were more successful recognizing that two poses of the same face were the same person if the poses had more common elements among them. Thus they had less trouble recognizing the profile picture of the man in the top sequence if they had first seen him in the three-quarters view rather than in the full-face view.

could discriminate between the faces of two different men regardless of whether they saw them full face, in profile, or in half-profile. Cohen (1977) likewise found that by 30 weeks infants could discriminate between similar poses of different people, and recognize as the same dissimilar poses of the same person. Thus by seven months, but not much earlier, infants seem able to recognize the invariant features in the patterns of faces even over changes in orientation.

These studies seem to indicate that at some point prior to seven months but not as early as five months, infants not only can remember a familiar display but can abstract invariant features of the display and thus recognize it as familiar even if presented in an orientation not seen before.

But what is it about a display that helps the infant to remember it when presented with a slightly changed version? Fagan (1978) found that a three-quarters view of a face helped the infant recognize the same face in profile more than did a full-face view, probably because there was more similarity of features between the first two. Thus the kinds of related instances rather than just the sheer number of them seem to determine recognition of displays. This is true not only for displays having inherent meaning such as faces, but also for geometric figures (Fagan 1977, 1978).

These studies by both Fagan (1976, 1977, 1978) and Cohen (1977) appear to be probing not only recognition of familiar objects but to some extent recall memory as well, inasmuch as the infant is classifying or abstracting features and therefore beginning to build concepts. When the infant makes the judgment that a new version of a face or geometric figure never seen before is an instance of an already familiar face or figure, there is more involved than mere recognition of the familiar. The invariant features learned from

concept of a face and to recognize a face as familiar even if seen in a new and unfamiliar pose. Thus Fagan (1976) found that seven-month olds could recognize as the same person different poses of the same face, and they the previous exposure must be remembered, compared to the new instance, and then evaluated on the basis of this comparison.

Obviously, the recognition of the familiar as familiar has implications for the social development of infants. As infants learn to recognize familiar people such as parents and other caregivers and familiar settings such as their own home and to perceive them as different from unfamiliar people and places, they also begin to form attachments to the familiar and to become uneasy with the unfamiliar. We shall deal with these social aspects of recognition memory in greater detail in chapters 11 and 12.

RECALL, OR REGENERATIVE MEMORY

Recall in infancy is difficult to ascertain, both because there is some doubt as to whether this kind of memory is possible before the beginning of symboling and because of the difficulties of designing ways to study it in individuals before they can talk. Few studies, therefore, exist to help evaluate possible instances of infant recall.

Short-Term Recall Short-term recall memory in infancy could be ascertained if it could be demonstrated that the infant is able to imitate or repeat a behavior at some time shortly after the appearance of the behavior in the infant or its modeling by someone else had ceased. The repetitive behaviors evident in the primary and secondary circular reactions described by Piaget (see chapter 9) may be considered examples of such imitations. If Piaget's ideas are correct, then some form of recall memory may exist as early as the second month after birth. Two studies suggests that recall may be present even in the neonate. A. N. Meltzoff and M. K. Moore (1977)

found that neonates would not only imitate such adult facial gestures as tongue protrusion but would also in some instances produce these gestures shortly after the adult had ceased modeling them. T. M. Field, R. Woodson, R. Greenberg, and D. Cohen (1982) demonstrated that neonates could imitate happy, sad, and surprised expressions of adults and that observers who saw the infants but not the adults could guess the expression the infants were imitating at a level far better than chance. These infant behaviors, if they occurred with some delay, could be interpreted as recall. Alternatively, however, it could be that the infant had already begun some portion of the imitation before the adult ceased and merely lagged in producing all of it. Furthermore, attempts at replication of the Meltzoff and Moore study have raised serious questions about its methodology and therefore about its conclusions. Thus it is a somewhat shaky basis for inferring the existence of recall memory in the neonate.

Long-Term Recall Long-term recall memory in infancy can be determined if the child shows even more delayed imitation. According to Piaget, such delayed imitation involves the symbolic encoding of a behavior never attempted by the infant but observed in someone else and its subsequent reproduction at some time quite removed from the earlier occurrence. This process does not happen until the last substage of the sensorimotor period, between 18 and 24 months of age. Before this point, according to Piaget, the child is not capable of the thought processes necessary to abstract a behavior, place it in long-term memory, and reproduce it at a much later time. While Piaget may be correct for long-term memory of a behavior, the Fagan and Cohen studies already mentioned suggest that long-term memory for a concept may appear much earlier, around seven months.

ASSOCIATIVE MEMORY

The presence of associative memory in infancy can be studied by means of classical and operant conditioning experiments. Conditioning depends upon associative memory, inasmuch as the association between the CS and the UCS, or between the response and its reinforcement, must exist in the infant's memory in order for it to emit the learned behavior. Since associations learned through classical conditioning seem to be retained for very long time periods, classical conditioning probably exemplifies long-term associative memory. Conversely, since responses learned through operant conditioning can be changed relatively easily, operant associations may be phenomena of short-term memory. Since operant conditioning seems somewhat easier to accomplish with very young infants than classical conditioning (see the previous section on learning) this classification of operant as involving short-term and classical involving long-term makes sense: one would expect short-term associative memory to develop before long-term associations can be made.

As discussed in the previous section on infant learning, young infants can learn through operant conditioning if responses that they already are able to perform, such as sucking or head turning, are used and if reinforcement is administered immediately. Short-term associative memory appears to be quite fragile for at least the first six months of life, since even a slight delay in the administration of the reinforcer prevents learning from occurring. Thus W. S. Millar (1972) found that a delay of three seconds prevented six-to-seven-month-olds from learning a hand-pulling response. A one-to-two-second delay produced some learning

but less than what occurred with immediate reinforcement. Millar then experimented with a spatial rather than temporal delay (Millar & Schaffer, 1972). Here the child was exposed to three conditions of reinforcement: after the child grasped an attractive container, blinking lights appeared either straight ahead, a little to the side, or far to the side of where the child was sitting. Infants six months old had the same problem with spatial displacement as with the three-second delay, being able to learn under the straight ahead and partial displacement condition but not when the reinforcer was far displaced. Infants of 9 and 12 months learned under all three conditions. Millar concluded that both the longer temporal and the farther spatial displacement involved greater memory capacity than the six-month-olds were able to exhibit. Only with increasing age beyond about eight months can the infant keep in mind an event no longer visible and tie it to a reinforcer that occurs either somewhat later or at a place relatively far removed from the event.

A form of long-term associative memory is measured by the use of the process of reactivation, or saving. This process refers to how a presumably forgotten association can be reactivated or relearned when the infant is briefly reexposed to the conditions under which it was learned. Thus prior learning facilitates relearning, showing the the association must have been stored in some manner in long-term memory. Studies of reactivation have been done primarily by Carolyn Rovee-Collier and her associates. You may remember the conjugate reinforcement studies involving the activation of a mobile through the infant's kicking that were discussed in the section on learning (Rovee & Rovee, 1969). The same mechanism was used for reactivation studies (Rovee-Collier, 1979; Rovee-Collier et al., 1980, Fagen, Yengo, Rovee-Collier,

& Enright, 1981). First, three-month-olds learned that kicking activated a crib mobile. According to Rovee-Collier, three-month-olds usually completely forget this type of an association within eight days if no longer exposed to it. After a two- or four-week delay, some of the infants were shown the moving mobile for three minutes 24 hours before testing, while others did not see it until the time of testing. It was found that this brief exposure, even without the opportunity to practice the behavior, was enough to reactivate the memory. At testing, the infants who had had reactivation successfully reinstated kicking in order to move the mobile. Those infants not exposed to reactivation did not remember and had to relearn completely the behavior.

In addition, reactivation seems to enable infants to remember an earlier learned discrimination between a mobile that responded to kicking and one that did not (Fagen et al., 1981). Infants remembered this discrimination 21 days after exposure if given the three-minute reactivation 24 hours before testing.

There is no question that infants can remember some objects, events, and people from early infancy on. Much early memory seems to be either recognition or association, with the status of early recall memory still somewhat in doubt. Much work still remains to be done for a more complete understanding of the origins and development of this process in the human infant.

Summary

1. Intelligence is a psychological structure that enables the individual to adapt to the environment. It has to do with how knowledge originates and becomes part of this structure.

2. Cognition is the act or process of knowing and is a function of intelligence. It includes learning, memory, symboling, and the higher-order process of problem solving.

3. Both genetic predispositions and environmental variables affect the development of cognition and especially learning. The influence of the genes is strongest early in life, and environmental, especially cultural, variables exert a greater effect with the increasing age of the child.

4. Classical conditioning involves the building of an association between an UCS and a CS so that the individual will respond to the CS. Classical conditioning in infancy is subject to constraints involving infant memory, lack of appropriate behaviors to use in conditioning, variability of infant state, the need for orienting to occur, and other problems resulting from the relative immaturity of the infant's neurological and motoric capabilities. If one can compensate for these constraints, however, infants can be successfully conditioned to respond to a limited number and kind of stimuli.

5. Operant conditioning is based upon the reinforcement, or consequence, that occurs after a behavior is emitted. If the effect is pleasant or satisfying, the likelihood of the repetition of the behavior increases; if not, it decreases. Operant conditioning can be demonstrated somewhat more successfully with younger infants than can classical conditioning. Younger infants, however, become conditioned much more slowly than do older ones. The opportunity to control contingencies of reinforcement seems to enhance learning in older infants.

6. Social learning based on vicarious reinforcement and especially on modeling appears to be important particularly in later infancy and toddlerhood. Few studies of social learning in infancy, however, have been done.

7. Memory in infancy can be divided into reactive memory (similar to recognition), regenerative memory (or recall) and associative memory.

8. Neonates seem to have some brief recognition memory, in that they can recognize an unfamiliar visual display as different from a familiar one. Between five and seven months, infants learn to abstract invariant features from a display so that they can recognize it even in an altered fashion.

9. Recall, except possibly for infant imitation of facial expressions, seems to develop somewhat later than recognition. Long-term recall probably does not occur until late toddlerhood. Associative memory, as demonstrated through the associations needed for conditioning to occur, begins to develop quite early. Short-term associations are learned earlier than long-term ones.

Participatory and Observational Exercises

1. Interview some parents of infants and toddlers. Can they describe any anecdotes that reveal association learning in infants (remember the example of Anne and the waitresses in white uniforms)? Almost all parents have similar anecdotes to tell. Do any of the anecdotes reveal discrimination learning? Have any of the parents used reinforcement and/or punishment in inducing the infant to learn a behavior? Ask them to describe what they have done and how successful they think it was.

2. Try to teach a 4-to-12-month-old to use an unfamiliar toy. Make sure the toy is age-appropriate. Model the use of the toy. Be sure the infant is paying attention and is properly positioned both to watch and to imitate your behavior with the toy and that you are positioned properly as well. Record what happens. If you can do this exercise with several infants of different ages, so much the better. Compare your results among the various in-

fants. Do older infants appear to learn more quickly than younger ones?

3. Try to induce a toddler to do something more frequently by reinforcing each instance of the behavior with a raisin (be sure to have parental permission). In addition, be sure before you begin that the behavior you will reinforce is one the parents don't mind the child showing more of! What happens to the frequency of the behavior over the course of your experiment? Record the frequency of the behavior before you start and after your use of reinforcement for a certain time period or for a certain number of instances of the behavior. Was there a change? How long did it take for the behavior to increase in frequency? Now stop giving out raisins. What does the child do? Describe what happens.

4. Interview parents about instances of social modeling, that is, instances in which their infant or toddler obviously imitated a behavior it observed in someone else. How old was the child? Whom did it imitate? What kind of behavior was imitated? How good was the imitation? How soon after the model produced it did the child imitate the behavior in question?

5. Talk to some adults (parents as well as nonparents) about infant intelligence. Do they believe that infants can think? In what ways do infants show thought or intelligence? Can infants produce intelligent behavior? Can they learn? What kinds of things can they learn? How early in life does learning begin? Do the adults think that intelligence is inborn? How much do they attribute to environmental factors? Are there differences in opinions expressed between parents and nonparents?

6. Observe several older infants and/or toddlers of somewhat different ages. Record the reactions of each child as a new skill emerges and is mastered.

DISCUSSION QUESTIONS

1. Since intelligence seems to have a large hereditary component, should the government have some say in who is allowed to have children and how many, so as to insure as intelligent a citizenry as possible?

2. Since environment also plays a part in intellectual development, should all toddlers be put into some specialized enriched environments such as preschools to further intellectual development and not leave this to chance in the home?

3. Is the use of behavior modification techniques morally acceptable? If so, what safeguards should be used to protect subjects?

Infant Intelligence II: Cognition and the Assessment of Intelligence

PIAGET'S THEORY OF INTELLECTUAL DEVELOPMENT

The major influence on the study of intellectual development in infancy from the structuralist point of view has been that of the Swiss psychologist Jean Piaget. Piaget was trained as a biologist whose early research involved fresh-water mollusks. The terminology he later used to describe psychological structures, functions, and events reveals the influence of this training. But he also read extensively in philosophy particularly in the area of **epistemology,** the branch of philosophy that deals with knowledge and its attainment.

After completing his doctorate in biology, Piaget went to work in Paris in the laboratory of Théophile Simon, the codeveloper with Alfred Binet of the first intelligence test. His work involved standardizing the French version of Cyril Burt's reasoning tasks by asking children to explain various tasks. Piaget found that a pattern existed, related generally to age, in the types of wrong answers given by the children he tested. He also found that the reasons they gave for their answers were based on a kind of logic very different from adult logic. This difference led him to believe that intelligence in children was qualitatively as well as quantitatively different from that in adults. That is, children gave the wrong answers they did and justified them as they did not only because they knew less than adults but because they viewed and understood reality in quite a different way.

Piaget therefore decided that his major interest lay in the field of **genetic epistemology,** the study of how intelligence originated and developed. He returned to his home city of Geneva in 1921 and spent the rest of his life, a period of almost 60 years, studying the development of intelligence in children.

Structure of Intellect

To Piaget, intelligence was inextricably linked to biology, inasmuch as he believed that human intelligence contained within it the most advanced form of all biological structures. As all other biological structures, in turn, interacted with biological functions, so the intellectual structures interacted with a set of psychological functions. To Piaget, intelligence had three aspects: structure, function, and content. See Table 9.1 for the explanation of each and how they interact with each other. Piaget was primarily interested in how the intellectual, or mental, structures, the internal organizational properties underlying thought, developed and how they interacted with and produced intellectual functions such as organization and adaptation. These two intellectual functions he labeled functional invariants, because he thought that even as in biological life adaptation and organization had to exist, so did they for intellectual life.

PIAGET'S INTEREST

The main thrust of Piaget's research and theory building thus has been to discover the structure of intellect. He realized very early that in order to study this structure from its earliest and most primitive level he would have to begin with the study of young infants. Fortunately around the time that he decided this, he and his wife became the parents of three children, and his intensive study of them became the basis of his early investigations of infant intelligence. These studies were later extended to include many more children at various ages throughout infancy and childhood. The major works in which he described the results of his research with infants were *The Origins of Intelligence in Children* (1952), *The Construction of Reality in the*

TABLE 9.1 PIAGET'S THEORY OF INTELLIGENCE

Aspects of Intelligence	Definition	Examples of Components	Change over Time?
Structure	A system of transformations which is self-regulating and relatively stable, through the maintenance of equilibrium (assimilation and accommodation) between functions. But the structure does change as a result of accommodation. Structure can also be defined as organizational properties of thought.	Stages of development	Yes, but slowly
Function	Characteristics of intelligent activity. This activity remains the same over time.	1. Functional invariants: a. organization b. adaptation 1) assimilation 2) accommodation 2. Other scheme-building.	No
Content	Behavioral data or actual events experienced and transferred to thought	Whatever is perceived or thought about	Yes

Child (1954), and *Play, Dreams and Imitation in Childhood* (1951). The dates cited here are of the American publications of the English translations; the original French versions appeared earlier.

ADAPTATION, SCHEME BUILDING, AND ORGANIZATION

Piaget developed the theory that as a result of action upon the environment, the structures of the individual's intellect change and develop. Thus action underlies and leads to thought. Basically, Piaget thought that three major functional processes occurred and interacted in the child in order to produce cognitive growth and alter the structure of the intellect. The first process is the adaptation of the organism to the environment. The second entails the building of inner or mental psychological structures called **schemes** based upon the individual's interaction with external reality. The third process, called organization, is the establishment of higher-order internal cognitive interrelationships between these internal psychological structures. These internal relationships are not exact copies of external reality but instead result from a constant interaction between input from external reality and from the internal structures. They are in a sense the individual's interpretation of reality based upon action.

MATURATION, EQUILIBRIUM, EXPERIENCE AND SOCIAL TRANSMISSION

According to Piaget, several additional basic processes in the individual are necessary for intellectual development to occur. One is the process of maturation, including the growth and development of motor, neurological, and endocrine (or glandular) systems. Another is the process of **equilibrium,** which entails the balancing and regulation of the adaptive and organizational functions. A third is experience, which grows out of action on the environment. There are two kinds of experience, physical and logico-mathematical. The former entails what the child learns about such properties as the weight, color, or shape of objects. The latter involves knowledge acquired from thinking about one's actions, such as realizing that if one has three red balls and three blue balls, the number of each color is equal. Obviously, in the young infant physical experience is much more important. Finally, social transmission, or what the child learns from other people about her or his particular culture and family, is also an important source of intelligence. Several of these processes will now be briefly explained and discussed.

Functions of Intellect

ADAPTATION

Adaptation in the Piagetian sense entails two separate, different, and yet complementary processes—assimilation and accommodation. Let us take a closer look at both and what they mean.

Assimilation   In the process of **assimilation,** external information is taken in and adapted to conform to the individual's already existing mental or intellectual structures. That is, new stimuli and new experiences are interpreted as conforming to previous experience or previously acquired knowledge. A biological example of assimilation is the digestion of food, whereby the various nutrients in the food become assimilated to, or become building blocks of, body organs and tissues. Assimilation in infancy occurs, for example, when a baby who has already learned to grasp a plastic cube or a rattle will use the same grasping motions in reaching for and obtaining a plastic ball. An instance of assimilation in a toddler might be the previously mentioned child who knew

that cows were large animals in pastures and applied the same name to a horse.

Accommodation   In the process of **accommodation,** on the other hand, inner reality, or one's own previous experience, is altered to conform to new information, new environmental input, new interactions. Biologically, the human eye accommodates to varying intensities of light by adjusting the size of the pupil, thereby regulating the amount of light allowed to enter the eye. The infant in our previous example has to adjust

The infant who has learned to grasp an object and bring it to the mouth will assimilate a new object such as this rattle by grasping it and mouthing it in a similar fashion. However, since the shape, size, and weight of the rattle are somewhat different from those of previous toys the infant has encountered, she or he will accommodate or adjust her or his grasping and mouthing to conform to the particular properties of the rattle.

the grasp to conform to the shape of the ball, which differs from that of the cube or rattle. The toddler learns that animals in pastures that can run fast and have flowing manes and tails are called horses, while those that have stockier necks and ropelike tails and that say "moo" are called cows. These two processes, therefore, can also be seen as roughly analogous to stimulus generalization (for assimilation) and discrimination (for accommodation) in a learning paradigm. Piaget applied them more widely, however, than would most learning theorists to include not only changes in behavior but also changes in the underlying structure of the mind, or intellect. Furthermore, he saw the individual as much more actively involved rather than merely subject to changing environmental stimulation, as would most learning theorists.

In the normal individual, these two processes, assimilation and accommodation, always occur together in a reciprocal, interweaving fashion, called **equilibrium** or **equilibration**. This process will be explained in detail a bit farther on.

ORGANIZATION

The function of organization refers to systems of relationships among elements. Any act of intelligence or thinking relates to this total interrelated system and helps to develop more and more complex relationships within it. Organization thus is the function or process whereby experience and knowledge are categorized and sorted out into meaningful segments or wholes that become progressively more complex. It also involves the establishment of higher-order relationships between these factors or systems. Thus, while adaptation involves change, organization involves stability in that the whole system is undergoing a kind of stabilizing pro-

cess whereby all portions of it become more tied to one another.

EQUILIBRIUM BETWEEN FUNCTIONS

Piaget posited that both assimilation and accommodation, and organization and adaptation, exist with each other in a balanced relationship called equilibrium. This concept of equilibrium is important in a consideration of Piaget's theory of intellect. To Piaget, equilibrium is a dynamic, ever-shifting balance between various aspects of intellectual functioning. It might be compared to the balance achieved by a circus tightrope walker, who must constantly readjust and recalibrate his balance as he proceeds along the wire. In the same manner, Piaget saw a constantly shifting balance between the two processes of adaptation—assimilation and accommodation—and between adaptation and organization. In addition, the total organism, the child, exists in a constantly changing equilibrium with the environment. This process of building and maintaining equilibrium, which Piaget termed equilibration, propels the individual to progress and change in relation to the environment. The process of equilibration produces various successive equilibrium states, or stages, that differ from one another in the degree and kind of equilibrium achieved. These states or stages will be discussed in more detail shortly.

Equilibration is, therefore, a self-regulatory process within the child that enables him or her to reach successively higher levels of mental development. Accommodation and assimilation each affect and interact with the other and in turn also interact with organization. These interactions produce a new state of equilibrium, which leads to changes and progress in intellectual functioning. For example, the infant learns both that previously acquired ways of grasping can be used to grasp the plastic ball and that they must be modified or changed somewhat. The resulting new skill represents an equilibrium that enables the child to proceed further and master successively more difficult grasping skills. Thus the individual must continually both reinterpret reality in the light of existing internal structures and change these structures to conform to changing input from external reality. Piaget envisaged this sequence as a continually ongoing, changing, dynamic process that enables the individual to adapt to successively more complex environmental situations.

Scheme

Another important Piagetian concept is that of a scheme, or schema. To Piaget, a scheme is an intellectual structure referring to a particular behavioral action sequence. That is, a scheme consists of an abstraction from an organized pattern of behavior that is frequently repeated. This abstraction, or thought, is part of the mental structure. A scheme involves both the basic intellectual structure underlying any overt actions and the actions used in engaging in a behavior. These actions may be physical activities or mental ones. Schemes are built by the processes of the functions such as accommodation and assimilation acting upon reality. The actions abstracted into a scheme will differ from each other in some small details. For example, each time a baby seizes upon the nipple of a breast or bottle, it may do so in a slightly different manner, depending upon position, degree of hunger, state, or other variables. The resultant sucking scheme is a mental abstraction based upon commonalities across all the various ways that the particular actions or functions, in this instance sucking, are performed.

Piaget has stated that in infancy, schemes are based upon physical, that is, sensorimotor, action. Very early ones are based upon reflex activities such as sucking, which become modified through the processes of assimilation and accommodation. Later on in toddlerhood and early childhood, schemes become increasingly based upon mental activity as the individual develops knowledge from concept formation, reasoning, and symboling, in addition to physical activity. He or she thus begins to interact with external reality in ways such as speaking, thinking, and writing in addition to sensorimotor interaction.

Some recent research has questioned the universality of actions as the basis of intellectual growth in infancy. For example, studies with thalidomide children in Canada have shown that even children who cannot manipulate objects because they have no hands develop the same kinds of schemes about objects at approximately the same times as do normal children (Gouin-Décarie, 1969). These children appear to develop the same concepts as do those who have hands but test them out in different ways than through manipulation.

Similarly, L. B. Cohen (1977) has found that older infants seem able to build visually based concepts without manipulating environmental variables in any way. When 30-week-old infants were shown various female faces in different poses, they were able to generalize to such faces in other orientations or to female faces they had not previously seen. Thus, the concept of sensorimotor action must be broadened to include visual action, that is looking, in addition to physical manipulation. Nevertheless, it appears that for most infants in many situations, physical interaction with the environment provides the usual first experiences upon which later intellectual structures are built.

Theory of Stages

The functional invariants, organization and adaptation, operate continually from birth on. But their processes of equilibration, which serve to build and modify intellectual structures, change in their complexity and in the relative emphasis given to the two functions in the relationship over time. They thus produce relatively distinct and discontinuous structural states or levels called stages. As the kind of equilibrium attained between external reality and the child's developing intellect becomes consolidated at a particular level, the child can move on to the next, more advanced series of equilibrations and hence to a new, more advanced intellectual stage. Piaget posited that these stages, or developmental steps, occurred in an invariant sequence, that is that stage 1 would always precede stage 2, and 2 would precede 3, and so on. However, although this order would result in a chronological sequence, that is, older children would be more likely to be in a more advanced stage than younger ones, the transitions from stage to stage were not tied to any particular chronological age but varied among children based upon the kinds of equilibrations done, which in turn depended to some degree on individual differences and experience. Thus, where ages are mentioned in relation to stages, they are always meant to be regarded as approximate ones and not in any way to represent definite transition times.

Piaget divided children's intellectual development into three broad stages, some of which had several subsidiary portions, or substages. The first stage, lasting from birth to about two years of age, was called the **sensorimotor stage** because the child was seen as acting upon the environment primarily through the use of the senses and motor capacities. This stage was subdivided into six substages, which will be discussed in detail a little farther on. The second stage, stretching from age 2 to about 11, was the stage of concrete operations. It was subdivided into a preparatory substage called preoperational, which lasted from age 2 to about 6 or 7, and the true concrete operational stage, which followed. During this period the child can think concretely but not yet abstractly about reality. Finally, during early adolescence, from ages 11 to 15, the child is in the third stage or the stage of formal operations, during which abstract, hypothetical thinking develops.

Sensorimotor Stage

The basic stage postulated by Piaget in the devleopment of intellect was the sensorimotor stage lasting from birth to about age two. During this stage, which is divided into six substages, the infant begins to interact with the environment, at first merely on a reflexive level, and advances until the beginning of true thinking can be discerned in the last substage. Let us consider these substages in detail.

SUBSTAGE 1: REFLEXES

During this substage, which lasts from birth through the first month, the infant modifies and adapts inborn reflex activities. Reflexes, or such behaviors as sucking, looking, and grasping, become modified through accommodation and assimilation as the infant practices them in interaction with the environment. As accommodation proceeds and the infant practices sucking, the sucking reflex becomes more efficient and more adapted to the particular shape of the mother's or bottle's nipple. The reflex also adjusts to the degree of sucking required to bring in needed nourishment, depending upon both the amount of milk delivered and the hunger state of the infant. The infant advances from passively responding to stimulation by producing the reflex behavior to actively seeking out the sources of stimulation, that is, the conditions under which the activity can be practiced.

Piaget noted some interesting aspects of this first substage. First of all, the infant seems to practice some behaviors even if there appears to be no reward, or reinforcement. For example, an infant will suck on an object such as a pacifier, its thumb, or a corner of a blanket, none of which appease hunger. Why would an infant do so? Piaget explained this behavior by positing that when a structure or scheme is available, there is a tendency in the organism to use or exercise it, that is, to perform a function with it. This process of exercising an available structure is called **functional assimilation,** since a function is being assimilated to the existing scheme. Thus, when the sucking scheme is available, the infant practices it even when no food reinforcement is forthcoming, simply because the scheme is available.

Two other kinds of assimilation, generalizing and recognitory, also begin to function during this earliest substage. Generalizing assimilation, which is similar to stimulus generalization in the learning-theory approach, involves generalizing a scheme or activity from its original object to various others. Thus, the infant's sucking on other objects in addition to the nipple is due to generalizing as well as to functional assimilation, as the infant extends the sucking scheme to other suckable objects. Recognitory assimilation is the first primitive kind of memory, through which the infant when hungry begins to differentiate between suckable objects that appease hunger and other suckable objects that do not. Using recognitory assimilation, the very hungry baby may refuse the

pacifier but accept the breast or bottle. Recognitory assimilation can be compared to an early form of discrimination learning.

During this first substage, the infant as yet has no conception of where the self ends and outside reality begins. It is as yet unaware of what contingencies it can control and which are beyond control. The infant at this time is entirely **egocentric,** or centered upon self. As it passes through subsequent substages by interacting with the environment, this egocentrism declines because the infant learns through experience the boundaries of self vis-a-vis the environment. Thus, for example, the infant learns that crying does not magically bring forth its mother; it merely serves as a signal that usually, but not always, summons her. The infant thus learns which contingencies can be controlled and which are under external control. This decline of egocentrism is called **decentration,** or the process of decentering.

SUBSTAGE 2: PRIMARY CIRCULAR REACTIONS

The second substage, which lasts from the end of the preceding one till about four months, is characterized by **primary circular reactions,** the first acquired adaptations to the environment. That is, the adaptations are now based on more than mere reflex actions. The infant is able to modify actions to some extent based upon the experiences of differing situations. It builds upon the reflex patterns of the previous stage by trying to prolong or repeat interesting results (hence circular reactions) that at first occurred inadvertently as schemes were exercised.

Activities during this period are still centered upon the child's own body; hence the use of the term primary for this substage. The infant engages in repeating such interesting activities for their own sake and not yet as means toward ends; that is, behavior is not yet goal-directed.

During this substage, the infant begins to show curiosity, which impels exploration, particularly visual exploration. Studies of visual perception that show the infant's growing attention to novelty and later to discrepancy support this Piagetian contention. The ability to distinguish novel stimuli is an indication of the growth of memory. The infant also begins to anticipate the occurrence of particular events from cues given through actions by others. This ability also is indicative of memory. Thus, the baby will anticipate feeding by beginning to make sucking movements and postural adjustments as soon as it is picked up by the mother.

Infants also begin to imitate behaviors, particularly the vocalizations, of others, if they are already able to produce these behaviors. If an adult utters a sound, the baby often attempts to continue or to repeat it, an example of a circular reaction that begins from without the baby but is then repeated by the baby. The child does so because it still cannot distinguish what originated from self and what from outside self. Some recent research appears to indicate that even neonates can imitate some adult gestures (Meltzoff & Moore, 1977). Other researchers have argued that this study was methodologically flawed and that its results cannot be replicated (Hamm, Russell, & Koepke, 1979; Hayes & Watson, 1979). Therefore, at present it appears that Piaget may have been correct to place the onset of the earliest true imitations in this one-to-four-month period and not earlier.

During this substage the infant also begins to coordinate schemes whose actions are based on separate sense modalities, an activity that Piaget called **reciprocal coordination,** and that others would call sensory integration. A particular object or event is assimilated to more than one scheme. For example, the mother is assimilated to both the looking and the hearing scheme; thus the child will search visually in the direction from which the mother's voice comes. The infant comes to associate particular properties of objects with each other: Mother looks like this and sounds like this and feels like that, and all of these aspects or qualities are part of Mother. As with imitation, some research suggests that cross-modal integration may be present earlier than in this stage. For example, we have already discussed Wertheimer's (1961) experiment in which neonates turned in the direction of a sound. Bower (1982) and Gibson (1969) also believe in a primitive integration of the senses from birth on, which would thus be present in Piaget's first substage. Obviously, this topic also needs further investigation before one can decide with certainty when integration begins.

SUBSTAGE 3: SECONDARY CIRCULAR REACTIONS

The third substage, which extends from about 4 months to about 8 to 10 months, is characterized by **secondary circular reactions.** The word secondary refers to the fact that the infant now begins to involve objects and events in the environment in activities, while the term circular reactions again indicates that the infant is repeating or prolonging behaviors that lead to interesting results. Since the activities now involve environmental results, they can be interpreted as being goal-directed and intentional, that is, as having ends beyond themselves. The child is able to discriminate between his or her own actions and the environmental results of these actions, that is, between the means and their ends. He or she can thus begin to anticipate the effects of his or her own behavior.

As they pass from one substage of the sensorimotor stage to the next, infants change in the way they interact with objects. This infant, who is in the third substage, tries out all available schemes in sequence on the book he or she is playing with, such as turning the pages and dropping it. Later, during substage 4, the infant may combine another previously learned scheme such as pushing with dropping, and perform the two as one coordinated activity. Later yet, in substage 5, he or she may experiment with all the possible different ways of dropping or throwing the book.

The actions during this period focus upon the infant's manipulation of objects. When a new toy or other object is offered, the child tries out on it all available schemes such as grasping, banging, mouthing, dropping, and shaking. If one of these actions produces a satisfactory or interesting result, the child will repeat the action in order to attain the result again. Piaget used as an example his son Laurent's discovery that when he waved his arm, a rattle attached to the crib rail began to shake and make a sound. Delighted with this fortuitous result, Laurent began to wave his arm systematically to keep the rattle moving and making noise. Not only did he keep on waving his arm, but he also waved it just enough to keep the rattle moving, and no more. To Piaget it was apparent that the infant had learned the connection between his own activity and the environmental effect and had accommodated his actions to produce the most efficient results with the least effort.

During this substage, the child can produce variations of the circular reactions that could not be produced before. One such is the deferred circular reaction, in which the child will begin an activity involving an object, lay it aside, and return later to finish the activity. Another is the abbreviated scheme, or abbreviated circular reaction, which consists of an abbreviated, sketchy version of a behavior that is used when the child glimpses the object on or with which the action is usually performed. For example, a child may shake her or his empty hand in a characteristic manner when seeing a rattle that is usually shaken with such a hand movement. Both of these activities testify to the increasing span of the child's memory. The abbreviated scheme is particularly impressive in regard to the child's developing memory capacity, since he or she must recognize the object and recall the action or meaning associated with it in order to produce such a scheme.

While Piaget thought that the child's development throughout the sensorimotor period would occur in much the same way regardless of cultural or social environmental input because of the basic biological determination of early behavior (that is, the work of the functional invariants and the process of maturation), some of his followers think that this is true only through the first two substages. Thus, J. McV. Hunt (1961) and Burton White (1975) argue that during substage 3, or secondary circular reactions, the child's intellectual development begins to reflect differential environmental opportunities for learning based upon sociocultural variables.

They contend that since the actions in the first two substages involve reflex activities and activities centering upon the infant's own body, any physically supportive and safe environment probably can provide the needed stimulation. But as the child begins to act on the environment, particularly on the human, social environment during the third substage, different levels and kinds of stimulation can begin to make critical differences in further intellectual growth. These differences become more pronounced as children become older and advance further through the various developmental stages.

As we have already discussed in the previous chapter in considering critical periods for learning, some support for this contention can be derived from the Harvard Preschool Project studies (White & Watts, 1973; White, 1978), which show differential intellectual effects on children related to differing parenting styles during the second half of the first year. Intelligence test scores from multiple testings also typically show greater divergence between children with increasing age, which could result from environmental effects. Other studies, however, such as those of Jerome Kagan (1972) with Guatemalan infants and those of institutionalized children done by Wayne Dennis (1960; Dennis & Najarian, 1957), seem to show that early intellectual deficits can be compensated for at later times and lead to essentially normal outcomes in children. Again, the evidence is not as yet compelling for either view.

SUBSTAGE 4: COORDINATION OF SECONDARY CIRCULAR REACTIONS

The fourth substage, marked by **coordination of secondary circular reaction,** begins at 8 to 10 months as the child puts together two secondary circular reactions, or schemes, to form a new scheme that it could not produce before. Furthermore, the child has a final end or goal in mind before it begins to produce the combination. Thus, behavior is no longer directed solely toward prolonging or reinstating an interesting occurrence, toward reaching an immediate goal or end. Instead it is pursuing an end that is not directly attainable using any one available scheme but that can be attained through a coordinated combination of two schemes.

This ability implies that the child must do problem solving that combines several partial solutions to derive a combined one that will work, rather than merely applying those solutions that have already been learned. At this time, accommodation becomes more important than assimilation, for problem solving involves adjustment of behaviors to environmental realities. Assimilation is still involved, however, in the generalization of the action of these combined new schemes on different objects and events from those for which they were originally developed.

Piaget describes an interesting example of the coordination of two such circular reactions. One of his little daughters knew how to grasp objects and also how to pull on objects but had never done both together. Piaget provided an attractive cigarette case that was too far away to grasp but that had a string attached to it whose end was near the child. His daughter pulled on the string until the cigarette case was close enough to grasp and then seized it, neatly solving the problem and attaining the desired end.

Coordinated secondary circular reactions include such behaviors as putting objects into receptacles and dumping them back out, dropping and retrieving objects, and imitating new activities performed by others. While previous imitation involved only those behaviors the child already was capable of performing, imitation at this stage involves learning behaviors that are somewhat new though still relatively similar to previously learned ones. In addition, the child has developed an awareness of physical relationships in space. When an obstacle comes between the child and a goal, he or she knows that the obstacle will have to be moved or else he or she will have to move or reach around the obstacle to attain the goal.

The child also has developed an awareness that just as her or his own actions can affect objects and people, so can those of others. The child will move the adult's hand to the proper place to enable the adult to grasp an object or will push the adult to get him or her to move aside. Through these actions the child begins to acquire the ability to use the help of the adult in attaining goals and solving problems effectively. A striking difference begins to develop between children who have ready access to adults, and therefore become very adept at such skills, and those with minimal adult contact as a result of institutionalization or disrupted environmental circumstances, who remain ineffective in their use of adults in problem solving and goal attainment.

The child in substage 4 is also able to remember events quite clearly and therefore to anticipate their recurrence based upon minimal cues. For example, the child who hears the sound of a car in the driveway will look expectantly at the front door, knowing from memory of other such events that the sound signifies the return of father or mother.

SUBSTAGE 5: TERTIARY CIRCULAR REACTIONS

In the 12-to-18-month period the toddler passes through substage 5, that of **tertiary circular reactions,** in which entirely new means of doing things are acquired through active experimentation. The child is interested in novelty for its own sake. When a new activity is discovered, the toddler will repeat the activity but not in the same way as before. Now there is repetition with purposeful variations based upon different accommodations to the environment. For example, having discovered that a particular object makes an interesting noise when dropped on the floor, the toddler will proceed to drop it from close to the floor and from high overhead, will hurl it down, and will let it slowly roll off the fingers, all to discover what differences of sound will result from these various ways of dropping. Thus the stage is characterized by an initial experiment and then additional circular reactions based upon but differing from the initial one; hence the term tertiary (third-order) circular reactions.

The child now builds entirely new schemes, not just those based upon combinations of already learned ones as in the previous substage. Completely new problems, whose solution does not derive from two partial ones already known, can, therefore, be solved. The solutions, however, are still arrived at through physical activity. Because during this time toddlers begin to walk and, therefore, can interact with many more things in the environment, they develop a much better idea of the relationships of various objects in space to one another and to themselves as also located and moving in space. Children also develop improved understanding of such physical properties as weight, balance, grouping, and the relationships between containers and the objects within them. They know which objects are hard and which are soft, which ones are heavy and which light, which ones bounce, and which ones can break.

Improved recall memory enables a toddler to develop a general sense of time sequences, knowing, for example, that naptime occurs after lunch and that Daddy comes home from work just before dinner time. The toddler also is able to imitate behaviors that are quite different from any previous ones. A totally new behavior may be produced after the child has observed someone else perform it just once. Social-learning theorists would say that social modeling becomes particularly important.

A major hallmark of this substage is curiosity. The child wants to find out about everything through active exploration. In addition, with the development of language, as soon as the child can ask rudimentary questions, requests for information begin to come thick and fast.

SUBSTAGE 6: BEGINNING OF THOUGHT

The sixth substage, from about 18 months to two years, is a transitional one between the sensorimotor stage and the stage of concrete operations and is marked by the **invention of new means through mental representations,** or the beginning of true thought. The child now discovers new ways to solve problems through the use of mental images. She or he no longer needs to act out physical schemes in solving problems and to proceed by phys-

During the last sensorimotor substage, symbolic play develops. This child is pretending to feed her doll an apple. She knows, of course, that dolls cannot eat, but she enjoys making believe that she is a mother feeding her child.

ical trial and error. Actions become internalized and represented in the mind. Thought precedes action rather than resulting from it. The child thinks a problem through to its solution and only then implements the actions necessary. For example, Piaget described how his daughter saw a ball roll underneath a sofa having a floor-length skirt. She immediately and correctly went to the place behind the sofa to which the ball had rolled in order to retrieve it. She had mentally figured out how and where the ball rolled and did not have to find it by trial and error.

Thus, the child can now begin to divorce thinking from ongoing here-and-now activity and begin to think in images and symbols dealing with the past and future and with people, objects, and events that are either present or absent. The beginning of the use of mental imagery and symbols in thought marks the transition from sensorimotor to conceptual intelligence.

The toddler in this stage can infer caus-

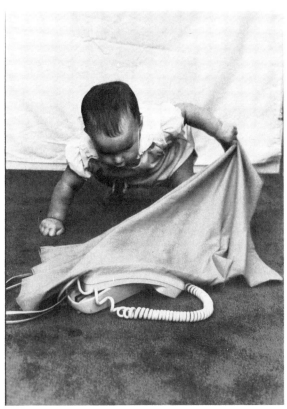

Development of the object concept. When an object is hidden from view, the young infant will behave as if the object had ceased to exist. Later, she is able successfully to retrieve a partially hidden object. After about eight months, even a totally hidden object is remembered and found successfully, as this infant is doing with the hidden telephone.

given the opportunity to watch as it is being hidden.

After about eight months, the child can begin to retrieve a totally hidden object. But he or she cannot yet account for the visible or invisible displacement of a hidden object. Thus, having successfully retrieved a rattle hidden under cloth A, the child will continue to seek it under cloth A even if he or she has watched the experimenter move the rattle from under cloth A to under cloth B. The

more experience the child has in finding the hidden object in its original hiding place, the more likely he or she is to continue to search for the object there (Flavell, 1977). The most reasonable explanation of this behavior is that while the baby now knows that a hidden object does not cease to exist, he or she cannot yet conceive of the object having an independent existence from the cloth covering it. The baby sees that the object is moved from under the cloth with which it is associated, but the intellect does not acknowledge the move.

By the time the child enters the substage of tertiary circular reactions, she or he begins to look for a hidden object in the place where it was most recently hidden, rather than in its usual hiding place. The object has assumed a permanence of its own, quite divorced from the place in which it usually was found or the covering or screen used to hide it. In the two-cloth problem, one-year-olds (and some children as young as 10 months) will search for and find the object under cloth B if they have watched it being moved from under cloth A. However, the child cannot yet account for an unseen displacement. If the object is moved while the child cannot see it, the child will not look under cloth B even if she or he has already searched under A and found that the object is not there. Similarly, if the experimenter has two cups, hides an object under one of them, and then moves the cups to each other's places, the child will search by the location at which the object was hidden, rather than under the cup where it was placed. Some researchers question whether the results of this last experiment reflect lack of the concept of object permanence or whether the child is reacting merely to spatial cues.

If other cues given the child are quite distinct, however, for example, if the two cups are of different colors, the influence of spatial cues diminishes, and infants as young as nine months are sometimes able to solve this problem of displacement in space (Goldfield & Dickerson, 1981). This ability improves greatly over the next seven months, until 16-month-olds solve such a problem correctly most of the time (Cornell, 1981).

During the last substage of the sensorimotor period, children achieve a complete understanding of the identity and permanence of objects. Other aspects of objects, such as transformations involved in changes of shape or of groupings of objects, do not develop until later on in the stage of concrete operations. The big advance made during substage 6 involves the ability to infer invisible displacements of objects. The two-cloth problem with hidden displacement is no problem at all to the substage 6 child. Children can make an organized search for an object that has seemed to disappear, searching for it in all possible locations in an ordered sequence until it is found. They even try the same game on an adult, assuming the role of hider and letting the adult search for the hidden object (Flavell, 1977).

Bower's Explanation of the Development of the Object Concept

Some recent researchers have questioned Piaget's explanations of the development of the object concept. Some question the methods he used. They contend that young infants know more about the nature of objects than Piaget's experiments tend to show and that motor immaturity rather than lack of understanding can account for many of Piaget's results. For example, in the classical Piagetian experiments using cloths to cover objects, it may be that the child knows that the covered object still exists but is motorically not yet skilled enough to move the covering cloth away.

Modern technology that was unavailable to Piaget in the 1920s enables present-day researchers to approach such problems in ways that can make up for the child's lack of motor maturity and test only for cognitive abilities. For example, objects can be made to move on mechanized tracks that enable them to go behind screens and emerge at selective speeds. Apparent objects that are projected by laser beams and that appear to be three-dimensional can be seen by infants wearing special goggles. Objects can appear to change into other objects through the use of mirrors and selective illumination. With such improved experimental methods, some researchers have shown results that often differ radically from Piaget's. Some of their experiments, however, have been unable to be replicated by others, and so their results are still controversial. Much of this work has been done by T. G. R. Bower and his associates (Bower, 1966, 1971; Bower, Broughton & Moore 1970a, 1970b, 1971; Dunkeld & Bower, 1977).

Bower's work questions the infant's understanding of the substance of objects, whether a hidden object continues to exist while hidden, and whether a particular object remains the same through changes of motion and location. We have already considered the first question regarding substance in the discussion of visually directed reaching and the avoidance of looming objects in chapter 7. In summary, these studies (Bower, Broughton, & Moore, 1970a, 1970b) seem to show that infants as young as seven days show surprise during visually directed reaching when they are unable to grasp what looks like a real object but is in fact a virtual object projected to appear three-dimensional. The visual looming experiments (Dunkeld & Bower, 1977) appear to indicate that the young infant has a notion of the solidity of objects as well as of their trajectories. Much controversy still surrounds these studies, however, both because of problems with replicability and because their results may be interpreted differently. The remaining two approaches will be considered in detail below.

EXISTENCE OF OBJECTS

Bower disagrees with Piaget's contention that for the young infant a hidden object ceases to exist. Rather, says Bower, the problem lies with the infant's motor inability to pick up the cloth covering the object. He experimented with this problem in two ways. The first experiment (Bower, 1966) involved dropping a screen in front of an object and then removing the screen. If Piaget is correct, the infant should show surprise if the object is still there once the screen is removed. If Bower is correct, the infant should show surprise only if the object is no longer there. Using change of heart rate as the indicator of surprise, Bower found a greater change when the object was not there after the screen was removed. He therefore concluded that the infant knew the object continued to exist even when it was hidden by a screen.

The second experiment involved tracking a moving object that went behind a screen and then reappeared at the other side of the screen (Bower, Broughton, & Moore, 1971). Again, if Piaget is correct, infants should stop tracking when the object goes behind the screen. Instead, Bower found that infants as young as eight weeks would visually anticipate the reappearance of the object at the other side of the screen. Further, Bower demonstrated that this continuation of tracking was not due to motor inability to

stop eye movements, for under other conditions, eight-week-olds could stop tracking when the object disappeared. He therefore concluded that eight-week-olds knew that the disappearing object still existed when hidden by the screen.

CONSTANCY OF OBJECTS

Even though younger infants apparently know that hidden objects still continue to exist, Bower believes that they have immature notions of the constancy of objects through changes in position and movement. He provides evidence that young infants believe that moving objects and objects at rest are not the same and that these infants specify the existence of objects by their motion or their location. Only after 20 weeks can the infant recognize the moving and stationary object as the same on the basis of its perceptual features.

Most of the experiments dealing with these ideas have involved the tracking of moving objects. Bower, J. M. Broughton, and M. K. Moore (1971) arranged an apparatus in which one object, such as a yellow duck, went behind a screen and another one, such as a green frog, emerged at the other side. When this sequence was shown to them, infants younger than 20 weeks would continue to track as though nothing had happened. Those over 20 weeks reacted by looking back to the place of disappearance as if they were seeking some explanation for what had happened. Again, it is not motor immaturity of tracking that is involved. For in a modification of the experiment, in which the same object emerged but either too quickly or on a different trajectory from the one on which it went behind the screen, infants younger than 20 weeks also looked back as if to check on what had occurred. Older infants appeared

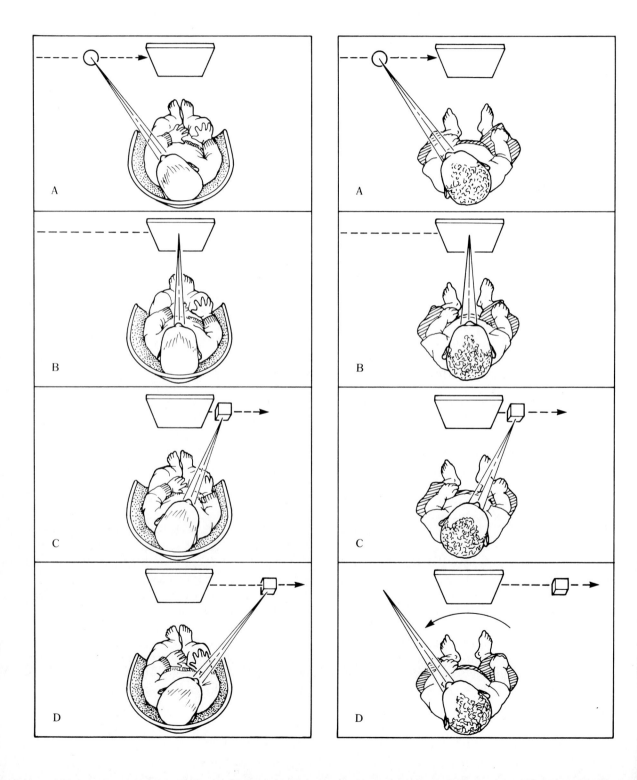

less bothered by changes of speed or trajectory as long as the object remained the same. The younger infant thus defines the identity of a moving object only by movement and does not consider its other features.

Bower demonstrated this difference in another ingenious experiment involving a toy train with flashing lights that moved from side to side and stopped at intervals in front of the seated infant (page 330) (Bower, 1971). The train would move from in front of the child, as in A, to a spot to the right of the child, as in B, and then back as in C. The infant would track the train visually as it moved back and forth. Then the train would move to the left of the infant, as in D, instead of to the right. Nevertheless, infants younger than four months would look to the right, as if expecting the train to be there, though it was quite obviously to their left. According to Bower, the young child's definition of the train was as follows: an object at A, motion, an object at B, motion, an object at A, and so on. There was no place in the child's mental framework for the "new" object at spot D, and it was, therefore, ignored.

Similarly, since the young child thinks an object appearing in several spots is a set of separate objects each defined by its place, it is not bothered by seeing several representations of its mother all talking and gesturing to the child at once. When using a series of mirrors and microphones to produce this effect, Bower (1971) found that younger babies looked and cooed at all the mothers without apparent disturbance.

But around 20 weeks, a drastic change takes place. Infants begin to identify objects by their features rather than by location or motion. The process happens at first for important objects such as the mother and later for less salient ones in the environment. Now place and movement become coordinated, inasmuch as a moving object and the object when it stops are known to be identical. Infants older than four or five months can correctly follow the movement of the train, regardless of whether it goes along the old path or a new one. Similarly, the same object seen at different times in different places is perceived to be the same. Therefore, older infants are disturbed to see multiple representations of their mother at the same time (Bower, 1971) or frogs coming from behind a screen in place of ducks. This identification of objects by their features rather than by place or motion sharply reduces the number of objects the child must contend with in the perceptual and cognitive universe.

Again, however, Bower's results have failed to be replicated by others. G. Gratch (1982) reports a study in which babies of 5, 9, and 16 months were exposed to the reappearance of the same moving object at the other side of a screen or else to a "trick" object that differed greatly from the first object in appearance. According to Bower, all these infants should have shown surprise or discomfiture at the appearance of the trick object; in fact, only the older ones did so and the 5-month-olds did not. This difference suggests that Piaget's notion that the substage 3 child does not remember the wholly hidden object may be more correct than Bower's.

These studies by Bower and his coworkers do represent highly innovative and creative ways of trying to determine the infant's knowledge of objects in spite of the immatur-

Bower's experiment with the object concept in infants. On the left, the younger infant tracks a moving object until it goes behind a screen, then anticipates its reappearance on the other side. When a different object emerges, the infant tracks that as if nothing unusual had occurred. But the older infant, shown on the right, sees the different object emerge and looks back to the place where the original object disappeared as if searching for it. Thus younger infants appear to Bower to react to movement, whereas older infants react to the perceptual features of objects.

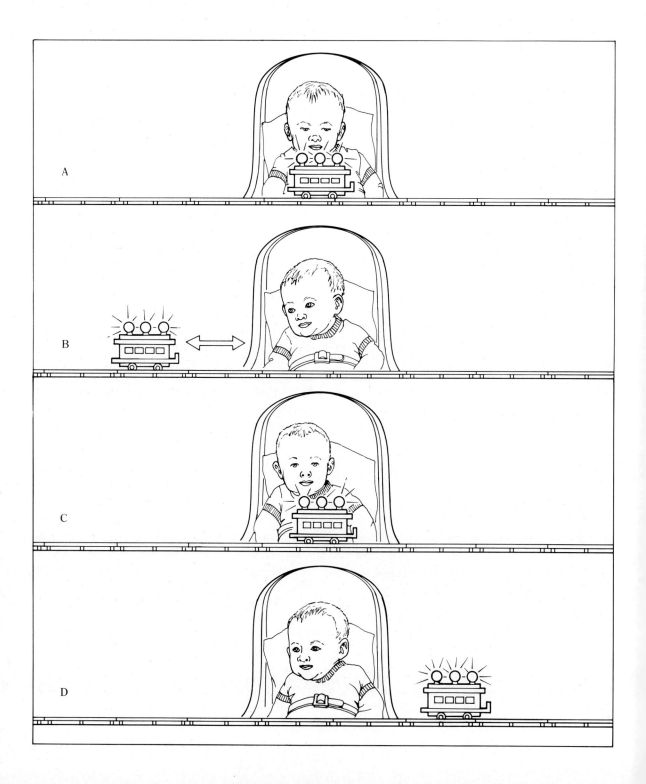

ities of behavior that have hindered previous researchers. The problem of replicability already alluded to does exist. Other researchers have reported that either infants do not perform for them the same behaviors that they did for Bower or their rates of performance are much lower than he has reported, sometimes no better than chance. Therefore, much more study is needed before the scientific community will accept Bower's modifications of Piagetian theory. Nevertheless, these studies raise provocative questions and have made a significant contribution to knowledge of the development of infant intelligence.

Enhancing Sensorimotor Learning

In the past most parents assumed that young infants did little except sleep, eat, and wet their diapers and that therefore the major parental responsibility was physical caregiving. The work of Piaget and his followers has clearly shown, however, that even the young infant is competent at many activities and begins to learn much from interaction with environmental events and people from birth onward. Consequently, in recent years, many parents have become increasingly interested in promoting activities with their infant that will enable the child to learn the most possible during the sensorimotor period.

Several recent books deal wholly with the subject of parental instruction during the sensorimotor period (e.g. Harnick, 1978; Lehane, 1976). We shall deal with the subject only briefly here and mention only a few activities appropriate for each substage. Table

9.2 also lists typical play and activities for each substage.

All during infancy, the child needs to be able to act upon the environment in ways appropriate to the particular stage of development. The infant should be exposed to various environmental objects with which to interact. These need not necessarily be expensive or "educational" toys, for clothespins, pots and pans, cardboard boxes, paper, and other ordinary household objects work equally well.

The young infant in substage 1, for example, should have interesting things to look at, placed to the side of the crib where they can be seen. Some are commercially available, but bright, large pictures cut out of magazines or even such items as newspaper headlines (which offer contour and contrast) are perfectly adequate. Because the infant learns much from touch, holding and cuddling it are also important. So is talking to the infant, for the child learns much from the tone of the parent's voice long before the words are understood.

In substage 2, objects that can be swiped at and grasped should be suspended where they can be reached. These objects can be commercially available suspendable crib toys or safe household objects made of wood, plastic, or metal hung on cloth, leather, or rope. During this substage, as the infant begins to track visually, a mobile that moves in response to air currents in the room is useful. Again, the mobile may be bought or made by parents out of paper cutouts suspended by thread from a wire coat hanger out of reach of the infant. During this substage also, parents can begin to demonstrate the use of ob-

Bower's disappearing train. The infant looks at the train standing straight ahead (condition A), and tracks it when it moves to position B, and back in front again in C. After several repetitions of this sequence, when the train moves to the opposite side as in D, the infant searches for it in its former position, even though it is clearly visible in the new one. Older infants, who no longer perceive objects as existing only in relation to motion, can track the train successfully, no matter in which direction it goes.

TABLE 9.2   SUBSTAGES OF THE SENSORIMOTOR STAGE

Sub-stage	Approx. Ages	Typical Behaviors	Object Concept	Play & Activity
1. Reflexes	0–1 months	Reflex behaviors or schemes practiced (functional assimilation) and modified	No awareness of distinction between self and environment. Infant does not recognize seen objects as real entities, only as images. Briefly looks to spot where an object disappeared.	Sucking, arm waving, visually following
2. Primary Circular Reactions	1–4 months	Reflexes become more coordinated and modified, adapted to environment. Hand to mouth coordination, beginning of eye-hand coordination. Repetition of an interesting behavior involving self. Beginning of curiosity and memory. Imitation of some behaviors of others.	Moving objects and the same objects at rest are perceived as different objects (Bower). Objects seen from different angles are perceived as different ones. Briefly looks to place where object disappeared. Unaware of existence of hidden object.	Sucking, swiping, and grasping, visual tracking and gazing
3. Secondary Circular Reactions	4–8 months	Eye-hand coordination improves. Repetition of interesting behaviors involving self and environment. Beginning of intention, goal-directed behavior. Abbreviated schemes show beginning of memory.	Begins to identify objects by features rather than location or motion. Infant can track trajectory of moving objects, can find partially hidden object, briefly searches for disappearing object.	Grasping objects, bringing them to mouth and mouthing them. Imitation of some adult actions and sounds. Dropping objects. Crumpling paper. Later in this stage infant transfers object from hand to hand.

jects to the baby in a slow and deliberate manner, although the infant will probably not yet be able to imitate any or many such behaviors.

During the four-to-eight-month period, the infant develops much more manual dexterity. Different objects to be handled in various ways should be provided. They may range from plastic or wooden blocks, doughnuts, rattles, and balls, to plastic measuring cups, spoons, and paper to crumple. As the baby begins to crawl and creep later in this substage or on into the next, the house should be baby-proofed and the infant allowed to explore. Baby-proofing includes securing electric outlets, putting away the antique ashtrays that were a wedding gift from Aunt Minnie, placing gates or other restraining devices at the top of open staircases, and removing potentially harmful objects. Incidentally, a recent government report indicated that some gates are dangerous: children have been hung up on them and have suffocated, so one must be sure to purchase a gate designed so this cannot happen and to install and use it properly.

TABLE 9.2   SUBSTAGES OF THE SENSORIMOTOR STAGE *(Continued)*

Sub-stage	Approx. Ages	Typical Behaviors	Object Concept	Play & Activity
4. Coordination of Secondary Circular Reactions	8–12 months	Organization of learning. Coordination of two schemes to reach a solution to a new problem. Infant can keep purpose or goal in mind through a two-step process and can anticipate actions and events. Develops means-ends relationships.	Infant searches for and finds vanished objects if it has seen them being hidden. Can find correct side of bottle to suck. Cannot find sequentially hidden object even if watches it being hidden.	Throws objects. Infant puts smaller objects into cup or box and dumps them out. Pulls at string to attain attached object. Imitates new sounds. Grasps and pokes. Picks up and plays with very small objects.
5. Tertiary Circular Reactions	12–18 months	Toddler tries out different ways of doing things: experiments. Interested in novelty for its own sake and not necessarily to attain a goal. Shows curiosity.	Toddler can find hidden object that is sequentially hidden if it watches. Understands some physical properties of objects: weight, substance, location in space, possible breakability. Toddler is aware of self as an object among others in space.	Drops objects in various ways. Toddler plays with blocks and pours water, macaroni, rice from container.
6. Beginning of Thought	18–24 months	Use of symbolic thought and of language to express thought. Deferred imitation. Toddler is able to invent new solutions by mentally combining schemes or by devising new ones.	Toddler can follow unseen displacement to find hidden object.	Symbolic play, using an object to stand for something else. Pretending. Toddler imitates previously observed behavior. Higher-level block play. Toddler begins to work with puzzles.

Babies like to imitate adult activities; therefore, it is useful to provide the baby with some activity that is similar to that carried on by the adult but that is also safe. For example, while the mother is cooking, the older infant can play with a pan and some spoons in the kitchen. Games involving hiding and finding objects, beginning with partially hidden ones, are useful in learning about object permanence.

During substage 4, at 8 to 12 months, the child becomes increasingly more mobile, as creeping, cruising, and perhaps walking begin. Now baby-proofing is even more important. The child needs, however, to be able to experience as much of the home environment as is safe. Confinement for hours on end in a playpen is not a good idea. One can do very little to act on the environment in a playpen, after throwing out all the toys one's mother put into it. Therefore, while a playpen is useful to confine the baby temporarily, such as when the parent is on the telephone, in the bathroom, or running the washing machine, it is not a good long-term environment for intellectual development.

When the infant learns that hidden objects or people still exist even though unseen, this knowledge can be used in playing games such as that old favorite, peek-a-boo.

The child needs to have objects that can safely be thrown, put into other objects, and manipulated in interesting ways. Balls, clothespins and plastic jars to drop them into, large plastic pop beads, boxes, and some types of cans are all good toys for this stage. Games involving imitation are fun for both parent and baby and teach many activities. Talking to the infant is very important as language use will begin during this time or shortly thereafter. Reading to the infant from a child's book can begin. Babies can learn to look at pictures of animals and objects and to identify them by sound, such as saying "meow" at a picture of a cat.

During the substage of tertiary circular reactions, at 12 to 18 months, toddlers begin both to walk and to talk. There now is much more of the world to explore, both through action and symbolically through language. The adult needs to provide experiences for both. As the toddler is taken for a walk, trees, flowers, stores, houses, and other environmental objects can be pointed out and explained. Colors and sizes of various objects can be noted, as for example, "Look at that very large red truck."

In the home, activities promoting more advanced hand use are useful. Dry macaroni and a jar to put it into, piece by piece, large crayons and sheets of newsprint to draw and scribble on, blocks to stack and to build with, are all good toys for this stage. Books to be read to the child become even more important. And the identification of pictures of objects with real objects they represent is a valuable skill.

During the final sensorimotor substage, at 18 to 24 months, more advanced toys such as puzzles made up of three or four pieces can be introduced. Toddlers enjoy problem-solving activities and symbolic play. Dressing up becomes a favorite activity. Guessing games and imitation are also fun for both parent and child. Water and sand play are good for learning about the qualities of various substances. Crayoning and even some painting can be introduced.

Piaget cautioned against doing too much didactic teaching to hasten the child's passage through the various stages. He thought that in most good home situations, infants and toddlers would be exposed to many experiences from which they could learn the environmental activities needed for intellectual development without much formal instruction. Thus, parents need to balance the provision of interesting activities and objects with the understanding that not every experience must have educational import. Often parents play with an infant or toddler not so much because it may lead to intellectual growth but because it makes the parent feel good or is satisfying to the child. Parents and other adults should not be unnecessarily concerned about having an intellectual goal in mind for everything they do with the infant or toddler.

BRUNER'S INTERPRETATION OF INFANT INTELLIGENCE

Jerome Bruner's main emphasis in the study of cognitive growth in infancy is on the development of motor skills related to problem solving that will later lead to the use of both tools and language. Bruner emphasizes the notion of competence, which consists of skills and their appropriate use. There are two kinds of competence, that which relates to mastery over tools and over spatially and temporally ordered events and that which involves interactions with other people.

According to Bruner (1968, 1973, 1976; Bruner, Olver, & Greenfield, 1967), activity that results in the building of competence is based upon four related processes: intention, skill, attention, and integration. These are roughly comparable to Piaget's functional invariants. Intention deals with the goal, or end point, the child has in mind. Skill is a loosely ordered sequence of acts that with practice increase in their coordination with one another. The child must also attend, that is be able to pay attention simultaneously to both the act itself and the goal toward which the action is to lead. Finally, an activity once learned is integrated into a more complex pattern of activities.

The actions involved in a skilled behavior also involve feedback and the self-correction based upon this feedback. Feedback is composed of three related portions: internal feedback describes the intended action before it is done; actual feedback comes from the nerves, muscles, and sense organs while the activity is being done; and cognitive feedback comes from knowing the results of the activity once it is completed. Because of this feedback during goal-directed behavior, the sequence of acts involved in attaining the goal becomes more efficient over time. In addition, once goals are attained, the acts may be put together into more complex, higher-order actions that are then directed toward more complex goals.

The outcome of these actions is an altered structure, which is an organized set of rules or a mental representation governing the behavior in question. Thus the structure is similar to a Piagetian scheme.

During infancy and toddlerhood, the young child goes through three stages of skill development, which Bruner has called the **enactive, ikonic,** and **symbolic** stages because they are based respectively on action, images, and symbols. Whereas Piaget saw qualitative differences in thought and therefore in action between stages, Bruner believes that behaviors developed in an earlier stage are still functional in any subsequent ones, even though other, higher-order behaviors have also developed. Thus he does not demarcate the stages from each other in quite as specific a manner as did Piaget.

Enactive Stage

The first stage, which encompasses approximately the first year, is called **enactive,** implying action, because Bruner posits that the child learns about the world primarily through physical activity upon objects. The child masters motor control and can do separate, isolated behaviors that are as yet not coordinated. For example, a sucking infant will stop sucking if something interesting comes into view, because it cannot yet coordinate the two activities of sucking and looking. Later, it will alternate the two behaviors, and finally it will be able to coordinate the two and produce them simultaneously. This coordination of two activities is accomplished through a mechanism that Bruner has labeled **place-holding**. This mechanism, which usually begins around four months of age, involves retaining in memory some reduced version of an ongoing or just completed activity while attending to and beginning another activity. Once the child can use place-holding, a smooth series of actions can be performed in place of uncoordinated separate actions performed sequentially. The child begins to put together two or more separate motor behaviors, such as learning to reach, grasp, and hold, to bring objects to the mouth, open the mouth, and suck or mouthe them.

These coordinated activities are put together into goal-directed behaviors designed to attain an objective. This procedure involves eliminating many available motor movements and using only those that lead most directly to the goal. Once limited, movements can be consolidated and mastered in the most efficient manner, a process called **modularization**. Once a skill becomes modularized, it no longer demands the child's undivided attention, and the child can go on to learn a new skill or strategy even while performing the old one. A good example of the modularization of an enactive skill in the adult is driving a car. Most adults do so relatively unconscious of the various detailed sequential steps involved, and they talk to passengers, listen to the radio, or mentally rehearse what they will do when they reach work or school, while safely driving to their destination.

Play, which Bruner describes as the development and practice of a variation on a behavior or action, also develops during the enactive stage. Play involves the matching of means and ends in a nonpurposeful manner. When a child has mastered the use of an object, he or she will proceed to use it in every other possible way. When a new action has been mastered, all sorts of objects will be subjected to this action. Play is thus the opposite of modularization, since it involves increasing rather than decreasing actions. While modularization makes some activities more efficient, play enables the individual to develop new activities and new ways of solving problems. Because of this aspect of play, Bruner believes that it is a vital precursor to the use of tools.

Ikonic Stage

When the infant ceases to see the world merely in a temporally related manner based on action and instead can make a mental map based on spatial relationships and images, it has reached the **ikonic stage**. The name derives from the Greek word ikon, meaning "image." Children usually enter this stage around the age of one year, but the transition from the enactive stage is slow, and some enactive ways of dealing with reality remain throughout life. For example, try to explain to someone how to unscrew a jar lid without using your hands!

The child's perceptions of the physical features of objects are the basis of ikonic thinking. The child focuses on only one perceptual feature, however, such as size, color, motion, or texture, at a time. Furthermore, the child's ikonic thinking is quite egocentric, in that she or he assumes that others have the same perceptions that the child has, even if located elsewhere or perceiving a different aspect of an object. The ability to visualize things in their spatial relationships does, however, aid the child in reaching for and grasping objects, finding hidden objects, reaching for objects behind obstructing barriers, and relating self to environmental variables involving such forces as gravity.

Symbolic Stage

Finally, toward the end of the second year, the child enters the **symbolic stage**. He or she can now think and express through the use of symbols what had been expressed first in actions and later through perceptual imagery. The major symbolic mode of representation is language. Bruner, however, sees the use of tools also as a form of symbolic representation and believes that there are strong cognitive relationships and parallels between language and use of tools. Both entail using two distinct but mutually interacting activities. Use of tools requires one hand to hold an object and the other hand to manipulate a tool to work on the object. Analogously, early language consists of a topic or symbolic object dealt with or held and successive comments about the topic. Given the role of play in the development of use of tools, and the close relationship between use of tools and language, Bruner sees it as no accident that only animals that play, the higher apes and humans, have developed any forms of use of tools and language. Some of the apes use twigs and thorns as tools to obtain food, and a few of them in laboratory settings have been taught the rudiments of symbolic communication through either sign language or plastic chips standing for words. Human children seem to learn both use of tools and language with a minimum of direct teaching by being exposed to environmental opportunity at the appropriate times.

Another important aspect of the symbolic stage involves the child's increasing ability to organize past experience into meaningful categories. This ability is necessary so that the child can use language to describe and recall these categories and need no longer depend on either action or perceptual imagery to deal with new instances of previously experienced matters.

PSYCHOMETRICALLY DERIVED STAGES OF COGNITIVE DEVELOPMENT

Support for the contentions of Piaget and Bruner that the human intellect develops in qualitatively different stages throughout infancy and childhood has been found through **psychometric** research, that is, research based on children's test scores (McCall, Eichorn, & Hogarty, 1977). Mental test data from infancy to age five accumulated on children who participated in the Berkeley Growth Study (Bayley, 1949) were analyzed to determine which mental functions remained stable over time and which ones changed. The analyses showed that there were discontinuities of behavior, indicating changes in the natures of the behaviors, at approximately 2, 8, 13, and 21 months of age. Since these transitions involved qualitative rather than quantitative changes, R. B. McCall and his coworkers thought that they represented transitions between discrete stages of mental development. The behavior changes found in test performance were based primarily on changes in the infant's understanding of the nature of objects.

Stage 1: Birth to Two Months

The infant is extremely responsive to environmental stimuli in stage 1 but does not yet actively explore the environment. It is unaware of any boundary between self and external reality and believes that objects are mere extensions of self. This stage parallels Piaget's first substage and part of his second.

Stage 2: Three to Seven Months

The infant actively explores the environment in stage 2, particularly if exploration results in changes in the object acted upon that the infant can perceive. While the infant begins to have some awareness of external reality as distinguished from self, it is still unable to determine what environmental events it can

control. This stage parallels Piaget's third substage.

Stage 3: Eight to Thirteen Months

In stage 3 the infant imitates the examiner during testing. The infant can distinguish means from ends in acting upon objects and thus realizes that environmental objects exist independently of its own actions. But the infant's understanding is still tied greatly to action. Late in this stage, some words begin to be used, but probably not yet in a symbolic sense. This stage corresponds to Piaget's coordination of circular reactions, or substage 4.

Stage 4: Fourteen to Eighteen Months

During stage 4 the child makes great advances in the use of language both in labeling and categorizing objects and events and in understanding the speech of others. He or she now understands the independence of objects from his or her actions quite well and can begin to associate two events or objects in the environment by developing a spatial map of their relationship without needing to act upon them. This stage corresponds to the Piagetian substage 5, of tertiary circular reactions.

Stage 5: Twenty-One to Twenty-Seven Months

During this last stage the child develops true symbolic relationships. Now he or she can relate objects to one another using conceptual categories, with no need either to act or to determine spatial relationships. Thus the child is mentally manipulating reality. This final stage corresponds to the Piagetian sensorimotor substage 6.

ASSESSMENT OF INFANT INTELLIGENCE

Introduction

The assessment of infant intelligence has concerned researchers for several reasons. First, they have sought to determine whether intelligence is a relatively fixed and stable entity within an individual or whether it changes in kind as well as quantity over portions of the life cycle. In other words, to what extent are individual differences in intelligence stable over time? Second, if intelligence is viewed not as a unitary entity but as composed of various factors, researchers have tried to determine what elements appear at what stages in the development of the individual and how they can be reliably measured. Finally, researchers have asked whether intelligence is indeed stable and therefore largely determined by heredity or whether it is subject to modification through environmental intervention.

Problems with the Concept

As we have seen in our discussions of both learning and conditioning and of Piaget's stages of infant intellectual development, infant intelligence appears to be largely based on the refinement and coordination of sensorimotor capacities. Later, intelligence appears to involve conceptual and symbolic thinking and mental problem solving. First, it is difficult to establish what, if any, the relationship between these capacities is and the extent to which development in sensorimotor areas may affect development of more advanced intellectual functions. Thus it is difficult to determine whether and to what extent the kinds of behaviors measured in infant tests relate to those measured in tests given later.

Second, the various abilities and skills that appear to make up infant intelligence cannot easily be aggregated either conceptually or as related test scores. Infant abilities neither cluster together into a general intelligence factor, or G factor, nor do they fit together into neat groups of related factors that together can be viewed as intelligence (Lewis, 1976). There are no necessarily equivalent levels of development in two or more functions at the same time. It cannot be concluded that because a child is at point x in one function, it will be at an equivalent point x in another. For example, at one point in time, a child may be ahead of others of the same age on motor functions but be behind them in language development. Neither are there consistent parallels over time in the development of separate factors that can be included together as forming intelligence. Thus the child with precocious motor development and average language development at one year may be ahead in language and average for motor skills at 18 months. Even within a particular function, the rate of development may be extremely uneven. For instance, a child may make dramatic changes in motor abilities during one month and change very little during the next.

Problems with Assessment

Those who test infant intelligence encounter unique problems in both test construction and test administration. First of all, young infants are unable to follow instructions. Rather than asking a child to produce a behavior, testers must either elicit the behavior using the child's ability to orient, habituate and dishabituate, and show preference, or they must wait until an infant produces a desired behavior spontaneously. Either situation is more difficult and can be more time-consuming than the standard testing situations that can be used with older children. Problems of state change and fatigue obviously also affect the use and success of infant assessment procedures.

There also appears to be little relationship between the performance of infants on tests and their behavior in social situations. That is, infants who do poorly on tests do not necessarily appear slower, or listless, or behind their age mates when observed in normal interactions with parents, other adults, or peers. Only extremely handicapped infants show a relationship between low scores on infant tests and retarded observed behaviors. Thus, for the nonhandicapped infant, poor performance on infant tests may often be a result of the testing situation rather than an accurate measure of intellectual ability.

Validity and Reliability of Infant Tests

For all these reasons, the predictive validity of infant tests is quite low. That is, there appears to be little relationship between scores on infant tests and scores on other intellectual measures used later on in childhood (Lewis, 1976). Thus the question of stability of intelligence cannot really be answered at this time. It is not known if intelligence appears unstable because it really does change or because instruments are not yet good enough to detect stability.

Furthermore, there appears to be little relationship among various infant tests given at about the same time or between repeated administrations of the same test over a span of time. In part this lack is due to fluctuations of infant state and in part to the rapid changes that infants undergo at some times during early development. In any event, the reliability of the tests is therefore also not very great.

In spite of these limitations, however, infant intelligence tests are used. For they do provide some limited diagnostic or predictive information, particularly for infants who deviate a great deal from the mean. In addition, they are more valuable when used to assess groups of infants rather than just one particular infant. They provide a relatively objective, standardized, and repeatable way of comparing groups of infants at the same time or a group with itself at a later date. Therefore, they can provide a data base for the evaluation of research and intervention programs dealing with infant groups.

Types of Tests

Most of the tests used in assessing infant intellect are related to or derived from intelligence scales used with older children. They grow out of the psychometric tradition of the mental-test movement. Therefore, they represent either downward extensions of other tests or the adaptation of measurement techniques used in other assessments to the particular intellectual and testing constraints of infants. The Gesell Developmental Schedules, the Cattell Scales of Infant Intelligence, and the Bayley Scales are all of this type. Although both Arnold Gesell and Nancy Bayley deny that their tests measure intelligence and stress that they measure development instead, the tests are considered by most of those who use them to be attempts at measuring intelligence in infants. More recent attention has focused on assessment from a Piagetian rather than psychometric point of view. The child's way of tackling problems rather than the correctness of outcomes is considered important in these tests. The Uzgiris-Hunt Scales are the most frequently used Piagetian measures of intelligence at present.

Gesell Development Schedules

Gesell and his associates at Yale have produced the Gesell Developmental Schedules (Gesell & Amatruda, 1947), an assessment device based upon their extensive observations of infants and children. The scales deal with the four areas of development identified by Gesell as important: motor, language, adaptation, and personal-social. The various items on the Schedules are assigned age-based norms derived from the percentages of children of various ages who succeeded at particular tasks. Thus developmental level of a particular child on various tasks can be ascertained.

Gesell always emphasized, however, that these tests were to be used as measures of development rather than of intelligence. He therefore discouraged the use of an overall score and advised test administrators to use only scores on individual items or at most those of subscales in assessing the developmental level of children.

Test items on the Gesell Schedules range from age four weeks to six years. Most items are observational, in which the examiner observes and records the child's behavior in interaction with specific toys and household objects provided in the test kit. A few items require parental report. Both descriptions of requisite behaviors and many illustrations of infant behaviors in various testing situations are provided in the manual to aid the examiner.

Cattell Infant Intelligence Scale

The Cattell Infant Intelligence Scale (P. Cattell, 1940) is a downward extension of the second revision of the Stanford-Binet Intelligence Scale. Items on the test are appropriate for ages 3 to 30 months. Psyche Cattell used test items from the Gesell Schedules that showed a regular increase in the percentage of children succeeding at them with increasing age, provided these items proved relatively independent of the effects of training in the home. Cattell thus attempted to make her test relatively free of cultural or class influences. She also thought that some earlier tests had relied too much on motor measures, which she did not believe related to later intelligence and therefore tried to avoid using. Cattell provided specific scoring criteria and instructions for the examiner, both patterned closely on those for the Stanford-Binet. Thus judging a child's performance could be relatively standardized.

Bayley Scales of Infant Development

Bayley's longitudinal study of children in the Berkeley Growth Project of the 1920s and 30s was the basis of the Bayley Scales of Infant Development (Bayley, 1969). A short scale of items based on the early study of these children was first published in 1933. These original scales were later expanded, and additional scales were added. A larger and more diverse sample of children than those in the original Berkeley study was used to restandardize the expanded instrument. Reworking and restandardization in the period 1958–1960 yielded an instrument that Bayley believed to be a new way of measuring infant development rather than a mere downward extension of an existing test, since she thought that it took into account the unique structure of mental abilities in the infant and was sensitive to variation in infant state.

The test is divided into three portions: mental, motor, and behavioral. The first two involve child actions indicating sensory and perceptual acuity, learning, memory, knowledge of objects, problem solving, vocalization, classification, generalizing, and the coordination of large and small muscle groups. The third involves the examiner's global assessment of the child's behavior during the test situation.

Like Gesell, Bayley emphasized that her instrument measured level of development rather than intelligence. Yet because test results are reported through the use of standard scores deviating from a mean or average score of 100, there is a temptation to interpret them as equivalent to later IQ scores that are reported in a similar manner.

The Bayley Scales are probably the best-standardized tests of infant performance that can be related to intelligence available at the present time. They are helpful in assessing developmental lags in either sensory or motor areas. They can also indicate the lack of stimulation in the infant's environment that prevents satisfactory progress. Therefore, these scales are widely used both to assess development in individual infants and to study the efficacy of various teaching, parenting, and other intervention programs by testing groups of infants and comparing results.

Uzgiris-Hunt Scales

Ina Uzgiris and J. McV. Hunt of the University of Illinois thought that most infant tests were based on the (to them) erroneous assumption that intelligence was a relatively unitary process whose rate of development was uniform or stable. These tests were based on other tests used with older children or with adults, merely using simpler items. Uzgiris and Hunt (1975) wanted to try a different approach, which assumed that the rate of development of infant intelligence was not linear. They reached this conclusion in part because there appear to be discontinuities and inconsistencies of behavioral development in children and in part because they re-

alized that different children were exposed to different environmental circumstances that could affect the rate of intellectual development. In place of the linear model, they assumed intelligence to develop at different rates during different times and to develop from the formation of a hierarchical set of competencies.

The Uzgiris-Hunt Scales, therefore, basically test sensorimotor intelligence according to the Piagetian formulation. There are six scales, each including a variety of tasks and subtasks. These consist of visual pursuit and object permanence, means for obtaining desired environmental events, vocal and gestural imitation, operational causality, object relations in space, and schemes relating to objects.

Test items used were drawn from situations described by Piaget in explaining his theory. For each test item, a series of possible infant behaviors is described, and those that are considered critical in order for an infant to achieve the objectives of the item are listed. A number of items may be presented to the infant several times; others only once.

These scales view infant intelligence not as an overall developmental quotient or in comparison to developmental norms set up for particular ages but as comprised of a series of separate developmental skills, some of which may interact in a hierarchical fashion. While the sequence is considered invariant, the rate of development of specific skills and the intermeshing of skills with one another is viewed as very much individualized. Each child is therefore used as the basis of comparison for herself or himself alone.

The measurement of infant intelligence is still an inexact science. Many questions whose answers were sought through such tests still have no definitive answers. Indeed, it may be that infant intelligence is such a changeable structure involving the interaction of so many functions, which begin and develop at such different rates, that even in the future there may not be many more answers than at present. That is, the major

stumbling block to understanding may be not the nature of the tests but the nature of infant intelligence itself.

Summary

1. The major theorist of children's intellectual development has been the Swiss psychologist Jean Piaget. Piaget's lifelong endeavor was to trace the development of genetic epistemology, that is, the origin of how humans know. In doing so he began logically with the study of infants.

2. Piaget saw intelligence as composed of structure, function, and content. The three major functions are adaptation, scheme building, and organization, and these in turn affect the developing structure of intelligence. In addition, maturation, experience, and organization also affect the development of the intellect.

3. Adaptation is composed of the reciprocal processes of assimilation and accommodation. Assimilation entails adapting outside reality to existing intellectual structures, while accommodation involves altering internal structures to conform to outside reality. These two functions exist in a state of dynamic equilibrium with each other.

4. A scheme is an intellectual structure that is the mental representation of a particular behavioral action sequence. In infancy, schemes are primarily based upon motor actions, but with increasing age they become based more upon mental activity.

5. Piaget believed that the child's intellect develops through successive stages of mental functioning that differ qualitatively from each other. During the stage encompassing infancy, which he labeled the sensorimotor

stage, there are six distinct substages of mental development. During these the infant progresses from being a reflexive organism to an individual capable of true thought.

6. One important aspect of intellectual development in infancy is the development of the object concept. The infant progresses from an initial "out of sight, out of mind" evaluation of objects to having some memory, being able to retrieve a partially hidden object and later a completely hidden one, and finally being able to account for unseen relocations of a hidden object.

7. T. G. R. Bower has proposed some alternative explanations of the development of the concept of object. While his methodology is ingenious, his work has been difficult to replicate by others, and therefore much doubt about his theories remains.

8. Jerome Bruner has developed a stage-based theory of infant intelligence that is somewhat different from that of Piaget but is basically in harmony with many of Piaget's ideas. Bruner's major concern is with the development of motor problem-solving skills that will lead to language and the use of tools in the developing infant.

9. Statistical analysis of data based upon the administration of the Bayley Scales to children in the Berkeley Growth Study has indicated the existence of qualitative discontinuities of behavior at times roughly corresponding to the stages posited by Piaget. These discontinuities are based primarily

upon the infant's changing understanding of objects.

10. Infant intelligence can be assessed through a variety of standardized testing instruments that attempt to measure both the growth of intellectual abilities within a child and the differences in these abilities among individuals. Infants are difficult to test because of immaturity and lack of verbal responses. Since the intellect changes greatly in a qualitative as well as quantitative manner during this period, the predictive validity of infant tests is not great. The most popular infant tests at present are the Bayley Scales and the Uzgiris-Hunt Scales.

Participatory And Observational Exercises

1. Observe infants and toddlers in each of Piaget's six substages of the sensorimotor stage. How does behavior differ from each stage to the next? What inferences can you make from watching the behaviors about different thought patterns underlying the behaviors?

2. Experiment with the development of the object concept by trying out Piaget's hidden object problems with as many infants of different ages as possible. Young infants will stop looking if you hide an object, even if it is partially visible. Infants between four and eight months should be able to retrieve a partially hidden toy. Notice how much more easily and quickly an older infant does this than a somewhat younger one. After eight months, a totally hidden object can be retrieved if the child can watch you hiding it. But the child cannot yet find the object if you hid it under one cloth and then move it under another, even if he or she watches. After age one year, the child can find it under the second cloth if he or she watches. Finally, older toddlers can account for even an invisible displacement. Try out various of these with infants and toddlers of various ages, and record your observations. Can you see an age-related development of the object concept?

3. Observe the administration of an infant test such as the Bayley Scales or the Gesell Developmental Schedules. Can you see why infant state is an important variable in testing? Did the infant become bored or fatigued? What methods did the examiner use to hold the infant's attention? Do the items appear to challenge the infant's skills? If you cannot observe someone administering such a test, try at least to find a test kit for one of the tests. Examine the materials used in the kit, and study the manual and directions for administration. What are some difficulties with test administration that seem apparent to you?

DISCUSSION QUESTIONS

1. Should infants and toddlers be taught various intellectual skills so as to pass through the various substages of the sensorimotor stage more quickly? Does teaching or coaching in fact speed up this progression? What value is there in faster progress?

2. Discuss examples of accommodation and assimilation that occur in your daily life. Does either predominate over the other in your current life stage?

3. Should infant intelligence testing be done? Why or why not? Under what circumstances? How can test results be misused? Can such misuse be prevented?

Language Development

INTRODUCTION

When Christopher was a year old, he began to say words. Some, like "Mama" and "Annie," were easy to understand. Some like "kikkie," were immature mispronunciations, in this instance for cookie. But some words baffled his family. He said "faddie," and pointed to either a flower or to his sweater. Evidently either the label could be used for both, or there were slight differences in his pronunciation to differentiate between the two that the family did not catch. Finally, several months later he invented the word "woy." This was an all-purpose word of dislike or negativism. It could mean "no," or "I don't want to," or even "I don't like you." The height of woy use, as well as the beginning of meaningful use of two-word combinations came the day Chris was mad at everyone. He exploded with the sequence, "Mama-woy, Daddy-woy, Annie-woy, Robbie-woy, Greggy-woy." It's a good thing that the dog was not around, or he might have been woy-ed as well! At 28 months, as the family was driving in the car, Christopher pointed to a purple plum tree in someone's yard and said, "That's my favorite tree." When asked what that meant, he replied, "I like it the best." He not only had the words right but understood the concept of favorite.

Christopher's early language development was thus quite typical of, if perhaps a bit more inventive than, that of all toddlers. He learned a number of single words, generally referring to people, objects, and actions in the environment. Some of these were at first difficult to understand because of immaturities of pronunciation. Like some children, he also invented a few of his own words that were unique and not just immature forms of adult words. Eventually, he put some words together into two-word combinations that were unlike adult forms. And finally, he went on to produce relatively complex sentences of three words or more that were very close to the adult models.

GENERAL IDEAS ABOUT LANGUAGE

Language is the major means whereby people communicate with one another. Thus it may be the most unique attribute of humans. We seem to be the only species able to communicate not only about experiences at hand but about those of our own past and those of others, even many generations ago. Therefore, we can learn from the experience of others and can follow the instructions of others. We use language to express our thoughts and feelings as well as experience. Recent experiments have shown that chimpanzees can be taught to communicate using either plastic shapes that stand for words or the manual alphabet employed by the deaf, but they cannot be taught speech because their vocal apparatus is unable to produce the sounds used in human speech. Furthermore, chimpanzees do not spontaneously begin to communicate with humans or one another through the use of linguistic symbols such as words. Nor can they "talk" about events in the distant past, hypothetical situations, or the very act of communicating itself.

By contrast, every normal human child (excepting those severely retarded or profoundly deaf), if exposed to the usual everyday companionship of people using language such as older children and adults, will during the first two to three years of life develop a relatively complete language without explicit instruction and will do so in very much the same way as all other children.

All human societies, from the most primitive to the most technologically advanced, have a language. The complexity of a language bears no relationship to the level of advancement of the particular culture using it (Greenberg, 1963). A relatively primitive culture may have a very complex language. For example, the !K'ung (formerly called bushmen) of the Kalahari Desert in Southwest Africa, whose culture is essentially a Stone Age one, have a highly complex and detailed language, including many different verb tenses and words denoting specific kinship relationships for which no equivalents exist in the languages of most advanced cultures.

Definition

Language is a form of communication that employs symbols. It may be transmitted from one person to another by speech or by some other means such as writing. It entails both one person's production of symbols, as in speaking or writing, and another person's intake of symbols through listening to speech or reading what has been written. Language consists essentially of a series of arbitrary spoken or written symbols that stand for particular objects, relationships, actions, or feelings. A **symbol** is a sign that is related to what it refers to only through conventions agreed upon in the language community in which it is used (Bates, 1979). It is arbitrary in the sense that there is no inherent relationship between the symbol and the referent. Thus a symbol that used to stand for one referent can by common consent be changed to stand for another. An example is the change in the meaning of the word "gay" that has occurred in American English in the last few decades. In addition, new symbols are constantly being added to every language as the tools and technologies used in everyday life change. Words such as "automobile" or "telephone" were unheard of 200 years ago, although they are made up of root words coming from ancient Latin and Greek. The word "motel" arose in the period after World War II as a contraction of the words "motor hotel," to signify a new kind of hotel that catered to those driving automobiles and that usually was located near a highway. "Microprocessor" is a brand-new word made up of roots previously used in different ways. "Chip," in the sense of the microchip used in computers and other electronic equipment, represents a new meaning for a word that previously had a different connotation.

Language enables the individual to use cognitive categories in communication. A person can label what he or she has categorized and thus has a means of organizing experience and sharing this organization with others. Thus language can also serve to aid both generalization and discrimination of cognitive and perceptual features of reality.

Four Systems of Language

Four systems exist in all human languages: semantic, syntactical, phonological, and lexical. Their specific forms differ, of course, from language to language. For example, all languages have a **phonology**, or sound system, but the particular sounds used may vary greatly among languages.

SEMANTIC

The **semantic system** has to do with the meaning of utterances in the particular language. It includes the meaning of words themselves and the meaning of the phrases and sentences formed from groups of words. For example, "dog" means a certain kind of animal. But how that word is used in a sentence affects the meaning of the sentence. The dog may be the doer or agent in the sentence, as in "The dog bit the boy." Or he may be the object or receiver of the action as in "The boy bit the dog." The meaning of these two sentences is obviously quite different, depending upon the functions of the words employed in them.

Basic individual units of meaning are called **morphemes.** A morpheme may be a word. Or else it may be an **inflectional** ending added onto a word that denotes special information about the word, such as that it is plural (as in the noun dogs) or that it is in the past (as in the verb walked). In these examples, the word "dogs" is made of up of two morphemes, dog and the inflectional ending s, which indicates plural. "Walked" also has two morphemes, the verb walk plus the inflectional ending ed indicating the past tense.

English uses few inflections. The main ones are those we have just singled out indicating verb tenses of regular verbs and the plural of regular nouns. In addition, some pronouns have different forms (such as she and her) to indicate agent, object, or other purpose in a sentence. Because of the few inflections in English, the meaning of an English sentence is largely dependent upon word order and the reader or listener can deduce the meaning primarily from that order. The above sentences involving the dog are good examples of this dependence of meaning on word order. Other languages such as Russian or Latin use many inflections that permit understanding of the meaning of a sentence regardless of the word order used. Therefore in such languages word order is much less important.

SYNTACTICAL

The **syntactical system** is concerned with putting words together according to the rules of **syntax,** or grammar, that is, arranging them to form phrases or sentences that convey meaning. All languages have a syntax, but they vary widely in the kinds and contents of rules that are employed. For example, depending in part upon how inflectional a language is, word order may be quite rigid or quite flexible. But in no language is word order completely arbitrary. All languages have certain rules for how words can be put together relating to word order, subject-verb agreement, and the like, in order to produce meaning.

PHONOLOGICAL

The **phonological system,** as was said, is concerned with the phonology, or sounds, used in a particular language. These units of sound are called **phonemes.** Each syllable in a spoken word is made up of one or several phonemes. Although a large number of possible phonemes can be made by the human voice, probably as many as about 800, most languages use only a limited number. The phonemes used in one language may be quite different from those used in another. That is one reason why many foreign languages sound so strange to English-speakers. English uses only about 45 phonemes; other languages may use more or fewer. This difference in the numbers and types of phonemes used is what causes difficulty in learning to pronounce a foreign language, for some of the sounds used in that language may be new to the learner. For example, most native English-speakers have trouble pronouncing the Spanish r or the German ch sound.

LEXICAL

Finally, the **lexical system** refers to the lexicon, or the total corpus of words that exist in a language. The lexicon of a language may be thought of as a listing of all the words that occur in the dictionary of that language. An individual child's lexicon consists of all the words the child knows and can use at a particular point in time.

Competence versus Performance in Using Language

It is important that linguistic competence and performance be distinguished from each other, although they are closely related. In addition, comprehension, or receptive language, and production, or expressive language, which also are related to them, need to be defined and explained.

COMPETENCE

Competence refers to what the child knows of language, that is, the degree to which he or she has absorbed the phonological, syntactical, morphological, and semantic and lexical aspects of his or her language (Dale, 1972; McNeill, 1970a). It is the child's plan for speaking and understanding words and word relations and depends upon the child's development of rules that pair up particular sounds with the meaning of the utterances formed of those sounds (Bloom & Lahey, 1973).

RECEPTIVE LANGUAGE

Receptive language, or the comprehension of language, depends upon language competence. The child takes in and comprehends the language of others as it is either heard or read by the child, because competence has provided the means whereby comprehension can occur.

PERFORMANCE AND PRODUCTION OR EXPRESSIVE LANGUAGE

Performance is the language the child is able to bring forth, in either speaking or writing.

Performance depends upon the existence of language competence and also is related to experience in the language environment. When the child is actually producing language, this aspect of performance is called production. It is the same as expressive language. Performance and production thus really are so closely related as to be just about equivalent to all but the trained linguist.

PROBLEMS WITH MEASUREMENT

Unfortunately, there is no direct way to gauge a child's language competence; it can only be inferred from measures of imitation, comprehension, and production or performance (Dale, 1972). Imitation can be tested by asking a child to repeat an utterance and determining how well she or he does so. Comprehension is tested by giving the child two pictures and a stimulus phrase or sentence and asking the child to point to the picture that goes with the phrase or sentence. Comprehension can also be inferred from imitation. Thus, if a child repeats a phrase or sentence the adult has uttered and does not produce an exact imitation but one that still preserves the meaning, it can be inferred that the child comprehended what the adult said (Slobin & Welsh, 1967). Finally, production is tested by showing the child a stimulus picture and asking the child to name or describe the picture. All of these methods enable one to build a theory regarding a particular child's language competence. The nature of these tasks, however, precludes their use before late toddlerhood.

Content, Form, and Use of Language

In studying the language of children, it is also useful to distinguish its content, form, and use.

Content is the meaning of the messages used by the child, what the child is actually talking about. Content refers to particular words and relationships expressed in speech.

The form of language refers to the semantic and phonetic units, that is, the units of meaning and sound that are used by the child, as well as to the syntax. In other words, what is the utterance built of?

Finally, the use of a language refers to the goal and function of language as a means of communication and also to the particular forms of language that are actually used. Is the goal to ask a question, give information, or keep a dialogue going? The particular forms of language used also vary with the social context in which the communication occurs. For example, most people talk in a different manner with their parents or siblings than with an employer, a professor, or their minister. These differences of form are also an aspect of the use of language.

Other Kinds of Communication

Humans as well as animals have kinds of communication other than language. These forms include eye contact, facial expression, gestures, body movements, and physical contact such as holding, caressing, and hugging. These forms of nonverbal communication serve to transmit feelings and information either in and of themselves or in conjunction with spoken language. Infants produce these nonverbal forms of communication and seem to understand those used by adults long before they understand spoken language or produce words of their own. Thus nonverbal communication is used by infants before words and continues to be used by all humans to supplement and enhance verbal communication or, in some instances, to substitute for it. For example, if you do some-

thing and someone gives you an angry look, you may not need to have that person tell you in words that he or she disapproves.

CHANGING TRENDS IN STUDYING LANGUAGE OF CHILDREN

Early Studies

When linguists began to study language, most of them at first did not show much interest in the language of early childhood and how communication begins. Instead they concentrated on the language of adults or older children. Some studies in the 1930s and 1940s consisted of a parent's description of the progress in spoken language of an individual child. That is, the parent recorded what the child said, at what age, and under what circumstances. The best example of this type is W. F. Leopold's study of the early language development of his daughter Hildegarde (Leopold, 1939).

Other studies dealt with the kinds of words that children first uttered and how these words began to be grammatically arranged. Researchers concentrated on the structures of the utterances (Bloomfield, 1933) or on the kinds of words and the frequency of the use of particular words. This latter type of study used the technique of distributional analysis, which determines what linguistic elements the child used, where in the child's speech they occurred, and how they related to other elements. Researchers recorded how many different nouns the child used, how many verbs, what kinds of verbs, and the like. They also looked at lengths and complexity of sentences. These methods gave researchers some insight into the child's theory of language at that point. Several children of the same age could be studied in this man-

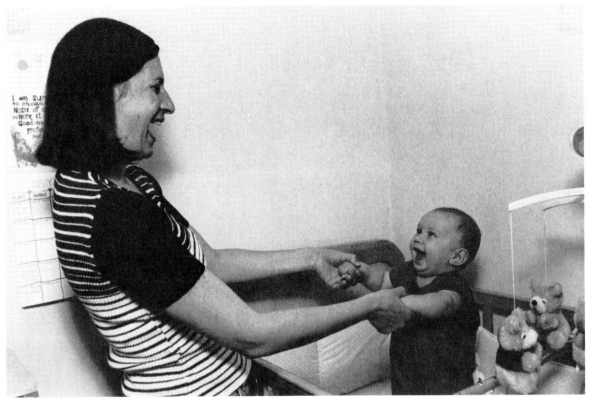

Infants and adults can communicate with each other through the use of gestures and facial expressions long before the infants can understand adult language or produce words. It is quite obvious that this mother and infant are communicating delight to each other.

ner, and the similarities and differences could be compared cross-sectionally. That is, one could determine how many words the average 18-month-old used or how long the usual sentence of a 24-month-old was. Alternatively, one could study how a particular language phenomenon developed over time, or longitudinally. For instance, how does the child begin to ask questions? How does the child begin to form plurals, and what are the steps in learning correct plural formation? If several children were studied in such a longitudinal manner, comparisons among them could help determine whether the steps of development were regular and occurred in many children or differed from child to child.

Transformational Grammar

In the 1950s and 1960s, the emphasis of linguists came to be on the development of grammatical relationships in language. How does the child absorb the particular grammatical rules of her or his language? One of the most influential theories was that of transformational grammar. It attempted to explain how children learned the transformations from deep to surface structures of language. Linguists such as Noam Chomsky (1965) looked at the relationship between the deep structure, or meaning, of the grammatical units of a sentence and the surface structure, or how this meaning was actually expressed in words. That is, there are universal meanings across languages that can be expressed in various ways in a particular language and in other similar or different ways in other languages. Thus the deep structure, since it remains the same, has to do with cognition, or understanding. The surface structure depends upon both the understanding of the deep structure and the ability to express this meaning in a way that is acceptable and understandable in the particular language of the child. For example, both the sentence "The dog bit the boy" and the sentence "The boy was bitten by the dog" have the same deep structure or meaning. They differ considerably in surface structure or how the meaning is expressed. By contrast, "The dog bit the boy" and "The boy bit the dog" have very similar surface structure, but differ greatly in deep structure or meaning.

Chomsky believed that the deep structure was universal across all languages. The surface structure, however, varied from language to language depending upon the syntax of the language. Therefore, in learning to use their native language, children had to learn the deep structure as well as the transformational rules that tied the deep structure to the surface structure in that particular language (Braine, 1976). Chomsky believed that children were capable of learning only those surface structures, whose deep structures they had already absorbed, through the process of imitating adult speech. If they did not yet grasp the meaning of the deep struc-

ture, exposing them to adult speech models would not help. He explained the immaturities of the language of children in terms of this slow learning of the deep structures.

But the studies of children's language up through the 1960s mainly emphasized the form of language, that is the units of meaning (morphemes) and units of sound (phonemes) and how they were arranged. These studies were primarily concerned with the development of syntax. They asked how the grammar the child apparently used differed from adult grammar and how the child eventually absorbed adult grammatical forms.

The emphasis of studies during the 1970s shifted away from the use of form alone. It came to be recognized that the meaning of the messages the child was using was more important than the particular grammatical structures the child used. It also became apparent that young children communicated far more than their command of language forms alone revealed and understood much more of adult communication than their understanding of grammar alone would explain. Therefore, more recent studies of children's language have tended to concentrate more upon the use, the content, and the context of language (Bloom, 1970). That is, what does the child mean to communicate, how does he or she do it, and in what circumstances? Linguists increasingly emphasized the development of semantics, or meaning of words and utterances, and the relationship of language to other forms of cognitive development. Where form was still studied in the 1970s, it was mainly to ascertain whether children learned word meaning from the form or grammatical aspect of these words or from the functional characteristics of the words in particular situations.

Present-day linguists generally think that the child who is learning language is able to figure out words and their relationships only within a familiar context of objects and events. These scholars therefore stress word meanings and the semantic relations between words more than the grammatical relationship (Brown, 1973; Bloom & Lahey, 1973). The social and physical setting in which words are used is also emphasized.

ISSUES IN STUDYING LANGUAGE DEVELOPMENT

Nativist versus Empiricist

Not surprisingly, the debate between the nativist position, which says the ability to produce language is an inborn mechanism, and the empiricist position, which attributes language development to learning, has been long-standing and heated. It began in the 19th century with the philosophers and scientists who argued about the relative importance of heredity and environment for human development. The argument about language centered on whether language was an innate feature of human existence that would unfold within each individual at the proper time or whether it was a learned behavior that was based upon adult modeling of words and sentences and the selective reinforcement of children's utterances that approximated adult sounds.

This argument became particularly heated in the late 1950s, as both learning theory and new theories of language development were becoming popular. Chomsky (1957, 1959) was the leading proponent of the nativist position, while B. F. Skinner (1957) and Arthur Staats (1968) were the major supporters of the empiricist point of view. There is evidence on both sides.

NATIVIST

The nativist view receives support from the fact that language appears to be an inborn human capacity found in no other species but always (except in extreme instances) found in humans. Early **babbling** (uttering repetitive sounds) of infants worldwide sounds remarkably the same, despite great differences between the sounds of the languages they will eventually speak. Babies of different language communities make the same sounds, including sounds that may not exist in the language they will eventually speak. Only after several months of babbling do infants begin to concentrate on the sounds that exist in the language around them and gradually cease using those of other languages.

Furthermore, children the world over develop language in the same sequence, although they end up speaking quite diverse languages. Thus babbling, **lalling** (less repetitive babbling), **protowords** (sounds approaching those of true words), and one-word and then two-word utterances occur in the same order whether a child is learning English, Russian, Swahili, or Chinese. Children make the same charming "errors" of language and produce the same kinds of two-word utterances that differ from any adult utterances they may have heard, regardless of the language they hear spoken.

Another piece of evidence in support of the innateness of language is the fact that in normal children its development correlates very closely with motor development, another mechanism relatively impervious to environmental influence (Lenneberg, 1969). Milestones of motor development such as walking and milestones of language development such as the first word occur at closely related times, although the practice of one may temporarily hinder that of the other. For example, most children begin to walk un-aided and to produce single words around the ages of 12 to 13 months. Children who are mentally retarded frequently walk much later than do normal children and do not begin to use words until the onset of walking, regardless of actual chronological age (Lenneberg, 1969).

Except for retarded children or those with hearing loss, there appears to be little significant difference in the way or the timing that very early language is learned between bright, average, and somewhat slower children. They all seem to learn the same kinds and numbers of words, in much the same way, and at approximately the same time at the beginning. For example, a child who began speaking in words a month earlier than another cannot necessarily be considered brighter. Later, of course, differences appear between brighter and slower children in the size of vocabulary and the length and complexity of sentences employed. These differences are partly due to the hereditary factor of intelligence, which affects language development. Differences can be enhanced, however, by environmental input such as the speech of adults so that learning obviously plays a part as well.

The most potent nativist argument is that young children produce utterances that they have heard no other speaker make and hence could not have learned through imitation of a model. They are also able to use words that they have never heard before in rule-bound ways in forming sentences and clauses (Berko, 1958).

Many of the nativist arguments supposed the existence of something in the child's brain that was wired or programmed by nature for the development of language (Nelson, 1973). Chomsky (1959) and David McNeill (1966) explained this innate development of language in the child through a hypothetical device in the human brain, which McNeill called the **Language Acquisition Device,** or LAD.

This LAD, according to Chomsky and McNeill, takes in the utterances made by those in the child's linguistic group and, because it is programmed with grammatical rules, is able to devise a grammatical system from the utterances. It thus sets up a series of hypotheses about the language the child hears. These hypotheses will help the child to understand new utterances when they are heard. At present, many theorists leaning in a nativist direction discount the hypothesis-building function of the LAD, as well as the emphasis on grammatical rules, but still think that some such sensitivity for language learning does exist.

EMPIRICIST

Evidence cited by empiricists includes the fact that children not exposed to human speech during their early years either develop no speech at all or do so only imperfectly if later exposed to speakers. Feral children (those supposedly raised by wolves or other wild animals) learned no or very little language when returned to human company. For example, Victor, the famous wild boy of Aveyron, was found in 1797 and raised from about age twelve by the French psychologist Jean-Marc Itard for five years. Victor learned only a few words and was unable to comprehend some of the generalizations and categorizations used in speech. Having learned after a great deal of effort and practice that a particular book Itard owned had the name "book," Victor was unable to generalize this name or label to other books whose appearance was somewhat different. Of course, it also is quite possible that Victor was mentally retarded, as well as cut off from human company for some time.

On the other hand, Genie, a child who had been isolated from almost all human contact between 20 months and 13 years, learned to communicate quite well in English (Curtiss, 1977). But the process took seven years, which is much longer than the time young children need to acquire language. Also Genie was in a relatively normal language environment before the age of 20 months and not totally separated from human company even during her period of isolation, so that some language learning could have occurred during those times.

Children exposed to some but not a lot of adult speech, such as those raised in understaffed orphanages or the children of deaf-mute parents, generally have somewhat retarded language and speech development. So do multiple-birth children who spend a great deal of time with each other and relatively little with adults (Zazzo, 1982). The most famous such case was that of the Dionne Quintuplets, all of whom were notoriously slow to learn language.

Another fact supporting the environmentalist position is that children learn the particular language spoken by adults in their environment, not a language related in some way to their genetic makeup. Thus, for example, Vietnamese children adopted in infancy by American families grow up speaking English, not Vietnamese. Furthermore, children learn the regional accents and expressions spoken in the part of the country in which they grow up. They also begin to differ, after the very earliest language has developed, in the content of their spoken and comprehended language, as well as in the size and qualities of their vocabularies, based upon factors such as their parents' socioeconomic class and educational level. These differences begin to be noticeable during the last half of the first year and at first are merely differences in the amount of vocaliz-

ing adults do to the child and the amount the child vocalizes back. They become larger with continued differential experience.

Hard-of-hearing babies develop language up to a point in the same way as babies who hear, but here too, differences become apparent in the second half of the first year. Without special training from parents and personnel of specialized schools, many hard-of-hearing children do not develop true language or else only very limited language. Thus, although there seems some inborn mechanism that triggers early prelanguage behaviors, it is apparent that a child must hear speech in order to begin to talk. Therefore, environment unquestionably plays a large role in language development.

RESOLUTION

In recent years the debate has assumed less of the either-or quality exemplified by Chomsky and Skinner. It is becoming increasingly obvious that the development of language is due to an interaction between inborn developmental tendencies and environmental input. There seems to be some innate predisposition to develop language, but it does not become activated unless the child has experience with language in the environment, preferably during the first two to three years. Neither heredity nor environment alone can account for the beginning and development of language. Both are necessary.

Continuity versus Discontinuity

Another unresolved issue is whether the child develops language in a continuous or a discontinuous fashion. The argument in favor of continuity rests upon the fact that the child learns some early words and continues to use them even after learning others. Furthermore, early prelanguage communication uses gestures. When words develop, the gestures often remain and are used in conjunction with the words.

Nevertheless, language seems to develop in something akin to stages, which would imply discontinuity. The child goes from no words to words, with various regular stages of oral communication coming between. In addition, some children cease babbling before real words begin (Bever, 1961), also suggesting some separation between various sequential aspects of language development.

Comprehension-Production Discrepancy

Another issue of debate centers on whether the disparity between comprehension and production is part of the nature of the acquisition of language or whether it is an artifact that merely occurs. Infants and toddlers seem to comprehend more than they can produce, and they comprehend some aspects of language long before they ever utter a word. This discrepancy continues on through childhood and can be found to exist even in adults. For example, most adults understand many words that they are unlikely ever to use in speech or writing. They also understand language overlaid by regional accents, but they usually are unable to reproduce these accents. Most Americans, for example, can readily understand a Southerner, a New Englander, or even someone from Britain or Australia, but they cannot mimic their particular way of speaking.

There also is some debate as to whether infants and toddlers really comprehend as much of language as had been assumed they did (Chapman, 1981). In part this possible lack of comprehension may be due to limited memory capacity. Some authorities argue that young children are reacting to the context of the situation in which words are uttered rather than to the words themselves. They react appropriately not because they understand the words but merely because they produce the usual behavior for that situation (Fischer & Corrigan, 1981). This behavior is similar to that of the pet dog or cat who acts appropriately to a situational cue but obviously has no understanding of human language. If this view is correct, the discrepancy, or asymmetry, between comprehension and production may not be as great as had been thought: young children may not comprehend a great deal more than they produce.

Language and Cognition

It has been assumed by most linguists that language development is closely tied to that of cognition. That is, many students have thought that the child will develop language only when cognitively ready and that he or she will understand and produce only those language forms whose underlying intellectual basis is already understood (Bates, 1976; Bates, Benigni, Bretherton, Camaioni, & Volterra, 1977; Nelson, 1973). Some aspects of young children's language, such as the content of their utterances and the meanings expressed by them, are probably more closely related to intellectual development than are the ways in which these are expressed (Stark, 1980b).

In the 1970s and 1980s, however, a number of studies, whose conclusions are still considered very controversial, have seemed to show that the link between cognition and language may not be as close as had been supposed (Sinclair, 1970; Corrigan 1978; Chapman 1981; Fischer & Corrigan, 1981).

K. W. Fischer and R. Corrigan posit a skill theory of language acquisition. According to them, skills are more specific than are cognitive stages, such as those of Piaget, and are learned through an interaction of the individual and the environment. Thus a skill may be at a particular level, while the child's development through the Piagetian stages may be at another. Skills can also be combined with one another to produce higher-order skills. As a result, the skills needed for language development and those for cognition are not necessarily the same ones, nor are both sets of skills necessarily attained at comparable ages or developmental levels.

At present, this controversy is far from settled. The supporters of a strong relationship between language and cognition agree that researchers must make sure the child really comprehends and is not just using contextual cues or rules based on frequency of occurrence. But they insist that since the child can only produce that which he or she already understands and can therefore talk knowledgeably about, language production at least is closely tied to cognition. Much of the research, which will be discussed in detail in the sections on one-word and two-word utterances, seems to support this position.

PRECURSORS TO SPEECH

Stages of Prespeech Sounds

Prespeech sounds develop in the infant in an invariant sequence during which there is a good deal of overlap between stages, beginning at birth and continuing through the first year of postnatal life (Stark, 1980a). This is a six-step progression as follows:

1. reflexive, crying, distress, and vegetative sounds having to do with eating (from birth on)
    2. cooing and laughing (1–3 months)
    3. exploratory vocal play (2–7 months)
    4. reduplicative babbling (4–8 months)

5. nonreduplicative babbling, jargon, and protowords, that is, sounds approaching true words (8–12 months)
6. referential words, that is, words referring to objects and events in the environment (around one year)

A Detailed Look

Let us now consider in more detail the infant's vocal productions during each of these stages of preverbal behavior. In addition, since human communication is a two-way process, we shall also consider the infant's responsiveness to vocal and verbal behavior of caregivers and others in the environment and the techniques adults use to foster vocal and later verbal interaction with the child.

REFLEXIVE, CRYING, DISTRESS, AND VEGETATIVE SOUNDS

At birth the baby is able to produce some sound. It can cry. We have already discussed in chapter 5 the early presence of distinctive types of cries that can be recognized by parents and that serve to communicate diffferent needs of the neonate. In addition to crying, the child can make gasping sounds, such as those that accompany the intake and expulsion of air, and vegetative sounds, such as murmurs and gurgles that usually accompany feeding. Moans and whimpers that indicate distress and may lead to full-scale crying are also produced.

The newborn appears remarkably responsive to the human voice. Condon and Sander (1974; Condon, 1975) have demonstrated that neonates move in rhythm to adult speech, a process they have called "interactional synchrony." Newborns move so not only for adult speakers of their own language but also for those of other languages. This latter ability is another piece of evi-

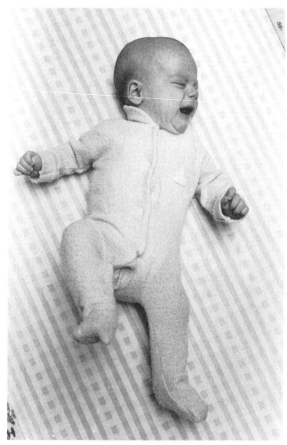

Crying serves as a major means of communicating hunger or other distress, pain, or boredom in the very young infant. Later on, as other means of communicating such as gestures and babbling develop, the infant needs to rely less on crying as a signal to caregivers and the amount of crying decreases.

dence for the nativist position. In the Condon and Sander research, which filmed baby behavior as the adult talked and then analyzed the synchrony that was evident when the film was replayed in slow motion, it was found that when the adult spoke quickly, the child's motions picked up speed in rhythm with the adult's voice. When the adult speech became slower, the baby's movements slowed down.

A crying baby will often calm to the sound of the parent's or other caregiver's voice, even without being picked up. Newborn babies prefer vocal music over instrumental music, again showing this sensitivity to the human voice (Butterfield & Siperstein, 1972). Neonates appear more responsive to higher-pitched than to lower-pitched voices. This is an interesting fact when one considers that female voices are generally higher than male ones, and that since earliest times the predominant number of caregivers of young infants have been female.

Since the essence of human communication appears to be an interaction between two or more partners, in which one will say something and then pause and wait for the other one to reply, and so forth, we should consider a completely nonverbal form of communication that begins in the neonate and is the first such interaction between partners. This is the "suck-jiggle" phenomenon described by Kenneth Kaye (Kaye & Brazelton, 1971; Kaye, 1977). When the feeding infant sucks in bursts, the mother pauses and waits. When the infant stops sucking, the mother jiggles the infant. If they are asked, mothers say they jiggle to induce the infant to resume sucking. In fact, Kaye has shown that if the mother did not jiggle, the baby would resume sucking more quickly. Thus the mother's jiggling appears to lengthen the pause between sucking bursts rather than to shorten it. The mother's jiggling, however, in alternation with the child's sucking serves to establish the first coordinated two-way interaction in which the infant participates. The mother believes that her jiggling causes the baby to recommence sucking, and so she feels that she is doing her part of keeping this communicative interaction going.

In addition, mothers and other adults treat infant behaviors that probably at first have no communicative intent, such as sneezing, yawning, or early sounds, as if they were replies in the ongoing dialogue between adult and infant. For instance, the baby will sneeze, and the mother will most likely say something like, "That sure was a nice big sneeze," as though the infant had meant to communicate something.

COOING AND LAUGHING

Sometimes as early as the third week, and generally by about one month of age, babies begin to make cooing sounds. At first they coo just before they begin to cry, but later they coo when they are content and satisfied and appear to be doing so just for the fun of it. Adults generally react favorably to cooing and vocalize back to the baby. In turn the infant responds with more cooing. This back and forth vocalization, which is an early form of the two-way communication typical of adult conversation, has been called a vocal circular reaction (Wolff, 1969). It is a form of the circular reactions described by Piaget, in which the child will hear a pleasing sound made by the adult or by itself and will try to prolong or reinstate it by repeating it.

Another early noncrying vocalization is laughing out loud, which usually begins around the fourth week after birth. At first, laughter is generally not spontaneous but is elicited by the adult's tickling the infant. It sounds like the onset of a crying cycle or the fussing that may precede crying, but soon it becomes distinguishable from these sounds. Usually babies laugh at being tickled only if they are in a good mood; if fussy or unhappy they will probably cry instead. As babies mature into the third month, they are more likely to laugh to express pleasure or joy.

By the third to fourth month (Stern, 1971, 1974b), the infant begins to exert some control over interchanges with adults by averting its gaze when there appears to be an overload of adult communicative stimulation (Brazelton, Koslowski, & Main, 1974). The adult will then attempt to reestablish communication by trying to draw the infant's gaze back to the adult face. In optimal adult-infant interaction, a cyclic coordination of both gaze and vocalizations takes place between infant and adult (Stern, 1974a). In this interaction, which D. N. Stern referred to as a game, each partner alternates roles, with first one being an active vocalizer and the other an attender, and then reversing the pattern. Although the groundwork for this type of interaction is laid even earlier than this period, it becomes more frequent as the baby goes on to the cooing and babbling stages of vocal development.

At this time or even earlier, adults begin to use a variety of techniques to attract the infant's attention or to draw it back after the infant has ceased attending. These include pitching the voice artificially high and exaggerating the intonation of a sentence. Often adults will call out the child's name as they begin a segment of words or will use an exclamation such as "hey," "yoo-hoo," or "look."

EXPLORATORY VOCAL PLAY

With increased age and maturity, the infant spends more time awake and finds time to practice sounds when it is not hungry or feeding, upset or fussy. The infant begins to entertain itself by producing new sounds and repeating them with some modification. This is vocal play. In addition, as in the preceding stage, the infant will respond to adult vocalizations by vocalizing back.

Vowel sounds, which grow out of the cooing of the previous stage, are produced first, followed by some consonant sounds (Bever, 1961). At first, there are periods of rapid change in the frequency and variety of these sounds. Just before the onset of babbling, the rate of change in sound production goes down drastically, as the kinds of sounds the baby produces become stabilized.

During this time, adults begin to show and offer items such as toys and household objects to the infant, referring to them by name (Escalona, 1973). By the time the baby is about six months, it in turn begins to show objects to adults by holding them out. A little later, when the baby is about seven or eight months, the adult will draw the child's attention to objects and events by pointing to them and will expect the child's gaze to follow to what is pointed at. Finally, near the end of the first year, the child, too, will begin to point out objects to the adult.

According to the theory of pragmatics proposed by Elizabeth Bates (1976; 1979), which relates the stages of a child's knowledge of language to cognitive development, the child's early signaling devices such as smiling and crying are important precursors to language in that they have an effect on the parent or other adult and thus foster interaction. Later (beyond the stage we are now considering) as the infant matures cognitively it is able to use nonverbal signals intentionally in order to focus adult attention on an object or to request certain objects or actions. The child begins to understand that adults can be used as agents in attaining and attending to environmental objects. Thus pointing is an important prelanguage aspect of communication, since it asserts to the adult that the infant knows an object is there and wants the adult to attend to it. In addition, the child will use the adult to obtain something by taking the adult's hand and reaching with it, tugging at the adult to get him or her to move, or handing an object to the adult to manipulate. As children learn words for objects, they will often accompany them for a while with the gestures they had previously used to point to or ask for these objects. According to Bates, as the child's knowledge of objects becomes more precise, he or she will become able to express in propositional statements made up of words the same performative sequences that he or she already has expressed through these actions. Thus most early two-word combinations will be requests or assertions, such as "more cookie" and "there Daddy," just as the earlier gestures had been.

REDUPLICATIVE BABBLING

Between 6 and 16 weeks, usually closer to the latter, babbling usually begins (Oller, 1981). Some infants, however, do not begin babbling until they are five or six months old. The entire babbling stage lasts about six to eight months; therefore, babies who babble earlier than others are likely to proceed from this stage to the next earlier also. The baby now begins to use sounds that have been produced earlier, as well as new sounds, to produce repetitive syllables such as a-la-la. The borders between the various stages of vocalization, however, are not clear and absolute. For example, when babbling begins, the child is still engaged in some exploratory vocal play, and both these forms of vocalization will occur side by side for several months. Eventually, babbling will predominate. Similarly, when true words begin, many children will continue to babble to some degree for a while, interspersing babbling sounds with words (Clark & Clark, 1977). Others will cease babbling entirely and have a quiet period with little vocalizing just before the first true words appear (Bever, 1961).

All children in all language communities produce early babbling sounds that are much alike. Contrary to popular belief, babies do not babble all possible sounds, but they do produce a large variety, including sounds not generally found in their own language community. Often babies can easily babble a sound that they may have trouble learning later as part of a foreign language. The English l and r sounds for speakers of Chinese or Japanese or the Spanish r sound for English-speakers are examples of such sounds.

Hard-of-hearing infants begin to babble at about the same time and in the same way as do normally hearing infants. The sounds made by the hard-of-hearing are the same up to about six months and then begin to differ. While normal babies increase both the amount of babbling and the number of sounds, the rate of babbling and the number of sounds both decrease in hard-of-hearing babies. This fact suggests that to produce early vocalizations, including the first stages of babbling, children do not have to have feedback provided by the sounds of their own voices or those of others. But after six months such feedback becomes crucial for further language development. While hearing children will babble and use other vocalizations not only for communication but also for pleasure, the hard-of-hearing will vocalize only for the sake of communication (Fry, 1966; Lenneberg, Rebelsky, & Nichols, 1965). Thus it seems likely that hearing itself babble provides not only feedback but also reinforcement to the normally hearing infant and therefore is used for pleasure as well as to communicate with those looking after it.

NONREDUPLICATIVE BABBLING

After several months of increased sound production, babies begin to concentrate on making those sounds that most commonly occur in the language used by the adults around them. Their babbling now begins to sound more and more like true language, as the intonational quality of the language as well as

its sound system are adopted. Around eight months, "da-da," though used inappropriately, appears. That is, the infant uses the word combination but does not refer to the father with it. Thus "da-da" is produced even by children who have no father in the household. A little later, "ma-ma" is said, also inappropriately. But by 10 months, both "da-da" and "ma-ma" are used appropriately in reference to the parents or other adults (Capute, Palmer, Shapiro, Wachtel, & Accardo, 1981).

Fewer purely repetitive syllables are now used. This more advanced kind of babbling is also referred to as lalling. The child now begins to use protowords, which are sounds approaching those of true words but not yet quite "there." Christopher's use of "faddy" to denote both the flower and his sweater would be an example of a protoword. So would "ma," which many children use to refer to milk.

Jargon, which may appear at this time or in some children only later in conjunction with true words, is an entire "sentence" made up of lalling sounds or such sounds intermingled with one or more protowords or true words. Jargon can be distinguished from earlier babbling in that it has the intonational qualities of true speech. Thus adults can guess the emotional tone or intent of the child's communication because the intonation will reveal anger, fear, pleasure, or surprise. They can tell that the child is asking a question by the rising pitch near the end of the "sentence" that is usual in English questions.

REFERENTIAL WORDS

Around the age of one year, babbling will decline in some children in preparation for the beginning of true word usage (Bever, 1961).

As indicated before, however, some children continue to produce lalling sounds and eventually combine them with protowords and/or true words into jargon that sounds like whole sentences even as they are beginning to use words. Some children will continue to babble for quite a while after they begin to use real words, and will alternate the use of these two forms (Clark & Clark, 1977).

During this last portion of the first year, infants become increasingly involved in the language of the adults around them. Sound games are played by parents and baby, in which parents model sounds and the baby tries to reproduce them. Other games involving words, such as peek-a-boo or pat-a-cake, are also favorites. The child learns to wave bye-bye on command. While at first gestural cues given by the adult are important in these games, the infant eventually learns the appropriate responses just from hearing the adult recite the words.

The infant also recognizes the sounds of a number of commonly used words, especially those referring to objects or people in the environment. Thus it understands references to Daddy, bottle, or ball. It will react appropriately to such sentences as "Where's the dog?" by searching for the family pet or "Here comes Mama" by looking expectantly at the front door.

Adults will comment a lot about what is going on around the child, referring to their own actions, the actions of the child, what is happening outside the window, and so forth. Since names of objects and people are easier for the child to understand than are pronoun referents, adults will often refer to themselves during these comments as "Mama" or "Daddy" rather than as "I" or "me," and to the child by name rather than as "you." A mother is more likely to say, "Now Mama is giving Susie a bath," than "Now I am giving

you a bath," or "Give the ball to Mama" than "Give the ball to me."

THE ONE-WORD STAGE

Beginning of Single-Word Utterances

At some time between 10 and 12 months, and most usually around the time of the first birthday, the child will utter her or his first real word. Usually it is a word that refers to an object or person in the environment, but occasionally it is one that signifies an action. Words such as Mama, Baby, ball, doggie, cookie, go, and look, are common first words. First words usually are acquired by direct imitation of adult speech. After the adult has said, "Here's the ball" when handing that object to the child numerous times, the child may say "ball" as the object is handed to her or him. These early words are probably not truly referential, however; that is, referring to the particular object regardless of context. Rather, they are accompaniments of the sensorimotor action, such as the handing of the ball. The child may merely have learned that it is appropriate to use that particular word in that particular context (Fischer & Corrigan, 1981).

After the first word is learned, a few other words follow in close succession, until the average 12-month-old has a vocabulary of about three to eight words, each used singly as an utterance. For several months thereafter additional words are learned relatively slowly.

Such a first word often is accompanied by the gesture that signified it in the preverbal period. For example, "bye-bye" is accompanied by a wave of the hand, "cookie" may include a pantomime of eating, and "bottle" one of holding the bottle and sucking.

Speech and Other Developmental Mechanisms

The onset of true speech is closely related to both motoric and cognitive development. The first word usually appears around the same time as the onset of walking (Shirley, 1959), but either walking or talking is at first practiced so much that the other temporarily is neglected (Netsell, 1981).

If motor development is appreciably ahead of that of language, either hearing loss or some other language problem may be suspected. Conversely, if motor development lags behind language development, then a motor delay, including the possibility of cerebral palsy, may be indicated (Capute et al., 1981).

Language and thought development appear closely related inasmuch as the young child seems able to talk only about those objects, relationships, and events that he or she understands. Therefore, the child's first words express the very objects, actions, or relationships that he or she already understands cognitively and for which gestures and similar communicative strategies have already been developed. These usually are people or objects that are physically present or relationships already observed (Chapman, 1978). At first these may very likely be contextual rather than referential, as has been indicated. Over the first few months of the second year, however, the child begins to use referential language. Now a particular term stands for an event, object, or action across situations or contexts. As the complexity of thought increases, the child is also increasingly able to express thought in more complex linguistic constructions. For example, as object permanence develops, the child can mention an object or person not immediately present. As the idea of quantity and number

develops, the child can begin to use plural endings or words such as "two," or "more." When memory becomes better, the child will refer to past events. As the concept of negation becomes understood, the child will begin to use such words as "no," "not," and "all gone." Later in the second year, as the child begins to sort events and objects into classes and categories, she or he will use verbal labels to express these classifications.

Children learn first the words that relate to what they already know about. In a study of 18 children, Katherine Nelson (1973) found that the most frequently learned and used early words were those referring to food and food utensils (such as cookie, milk, bottle), parts of the body, the names of people and pets (including Mama, Dada or Daddy, the child's own name, or the referent baby), articles of clothing, household items (such as items of furniture like chair or table, cleaning tools like broom, the radio, and television), and the names of toys (such as ball or doll).

Theories

Many researchers of children's language through the early 1970s, who were concentrating upon syntactical development, thought that the child's one-word utterances were **holophrastic,** meaning that the one word stands for a whole sentence or phrase. Holophrastic speech was taken to indicate that the child already had the semantic and syntactical structure of whole sentences in mind but was able to produce only one word, probably because of memory limitations (McNeill, 1970a). David McNeill believed that at the single-word stage the child already had in mind the content, though not necessarily the syntax, of a full sentence and was trying to express complex ideas closely linked to action and/or emotion by the one spoken word. He thought that all children everywhere learn language via a series of hypotheses that they construct about the nature of sentences. The first of these hypotheses, he believed, is that a sentence is composed of one word, and therefore children begin their construction of sentences with one-word utterances.

This idea has been discounted lately for two reasons. First, since children at the one-word stage have a good memory in other regards, it is questionable whether they produce one-word utterances because of memory deficits. They are able, for example, to reel off long strings of jargon or to do a series of sequential sensorimotor tasks without a memory problem. Second, as linguists have become more interested in the content and use of language, they have tended to interpret these early utterances in the light of the child's cognitive immaturity. They believe that the child says only one word at a time because he or she as yet lacks the cognitive complexity to build more complex utterances (Bloom, 1973).

Based on a long-term study of language development in her daughter Allison, Lois Bloom concludes that the one-year-old child knows little or nothing about sentences or sentence formation but does have some knowledge about the people, objects, and events in the environment. Therefore, the child's one-word utterances deal with these and have no syntactical relationship to later sentences as such. Bloom points out that even the later two-word utterances that the child will produce show a very limited understanding of semantic (meaning) or syntactical (grammatical) notions. Therefore, she reasons that the earlier one-word utterances must be based on at least as limited, or perhaps even more limited, a set of knowledge.

Much of the child's understanding of adult language comes from either the context in which it is produced or the gestures and vocal stress or intonation used by the adult, rather than from the grammatical and semantic relationships of the words in the adult's sentences.

P. M. Greenfield and J. H. Smith (1976), in their study of the language development of two toddlers, have concluded that in using one-word utterances children are not referring to the object itself as they name it but rather to the role the object plays. Does it move? Is it a place? Is something done to it? These researchers have derived five roles that children seem to ascribe to the words they use. These roles are 1) movers, which include both animate (such as people or pets) and inanimate objects that move (such as cars and trucks), 2) moveables, or objects that are affected by an action, 3) possessors or recipients of objects, 4) places, and 5) instruments that are used to do something. There is some evidence that not only do children use one-word utterances in this manner, but that as they expand to using two-word combinations each word still conforms to one of these same roles.

Transition to Two-Word Utterances

Around the age of 18 months, many children enter a transitional phase in which they begin to utter two words but usually maintain a space between them. These are not yet true two-word utterances in which the two words are tied together to express some kind of meaningful relationship according to rules. Instead the child seems to recognize several aspects of a referent and comments on these by using successive individual words, each referring to one of these aspects (Leopold, 1939). The child may look at a big brown teddy bear and say "big"——"bear." But that is not the same as the later "big bear." For one thing, word order is not yet fixed

(Bloom, 1970). The child may say "bear" ——"big" instead. For another, often a very definite space occurs between the two words, which is not found in true two-word utterances. Sometimes these early utterances that consist of more than one unrelated word are simply rote productions of successive words that the child has memorized but that convey no meaning through their relationship (Nelson, 1973).

Some researchers such as M. D. S. Braine (1976) believe that the variable word order used during this period reflects a groping pattern on the part of the child. That is, the child is attempting to express meaning but does not yet know the formula by which words are ordered. Therefore the child will sometimes use one word order, "get . . . doggie," and sometimes another, "doggie . . . get." Once the child has figured out the formula by which word position is assigned, he or she stops groping and uses a fixed word order. Braine also believes that some children may learn two separate formulae for the same two words in different contexts or at different times. Then the child will sometimes produce one formula and sometimes the other, each resulting in different word order.

Other researchers such as Melissa Bowerman (1976) and Lois Bloom (Bloom, Lightbown, & Hood, 1975) disagree with the idea of formula learning, because they think that the child does not yet have sufficient knowledge of syntax to combine words even by groping. Bloom (1973) thinks that some children, such as her daughter, progress from single-word utterances to utterances that consist of a single true word that the child has already used plus an indeterminate word of the child's own invention. Christopher's use of "woy", his own indeterminate word, in such constructions as "Mama-woy" would be an example. Bloom says that after a period of using real plus indeterminate words, the child will begin to use two- and three-word utterances made up of true words in which the words appear to have no syntactical relationship. Bloom interprets these, much as Leopold did, as successive independent comments about ongoing events or interesting states. The words are said with pauses between them, and all are stressed equally.

Different Styles of Language Learning

There is some evidence that different children acquire words in different ways (Peters, 1977). Analytic children appear to learn one word at a time, usually by referring to or labeling particular objects or people they are already familiar with. Other children seem to use a gestalt or configurational approach, in which they try to use a whole utterance, or as much of it as they are able to produce, within the context of a conversation.

Mean Length of Utterance

Since children vary greatly in the rate at which they acquire language beyond the one-word stage, chronological age becomes a less useful indicator than it had been with younger children. In describing language production during the child's second year, **mean length of utterance,** or MLU, is the most used indicator of linguistic maturity. MLU is a measure of the mean number of morphemes, or units of meaning, used in the child's speech. Morphemes, it was noted, are words as well as inflectional endings that can be attached to words. For example, "dog" is one morpheme in length, but "dogs" is two, the word dog plus the inflectional ending s that denotes the plural. At the one-word stage, the child's MLU is close to 1.0, though probably a bit higher, since some of these one-word utterances may consist of two morphemes. As two-word utterances begin to be used, the child will continue to make some one-word ones but also some two-word ones, and the MLU may climb to 1.7 or higher. MLU is a good indicator both for tracking an individual child's increasing language production and for comparing the rate of increase among several children. MLU tells only about the number of morphemes used, however, and nothing about the semantic complexity or level of meaning of what the child is expressing, which to some degree is independent of the number of morphemes.

THE TWO-WORD STAGE

Beginning of Two-Word Utterances

At some time not too long beyond 18 months, true two-word utterances begin to appear. The space between the words has disappeared, and word order becomes more regular, though it may differ from child to child and within a child from situation to situation. The word order used by the child may also differ from the usual adult word order. The child continues to use some one-word utterances. He or she may even on occasion produce what appears to be a three-word one, made up of a two-word utterance plus a single-word utterance. With a relatively small total number of words, the child can now begin to express an amazing number of ideas. Not surprisingly, this development occurs just about the time that the child enters the final, or sixth, substage of Piaget's sensorimotor period in which true thought begins.

Shortly after the beginning of two-word utterances, the child also enters a period in which new words are learned rapidly. Between 18 and 24 months, total vocabulary increases at a fast rate, so that the 24-month-old may know between 50 and 100 words or more (Capute et al. 1981).

Early Explanations

Earlier linguists had stressed the structure of two-word utterances. They had tried to build a children's grammar by analyzing the word combinations, assuming that the children who were speaking these word combinations already had some rudimentary ideas of grammar on which to base them. Thus they divided early utterances into two grammatical classes, or groups, of words. These two were pivot words, or functors, and open words, or contentives (Braine, 1963; Brown & Bellugi, 1964; McNeill, 1970b). Pivot words were thought of as similar to later verbs, prepositions, adjectives, and adverbs. Open words were similar to nouns. Thus in the phrase, "more cookie," "more," later to be recognized as an adjective, served as a pivot word. "Cookie," later to be a noun, served as an open word. One major problem these researchers encountered was that only a small percentage of two-word utterances produced by young children could be made to fit into the pivot-open model (Bloom, 1970); others could not be assigned to any grammatical categories, as for example, "Mama chair." Both these words are open words; there is no pivot word. In addition, the same two-word combinations could have the words playing different roles or assuming different grammatical functions depending upon altered context. For example "Mama chair" might refer to a particular chair that belonged to mother, that is, Mama's chair as distinct from the chair belonging to someone else. In this context, "Mama" would be a pivot word, and "chair" an open word. But the same two words could be a comment upon seeing mother sit in a chair, such as the later sentence, "Mama is sitting in the chair." Here are two contentives again. Or else it might refer to mother bringing a chair into the room, as in "Mama is bringing the chair," or "Mama is carrying the chair." Finally, there seemed to be no continuity between these supposed early grammatical structures and later grammatical constructions. This discontinuity called the earlier structures into question. For it seems unreasonable to suppose that the child would build one grammatical system and then later abandon it and build an entirely different one.

Other researchers such as Braine (1971, 1976) believed that some early awareness of grammar must begin during the two-word stage, growing out of the earlier groping pattern. Each child uses a particular grammatical formula he or she has evolved. Some children always put a word for action first, as in "runs doggie," while others always put it last, as in "doggie runs." Unfortunately for this theory, as children's language was analyzed more fully, it was found that children did not stick to particular formulae but changed word order frequently, depending upon the context.

The Semantic View

Many present-day students of children's language think that the child's two-word utterances express semantic rather than grammatical relationships (Schlesinger, 1971; Bowerman, 1973). That is, they have to do with the meaning of the situation the child is commenting on, rather than being a group of words related in a grammatical manner. The child develops notions of such things as agent, possessor, or action long before those of subject, verb, or direct object. The child realizes that people or animals do things, that is, are agents. Only much later does he

or she figure out that agents are usually the subjects of sentences. These agents perform certain actions, and again the child is aware of these actions—runs, says, gives—long before he or she realizes that they are verbs. Finally, the person owns, or acts in certain ways on, other things. These later become objects in the grammatical sense. So the child says "baby eat" and "eat cookie" and later "baby eat cookie" and is aware of who is doing what to what, that is, the semantic categories. The grammatical relationships evolve only later from semantic ones, rather than being the basis upon which word groups are at first constructed.

For example, Bloom believes that two-word utterances can express functional relationships based upon notions of existence or nonexistence, occurrence or recurrence (such as "no candy", "more banana" or "this doggie"). Or else they can express beginning grammatical relationships based on conceptual relationships between persons, objects, and events (such as "Mama sock," which expresses a subject-object relationship, that is, (Mama has a sock, or a possessive one, such as Mama's sock). She believes that functional relationships are learned somewhat earlier than are grammatical ones but that both types are closely linked to the ongoing situational context as well as to the child's own actions.

In a still controversial study of the language development of four children (Bloom et al. 1975), Bloom has added to these two categories of two-word constructions a third that expresses verb relations. These two-word sentences describe either events or actions (such as "cookie allgone" or "Mama get"). After building these three types of two-word utterances, the child goes on to develop semantic categories such as agent, action, or object of action and to begin to understand that some words will fit into one or several of these categories, while others will fit only into one specific one. Thus a noun such as "Mama" can be either an agent (as in "Mama bring") or an object of an action (as in "get Mama"). But a verb such as "get" can only express an action and cannot be an agent. The child thus builds a rudimentary grammar out of semantic relationships that she or he has learned to express.

C. J. Fillmore (1968, 1971) distinguishes semantic concepts from grammatical relations. He believes that while there is a grammatical base to early children's language, it is related to the roles words play. This research has developed what are called case grammars, which appear to be related to later more adult grammars. According to Fillmore, nouns can have varying case roles that foreshadow those used by adults in expressing semantic relationships. In any statement, only one noun can occupy a particular case role. These case roles are similar to the role categories that Greenfield and Smith found used at the one-word stage, but here they are used in combinations of two or more words.

Case roles are difficult to explain to speakers of English, since English nouns have no case endings and their case has to be inferred. In those other languages in which nouns have case endings, it is easy to see what roles they play just by looking at the written endings or hearing them spoken. Therefore let us use pronouns, which have cases even in English, as examples. When the pronoun that refers to self is used as a subject of a sentence, the subjective case form, I, must be used. When the pronoun refers to the object of the sentence, the objective case form, me, rather than I, must be used. In children's speech, several cases can be used for nouns. They include the agentive case, referring to the agent, or doer, of something.

This word is usually the name of a person or animal, such as Mama, Daddy, Susie, or Rover, or of impersonals such as man or dog. The instrumental case refers to an inanimate object used to perform an action. For example, if Mother is using the broom to sweep the floor, and the child is using the word broom to comment on the action, "broom" would be in the instrumental case. The case of experiencer refers to the person or object being affected by the action of the verb but not actually performing an action. The word Johnny in "Johnny is sleepy" would be in the experiencer case. The goal case refers to an object or state that results from an action, such as "Mama baked cookies," in which "cookies" is in the goal case. Finally, the locative case refers to position or location of an object or person. For example, in the sentence "Daddy is home," "home" is in the locative case.

Thus, it can be seen that words that were in the mover role in one-word utterances are now used in the agentive case, movables become goal, or objective, case, possessors or recipients are in the experiencer case, places become locative case, and instruments are instrumental case (Clark & Clark, 1977).

Not all of these cases, however, are used with the same frequency by all young children. There is wide individual variance among children. Also, cases that are cognitively easier are used more generally and earlier by most children than those that are more difficult conceptually. Agentive, objective, and locative cases are at first used far more frequently than is the experiencer case. The instrumental case is used the least and last of all.

Other supporters of the case-grammar concept include Bowerman (1973) and I. M. Schlesinger (1971). Bowerman believes that children learn the relationships between words that are in fact nouns and verbs in adult speech by deducing that nouns express agent, objective, location, or instrument. Thus they learn semantic concepts first and base their grammatical learning upon these. Schlesinger basically agrees with this point of view and adds as evidence for it the regularities of early speech across children. These regularities occur, he believes, because children acquire positional rules (that is, rules of where in a sentence a word should appear) based upon the semantic quality of words and thus do so in the same way.

The present-day emphasis on semantic and contextual rather than syntactical relationships in attempting to explain the development of language in young children is surely not the last word as researchers continue to investigate unanswered questions.

Uses of Two-Word Sentences

Children use two-word sentences primarily for two functions, to comment on an ongoing situation and to request something. Both of these verbal functions grow out of the gestures Bates found children using to perform the same functions in the preverbal period. Comments may be negations such as "no cookie." Often two-word comments consist of a word the adult and child have already used, plus the child's additional comment about it. After the adult acknowledges the child's input, the child may proceed to another comment about the same subject. Thus the child may say "cookie good." When the adult agrees, the child may go on to "more cookie," or "cookie allgone." Requests are usually either for information, such as the location of an object or person ("where Daddy?") or else for an action that the child wants the adult to perform ("take shoe").

The relationships expressed in these sentences are appropriate to the ongoing sit-

Children learn to use their native language by listening to the speech of adults. They learn additional language constructs from being read to, because certain words and grammatical combinations are more likely to be found in written language than in everyday speech.

uation. Therefore, in spite of the limited number of words the child can use, and the constraints imposed by the length of the utterances, the adult has no trouble interpreting what the child means if the adult is present in the situation. Only those listening later to an audiotape who were not present in the original situation may have trouble figuring out the child's meaning. The word order the child uses generally is also essentially the correct one for the child's own language. That is, although many words that would be used in adult speech are left out, or rather have not yet been put in, those that the child does use are in their correct location. For example, in English the usual word order is agent-action-object (as in "The baby eats the cookie"). The child will use agent-action ("baby eat") or agent-object ("baby cookie") or action-object ("eat cookie"). He or she is unlikely to use object-agent ("cookie baby"), object-action ("cookie eat"), or action-agent ("eat baby") combinations, which generally do not occur in adult English. However, in learning languages in which adult speech would place the object or action before the agent, children learn two-word combinations that follow that particular word order appropriately.

Adult Speech to the Child

Around the time that the child produces the first two-word combination, adults tend to modify their speech to the child from a kind of baby talk to a form of simplified adult speech (Phillips, 1973). The child's use of these protosentences evidently signifies to the adult that the child is now truly becoming a verbal communicator. The adult is careful, however, to adjust speech to the perceived immaturities of the child's understanding. Sentences are far shorter and less complex than those used in adult discourse. The most common referents for particular objects are used in such speech. For example, the adult is more likely to say "dog" than "beagle" in talking to the child. Pitch is generally still higher than in conversations between adults, though lower than the artificially high pitch previously used to draw the young baby's attention. The most important words are enunciated clearly and given more stress. Although name referents such as Mama or Baby are still used, the adult increasingly begins to use pronouns such as I, you, or we.

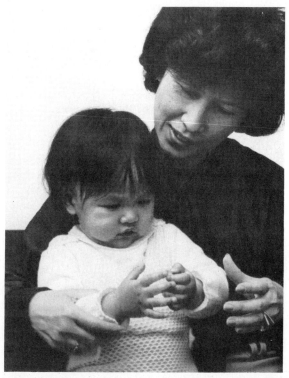

Adults adjust their speech to the child's immature understanding by using shorter, more simplified sentences than they would in speaking to other adults. They also expand on the child's utterances by adding information and by using correct grammatical versions of the child's immature utterances. But they do not directly correct the child's immaturities of grammar or pronunciation, only errors of fact.

The adult will typically reply to the child's two-word (and later three-word) utterances by expanding upon them, adding both words and information that the child did not use. If the child says "Truck coming" the adult is likely to reply, "Yes, a big truck is coming." The adult also, however, will add some new information, such as "That is the garbage truck." Note that the adult first repeats what the child has said, keeping the child's word order but inserting words that should be there in adult speech which the child is not yet using. Then some new piece of information is added, so that the adult is not just parroting back the child's speech but is adding her or his own comment as well.

Adults tend to overlook the child's immaturities of grammar and pronunciation. They will correct only errors of fact or gross errors of pronunciation (Brown & Hanlon, 1970). But in expanding on the child's sentence they do so using correct grammar. Thus if the child says "truck comed" the parent is likely to reply, "Yes, the big truck came." If the child makes an error of fact, such as saying "yellow truck comed," and the truck in fact is red, or the vehicle is a car and not a truck, the adult will offer a correction, such as "That truck is not yellow, it's red" or "That's not a truck, it's a car."

In addition to expanding and commenting, adults often use two other techniques in eliciting continued speech from children, prompting and echoing (McNeill, 1970a; Dale, 1972). In prompting, the adult rephrases a question to which the child has not responded in order to elicit the response. If the adult had asked, "What are you eating?" and received no reply, he or she may rephrase this into "You are eating——what?"

Echoing is the process whereby the adult will repeat the intelligible portion of a child's partially unintelligible phrase, in order to induce the child to repeat more clearly what had not been understood. If the child says, "I want (unintelligible)," the adult will come back with "You want——what?" or "you want——whom?"

LATER ACQUISITION OF LANGUAGE

Much of what the child learns beyond the two-word stage occurs after the age of two years and is thus beyond the scope of this book. But some brief comments on increased semantic and syntactical competence that occurs in the child after the acquisition of two-word phrases are included here.

Early sentences that are longer than two words are at first likely to be combinations of either a word plus a two-word phrase or else two two-word phrases put together. Pronouns may begin to be added at this time, particularly "I" in reference to self. "See truck" now becomes "I see truck."

As the child passes from two-word to three-word or longer sentences, inflectional endings start to be used. This fact appears to be equally true for children learning relatively noninflectional languages such as English and for those learning more inflectional ones such as Russian (McNeill, 1970a). For example, in Russian, case endings are added to adjectives to show whether the word they are describing is masculine, feminine, or neuter. At the two-word stage, Russian children generally use only one case ending with all adjectives, regardless of the gender of the noun each modifies. But at the three-word stage, they begin to alternate the use of several case endings of adjectives, although at first they don't always use the correct one.

Plural indicators, such as the terminal "s" in English, also come into use. Verb endings denoting tense, which occur in both Russian and English, and of course in other languages as well, appear. The child will say "I walked" in referring to something already done, where earlier he or she might have said "I walk" referring to either past or present indiscriminately. The various semantic and syntactical forms of the same ending sound may not, however, appear at the same time. For example, the terminal "s" denoting the plural (such as in "dogs") is acquired long before the terminal "s" denoting the third person singular ending of a verb (such as "walks") (Bellugi, 1964).

As children begin to form verb endings and plurals, they will at first learn the correct form for those that are irregular by hearing adults using them correctly and mimicking them. For a time the child will correctly say, "I came" and "Mama saw" as well as use plurals such as "sheep" or "mice." As children absorb the rules for forming verb tenses and plurals, they stop using these correct formations of the irregular words and attempt to regularize them. This process is referred to as rule overgeneralization. It produces some of the charming aberrations of child language that adults enjoy laughing about, such as "I comed home" or "I seed the mouses." Later yet, the child will realize that some of these words form the plural or the past in an irregular manner and will return to the correct usage.

Overgeneralization is an important phenomenon for students of children's language because it provides evidence that children have internalized, or learned to use, the rules pertaining to their native language. For if they used only the proper form of plurals and past tenses where appropriate, it would be impossible to determine whether they were just copying what they had heard or had absorbed the rules. When a child applies a rule in the situation in which it does not hold, or uses a construction he or she has never heard adults use, researchers are led to the conclusion that the child must indeed have learned such a rule.

As the child's cognitive skills and experience increase, his or her language shows a concomitant refinement. Negation, or nonexistence, which had earlier been expressed simply as "no" or "allgone" (as in "no cookie" or "milk allgone"), now can be expressed in many different ways. The child may still use "no" but also uses "not" or

"don't." The use of questions increases. Questions involving location ("Where's the doggie?") or identity ("What is this?") precede those involving more complicated intellectual notions such as causality ("Why is it raining?").

LANGUAGE DEVELOPMENT OF THE HARD-OF-HEARING CHILD

There appear to be optimal maturational stages during which speech and language learning occur most easily. The closer to the normal developmental timetable related to speech and hearing that the hearing-handicapped child can attain milestone skills, the more likely he or she is to develop functional speech (Pollack, 1970). In contrast to the child with normal hearing, however, the child with a hearing loss will not have a hearing age that is the same as her or his chronological age (Pollack, 1970). Rather the hearing age will date from the time that a hearing aid is first worn and sounds are perceived. So on the one hand, children who are hearing-impaired should be expected to reach speech milestones not according to their chronological age but according to their hearing age. On the other, the closer together these two ages are, the more language and speech learning are facilitated. Therefore, the need for early identification of hearing problems and the early use of a hearing aid becomes clear.

The early language development of the hard-of-hearing child is remarkably like that of the child with unimpaired hearing. Crying, other early sounds, cooing, and laughing all occur just as they do in other children. The cries of the hearing-impaired may be higher pitched than those of the unaffected child, but essentially, early sound production appears normal (Jones, 1965). Babbling begins at the appropriate time and continues normally till about 24 to 26 weeks of age. At this time, as normal infants begin to use feedback from their own babbling and from the language of the adults around them to make sounds that are increasingly similar to those in their native language, babbling in the hard-of-hearing child without special help will diminish and finally cease.

As babbling progresses, the child must be exposed to auditory feedback from babbling. Recorded sounds of the child's own babbling and that of others, played to the child on a tape recorder, are useful. So is the repetition back to the child of her or his babbling sounds by adults (Mavilya & Mignone, 1977).

In order to learn to speak words, the child must also learn to localize sound, that is, be able to locate its source. Adults must always point out to the child the sound source when playing listening games. Thus the child will begin to associate sounds with their source. He or she must also be able to discriminate between sounds. And finally he or she must begin to reproduce those sounds.

Hearing in the hard-of-hearing child can be fostered by exposing the child to experiences such as learning the awareness of loud versus quiet sounds, learning to attend to a variety of sounds, associating objects with the sounds they make (which trains in localizing sound sources) and recognizing sounds (developing a knowledge of what they mean) (Pollack, 1970). Adults should use a minimum of gestures when speaking to the child

so that the child does not try to guess from context what the adult is saying but is forced to concentrate on listening.

Just as the normally hearing child first learns a word by associating it to an experience, so will the hard-of-hearing child if adults talk to him or her as experiences are occurring. Parents must be sure to talk to the child while doing routine chores such as bathing and dressing him or her, while out for walks, and at the dinner table. Particularly during the early part of the second year, naming objects and events to the child as they occur becomes extremely important. Adults should not just repeat the name of an object but should use short phrases with the name in them. Adults should keep sentences short and meaningful and linked to the activity or object the child is involved with (Northcott, 1972, 1977). When the child begins to produce short utterances, expansion of these into slightly longer ones is also important, just as for the normally hearing child.

Many hearing-impaired children whose condition is diagnosed relatively early, who use a hearing aid to help residual hearing, and whose families work conscientiously with them in speech development attain normal or near normal speech and language functions. A series of lesson plans for parents to use in teaching their hearing-impaired child can be obtained from The John Tracy Clinic, 806 West Adams Boulevard, Los Angeles, CA 90007.

Summary

1. Language is symbolic communication transmitted by speech or writing. Any language is composed of four sets of components or aspects: semantic, or meaning; syntactical, or grammatical; phonological, or sound; and lexical, or the total corpus of words used in the particular language.

2. Children know or understand more of

language (language competence) than they are able to produce (language performance). Thus infants understand some of adult speech long before they are able to utter any words. Even older children and adults generally understand more complex language forms than they produce.

3. Early linguists were not particularly interested in the study of the beginnings of children's language. When some interest was shown beginning in the 1950s, it generally centered on the form, or structure, of children's language, that is, the development of syntax, or grammar. More recent study from the 1970s on has concentrated on the use and content of early language, that is, the meaning conveyed by the child.

4. Early sounds that are precursors to speech include crying, vegetative sounds, exploratory vocal play, cooing and laughing, and babbling. Finally, around the age of one year, true referential speech begins.

5. First words usually are learned in direct imitation of adult speech and accompany actions with objects in which the adult has labeled these objects. Soon the child begins to use other referential words dealing with objects, toys, people, and pets in the environment.

6. One-word utterances probably are not holophrastic, that is, referring to a whole sentence or idea, but limited because of memory deficits to only one word. Instead, the child probably is referring to the role the particular object named is playing within the context of the child's comment on it.

7. Around the age of 18 months, the child begins to utter two-word combinations. At first these are separate one-word utterances produced in sequence. Later they become true two-word utterances in that the two together convey a particular thought.

8. Linguists of the 1950s and 1960s analyzed these two-word combinations to discover if the child had formed them according to a rudimentary grammar. More recent emphasis has been on the semantic relationships expressed by two-word utterances. They can express functional relationships such as existence, occurrence, possession, or agent acting upon object. Children use two-word sentences either to comment on the ongoing situation or to request something from the adult.

9. Adult speech to the young child is adjusted both in the words used and the length of sentences to the immaturities of the learner. Adults tend to comment upon the child's two-word utterances by expanding upon them. They will not correct the child's immaturities of expression or pronunciation but instead will demonstrate the proper usage. Only if the child makes an error of fact will an adult provide correction.

10. As the child begins to use three-word combinations, usually after the age of two years, he or she also begins to use inflectional endings such as plural indicators and verb tenses. At first, children will use irregular plurals and verbs correctly, but later they overgeneralize the rules to produce regularized versions of the irregulars such as "comed" or "sheeps." Still later, these irregulars are again formed correctly.

11. Hearing-impaired children proceed through the early stages of preverbal sound production like normal children. They need, however, to be exposed to the sounds of their own babbling via amplification, to learn to seek the sources of sound, and to hear a lot of adult speech associated with tasks and objects in the environment. The use of a hearing aid from as early as is possible is vital for adequate language development in the hearing-impaired child.

Participatory and Observational Exercises

1. Observe parents or other caregivers in early communicative interactions with an infant. Watch several such interactions or several adult-infant pairs if possible.

a. Can you see the suck-jiggle phenomenon during feeding? Besides jiggling, what other communicative techniques does the adult use?

b. How and when does the infant break off eye contact? How does the adult try to reinstate it?

c. Watch and listen as the adult talks to the infant. What infant behaviors does the adult use as if the infant were participating in a dialogue? Record the "dialogue," giving both the adult's words and the infant behaviors the adult uses as if they were words.

d. Can you observe differences in communicative strategies between different adults as they talk to infants? Are some more effective communicators than others? Explain.

2. Observe infants of varying ages in a group setting such as a day-care center or church nursery, or else make home visits to several infants of different ages.

a. Observe and record all vocal behavior for each infant. At what ages are crying, cooing, reduplicative and nonreduplicative babbling, and jargon used? When can you begin to hear intonation in the child's vocal productions? When does vocalizing begin to sound like language? Are any real words produced?

b. What gestures, facial expressions, and other nonverbal techniques does each child use to convey communicative intent? De-

scribe these as you observe them. Do you or other adults have any trouble figuring out the child's meaning?

c. Relate your observations both to the progression with increasing age that occurs in vocal and verbal behavior in all children and to individual differences among the children you have observed.

3. Listen to, and if possible record, toddler speech. What kinds of words do toddlers use? How long are their "sentences?" What do adults reply to toddler speech? Are there instances of expansion by adults? Do adults correct the toddler's speech, and if so, what kinds of things do they correct? Record the adult speech as well.

4. If possible, listen to toddlers speaking to each other. How does toddler speech to peers differ from that to adults?

5. Interview parents of toddlers. Do they remember their child's first word? What was it? How old was the child when the first word was used? What other words came next? Did the child make up any of her or his own words? What were they? How did the adults figure out the meaning of such words? What examples of charming or colorful "errors" of speech can parents remember their child making?

DISCUSSION QUESTIONS

1. Should adults use baby talk in talking to an infant or toddler? Why or why not?

2. Is it important to talk to an infant who is too young to understand what you are saying?

Socioemotional Development

CHAPTER 11

I can vividly remember my daughter Anne's first social smile. It was Christmas Eve. As I bent over her crib, Anne's face lit up in a joyful smile that obviously was directed at me. With that smile I felt myself "hooked" on motherhood as surely as a drug addict becomes "hooked" on his supply of drugs.

The human infant begins life already uniquely prepared to express its feelings and to begin social interactions with those who care for it. The social smile is perhaps the young infant's most dramatic social technique to attract and keep the attention of other people. From birth on, however, the infant is capable of using other expressions to initiate overtures to adults and to respond to theirs. Distress and contentment can be shown by the neonate. Visual attention, crying, and other sounds serve to attract adults to provide caregiving and attention. Later in infancy such additional behaviors as the expression of happiness, glee, wariness, fear, affiliation, and curiosity will follow, for the infant is, above all, a social and emotional being. It depends upon interaction with others not only for physical survival, but also for the development of its intellectual and communicative abilities and for emotional support. Perception, cognition, and language all develop within the social context of the infant's interactions with the people around it, especially the parents. The warm, loving relationship that is mutually established between infant and adult is as critical for the infant's healthful emotional development as is food and warmth for its physical well-being.

In a consideration of socioemotional development in infancy, a number of terms that are used should first be described and defined. First of all, there is the concept of affect. **Affect** is the same as feeling. It usually is taken to include such feelings as pleasure and discomfort. In the very young infant, af-fect may have a purely physiological basis, that is, it comes about because of various physical states within and around the infant, with little or no voluntary control by the infant. At first, affect is expressed primarily in nonsocial situations, as for example the very earliest smiling that occurs to internal cues or to nonsocial stimuli such as toys. **Emotions** include not only affect but also the intellectual or cognitive interpretation of the situation in which these feelings are expressed (Sroufe, 1979). Thus they are somewhat more advanced than mere affect and arise somewhat later, probably around the two- to three-month period. Since most situations in which emotions are expressed are social ones, that is, involving other people, emotion usually also involves social factors. Therefore we could say that emotions are expressions of affect that take into consideration both cognitive and social situational variables. Although emotions are thus more advanced or of a higher order than is affect, most writers use emotions and affect, or the adjectives emotional and affective, in a relatively interchangeable manner.

While social interactions between infant and parent probably always have an affective or emotional component, they are not totally emotional in nature. For example, such social devices as mutual gazing, vocal or physical play, exploration of the environment while in the presence of the parent, or various expressions of communicative intent between the two have aspects that are above and beyond the mere expression of affect or feeling and its interpretation. Therefore social and emotional, although they interact, are not the same. In recognition of this interactive situation, this chapter uses the term **socioemotional** in describing the development of the infant's emotional states in interaction with the social situation.

Emotions can serve a communicative

function. The relation to communication is complex. In part, emotions indicate internal states, representing pain, anger, or joy. In part they reflect qualitative responses to social situations, such as adverse reactions to strangers. As the infant expresses emotions, these affect the behaviors of those around it as well as its subsequent behaviors. When emotional expression deviates from the expected, as, for example, in blind or severely retarded infants, parents and other caregivers often report that their reactions to the infant are disturbed and troubled.

Early studies of infancy emphasized the influence of the adult on the social behavior of the infant and pretty much ignored the contributions of the infant to the relationship. Early students of social behavior believed that infant socialization proceeded merely as a result of adult behaviors toward the infant. More recently, beginning with the work of Richard Bell (1968), researchers have become aware of the two-way nature of such relationships, with each partner exerting an effect upon the behaviors of the other. And they now realize that the infant takes a very active role in this interaction. Social interaction thus involves a dyadic relationship to which each partner contributes in alternation with the other and depends upon feedback from the other to modulate her or his next response. Since the infant evidently is born with some capacities for social interaction already operational, as if pre-wired by nature to begin to act and react in a social manner to caregivers as soon as born, one is led to infer that such interaction must be of great importance for the survival and normal development of the child.

The importance of social and emotional interaction with adults for the psychological and physical well-being of the infant has been apparent at least since the famous experiment conducted by the Holy Roman Emperor Frederick II in the 13th century. As described by the friar Salimbene (Ross & McLaughlin, 1949), the chronicler of his reign, Frederick was trying to determine the original language of humanity by seeing which language children would begin speaking if they were exposed to no speech at all. He hired some foster mothers for a group of motherless infants and forbade them to talk to the children or otherwise interact much during caregiving procedures. Unfortunately, he did not find the answer to his question because the children all died in early infancy in spite of what was presumably good physical care. Salimbene correctly attributed their death to the fact that they "could not live without the petting and joyful faces and loving words" of adults (Ross & McLaughlin, 1949, p.366).

Although the importance of social interaction with adults was thus recognized long ago, scientific study of the socioemotional development of infants did not begin until the end of the 19th century, and has been prominent only since the 1940s.

THEORETICAL APPROACHES

No single theoretical approach appears able to explain adequately the various constructs or ideas involved in infant social and emotional development. That is, each of the various theories seems adequate to explain some aspects but is unable to account for others. Therefore, there is no one strong theoretical base for the explanation of social and emotional development in infancy. The various theories, however, are not necessarily antithetical or mutually exclusive.

Theoretical approaches to socioemotional development include psychoanalytic and psychosocial ones such as those of Freud and Erik Erikson and classical conditioning and operant conditioning, especially social-learning theory, approaches. Additionally there are theories based on cognition and ethological theories that relate social development to the evolutionary development of the human species.

A brief overview of several of the most important theories that attempt to explain the growth of mutual responsiveness, interaction, and affection between infant and adult as well as infant and peers is presented here. Most of the theories relating to socioemotional development focus primarily upon the growth of emotions. They center especially upon the construct of **dependency,** which later with the recognition of the two-way nature of social development came to be called **attachment.** In addition, the theories attempt to explain other emotional expressions such as why older infants become wary and often frightened of strangers. The theories also investigate the reasons why secure attachment to the primary caregiver sometimes does not occur and what the consequences of this lack of attachment might be.

Psychoanalytic Theory

The psychoanalytic viewpoint emphasizes the causes, or antecedents, of particular behaviors shown by the child and is less concerned with the goals or adaptive purposes of the behaviors. According to Freudian **psychoanalytic theory,** the infant at birth is unable to recognize any reality beyond itself. Freud posited that the infant possesses from birth on a basic motivational function, the **id,** which attempts to achieve immediate gratification of its needs. The infant has a set of needs that must be met, such as those for food and dry diapers. The unmet needs result in a high level of drive. The alleviation of these needs make the infant feel satisfied or gratified. The mother, who is most likely to provide the food, dry diaper, and comforting that meet the child's needs, becomes associated with the provision of satisfactions and thus serves as a strong tension reducer or drive reducer for the child. An especially important function of the mother is providing milk, via breast or bottle, since milk not only is drive-reducing but also gratifies the child's oral need to suck. Over time, the infant thus builds a strong relationship with the mother because she is the object that both gratifies its needs and serves a drive-reducing function.

At first, the young infant feels that it is in complete control over the mother. It is unable to recognize that the mother is a distinct, separate individual and believes that what the mother does is due to the infant's actions. Gradually, as the infant realizes that the mother is not always responsive to its summons, it learns that the mother is a separate person who cannot be completely controlled and who in turn exerts a lot of control over the child. As a result, the mother does not always serve a drive-reducing function. For example, in trying to make the child conform to family time patterns such as sleeping through the night or not demanding feeding just as the family begins its dinner, and later in controlling such functions as elimination, the mother imposes constraints that may increase rather than decrease the child's drive states.

Because of these externally imposed controls and the increased drives that result from them, the second of Freud's dynamic functions, the **ego,** begins to develop. The ego is that portion of the developing self that deals with reality around the child. Thus the ego represents self in reality and develops out of the fear of punishment or threat through the socialization process. It attempts to control the id by trying to control the ways in which needs are gratified, that is, it tries to reduce drive in socially acceptable ways. The ego develops slowly during infancy, as the infant learns more about social and environmental constraints and how to conform to them. The third of Freud's principles, the **superego,** which is roughly analogous to conscience, does not develop until after infancy and toddlerhood and thus will not be dealt with here.

The development of the ego is most strongly affected by the type of the infant's relationship with the mother. The quality of mothering is, according to Freud, crucial for the normal development of the ego. For this reason, psychoanalytic theorists have shown much interest in the study of the effects of indifferent mothering, separation, and institutionalization upon the development of the child's ego. If the relationship is a good one, then because the mother is both a powerful person and one to whom the child has become attached due to her own need gratifying functions, the older infant and toddler begins to identify with her, that is, to try to imitate her behavior as a means of being like her.

Psychoanalytic theory posited that later socioemotional developments such as wariness and fear of strangers and distress and protest at separation from the mother were not just indicators of maturational stages through which all children passed. Instead, they depended upon the quality of mothering the child had received up to that time. The child who had been raised in an atmosphere of security and freedom from anxiety would be less likely to show distress than a child who had been exposed to many frustrations.

Erikson's **psychosocial** theory differs somewhat from Freud's in stressing more the development of the child's ego over that of the id and in emphasizing the importance of culture in determining child-care practices. Erikson also believes that while early experiences are important, the child can grow out

of and overcome frustrations and deprivations of early infancy and still develop relatively normally. He sees the individual as possessing some self-righting or self-healing tendencies that Freud did not. Erikson posits that, in early infancy, there is a stage of the development of basic trust in others because the infant's needs are regularly met by adults such as the mother. Consequently, the infant comes to expect that the world around it is basically a good, friendly place and that people are to be trusted and relied upon to meet its needs. But if the young infant's needs are met after much delay or not at all, it will instead develop an attitude of mistrust in people. The trusting child will later develop a sense of her or his own competence and ability to master problems in interacting with others and in the environment, while the mistrusting child will be unsure of her or his own capabilities, and of the willingness of other people to meet her or his needs.

During the toddler period, according to Erikson, the child enters a second stage, when it may develop a sense of autonomy because it feels some control over the self and the environment. If adults do not let the child show some independence, however, or if the child is held up to ridicule for what it does, a sense of doubt and shame, entailing feelings of incompetence and unworthiness, will develop.

One problem with the emphasis on the intensive mother-child relationship posited by Freudian and Eriksonian theorists is that it is based solely on Western (that is, European and North American) patterns of infant care. In other cultures, child care is often shared among many maternal figures, including grandmothers, aunts, and neighbors. Indeed this pattern is becoming more usual even in the West at present as more women are in the labor force. Yet children raised under such conditions also show a similar development of the ego, and later the superego. Thus the exclusive focus on the mother may be in error.

Furthermore, in some cultures, shame and ridicule are extensively used during the child's second year to assure obedience and adherence to group standards. Yet, contrary to Erikson's ideas, such children do develop a good deal of autonomy.

Another related critique of psychoanalytic explanations arises because even in nuclear families the infant becomes attached to people that do not serve much of a drive-reducing function as well as to those who do. Typically the infant becomes as attached to the father, who provides little or no food or dry diapers, as to the mother, who does. Similarly, infants in day-care centers or homes form primary attachments to their parents, with whom they interact only for short periods daily, rather than to the day-care staff, who provide most of the food and alleviation of distress.

Furthermore, in spite of Freud's emphasis on the importance of the early emotional relationship between mother and infant, infants denied this relationship because of illness, foster care and later adoption, or wartime separation, often make relatively good social adjustments later in life. People seem to be more plastic and self-restoring in spite of distressing early experiences than psychoanalytic theory, particularly that of Freud, predicts. Thus today, drive reduction is no longer considered an exclusive motivation principle for the development of socioemotional relationships in infancy. There seems to be some support, however, for the notion that securely attached infants will adjust more easily to temporary separation from parents and to the presence of strangers than will less securely attached ones. We shall discuss the research done with this construct in greater detail later.

Classical-Conditioning Theories

Like the psychoanalytic theory, explanations of social development based on learning theory, whether classical or operant in their emphasis, tend to focus on the causes of behaviors rather than on their consequences. Classical-conditioning theories to help explain socioemotional development became prominent at the same time as they were used to demonstrate learning in the infant, that is, during the 1920s. We have already discussed in the section on learning the experiment conducted by John B. Watson and Rosalie Rayner (1920) in conditioning fear in a child and the opposite one of counterconditioning and thus eliminating fear done by Mary Cover Jones (1924). Watson and his contemporaries believed that many social behaviors were learned through pairing of unconditional and conditional stimuli, just as he experimentally demonstrated using the loud noise and the white rat. Therefore, Watson attempted to explain much of the socioemotional behavior of the infant such as crying, smiling, and fussing in terms of conditioning done unwittingly by the parents through the circumstances under which they responded to the child. He cautioned parents against showing undue affection (such as hugging or kissing the child) because the child could learn bad habits, such as habitual crying or attempting to get attention, from such parental behaviors. In addition, he advocated keeping the child on a strict schedule for sleeping and eating and warned against exposing the child to excessive social as well as nonsocial stimulation.

While classical conditioning can certainly explain the development of a conditioned association producing emotions such as fear of certain objects once fear reactions to others already exist, it is unable to explain the origin of fear as such or the relatively sudden onset of fear of strangers (who usually are not accompanied by sudden noises as was the rat in Watson's experiment). Classical-conditioning theory also is at a loss to explain why children who are picked up promptly eventually cry less and seem to be less "spoiled" than those attended to according to Watson's strict schedules. While classical-conditioning theory can explain attachment to the mother, since she provides food or other comfort and thus becomes a conditional stimulus by being paired with the unconditional stimulus of food, it cannot explain any better than can psychoanalytic theory the attachment that is formed to the father or siblings who presumably are not paired with such stimuli.

Operant-Conditioning Theories

Theories based on operant, or instrumental, conditioning explain the attachment of child to an adult in terms of the reinforcing properties of the adult. That is, because the mother provides primary reinforcement such as food or the alleviation of discomfort, she becomes paired with these conditions and herself becomes a strong learned, or secondary, reinforcer. After a while, even when she is not providing food or other tangible comfort, the mere presence of the mother, her face and her voice, all serve as secondary reinforcers to the infant. Again, one problem encountered by this approach also is to explain the attachment to those who are not paired with primary reinforcers and therefore cannot become secondary ones.

Operant-conditioning theory also is at a loss to explain why the reinforcement of crying appears to result in less crying than the attempt to extinguish it by ignoring the crying (Bell & Ainsworth, 1972). Of course, as we have discussed in chapter 5, there are some methodological criticisms of the Bell

and Ainsworth study that cast some doubt on their conclusions.

Social-Learning Theory

Social-learning theorists are largely concerned with the learning of social behaviors through the use of modeling. Since the adult functions as a strong social reinforcer, the child tends to imitate the behaviors of the adult. Many emotional reactions as well as social behaviors are thought to be learned by the child through observation and subsequent imitation of adult behaviors.

Social-learning theory, however, similarly to psychoanalytic and classical- and operant-conditioning theories, cannot adequately explain why the father who interacts so much less with the infant is as strong a social reinforcer as is the nonemployed mother who is home with the child all day, and why he also functions as an important social model. It also is unable to explain why working parents, who spend little time with the child, are also greater models for child behavior than day-care workers who are with the child longer and who presumably have greater secondary reinforcing properties. Social-learning theory cannot adequately account for the beginning of emotional expressions such as smiling, which occur first in nonsocial contexts. And it can not explain why separation protest occurs in the older infant.

In addition, and unfortunately for both the various learning and psychoanalytic theories, some studies done in the 1960s by Harry and Margaret Harlow (Harlow & Harlow, 1966, 1969) using monkeys appear to refute both these explanations for the development of attachment.

Harlow and Harlow separated baby monkeys from their mothers shortly after birth but provided mother surrogates, which

The Harlows' experiments with wire and terry cloth mother surrogates showed that contact comfort was more important than the provision of food for the development of attachment. Most monkey infants would spend their time clinging to the soft terry cloth mother and only go to the wire mother, which held the feeding bottle, long enough to satisfy hunger. This infant monkey is trying to get the best of both, by clinging as much as is possible to the cloth mother while getting a few sips of milk from the bottle on the wire mother.

were wire contraptions with schematic faces to which nursing bottles filled with milk could be attached. In one experiment, baby monkeys were given a choice between a wire "mother" that had a bottle available for sucking milk and one covered with terry cloth that did not provide milk. The infant monkeys spent only enough time clinging to the wire mother to satisfy hunger but would spend the rest of the time clinging to the soft cloth mother. Since the wire mother pro-

vided the food, both psychoanalytic and learning theories would have predicted that she would become the attachment object for the baby monkey. Instead the cloth mother, who provided contact comfort but not milk, obviously filled that role. In other ways besides clinging, the baby monkeys also clearly showed their preference. For example, when a mechanical toy that made noise was brought into the room while a monkey was playing on the floor, it would scamper to the cloth rather than the wire mother and cling as if seeking protection and reassurance. When put into a new and strange room with both the cloth and wire mothers, the baby used the cloth mother for reassurance in the strange environment. In neither instance did any of the Harlows' monkeys run to the wire mother.

Conditioning and social-learning theories are useful in helping explain the reasons for some emotional reactions. They also emphasize the importance of social models. Because of the inability of either of these theories to explain attachment adequately, however, and because neither learning nor psychoanalytic theories can adequately explain some other social behaviors, attention in recent years has turned more to ethological and cognitive theories in seeking such explanations.

Ethological Theories

Ethological theories are less concerned with the causes of behaviors and more with the way behaviors result in adaptation to environmental circumstances. These theories were originally based upon the study of animal behaviors and their utility for species survival within the animals' environment. In an analogous fashion, the behaviors of human infants and nurturing adults came to be seen as evolutionary adaptations to human environmental circumstances that help assure the survival of our species. Human attachment specifically and socioemotional development in general are seen as a species-specific variant of animal behaviors. The major theorists of the ethological position have been John Bowlby in Britain, who began with a psychoanalytic perspective but began to adapt it to an ethological one on the basis of cross-cultural studies of attachment (Bowlby, 1951), and Mary Ainsworth (1973) in the United States.

According to ethological theory, human attachment behaviors are variants of imprinting, following, and other animal behaviors that enhance the survival chances of the infant by assuring the proximity of infant to mother. Many animal species have a short critical, or sensitive, period after birth during which the mother is responsive to and accepting of her infant, and the infant in turn learns to follow the mother, to remain with her, and to adapt its behaviors to hers.

In many animal species, if the infant is removed from the mother at birth and later returned after some period of separation, the mother will reject the child and refuse to nurture it. Similarly, the infant often will not learn to respond appropriately to the mother after such a separation even if it is not rejected by her. If the separation is relatively brief, the relationship may be altered or disrupted for a time, but it is usually not completely precluded. But if the separation is longer, either partner or both may be unable to establish the relationship and the infant dies.

Since the human infant is born more helpless than those of other species and has a longer period of infancy, and since the infant does not have to be able to stay with and follow the mother in a moving herd, ethological theorists believe that rather than one brief critical period as in animals, the human

infant has longer sensitive periods during which the infant is uniquely responsive to particular social stimuli. Such processes as attachment, though they may begin at birth, become established only over a relatively long time period. If not established during this relatively long sensitive period, however, they may not develop later.

Bowlby and Ainsworth both believe that the infant uses five kinds of behaviors as systems, or means, of establishing and maintaining proximity to the mother, which is part of the process of attachment. These behaviors are crying, smiling, sucking, clinging, and following. Since the infant is helpless at birth and for a long time thereafter and cannot follow the mother, the first four of these systems are designed to summon the mother or to make sure that she remains with the child once she has arrived. Two of the five systems entail signal behaviors and the other three involve active ones. Smiling and crying are signals to the mother and serve as means of activating her reciprocal behaviors such as approaching, picking up, smiling, or gazing back. The infant also shows active behaviors such as sucking and clinging to maintain the mother's presence. At first the very young infant is more able to use signaling behaviors, but over time it uses the active behaviors as well. The last of the active behaviors, following, only becomes operative as the infant begins to move about, first by crawling and later by walking. It does not serve to summon the mother or to keep her there but instead involves the child's active endeavors to maintain proximity to the mother wherever she goes.

All of these behaviors appear to Bowlby and Ainsworth to have been particularly useful to insure infant survival and to protect the infant from predators during the dawn of human existence when our ancestors may have roamed the grassy plains or forests of the world much as the great apes live at present. For example, the infant's cry would have been an important clue of its whereabouts to the mother if they had become separated in tall grass or underbrush. Since prolonged crying might also summon predators, the cessation of crying when found and picked up by the mother also would have had obvious survival value. While humans no longer live out in the wild among predators, such behavioral patterns have persisted among human infants. Some of them still have some survival value, given the helpless state of the infant at birth and for many months thereafter, since they still serve to establish and maintain the close bond between mother and infant, and thus ensure her care.

Criticism of the ethological approach notes that humans are very different from animals that have critical periods such as geese or ducks or goats or sheep. Comparing the development of social behaviors in humans to such behaviors as following the mother in other species is thought by critics to be based on risky assumptions. Furthermore, some research suggests that even if sensitive periods do exist, the human infant can learn particular social behaviors at times beyond these sensitive periods as well. Human infant behavior thus is much more plastic than is animal infant behavior, with more room for later amelioration of early deficits. And human adult behavior towards infants, since it is controlled not only by instinctual patterns but also by cognition, is also more flexible than the behavior of adult animals.

Furthermore, if one is dealing from the ethological perspective, comparisons to closely related animals such as the apes appear to be more useful than those to more distantly related ones such as herd animals or fowl. And in ape society, modern research has found that the usual mode of caregiving involves multiple mothering, in which all adult and juvenile females of a pack will cooperate in the care of infants. Consequently, the infant ape becomes attached not only to its biological mother but to many nurturing females.

Cognitive Theories

Theories of cognition posit that social attachment between infant and adult caregivers develops because the adult provides in his or her appearance and behavior a constantly changing and therefore interesting cognitive array for the infant to study and try to understand. Human beings become the objects of an infant's attachment because they regularly and dependably provide varied and interesting stimulation to the child. At first this stimulation is primarily directed to the child's perceptual processes—visual, auditory, or tactual—but later on the cognitive and language processes come into play as well. Babies become attached to other people because people are more interesting for longer times than anything else in the environment.

Cognitive theories stress that the infant actively reorganizes past social experience upon the basis of its correspondence to new social input. Thus the process of accommodation is continually occurring.

Since each theory has some merits and serves to explain some aspect of infant social development, many researchers at present assume an eclectic approach, drawing upon any or several of the theoretical positions that appear useful.

MAJOR ISSUES

Besides the various theoretical bases for the development of social and emotional capacities in infants, some other areas of dispute or contention exist. Let us briefly consider several of these.

Normal versus Abnormal Development

The issue of normal versus abnormal development concerns what aspects of social interaction with others are considered critical, whether specific times for these are more important than others, and what the possible outcomes of differences in these variables might be. Therefore, it includes such issues as the effects of long-term and short-term separation, the qualities of parenting, two parents versus multiple parenting, out-of-home care, and institutionalization. Some theorists cite studies of children reared under good physical conditions but with minimal social interaction with either adults or peers who showed high rates of disturbance and even death to demonstrate the importance of the warm relationship with primary caregivers. Other theorists, however, cite studies of improvement in social and intellectual functioning as a result of changes in the environment to show that even such deficits can be overcome. Modern researchers also question the attribution of death of institutionalized children to social deprivation and often cite the likelihood that physical factors may have been involved after all (Kagan, 1979).

The possibility that **bonding,** the establishment of the early tie of affection of the parents for the child, is especially facilitated in the first few hours after birth, is also being explored. Some researchers believe that this is the optimum time for the initiation of social interaction between parents and child, while others, though agreeing that it can be beneficial, do not see it as a unique time. They think that such bonds can be established later with no serious consequences for the relationship.

Sensitive Periods

A closely related issue, as the subject of bonding can demonstrate, is the debate on whether critical, or sensitive, periods for infant social development exist or whether the human infant is extremely plastic and able to profit from social interaction whenever it occurs. The idea of sensitive periods derives, of course, from animal studies of imprinting and similar behaviors.

Some researchers believe that there are times of maximum sensitivity in either infant or adult or both in which to foster particular social interactions. For example, the supporters of early bonding believe that in the first few hours after birth the sight, sound, smell, and feel of the infant uniquely sensitize the parents to develop feelings of care and nurturance for the baby. They also assert that this time affords to the alert baby the chance to begin to see and hear and feel the caregivers when the infant is uniquely susceptible to such stimulation.

Most of the psychoanalytic theorists believe that the first few months of life are of critical importance in the establishment of relationships with the mother and that therefore the mother's continued presence as the primary caregiver is most important during this time. Still other theorists believe that it is during these first few months while the infant is still relatively unselective in social responsiveness that care by surrogate parents such as day-care staff or baby-sitters is best initiated.

Nature versus Nurture

The discussion of critical periods versus a smooth curve of social development also leads to consideration of how canalized, or genetically preprogrammed, social and emotional development of the infant might be and how much, conversely, such development is subject to environmental influence. Cross-cultural studies of infants under varying child-rearing conditions seem to show not only that environmental factors greatly affect the times that many early social behaviors are manifested but also that eventually all normal infants learn the various social behaviors necessary for competent interaction. As in most of the nature-nurture controversies, it appears that neither is exclusively responsible but that the two factors interact.

Level of Analysis

How does one study infant socialization? What is the proper level of analysis? The studies done in the 1940s and 1950s concentrated on what the parental actions did and what the consequences of these actions were. More recently researchers have become increasingly aware of the dyadic, interactive nature of social development. Thus they have begun to study social behaviors in dyads. But which dyad? Obviously mother and infant, but what about father and infant? Siblings and infant? Peer interaction among infants? What about the triadic relationship that occurs when mother and father both interact with the infant? Is maternal behavior different in the presence of the father? Is paternal behavior different in the presence of the mother? Does the baby react differently to the presence of either or of both together? Recent emphasis on the family as a system leads to the conclusion that any interaction of infant and parent cannot be studied in isolation but only as part of the whole family system. Accordingly, many efforts at present are directed toward finding out how relationships between infants and others vary depending upon the individuals present in the total interaction and what roles each assumes.

METHODOLOGICAL ISSUES

The question of the proper level of analysis of infant social behavior leads to further questions regarding methodology, such as the types of studies, the location, and the time periods in which the studies operate.

Types of Studies

In studying something as situationally dependent as infant socioemotional behaviors, researchers must face the problem that laboratory settings could drastically alter manifestations of such behaviors because of their unfamiliarity to the infant. This fact is, of course, more true for older infants than for very young ones. For example, the child's reaction to the departure of the mother or the appearance of a stranger may be very different in the unfamiliar laboratory from what it might have been in familiar home surroundings. On the other hand, studies in the home are subject to all the vagaries and interruptions of daily life. It is difficult to standardize conditions over time and to avoid interruptions from family members, neighbors, or the telephone. Because of this difficulty and because children's homes differ greatly from one another, children observed at home are much less subject to the research controls that insure a standardized situation. Researchers are faced with difficult decisions regarding the setting, which will affect both the generalizability and validity of their results.

Time Frame of Studies

Widely differing infant social behaviors may signify the same emotions at different time periods. The young infant who stops crying quickly when picked up may develop into the toddler who is exploratory and curious. On the face of things, these two behaviors appear unrelated. But they may be manifestations of the same emotion or trait that is shown by different behaviors at different ages or developmental periods. Only if the same children are studied longitudinally, over an extended time period, will such a relationship between earlier and later social behaviors become apparent. If cross-sectional methods are used, the two behaviors appear discrete, and no relationship between them can be discerned. For this reason, studies of social and emotional development have tended to be longitudinal rather than cross-sectional.

A longitudinal design, however, carries with it its own set of weaknesses. One must wait a long time for all data to be collected, hence results are not known for many months or years. The numbers of infants that can be studied in this way usually are quite small, generally smaller than in cross-sectional studies. In addition, there is attrition of numbers as children's families move away, lose interest, or just lose contact with the researchers.

Methods and Problems

Because of the problems of laboratory settings as well as the time and effort involved in longitudinal study, and because it is felt that parents know their infants and in many instances can interpret their behaviors better than can researchers, many studies of social behavior are indirect. That is, instead of studying the infant or the infant-parent dyad or triad directly, researchers often use questionnaires or rating scales filled out by parents. The technique of parent questionnaires goes back as far as G. Stanley Hall at the turn of the century. The obvious problems with questionnaires and rating scales are those of memory and rater generalization,

aquiescence, social desirabilty, and differences of interpretation. First, parents may remember some aspects of an infant's behaviors that seem salient to them and forget others. This is particularly so if some time has elapsed between the behaviors and the time of recording. They also generalize past behaviors to some degree based on more recent ones. Second, parents may answer what they think the experimenter wants to hear, the process known as acquiescence. Third, they may answer in ways that they believe to be socially acceptable or that will show their baby as bright and ahead of its peers, rather than truthfully. For example, they might indicate that the baby cries only a little when in fact it might cry a lot. But the parent might believe that a truthful answer would reflect negatively upon her or his parenting skills and therefore tries to cover up the fact. Finally, some parents may interpret events differently from others. For example, what one parent may rate as "extremely active" behavior on the part of an infant may appear only "average" to another.

In addition, there remains the question whether experimental studies in a laboratory are preferable to naturalistic observations. Each type of study possesses some merits, but each has its drawbacks. As already indicated, infants in the unfamiliar laboratory setting and exposed to unfamiliar social stimuli may behave very differently from their usual behavior under familiar circumstances. Home studies are, however, more difficult to conduct under standard circumstances. Observational studies are slower and more difficult to do and are less standardized, but they may yield more interesting and environmentally valid information than do many experimental studies. Researchers must have some clear ideas of what types of social behaviors they are interested in and under what kinds of circumstances these can best be observed and measured. They must then choose the settings for their studies to maximize the advantages and minimize the disadvantages of the two methods.

The foregoing discussion has, it is hoped, led you to an awareness that social and emotional behaviors in infants are diverse and difficult to study. Because they interact with perception, cognition, and language, they are difficult to isolate and study in and of themselves. Each method of study can produce some kinds of answers but precludes others. Now that we have considered some of these, let us turn to some specific topics in infant social development in greater detail.

EARLY SOCIAL DEVELOPMENT IN THE FAMILY

Different Kinds of Families

Infants in all cultures develop socially within the context of the family, though the compositions of families may differ greatly across and within cultures. In Europe and North America, the nuclear family of two parents plus the child or children is most usual. The infant interacts the most with its parents, particularly with the mother, and with siblings if there are any. Single-parent families, particularly those in which the mother is the parent present, are becoming more numerous, however. In other cultures such as in most of Asia, the extended family, which includes in addition to the nuclear family the grandparents and/or the aunts and uncles and their children, is the norm. In such a family, the infant learns to relate to a multiplicity of family members and/or caregivers. Early relationships between infant and parents (and siblings, grandparents, or other family members) are important because they become the basis for attachment, the lasting

emotional bond between child and caregiver(s). Individual rhythms and temperament of both infant and caregiver(s) and how well they become coordinated affect how smoothly these growing relationships are established. The child's later acceptance of strangers and relationships with peers are based in large degree upon the quality of the early interactions within the family.

Because most study of social development in infancy has until quite recently been limited to Western cultures, it is sometimes not clear whether a pattern seen in Western cultures is universal or whether it is idiosyncratic to those cultures. To put it another way, researchers are not yet completely certain as to what aspects of human social development occur primarily because of genetic-developmental mechanisms and which ones are due to cultural influence.

Early Interactions of Infant and Attending Adult

BONDING

The term used to describe the close emotional tie established by the mother (and sometimes the father) towards the newborn baby in the first days of life is **bonding.** Some students of early socioemotional development classify bonding as the precursor of, or else the earliest portion of, the attachment process; others see it as a different and unrelated mechanism; and still others deny that such a dynamic exists at all. Many researchers believe that bonding becomes uniquely established during the neonatal period and, therefore, is based upon the sight, sound, and touch of the infant and is enhanced by gazing and extended skin-to-skin contact. There still exists some controversy, however, even among those who believe that bonding really does take place, over how critical this phenome-

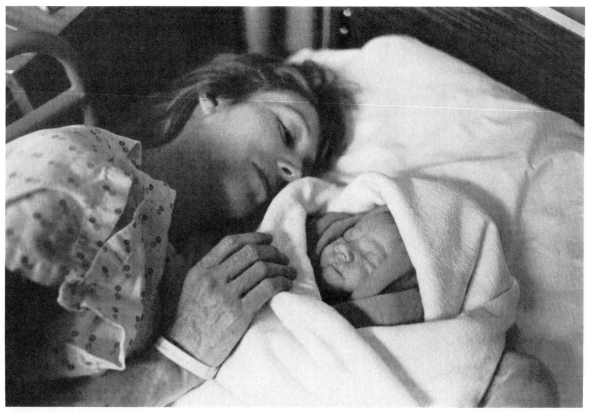

Early close interaction between parents and the neonate seems to help promote the development of an affective bond between them. Many hospitals now permit mother and child to spend an extended time period together beginning shortly after birth.

non is to the establishment of emotional relationships between infant and parents.

Causes of Bonding It has been shown that the appearance of the newborn, especially the "cute baby" appearance (Lorenz, 1943), as well as eye contact by the infant may be important release mechanisms that trigger nurturant behavior in adults (Robson, 1967). Characteristics typical of the appearance of the newborn, such as the relatively large eyes, the small face and high forehead, and the small trunk and limbs all reinforce

the perception of appealing looks and helplessness by parents and other adults (Eibl-Eibesfeldt, 1971). Some have hypothesized that the higher incidence of child abuse that occurs with premature infants may be due in part to the premature child's lack of appealing appearance and the consequent failure by the parents to establish nurturant and caregiving behaviors.

Importance of Bonding In the last few years, some researchers have been investigating the importance of very early interaction between mother and newborn infant and sometimes between father and newborn as well (Klaus & Kennell, 1976, 1982; Kennell, Voos, & Klaus, 1979). These studies are concerned more with the effects of early contact on the development of nurturant responses in the adult and hence the subsequent quality of infant care than they are with the direct effects upon the infant. That is, this early and extended contact appears to be more important for the establishment of adult feelings and behaviors toward the infant than for any development of specific behaviors and feelings in the neonate.

Drawing an analogy from the necessity for close interaction between mother and baby in the first few hours after birth in some animal species, Marshall H. Klaus and John H. Kennell investigated whether a similar relationship existed in humans. During the 1970s they began to report that their studies of human mothers and babies appeared to show bonding phenomena similar to those found in animals.

Prenatal Beginnings According to Klaus and Kennell, maternal bonding to the infant seems to begin before birth, especially as the mother becomes more aware of the growing child within her. A study by Kennell, Slyter, and Klaus (1970) found that human mothers appear to begin to feel specific attachment to their babies even before birth. In studying the reactions of mothers of neonates who had died before their mothers could see or touch them, they found that these mothers grieved extensively in spite of the lack of any real contact. On this basis they concluded that some bonding must occur even before birth. They did find, however, that mothers who had touched or held their babies before their early death grieved even longer and more intensely than those who had not. Thus contact with the "real" child seems even more im-

portant than feelings during the prenatal period for the establishment of the affective bond in the mother.

Maternal Behaviors When given their normal, healthy baby to hold for an extended period after birth, mothers go through a regular and predictable sequence of behaviors. They begin by tentatively touching the baby's extremities and later the whole body with their fingertips. Then they begin to stroke the baby. After this they will often pick up the baby and hold it close up while gazing into its face. Finally, mothers may massage their babies using the whole hand and may hug and cuddle them as well.

Long-Term Implications Further study of mothers of normal infants who had the opportunity to spend some time touching, holding, and looking at their babies after birth found that even a relatively brief period of extra contact appeared to have long-lasting effects upon the behaviors of these mothers (Kennell, Jerauld, Wolfe, Chesler, Kreger, McAlpine, Steffa, & Klaus, 1974; Klaus, Jerauld, Kreger, McAlpine, Steffa, & Kennell, 1972; Ringler, Kennell, Jarvelle, Navojosky, & Klaus, 1975). In an intensive, long-term study of the effects of early interaction (Klaus et al., 1972), 14 mothers had the usual brief contact with their babies after birth, while 14 others had an extra hour of contact with the infant within three hours of birth and five extra hours daily for the next three days. At one month these high-contact mothers spent more time holding and looking at their babies than did mothers exposed to the more usual hospital routines. They also spent more time caressing the baby and while looking tended to hold the baby in the **en face position,** which involves holding the baby close to the mother's face and gazing directly into its eyes (Hales, Trause, & Kennell, 1976). Further follow-up at one year and two years of age found continuing differences in maternal attachment and in the use of language with the infant, favoring the extended contact group. A long-term follow-up of the same group showed intelligence and language differences also favoring the early- and extended-contact children as late as age five (Klaus & Kennell 1976, 1982).

A similar study of low-income, first-time mothers who had early and extended contact immediately after birth and extended periods of shared time while in the hospital found that they were more likely to continue breast-feeding after hospital discharge, brought their children more frequently to well-baby clinics, and were more likely to keep their immunizations current than were matched controls who did not have such contact (O'Connor, 1977; O'Connor, Sherrod, Sandler, et al., 1978). Furthermore, a long-term follow-up of the same group found a significantly lower incidence of child abuse than was true for controls (O'Connor, Vietze, Sherrod, et al., 1980). Both the experimental and control groups were quite small, however, and results must therefore be approached with caution.

A Swedish study (Winberg & de Château, 1982) demonstrates that even very brief extra contact appears to make a difference. In this study, some mothers had 15 to 20 minutes extra contact, being allowed to hold their naked baby immediately after delivery, while a comparable control group did not. This extra contact resulted in observable differences in maternal behavior and in child abilities. Extra-contact mothers breast-fed babies longer before weaning them than did the controls. When the child reached age one, these extra-contact mothers still displayed more touching, caressing, and holding than did the controls. Interestingly, the differences between

the groups were greater for boys than for girls, suggesting that early contact was even more necessary for the former. Tests at age one showed the experimental children ahead of controls in gross motor and language development. By age three, however, the children's test results did not differ, indicating that the differential effects wore off over time. Jan Winberg and Peter de Château do not attribute the differences at age one solely to the brief postnatal experience itself. Rather they think it set the stage for many later mutual interactions that were able to proceed more smoothly because of it. They believe that it is the accumulation of these interactions that resulted in the differential behaviors shown by both mothers and children.

Bonding with High-Risk Infants Similarly, Klaus and Kennell (1976, 1982) report that mothers of premature or ill babies that require care in high-risk nurseries and are therefore separated from maternal contact often feel incompetent in mothering their infants even after they no longer need to be isolated in high-risk settings. Some mothers even reported that they would momentarily forget that they had a child at all. A number of researchers, therefore, have initiated programs in which mothers are encouraged to visit, touch, and help care for their infants even while these are in the intensive-care nursery. When the condition of the baby improves, mothers take over more and more of the caregiving tasks with the baby. This contact appears to improve caregiving skills as well as the growth of attachment on the part of the mother. The behaviors of such mothers toward their babies can later be compared to those of mothers not afforded this opportunity.

For example, P. H. Leiderman (1969) found that later mothering behaviors were greatly enhanced if mothers of premature infants were allowed to handle them instead of just looking at them. A later study (Leifer, Leiderman, Barnett, & Williams, 1972) compared three groups of mothers, one of full-term babies and two of premature babies. The mothers of the full-term babies all had early contact with their offspring. One group of mothers of the premature babies only watched their babies, while the other group were also allowed to handle theirs. The greatest evidence of maternal attachment to the infant was found in the group that had normal full-term babies. No differences in early attachment behaviors were found between the two groups of mothers of premature infants. Later follow-up studies revealed, however, that the mothers in the group who had been able only to look at their offspring had higher later rates of divorce and of surrendering the infant for adoption than did mothers who had also been able to handle their babies. Thus, even if early attachment behaviors do not differ between mothers with high and low contact, prolonged and profound separation from the infant, with only visual contact allowed, seems to be related to other areas of maternal stress or maladjustment. This separation of mother and infant may contribute to the severity of other interpersonal problems that the mothers may later encounter.

Paternal Bonding   It is interesting that not only the mother, but the father as well appears to undergo this bonding process if he is exposed to the baby shortly after birth (Greenberg & Morris, 1974; Miller & Bowen, 1982). Fathers who saw their newborns and were given the opportunity to interact with them described their babies as "perfect" and expressed feelings of elation and the desire to hold and look at their infant (Greenberg & Morris, 1974). Presence at the delivery of the infant relates to increased looking and talking to the newborn by fathers, but it does not

increase the amount of touching and holding over that of fathers who saw the baby only shortly after birth (Miller & Bowen, 1982). Fathers, just like mothers, interacted with their newborn infants in a regular and predictable sequence. First they hovered over the child and pointed to its features. Then they established eye-to-eye contact and began to touch the baby with their fingertips (McDonald, 1978). Finally they touched the baby with their palms and rubbed them with the backs of their hands (Roedholm & Larsson, 1979).

Disputes over Bonding   Some cautions must be expressed in evaluating the importance of early bonding. First, the samples in all the above studies are quite small. The treatments are not all equal. In some instances, contact began immediately after birth, in others as late as eight hours after. The length of contact time varied also, with some mothers having their babies with them for frequent, long intervals and others for less frequent and/or shorter ones. There have not been enough comparable studies with large enough numbers of cases to draw firm conclusions.

Second, other research (Rutter, 1979), as well as common-sense observations of parents and infants, has demonstrated that bonding can be established quite well even beyond the newborn period. For example, babies placed for adoption several weeks after birth and their adoptive parents usually adapt to each other beautifully within several days in spite of the lack of early contact. Many mothers separated from their infants because of the illness of either mother or infant still establish good relationships and become competent parents. Similarly, fathers who are not present at delivery or who may have very limited contact with their newborn in the first few days generally also develop close relationships later. Other research has found no difference in maternal behavior between mothers with high contact and mothers with low contact (Svejda, Campos, & Emde, 1980).

Furthermore, what differences in maternal behaviors there are seem to have little permanent effect upon the behaviors of the child. Either as early as 10 months (Wachs & Cucinotta, 1972) or at least by three years (Winberg & de Château, 1982), children behave quite similarly even in those areas where early contact had previously made a difference.

Then there is the possibility that the experimental intervention by researchers, rather than the actual extra exposure to the neonate, may have affected maternal behaviors. That is, a kind of Hawthorne effect may have occurred. In other words, mothers responded to the extra attention of being part of a study by behaving differently toward the infant than they might otherwise have. This difference is possible particularly in studies of low-income groups such as the O'Connor one, since such mothers typically feel ignored by the medical and hospital establishment and might thus be most susceptible to extra attention.

Bonding in Industrial versus Nonindustrial Societies   Finally, studies of nonindustrial societies have shown that, contrary to folklore about such societies, there exists in few of them any extended early contact between mother and infant (Lozoff, 1982). They are usually separated for a time after birth as either or both are washed and dressed. In some of these cultures the infant is later placed in the mother's bed; in others it is put in a separate basket or cradle, which is kept close to the mother.

In all of these cultures, however, mother and infant are given a time of relative isolation from the everyday world. Furthermore, the mother is not expected to return to her usual tasks for several weeks after delivery, while friends or relatives take over her household work and other tasks. This practice too runs counter to folklore of the primitive mother who gives birth and then immediately resumes her daily work. Thus, even though there may not be early and extended skin-to-skin contact, mothers and babies spend much time together in the first weeks after birth. Furthermore, babies are generally fed frequently on a self-demand schedule, and mothers spend much time holding them and are very responsive to their needs.

Betsy Lozoff (1977, 1982), therefore, believes that the phenomenon of early bonding may be important only in industrial and postindustrial societies such as those of North America and Europe in which mothers are expected to resume their work at home or in the work place shortly after the return from the hospital. Furthermore, in Western cultures, even after they are brought home from the hospital, infants are often kept in cribs in separate rooms and hence in relative isolation from the mother and are fed on a less frequent schedule. Consequently, Lozoff thinks that early bonding may not be necessary in nonindustrial cultures since they provide many opportunities during early infancy for the development of a close relationship between mother and infant. Only if later contact is relatively restricted as it is in Western culture does early bonding assume such an important function in the establishment of the relationship between mother and infant.

Perspective on Bonding   Regardless of whether early bonding is eventually found to be critical or not, certainly the practice of allowing parents and infant some close and intimate time together after birth appears to be rational and humane. Whatever can help parents to establish a close relationship with their child can only be beneficial. Thus, changes in hospital practice such as allowing mother, father, and infant some time alone together shortly after delivery, the practice of rooming in, and unlimited visitation by fathers (and sometimes by siblings as well) are to be applauded.

MUTUAL RHYTHMICITY

The Neonatal Period   The newborn infant appears to be "pre-wired" by nature for social encounters, since it exhibits social competencies so early that no explanation involving learning is adequate. The neonate is already able to summon attention by crying and is able to gaze at the adult and to some extent to track her or him visually. An important task of the first few days after birth for both mother (and father if he is helping) and baby is to develop a mutual rhythm, that is, to adjust their styles of activity to each other.

At first the infant probably exerts more control over the behavior of the mother than she does over that of the infant (Moss, 1967). That is, the infant's signaling is more likely to summon and keep the mother near than any maternal behavior is able to control the infant. A contingent relationship, in which the mother's behavior is dependent upon, and highly responsive to, signals from the infant is most characteristic of the first few weeks of life (Yarrow & Pederson, 1972).

The "Suck-Jiggle" Phenomenon   One of the earliest maternal responses that appears contingent upon infant behavior is what Kenneth Kaye (1977) has termed the "suck-jiggle" phenomenon, noted in chapter 10. The young infant sucks in bursts and then will pause for a few moments before resum-

ing sucking. During this pause, the mother typically will jiggle the infant. When asked, mothers say they do so in order that the infant will resume sucking. In fact, experimental evidence shows that the infant will resume sucking sooner if not jiggled (Kaye & Brazelton, 1971; Kaye, 1977). The jiggling thus retards rather than facilitates the resumption of sucking. It is difficult to see why mothers do it, except that it provides an early means by which both partners in the relationship learn to take turns and to adjust their rhythmic behaviors to those of the other.

Interactional Synchrony   A striking example of the infant's evidently inborn capacity to engage in social interaction is that of interactional synchrony (Condon & Sander, 1974; Condon, 1977). Infants as young as one to four days have been found to move their arms and legs in synchrony with an adult voice. When the adult spoke quickly, the infant moved quickly. But when the adult spoke slowly, infant motion slowed down to match adult speech. Interactional synchrony exists among adults as well; in fact we become disturbed if the listener moves "out of sync" with us as we talk. But it does not appear to be a learned behavior, for the newborn infant can track variations in adult speech and move in response to them almost as well as can an adult.

Awareness of Contingency   Some researchers believe that the origin of social responsivity occurs when the infant begins to perceive that a contingent relationship exists between its own behavior and some event in the world outside the infant (Watson, 1978). That is, the infant becomes aware that what it does has an effect on outside reality since the infant's actions such as crying or smiling result in actions by caregivers.

However, some environmental events also occur noncontingently. For example, the caregiver may attend to the infant even when it has not signaled, or at other times may not respond or may delay in responding to the infant's signals. John S. Watson believes that such noncontingent events actually hasten the learning of contingency relationships, because infants appear to learn contingencies most quickly when the rates of occurrence of contingent and noncontingent reinforcement are about equal (Watson, 1978).

Beginnings of a Transactional Relationship: Mutual Gazing The word relationship, which implies a long-term encounter between partners, is better in describing these phenomena than is the word interaction, which implies a much briefer encounter between the two (Stern, 1982). Transactional, in turn, refers to what happens in the relationship over time. Thus the quantity of interaction or the amount of time spent in each is less important than the kinds of sequences in which such relationships occur (Schaffer, 1977). The process of the developing relationship, rather than the outcome of any particular encounter, seems to be the critical component in the building of the relationship.

At first this growing relationship between mother and infant consists mainly of the mother responding to whatever behavior the infant emits as if the infant were in fact attempting to communicate (Schaffer, 1977). A good example involves the phenomenon of mutual gazing, which begins when the infant is between the ages of three and six weeks (Stern, 1974). The mother will gaze at the infant for long time periods, while the infant may glance at her only occasionally. The mother will look away only if the infant's gaze is averted and look back immediately if the infant's gaze should return (Fogel, 1977). Her gazes thus provide a "frame" around the gazing behavior of the infant. When the infant looks away, the mother may attempt to redirect the infant's gaze to her through a change of loudness or pitch of the voice, face or limb movement, contortion of facial features, or by touching the baby (Kaye, 1975).

The sensitive mother is aware, however, that the infant may be looking away because it has already had too much visual stimulation. The adult, therefore, will not persist in such efforts to redirect the infant's attention for very long. Less sensitive mothers may either not try to redirect the infant's attention at all or else try to do so long after the infant had indicated an overload of stimulation. Just how and why some mothers develop such a unique sensitivity to their baby's cues and why some do not is still a matter of speculation (Kaye, 1975).

An interesting aspect of the mutual gaze phenomenon is that the infant prefers eye contact to contingent behavior without eye contact. In an ingenious experiment done by Hanuš and Mechtild Papoušek (Papoušek & Papoušek, 1974), infants were allowed to watch a videotape of themselves in which they gazed at the camera, and hence at the observing infants, but with actions that had no relationship to what the real infants were currently doing. Alternatively, they could watch an instantaneous picture of themselves, in which the mirror image moved when they moved, and therefore behaved contingently, but which did not provide eye contact. Infants overwhelmingly preferred the eye contact condition. Thus being able to look at the "other" person's eyes seems to be more important to infants than to control the contingencies of movement of the "other."

Other Reciprocal Interactions The mother perceives any vocalization produced by the infant, like its gaze, as communicative in intent, and she in turn responds by further vocalization. She treats sneezes, coughs, and gurgles as if the infant were using them to say something to her. The mother is thus controlled by the infant's behaviors, as she begins to organize her responses to alternate with the behaviors emitted by the infant in a synchronized, rhythmic way (Newson, 1977).

The infant also begins quite early beyond the neonatal stage, however, to adjust to maternal patterns. It is able to do so because it is more able to assume voluntary control over some functions that had at first been entirely under internal biological control, such as its patterns of attention, hunger, and sleep. Infant state changes, which at first are entirely biologically controlled, become remarkably sensitive very early to caregiver influence. Entrainment, the adjustment of behavioral organization to outside influence, proceeds quickly.

That the infant adjusts to activities of the caregiver can be ascertained indirectly from what happens when young infants in foster care are changed from one foster home to another. There generally is a period of upset, even in infants too young to recognize that the new caregiver is a stranger, because of the change in caregiver rhythmicity. Over a period of several days or weeks, the infant adjusts to the rhythms of the new caregiver. The temporal conditioning study done by Dorothy Marquis (1941) in which babies were switched from a three-hour to a four-hour schedule or vice versa demonstrates the same phenomenon. The fact that babies fussed and cried at the old time of feeding shows they had already adjusted their rhythms to those imposed by caregivers; that they adjusted to the new schedules over several days was indicative of their ability to adapt to a new pattern.

Maternal Contributions to Interaction
In the rhythmic interactions between mother and infant, such as the jiggling phenomenon, interactional synchrony, and the mother's attribution of communicative intent to some of the visual and vocal activities of the infant, can be seen the beginnings of the turn-taking behavior characteristic of adult dialogue. The mother must attend much more to the behavior of the infant than she would with an adult partner, since the timing of her responses is critical in keeping the infant on task in this incipient dialogue. That is, if in an adult dialogue one partner misses a cue or delays in responding, the other adult partner can compensate for such an omission. When a young baby is the partner, it cannot yet do so. The adult must be more sensitive and have a much better sense of timing for the adult-infant dialogue to succeed.

The mother interacts not only through mutual gazing but also by imitating behaviors emitted by the infant (Schaffer, 1977). These behaviors include vocalizing, gesturing, making body movements, and making facial expressions (Newson, 1977). The mother thus helps to bring about a very predictable form of interaction, which is always "baby does something and mother repeats it." In a sense this maternal behavior provides a "mirror" (Papoušek & Papoušek, 1977) through which the infant can see its own behavior, especially since the mother exaggerates, slows down, and often repeats several times the actions of the infant to ensure that the child can obtain and assimilate as much information as possible (Schaffer, 1977). This repetition serves to help the infant learn what a response should be and when it should be emitted. It also helps to hold the infant's attention and provides predictability in the dialogue. The infant in turn may repeat the mother's behavior, which tells her that the infant has processed the information and enbles her to predict and anticipate the infant's later behavior (Fogel, 1977).

A Basis for Communication
The infant, therefore, becomes involved in the two-way process that is the essence of communi-

cation long before it is able to communicate much in the way of content (Newson, 1977). That is, the means of communication are well established before what the baby communicates becomes very clear or important. But since the signals of the infant and the mother's responses to them are unique to the pair and have been built by them over time, they may not be obvious to other people, who often must ask, "What does it mean when she does thus and so?" Thus parents, especially mothers if they are the primary caregivers, know when the child is communicating hunger, fatigue, or boredom, but the casual visitor cannot figure out what it is the baby means.

As the infant becomes older, it begins to realize that this interactive behavior has communicative value, that is, that it can convey some kind of information and therefore can be used even more effectively to influence the behaviors of others. As the child is more able to separate self from the outside world and can distinguish means from ends, he or she can begin to communicate intention in addition to need. He or she does so by following the gaze of another, directing the gaze of another, pointing, gesturing to signify demand, and finally, using words (Schaffer, 1977).

Thus, out of the early rhythmic interactions between infant and caregiver develops what will be the system of interpersonal communication best typefied in the older child and adult by the process of speech.

SMILING

As noted, one of the most powerful means of obtaining and prolonging social attention from caregivers and others is social smiling. According to our discussion of smiling in chapter 5, early smiles seem to result from internal stimulation. Exogenous smiling, resulting from factors outside the child, devel-

ops in the first couple of months after birth, as the child smiles at the sound of a bell or the sight of a familiar object. Around two and a half to three months, smiling in response to a social stimulus, which is usually the face of a person, begins (Emde, Gaensbauer, & Harmon, 1976).

While early endogenous and exogenous smiling may be related to infant state, social smiling is very clearly a voluntary activity that has both cognitive and motivational components. The infant has learned that smiling will bring about attention and reciprocal smiling from others and thus uses smiling to control their behaviors. While younger babies smile indiscriminately at both strangers and familiar people, older babies prefer familiar faces. They will smile more frequently and longer at their mothers than at strangers and will express pleasure at the mother's presence by acting excited, cooing, and making hand and arm movements (Sroufe, 1979). Blind babies react with smiling in the same way as do sighted ones, except that they smile at the sound of human voices rather than at the sight of faces (Fraiberg, 1974). Familiar voices, especially that of the mother, come to elicit more smiling in blind babies than do unfamiliar ones.

The baby's social smile serves as a very powerful reinforcer to the caregiving adult. Such smiling not only expresses infant emotion but is a very important aspect of the infant's social overtures to the caregiver. It tends to prolong adult attention to the infant.

Infant Temperament

ORIGINS OF TEMPERAMENT DIFFERENCES

One area of interest for both researchers and parents of infants has been the extent to which infant styles of social behavior may be determined by individual temperament char-

Social smiling by the infant is a powerful reinforcer that can control adult behavior.

acteristics that appear at or shortly after birth and thus are presumed to be inborn. Conversely, if differences of infant temperament style are not inborn, do they result from differing caregiving styles? Evidence exists for both views.

THE NEW YORK LONGITUDINAL STUDY

The major investigators into temperament and its possible origin in early infancy have been Alexander Thomas and Stella Chess through their New York Longitudinal Study (NYLS) begun in 1956 (Thomas, Chess, & Birch, 1968; Thomas & Chess, 1977). Thomas and Chess have studied a group of 141 New York City children over a 20-year period from infancy to adulthood. Since this sample consisted almost exclusively of upper-middle-class children, 95 working-class children were later added to the study, as were some mentally handicapped children, some who had been born prematurely, and a group of children who had contracted rubella prenatally and suffered from some handicapping conditions as a result.

Unfortunately, information about early

infancy was gathered from retrospective parental reports several months later rather than from actual observation of the infants. It is thus subject to distortions resulting from faulty memory as well as parental attributions of cause for behavioral differences. Parents might have interpreted as evidence of inborn characteristics behaviors that might in fact have resulted from parental behaviors toward the infant. Information on development beyond early infancy was gathered from observations of the children as well as from interviews with parents, preschool and elementary teachers, and, after they became verbal, the children themselves. The later data are probably more reliable than those on early infancy. Even the early parent report data, however, showed remarkable consistency with later observational data regarding the styles of behavior shown by the children. This may mean that temperament is indeed consistent from early infancy onward and that parents' recollections are basically accurate. Conversely it could mean that parents generalized from later observations to their reports of earlier memories.

THREE TEMPERAMENT TYPES

Thomas and Chess isolated nine areas, or dimensions, according to which temperament differences were already evident in infancy. These include 1) level of motor activity, 2) rhythmicity, or regularity; 3) approach or withdrawal in the presence of a new stimulus; 4) adaptability to a new or changed stimulus; 5) threshold of responsiveness to stimulation; 6) intensity of reaction; 7) pleasant versus unfriendly quality of mood; 8) distractibility; and 9) attention span, or persistence. Each child was rated on each of these nine dimensions on a three-point scale ranging from showing very little of a quality to showing an extreme degree of it. After a factor analysis of the nine variables was done,

three distinct groups of children were identified who differed from one another on how these variables clustered.

The first of these groups is that of the easy child. Such a child has a regular, positive approach to new stimuli. He or she adapts easily to change and to various caregiving regimens and generally shows a mild or moderate mood which tends to be pleasant. About 40 percent of the children studied by Thomas and Chess were categorized as easy children.

The second group is that of the difficult child, who manifests irregular functions in such areas as eating and sleeping patterns and tends to respond negatively and with withdrawal to new stimulation. She or he is slow to adapt to change and displays rather intense moods that are often negative. About 10 percent of the NYLS sample were found to be in the difficult category.

The third group consists of children they labeled slow-to-warm-up. Such a child is characterized by a combination of mildly negative responses to new stimuli as well as slow adaptability. More regular and less intense than the difficult child, however, the slow-to-warm-up child can, with repeated exposure to a new or changed situation, finally adapt in a positive manner. About 15 percent of the study sample fell into this category.

The remaining approximately 35 percent of the children in the NYLS did not clearly belong in any of the three categories but were of mixed or unclear temperament styles. Thomas and Chess maintain that temperament styles identified early in life seem to have lasting effects upon the children's development and adjustment to environmental variables.

PARENTAL REACTIONS

Furthermore, the children's temperaments in turn affected parental attitudes and behaviors and thus influenced the interaction between parents and children from infancy onward. For example, parents of easy children tend to feel reassured and confident of their parenting abilities because their children react so positively and mildly to their actions. The parents' behaviors toward the child reflect their relaxed, happy attitude, and the child in turn keeps on responding positively. By contrast, difficult children bring about parental anxiety because the parents believe that it is their own inadequacy and ineptness that cause the children's extreme behaviors. In fact, since parents often act inconsistently owing to their uncertainty in the face of the child's unpleasant behavior, the parents of a difficult child may indeed contribute to making the child even more difficult to manage. Thomas and Chess believe, however, that the root cause of the problem ultimately is the child's temperament and not the parental behavior, which merely interacts with what the child presents to begin with.

Since the slow-to-warm-up child expresses negativism less intensely than the difficult child, this child usually does not present a problem to parents during infancy and toddlerhood. The parents tend to feel almost as positive and self-assured as those of the easy child during these early stages. Only when exposed to many new environmental stimuli at once, such as upon entry into nursery school, does the slow-to-warm-up child show some problem behaviors. These are seldom as severe as those of difficult children and tend to resolve themselves over time.

AT-RISK CHILDREN

Thomas and Chess, therefore, believe that individual temperament styles play a large part in determining personality and social development. The reason is that they interact with environmental factors, including paren-

tal actions, that can help lead to normal or abnormal development.

Being a difficult child in infancy and early childhood places one "at risk" for later problems. Thomas, Chess, and Korn (1982) attribute this sequence to the fact that temperament in childhood interacts with environmental factors within and without the family. The demands for adaptation to such environmentally imposed events as sleeping and feeding schedules, toilet training, and relationships with adults and peers are especially trying for the difficult child. In turn, parents feel inadequate and guilty because of the child's behaviors, resulting in further disturbance of the relationship. Later the child develops similar difficulties with other people such as peers and teachers. Some difficult children eventually make a good adjustment and develop normally, but others do not. For example, in a portion of their long-term follow-up (Thomas, Chess, & Korn, 1982) they found that behavior problems were more likely to develop with difficult and slow-to-warm-up children than with others during school age. Furthermore, a significant correlation existed between young adults who had psychological disorders and those who had been difficult children. This correlation does not mean that all difficult children grow up to have behavioral disorders; only that those who do also generally had been difficult children earlier. Thus Thomas and Chess believe that child temperament interacts with familial and extrafamilial environmental factors to produce particular levels of adjustment to interpersonal situations.

The stability of temperament in infancy as perceived by parents may be measured by the Carey Scales (Carey, 1970; Carey & McDevitt, 1978), which were based on the research of Thomas and Chess. These scales are used by researchers who ask parents to rate the temperament characteristics of infants and toddlers.

EXOGENOUS EXPLANATIONS

Other researchers think that temperament is not an inborn attribute but the result of the perceptions of parents and other caregivers, which lead them to act toward the child in certain ways that affect the child's behavior and attitudes (Bates, 1980). One can then, of course, inquire what the perceptions of the adults are based on, if not the child's behaviors.

Evidence exists, however, that parental, particularly maternal, behaviors toward the infant are to a great extent the determiners of infant behavioral styles. These studies have been done primarily by Mary Ainsworth and her associates. For example, Sylvia M. Bell and Ainsworth (1972), in a study of infant crying, found that babies of responsive mothers who picked them up and cared for them quickly when they cried tended to cry less overall than did babies of less responsive mothers. This finding not only runs counter to the behavioral point of view, which would lead one to expect that the reinforcement of crying would lead to more crying, but could also explain the origin of difficult children. They could be children of less responsive mothers, who therefore tend to cry and fuss more. A subsequent study (Stayton & Ainsworth, 1973) found that mothers who were more unresponsive to their children's cues throughout infancy had children who showed more protest at separation from the mother during the last quarter of the first year than did children of more responsive mothers. Thus Ainsworth believes that a secure relationship, resulting in what Thomas and Chess probably would call a child with an easy temperament, comes about because of greater maternal sensitivity and responsiveness and not because of any inborn factors in the child. Conversely, maternal anxiety and lack of responsiveness could result in what Thomas and Chess term a difficult child.

AN ATTEMPT AT RESOLUTION

This controversy is a "which came first, the chicken or the egg?" situation. There is probably some truth to both views. Anyone who has ever spent some time in a nursery for newborn babies can attest to the fact that infants from birth on seem to show great variation in individual rhythmicity and sensitivity to stimulation. Some babies appear fussy and upset, and others seem to accept peacefully whatever happens. Some of these differences may be due to factors of the delivery such as the amount and kind of anesthetic used or the length and difficulty of labor. But not all of them. There is a strong indication that some inborn differences are being expressed through these differential behaviors.

On the other hand, parental attitudes and behaviors undoubtedly affect the infant's repertoire of responses. Even a child who reacts mildly may become more demanding if needs are not met promptly, and a more fussy baby can be calmed through prompt attention by sensitive and self-confident parents. Finally, since we have here a continuing transactional relationship between two partners, the behaviors of each in turn influence any subsequent behaviors of the other. The result is a cycle of behaviors with each constantly changing and affecting the other.

Regardless of whether temperament is inborn or is dependent upon parental actions, individual differences among children and how they react inevitably influence the parent-child relationship and therefore the entire socioemotional development of the child.

BEHAVIORAL SYSTEMS IN SOCIOEMOTIONAL DEVELOPMENT

Emotion can be defined as the meaning attached by the infant to its transactions with people, objects, and events in the environment (Sroufe, 1979). Cognition and affect interact in emotion, since intelligence can organize and interpret affect, and since affect in turn can influence thought. Early affective behaviors are at first diffuse in the young infant. They may occur or not, or be mild or extreme, depending upon the state of the infant as well as situational variables. A little later, as they develop into emotional behaviors, they become more specific and coordinated. These behaviors become organized over time into distinct hierarchical patterns of actions. That is, certain groups of the behaviors tend to occur together in an organized, predictable manner. Later still, during the second half of the first year and thereafter, these patterns are further organized to become definite systems of behavior (Sroufe, 1979). These various systems are groups of organized behaviors that have certain goals, functions, and feelings attached to them. They interact with one another in predictable, regular ways and in a dynamic balance. Certain behaviors such as looking or smiling are present in several of these systems. These systems include attachment, wariness and fear, exploration, and **affiliation.**

In addition to the systems, which are comprised of behaviors, it is helpful to think of attachment, fear, or the others as explanatory constructs as well. That is, the specific behaviors involved in attachment, for example, can vary somewhat from infant to infant or within the same infant over time. The construct of attachment, however, as an explanation for the development of a strong bond between infant and parent, goes beyond any specific behavior or behavioral system. We shall deal here with both the explanatory constructs and with the behavioral systems.

Attachment

The construct of **attachment** refers to the formation and continuation of a strong and last-ing emotional bond between the child and the parents and between the child and other primary caregivers or close individuals such as grandparents and siblings. The term also refers to the behavioral system through which this tie is operationalized (Sroufe & Waters, 1977). Attachment implies a reciprocal relationship in which both infant and adult show the emotional feelings and behaviors that serve to promote proximity. This reciprocity distinguishes attachment from **dependency,** which implied a one-way relationship with the child dependent upon the parent but did not account for parental attachment to the child. The earlier researchers who had labeled this construct dependency had defined it as a trait that inhered in the child. The child was seen to be either strongly or less strongly dependent upon the parents, usually the mother, in some quantitatively measurable way. The more recent view stresses qualitative and situational factors to a greater extent and sees attachment as an affective and behavioral outcome of the interaction between parent and child rather than as a quantitative trait within the child alone.

The behavioral system of attachment is also related to the other behavioral systems such as wariness and fear, exploration and curiosity, and affiliation (Ainsworth, 1973; Bowlby, 1969). Affiliation refers to friendly social interactions without trying to attain or maintain proximity. For example, when a child is interacting with someone other than an attachment figure by smiling or vocalizing but stays at a distance, this behavior could be called affiliative. Occasionally, affiliative behaviors are shown even toward attachment figures. Each of these systems interacts with the others and each can affect the others, heightening or depressing their activity. For example, if the child is in a strange situation, the rise of fear and wariness feelings and behaviors will most likely also increase attachment behaviors, as the

Attachment is the strong emotional bond between the infant and other family members such as parents and siblings. This infant is secure in the warm relationship with her mother.

child tries to remain near the parent, and will probably decrease affiliation.

Attachment behaviors shown by the infant include expressions of pleasure at the presence of the parent such as smiling and other reactions of greeting, seeking and maintaining proximity with the parent or other attachment figure, and the security gained from the presence of the caregiver (Ainsworth, 1973). Later, in the somewhat older child, even the memory of the caregiver while the child is temporarily away from this person helps preserve attachment.

The existence of the attachment bond can often only be determined in situations that are stressful to the child. That is, even a child who is securely attached may not evidence this feeling behaviorally in a familiar situation and with the mother nearby. Only when the child is in a strange place, or if the mother leaves, and some of the other behavioral systems come into play as well, are attachment behaviors enhanced, enabling the observer to determine their existence and degree.

Earlier in this chapter we considered the various theoretical explanations offered for the development of the construct of attachment. The ethological view offered by Ainsworth and Bowlby (Bowlby, 1969; Ain-

The securely attached child is also able to detach. That is, he or she does not cling to Mother but instead feels able to freely explore the environment while Mother is present.

sworth, 1973; Bell & Ainsworth, 1972; Stayton & Ainsworth, 1973; Stayton, Ainsworth, & Main, 1973) appears the most satisfactory at the moment. In their view, attachment behaviors are seen as having originally had survival value in that they assured the proximity of mother and child and thus enhanced the survival chances of the child in a hostile environment. The infant's signaling and trying to maintain proximity and the parent's wanting closeness to the child both helped to protect the child from dangers. Furthermore, attachment will later lead to **detachment,** the ability of the child to use an attachment fig-

ure such as the mother as a secure base for exploration of the environment. This detachment process also is important for the eventual survival of the child as it enables her or him to begin to interact with other people and environmental objects and events, and not to remain bound only to one or a few primary attachment figures as infancy is outgrown.

The ethological explanation also dovetails nicely with cognitive viewpoints such as that of Piaget that describe the infant's growing intellectual capacities. For example, the reason that the older infant who has achieved object permanence will protest at the absence of the mother is that it knows the mother still exists even if unseen. A little later, as memory develops even more, such a child will tolerate a brief separation because the memory of the mother will be sufficient to support the child for a while. That is, the child can tolerate a brief separation from the mother because he or she can remember the mother and knows that she still exists. We shall therefore also consider the cognitive aspects as we discuss the development of attachment.

Bowlby and Ainsworth have postulated a four-stage process in the development of attachment:

FIRST STAGE

There is first a stage of undiscriminating social responsiveness, lasting from birth through the first two or three months. During this period the infant attends to any persons that are nearby through visually fixating and tracking and through listening. If picked up and held, the infant will make postural adjustments and will attempt to root and suck and sometimes grasp with the hand in order to maintain contact. Additionally, the infant cries and later smiles at the adult.

During this first stage the infant is responsive to any and all adults. The parents and other people looking after it are not yet singled out in any particular way. While the infant likes adult company, it is not yet particular about which adult; anyone will do. This stage corresponds to the first and part of the second substages of the sensorimotor period as postulated by Piaget. In these stages the child cannot yet distinguish the boundaries between self and others and cannot yet use the environment to build cognitive categories or schemes. It is therefore not surprising that the infant also does not distinguish between familiar and unfamiliar people but is responsive to social overtures from a variety of adults.

SECOND STAGE

Next is the stage of discriminating social responsiveness, which lasts from two or three to about six months. The infant begins to discriminate between familiar people such as parents, grandparents, and siblings, and unfamiliar ones. Just how the infant builds such discriminations while so young is not yet understood. It probably comes about from a combination of visual, tactile, and auditory stimuli that together signify a particular person. The infant behaves far more responsively to familiar than to unfamiliar people, expressing both positive and negative emotions more vehemently to them. The baby will vocalize and smile much more to familiar people and will show joy and greeting behaviors such as body and arm movements when they appear.

This stage parallels the latter portion of Piaget's substage of primary circular reactions and all of secondary circular reactions. Since during these substages the infant begins to involve people in cognitive schemes,

begins to identify them by feature rather than location, and tries to prolong schemes having interesting results, the increased responsiveness to people and the ability to distinguish the familiar from the unfamiliar is not surprising.

THIRD STAGE

The third stage is that of active interaction in seeking out proximity and contact with the attachment figure. In other words, the child tries to remain near to or touching the adult. The child also begins to protest separation from the attachment figure. This stage lasts from about seven months to approximately the beginning of the third year. Early in this stage, the child begins to move about, first by creeping and then by walking. Thus she or he can successfully establish and maintain proximity to the mother by creeping and later walking to her or following her if she moves. This ability to move about also aids in the detachment process, as the child can move away from the attachment figure and then return at will. During this period, the child begins to use her or his signals to the adult not only to summon or to prevent the adult from leaving but also to elicit a response from the adult. Thus, signaling behavior begins to have not only attachment but communicative intent at this time.

During the early portions of the stage, the child begins to adapt his or her behavior based upon feedback from the adult. Attachment behaviors can be altered to conform to situational variables and to the adult's actions or reactions. Bowlby refers to this adapted child behavior as "goal-directed" behavior (Bowlby, 1969). It occurs during the Piagetian substage of the coordination of circular reactions, during which child begins to put together two previously learned schemes to form a new one. During this substage the infant also begins to achieve object permanence. It is not surprising that now the child is able to adjust behavior based upon the adult's reactions and to begin the process of detachment. Later portions of Bowlby's third stage of the attachment process extend over into the last two sensorimotor substages.

FOURTH STAGE

Finally, after age two, the child reaches the stage of goal-corrected partnerships, during which he or she begins to develop hypotheses about the intentions and goals of the mother and other attachment figures and plans how to induce adults to modify their behavior to suit the child's wishes. Since this stage falls beyond the ages dealt with in this book, no more will be said about it here.

Ainsworth and Bowlby believe that it is in the third stage, after the age of seven months, that true attachment develops. Some behaviors that will lead to attachment, such as smiling and greeting, are present earlier. But true attachment does not occur until the infant can both discriminate primary attachment figures from other people and can realize that they exist independently of their presence in the infant's life space. Both these skills are cognitive ones, but they are prerequisites for the development of the social and emotional behaviors relating to attachment.

Other Research

A study similar to those done by Bowlby and by Ainsworth and with similar conclusions was that of H. Rudolph Schaffer and Peggy Emerson (1964) in Scotland. These researchers were especially interested in infants' reactions to brief, temporary separations from the mother or other caregivers. They believed that the strength of the in-

fant's attachment could be determined from the degree of protest at separation.

Schaffer and Emerson found that satisfaction of physiological needs, such as for food or dry diapers, was not the basis for attachment, since infants became attached to individuals (such as their fathers) who did little or nothing to satisfy these needs. It should be noted that this study was done in the 1960s when fathers were generally less involved in caregiving than they are at present. Furthermore, familiarity alone was not the basis for attachment either. Often infants became more attached to people with whom they spent less time, such as their fathers or employed mothers, than they did to those who were with them for much longer time periods, such as day-care personnel or baby sitters.

Schaffer and Emerson postulated the existence of some stages in the development of attachment processes that are quite similar to those proposed by Ainsworth and Bowlby. According to the former, the infant at first is asocial, then becomes indiscriminately social to all, and finally shows social attachment only to a small group of persons. They believed that this stage of specific attachments generally began around seven months of age, although some infants began it as early as five months, and some did not reach it until about one year.

One additional aspect of attachment that deserves mention is **separation protest,** or separation anxiety. Although these two terms are generally used interchangeably, separation protest refers more to the behavioral aspects, while separation anxiety is an emotional term. Earlier researchers had tended to view separation protest and fear in the presence of a stranger as the same phenomenon. Researchers now realize that these are portions of two different systems, though they tend to occur together and their effects may interact. Separation distress occurs more erratically than fear of strangers. It is also more dependent upon the situational context, such as whether the child is ill or not, or if he or she is being left in a strange or familiar place. Separation may, however, sensitize the child to a stranger and make the fear reaction more acute, as when the stranger appears and then the mother leaves the child alone with the stranger (Emde et al. 1976).

Schaffer and Emerson (1964), who were investigating both attachment and separation in their study, found that young babies, between the ages of about five and six months, protested by crying and other signs of distress if left alone by anyone, familiar or unfamiliar. That is, during the time of indiscriminate attachment, they simply liked to be with people, regardless of who these people were, and disliked being left alone. During the stage of specific attachments, especially around 9 to 10 months, babies protested most vehemently when being left by the mother but not necessarily when left by others. This high degree of separation protest then leveled off, but it reappeared strongly again around 18 months of age.

In a study of long-term versus short-term separation, Leon Yarrow (1967) found that short-term separation, such as when the mother went shopping and left the child with a friend or a sitter, resulted in some protest but not anxiety. That is, the child protested with crying, attempts at following, and similar distress reactions but did not show any long-term emotional upset. Long-term separation, such as when the child was hospitalized for an extended period or when transferred from the familiar foster home to a strange adoptive home, resulted in symptoms of anxiety such as disturbances of eating and sleeping, lack of affect, and withdrawal, particularly in children between five months and one year.

Wariness and Fear

Although Ainsworth and Bowlby see wariness and fear as closely related aspects of the same system, they may be two separate systems since they develop at different times (Bronson, 1972). Wariness is a relatively mild negative reaction to what is unfamiliar or unknown, which usually begins to appear sometime before the age of six months. Thus four-month olds smile less at a stranger than at the mother and between four and six months will stare intently at a stranger instead of smiling (Emde et al., 1976). By six months a stranger will receive what Emde calls a "sobering" look, as the infant looks a bit uncertain whether to cry or not and certainly exhibits a slightly negative reaction. A little later, around seven months, the infant may fuss or frown at the stranger.

Reactions of fear, which are more forceful than wariness and generally involve crying at the stranger and an increase of attachment behaviors toward the person looking after the child if present, begin later than wariness, generally between seven (Schaffer & Emerson, 1964) and nine months (Bronson, 1972). Cross-sectional studies usually show only some babies and not others reacting with fear. For example, in a study done by Yarrow (1967), only 29 percent of babies at nine months cried at the appearance of a stranger, and of these half showed what was termed mild distress. When studied longitudinally, however, all babies appear to show reactions of fear to strangers (Emde at al. 1976). These fear reactions may range from mild to forceful, depending upon the individual baby and also the situation. Babies seem to react more negatively to strangers if they

Between seven and nine months, infants begin to react with wariness and fear to the presence of strangers. They are more distressed if they encounter the stranger in an unfamiliar place or if the parent leaves them alone with the stranger. Even though Mother seems happy to be showing her child off to the unfamiliar man, this infant is distressed by the encounter.

are in a strange place or separated from an attachment figure than when in familiar surroundings or in the presence of a parent. Greta Fein (1975) found little fear of strangers expressed by toddlers when the experiment was conducted in a homelike setting and the parent remained present and chatted comfortably with the stranger. In other words,

separation and unfamiliarity heighten the probability of the expression of either wariness or fear.

Experience also seems to play a part. Babies who have had more opportunity to interact with strangers develop fear of strangers later and less acutely than those who have had little such opportunity (Schaffer, 1966).

Fear of strangers seems to peak at around 12 to 13 months (Rheingold & Eckerman, 1973) and then declines slowly. By ages two to three, most children interact quite happily with strangers. For example, most children who attend nursery school like to do so and adjust well to their peers and teachers there. The fear of strangers that normally occurs in toddlers around the age of one does not seem to have any lasting effect.

Affiliation

The system of affiliation refers to friendly social interaction with other adults or with siblings or peers who are not attachment figures as well as with attachment figures at times when proximity is not sought. For example, a child may interact pleasantly with a stranger while seated on the mother's lap or may play next to a peer friend in a familiar room. The child does not seek to be close to or in contact with the other person yet is pleasant and interested in the interaction. Affiliative behaviors are usually seen only in older infants and toddlers. They usually occur only in situations in which attachment figures are available and there is little or no fear exhibited. But affiliative behavior can turn to fear if the mother suddenly leaves the child alone with the stranger with whom the child has been interacting.

Exploration and Curiosity

The system of exploration and curiosity is related to the detachment aspect of the attachment system. It develops in the infant and toddler who is able to move about independently and who has achieved object permanence and some long-term memory. The former is obviously important so that the infant can physically move around to explore the environment. The latter are needed since

the child will begin to explore away from the physical presence of mother or father only when the child can remember and realize that this attachment figure still exists even if not present physically and that therefore the child can return to her or him at will.

Securely attached infants and toddlers, who have learned that the mother or other caregiver is reliably available and will meet their needs, can detach and explore more easily than those who are less securely attached. Such securely attached children will play away from the mother, glancing over at her once in a while to make sure she is still there. Later they will go into another room or out into the yard, away altogether from her physical presence, returning once in a while to check on her whereabouts. By contrast, insecurely attached children will cling to the mother and refuse to explore.

Practical Implications

The fact that infants become securely attached to their parents even when others such as sitters or day-care personnel provide a large amount of the caregiving should be reassuring to working parents who worry about establishing affective bonds with their children.

Furthermore, the data on fear and wariness seem to suggest that if infants are to be placed in care arrangements involving sitters or day-care staff, such arrangements are best made before the child begins to show separation protest or fear of strangers, such as before 7 to 9 months, or else between one year and the second peak of separation protest at 18 months.

Although the Yarrow studies of separation anxiety dealt with long-term or even permanent separation rather than with the child in day care who returns home every night, they too suggest that the best times for placement in day-care centers or with baby-sitters might be before the ages where separation anxiety becomes great, that is, in the first few months of life. If such placement is not made then, it is probably best to wait until both separation protest and fear of strangers have begun to decline, at some time later during the second year of life.

These same studies also suggest that adoption is far less traumatic for the infant if it takes place before specific attachments are established and before separation anxiety becomes involved. Early surrender of adoptable children by their natural mothers, and the expediting of legal arrangements so as to ensure only a short stay in foster care before permanent placement, are all to the benefit of the sound development of the infant.

THE FATHER'S ROLE

In some other cultures and at different historical times, fathers have been more involved with the care of infants and toddlers than has been traditional in the United States. Therefore, the recent interest of some American fathers in participating more actively in their young children's lives can be viewed as something other than a temporary aberration.

Indeed, as changes have taken place in medicine, technology, and economics, roles of men and women can change quickly and drastically. An example of such change is the invention of bottle-feeding of infants, which enabled fathers (as well as other nonmaternal caregivers) to increase their participation in child care. Another change is the advent of safe and reliable methods of birth control, which for the first time in history have freed women from lifelong childbearing and have enabled couples to plan how many children they wanted and when to have them. Other

such changes include the increasing employment of women, including the mothers of young children, which has thrust many fathers into a role of shared caregiving whether they prefer it or not. Under the influence of such changes or perhaps in addition to them, an increasing number of fathers have shown interest in their young child's development.

These socioeconomic changes plus changes in theories of attachment regarding the mother have led researchers seriously to reconsider the roles of both parents.

In the past, parental roles were often regarded as narrowly circumscribed by biology and economics, and as complementary to each other. The mother was seen as the expressive partner, showing affective, nurturant involvement with the family (Parsons, 1955). The father, on the other hand, performed the instrumental function of family breadwinner. Today there is increased recognition that both parents perform both expressive and instrumental functions, and roles have therefore become less narrowly defined and fixed.

Also, the psychoanalytic drive-reduction theories popular in the 1940s and 1950s focused on the unique importance of the mother as the provider of food to the infant. As these became less credible in part due to the studies of the Harlows with monkeys and mother surrogates, as well as through the increasing emphasis on ethological theories, this centering on the maternal role as unique lessened. Under the influence of the women's movement, gender roles and gender-role learning began to be studied in more detail. Researchers began to realize that many individuals were not as narrowly constrained to particular roles as Parsons had suggested. Indeed, the androgyny studies of Bem (1977) have demonstrated that well-adjusted individuals of either sex share some of the qualities usually attributed to the opposite sex. Thus well-

Many fathers today play a much more important part in the care and nurture of their young children than was the case in the past. Some fathers even care for their children at work.

adjusted men show not only such "typically masculine" qualities as independence, industry, and assertiveness, but also such "typically feminine" ones as compassion, empathy, and nurturance.

In the last 10 to 15 years, at a time when many modern fathers were asking for an increasing role, researchers also became interested in the father's contributions to the life of his young child, and whether these differed from or were similar to those of the mother in any critical ways. Before the late 1960s, the only studies involving fathers were those dealing with their absence (Lynn & Sawrey, 1959). Since then, a variety of studies of the quality and quantity of father-infant interactions, the influence of the father on mother-infant interactions, the stability versus change over time of the father-infant relationship, and the attachment of the infant to the father have been reported. Much more is beginning to be known about these topics. In addition, a variety of popular and technical books and special issues of psychological and family journals have highlighted the role of the father.

Role in the Prenatal Period and at Birth

Beyond the fact of conception itself, the father's role in the prenatal period has been studied little. It appears obvious that his attitude toward the pregnancy will affect his partner's feelings and attitudes, but beyond this little has been explored. In some tribal cultures, a phenomenon called the **couvade** occurs in expectant fathers. They tend to exhibit some of the same physical and psychological symptoms of pregnancy that women do, as for example, morning sickness, feelings of heaviness, and abdominal contractions. During their wives' labors, the husbands often take to their beds with physical symptoms resembling labor.

American expectant fathers sometimes report that they too have symptoms such as dizziness, nausea, food cravings, and feelings of heaviness in the breasts or abdomen that are often associated with pregnancy. It is assumed that these physical symptoms in men have psychological bases. They may be due to anxiety over the incipient birth and the new triadic relationship that will replace the dyadic one with the birth of the baby. Or they may be due to empathy for the mother. They may also, however, be an expression of the father's wish to have a role in the pregnancy and the birth and to indicate that this period has profound significance not only for his partner but for him as well. For the expectant father's feelings are often overlooked.

Evidence indicates that the father's ability to assist the mother during pregnancy and childbirth has a positive effect upon both partners. Fathers who attended prenatal classes with their wives were more supportive of them during labor (Jordan, 1973). Those who attended Lamaze classes showed a higher degree of involvement in the pregnancy and more concern for their wives than those who did not (Wapner, 1976). Of course it could have been this involvement that led them to attend the classes in the first place. Such class attendance, however, seems to have no effect upon father-infant bonding after birth, since fathers not present at birth but exposed to their infants shortly thereafter behaved toward them very much as those did who had been present (Miller & Bowen, 1982).

As we discussed earlier in our consideration of bonding, fathers present at the birth of their infant or exposed to them soon after birth report feelings of elation, of wishing to touch and hold the infant, and they describe their offspring as beautiful and perfect (Greenberg & Morris, 1974). Such fathers also do more looking at and talking to the infant (Miller & Bowen, 1982) than those not present at birth.

Early Postnatal Interaction

While many of the earlier studies of social development in early infancy had focused upon the mother-infant dyad, more recent studies have concentrated upon the triadic relationship of father-mother-infant, or upon the father-infant dyad as compared to the mother-infant one, and finally upon the effects of either the father or the mother on the dyadic interaction of the infant with the other (Parke, 1979). Any of these relationships is seen as forming an interactive network in which each affects the behaviors of the others and is in turn affected by theirs. The father is now understood not only to affect the infant directly through his interactions with the child but also indirectly in that he influences the behaviors of the mother.

To determine what this triadic relationship is like, Ross D. Parke and his coworkers (Parke, O'Leary, & West, 1972) studied the

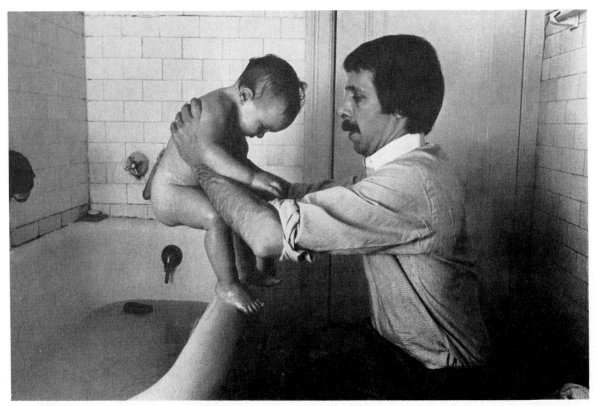

Fathers interact with their infants somewhat differently than do mothers. They spend relatively more of their time in play and less in caregiving than do mothers, and play with their infants in a more active, physical manner. This father is managing to combine a caregiving function such as bathing with some active play as well.

relationship of father, mother, and infant as observed in the hospital in the first few days after birth. The father was found to be just as involved with the newborn as was the mother. In fact, he tended to hold the baby more than she did. When Parke and D. B. Sawin (1975) studied one-to-four-day-old infants interacting with their parents, they found that fathers spent more time talking to and looking at their babies than did mothers. Mothers spent more time tending the babies than did fathers, but fathers did some tending also. Fathers who bottle-fed their babies spent slightly less time at it than did mothers, but

their infants consumed almost equal amounts of milk.

Because these studies had been done with a middle-class sample with Lamaze training, Parke and S. E. O'Leary (1976) replicated them with a lower-class sample who had no prenatal training and in which the fathers did not attend the birth. These fathers also turned out to be just as involved as the mothers and tended to interact with the infant both when the mother was also present and when they were alone with the child.

Thus fathers of young infants seem to be both as interested in them as are mothers and as competent in providing care if they are given the opportunity to do so. Furthermore, the presence of the father seemed to affect the behaviors of the mother toward the infant. When father was present, the mother showed more interest in the infant and did more smiling and cuddling than when the father was not there (Parke & O'Leary, 1976).

Later Interactions

As infants grow beyond the neonatal period, the quality of father-infant interactions begins to differ from that of mother-infant ones. First, although fathers can and do continue to participate in some caregiving tasks, they tend to spend more of their interaction time playing with the infant (Rendina & Dickerscheid, 1976). Fathers pick up their baby more often to play with it or because they believe it wants to be held; mothers do so more often for caregiving (Lamb & Lamb, 1976). Of course the fact that most fathers typically are away from home at work most of the day may help to explain this difference.

Second, when fathers play with their babies, their play differs from that of mothers. This difference is already apparent when the baby is only three weeks old (Parke & Sawin, 1977). Fathers tend to use more physical, energetic, unpredictable, and unusual play, while mothers tend to use conventional games and toys and rhythmic activities and later to read to the child (Clarke-Stewart, 1977; Lamb, 1977a; Yogman, Dixon, Tronick, Als, Adamson, Lester, & Brazelton, 1977; Yogman, 1981). Babies of either sex seem to enjoy play with their fathers more than play with their mothers (Lamb & Lamb, 1976). By 20 months, infants have developed different expectations of play and expect fathers to play with them more frequently than mothers. By 30 months, toddlers show markedly more interest in playing with fathers than with mothers (Clarke-Stewart, 1977).

Fathers treat male and female children somewhat differently, using more action play with boys than with girls (Pedersen & Robson, 1969). When firstborn infants are very young, two to four weeks, fathers talk more to girl babies than to boys (Rebelsky & Hanks, 1971). But by three months, they talk more to sons than to daughters. They talk more to firstborn sons than to firstborn daughters but talk to later-born offspring of either sex equally (Parke & O'Leary, 1976). Thus, fathers seem to be more involved and involved earlier in the gender typing of infants than was previously thought.

The presence of the father continues to affect the mother-child relationship beyond early infancy. In a study of children from 15 to 30 months of age, it was found that if the father is present, the mother tends to talk less responsively to her toddler and also plays less with the child than if the father is not there (Clarke-Stewart, 1978). It is as if the mother expects the father to "pick up the slack" when he is available.

Quantity of Interactions

Although fathers show interest in their infants, they spend far less time interacting with them than do mothers. In part, the reason is that the birth of a baby often fixes parents, at least temporarily, in a more traditional life-style: the mother often quits outside employment and stays home to care for the baby; the father becomes the only breadwinner (Cowan, Cowan, Cole, & Cole, 1976). Thus, the father's lesser involvement may reflect not so much his choice but the fact that he must be out of the home and in the workplace for extended time periods each day.

Whatever the cause, fathers spend considerably less time with their infants than do mothers. Indeed, one study found that they spent only 38 seconds (!) per day talking to their infant between the ages of two weeks and three months and talked to them an average of only three times during that period (Rebelsky & Hanks, 1971). Of course, they may have attended to their children in some nonverbal way as well, but most adults have a tendency to talk to an infant if they are otherwise attending to it. As the babies became older, the father's talk tended to decrease from this already tiny amount. Because it seems almost ludicrous that fathers would interact so little with their infants, this study has been questioned by others. More recent work does not support its conclusions.

For example, a more recent study by Milton Kotelchuk found that fathers spend more time with their infants than Rebelsky and Hanks found but still considerably less than do mothers (Kotelchuk, 1976). Middle-class fathers spend a little more than three hours a day in the presence of their infant, while mothers spend more than nine hours with them (Kotelchuk, 1976). Of the fathers in this study, 75 percent took no responsibility at all for tasks such as feeding, bathing, or diapering. Since mothers spent more time overall with their infants, they devoted a greater total amount of time to play with their infants than did fathers. Since mothers also had to do the bulk of caregiving the fathers tended to spend a higher percentage of their time with the infant engaged in play. The study by I. Rendina & J. Dickerscheid (1976) that has already been described found a similar pattern: while fathers spent about

three times as much time on play as on caregiving, they spent relatively little of their overall time with the infant (but more than Rebelsky and Hanks's 38 seconds). Social class affects caregiving. Middle-class fathers spent more time looking after children than did lower-class ones (Lamb, 1977b), probably because gender roles seem to be less rigidly defined among the middle class.

Attachment of Infant to Father

There is some question whether attachment to the mother is stronger than that to the father when attachment begins to manifest itself in the second half of the first year (Cohen & Campos, 1974) or whether infants become just as strongly attached to their fathers (Lamb 1976 a,b,c). At any rate, by 18 months there is no difference in the strength of attachment to either parent (Schaffer & Emerson, 1964). Either one is preferred over a stranger (Kotelchuk, 1972), although in a stressful situation in which a stranger and both parents are present the mother is preferred over the father (Lamb, 1976a). Mothers seem to be a more secure base for detachment, however, since toddlers tend to explore farther from the mother than the father. If fathers have been involved a lot in caregiving, infants tend to express greater preference for the father and less protest at separation from them than if fathers have done little caregiving. Infants with highly involved fathers showed less fear of strangers than did those with fathers of low involvement (Spelke, Zelazo, Kagan, & Kotelchuk, 1973).

Summary

1. Psychoanalytic, ethological, learning, and cognitive theories all have attempted to explain social development in infancy. While each is able to account for some aspects of infant social behavior, no one theory appears adequate to explain all.

2. Some issues in the study of infant social development include whether there exist sensitive periods for the establishment of particular social behaviors, whether social development is primarily preprogrammed by nature or whether it depends more strongly on environmental influences, and in what manner such development is best studied.

3. The early period right after birth appears to be an important time for the establishment of the mother's and father's bonding behaviors toward the infant. There is some evidence that at least in industrial cultures early and extended contact between mother and infant can have important beneficial results that extend over the first few years of the child's life. It is important that parents of babies in high-risk nurseries be afforded the opportunity to interact with their ill baby in order to establish this bond.

4. Infant and mother appear to operate in a mutually rhythmic pattern as can be seen in the suck-jiggle phenomenon of nursing, interactional synchrony, and the development of mutual gazing. Mothers also imitate infant behaviors back to their offspring.

5. Social smiling is a powerful social reinforcer of adult attention, which the infant uses most effectively.

6. Infant social behaviors may be affected by inborn temperament characteristics that remain relatively stable throughout childhood. Thomas and Chess have found that infants and children can be divided into three basic types: easy, difficult, and slow-to-warm-up. These temperament characteristics in the child interact with and influence parental, peer, and teacher behaviors toward the child.

7. Attachment is the strong and continuous emotional bond that becomes established between infant and parents as well as with others such as siblings and caregivers. At-tachment does not seem to depend upon the alleviation of discomfort or the provision of food, since fathers or working mothers become attachment figures in preference to day-care workers or baby-sitters.

8. According to Bowlby and Ainsworth, attachment develops in a series of stages. At first the infant is socially responsive to all adults. Later the infant is more responsive to familiar people, such as parents or siblings. Then as the infant begins to move about, it tries to maintain proximity with the attachment figure. Finally, after age two, the child begins to form hypotheses about the social intent of the adult.

9. Particularly in strange environments or in the presence of strangers, older infants may show separation protest if the parent or other attachment figure leaves. Infants who are securely attached can, however, begin to detach and explore the environment as they become older if the attachment figure is close by or the child can remember her or his existence while separated.

10. Wariness and fear in the presence of strangers develop as infants are able to distinguish the familiar from the unfamiliar. Fear of strangers seems to be greatest around one year of age. Children differ greatly in the expression of this fear.

11. Fathers are important in the lives of their infants because they interact with them in some ways differently from mothers and because they affect the mothers' behaviors toward the infants.

12. Although fathers generally spend far less time with infants than do mothers, they appear equally competent in caregiving. They spend proportionally more time playing with infants and less time caregiving than do mothers.

13. Fathers seem to treat sons and daughters differently from early in infancy onward, thus contributing significantly to gender role learning. They play more creatively with children of both sexes than do mothers, and children seem to enjoy play with the father more.

Participatory and Observational Exercises

1. Observe several young infants with their parents or other caregivers. How does each infant use any or all of the five behavioral systems (crying, smiling, sucking, clinging, and following) to maintain proximity with the caregiving adult? Which of the systems is more likely to be used by very young infants? By older ones? Give details of your observations.

2. Interview some new parents soon after mother and baby have come home from the hospital. How soon after birth could they hold and watch their baby? How do they describe their bonding experience? Then interview a couple who are adoptive parents. How old was the child when adopted? How and when did they feel their attachments to the child develop? How different do they perceive their experience to be from that of parents who have had the opportunity of bonding soon after birth?

3. Observe infants of varying ages and their responses to the appearance of a parent and/or a stranger. How do the same infants react when the parent leaves and they are left alone with the stranger? You are probably the stranger in these situations. Can you differentiate the various stages of attachment from the behaviors of infants of varying ages? Remember that younger infants (up to two or three months) generally are undiscriminating, that is, they like to interact with any adult. From two to three until about six months they discriminate, preferring parents to strangers but still interacting with strangers. After seven months, infants begin actively seeking out attachment figures and finally may become wary or fearful with strangers around the ages of 11 to 12 months. Can you determine in which of these stages each infant you observe is? Describe each infant's behavior in the various situations.

4. Visit a day-care center at the time when parents are leaving their children for the day, probably quite early in the morning. Observe how each child reacts to being left at the center. Are there age-related differences? Check with caregivers to find out how long each of the children you have observed has been attending this center and how long each has been under the care of this same caregiver at the center. Are there differences in child behavior depending upon how familiar the child is with the setting and the caregiver?

5. Observe a group of toddlers in a play situation. Watch how adults (mothers and fathers) discipline the children. Notice the different methods used by different adults. How do different discipline methods seem to affect the behavior of the children?

6. Watch some adult-toddler interactions. Can you relate examples of adult sensitivity (empathy) toward the feelings of the toddler? How were they expressed? Were there any examples of sensitivity toward the feelings of the adult by the toddler? How were they expressed?

DISCUSSION QUESTIONS

1. Express some of your beliefs about adult-infant (or adult-toddler) relationships in the areas of attachment, discipline, and personality development. Compare them with those of your classmates.

2. Do your beliefs reflect more of an adherence to the environmental or the genetic points of view? Why do you think you hold such beliefs?

The Infant in the Social Context of Family and Society

INTRODUCTION

Infants as social beings develop within the context of the family, peers, and society. Their development is influenced by many larger forces outside them, such as social trends, economic conditions, and political decisions made by those in power. In addition, the life of an individual infant can be affected by particular social circumstances such as the conditions under which it is born, separation from the family on a short-term or long-term basis, illness, and physical or mental handicap. All of these situations and conditions interact to have a profound effect upon the social and emotional development of an infant. In this chapter we shall first consider the history of parenting. Then we shall discuss some of the social trends and forces that affect infants. After that, we will consider infant day care. Then we shall focus on some of the serious social malfunctions in the adult-infant relationship that greatly hamper the development of some infants. Finally, we shall deal with the education of parents for successful parenting.

A CONSIDERATION OF PARENTING

Parenting in the Past

What about parenting in the past? Although historical evidence is meager, it appears that many people were neglectful and even cruel parents (De Mause, 1974). Abandonment, infanticide, child abuse, and the giving or selling of children to strangers were widespread practices not only in the ancient world but also in Europe and North America until the 19th century. Not only were such practices widespread, but they were accepted as inevitable. It appears that many children did not live beyond infancy or early childhood, and

many others who survived suffered lasting effects from inhumane treatment. Undoubtedly, many people spent their lives psychologically damaged by abusive or neglectful practices of their parents or of others to whom parents had relegated their care. But in the modern world, with increased understanding of the importance of early social interaction with caregivers and its influence upon later development, society has come to abhor such practices. Today, educators and behavioral scientists, as well as parents, believe that the education of parents and other caregivers to improve adult-child interaction is important.

Families in the past, however, had one advantage that many modern families do not have. Their child rearing was often done in a more public context, within a network of extended family or other kin, neighbors, household or farm employees, and friends. Thus parents, especially mothers, had the advantage of the experience and companionship of other parents to draw on. In addition, caregiving was shared by many adult women in the family or household. Thus children with cruel or inept parents had a chance to be cared for by some effectual and loving adults as well.

Isolation of Modern Parents

By contrast, modern North American parents, especially mothers who are not employed, are singularly alone in their child-rearing tasks. Fathers usually work away from home, and thus caregiving mothers are often left with just the infant for most of the day. With smaller families and increased geographic mobility, a family may live far away from any relatives. Since cooking, washing, and other household tasks are usually done within the home rather than communally, the opportunities for parents to mix with others while performing either home maintenance or child caregiving tasks are greatly diminished.

Importance of Parenting

In addition to these changes in family life patterns, modern parenting has become a more complex enterprise. People today expect far more from children than their ancestors did in the past. In an agrarian or relatively nontechnical society, there was a place for most people regardless of intellectual endowment or mental health. There was little need for excellence or intellectual ability among the vast majority of the people, who were governed by a small intellectual elite. Therefore, early stimulation of the child's intellectual potential was neither needed nor emphasized. Most people were able to become moderately successful adults and to perform the relatively simple tasks they had to do without the benefit of interesting toys or having adults read to them.

By contrast, in the postindustrial technological cultures of present-day North America, Europe, and Japan, much more emphasis is put on intellectual development. Education is vital, and the person who does not finish at least high school may be economically disadvantaged for life. It is known that early intellectual stimulation in the home seems to influence later achievement in school. Many authorities consider the first few years the most critical in a child's life. Indeed, massive intervention programs such as Head Start are designed for the very purpose of offsetting an unstimulating early home environment and giving children from such environments a chance to succeed in school and later in adult life. Thus what parents or parent substitutes do with and to the infant in these early years is considered extremely important.

Longer Time Spent Parenting

At the same time, parenthood takes much longer with respect to the nurturance of any one child. In the past, children often were apprenticed or went to work as young as six or seven years of age. The law, the church, and employers all considered such children adults, and they were expected to assume adult responsibilities. Thus, parents were charged with the care of each of their children for a relatively short period of time. By contrast, parental responsibility for a child today may extend until such a child finishes college or even graduate or professional school. Although legally adult at either 18 or 21, depending upon state law, many young people today are not economically independent until age 22 or later. Of course, with fewer children in the modern family and with increased life expectancy, most modern parents spend a smaller proportion of their total lives in parenting tasks than did their ancestors who had larger numbers of children and who often died at younger ages. But for any one child, the total number of years spent in parenting has risen dramatically within the span of only a few generations. Parenting has become a much more time-consuming and weighty task.

SOCIAL CHANGE IN CONTEMPORARY NORTH AMERICA

Recent and continuing social changes have profound effects upon the infants born and raised in American families. These changes include the decline in the overall birth rate, the long-term lowering of the marriage rate, the increase of adolescent pregnancies, the high divorce rate, the increase of single-parent families, and changing roles of both mothers and fathers, especially as a result of the increase in the number of working mothers (Huntington, 1979).

Economic changes also affect these social changes. Four economic changes that affect infants and their families have been the high rate of inflation in the late 1970s and the early 1980s, the high interest rates for housing that put either rental or purchased homes beyond the reach of many couples during the typical childbearing years, the high level of unemployment, which meant the loss of jobs for many parents and prospective parents, and finally the great cuts in social programs made by the Reagan administration in an effort to curb government spending and lower the inflation rate. (The pattern in Canada has been similar to that of the United States, except that a greater number of social programs benefiting children remains.)

The implications of these economic changes for the social development of infants in families are quite obvious. Inflation means that families find it increasingly difficult to maintain economic stability; to provide basic housing, food, and medical care for their children; and to depend upon only one breadwinner to provide enough income. Inflation is partly responsible for the great rise in the employment of women in the last decade or so. Because of the increased cost of housing, many families are postponing children while both spouses work to afford the home they wish. Some are planning on no children at all. Unemployment has caused many to rethink how many children, if any, they can afford to have. It also has caused many wives to work to supply at least one paycheck if the husband is out of work. At the same time, many working women, like working men, have lost their jobs and their significant contribution to family economic welfare. Finally, the cutbacks in social programs have pushed many borderline families, particularly single-parent families, back below the poverty line and have affected the education and health care available to children in those families.

We have dealt with the effects of these economic changes only briefly, since this is a textbook about infants and not economics. However, their pervasive influence upon the well-being of infants and their families means that we should not overlook them.

Some of the information about families and how they are changing comes from demographic surveys such as the census that tell us about rates of, and ages at, marriage, the divorce rate, the number of children born each year, and similar statistical information. Let us begin by considering this information.

Marriage Rates and Ages

Since the majority of babies are born to married couples, an important factor affecting how many babies will be born and the kinds of families into which they are born is the marriage rate. In addition, age at marriage can give some indication about whether children may result, based on the assumption that if a couple, and especially the woman, marries at a younger age, they have a greater chance of having children.

The marriage rate calculation is based upon the proportion of people within a particular age span that marry during a given year. The American marriage rate had risen sharply in the period immediately after World War II as servicemen returned home and couples who had postponed marriage finally were able to marry. The rate then declined somewhat, rose again slightly in the late 1960s and early 1970s, declined again, and began rising again in 1976. From 1976 to 1982, the last year for which data are available, the marriage rate rose a little each year.

In 1982 it stood at 10.8 per 1000 of population (U.S. Life Expectancy, 1983). This figure is 16 percent higher than in 1975 and represents 2,495,000 couples who married in 1982. No one can say whether this steady rise will continue, or whether the marriage rate will again begin to decline. Nor can anyone predict whether this rise will result in a rising birth rate. If marriage rates should continue to rise, however, the total birth rate may also rise somewhat.

The vast majority of Americans marry at some time in their lives. In 1982, more than 90 percent of women over 30 and 85 percent of men of the same age had been married at least once (Rich, 1983). Americans appear to be marrying later, however, which probably will result in smaller families. For example, in 1950, 66.7 percent of all women aged 20 to 24 were already married. By 1960, 72 percent of 20- to 24-year-olds were married (Commerce News, 1982). But by 1980, only 46 percent of this age group were married (Rich, 1983), and 50 percent had never been married (the other 4 percent presumably were widowed or divorced). The comparable rates for never having been married at 20 to 24 for men were 69 percent in 1980 versus 53 percent in 1960 (men tend to marry later than women). Another way of looking at the situation is age at first marriage. In 1950, the average age for women at first marriage was 20.3 years; by 1980 it was 22.1 years. Thus the average bride of 1980 was almost two years older than that of 1950. So it appears that at present increasing numbers of people are either postponing both marriage and childbearing until later, or else are having children before marriage or outside marriage.

As an indication that many more are choosing the latter of these alternatives, the proportion of out-of-wedlock births to total live births has more than tripled for women in the 15 to 24 age range from 1950 to 1979 (Commerce News, 1982). That is, out of the total number of births in 1979, three times as many were to unwed mothers as in 1950. This increase plus the increase in divorce and desertion explains to a large extent the great increase of single-parent households in the United States today.

Divorce

The divorce rate, which also skyrocketed for a brief period after World War II and then declined somewhat, rose every year from 1962 to 1981, until the 1981 divorce rate was triple that of 1962. By 1981, one in three marriages overall apparently would be terminated by divorce. But the divorce rate dropped in 1982. About 3 percent fewer divorces occurred that year than in 1981 (U.S. Life Expectancy, 1983). Since no data for later than 1982 are yet available, it is not known if this drop is a temporary quirk or the beginning of a trend. Even if the latter, the divorce rate is still very high and affects children. Of course, some people who divorce have no children, and others divorce after their children are grown. Nevertheless, a significant proportion of divorces result in children being raised temporarily (until the parent remarries) or permanently in a single-parent household.

Single Parenthood

Single parenthood is not an entirely new phenomenon. In every period of history some unmarried people have had children. In addition, although until the end of World War II the divorce rate was quite low, many more parents used to die while their children were young. Single parenthood as a result of widowhood was quite common until the 20th century (Bane, 1976), although the majority

Single-parent families, especially those headed by women, have become far more common in recent years because of higher rates of divorce, desertion, and out-of-wedlock births. Single parents can be competent and loving caregivers and can do an excellent job of raising their children. However, single-parent families headed by women often are forced to exist in poverty, and these families are subject to all the problems that this condition brings with it.

of widows or widowers tended to remarry eventually. Some spouses in the past have also deserted the marriage, leaving the remaining parent with the task of raising the children alone. In recent years, the desertion rate has gone up. And while in the past almost all deserting parents had been fathers, in recent years the desertion rate of mothers has risen sharply. This rise for women probably reflects some societal changes regarding roles, as well as the increasing educational and economic opportunities available to women.

We have already mentioned the increase

in out-of-wedlock births. Because of these, and because of divorce and desertion, the proportion of children living in single-parent households rose from 12 percent in 1970 to 20 percent in 1980 (Commerce News, 1982). In other words, one child out of five in America today is raised in a home with only one parent present. Although some divorced parents remarry, and some mothers who give birth out of wedlock marry later, the majority of children of divorced or unwed parents spend all or most of their growing years in a home with only one parent.

The vast majority of single-parent

households in America today, about 90 percent, are those headed by mothers. But the proportion headed by fathers is slowly increasing, both because more divorcing fathers are requesting and obtaining child custody and because somewhat more mothers are either deserting or do not want custody (Orthner, Brown, & Ferguson, 1976). By 1980, 40 percent of all black families and 12 percent of all white families were headed by women (Rich, 1983).

Many of these families headed by women are among the poorest families in America today. Often the mothers cannot obtain work because of their lack of education and training or because of their child-care responsibilities. Those who do work tend to cluster in the lowest-paid occupations and have to absorb the cost of child-care from their already meager wages. In 1979, 31 percent of single-parent families headed by women had incomes of $5,000 or less, well below the official poverty level. With increased unemployment and the curtailment of social programs since then, that proportion has undoubtedly risen.

Consequently, in terms of housing, food, clothing, medical and dental care, and education, many children of single-parent families are far less advantaged than those in which two parents are present. In addition, some single parents may be faced with such psychological problems as lack of emotional companionship and support. For these there may often be no backup from anyone else in the demanding physical and psychological task of raising a child.

Aside from the economic burden on many single-parent families, the available evidence appears to show that in other respects children do not necessarily suffer from such an arrangement. The psychological stresses that come from living in a home with two parents who do not get along may be alleviated by their separation. Living with only one parent after a divorce may be better for a child than living with two parents locked in constant dissention (Hill, 1968). Furthermore, many single parents, whether divorced or unwed, often have a supportive network of extended family or friends who offer both emotional and financial help. Often the family itself is more complex than the label "single-parent family" indicates and may include grandparents, aunts and uncles, or nonrelated adults such as boarders who provide nurturance and both psychological and economic support for the child and parent. Nevertheless, because of the pervasive economic and social problems faced by many single-parent families, a child raised in such a setting may be more "at risk" both physically and psychologically than one raised in a family with both parents present.

Birth Rate

Except for the relatively brief period from 1945 to 1957, the number of children born to the typical American family has declined steadily since colonial days (Bane, 1976). The colonial family usually had eight or nine children, that of the 19th century about five, and during the early 20th century and in the brief boom after World War II the average family had three or four (Bane, 1976). Of course, infant and child mortality has declined steadily during these years as well, so that actual family size has varied less than the number of births per family would indicate. Today, the married woman in the 18- to 24-year range is expected to produce an average of only 1.8 children (Rich, 1983). This figure is below the level for natural replacement of the population, in other words, below zero population growth. If this trend continues, further increases in the United States population will be due solely to im-

Family size in the United States has been declining since colonial days, except for the brief baby boom following World War II. The 19th-century and early 20th-century family, such as this one, usually had four to five children.

migration. The trend to smaller families is supported by interview data with modern young couples, who consider two children as the ideal (David & Baldwin, 1979).

The decline in the overall birth rate from its height in the 18th and 19th centuries, although calculated in a somewhat different manner, based upon the number of births per 100,000 population, shows the same trend. The birth rate reached a low point of 14.8 per 100,000, the lowest ever, in 1975 and 1976 (Statistical Abstract of the United States, 1979). Since then it has risen only slightly. In 1982, the most recent year

for which data are available, it was 16 per 100,000 with a total of 3,704,000 babies born in that year (U.S. Life Expectancy, 1983). The drop in the birth rate seems to be due primarily to the limiting of family size by families having children, rather than to a marked increase in voluntary childlessness (although economic trends of the last few years, which have not yet been reflected in demographic data, may have begun to alter this). When a large sample of wives was interviewed in 1975, only 5 percent indicated that they wished no children at all (Bane, 1976). Involuntary factors such as infertility, divorce, or death of spouse usually result in an additional 5 percent not having children. This 10 percent childlessness rate among married women is close to the percentage who have not borne children throughout American history (Bane, 1976). The vast majority of young American adults thus marry and have children, just as their ancestors did. The difference is that they are having fewer children.

Much of the decline in the birth rate can be attributed to economic conditions. It costs a lot to have a child and to raise it to adulthood at present, whereas in the past a child was an economic asset, who contributed to the family welfare. With both parents often needing to work, it is increasingly difficult to plan for children, to forego the extra income even temporarily, and to work out good alternative caregiving arrangements for the children when the mother returns to work. The reduced size of homes and apartments also may help persuade families to limit the number of children.

In addition, the increase in the employment of women, coupled with higher educational levels for many women, often makes those in business and the professions reluctant to interrupt a career. The fact that women are finding fulfillment in many things in addition to or in place of motherhood may have influenced the birth rate. Finally, once a couple has decided to limit their family in its own best interest, improved and varied methods of birth control have made such limitation easier than in the past.

What are the implications of this lowered birth rate for infants born today? Like their grandparents born in the 1930s or early 1940s, but contrary to their own parents who were born during or after the postwar baby boom, today's babies will grow up in families with few or no siblings and in a society populated more by adults rather than by peers (Bane, 1976). If there are siblings, they may

Many present-day families are limiting themselves to just one or two children. This one-child family is quite typical. Furthermore, increasing numbers of well-educated women are now waiting until they are in their thirties to have their first or only child.

be quite a bit older or younger than the child in question. Since the mother may be working, however, the child is likely to be exposed to same-age peers with a baby-sitter or in day care. Since the birth rate among the disadvantaged is somewhat higher than among the middle class, and since many rural and urban poor live in extended family households, poor children are more likely to have siblings or peers of about the same age range in the home than are middle-class youngsters.

The median age of the American population is steadily increasing and will continue to increase. In 1979 it stood at 30, an increase of 2.1 years since 1970 (Schmid, 1980). This situation will be a mixed blessing for today's infants as they grow up. On the one hand, they will find less crowding in schools and less competition for college entrance and for employment than did their parents. On the other hand, a larger proportion of the total will probably have to serve in the military. They also will have to provide an increasing amount of support for their elders as these reach retirement. The problems in recent years of keeping the Social Security system solvent are one indicator of even greater problems to come as there are fewer young people in proportion to older ones.

Working Mothers

The increase in working mothers of small children is in part related to the increase in single-parent families, in part to the pressures of inflation and the escalating cost of housing, as well as to the unemployment of many men that has forced their wives to seek work. In addition, the increasing educational level of many women and those aspects of the women's movement dealing with equality and with self-fulfillment certainly have played a part in impelling women either to seek employment or to continue it even after marriage and children.

For many centuries, of course, women have done more than housekeeping and childcare, but they usually worked in the home or on the family farm rather than in a work place removed from the family. From the time of the Industrial Revolution, however, poorer women have frequently labored outside the home, in factories and other work places, while middle-class women increasingly were restricted to the role of housewife after marriage. The impact of World War II and especially the economic and social developments of the last 20 years have changed all that. Now not only poor women, but women of all social classes are in the work force in ever-increasing numbers.

Women in the labor force increased by 173 percent from 1947 to 1980 (Rich, 1983). By 1980, the total female labor force stood at 46 million. This figure represented slightly more than 41 percent of the total labor force in the United States and meant that about 52 percent of the adult female population over the age of 16 were in the work force (Rich, 1983). Furthermore, an increasing proportion of working women are the mothers of young children. In 1970, 29 percent of children under six had employed mothers. But by 1980, this figure had risen to 43 percent (Commerce News, 1982). More than 4 out of every 10 preschoolers have a working mother and thus presumably must be cared for by someone else during a portion of every working day.

Changing Role of the Mother

The biggest change in the maternal role has been that for many women mothering has become a part-time rather than a full-time occupation because they continue in or return to the labor force while their child is still very young. This role change in turn has affected that of the father, who may have to increase his involvement either with the child or with household tasks such as cleaning and cooking or perhaps with both. If there are older siblings in the family, they too may become more involved just like the father. In addition, others outside the nuclear family, such as relatives, friends, or baby-sitters, or the staff of day-care centers and nursery schools, may become more important in the care of the infant or toddler as the time involvement of the mother lessens.

In addition to the great increase in the proportion and absolute number of mothers in the work force, the pattern of married female employment over the life cycle has changed. In the past, women entered the work force, if at all, only briefly before marriage and then dropped out for the rest of their lives or at least until their children were grown. Only single women tended to work as long or almost as long in the course of their lives as did men. In the past 15 to 20 years, this pattern has changed markedly. There are now two peaks of female employment, one as before among younger women before marriage or before the birth of children but another that begins around age 34 and rises to its greatest height around age 45. This peak represents those women who return to work after the last child is in school. In addition, however, an increasing number of women do not leave the work force at all, even when they have children, or do so only briefly for a short or extended maternity leave.

A number of factors contribute to this latter pattern. Women at lower income levels, particularly single parents, may not be able to take off more than a brief period from work because of economic hardship. Also, since employers in many of the fields in which such women cluster do not give maternity leaves, such women are forced to leave their jobs and then to look for others after the birth; they cannot afford the luxury of waiting but must begin the job search soon.

At the same time, many well-educated women also resume work after only a brief leave but for a different set of reasons. Many of them are highly trained business and professional people who are difficult to replace even temporarily because their skills are scarce and badly needed. Others may be working in such rapidly changing fields that they cannot risk letting their skills become obsolete while they are out of the work force caring for young children.

These developments have made the study of how and if maternal employment affects infants and young children an important field of study. In spite of myths to the contrary, usually based on false analogy to studies of institutionalized or hospitalized children, well-conducted research has found few effects of maternal employment as such (Etaugh, 1974). When other factors that play a part in the mother's decision to work such as single parenthood, divorce, poverty, or type of employment available are accounted for, the fact that the mother is working does not appear to be in any way detrimental to the child's physical or psychological development (Hoffman & Nye, 1974).

What does seem to be a crucial variable is the mother's level of satisfaction with what she is doing (Hoffman & Nye, 1974). Employed mothers who are happy with their jobs and homemaker mothers who enjoy that role have children who are better adjusted and happier. By contrast, either working mothers or homemaker mothers who are unhappy tend to have less well-adjusted and less happy children. Thus it is the mother's own satisfaction rather than her employment or lack of it that seems to be critical in influencing the child's level of adjustment.

Shared Parenting

A "mini-phenomenon" of the 1970s and 1980s (since the numbers, though increasing, are still very small) has been the increase of shared parenting, that is, parents sharing the major caregiving tasks by using a split work schedule and in some instances by reversing the usual roles. In this latter instance, the mother goes to work outside the home and the father assumes the role of "househusband," caring for the home and the offspring. This role switch has had some modest popularity in Sweden and also has been tried by some couples in the United States. It works well if the father is in an occupation where he can do some of his work from the home and can watch the child while doing so. It also works at times of economic stress when the woman is in a field that needs employees while the man has difficulty finding work, by ensuring that there will be at least one income for the family.

Age At First Pregnancy

Some alarming trends are taking place in the matter of age at first pregnancy, both upward and downward. The most usual childbearing ages in the past had been within the 18- to 24-year age span. At present, although the teenage pregnancy rate declined during the 1970s (Williams, 1982), a large number of first pregnancies still occur among younger adolescents. Many girls of 15 and 16, and some even as young as 11, are bearing children. By 1973, one baby out of every five was being born to an adolescent mother (Huntington, 1979). This phenomenon, which interacts with some of the other factors we have discussed, such as single parenthood and poverty, often will have undesirable consequences for the children born thus.

First of all, very young girls are not physically prepared for childbearing, as was discussed in a previous chapter. For example, babies born to very young mothers are more likely to be premature, of low birth weight, or to have other problems during gestation or birth. Second, many adolescent mothers tend to be unmarried, to have a low educational level (and seldom complete their education after the birth of the baby), and to be of low economic level. Consequently, the vast

majority rely on the meager benefits of public assistance for their livelihood. Their children are most likely to be raised in poverty, with little in the way of proper nutrition or preventive medical care. Being the child of an adolescent mother places the child at risk for developing a variety of physical and psychological problems.

At the same time as the increase in adolescent childbearing, well-educated women are increasingly postponing childbearing until their thirties (Williams, 1982). First births to women aged 30 to 34 rose by 66 percent in the span from 1970 to 1979, and another 15 percent from 1980 to 1983 (Schmid, 1984). This over 30 group was the only group of women showing a significant increase of births since 1980. Although in the past many women, having a higher birthrate, gave birth to their later children during their thirties, the increase of first births to this age group is a new phenomenon. Medical advances have made the procedure relatively safe for older mothers, and the use of amniocentesis and selective abortion has decreased the risk of producing a defective child. But it is not yet known in what ways, if any, these women and their husbands differ from younger ones in how they raise their children. It is known that twice as many of these older mothers had managerial or professional jobs than did those under 30, and they tended to have much higher family incomes than did the younger ones (Schmid, 1984). Thus researchers have no idea what the psychological consequences of older first parenthood combined with these other variables might be for either the child or the parents.

Conclusion

Infants at present are being born into smaller families than at just about any time in the nation's history. They are very likely to be only children or to have only one sibling. Their mothers are quite likely to be very young, perhaps even teen-agers, or else over the age of 30. In addition, the picture for infants born in the 1980s is mixed as far as the impact of social forces is concerned. On the other hand, American society is more concerned than ever before about problems that had largely been ignored in the past, such as child abuse. More parents are interested in learning about child-rearing methods that will help their children grow into secure and happy adults. Fathers are more involved with the care and nurture of their young children than in the past.

On the other hand, problems still abound. Especially if their mothers are very young, today's infants are fairly likely to be raised in a home with only one parent present. Even if born into an intact, two-parent family, a modern infant has a relatively large chance of losing one parent through divorce or desertion. An increasing number of children are being born into families who are quite poor and whose chances of escaping poverty are remote. Finally, whether born into or raised in a two-parent or single-parent family, the infant is quite likely to have a mother who goes to work while the child is still quite young and who has trouble finding adequate child-care arrangements while she works. Thus in considering the state of infants in present-day America, the state of their families and of the society in general must also be considered, since these conditions have the most profound effects upon the well-being of infants.

PEER AND SIBLING RELATIONS

Background

Until recently, little attention was paid to the social influence of peers in the lives of infants and toddlers. There may be little evolutionary precedence for peer and sibling interactions, inasmuch as for many millenia people lived in small bands and so few children survived early infancy that interaction with a similar-aged peer outside the immediate family was highly unlikely (Mueller & Vandell, 1979). Since infants were weaned late, biology, custom, and necessity dictated a wide spacing of children, a practice that generally precluded interaction with closely aged siblings. As civilization developed and resulted in larger groups of people living closely to one another, and as infant mortality decreased, it became more likely that infants would be exposed to other peers close to them in age.

In more recent times, however, other factors that again tended to isolate infants came into play. For example, most infants in North America and Western Europe since at least the 17th century have been raised in nuclear families, again making interactions with peers more unlikely. The decreasing birth rate has militated against the presence of closely aged siblings, as parents who have fewer children also tend to space them more widely.

In recent decades, however, group care of infants has become more common in many cultures including that of North America, and some infants are therefore increasingly spending time with peers of similar age. Therefore, research on the roles of peers in the social development of infants has begun. Researchers increasingly want to determine whether the peer group may perform an important function either similar to or different from that of adults in the social lives of infants and toddlers.

Definition of Peers

Peers are usually defined as children close in age who interact with the child in question

(Mueller & Vandell, 1979). Siblings can play the part of peers if they are relatively close in age to the infant. But if they are quite a bit older and helping to tend the child, then their role is more like that of surrogate parents.

Peer Relations in Infancy

Very young infants have little or no understanding of a peer as a social being. This is not surprising since the young infant has no clear ideas of the boundaries between self and the outside world and no understanding of what it can control and what is beyond control. Early interaction with adults such as the mother is easier than peer interaction. The mother is better able to adjust her responses to the competencies of the infant and to make allowances for the child's immaturity, while a peer is unable to do so (Lewis, Young, Brooks, & Michalson, 1975). Thus parent-infant social interaction begins much earlier in life than does peer interaction. Furthermore, young infants still lack some of the physical and intellectual skills needed in order to participate in peer interaction. As they master more of these skills, such as gazing and noncrying vocalizations, they begin to interact with peers if these are available. But they may not realize the difference between a peer and a moving toy. They may not yet understand that peers are people! After about six months, infants seem to become more actively involved with each other (Buehler, 1933). They smile at each other, reach out, and may try to follow after a peer. Even these early interactions may be at some level that is not yet truly social, in which the peer is regarded as just another interesting or familiar object in the environment.

By the time infants are 9 to 12 months old, their behaviors toward peers have taken on a truly social quality. At this time they seem to begin to understand that peers are truly people. They offer objects to peers and in turn take those offered to them. They also begin to play social games such as peek-a-boo, to wave at the peer, and to vocalize with the apparent anticipation of reciprocal vocalization.

In a study of peer relations of nine-month olds (Becker, 1977), pairs of infants who were previously unacquainted with each other met for 10 consecutive days in play sessions with both mothers present. A group of controls met in pairs only on the 1st and 10th days. Becker found that even early in the study, infants interacted more with one another than with their own or the other mother or with toys that were provided. Over the 10 days, the amount of peer interaction increased steadily. By contrast, the amount of interaction did not noticeably increase among the controls between the 1st and the 10th day, indicating that both practice and familiarity, but not maturation, probably contributed to increasing interactions. Practice may be even more important than familiarity, however, since when in an 11th session an unfamiliar peer was substituted for the familiar one, the higher degree of interaction learned with the familiar peer generalized to the new peer.

Peer Relations Among Toddlers

By 13 to 14 months, children imitate one another's behavior. They also gesture to one another, point, lean on one another, and babble or talk to one another (Lewis et al., 1975). Life is not all sweetness and light, however, because around this time toddlers also begin to fight over the possession of toys. They may hit one another and pull hair in an effort to keep or regain possession of a treasured object (Mueller & Vandell, 1979).

As the second year goes on, toddlers increasingly like to interact with peers. Both the amount of mutual play and the total

Peer interaction among toddlers provides much satisfaction, especially if the peers are familiar. What could be better than sharing a birthday party with a friend?

length of time spent playing together increase as children approach age two (Lewis et al., 1975). When put into a situation with a stranger, who may be either a peer or an adult, they overwhelmingly prefer to be with the strange peer (Lewis et al., 1975). In such a situation, the toddler will seek proximity with the mother or at least maintain frequent eye contact with her, but will interact with the other child. By contrast, an adult stranger is treated far more warily than the strange peer and is likely not to be interacted with at all.

But toddlers prefer to interact with familiar peers and to interact longer with them. Previous peer experience, such as through attendance at a play group or in day care increases peer interaction, even if the peers are unfamiliar, that is, different children from those previously encountered (Mueller & Brunner, 1977). Again, this indicates that peer behaviors once learned can be generalized to new peers as shown in the study by Becker with slightly younger children.

Sibling Relations

Little work has been done to explore social interaction between infants or toddlers and their older siblings. The few studies that have been reported indicate that infants interact little with their siblings if put in a strange laboratory situation (Lamb, 1978a & b). In the familiar surroundings of the home, however, infants interact with siblings a good deal more (Abramovitch, Corter, & Lando, 1979).

Mothers versus Peers

Researchers question whether toddlers prefer to interact with their mothers or with peers. W. Bronson (1975) found that when unfamiliar one-to-two-year-old peers were put together, they spent a lot of time looking at one another but did little to seek one another out for social contact beyond echoing some vocalizations or imitating some motor activities. These same toddlers were much more likely to engage their mothers in social interactions. Bronson speculated that such children are more interested in comprehending their environment than they are in social interactions as such. Age mates are only useful and interesting insofar as they are social objects in the environment on whom the toddler can try out her or his expanding motor and intellectual skills. But when mothers are also present, they function much more effectively than peers in the child's experimentation with the environment, and toddlers thus prefer to interact with them.

Michael Lewis and his associates (Lewis et al., 1975) also think that peers and the mother perform very different functions but that peers are therefore preferred in some situations. "Mothers are good for protection, peers for watching and playing with" (Lewis et al., 1975, p. 57). Children evidence more motor behaviors directed toward peers but vocalize more to their mothers.

But overall, the total amount of interaction with peers seems to exceed that with

Interaction between infants and their siblings has not been the subject of much study. However it is obvious that this infant and older brother are enjoying each other's company.

adults. For example, Carol Eckerman, Judith Whatley, and Stuart Kutz (1975) brought together pairs of unfamiliar peers in a playroom situation while their mothers were present. Three age groups, 10–12 months, 16–18 months, and 22–24 months, were used in the study. Peer-to-peer interactions occurred in more than 60 percent of their observations at all three age levels. As children became older, social play using a shared toy as well as physical interaction with one another increased, and solitary play decreased.

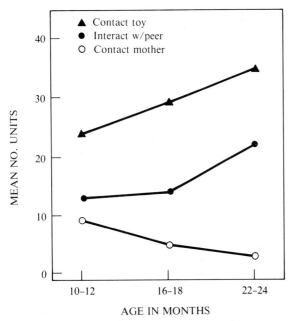

Object, Peer, and Mother Interaction of Toddlers. In a novel play setting, toddlers in all three age groups were most likely to play with a toy. The next most likely behavior was interaction with a peer, and the least likely was interaction with Mother. The older the toddlers, the greater their interaction with toys and peers. Interactions with Mother among older toddlers were fewer than among the younger ones.

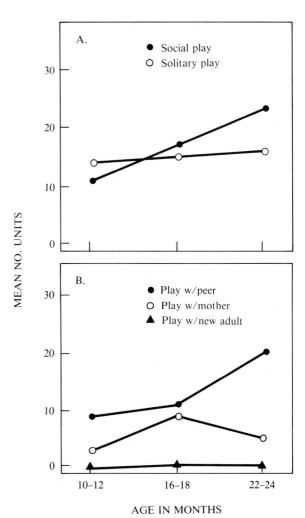

In the same experiment, older toddlers also showed an increasing amount of social play and a decreasing amount of solitary play as compared to younger ones. At all three ages, toddlers were most likely to play with a peer, in preference to play with Mother or an adult stranger. However, Mother play was preferred over that with the stranger. Interestingly, 16- to 18-month-olds played more with Mother than did either older or younger toddlers.

These researchers were especially surprised at how little the children interacted with their mothers as compared to their interactions with the peer. Given the choice, they overwhelmingly chose to interact with the peer, if they interacted with anyone at all. But these researchers also noticed that peer-to-peer interactions were similar in quality to interactions between the child and a familiar adult such as the mother. They concluded that toddlers perceive their peers as people and not as similar to objects in the environment. Toddlers seem to model their behaviors toward peers on those they have already learned to use with adults and in turn seem to expect responses similar to those given by adults. Whether this interpre-

tation or those of Bronson and the Lewis group are more correct remains to be seen.

Not surprisingly, young children also seem to prefer peer interactions to those with adults other than mothers. For example, a study of infants and toddlers in day-care centers (Finkelstein, Dent, Gallacher, & Ramey, 1978), found that as children became older and were able to locomote, vocalize, and otherwise interact socially, they tended to spend increasing amounts of time with one another and correspondingly less with day-care personnel.

Peers as Substitutes for Adults

Both human and animal studies have found that in the absence of nurturant adults, peers can serve as important social substitutes for adults that lessen somewhat the effects of isolation from adults. While the children involved do not grow up as normally as those exposed to adult influence, the peers provide important social stimulation.

Some of the studies with rhesus monkeys done by Harry Harlow and Margaret Harlow (Harlow & Harlow, 1962) involved infant monkeys raised only with peers as compared to those raised by their mothers in an environment that included other mothers and infants, and those raised in total isolation. Not surprisingly, those raised in total isolation for six months or more reacted with extreme fear and antisocial behavior when exposed to other monkeys. Their behaviors closely resembled some of the psychotic behaviors found among extremely disturbed humans. They would cower in a corner in fright, tremble, or engage in self-mutilating behaviors such as biting themselves or banging their heads against the wall. If such monkeys were placed with younger peers after the six-month isolation, they tended to improve over time (Novak & Harlow, 1975). If placed with same-aged peers who had not been isolated, they did not improve, probably because the social behaviors of these peers were already too advanced for the isolated monkeys to profit from them.

Monkeys raised from birth separated from the mother but with a peer group tended to cling together for mutual protection or to enjoy the contact comfort of one another's bodies. As they grew up, they tended to play much less aggressively with peers than did monkeys who had been raised by mothers. Their sexual development, however, was no different from that of normal monkeys.

Since researchers cannot ethically subject humans to such gross deprivation, the only similar human situation occurred as a result of the upheavals of World War II. As reported by Anna Freud (Freud & Dann, 1951), a group of six children who had been born in a concentration camp and separated from their parents as toddlers and spent their time only with one another were found at the end of the war. These children, when liberated, could not tolerate separation from one another, even for a short time. If one child was temporarily removed from the group, the others became quite agitated and would not calm down until the child returned. The child who was removed reacted to this separation much as would a normal child at separation from the mother. Thus it appeared that the children served not only as playmates but as primary attachment figures for one another. They looked out for and helped one another, as adults usually look after children, to the degree that they could.

Surprisingly, as Anna Freud followed up these children after their liberation, they seemed to develop relatively normally during childhood. As they spent more time with the same nurturing adults, their dependence upon one another lessened and they began to relate to the adults as well. This situation demonstrated that among humans also, peers seem able to substitute to some extent for the absent adults.

Even if isolation from adults is not total, peers seem able to substitute for adults who are present only to a limited extent in children's lives, such as if children are confined in institutions. Wayne Dennis and P. Najarian (1957), in studying babies in a foundling home in Iran where caregivers were few and far between, found that at age two these children who had up to that time been quite isolated were behaving in a retarded manner. After age two, however, they were allowed to mix freely with age peers. As they played with other children and explored their environment, these children began to act less retarded and by age five appeared quite normal, except for somewhat retarded language development. It appears that, except for language, in which a model who speaks better than the child is needed, these children were able to substitute peer interactions for adult ones quite successfully.

In summary, it appears that when given the choice, infants and toddlers like to interact with peers, in some instances preferring them over adults. While it is still debatable whether the peer interaction differs from adult-child interaction or is similar to it, children seem to profit from interactions with others their own age. Indeed, in the absence of much adult contact, that with peers may provide a viable substitute. These findings should reassure both parents and child-care providers at a time when more children than ever before are spending a considerable portion of their lives in group care.

INFANT DAY CARE

As more mothers of young children are in the labor force and unable to care for them in their own homes on a daily basis, the need for various kinds of alternative care for infants and toddlers either out of the home or in the home but with a caregiver other than the mother has become much greater than in the past. This need in turn has resulted in the establishment of various alternative child-care arrangements such as care in the home by a relative or by a baby-sitter, or out of home care by a baby-sitter in the baby-sitter's home, or day care in either a day-care home or center. As such arrangements have proliferated, both the parents who patronize them and researchers in child development have become concerned about the effects of such care on children. Both groups want to know if the presence of the mother in the home is a critical variable or if children can develop normally both socially, intellectually, and physically in other situations. They are concerned with what kind of group care under what circumstances offers the best out-of-home environment for the child. In addition, parents and researchers are interested in the possible benefits of day care for children from homes in which there are many problems or in which the intellectual climate is deficient for optimum development. Finally, they question what kind of alternative care, begun when, and how often, is best for the child whose mother works outside the home.

Historical Perspective

Little is known of the history of nonmaternal care of children other than the history of day care, and little is known even about that (Baxandall, 1975). In the past even as now, most day care that did exist was for somewhat older children, and the degree of involvement of infants in such arrangements can only be guessed. Day care in the United States has generally been in private hands. A few day-care centers have been sponsored by government agencies, usually at the local and sometimes at the state level. Federal involvement, when there has been such, has generally been in the form of underwriting the cost of certain classes of children in private, state, or municipal day-care centers or of providing matching funds for support of a center if other levels of government or private individuals raised the rest of the money. This pattern differs from that in many other countries, particularly in Western Europe and the Communist sphere, in which national governments actively sponsor day-care facilities for children.

While some children have obviously always been cared for by others while their mothers worked, organized group care of young children did not begin until late in the 19th century when philanthropic upper-class women began to set up day-care centers in some of the large cities to take the children of the working poor and of recent immigrants (Baxandall, 1975). In the early 20th century, social workers began to show interest in day care, perceiving it to be an important part of the total social-welfare movement. Some municipal funding became available for day-care programs as part of other social services provided by some of the nation's cities. Social workers were the first to train workers for day care, treating them as a separate group of paraprofessionals for the first time.

The federal government became involved in day care during the Great Depression of the 1930s, when under the Works Progress Administration (WPA) program, which provided work to the unemployed, day-care centers were set up. They served to employ out-of-work teachers, to care for the children of mothers who were working because their husbands were out of work, and also to use commodity foods that the government had bought from farmers to relieve them of surpluses. This federal involvement

continued into World War II, with the passage of the Lanham Act, which provided federal matching funds for day care for children of mothers employed in the defense effort. With the end of the war, some states and municipalities, recognizing that working mothers were still in need of child care, continued to operate some of these centers, but the majority closed.

During the late 1940s and the 1950s, social pressure on mothers to remain at home with their children was strong. There was some private day care, but most out-of-home care was probably given by individual babysitters, friends, or relatives.

Day care assumed increasing importance in the 1960s, however, and has continued to be an important issue for working mothers. First, increasing numbers of women have been entering the labor market. Second, the importance of early education, particularly for children from disadvantaged homes, began to be recognized. This was the era of the Great Society programs, during which Head Start began. Day care that had an educational component and began while the child was very young was viewed as possibly helpful for such children in preventing later school failure. Finally, the federal government beginning in the 1960s again made some contribution to day care, in the form of support for day care for former, present, or incipient welfare recipients under Title XX of the Social Security Act of 1962.

Even with some continued federal support at present, the bulk of day care remains in private hands, with some regulation by state government, particularly for safety and health, and some federal supervision of centers that still receive federal aid. It seems quite obvious that at a time of shrinking public service funds, there will not be any expansion of either federal or state support of day care in the near future. Thus day care appears destined to remain a privately run enterprise subject to some government supervision.

Day Care and Alternate Forms of Care

Care for infants and toddlers by someone other than the mother exists primarily because it is needed. It is needed because increasing numbers of mothers are in the labor force. The vast majority of women who work outside the home do so for exactly the same reason men do: to provide food, clothing, shelter, medical care, and other necessities of life for their families and themselves. Many women work because they are heads of households. They have no husbands because they are divorced, widowed, or deserted or were never married. Many of these women have children to support. Many married women work because their husbands are too ill or disabled to work, cannot find work especially at times of recession or changing employment patterns, or earn too little to support a family without the wife's help. Finally, many women who are better educated and have held responsible and challenging employment before having children are reluctant to stop working when children come. Although they might not have to work for economic reasons alone, they prefer to do so, and thus their children also need some type of alternate care.

What sorts of numbers are represented by these facts? In 1978, there were 9 million children under three in the United States. Of the 7.8 million mothers of these children (obviously some mothers had more than one child under three), 39 percent, a total of 3.1 million mothers, were in the labor force (Ruopp, 1979). By the 1980 census, there were 10 million children under the age of three. While there is no comparable infor-

mation for employment of mothers of children under three from the 1980 census, it is known that for children under the age of six, 45 percent of the mothers were working (Women at Work, 1983). Thus it is quite likely that the labor force participation of even mothers of children under three was at the level of the earlier 39 percent or perhaps even higher.

Many of the children of these working mothers are being cared for in their own home by a relative such as the father or grandmother. Others are cared for at home by an employed nonrelative such as a neighbor or baby-sitter. The proportion of those cared for by relatives and those cared for in their own homes has declined. During the 1960s, almost half of the preschool children of working mothers were cared for at home (Low & Spindler, 1968); by 1975 this figure had declined to one-third (Ruopp, 1979). Care by relatives also seems to be declining: the 1968 study found 48 percent of children of working mothers cared for by a relative and 52 percent by a nonrelative (Low & Spindler, 1968); this latter figure rose to 56 percent by by 1975 (Ruopp, 1979).

Child care outside the home may be in a professionally staffed day-care center, in a day-care home run by a housewife, or with a baby-sitter. For older children, day-care homes provide about 75 percent of the care and centers only 25 percent (Ruderman, 1968). The difference is even greater for infants: in 1969, only 2 percent of the children under age three of working mothers were in day-care centers (Ruopp, 1979). Three factors account for this difference: cost, availability, and preference. First, center-based infant care is too expensive for many parents—usually from $2,000 to $5,000 per child per year (Ruopp, 1979). Secondly, in part because of the expense and also because infant care is more demanding and difficult and requires separate facilities, not many day-care centers offer infant care. The majority do not take children under age two or those who are not toilet trained (which also eliminates younger children). Finally, the majority of parents seem to prefer the proximity and convenience, lower cost, and homelike atmosphere offered by family day-care homes, in which a small number of children, usually not more than six, are cared for by a housewife alone or with part-time or full-time assistance. There is little difference between a day-care home and a baby-sitter who takes children into her own home, except that a sitter usually looks after fewer, perhaps only one or two, children. Many, though not all, family day-care homes are licensed or regulated by state agencies and must conform to basic safety laws, while baby-sitting is entirely private and uncontrolled.

Effects of Day Care

BACKGROUND

One concern regarding out-of-home care for infants or toddlers is the possibility of detrimental effects upon the social, emotional, and intellectual development of the child. Before any real research was done in this area, experts in child development who were heavily influenced by Freudian psychoanalytic theories in the 1940s and 50s had decided upon the evidence of maldevelopment in institutionalized children that the presence of the mother in the home was absolutely necessary for the welfare of the child. The fact that long-term hospitalization or institutionalization was quite different from out-of-home care for a number of hours each day, with a return to home and family each night and for weekends, appears to have escaped these individuals. As a result, women's magazines and books on parenting and child care written for the lay public generally also had a negative view of child care by anyone other than the mother (Etaugh, 1980).

More recently, research on day care rather than institutionalization has not demonstrated such negative results. For example, Jay Belsky and Laurence D. Steinberg (1978) presented an exhaustive review of day-care studies and concluded that no harmful effects can be found and that day care may be better for some children than home care. This evidence must still be approached with caution, however, because most studies of out-of-home care have been conducted in university-based or university-sponsored model programs. These programs typically have excellent facilities, much equipment, good adult-child ratios, and well-trained staffs. They have consultant help available. Usually their programs have a strong educational component based on a well-developed infant and toddler curriculum. For all these reasons, the day care that has been studied probably differs to some extent from what might be "typical" day care. It is hazardous to generalize from the favorable results found in such demonstration programs to day care in general. Nevertheless, the findings in favor of good day care should give support to parents who need or want to work, who are concerned about the effects of care for their children, and who can locate quality care.

In part because of encouraging research results and in part because of the changing outlook on maternal employment, the popular literature in the last decade or so has also shown day care in a more favorable light (Etaugh, 1980). Articles concentrate less on warning mothers of dire consequences and instead stress the positive value of day care as well as what to look for in choosing quality care.

Most out-of-home care for infants and toddlers of working parents is done by relatives, friends, or babysitters in their own homes. Day-care homes, which care for up to six infants in a homelike atmosphere, are also used. This infant, who is used to the regular caregiver, does not seem to mind her mother leaving for work.

EARLY STUDIES

Before the late 1960s, the effects of day care were not directly studied. What little research was done was on the effects of maternal employment. And this research generally dealt with older children rather than infants and toddlers. Extensive reviews of the litera-ture on maternal employment by Lois M. Stoltz (1960) for the period before 1960 and Claire Etaugh (1974) for the 1963-1972 period found little relevant research dealing with children under nursery-school age. Stoltz reported no studies on infants and toddlers in the pre-1960 period. Etaugh found several for the later period, mostly studies of attachment to the mother under varying degrees of maternal availability but also a few dealing with group care of infants.

RECENT STUDIES

Because of the increased use of day care and other child-care arrangements during the 1970s and 1980s, particularly for younger children, a considerably greater number of studies have been done in this time period. The review by Belsky and Steinberg (1978) already mentioned provides a good overview of the first half of this period. The studies have dealt not only with attachment to parents and caregivers, but also with intelligence, social and emotional development, and with characteristics of group care situations that affect the welfare of the child.

Attachment   The early attachment studies, such as those done by Mary D. Ainsworth with Ugandan infants (Ainsworth, 1963), and Schaffer and Emerson's (1964) Glasgow study, found that attachment to the mother was unrelated either to multiple caregiving or to the amount of maternal absence but was related to maternal responsiveness to the infant at times when the mother was present. More recent studies have reached similar conclusions. In general, children in day care are as much attached to their parents as are children reared at home (Caldwell, Wright, Honig, & Tannenbaum, 1970; Kagan, Kearsley, & Zelazo, 1978; Ragozin, 1980).

Even Israeli children reared in a children's house in a kibbutz who only visited the home of their parents for about 30 hours a week were not significantly different from home-reared American children in regard to maternal attachment (Maccoby & Feldman, 1972). In comparing 20 young kibbutz children to an American home-reared sample of 48 on their reaction to strangers, maternal separation, and being left alone, Eleanor E. Maccoby and Shirley S. Feldman found very few differences between the two groups. Kibbutz children just like American children did not like to be left alone or with a stranger and were likely to cry in either situation. In fact, American children showed somewhat more tolerance of the stranger than did kibbutz children. Both groups demonstrated attachment to their mothers by showing them toys, looking at them, and trying to remain close to them. Children in either group often cried when their mother left the room. Maccoby and Feldman speculated that the two groups behaved so similarly either because in both cultures there was much maternal contact during the early bonding period and that this was more critical than later exposure to the mother or that the quality rather than the quantity of maternal interaction is the important variable. And the quality of mothering in the kibbutz was comparable to that in the home. Alternatively they hypothesized that for attachment to develop, a minimum amount of maternal contact, which was provided in either culture, is sufficient. In any event, regardless of the reasons for the similarities, Maccoby and Feldman concluded that "the similarities in behavior of the two groups of children are more notable than the differences."

Some attachment studies also have focused on the formation of attachments to regular caregivers other than the parents. Such caregivers would include regular baby-sitters, day-care personnel, or the **metaplot** ("child-rearers") of the Israeli kibbutz. These studies have concluded that the pattern of forming attachments toward such adults is similar to the process for parents but is less intense (Farran & Ramey, 1977; Kagan,

Kearsley, & Zelazo, 1978). In preference studies, when both the mother and a regular other caregiver are present, the infant prefers the mother (Farran & Ramey, 1977; Kagan, Kearsley, & Zelazo, 1978; Ricciuti, 1974). When left alone by the other adult, the child's distress is quite similar to that when the mother leaves (Ricciuti, 1974). Furthermore, both the day-care children and those raised on the kibbutz (Fox, 1977) distinguish clearly between their parents as primary attachment figures and other caregivers as secondary ones. Thus the use of such caregivers does not disrupt or diminish attachment to parents (Belsky & Steinberg, 1978).

Socioemotional Development The evidence on socioemotional development is mixed. Some studies find that there are no differences between home-reared and day-care children, while some find differences in social patterns but not any clear indication that either one is better than the other. For example, in a study of Swedish 12-to-18-month-olds, M. A. Cochran (1973) found that home-reared children interacted more with adults and did more environmental exploration than did day-care children. Day-care workers, however, allowed the children more opportunity to explore than did parents, who were more restrictive. On the other hand, the New York City Infant Day Care Study (Golden, Rosenbluth, Grossi, Policare, Freeman, & Brownee, 1978) found no differences in social development rates or patterns between the home-care and day-care groups.

The study by J. Kagan, R. B. Kearsley, and P. R. Zelazo (1978) assumed that day care beginning at an early age and the resultant exposure to peers would enhance and accelerate social development, especially cooperative peer play. When these researchers analyzed their data, however, they found that day-care infants developed socially at the same rates and in the same way as did home-reared ones.

On the other hand, Henry N. Ricciuti (1974) found that day-care toddlers were more peer-oriented than were home-raised ones. Day-care children are also more aggressive and less cooperative (Schwartz, Strickland, & Krolick, 1974). However, when J. Macrae and E. Herbert-Jackson (1975) asked day-care staff to rate two-year-olds who had been in day care for more than 13 months and those who had been in day care less than 6 months, they rated the former group higher in the ability to get along with peers, cooperation, problem solving, ability to abstract, and playfulness. Thus either earlier entrance or longer exposure to day care does seem to enhance social development for some children; at least day-care workers believe that it does.

Intellectual Development Research into intellectual development shows few if any differences between children in day care and those reared at home and, for disadvantaged children, a positive effect if they are in day care. Middle-class children evidently do as well intellectually in either setting. But day care seems to prevent or at least ameliorate the drop in IQ test scores typically found in disadvantaged children after the age of 18 months (Golden & Birns, 1976). In a study of deprived, lower-class children, Bettye M. Caldwell and L. E. Smith (1970) found that when enrolled as infants in a quality day-care program these children had higher developmental quotients than did controls left in their unstimulating homes. These differences had persisted when the children were retested at age four. P. Mills (1975) compared 15 high-risk babies who attended a quality infant day-care program, 15 who remained at home, and 30 nonrisk infants from the same area who also remained at home. The high-risk children in day care did better on developmental tests than those who remained at home. The nonrisk children who had remained at home did equally well. C. Ramey and F. Smith (1976) report similar results. The New York City Infant Day Care Study (Golden et al., 1978), which assessed the impact of day care on poor black and Hispanic infants, also found that day care helped intellectual development. Day-care children did better on IQ tests and on tests of verbal ability than did comparable infants who remained at home. This study is especially important, inasmuch as it is the only one that studied infants in a variety of community-controlled day-care settings and not just in special demonstration programs. Thus some lower-quality programs as well as better ones were included. The fact that even in less than optimum settings the children still made intellectual gains is reassuring.

Of course to some extent these improved IQ scores may be an artifact of the testing situation rather than a real difference in intelligence, since day-care children, having been exposed more to nonfamiliar adults and to out-of-home situations, may be more cooperative and hence score better in a testing situation than children raised at home (Ramey & Campbell, 1977). The importance of a stimulating out-of-home environment for the intellectual development of disadvantaged children should not, however, be minimized.

Although a good deal more study, especially of nondemonstration day-care centers and of family day care, needs to be done, the research evidence available does not seem to show much difference between children raised in the more traditional fashion by the mother in the home and those who receive day care. Where differences occur, they are usually mixed and not all in favor of one or the other child-rearing style. The one exception is in-tellectual development of disadvantaged children, which appears enhanced by day care. Thus it may be cautiously concluded that other variables, such as socioeconomic level, the intactness of the home, the relationship between parents, and the mother's satisfaction with her role as homemaker or working mother are more important determinants of infant outcomes than is the kind of care provided.

Characteristics of Good Infant Day Care

The following discussion is based primarily upon studies of infant care in centers (Auerbach & Freedman, 1976; Children at the Center, 1979; Cohen, 1977; Dittman, 1973; Herbert-Jackson, O'Brien, Porterfield, & Risley, 1977; Silverman, 1979). But to an extent it applies also to day-care homes. Good infant day care depends primarily upon the people who provide the care. The personalities of the staff, their level of training, and the ratio of adults to infants are all critical. Secondly, good care depends on the physical setting, the availability of toys and play equipment, the chance for children to be both with a group and alone, and the utilization of indoor and outdoor space. Finally, the quality of the relationship between the family and the day-care center must be considered. We shall consider each aspect in some detail.

STAFF

Obviously, a person working with infants and toddlers must be a warm and loving individual who enjoys young children. The person must be mature enough to be able to meet the needs of the children, not just her own needs. (Although some workers in infant day care are men, the vast majority are women. Therefore the female pronoun will be used throughout this discussion in referring to the caregiver.) Flexibility in dealing with infants is necessary, inasmuch as infants are highly individualistic people with their own differing styles. Unless the caregiver can attune herself to these differences and treat each child according to the child's own individual rhythmicity, the child's already developed pattern of interaction can become disrupted. Thus the caregiver must be sensitive to individual differences of temperament, activity level, reactivity to stimulation, and cue-giving ability. Because it is impossible to learn these variables about very many children at once, it is important that caregivers, especially for young infants, work with only a small number of them and that they are regularly with the same infants.

One important caregiver characteristic is the ability to adjust to the growing independence of the children. The person must be ready to change her patterns of interaction over time, so as to encourage the development of self-help skills, environmental exploration, and social interaction with other children and adults. Often this adjustment must be at the expense of order, routine, and a tight schedule. Thus the caregiver must be flexible. At the same time, caregivers must be able to plan, organize, and maintain some routines, in order to provide regularity and predictability in the children's lives. The ability to be both organized and yet flexible is no small feat!

In addition, caregivers must be able to relate to infants both physically and verbally. They must enjoy handling, cuddling, and holding babies, as well as talking and singing to them. Furthermore, each caregiver must be capable of relating to all the children in her care, not just one or two favorites. This evenhandedness is very important. A mother in the home almost always has only one infant to interact with, but in group care the staff sometimes tend to interact with the most appealing or most responsive child and pretty much to ignore others who are placid, content or less appealing. This tendency must be avoided if quality care for all children is to be provided.

The infant caregiver must also have reasonable expectations about what the infants in her care can and cannot do. On the one hand, she must allow children to develop those skills they are ready for. On the other, she cannot expect so much that she and the children will be disappointed when failure occurs. The caregiver must be firm and yet loving, able to exercise authority without demanding complete control. She adjusts discipline to the level of understanding of the children, avoiding arbitrariness and minimizing punishment. An excellent summary of desirable caregiver characteristics developed by Armita L. Jacobson is found in Table 12.1.

ADULT-CHILD RATIO

Most studies reporting either benefits to children from attendance at day care or equivalent outcomes for home care have used ratios of about one adult to every three or four infants (Caldwell & Smith, 1970; Children at the Center, 1979; Fowler, 1975; Heber & Garber, 1975; Kagan, Kearsley, & Zelazo, 1978). This ratio usually increases to 1:5 for toddlers. Since some infants and toddlers are not regular in attendance because of illness, a ratio of 1:5 for infants and 1:6 or 7 for toddlers is probably more realistic. In practice, however, since infant and toddler day care thus becomes very expensive, many day-care centers and homes are run with much worse adult-to-child ratios. This situation affects not only the quality and quantity of physical care but also the personal interaction needed for the optimal development of the children.

A high degree of adult involvement is

TABLE 12.1   CHARACTERISTICS OF COMPETENT INFANT CAREGIVERS

Desired Caregiver Characteristics	Cues to Desirable Caregiver Characteristics
1. Personality factors	
A. Child-centered	1. Attentive and loving to infants
	2. Meets infants' needs before own
B. Self-confident	1. Relaxed and anxiety free
	2. Skilled in physical care of infants
	3. Individualistic caregiving style
C. Flexible	1. Uses different styles of caregiving to meet individual needs of infants
	2. Spontaneous and open behavior
	3. Permits increasing freedom of infant with development
D. Sensitive	1. Understands infants' cues readily
	2. Shows empathy for infants
	3. Acts purposefully in interactions with infants
2. Attitudes and values	
A. Displays positive outlook on life	1. Expresses positive affect
	2. No evidence of anger, unhappiness, or depression
B. Enjoys infants	1. Affectionate to infants
	2. Shows obvious pleasure in involvement with infants
C. Values infants more than possessions or immaculate appearance	1. Dresses practically and appropriately
	2. Places items not for infants' use out of reach
	3. Reacts to infant destruction or messiness with equanimity
	4. Takes risks with property in order to enhance infant development
3. Behavior	
A. Interacts appropriately with infants	1. Frequent interactions with infants
	2. Balances interaction with leaving infants alone
	3. Optimum amounts of touching, holding, smiling, and looking
	4. Responds consistently and without delay to infants; is always accessible
	5. Speaks in positive tone of voice
	6. Shows clearly that infants are loved and accepted
B. Facilitates development	1. Does not punish infants
	2. Plays with infants
	3. Provides stimulation with toys and objects
	4. Permits freedom to explore, including floor freedom
	5. Cooperates with infant-initiated activities and explorations
	6. Provides activities which stimulate achievement or goal orientation
	7. Acts purposefully in an educational role to teach and facilitate learning and development

A. L. Jacobson (1978), Infant day care: Toward a more human environment, *Young Children 33* : 14–21.

needed first because the young infant is both physically and psychologically dependent upon the caregiver. Infants need to be individually bathed, dressed, fed, and diapered. Many of these activities must be done repeatedly, and no automated or mechanized way

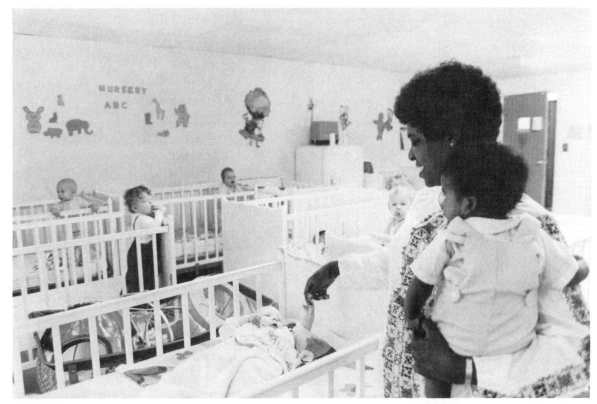

Recent research has shown that infants in good day care with loving, well-trained caregivers develop socially and cognitively as well as do those left at home in good homes. However, not all infant day care is of good quality. Although the caregiver in this picture seems to enjoy working with young children and shows warmth toward them, she appears to have more of them to care for than she can handle. Furthermore, these children seem to be confined to their cribs during awake time, when they should be allowed to play freely in a playroom.

to do them exists. Second, the young infant needs social interaction to thrive both socially and intellectually. Each child needs much individualized caregiver attention: smiling, talking, playing, and later reading to the child. And since it is important for each child to have one or only a small number of major adult caregivers who regularly meet his or her needs, these tasks cannot be shared with many other people.

Inevitably, as financial considerations force fewer caregivers to work with more children, each child's experiences with a nur-

turing adult become more diluted, and the possibility of harmful effects from group care increases.

CAREGIVER TRAINING

Even a caregiver who possesses the qualities of warmth and nurturance just discussed can profit from training in various child-care routines, child development principles, and health and safety measures (Children at the Center, 1979). Although many caregivers have had children of their own and thus have experience in infant care, they may not have had previous experience with dealing with several similar-aged infants or toddlers at once. They may not be aware of individual differences, of the need to attend to all equally, and of the programming needed to effect this goal. Many center-based day-care programs provide for preservice or inservice training of their employees. State regulations in many instances also mandate such training for a center to achieve or maintain licensure. Unfortunately, proprietors of day-care homes, who are generally also the major or only caregivers there, usually are not afforded the opportunities for such training, nor do states require them to have it.

What kind of training is needed? First, day-care workers need to know some basic information about infant development (Children at the Center, 1979). They must have a basic understanding of what the young infant is like, what it is capable of doing, and what is beyond its capabilities. Caregivers must learn the basics of physical and motor development and the ways the infant can use various sense modalities. They must also learn about how the growing intellect of the child changes and develops over time and how the child's growing language ability needs support. Day-care workers also need to know about individual differences among children and the range of behaviors that are normal, as well as those that are clearly deviant and may require further professional evaluation.

Second, staff members must learn about various practices and activities that foster the development of each of these areas. They must learn about the importance of interesting things to see, the use of toys and play equipment, talking and reading to children, and other means to foster the optimum development of each child. They need to be taught activities to engage in with the children in their charge. These activities may be

called an infant and toddler curriculum. A number of the experimental day-care programs for infants that have been developed by universities have issued curriculum guides. They may include a graded series of activities for caregiver-infant interaction that foster the development of motor, intellectual, language, and social competencies.

Third, day-care staff need training in health and safety practices involving infants and toddlers. They must acquire some understanding of symptoms of illness or physical distress, what to do in a medical emergency, and when to summon a doctor or nurse. They must learn some common safety practices dealing with the preparation, storage, and handling of food and those relating to the feeding, diapering, and cleaning of the children. They must learn what to do in an emergency such as a power failure, a fire, or a storm. In addition, caregivers should have some basic understanding of infant and toddler nutrition and of typical eating patterns of young children and the changes in these over time.

RELATIONS WITH HOME AND FAMILY

Good day care for infants and toddlers must take into account the individual needs of the families of the children. This consideration includes adjusting scheduling to family needs when possible; communicating information about the child to the family; cooperating with the family in satisfying its particular cultural, religious, or health needs; and serving to support families in their provision of the child's care at all times when the child is not at the day-care center.

Parents should be informed of the day-to-day progress of their own child as well as any high or low points encountered on that particular day when they come to pick up their child. In turn, day-care personnel must listen carefully to parents' reports about what has happened at home, or the child's mood on a particular day as perceived by the parents, when the child is left off at the center in the morning. Such attention should make the child's transitions from home to day care and back to the home as smooth as possible.

Caregivers must also be careful to behave supportively of the parents and help maintain the parents' confidence in their own ability to understand and care for their infants. Many parents still have some feelings of guilt or at least ambivalence over leaving an infant or toddler to the care of someone else. In addition, they may feel unsure and defensive when faced with people they presume to be experts in child care. Wise day-care workers will help parents bring their feelings out into the open and discuss them. They will also reassure parents and instruct them in techniques of child care or child management if this is requested or seems appropriate.

PHYSICAL SETTING

Good infant day care can be provided in many different settings, varying greatly in location, size, and type of facility. All good infant day care, however, meets certain criteria relating to physical setting.

First, the setting should be esthetically pleasing for the benefit of the children, staff, and parents. There should be bright colors, interesting things to see, cleanliness, and comfort.

Second, it should be physically safe. This means adequate ventilation, heating, and cooling, the availability of exits in case of fire, and no exposed hazards such as unguarded stairs.

Good day care also is relatively uncrowded. Each child should have adequate

sleeping space as well as play space, and the two should be physically separate so that awake children do not bother sleeping ones. The exact space requirements change over time, as crib-bound young infants need relatively little space, while creepers and toddlers need quite a bit more. Space used by awake infants and toddlers should be arranged in such a way that different age groups can watch one another at play and interact on occasion. Younger infants, however, need to be protected from older and stronger toddlers by some physical barrier unless there is continuous adult supervision.

Third, day care needs to provide opportunities for children to be alone as well as with a group. Space should be utilized in such a way that adults can watch even those playing alone, so that they can intervene in case of danger.

Fourth, since day care for most infants and toddlers keeps them for all or most of the day, it is important that outdoor as well as indoor play experiences are provided. Not all infant day-care homes or centers have private outdoor play space such as a yard or playground. But creative use can often be made of a nearby community facility such as a park. Of course in all outdoor situations, adequate adult supervision is most necessary.

EQUIPMENT

Closely related to setting is equipment. It can be divided into that necessary for physically caring for the children and that needed for the children's play.

Physical equipment includes such items as cribs, playpens, changing tables, infant seats, bathing equipment, and high chairs as well as small tables and chairs at which toddlers can be fed. It also includes storage space for the children's clothing and personal possessions, as well as for food, linens, diapers, and other supplies. In addition, in centers that cater to larger numbers, low dividers to separate temporarily one group of children from another are useful.

Play equipment quite obviously includes toys suitable for children of different ages. These include interesting things suspended at the sides of the cribs for young babies to look at. Later, manipulable objects for babies to swipe at and finally grasp should be provided. Crib sides should be left free of dividers so that infants can watch other infants and adults during the day. When possible, slightly older infants should spend part of their awake time sitting supported in infant seats so they can watch activities in the center or home, rather than being left in cribs where there is much less to see.

As infants and toddlers develop, additional toys that foster large and small muscle development and intellectual growth must be provided. These include manipulable toys such as blocks, beads, and puzzles, push and pull toys for beginning walkers, indoor and outdoor climbing equipment, and stuffed dolls or small animal toys. There should be enough toys so that squabbles over possession do not occur frequently, although sharing is encouraged among older infants and toddlers.

All toys should be safe: not too small, with no sharp projections or removable small parts, painted with nontoxic paint. They should be available in age-appropriate areas of the center. Large wooden play equipment should be smoothly sanded and free of splinters. All toys and other equipment must be checked periodically to make sure they remain in usable and safe condition, and they must be repaired or replaced promptly if not.

HEALTH AND SAFETY

Good infant and toddler day care must provide as well as possible for the health and safety of both the children and the staff. How

this is done will of course vary greatly depending upon the kind and size of facility, the number and ages of the children, and the number of staff involved. But all places that care for young children should meet local and national fire code standards for number and location of exits, fire alarm or smoke alarm systems, and fire prevention and containment devices such as fire extinguishers. Furthermore, all day-care facilities must be kept clean of insect and rodent infestation.

Adequate bathroom space for children to use the toilet and be washed and bathed, as well as for adult use, must be provided. The kinds and number of such facilities obviously will differ from a center catering to many children to a day-care home caring for two or three.

All equipment, furniture, and supplies must be checked periodically to make sure they are safe and in proper working condition, and that they are clean.

All children in a day-care center or home should be routinely checked each day for physical health. Parents should be urged to keep a child home at any sign of illness. In addition, it is wise for a day-care center or home to have a preexisting arrangement with a physician and/or hospital, or with each child's own family physician, for the provision of emergency medical care. Parental permission for securing such care should be obtained when the child is enrolled. Each center or home should also have some space available in which to isolate a child who becomes ill during the day so that other children are not exposed to infection.

Parental Responsibility

Ultimately, good day care for infants will exist only if parents insist that it does. If parents patronize quality centers and avoid bad ones, the latter must sooner or later either reform or go out of business. Thus it is incumbent on parents to know about the center their child attends and to check on it periodically. No parent should send a child to a day-care center he or she has not visited for an extended time period. Good centers encourage parental visitation, both before a child is enrolled and during the child's stay. They have nothing to hide.

Furthermore, parents can help a center maintain quality by providing helpful suggestions, serving on policy committees, and helping centers in their relations with various governmental agencies and the community at large. If both parents and day-care staff can agree that their joint aim is the best possible care for the children, then they should be able to work together to foster this aim.

Concluding Remarks

The employment of women, including mothers of young children, will most likely increase rather than decrease. The number of single-parent families also is unlikely to decline. Consequently, it seems reasonable to conclude that the needs for out-of-home care for infants and toddlers will not diminish in the foreseeable future. At the same time, the withdrawal or curtailment in the early 1980s of both federal and state funds from a variety of social-service programs makes any increased governmental support of day care extremely doubtful. Thus American day care appears, for the immediate future, to remain a private enterprise subject only to some state or local supervision for safety. Responsibility for the quality of day care will fall entirely on individual operators, voluntary day-care associations, and most especially the parents who elect to send their children to particular settings. But if parents are to choose day-care facilities intelligently, they must have information about what quality

day care is and the extent to which a particular center or home measures up to these standards. This information is not easy to obtain.

A second problem revolves around the issue of cost. Privately run day care obviously must return some profit to the owner or operator, as well as pay salaries and pay for equipment and supplies. Only in publicly owned, government-subsidized facilities can day care be provided at cost or below. Yet many working parents do not have unlimited funds to pay for day care. Thus quality day care that also provides a reasonable profit may be pricing itself out of the market in favor of inferior day care that is able to cut corners and save money. Is this inferior day care what we as a nation want our children to have? There are no easy answers to these problems, particularly at a time of mounting government deficit spending. But ignoring them will not make them go away.

SOCIAL PSYCHOPATHOLOGY

Occasionally, the transactional relationship between the infant and caregiving adults, including parents, becomes distorted to the degree that extremely maladaptive behaviors by either the child or the adults are the result (Sameroff & Chandler, 1975). The origins of these distortions may lie in the social environment outside the child, especially in the parent, and include the developmental history and personal-social situation of the parent or other caregiver, such as her or his marital, educational, and socioeconomic status. Parents who themselves had disturbed childhoods, teen-age parents, and those who are economically poor or unmarried are more at risk than are others. Additional parental factors that may adversely affect the children include separation from or loss of the parent as a result of parental illness, desertion, or death and the absence of societal support systems for the parent, which means that the troubled parent does not have either family or social agencies able or willing to provide help.

Alternatively, the problems can originate from the physical-biological risk status of the child at birth and in early infancy, such as preterm birth or illness. They may also be caused by an otherwise normal child's inability to provide clear clues of wants and needs to the caregiver or by the child's apparent lack of responsiveness to caregiver efforts (Barnard, 1977). Children also are more at risk if they have difficult temperaments, such as being irritable, difficult to console, fussy, or overly active. Finally, the child may be suffering from the cluster of social withdrawal symptoms called infantile autism, which appears to be an inborn condition of unknown origin.

The two sets of inputs, from child and parent, interact over time in such a way that if there are weaknesses or trouble spots on both sides, maldevelopment or malfunction is more likely to occur. If either the child's or the parent's input to the relationship is normal, even though that of the other is not, the chances for trouble are much reduced though not entirely eliminated. For example, a mature, middle-class, well-educated parent may adjust to the birth of a premature, critically ill baby or one with handicaps somewhat better than an unmarried, poor, teenage parent from a deprived economic background. This relationship has been called the "continuum of caretaking causality" by Arnold Sameroff and Michael Chandler (1975). That is, a range of possible parental responses interacts with the state of the child to produce either normal or deviant outcomes in the child's development.

Major problems that may arise from the disruption, for whatever reason, of the transaction between child and adult include failure to thrive, child abuse, and the child's reactions to long-term separation or institutionalization.

Failure to Thrive

Failure to thrive is characterized by little or no weight gain and by stunting of physical growth over time in a child who appears to be normal otherwise or who, although born prematurely, seems at first to have recovered from this complication with no apparent ill effects. The immediate cause of failure to thrive may be parental neglect. Parents do not provide adequately for the child's nutrition or general health as well as for its emotional well-being. In addition, failure to thrive can also come about from improper or inappropriately timed care (Sameroff & Chandler, 1975). For example, parents may not realize that a bottle-fed infant needs more milk as time goes on and continue giving only the small amount they were advised to offer to a neonate. Or they may feed a child primarily or only at times when the child is too tired to ingest sufficient food.

Upon hospitalization, such children usually show remarkable recovery, gaining weight appropriately and often showing considerable physical as well as social growth. When they return home, their condition usually worsens again, and often repeated hospitalization is necessary.

Thus failure to thrive appears quite clearly to be not a physical problem as such but to have largely a social origin. Parents of such infants often are quite unstable in their personal lives. There is a high incidence of marital problems and of alcoholism in families of such children. The parents often are unreliable workers who are frequently out of jobs and thus unable to provide consistent financial support. Even when adequate physical caregiving is provided, such parents often lack the emotional warmth and the ability to relate to their children. They may be depressed over the birth of the child and unable to cope with the physical and emotional demands the child makes upon them. Thus, although they provide routine physical care, they do not show emotional involvement, and the child may not develop properly.

The condition is also, however, related to variables in the child. He or she may be a fussy eater, who takes in little food and tends to spit it up (Galdston, 1971). He or she may be subject to allergic reactions and intestinal upsets such as diarrhea, which make feeding and other aspects of caregiving much more difficult for the parent. The child's temperament may also be what Thomas and Chess (1977) have described as difficult: irritable, fussy, crying, unable to adjust, overly active, and hard to console. This temperament may interact with the parents' inability to express their feelings to the child.

Since failure to thrive occurs more frequently in children who were premature or sick at birth and who were therefore separated from their parents longer, inadequate bonding may be a cause. In addition, such children often were unwanted, and the psychological as well as physical burden of this problem child may be more than the parent is able to handle.

Child Abuse

More serious than the neglect that can result in failure to thrive is child abuse, which is gross physical or psychological trauma or both inflicted upon the child. Abused children may be beaten, thrown, burned with hot objects or on stoves, scalded with hot water, or in other ways grievously hurt. Psychological abuse may include total or partial isolation of the child from the family, verbal abuse, or an extreme lack of feeling. In older children, the results of physical abuse, since they involve bruises, broken bones, burns, and other injuries, are of course easier to spot than are the results of psychological abuse, as such children are likely to be seen in public by other concerned adults such as teachers or neighbors. Since infants spend most of their time at home and without many social contacts, even their physical abuse is often harder to discover.

It has been estimated that between 1.4 and 1.9 million children in the United States annually experience physical injury as a result of violent behavior by parents (Straus, Gelles, & Steinmetz, 1979). While older children are subject to child abuse as well, a large proportion of abused children are under the age of three (Gelles, 1973). About 6.5 percent of abused and neglected children are under the age of one year; almost 22 percent are between the ages of one and three (National Analysis of Official Child Neglect and Abuse Reporting, 1979). Thus child abuse is a major social problem. Abused children who survive the period of infancy often show long-term physical and psychological damage such as mental retardation, speech problems, growth failure, and emotional maladjustment. These disabilities prevent them from the full enjoyment of life and exact a social cost from the community, which must provide long-term care or special education.

Many infants die of child abuse each year in the United States. The number is difficult to document, since most abuse is disguised as accidental injury, and since post-mortem examination of infants who die under suspicious circumstances is sometimes not done. But it has been estimated that a larger number die each year as the result of abuse than of all illnesses and accidents combined.

Parents who abuse their children are highly likely to have been themselves abused or neglected as young children (Spinetta & Rigler, 1968). Therefore, they have probably not had adequate opportunity to learn appropriate parenting skills from competent role models. They also have little knowledge of what is normal in child development or child-parent relationships. In addition, they have high rates of marital instability, including divorce and desertion. They are often anxious, hostile, and lonely people, unable to make friends and isolated from a family network (Johnson & Morse, 1968). Their personality characteristics include rigidity, compulsiveness (Fontana & Bernard, 1971), and lack of self-esteem (Blumberg, 1974). Just as with neglectful parents, they have an unstable work history and are often unable to support their families.

Child abuse seems to be more prevalent in families of lower socioeconomic class and less education (Pelton, 1978). Of the instances of child abuse reported nationally in 1979, 47 percent occurred in single-parent families, and 48 percent occurred in families that were on some form of public assistance (National Analysis. . . , 1979). Of course these two categories tend to overlap, so one must not add the two figures to obtain some kind of erroneous total. In part, however, this apparently higher incidence of child abuse in lower-class families may be due to middle- and upper-class parents' greater ability to hide the condition by consulting private physicians rather than public clinics for help with the child's injuries, and their greater sophistication in devising explanations for the child's injuries that seem to absolve them of responsibility. Child abuse occurs in families of all socioeconomic and educational levels, but it is more prevalent among families that are exposed to other stresses as well.

Abused children are more likely to have been of low birth weight and to have had some difficulties at the time of birth as indicated by lower Apgar scores (Goldson, Fitch, Wendell, & Knapp, 1978). Regardless of birth weight, abused children are also more likely to have somewhat retarded motor and social development than do nonabused ones (Goldson et al., 1978). Abused infants also seem to contribute to their own abuse by posing special problems relating to feeding and sleeping. Of course this behavior does not justify the abuse, but it does help to explain it. These infants cry a lot and their cries are interpreted by adults as extremely irritating. They may be socially somewhat deviant even before the abuse occurs. Often other children in the family are treated relatively well, and only one particular child is singled out for abuse. Like children who fail to thrive, abused children are more likely to have been premature or ill at birth or otherwise have presented early problems.

Abusive parents may have a distorted perception of the abused child, projecting onto it their own negative feelings and then using it as a scapegoat (Green, Gaines, & Sandgrund, 1974). They may interpret the child's crying as rejection of themselves and overreact to it. They also expect more of the infant than it is developmentally ready to do and punish it severely when it does not live up to standards (Smith & Hanson, 1975). For example, they see the infant's inability to sleep through the night, or the occasional accident during toilet training, as personal affronts on the part of the child.

Because child abuse, particularly of infants who are unable to report it or to seek help, is such a pervasive and serious problem it deserves societal attention. Understanding the characteristics of the potentially abusive parent and of the child, so as to predict and try to prevent possible abuse, is important. In addition, education of parents in what reasonable expectations they should have of their child should help reduce child abuse.

Institutionalization

For many years, the death rate of children put in institutions such as foundling homes, orphanages, and hospitals for extended time periods was much higher than that of children reared at home. Until this century, this high mortality rate could be attributed to poor sanitation, lack of knowledge about infection, and poor nutrition. However, even with the advent of better medical, nutritional, and sanitary practices in the 20th century, the death rate for such children remained fairly high. In addition, many of those who survived such long-term institutionalization showed disturbing psychological results: they were often listless, socially unresponsive, or mentally retarded.

In the 1940s, psychoanalytic theorists such as Margaret Ribble (1944) and René Spitz (1945, 1946) concluded that the cause of either death or at least adverse development was the lack of a warm caregiver. They noticed that the infants they studied were cared for in a mechanical, impersonal way by overworked staff who had too many children in their charge. The children were often isolated from others and spent many hours alone in their cribs staring at the ceiling. Bottles were propped up for feedings. As a result, the infants appeared retarded in both motor and social skills, and the longer they remained in the institution, the more they fell behind. Many of the children died for reasons that could not be ascertained, that is, they were not physically ill or injured. Spitz coined the term "hospitalism" to describe

this cluster of physical and psychological symptoms that could result in the unexplained death of such children. Like Ribble, he attributed them to lack of social stimulation.

In an interesting study by Spitz and Katherine Wolf (1946) some children who had been institutionalized with their mothers were taken from them at age six months and thereafter had either no contact or only a brief weekly contact with them. After apparently normal development up to this point, some strikingly deviant behaviors began to show up after separation. Babies who had previously been friendly and sociable began to cry a good deal, without apparent cause. Later they would withdraw from social contact with caregivers, paying no attention to people who tried to interact with or care for them. They looked away and would not make direct eye contact. Along with these behavioral changes, the infants also showed loss of appetite and weight, poor sleep patterns, and greater susceptibility to infections. After about three months of this situation, the crying disappeared, but the babies spent most of their time either lying in what Spitz and Wolf described as a "frozen" state, paying no attention to their environment, or else playing with some part of their own bodies in a stereotypic and repetitive manner such as rocking themselves or banging their heads.

John Bowlby (1952), in a report to the World Health Organization on children separated from mothers and other caregivers used the term "maternal deprivation" to describe the same condition. Bowlby found, however, that this condition could occur even if the mother or other adult were present but was unable to establish a positive, nurturant relationship with the child.

These studies were cited in the 1950s as evidence of the importance of full-time mothering. Mothers were warned that if they did not devote themselves totally to their children, their offspring might suffer the same dire outcomes as those in institutions.

Later researchers have pointed out the weaknesses of the studies and of the assumptions of Ribble, Spitz, and Bowlby. For example, Leon Yarrow (1961) and Lawrence Casler (1961) have pointed out that such institutionalized children separated from primary caregivers were deprived not only of social-emotional but also of sensory and cognitive stimulation. It is true that there was no close relationship with a caregiver, but also there was little to see, hear, or play with. Thus it is difficult to determine to what degree the subsequent behavioral deficits were due to social factors and how much to these others. In addition, some people still think that undiagnosed physical illnesses caused many of the deaths attributed to hospitalism.

More recently, a different explanation has been proposed by Michael Rutter (1979, 1982). He has argued that the problems encountered by institutionalized children devolve from the fact that they are prevented from forming attachments to primary attachment figures such as their mother or even a regular caregiver who regularly spends much time with the child. Thus the children feel powerless over their environment and feel that their efforts will make no difference. He cites the apparently normal development of children separated from their families in Britain during World War II as evidence. When these children who already had formed such primary attachments were evacuated to the countryside because of the danger of air raids, they developed normally and adjusted well both to their temporary placements and to eventual reunion with their families. In this connection it is interesting that the children studied by Spitz and Wolf (1946) were removed from their mothers at six months, before secure attachments would have been completed. This fact lends support to Rutter's contention.

Thus it appears that if children can form attachments to nurturant adults early in their lives, if these attachments are not disrupted at too early an age, and if the children are given personalized and warm care, they can tolerate even some separation.

Infantile Autism

Another disruption of the relationship between infant and caregiver, but one that seems to originate from within the child, is the condition called infantile autism. It consists of a cluster of symptoms including a profound failure to develop social relationships, abnormalities of language development and language usage, and compulsive, stereotypic, and ritualistic behaviors, all of which originate before the age of three (Rutter, 1978). Not all of these symptoms are necessarily present in a given child, and the severity of the symptoms can vary greatly among children. Young autistic infants tend to stiffen and pull away when held rather than conform to the body of the holding adult. When older, these children treat adults and peers as if they were objects. They typically avoid social contacts, avert the gaze, and resist attempts by the adult to touch or cuddle them. They do not learn communicative language, and if language develops at all, such children use it to echo the words and expressions of others or in stereotypic, self-centered ways. Autistic children tend to play with their own bodies rather than with toys. They may use repetitive, self-stimulating, and sometimes self-mutilating behaviors such as flapping the hands, rocking, or head banging. If they use toys, they do not play with them appropriately but rather use them as part of self-stimulation, such as hitting themselves with a toy truck.

The psychoanalytic explanation for autism proposed by Leo Kanner (1943), who first described and labeled the condition, was that parents of children showing these symptoms were cold loners who provided inadequate parenting and whose children therefore did not bond adequately. This view has often been referred to as the "refrigerator mother" theory. It appears inadequate, inasmuch as many parents of autistic children are not cool and aloof and families of such children often include several other quite normal children. More recent explanations have tried to link autism to sensory or to neurological dysfunction (Schreibman, Charlop & Britten, 1983). It appears to be an inborn rather than environmentally induced condition, but no one knows as yet for sure what its cause or causes might be.

Whatever the origin of autism, it certainly affects the relationship between parents and child. Although definite diagnosis of the condition is usually not made until the child is two years old or older, the condition appears to be present from birth on, and the child manifests unusual behaviors beginning early in infancy. In addition to lack of cuddliness and avoidance of eye contact, the child may be unresponsive in other ways to the presence of the parents or other caregivers. There may be no social smiling and no attempt to interact and to communicate. This lack of reinforcement for parental attempts at interaction with the child is difficult for parents, who often question their parenting skills and may feel confused and guilty about apparent mistakes in their ways of treating the child.

While moderate success has been reported in altering some of the most obvious self-mutilating or irritating behaviors of older children through stringent use of behavior modification techniques, no real cure for the condition is available. Thus the outlook for families of autistic children is rather bleak. About all that they can do is to try to suppress some of the most noxious behaviors and learn to live with the child without self-reproach or guilt.

EDUCATION OF PARENTS

Parent education has become an important issue in modern North America because of problems such as child abuse that can result from parents' having learned few skills relating to parenting and lacking adequate role models for their behaviors. In addition, many young parents today raise their children away from older family members on whom they can call for advice and guidance and thus need help from other sources. Finally, the very acts involved in successful parenting today are more difficult and complex because so much more is expected of children than in the past.

When we speak of parenting in this section, we are concerned less with physical caregiving tasks such as feeding, bathing, dressing, and putting to bed and much more with the social-emotional and intellectual aspects of the interaction between parent and infant.

Learned Parenting Behaviors

Human parenting behaviors appear to be largely based on learning. What people do with their children depends to a large extent on how they were treated when they were children and on their observations of other parents and children around them. In addition, in the modern world people learn some parenting behaviors from the media: television, radio, newspapers, magazines, and books.

It is important to note that since parenting behaviors are learned they do not automatically result from the biological act of becoming a parent. It cannot be assumed that because parents have produced a child they therefore have acquired the behaviors and attitudes needed for successful parenting. Biological parenthood is not just the same as psychological parenthood.

Parenting Skills

Realizing the complexity of all the acts that together constitute good and effective parenting, the importance of parenting to the development of the child, and the lack of alternative ways to learn many parenting skills, much research today is focusing on defining good parenting and devising means to teach these skills to parents.

THE NCAP STUDY

Research by Kathryn Barnard and her associates in the Nursing Child Assessment Project (NCAP) at the University of Washington (Barnard, 1977) focused on parenting skills needed for successful early interaction between mother and child. Three important parenting skills were isolated. They included sensitivity to infant cues, alleviation of infant distress, and the provision of situations that foster the infant's social and intellectual growth. These behaviors can be observed to occur in competent mothers especially during feeding and teaching situations.

In feeding, a competent mother will correctly read the child's cue of hunger and will then position the child so that it can feed comfortably yet maintain eye contact with her. She will be relatively free of tension and able to interact with the infant appropriately.

In teaching, which generally does not begin until the latter half of the first year, such a mother will give clear instructions that are age-appropriate and understandable. They may include verbal instructions,

modeling of the appropriate behavior, or a combination of the two. The mother also provides positive feedback to the child, which means more praise than criticism. This feedback is contingent, however, meaning that it depends upon the child's level of performance; thus the child is apprised of how well she or he is doing, so she or he can assess and improve performance.

Important for a successful teaching-learning experience are the mother's timing and her sensitivity to the child's performance. Timing involves initiating a task when the child is attending, allotting sufficient time to finish it but not so much that boredom or fatigue ensues, and providing feedback at the appropriate time. Sensitivity involves setting appropriate performance standards based on the child's ability and maturity, positioning both child and materials in such a way that they can interact effectively, adapting the level of teaching to the child's improving performance, and responding to the child's attempts at task mastery.

When the NCAP study compared children who scored well on mental tests at 12 and 24 months with those who did not, and retrospectively reviewed data gathered on earlier maternal behaviors as well as infant characteristics, the maternal behaviors outweighed all infant circumstances other than neurological status at birth. In other words, the study strongly suggests that maternal behaviors rather than inborn abilities or predispositions in the child are the major influence upon the child's intellectual development in the first two years.

THE HARVARD PRESCHOOL PROJECT

In contrast to the NCAP study, which found maternal behaviors in the first few months to be the most critical, the Harvard Preschool Project (White, 1969; White & Watts, 1973; White, 1978; White, Kaban, & Attanucci, 1979) has pinpointed maternal behaviors in the 10-to-18-month period as most important for the child's optimal intellectual and social development.

This research effort attempted to trace the origin of competence in children. It began with a study of three-to-six-year-olds. But Burton L. White and his coworkers found that competent and noncompetent children could already be clearly distinguished at age three. Therefore, later research focused on the origins of these competent behaviors in one- and two-year-olds. Behaviors exhibited to a much greater degree by competent three-year-old children included language fluency and intellectual abilities such as to discern discrepancies, anticipate consequences, deal with abstractions, make interesting associations, and see things from another person's point of view.

Activities called executive, which competent children also possessed, included being able to plan and carry out multistep activities, use resources effectively, and pay attention. Finally, competent children possessed many social abilities, including obtaining and keeping adult attention in socially accepted ways, asking questions and seeking help of adults, expressing affection and hostility toward adults and peers, both leading and following peers, competing, and showing pride in accomplishments.

White and his associates were interested in which parental styles in infancy and toddlerhood helped children later become competent in these ways. They observed groups of one- and two-year-olds in interactions with their mothers in the home. On the basis of these observations, they isolated differences in maternal behaviors that affected whether or not their children would later be judged as possessing these competent behaviors.

White thinks that the critical period for establishing children's competence is between 10 and 18 months. Before 10 months, adequate physical care and emotional warmth seem to him sufficient for the baby's development, and most normal parents appear able to provide these quite adequately. But three critical developments in the child just before its first birthday begin to make extra demands upon adults that some respond to more successfully than others. These are the onset of walking, the beginning of language use, and the child's increasing awareness of self as an independent being in a social setting.

Mothers of competent children tended to spend more of their time interacting with their children than did those of less competent ones. They also spent relatively more of this interaction time on intellectual activities than caregiving. They were able to adjust their behaviors to the growing curiosity and abilities of their children much better than did the mothers of less competent children, by substituting activities requiring more intellectual participation for earlier simpler ones.

These mothers also were far ahead of the others in how they designed the child's environment. They protected the child from danger yet provided much access to interesting areas of the home and the outdoors and permitted the child to interact freely with objects, people, and events. By contrast, mothers of less competent children restricted the child's access to the environment. Mothers of competent children did not hover over the child or overwhelm her or him with attention, but they were available to the child when needed. They tended to interrupt their other tasks on occasion to ask a question, propose an activity, or make a pertinent comment. By contrast, mothers of less competent ones either were relatively unavailable or else interacted so excessively with the child that the child could not initiate or carry out any activity without the mother.

CONCLUSIONS

Thus parental behaviors in early childhood that appear important in establishing the child's beginning social and intellectual competence seem to include sensitivity to the infant's needs and to her or his increasing competence over time and the ability to structure teaching to maximize the child's learning. In toddlerhood, continued sensitivity to the child's changing and increasing capabilities remains important. Mothers need to devote more time to intellectual tasks with their children and not concentrate merely on caregiving. But at the same time they must be careful to structure the environment to maximize the child's potential to learn alone, without too intrusive maternal interaction. Parenthetically, it should be noted that both these studies dealt with mothers, since they were their children's primary caregivers. Nevertheless, the appropriate behaviors shown by these mothers obviously are useful behaviors for fathers and other caregivers to demonstrate as well.

Parent Education Projects

BACKGROUND

Based on preliminary results from the above and similar studies, and from studies of the apparent causes of child neglect and abuse, some pilot projects in education for parents considered to be especially at risk have been carried out. Researchers have realized that environmental influences such as poor housing, and personal instability influences such as lower educational level of parents and higher rates of single-parent families are more likely to affect parenting variables in parents of lower socioeconomic levels and especially of racial minorities. Therefore, many of these studies have been done with poor parents, especially with black parents. In addition, some have focused on other at-risk populations such as mothers considered to be mentally retarded or very young mothers.

Philosophically these projects vary widely. Some are based on the theory that parents want to be good parents and only need the help and support of others to learn how to maximize their children's social and intellectual development. According to this viewpoint, parents are taught effective parenting skills, which they can then apply in their own homes. On the other hand, some projects are based on the notion that the early development of the child is so important that it cannot be entrusted to amateurs such as uneducated parents. Infants in these studies therefore spend much of their time outside the home in the care of professional infant educators. Finally, some projects provide some parent education and some group experience for infants under professional tutelage.

It must be recognized that most of these projects, just like the previously discussed day-care projects, are research and demonstration projects under the auspices of universities or private foundations, which serve only small, select populations. Many more parents and infants who might profit from such services do not have the opportunity to utilize them. Furthermore, the amounts of data available from these projects vary greatly. The data may take a variety of forms such as observations, parent questionnaires, standardized tests, interviews, and teacher ratings. Thus many sets of data within and between studies are difficult to compare. Let

Parents can be effective teachers of their young children by providing experiences and toys that help the child's mental growth and by talking and attending to the child in a consistent and loving manner.

us first consider a few studies that have emphasized parent training.

UNIVERSITY OF ILLINOIS PROGRAM

The earliest program that concentrated on teaching parents how to teach their children is probably that sponsored by the University of Illinois. It was begun in the 1960s by Merle Karnes and her associates (Karnes, Studley, Wright, & Hodgins, 1968; Karnes, Teska, Hodgins, & Badger, 1970; Karnes, Zehrbach, & Teska, 1973) as part of the compensatory education movement then current. While

other researchers concentrated on compensatory education for young children or adolescents, this group focused upon the mothers of infants as the most important socializing influences on children. The thrust of the program became training parents in teaching skills to be used with their children and such other skills as would increase their own self-esteem and competency and therefore enhance their abilities to care for their families and to teach their children.

Low-income mothers recruited through referrals from the local welfare department participated in two-hour weekly training sessions with project staff for a period of seven to eight months. The staff also made monthly home visits. Later they increased the visits to twice weekly. In addition, staff were available to mothers for consultation and more frequent home visits if desired. They trained parents in learning how to teach skills or tasks in small steps, using positive reinforcement and minimizing mistakes, establishing a climate of mutual respect between child and mother, and changing tasks when the child appeared bored or fatigued so as to emphasize that learning was fun and not a forced activity. They also taught mothers songs, poems, stories, and fingerplays and ways to make and effectively use toys and equipment with the children. In addition, the staff made available a lending library of books and toys.

When compared to similar children (no real control group was used in the project) as well as to their own older siblings, project children showed considerably higher IQ test results. In addition, mothers exhibited more self-competency in dealing with problems, and the families appeared generally headed in a more positive direction.

YPSILANTI-CARNEGIE INFANT EDUCATION MODEL

A brief 16-month parent education project called the Ypsilanti-Carnegie Infant Education Model was funded by the Carnegie Corporation and administered by the High/Scope Educational and Research Foundation, which had a long history of developing and administering a model Head Start program for disadvantaged minority children (Lambie, Bond, & Weikart, 1974, 1975; Weikart, 1975). The study proceeded on the assumption that the home culture of low-income minority children differed from the school situation in certain significant ways that predisposed such children to school failure. These children needed to learn not only the skills important for their own culture but also those needed in the school culture. Because the mother was seen as the most effective person to teach the skills needed for eventual school success, the project concentrated on helping mothers teach their children by supplying the mothers with information, teaching methods and resources, and help with meeting some of the stresses of daily life under deprived circumstances.

A professional educator made weekly home visits in which she helped parents clarify and plan their own goals for the children. These home visitors supported mothers in their belief that they were their own children's primary educator. Home visitors helped the mothers to evaluate the effectiveness of their teaching strategies and demonstrated alternative ones if mothers desired them.

Mothers of the infants in this study were found to provide much more supportive verbal interaction with their children than comparable mothers who were not trained by home visitors. On intelligence tests at age three, their children did better than comparison peers and also showed greater language development.

While these two projects show that maternal education alone may help children to achieve the kinds of competence needed for later success, other projects have used a two-pronged approach: parent education plus group experience for the children under the guidance of a trained professional or paraprofessional.

UNIVERSITY OF FLORIDA PROJECT

The University of Florida has been engaged in a variety of research and demonstration projects involving parent and infant education begun originally by Ira Gordon and subsumed under the Parent Education Project (PEP) since 1966 (Gordon, 1975; Gordon, Guinagh, & Jester, 1977).

This group of researchers also believed that the family was the most important influence on the young child and therefore decided that intervention with the family as early in the child's life as possible was most important. They believed that intervention would be maximized if it included both teaching of the mothers and group experiences for the children. Because they thought this intervention would be most effective if carried out by people similar to the children's mothers, they used trained paraprofessionals from the same area as the mothers, a low-income rural area in Florida. Mothers and children were divided into eight different groups; each group had a different intensity of interaction with trainers or spent a different amount of time in the project. Some children and mothers received services for only three months, others for as long as three years, and others were controls who received testing only.

Paraprofessional staff were trained before the project began and in continuing in-service sessions. They learned techniques of teaching mothers how to teach their children, the importance of maternal teaching, and the reasons why particular activities should be done with the children.

When children were three months old, home visitors began to make regular weekly visits during which they demonstrated a teaching skill and then had the mother show she had mastered it also. The visitor also left a one-page curriculum for the mother to use in implementing the newly learned skill with her child during the coming week.

When the children reached age two, they began to take part in a preschool experience for two hours twice a week. It took place in a home learning center located in a spare room of the home of one of the mothers. Ten children, the host mother, and the home visitor attended each session.

Testing on a variety of instruments up to the age of six showed that the biggest gains were made by the children who had been enrolled in the full three years of the program. Even those enrolled for only one or two years did better on various tests than did children who received no intervention at all. Furthermore, when videotapes made of mother-child interactions were analyzed by the Florida team, they found that the behaviors of trained mothers resembled those of mothers of competent children identified by the Harvard Preschool Project. By contrast, untrained mothers tended to dominate the child without allowing her or him to respond, continued activities beyond the time the child had lost interest, or else interacted very little with the child. Furthermore, trained mothers talked more to their children and used appropriate language much more than did control mothers; they also concentrated their talk more on instruction rather than on idle chatter.

SYRACUSE UNIVERSITY PROGRAM

The Family Development Research Program at Syracuse University is another example of a mixed parent-training plus infant education approach. It was begun under the leadership of Bettye Caldwell and later continued by Alice Honig and Ronald Lally (Honig & Lally, 1972; Lally & Honig, 1975). This group of early childhood specialists believe that the most effective intervention strategy is to involve both mother and infant, so that the mother's improvements in self-concept, teaching ability, and general competence can continue to influence the child's learning after the end of the project. In order to maximize the child's exposure to a learning environment and to foster social interaction among children, group experiences are also provided for the children.

Parents entered the project from three to six months before the baby's anticipated birth. The prenatal training program focused on health and nutrition. A home visitor, who as in the Florida project was a trained para-professional from the mother's neighbor-hood, began weekly home visits at this time. After the child's birth, the emphasis in these home visits changed to demonstrations of good mother-child interactions that would foster the child's intellectual and social development.

When children reached six months of age, they began to attend daily a center-based, half-day learning program. A trained teacher taught each group of four children, using a curriculum based on the theories of both Piaget and Erikson. After age 15 months, and continuing until age five years, children attended a full-day program structured into multiage groups similar to the Infant School model used in Britain. The home visitor pro-gram continued during this whole period up to the time the children were five. Home vis-itors taught the mothers to work with the children on the same skills that were being taught in the school program, so that home learning would reinforce and augment that done in school. The program also maintained a toy and book lending library. Adult-level books on child care, child development, and family life were also available.

The original study used 108 infants and their families from low-income homes in the area of Syracuse, New York. Half were en-rolled in the program while half served as controls and were tested only. In addition, a group of middle-class infants were used as a comparison group for testing purposes to as-certain how close to middle-class norms the program might raise disadvantaged children.

Testing at 12 months showed that proj-ect children did as well as the middle-class group and much better than controls. At 36 months they did better than controls, but slightly worse than the middle-class group on intelligence tests. Behavioral measures also showed that project children did sub-stantially better than controls. Furthermore, parents reported that the use of home visi-tors, the placement of the child in the edu-cational program, and the availability of toys and books all were extremely helpful. They felt that the modeling and advice of the home visitor helped them get better control over their own lives and in managing their families.

The two remaining programs to be con-sidered concentrated on educating the child in a setting away from the home and made only minimal efforts to involve parents or teach them how to teach their children.

INFANT EDUCATION RESEARCH PROJECT

A study called the Infant Education Research Project was carried out with a group of in-fants from low-income families in Washing-ton, D.C. (Schaefer & Aaronson, 1977). A group of infant boys received tutoring and testing; a control group was tested only. The program began when the children were 15 months old and was terminated when they reached age three. Tutors who were college graduates visited each experimental child for an hour daily. Although mothers were en-couraged to participate in tutoring sessions and to help teach their children, the primary focus was on interaction between tutor and child.

The curriculum emphasized language development and was individualized for each child based upon his interests, progress, and family situation. Children were tested before the beginning of the program and at intervals during and after it. While there were no differences between experimental and control children at the beginning, the IQ of experimental children remained high while that of the controls began to drop. At the end of the program, when the children were 36 months old, there was a mean difference of 16 IQ points. Follow-up after the end of the program, however, showed a slow decrease in IQ of the experimental children up to the age of school entrance. The controls remained low until they began school at age five but then made gains that put them at the level of the experimental group by age six. Thus it would seem that early intervention must be continued right up to school entrance if gains made are to be maintained. The study also suggests, however, that interventions even as late as the kindergarten year have some beneficial effects, supporting the major premise of the Head Start program.

MILWAUKEE PROJECT

A second example of a total child instructional program is the Milwaukee Project, which has aroused a lot of controversy. This project (Heber & Garber, 1975; Trotter, 1976) has been faulted by other researchers for possible methodological errors in assigning children to experimental and control groups and because the few reports that have been issued do not contain statistical data but report results only in graphs and percentages. Nevertheless, the approach used certainly was innovative and the results of the project seem so impressive, if true, that it deserves mention but with a great deal of caution.

The Milwaukee Project began in the 1960s, and the children were still being followed up in the mid 1970s when they were in grade school (Trotter, 1976). The basic premise was that most of the incidence of mental retardation found among lower socioeconomic groups was cultural-familial. That is, retardation was passed on from generation to generation because the unstimulating home environment was not changed, rather than for any genetic reasons. If the child's environment could be drastically altered for the better, this kind of retardation would in all likelihood be prevented. The researchers from the University of Wisconsin thought that the home of such a retarded mother was an even less stimulating place than that of a low-income family of normal intelligence (which they considered unstimulating as compared to a middle-class home). Therefore the project was designed to provide massive interventions, beginning very soon after the birth of the child.

Forty black inner-city mothers who had tested IQs of 75 or below (and so were considered mentally retarded) were selected for the study. Half of these mothers and their infants became the experimental group; the other half were controls. Beginning a few days after birth, home visits were made daily by a team of a professional and a trained paraprofessional. These visitors took over most of the child caregiving functions after a short period of acclimatization. Around the age of three months, infants began a center-based program five days a week. It was an enormously rich program in terms of adult-child interaction. At first there was one adult for every infant, after 12 months one for every two, and at 18 months group experiences began. Finally, from 24 months until school entrance, children attended a daily preschool class.

While children were in the center-based program, their mothers were being trained to develop skills that would enable them to seek and find employment and to enhance their homemaking skills. This training included basic literacy, basic mathematics, home economics, and child care. After training, they were paired with skilled employees for on-the-job training in a nursing home.

On various developmental and intelligence tests, no early differences were found between experimental and control infants. But beginning at 18 months, the experimental infants began to outstrip the controls, and at 22 months they were from 4 to 6 months ahead of them in most developmental areas. They also did better on language skills, testing one and a half years ahead of controls at age four and a half.

The most recent follow-up reported, when the children had finished the third grade, showed that experimental children tested 20 to 30 IQ points above controls and were well into the normal range three years after the conclusion of the program (Trotter, 1976).

Although the results must be approached cautiously, they appear too promising to be completely dismissed. Such a program, however, with its high adult-to-child ratio would be enormously expensive to operate on anything more than an experimental basis. Probably projects utilizing both paraprofessional trainers and the mothers themselves as teachers of their children makes much more economic sense.

CONCLUSIONS

In looking over the methods and outcomes of the various parent training and infant education models discussed, some conclusions can be reached. First, it seems quite feasible to train mothers to do a better job of meeting their infants' social, intellectual, and emotional needs than they could if they were not trained. Second, interventions, whether they be at home or at a center, by parents, home visitors, or center teachers, do make a difference. The effects of short-term interventions appear to diminish over time in most instances; those of interventions lasting until the child begins school appear to have a more permanent effect. Third, paraprofessionals from the same background as low-income mothers can be trained to work with mothers and infants and do an excellent job. Indeed, paraprofessionals who are of the same ethnic group and know the mother's cultural and social background may have an advantage over professionals who are unfamiliar both in establishing rapport with parents and in knowing how best to instruct them. Finally, for the most cost-effective and long-term results, parent training as well as child training is needed. Not only do trained parents actively teach the child and maintain the gains a child may make from a center-based program, but they also can apply the skills they have learned with any subsequent children they may have, as well as with other unrelated children they may care for. Furthermore, parent training affects not only the parent's interactions with the child, but also her self-concept, managerial skills, ability to use community and governmental resources, and skills needed to cope more effectively with the everyday problems of family life.

Summary

1. The marriage rate in the United States, which had been declining, has risen slightly every year since 1976. People are marrying at somewhat later ages than before, however. The divorce rate, which had been increasing each year since World War II, dropped slightly for the first time in 1982. Thus one can cautiously say that more people are marrying, though later, and fewer are divorcing.

2. Single parenthood, however, is on the increase. In part this rise is due to the increase in out-of-wedlock births, and in part it is the result of the still high divorce rate, as well as desertion by a parent. Most single-parent families are headed by women, and a large proportion of these are living in poverty. Many single-parent mothers bear children while they themselves are still adolescents. Their extreme youth damages their chances for education and economic improvement as well as the quality of their relationship with the child.

3. The number of children in the American family has been steadily declining since colonial days, except for a brief increase during the "baby boom" era after World War II. The average number of offspring for women today is 1.8 children which is below zero population growth. The decline in the number of children per family can be attributed in part to the rising cost of bearing and raising children and in part to the increased employment of women.

4. Increasing numbers of American women are working outside the home. At present 52 percent of adult women are in the work force. A significant proportion of these are mothers of young children. This fact has implications for child care.

5. For many women, the maternal role is changing to a part-time one as they tend to have fewer children and to return to work earlier after giving birth. Research evidence indicates that the most important variable affecting the adjustment of the child is not whether the mother is employed or not but whether she is happy with what she is doing, be it employment outside the home or full-time homemaking.

6. Infant-peer interaction has been studied little until recently. Research suggests that young infants treat peers as if they were objects but that by 9 to 12 months they behave socially toward peers. Toddlers imitate one another's behaviors, play together, and fight for possession of toys. They prefer familiar peers over unfamiliar ones but will interact with unfamiliar ones as well. Given the choice of interaction with peers or their own mothers, toddlers in general will interact with peers. If young children are deprived of adult interaction through situations such as living in poorly staffed institutions, the presence and availability of peers can to some extent compensate for the lack of adult interaction.

7. With the increase in the number of mothers working outside the home and the rise in the number of single-parent families, the need for infant day care is also increasing. Some of this care is provided by relatives or baby-sitters in the infant's own home, but increasingly infants are being cared for in group settings such as day-care homes and day-care centers.

8. Good day care appears to resemble good home care in the social-emotional and cognitive results for infants. Day-care infants are as much attached to their parents as are those who remain at home. Disadvantaged children show positive intellectual improvement from day care, which seems to prevent the drop in intellectual ability usually seen in such children left at home.

9. Good infant day care depends upon well-trained, warm and loving caregivers, a good adult-to-child ratio, a physically safe and pleasing environment, and the provision of adequate and appropriate toys and other play materials. These requirements make good day care expensive to provide and mean that without some outside support, quality day care may be too expensive for many families.

10. Disruptions and distortions of the infant-caregiver relationship as well as difficult health or temperament characteristics of the infant can result in maladaptive behaviors by either child or parent that further distort such a relationship. These results include failure to thrive, child abuse, the child's reactions to long-term separation, and infantile autism. Physical abuse of infants is an especially serious problem since infants are unable to communicate verbally and are infre-

quently in public situations in which such abuse can be recognized.

11. Parent education and parent-infant projects have demonstrated that parents can be taught to meet more effectively their infants' social-emotional, intellectual, and caregiving needs. The most successful parent education and infant intervention programs have been those that have lasted for relatively long periods, sometimes even until the child begins school. Parent training is an excellent investment since a trained parent can use the skills already learned with any subsequent children and also can teach them to others.

Participatory and Observational Exercises

1. Interview a couple who are parents of an infant or toddler and who both work at different times and share the caregiving role. Or interview a couple in which the wife works and the husband is a househusband who cares for the infant or toddler. What adjustments to new roles has each had to make? What skills have they had to learn? What has been the reaction of friends and relatives to their "different" life-style? Has the role sharing or role switch affected their relationship to each other? How satisfied is each with the arrangement?

2. If any of the infants you have been observing for earlier chapters have an older sibling or siblings, observe the infants at some time while they are interacting with such a sibling. What is the interaction like with a sibling who is only little more than a toddler? How does the sibling act toward the infant? In what ways does the interaction differ if the sibling is somewhat older? How does the infant react to the presence and attention of the sibling? How does the play of a sibling

with an infant differ from adult play with the infant?

3. Observe infants and toddlers in a day-care center during a relatively structured activity such as feeding or (with toddlers) a group sharing experience. What social interactions and experiences is the child exposed to? How do adults affect the child's behaviors in such situations.

4. Now observe the same infants and toddlers in free play situations. What differences in social interactions and experiences do you observe from the structured situations? What is the influence of the adults in this kind of situation?

5. While you are at a day-care center, pay attention to the caregivers. What personal characteristics do they demonstrate in their interactions with infants that make them good, competent caregivers? What characteristics do you consider negative or having room for improvement? Explain. If you were a working parent and had to put an infant or toddler in a day-care center, would you choose this one? Why or why not?

6. Interview several caregivers in day-care centers. Why are they doing this work? What are the qualifications for the job? What levels and kinds of training have they received? Do they receive any systematic in-service training? What are they paid? Do they belong to any professional organizations devoted to the education or care of young children?

7. Interview a single parent of an infant or toddler. What aspects of life appear to be more stressful for a single parent than for one who has a partner? In what ways does the child add to these stresses? What support network of friends or relatives does the parent have available?

8. Interview a young (under age 18), unmarried mother of an infant. You may be able to interview one through a high school counselor or through an agency for unwed mothers. Why did she continue the pregnancy and have the baby and why is she keeping the baby (if she is)? If not, what are her reasons for giving it up? What are the mother's plans for the infant? What about plans for herself? Did she complete high school? Is she planning to complete her education? How? When? Is she employed? Does she plan employment? What kind? How realistically does this parent plan? Based on her answers, do you think that this parent shows some understanding of what infants and toddlers are like, that they are individuals with wills and minds of their own? Or does she perceive them as cuddly playthings that will gratify her own needs?

9. Find out what social-service agencies that offer services to infants and their families exist in your home community or the community in which you are going to school. What kinds of clients does each have? What

services does it provide? What charge if any is there for services? What are the sources of funding for the agency? Visit one of these agencies and interview one or several of the professionals who work there. If you are allowed to, interview some of the clients that are parents of infants. What are the perceptions of each about the quality of services provided and the importance of these services? What services are not provided that they think should be?

DISCUSSION QUESTIONS

1. Do you think parental feelings and behaviors are inborn or learned?

2. Should children be removed from abusive parents? If so, whose responsibility is it to remove them and to care for them?

3. Should unmarried mothers continue to receive aid to families with dependent children for additional children that they have? Should sterilization be mandatory before aid is given? On what reasons do you base your opinion? Explain.

4. Argue in favor or against the following: "All infants and toddlers should be raised in their own homes, by their own parents, with the mother being a full-time homemaker." What facts can you use to justify your position?

5. Should the federal government provide day care for all who need it, based on ability to pay and subsidizing the difference between what is paid and actual cost? Why or why not?

6. Should mothers of young children work outside the home? Should fathers share in child care? Discuss your own and your classmates' opinions on these subjects.

Postscript

At the end of this volume we have a chance to pull together some of the themes we have encountered throughout the chapters and draw some conclusions.

INCREASE OF KNOWLEDGE

There has been an explosion of knowledge in the field of infant development in the last 20 years or so. More serious inquiry has been made into both prenatal development and the developments in the first year or two after birth than in any time in the past. The effect seems to be snowballing, for as more courses are taught, books are written, and research is pursued, this material whets the interest of additional students, writers, and researchers. And they in turn produce more. This increase in knowledge has enabled those interested in infants—developmental and other psychologists, health-care professionals, educators, and parents—to gain a much clearer understanding of what is myth and what is fact, what is known with some degree of certainty and what is still open to speculation.

LESS DOGMATIC RELIANCE ON EXTREME THEORIES

Clearer understanding, as well as an appreciation for how much is still unknown, has led to a decrease in either-or remarks and a general toning down of extreme positions. Therefore, comparing the state of knowledge about infancy and toddlerhood today with what was known 20 or 30 years ago, not only do scientists know more but some of the old dogmatism seems to have died a merciful death. Few scientists today make as extreme statements as did some in the past. They are much more cautious and more likely to call for further study before coming to definite conclusions.

For example, the extreme arguments of nature versus nurture seem quite out of place today. Almost no one at present would argue as Locke did that the individual was born as a blank slate or as Watson did that by environmental manipulation he could produce whatever kind of person he chose. On the other hand, few people seriously believe, as did the members of the eugenics movement in the 1920s, that genetic determination is the only important aspect. Ideas of master races and inferior groups are largely seen as nonsense perpetuated only by bigots. Although differences among individuals based on genetic determination obviously exist in a variety of physical and psychological characteristics, it is quite clear that environmental influence can serve either to decrease or enhance those differences, making variously endowed individuals either more alike or more different. At present, informed people are very much aware that individual development results from a constant interplay between the basic genetic blueprint, which imposes the upper limit to the expression of a trait or function, and environmental effects and events, which determine how close to this limit the individual will come. They understand that both heredity and environment have unique importance and that while little can be done about heredity once a child is conceived, society can support and enhance the inherited capacities through the provision of a good environment.

APPLICATIONS TO FAMILY LIFE AND TO CHILD REARING

No longer do experts tell mothers they must remain at home with the baby and that substitute care will produce great harm, as many psychoanalytic theorists, and even Dr. Spock, did earlier. No longer is day care condemned out of hand. People have learned to be more moderate, to see multiple, interactive causation rather than a linear, cause-and-effect situation.

Scientists also have a clearer understanding, gained largely from cross-species studies by ethologists and cross-cultural ones by anthropologists, of what are uniquely human attributes and in what ways we humans are quite similar to our closely related animal relatives. Thus some of the apes, not just humans, have been found to use gestures in communication and tools in gathering food. On the other hand, spoken language and hypothetical thought seem to be produced by the human intellect alone.

Cross-cultural studies as well as the study of children in various child-rearing situations within American culture have shown that infants can adapt successfully to a wide variety of caregiving methods and styles. In-

fants are able to adjust their tempos to conform to that of caregivers. Infants appear to thrive in a great variety of situations as long as these are basically supportive of their physical and psychological needs. Thus infants raised by multiple caregivers in extended families, by child-care workers on a kibbutz in Israel, by single parents, by married couples who share caregiving, and by parents with the addition of baby-sitters or day-care personnel all can develop as well as those raised in the more "typical" nuclear families in which the father works outside the home and the mother remains at home to care for the child. The importance to the infant of people other than the mother, such as the father, siblings, and peers, has also come to be recognized.

RECOGNITION OF THE IMPORTANCE OF INFANCY

Modern research and demographic change have resulted in a greater emphasis on infancy and toddlerhood as unique and important life stages. Research has enabled people to understand better than ever before how quickly both physical and psychological development of the individual proceed. It is now known that the infant is a fully formed miniature child as early as the eighth week after conception, often before the mother is aware that she is pregnant. It is known both that development usually proceeds quite normally and also that certain disease organisms, chemicals, and genetic or chromosomal aberrations can have devastating effects upon the infant as it develops prenatally or after birth.

Informed adults can begin to appreciate what the world must appear like to the neonate but also how well-equipped the neonate is to interact with the people and events of that world. But they also have greater knowledge of how vulnerable the infant can be to environmental conditions such as abuse and neglect, malnutrition, or disease.

It is known how very quickly the infant is able to use perception and cognition to make some limited sense of the environment and how rapidly its store of knowledge grows. All this information has led researchers, parents, and other caregivers to emphasize infancy more than ever before.

FEWER CHILDREN IN EACH FAMILY

At the same time, many families not only in North America but in many other parts of the world are limiting the number of children they will have. An extreme example of this trend is the People's Republic of China, where by government policy each couple is allowed to have only one child and is subject to penalties if they have more. Such limiting of the numbers of children means that more parental attention is focused on the one or two children in the family. Parents want to make sure that they do the best job possible with the few children they have. Many parents are having these fewer children when they themselves are already older and financially and psychologically more set in their ways. What differences, if any, this trend will bring about in the children can only be guessed at present.

CHANGING PRACTICES IN CHILDBIRTH

The emphasis on doing the best possible for the fewer children born begins with prenatal development and birth. Parents, childbirth educators, health-care professionals, and others involved with the processes involved in pregnancy and birth have been looking carefully at formerly accepted practices. Both pregnancy and childbirth are today regarded as much more normal and natural functions than in the recent past, when they were often considered a kind of illness that had to be rigorously managed medically. As a result, modern childbirth is generally managed in a more humane manner. Both parents are actively involved, and individual preference regarding the management of the birth can often be accommodated. The opportunity for bonding, the use of rooming in, and the increased time fathers and often siblings are allowed to spend with the neonate all express this more enlightened approach.

USES AND ABUSES OF TECHNOLOGY

Great advances have been made in scientific knowledge regarding prenatal development, birth, and infancy. Some of these advances, however, may also have created some problems that did not exist before. For example, the use of amniocentesis and sonography in prenatal diagnosis enables many parents to know long before birth whether their child will be normal or not. It also presents them with the necessity of deciding whether to terminate or continue the pregnancy. The use of fetal monitors in labor can detect real problems, but it can also lead to the overuse, in unnecessary situations, of emergency procedures such as cesarean section that pose an additional risk of their own.

Then there is the interplay between technology and morality. Technological developments in and of themselves are morally neutral. They are merely ways in which sci-

ence progresses. But their use and its implications often raise significant moral issues.
For example, reimplantation of a fertilized
ovum, the transfer of such an ovum to a host
mother, artificial insemination, and the use
of sonography and amniocentesis to spot genetic or developmental disorders are all technological advances whose use creates moral
problems for many people. Is transfer to a
host mother justifiable? Under what circumstances? What about abortion? Is it justifiable if the child is malformed? The "Baby
Doe"cases in Indiana and New York in 1982
and 1983 involving the withholding of treatment from infants born with multiple handicaps are another example of the moral issues
that arise from technological advances. Until
recently the medical techniques that can be
used to prolong the lives of such children
were unavailable and therefore the problem
would most likely not have occurred. Now
that such children can be kept alive for extended time periods, the issue of quality of
life arises. Should life be prolonged just for
its own sake, or should the individual have
some opportunity to enjoy it?

IMPORTANCE OF INFANCY
FOR THE FUTURE

Finally, although informed adults know
something about the resilience of infants,
they also have a clearer understanding of
their vulnerability. And because the future of
the country and of the world will ultimately
be in the hands of the children who are now
infants and those not yet born, each citizen,
not just parents, should have a profound and
abiding interest in the children's optimum
development. As citizens, we may differ on
what should be done about child abuse, teen-

age pregnancy, children raised in poverty,
single parenthood, the high divorce rate,
malnutrition, and insufficient preventive
medical care. But all these conditions affect
infants and present problems that we cannot
ignore if we wish to raise our infants in the
best physical and psychological conditions
possible.

As the author, I wish I knew some quick
and easy solutions. Unfortunately, in real life
there are few. But we must all think and
question and begin to search for solutions,
even if it is difficult. To some degree, we all
share the responsibility for this and every
generation of young children that is to follow, whether they are our own children or
not. They are too valuable a resource to be
neglected.

I hope you have enjoyed reading this
book and that you have learned from it. Because the state of knowledge about infancy is
in a continuous process of change and development, all the answers are not yet known.
Much of the evidence gathered in different
studies is often conflicting. Other areas are so
new that they have barely begun to be
explored.

For all these reasons, this book should
serve only as a beginning in your study of infants and toddlers. I hope it will stimulate
you to go on to read other books as well as
some of the research literature about infancy
that is now so readily to be found in various
developmental, psychological, and medical
journals.

I have learned much from writing this
book, not only about infants, but also about
myself. Perhaps that is as it should be. We
learn about ourselves as adults, how we
came to be as we are, by reflecting first upon
infancy, the fundamental stage through which
we all have passed and where we all had our
beginnings.

Glossary

Abruptio Placentae. A condition in which a normally situated placenta abruptly separates from the uterine wall after the 28th week of pregnancy, causing bleeding that can be life-threatening to the mother and that often leads to the death of the fetus.

Accommodation. A change in cognitive schemes, or schemas, to adjust to environmental demands.

Active Sleep. In the neonate, the same as REM sleep. The infant makes gross limb movements, facial grimaces, and stretching movements. The eyeballs also move rapidly.

Affect. Feeling. A portion of emotion. The term is often used interchangeably with emotion.

Afferent. Leading or conducting toward some point.

Affiliation. Friendly social interaction with other people, without the attempt to attain or maintain proximity to them.

Alpha Waves. Characteristic electrical activity of the waking-state brain as reflected on an EEG. This pattern consists of waves varying in frequency between 8 and 13 waves per second.

Alveoli. Microscopic air sacs in the lungs in which the transfer of gases takes place.

Amino Acids. Organic acids that make up the structure of proteins.

Amniocentesis. A procedure in which cells from the amniotic fluid are extracted to test for chromosomal abnormalities and/or gender determination of the fetus.

Amnion; Amniotic Sac. A membrane that forms a sac containing amniotic fluid around the developing fetus.

Amniotic Fluid. A salty fluid formed within the amniotic sac that serves to cushion the developing fetus.

Analgesics. Drugs used to decrease pain by causing the brain to interpret pain sensations as something other than pain.

Androgens. Male hormones.

Anemia. A deficiency of red blood cells and/or hemoglobin in the blood.

Anencephaly. A prenatal developmental defect in which the cerebrum of the brain fails to develop. It is usually incompatible with life.

Anesthetics. Drugs that either produce unconsciousness or cause loss of sensation in the nerves, blocking transmission of pain sensations to the brain. Anesthetics are stronger than analgesics in their effects.

Anesthesiologist. A physician specializing in the administration of anesthetics.

Anoxia. A lack of oxygen during the birth process, which may cause brain damage or death of the fetus.

Antibodies. Proteins produced by the body which inhibit the growth of or destroy foreign organisms such as disease organisms in the body.

Anticoagulants. Drugs used clinically to prevent or retard the clotting of blood. They are used in the treatment of conditions associated with blood clots and also in blood transfusions.

Aorta. The main artery that carries blood away from the heart.

Apgar Scale. A screening test administered at one and five or ten minutes after birth to determine the physiological state of the newborn infant.

Apnea. Interruptions of breathing lasting for more than 30 seconds, which may cause brain damage in the infant.

Asphyxia. A lack of oxygen and an excess of carbon dioxide in the blood, which may lead to unconsciousness or death.

Assimilation. The process of adapting or modifying environmental input to fit existing schemes.

Associative Memory. The remembering of an association between two events.

Asymmetrical Reflex. A reflex that is manifested by different movements or the lack of unity of movements by portions of the left and right side of the body.

Ataxia. A condition in which there is defective muscular control and coordination, with resultant irregular and jerky movements.

Atherosclerosis. A disease of the arteries in which fatty plaques develop on the inner walls, causing gradual but irreversible narrowing of the arteries and accompanying restriction of blood flow. A heart attack or stroke occurs when blockage resulting from atherosclerosis develops in a blood vessel leading to heart or brain.

Attachment. The lasting bond between infant and caregiver.

Auditory. Relating to hearing or to the organs of hearing.

Autonomic Nervous System. The portion of the nervous system that controls involuntary body functions such as the glands, smooth muscle tissue, and the heart.

Autosome. One of the 22 pairs of chromosomes possessed equally by male and female humans that do not affect gender. All the chromosomes except the sex chromosomes.

Babbling. The use of repetitive syllables in vocalizing.

Behavioral Genetics. The study of the interaction of genes, human evolution, and human behaviors.

Behaviorism. A school of psychology whose major premise is that behavior occurs as a result of stimulus-response connections.

Bile. A secretion of the liver, which aids in the digestion of fats.

Bilirubin. The orange or yellowish pigment found in bile that is produced from the breakdown of hemoglobin of the red blood cells.

Binocular. Referring to both eyes.

Binocular Disparity. Same as stereopsis: an object is perceived slightly differently by each eye, since each eye sees the same object from a slightly different angle because of the distance between the two eyes.

Binocular Parallax. The two aspects of binocular parallax are convergence (the angle between the eyes as they focus on an object) and binocular disparity (see above). Binocular parallax is the basis for binocular cues for depth perception.

Blastocyst. The hollow sphere of about 200 clustered cells that comprise the zygote at the time of implantation in the uterus.

Bond; Bonding. The establishment of feelings of affection between the mother (or other caregiver) and the infant.

Brain Stem. The entire brain except for the cerebellum and cerebrum.

Branchial Arches. The five pairs of arched structures that develop into portions of the neck and facial structures in the embryo.

Braxton-Hicks Contractions. Occasional, painless uterine contractions that are often mistaken for true labor; also called false labor.

Breech. The situation in which the fetus presents for birth either buttocks first or feet first.

Brown Fat. A special kind of fat needed during the neonatal period to produce heat as it is metabolized.

Calories; Caloric. A measure of the ability of a substance to release heat when oxidized. As commonly used in foods, a calorie (technically, one kilocalorie) has the ability to raise the temperature of one liter of water one degree celsius when it is oxidized.

Carbohydrates. Organic compounds consisting of carbon, hydrogen, and oxygen, such as the starches and sugars.

Caries. The gradual decay or disintegration of a bone or tooth. Dental caries may be caused by vitamin deficiencies as well as by the formation of bacteria-containing dental plaque.

Carpal Age. The maturational age of a child based on development of the bones of the hand.

Casein. A protein derived from milk that is used to make cheese. It is found in greater quantities in cow's milk than in human milk and is often difficult for human infants to digest.

Cataracts. A condition in which the normally transparent lens of the eye becomes opaque over time, resulting in gradually diminished vision.

Central Nervous System. The neural tissue that makes up the brain and spinal cord and is responsible for intellectual activity and voluntary movement.

Cephalo-Caudal. The direction of growth and development that proceeds from the head toward the lower extremities.

Cervix. The narrow lower end of the uterus, which connects the uterus and vagina.

Cesarean Section. The surgical procedure of delivering the fetus through an incision in the mother's abdomen and uterus.

Childhood Schizophrenia. A severe form of schizophrenia that appears during childhood, usually between the ages of 2 and 12.

Chorion. The outer membrane of the protective sac that surrounds the developing zygote.

Chromosome; Chromosomal. A threadlike substance found in the cell nucleus, which contains the genes. The name means "colored body" and comes from the fact that chromosomes appear dark in stained slides of the cells.

Circadian. Referring to cyclic biological changes or rhythms based on the 24-hour cycle of the day.

Classical Conditioning. The learning of an association between two previously unrelated events, so that the response to the original event, or unconditional stimulus, also is produced to the new event, or conditional stimulus.

Cleavage. The process of cell division that occurs in the fertilized ovum.

Clitoris. Part of the female genitalia, composed of erectile tissue and covered by a hood. It is the female analog to the male penis and is extremely sensitive.

Cognition; Cognitive. The act or process of knowing. It is one of the major functions of intelligence.

Cohort. A group of people born during the same period of time.

Colic. A severe cramping of the intestines or rectum.

Colostrum. The secretions from the breast the first two or three days after delivery, which precede true milk. Colostrum is composed of serum and white blood cells and contains antibodies against disease.

Concept; Conceptual. A set of attributes, characteristics, or classificatory statements common to a group of objects, symbols, or other mental representations. Concepts represent ways of organizing knowledge. Conceptual refers to concepts but can also refer to the process of conception, the fertilization of the ovum by the sperm.

Conceptual Age. The age of the embryo or fetus based on the time of conception or fertilization.

Conditioning. The process of learning new associations.

Congenital. Present at or from birth.

Conjoined Twins. Monozygotic twins that are united, usually at the hips or buttocks, because of incomplete separation of the two cell masses during the process of twinning. Also known as Siamese twins.

Convergence; To Converge. The angle formed between the two eyes as they fixate on an object in the visual field. Focusing the eyes so that only one image of the object is seen.

Coordination of Secondary Circular Reactions. Substage 4 of Piaget's sensorimotor stage, lasting from 8 or 10 months to about one year. The child puts together two previously learned secondary circular reactions to form new schemes in order to solve a problem or attain a goal.

Corpus Luteum. The yellow body formed on the wall of the ovary by the ruptured follicle that remains after the egg is released. The corpus luteum produces progesterone and estrogen and continues a pregnancy until the baby's placenta takes over hormone production.

Cortex; Cortical. The layer of gray matter that covers most of the surface of the cerebrum of the brain.

Counterconditioning. Eliminating unwanted behaviors through the use of extinction or punishment while simultaneously promoting the acquisition of new and appropriate behaviors.

Couvade. The manifesting of some of the physical symptoms associated with pregnancy and childbirth by the expectant father.

Crawling. Movement on all fours with the abdomen touching the floor or other surface.

Creeping. Moving on the hands and knees with the abdomen lifted off the floor or other surface.

Critical Periods. Times when the environment has a strong influence, either positive or negative, on the development of the young organism.

Cross-Sectional. A method of study using two or more groups or individuals at one time and making comparisons between them.

Crossing Over. The exchange of genes between chromosomes prior to cell division.

Crowning. The appearance of the infant's head at the opening of the birth canal during birth.

Cruising. Walking sideways while holding on to furniture or other stationary objects to maintain balance.

Crystallized Intelligence. Mental ability based on stored information acquired through learning.

Cutaneous. On, of, or affecting the skin.

Cystic Fibrosis. A disease that primarily affects the pancreas and lungs, causing difficulty in digestion and breathing. It is hereditary and chronic.

Decentration. The process that begins early in the sensorimotor stage in which the infant learns which contingencies it can control and which not. Decentration leads to a decline of egocentrism.

Decidua. The membrane that lines the uterus during pregnancy and is shed at birth.

Decidual. Relates to something that is shed. Thus the decidual membranes are shed at birth, and the decidual, or baby, teeth are shed as the permanent teeth appear.

Dependency. The term used in earlier times to describe the infant's attachment to the parent. As attachment came to be seen as a two-way process, the term dependency has been used less.

Detachment. The process of separation and distancing that the securely attached child is able to use in relation to the attachment figure.

Development. Orderly and progressive changes over time due in part to physical growth, to maturation of the mental and physical structures, and to the interaction of the individual with the environment.

Dilation Phase. Part of the first stage of labor in which the cervix expands to a diameter of about 10 cm.

Discrimination; Discriminate. The process whereby overgeneralization is corrected for, as two ideas or concepts are differentiated.

Dishabituation. Response increment resulting from a change in a stimulus.

Dizygotic; DZ. Refers to fraternal twins, two individuals born to the same mother at the same time but developed from two distinct eggs.

Deoxyribonucleic Acid; DNA. A substance that transmits the hereditary characteristics of the individual.

Dominance; Dominant. Refers to a gene that is evident in the phenotype, or appearance, of the individual whether paired with another dominant gene or a recessive one.

Down's Syndrome; Mongolism. A chromosomal condition in which there are three rather than two chromosomes on the 21st set. This condition results in mental retardation as well as some physical abnormalities.

Ductus Arteriosus. A blood vessel connecting the main pulmonary artery and the aorta in the fetus, which ceases to function at birth.

Dystocia. A difficult or slow labor caused either by the mother's pelvic size, the size of the baby, or irregular, weak uterine contractions.

Eclampsia. A disorder that may occur late in pregnancy whose symptoms include edema, high blood pressure, and convulsions.

Ectoderm. The outer layer of the embryo, which develops into skin, hair, nails, nervous system, and sensory cells.

Ectopic Pregnancy. A pregnancy in which the fertilized ovum does not reach the uterus but instead implants and begins to develop in either the abdominal cavity or in one of the fallopian tubes.

Edema. Excessive fluid retention in body tissues, especially during pregnancy.

Electroencephalogram; EEG. A graphic record of electrical activity of the brain.

Effacement Phase. Part of the first stage of labor in which the thinning and beginning dilation of the cervix of the uterus take place.

Ego. Freud's second psychodynamic function (after

the id). The ego is the reality principle, which tries to control the id by trying to control the means of need gratification.

Ejection Reflex; Let-Down Reflex. The reflexive flowing of the mother's milk in response to the infant's sucking and sometimes to the sight or sound of the infant.

Electrolyte. Any liquid or solution capable of conducting an electric current.

Embryo; Embryological; Embryology. Refers to the developing human from the time of implantation until eight weeks after conception. Comes from a Greek word meaning "swelling." The term is sometimes used to refer to the whole period of prenatal development, that is, embryology is the study of prenatal development from conception to birth.

Emotion. Affect plus intellectual and social interpretation linked to the affective state; the meaning attached to affective transactions with people, objects, and events in the environment.

Enactive Stage. According to Bruner, this is the primary stage of intellectual development in which an infant learns about the world through physical activity upon objects. It extends through the first year of life.

Endoderm. The inner layer of the developing embryo, which becomes the gastrointestinal tract, respiratory system, pancreas, and liver.

Endogenous. Growing from within; having an effect from within.

En Face. Positioning of the infant so that it is held up close to the mother's (or other caregiver's) face with the adult gazing at the infant's eyes.

Entrainment. The regulation of biological rhythms through external stimuli.

Enzyme. A complex protein that produces chemical changes such as those in the digestion of food.

Epigenesis. The reorganization of prior levels of development so as to progress to the next level.

Episiotomy. A small incision made into the perineum during childbirth to prevent its tearing.

Epistemology. An area of philosophy that deals with how knowledge is attained.

Equilibrium; Equilibration. According to Piaget, a self-regulatory process within the individual involving a dynamic balance between assimilation and accommodation.

Ethology; Ethological. The study of animal behavior.

Exogenous. From outside the organism; originating from the external environment.

Experimental. A type of research or study design in which the variables that are studied can be manipulated and the environment can be controlled by the experimenter.

Extinguish; Extinction. The reduction of frequency of a learned response or behavior over time as a result of lack of reinforcement.

Fallopian Tubes. The two tubes through which the ova are conducted from the ovaries to the uterus.

Fats. The principal oily, water-insoluble material in food, also known as triglycerides. Fats are the most concentrated source of energy in the body.

Fatty Acids. Organic acids that are derivatives of hydrocarbons and are found in animal and vegetable fats.

Fertilization. The penetration of an ovum by a sperm.

Fetus; Fetal. The unborn developing human from the end of the embryonic period at eight weeks until birth. Comes from a Latin word meaning "offspring."

Fetal Alcohol Syndrome; FAS. A cluster of symptoms including small physical size, mental retardation, and facial, limb, or organ abnormalities resulting from maternal consumption of alcohol during pregnancy.

Fetal Monitor. A device attached via sensors that are located on the laboring mother's abdomen that monitors the fetus's heart rate and uterine contractions and can indicate fetal distress.

Fluid Intelligence. Innate intellectual capacity based on inherited potential.

Folates. Chemicals of the B vitamin group that are necessary for the infant's proper development both prenatally and after birth.

Follicle. A small cavity or sac.

Follicle-Stimulating Hormone; FSH. A hormone that causes the ovum to ripen in the ovary.

Fontanels. Soft spaces between the bones of the skull that permit compression of the infant's head without damage during passage through the birth canal. They are found in all infants and disappear as the bones of the skull fuse.

Foramen Ovale. The opening between the two atria of the fetus's heart, which usually begins to close shortly before or after birth to permit efficient separation of oxygenated and deoxygenated blood after birth.

Forceps. Tonglike tool with large, curved blades sometimes used to pull the baby out of the birth canal.

Forebrain. The anterior portion of the embryo's brain.

Fovea. The area at the center of the retina of the eye containing the largest concentration of cones, which are receptors for color vision.

Function. Refers to the use or activity of a structure. Psychologically, functions are processes through which psychological structures operate.

Functional Assimilation. According to Piaget, the process of exercising an available structure, through which a function is being assimilated to an already existing scheme.

Galactose. A simple sugar derived from lactose.

Galactosemia. An inherited disease resulting from the lack of an enzyme needed to break down galactose into glucose.

Gamete. A reproductive cell, that is, the sperm or the ovum.

Gamma Globulin. One of several proteins referred to as immunoglobins that take part in the body's immune response to bacteria and other foreign substances. It is the most prevalent of these antibodies and congenital absence of it often results in death in early infancy. It may be administered by injection to individuals who have been exposed to certain diseases in order to aid in their warding off those disease agents.

Gavage; Gavaging. The process of feeding liquid nourishment directly to the stomach via a tube. It is used when a newborn cannot suck forcefully enough or cannot coordinate sucking and swallowing.

Gene. The unit of hereditary material in the chromosomes that governs the development or occurrence of one trait or function.

Gene-Splicing. Splitting strands of DNA from two origins in separate genes and recombining them to form a new combination of genes.

Genetic Epistemology. The study of how intelligence originates and develops.

Genetics. The study of the heredity and variation of organisms.

Genotype. The genetic composition possessed by an organism. The genotype may or may not be observable in the phenotype, or appearance.

Gestalt. German word for "shape" or "configuration." Refers to a school of psychological thought dealing with how configurational properties of environmental events are perceived and acted on.

Gestation. The time of development from conception to delivery of the fetus.

Glaucoma. An eye disease in which the pressure within the eyeball increases and there is a progressive loss of vision.

Glial Cells. Cells that are very prevalent in the brain and spinal cord, which provide structural and nutrient functions to the nerve cells.

Glucose. A simple sugar composed of 6 carbon atoms, 6 oxygen atoms, and 12 hydrogen atoms. It is in the form of glucose that all carbohydrates are absorbed from the digestive tract and circulated in the blood for use by body tissues. Other carbohydrates are converted to glucose through the action of digestive enzymes.

Gonadotrophic. Having an affinity for or influencing the gonads.

Gonadotropin or Gonadotrophin. A hormone that stimulates the gonads.

Gonads. Either of the two sex glands, the ovaries or the testes.

Gonorrhea. A venereal disease whose symptoms include an inflammation of and discharge from the mucous membranes of the genitals. It can cause blindness in the infant who passes through an infected mother's birth canal.

Habituation; Habituate. The decrease of responsiveness to a stimulus in the external environment that occurs after continued exposure to it.

Hemophilia. A hereditary disease characterized by prolonged and heavy bleeding from even minor injuries because of the lack of blood-clotting factors.

Heterozygous. Having different alleles of a gene present at the same position on two paired chromosomes, for example, one gene for brown eyes and another for blue.

Holography. A photographic method that produces three-dimensional images with the use of laser light.

Holophrastic. The notion that a single word uttered by the young child stands for a whole sentence or phrase.

Homozygous. Having matched alleles of a gene at the same locus on paired chromosomes, for example, two genes for blue eyes.

Hormone. A glandular secretion that produces specific responses in different parts of the body.

Huntington's Disease. A progressive hereditary disorder marked by increasing mental deterioration.

Hyaline Membrane Disease. A respiratory disorder of preterm infants in which the alveoli of the immature lungs are lined with an abnormal membrane of protein that hinders the exchange of gases.

Hydrocephalus. An accumulation of fluid in the skull, which causes the head to enlarge and through pressure on the brain can lead to mental retardation.

Hypertension. Abnormally high blood pressure, especially in the arteries.

Hypoglycemia. Abnormally low blood sugar.

Hypoxia. An abnormal condition that results from a decreased supply or utilization of oxygen by body tissues.

Id. The basic motivational principle posited by Freud, which seeks out gratification of its impulses.

Ikonic Stage. Bruner's second stage of cognitive development, during the second year of life, in which the child begins to perceive the world in terms of a mental map based upon spatial relationships and perceptual features of objects.

Implantation. The process whereby the fertilized ovum, or zygote, becomes attached to the uterine wall.

Infant; Infancy. The child during the period of development from birth to age one year. Comes from a Latin word meaning "without speech."

Infanticide. The socially approved or condoned killing of infants.

Infantile Autism. A form of schizophrenia which is a psychosis that begins early in life and whose symptoms can include unresponsiveness, lack of communication, bizarre repetitive movements, and a requirement of unchanging routines.

Inflection; Inflectional. Endings added onto words that denote verb tenses, plurals of nouns, cases of pronouns, or (in languages that have them) cases of nouns.

Inorganic. Chemicals whose structure does not include carbon.

Intelligence; Intellect; Intellectual. The capacity to learn, understand, or apply knowledge. The ability to adapt and to deal effectively with the environment.

Interactional Synchrony. The synchrony that exists between a listener's movements and the syllables in the speech of a speaker. Has been found to occur already in very young infants.

Intramuscular Injection. An injection made into a muscle.

Intravenous Injection. Injection made directly into a vein.

Invention of New Means through Mental Representations. Substage 6 of Piaget's sensorimotor stage, during which true thought begins and mental imagery rather than action begins to be used in problem solving.

Jargon. A "sentence" made up of lalling, protowords, and perhaps a few true words that has the intonational qualities of speech.

Ketones. Acids that are the end products of fat metabolism in the body. They may harm the developing fetal brain if excessive amounts are produced by the mother during pregnancy.

Kinesthetic. Relating to the ability to detect or perceive movement through end organs of sense in the muscles and joints of the body.

Klinefelter's Syndrome. A chromosomal abnormality in males in which an extra *X* chromosome is present. The individual thus has an *XXY* genotype and shows symptoms including underdeveloped testes, infertility, and possibly mental retardation.

Kwashiorkor. A nutritional disease associated with a lack of protein in the diet.

Labia. The outer and inner layers of tissue surrounding the vulva, or opening of the vagina.

Lactation. The production and secretion of milk.

Lactoalbumin. The major protein found in human milk. It is the protein found in the whey of milk products and is considered a protein of higher biological value than casein.

Lactoglobulin. A protein found in the whey of human milk.

Lactose. A milk sugar, which yields glucose and galactose.

Lactose Intolerance. An inability to digest the lactose found in milk, which produces symptoms of abdominal cramping and diarrhea.

La Leche League. A group that offers information and support to women who are interested in breast-feeding their infants. Branches exist in many parts of the United States.

Lalling. The babbling of a limited number of syllables that consist of sounds that are present in the language the child will learn to speak. Also referred to as nonreduplicative babbling.

Lamaze Method. A method of prepared childbirth in which both the mother and father (or a labor coach) are instructed in breathing and relaxation techniques to help ease the birth process.

Language Acquisition Device; LAD. A hypothetical structure in the brain programmed for language learning.

Lanugo. The soft, downy hair that covers the skin of the fetus. Traces of it may be present at birth.

Learning. The function through which knowledge or information is acquired. Learning can be inferred from a change of behavior that is not due to maturation, fatigue, or the influence of agents such as drugs.

Lexicon; Lexical. The total corpus of words that exist in a particular language.

Lightening. The process whereby the fetus's head moves down into the pelvic inlet in preparation for birth.

Linoleic Acid. An unsaturated fatty acid that is considered to be essential in animal diets and particularly is needed in infant nutrition.

Lithotomy Position. A position in which a person lies on the back with the thighs flexed on the abdomen and the legs on the thighs; the most usual position used for childbirth in the United States.

Longitudinal. A method of studying one individual or a group of individuals over time with repeated measurements of particular variables.

Macrosomia. A condition in which an abnormally large body is formed. In fetal development this can occur to babies of diabetic mothers.

Mammal; Mammalian. An animal characterized by having teats and glands that secrete milk to nourish the newborn.

Mandible. The bone of the lower jaw.

Marasmus. Emaciation that occurs as the result of starvation or acute disease.

Maple Syrup Urine Disease. An inherited metabolic disorder in which the body is unable to break down three amino acids. As a result the nervous system rapidly deteriorates during the first few months of life, and an early death ensues.

Mean Length of Utterance; MLU. The mean number of morphemes, or units of meaning, used by the child in speech at a particular time.

Mechanistic. A viewpoint stressing learning based on environmental factors. The individual is viewed as reactive and likened to a machine that responds to environmental input.

Meconium. The first feces of the neonate, composed of sloughed-off cells from the digestive system as well as cellular material swallowed by the baby in the amniotic fluid. It is greenish black.

Meiosis. Cell division in the reproductive system that reduces the number of chromosomes in the formation of gametes, the sperm or egg.

Menarche. The onset of the first menstruation in the girl at puberty.

Menopause. The cessation of the menstrual periods in women, usually between the ages of 45 and 55.

Menstrual Age. The age of the developing embryo and fetus as calculated from the time of the onset of the mother's last menstrual period before pregnancy.

Mesoderm. One of the three germ layers of the embryo. This layer forms the connective tissues, muscles, skeleton, circulatory, lymphatic, and urogenital systems.

Metabolism; Metabolize. All of the chemical and physical processes in the cells of an organism that provide energy for bodily processes to occur; consists of anabolism (a building-up process) and catabolism (a breaking-down process).

Metapelet; Metaplot (pl.). Child-rearer or child-care worker on a kibbutz, or collective farm, of Israel.

Methadone. A drug similar to morphine useful clinically in the treatment of intractable pain. Also used in treatment programs for heroin addicts but is a powerful addictive drug itself.

Microcephalic. Having an abnormally small head. Usually associated with underdevelopment of the brain and mental retardation.

Minerals. All solid materials except those containing carbon. In foods, those inorganic substances that are necessary for body function.

Mitosis. Cell division in which the number of chromosomes is preserved.

Mixed Dominance. The situation in which offspring show phenotypes that are half-way between those of the two parents; for example, if one parent flower is red and the other white, the offspring are pink.

Model; Modeling. A person who demonstrates a behavior that is observed by another. The process whereby the behavior of another is observed and imitated.

Modularization. According to Bruner, this is the consolidation and mastery of a skill so that it can be performed in the most efficient way possible.

Monocular. Pertaining to one eye.

Monozygotic; MZ. Referring to twins who develop from the same fertilized egg which splits at an early stage of cell division into two separate organisms; identical twins.

Morpheme. Unit of meaning in language; either a word or an inflectional ending on a word.

Morula. The solid mass of cells resulting from the early cell divisions of the fertilized egg, derived from the Latin word for "mulberry" because of its resemblance to that fruit.

Motion Parallax. The apparent motion of a stationary object against a stationary background as the observer moves her or his head.

Motivation. Wanting or needing something that results in a desire to act.

Mullerian Ducts; Mullerian System. Embryonic tubes, which in the female develop into the oviducts or fallopian tubes, uterus, and portions of the vagina.

Mullerian Inhibiting Substance. A hormone secreted by the testes of the male fetus which inhibits further development of the female structures.

Muscular Dystrophy. A chronic inherited disease that involves the progressive atrophy of the muscles.

Mutation. An alteration of the genes or chromosomes. May occur spontaneously or as a result of exposure to radiation or certain chemicals.

Myelin; Myelination; Myelinated. A fatty sheath covering major portions of nerve cells that enables nerve impulses to be transmitted more quickly and accurately. The process by which this sheath is formed.

Narcotics. Drugs used to depress the central nervous system in order to relieve pain or produce sleep.

Nature. The hereditary influences upon development.

Neonate; Neonatal. The newborn. Refers to the period from birth through the first four weeks after birth.

Neonatologist. A physician specializing in the care and treatment of the newborn.

Neurons. Nerve cells consisting of a body, an axon, and one or more dendrites.

Nondisjunction. The failure of a pair of chromosomes to separate during meiosis, causing one daughter cell to have both chromosomes and the other to have none.

Non-REM Sleep. Quiet sleep in the neonate. Few movements occur, and the eyeballs do not move. In older children and adults, there is more movement during non-REM sleep than during REM sleep.

Normative. Based on averages, established norms, or standards.

Notochord. A gelatinous rod that provides early back support in the embryo and is later replaced by the spine.

Nucleus. The vital part of the cell, which is essential for growth, metabolism, reproduction, and transmission of characteristics.

Nurture. The environmental influences on development.

Observational. A method of research in which individuals are watched but no experimental intervention is done.

Obstetrician. A physician specializing in the treatment of women during pregnancy, childbirth, and the first few weeks after birth.

Oogenesis. The process of the formation of the ovum.

Operant Conditioning. The forming of an association between a behavior emitted by an organism and a subsequent environmental event. If this event is rewarding or reinforcing, the behavior is likely to recur; if neutral or punishing, it is less likely to recur.

Organismic. A viewpoint stressing the structures within the individual, who is viewed as an active seeker for information, impelled by species-specific maturational factors.

Orienting. Response to the initiation or change of a stimulus evidenced by attention to the stimulus.

Ossification. The formation of bone. In prenatal and early childhood development it refers to the conversion of other tissue such as cartilage into true bone.

Ovary. An almond-shaped part of the female reproductive system. The two ovaries are located on the two sides within the lower abdomen and are responsible for the production and storage of ova, or eggs.

Ovulate; Ovulation. The ripening and discharge of an ovum from the ovary.

Ovum. The egg, or female germ cell, or gamete.

Oxytocin. A hormone released by the pituitary gland that stimulates uterine contractions helping to induce labor and that also stimulates the mammary glands to produce and release milk.

Parity. Refers to the number of children a woman has borne.

Pediatrician. A physician specializing in the care and treatment of children and adolescents.

Pellucid Zone. The clear outer layer covering the developing ovum before fertilization.

Pelvis; Pelvic. The bony structure below the abdomen through whose opening the baby must pass in emerging from the mother's body at birth.

Penis. The male sexual organ, which is mainly composed of erectile tissue.

Perception; Perceptual; Perceives. Perception is that form of cognition that takes in, processes, and interprets sensory information.

Perinatal. Occurring in the period around the time of birth; before, during, or after birth.

Perineum; Perineal. The area between the vulva, or opening of the vagina, and the anus in the female, or between the scrotum and the anus in the male.

Phenotype. The observable physical characteristics of an individual.

Phenylalanine. One of the amino acids, of which proteins are composed, that the child with phenylketonuria is unable to metabolize properly.

Phenylketonuria; PKU. A genetic disorder characterized by the inability to metabolize phenylalanine. This substance then damages the central nervous system and causes mental retardation. With a special diet the damage can be prevented or minimized.

Phonemes. Units of sound in a language. Phonemes vary from one language to another.

Phonetic. Relating to phonemes, or to the sound of words.

Phonology; Phonological. The sound system of a language.

Pica. The eating of nonnutritive substances. It sometimes occurs during pregnancy when the woman develops cravings for substances not fit as food and in young children.

Pituitary Gland. The "master gland" located at the base of the brain, which releases hormones that control and activate other glands.

Place-Holding. According to Bruner, the mechanism whereby two activities are coordinated by retaining one briefly in memory while initiating the other. It begins around the age of four months.

Placenta. The structure through which the developing embryo and later the fetus is nourished while in the uterus.

Placenta Previa. A condition in which the placenta implants too low in the uterus and separates too early in labor, causing uterine bleeding and the cessation of oxygen supply to the fetus. Hence it poses great danger to both fetus and mother.

Polar Body. A small unusable cell containing extra chromosomes that is formed during the meiotic division of the ovum.

Polydactily. The condition of having supernumerary fingers or toes. It is an inherited condition and occurs more frequently in blacks than in Caucasians.

Polygenic. Caused or determined by more than one gene pair.

Postmature. A baby born more than two weeks beyond the due date.

Postnatal. The period immediately following birth.

Preeclampsia. A toxemia of pregnancy whose symptoms include increasing hypertension, headaches, and edema of the legs. If not properly managed, preeclampsia may become true eclampsia.

Preformation. A theory that assumed that a completely formed miniature infant was already present within either the father or the mother. The father's semen either transferred this infant to the mother or triggered its growth.

Prenatal. The time from conception to birth.

Preterm. An infant born before 35 weeks of conceptual age.

Progesterone. The hormone that prepares the uterus for the implantation of the fertilized egg. It is secreted by the corpus luteum and later by the placenta. It later serves to maintain the capacity of the uterus to hold the developing baby.

Prostate Gland. A gland located at the upper end of the penis that secretes a fluid that forms part of the male ejaculate.

Prosthetic. The replacement of a missing part by a man-made substitute.

Prostoglandins. Substances produced by most body tissues that are similar to hormones, vitamins, and enzymes. They have many roles, most of which are as yet relatively unknown. One of their roles is to help trigger the onset of labor.

Proteins. Any of a class of complex nitrogenous compounds, which occur naturally in animals and plants. Proteins are composed of amino acids, which are essential for the growth and repair of animal tissue.

Protowords. Sounds approaching those of true words.

Primary Circular Reactions. The second substage of Piaget's sensorimotor stage, lasting from about one to four months. During this substage the infant begins to modify actions based on experience and begins to prolong or repeat interesting activities centered upon its own body.

Proximo-Distal. The direction of development of the body from the midline outward.

Pseudoconditioning. A situation in which an environmental event causes a heightened motivational or arousal state in which many behaviors, including the one being conditioned, occur.

Psychoanalysis; Psychoanalytic. Freud's theory of psychosexual development, which posits that most human behavior is governed by unconscious motivation. The goal of psychoanalysis, a treatment procedure initiated by Freud based on this theory, is to bring what is unconscious to consciousness through the use of dream analysis, free association, and the recall of childhood memories.

Psychobiology; Psychobiological. The study of behavior as based on the interaction between psychological and biological determinants.

Psychodynamic. A theoretical position placing emphasis on inner drives and goal-seeking behaviors based on these drives.

Psychometric. A method of objectively assessing individual differences using standardized mathematical procedures such as mental tests.

Psychosexual. Based on Freudian theory, the idea that cognitive, emotional, and social development are associated with stages of sexual sensitivity in children.

Psychosocial. In Eriksonian theory, the resolution of predictable tensions among an individual's biological and emotional needs and societal expectations.

Puberty. The time at which an individual becomes physiologically capable of sexual reproduction.

Quickening. The first movements of the fetus that are felt by the mother.

Quiet Alert State. The state in which the infant is awake, attentive, and especially responsive to visual, auditory, and tactile stimulation.

Quiet Sleep. The same as non-REM sleep in the young infant, during which little movement occurs.

Reactive Memory. The infant's version of recognition memory.

Recall Memory. Remembrance of an object, person, or events in the absence of such an object, person, or event.

Recessive. A gene whose traits do not appear or are not expressed if it is paired with a dominant gene. They are only expressed if it is paired with another recessive gene.

Recognition Memory. Remembrance of an object, person, or event when it is again presented as one that has been encountered previously.

Recommended Dietary Allowances; RDA. A compilation of recommendations by the Nutritional Research Council of the National Academy of Sciences of the amounts of nu-

trients that should be consumed by normal, healthy populations of individuals in order to avoid nutritional diseases.

Reflex. A response to stimulation that occurs automatically or involuntarily.

Reflexive Substage. Substage 1 of Piaget's sensorimotor stage, lasting from birth to about one month, during which the infant modifies and adapts inborn reflex activities.

Regenerative Memory. A portion of infant memory similar to recall memory.

Reinforcement. The consequences provided after a certain behavior is emitted.

REM Sleep. Sleep in which the eyes move rapidly. In older children and adults, it is at this time that dreams occur, and body motion is absent. In young infants, REM sleep is also called active sleep, as much movement does occur. It is probable that infants also dream during REM sleep. At least it is a time of increased cortical activity.

Retina. The light-sensitive layer at the back of the eye on which light rays are focused before information from them is transmitted to the brain.

Rh Incompatibility. A condition that results from an Rh negative woman carrying an Rh positive fetus, some of whose blood enters the mother during the birth process and causes the production of antibodies. These antibodies will be activated and destroy fetal blood cells in a subsequent pregnancy involving an Rh positive child.

Scheme; Schema; Schemes. According to Piaget, inner psychological intellectual structures referring to particular behavioral action sequences. Mental representations or blueprints of particular physical, and later mental, activities.

Scrotal Sac; Scrotum. The pouch that contains the male testes.

Secondary Circular Reactions. Piaget's third substage of the sensorimotor stage, lasting from 4 to about 8 to 10 months, during which the infant involves objects and environmental events in activities repeated for goal-directed purposes.

Sedatives. Medications used to soothe or tranquilize. They are milder than analgesics and anesthetics.

Semantic System. Deals with the meaning of utterances; the words or phrases used in sentences.

Semen. The secretion discharged by the male during sexual activity, which contains the sperm.

Seminal Fluid. The fluid portion of the semen produced by various glands; the semen except for the sperm.

Seminal Vesicles. Two saclike structures located behind the bladder in the male in which sperm and fluid are temporarily stored.

Sensation. Responsiveness of sensory end organs to outside stimulation. The sensory capacity to react to such stimulation.

Senses. Sight, hearing, smell, taste and touch, as well as sensitivity to pressure, pain, motion, temperature, hunger, and thirst.

Sensitive Periods. A time in development when a stimulus is likely to have the greatest effect because the developing organism has heightened sensitivity to it.

Sensorimotor Stage. Piaget's basic stage, lasting from birth to about 24 months, in which the child acts on the environment and learns about reality by using the senses and motor activities.

Sensory End Organs. The receptors that receive sensory information. Especially the eye and the ear.

Separation Distress; Separation Protest. The child's negative reactions to the departure of an attachment figure.

Sickle-Cell Anemia. A hereditary, chronic type of anemia characterized by crescent-shaped red blood cells that are deprived of sufficient oxygen and tend to clump in the capillaries. It is due to a defect in the structure of hemoglobin and is most prevalent in blacks and people of Mediterranean ancestry.

Sleep Spindles. A characteristic electrical pattern seen on an EEG in the first stages of light sleep. They vary in frequency between 14 and 16 waves per second and occur in bursts.

Small for Date. Same as low birth weight: babies of birth weight below 2500 g who are born after 35 weeks or more of gestation.

Social-Learning Theory. A form of learning theory that concentrates on what an individual learns from watching the behaviors of others.

Socioemotional. A term describing the interaction of emotions with the social situation.

Somites. Segments in the developing embryo that give rise to the muscles.

Sonography. The process in which sound waves are bounced off various portions of the mother's abdomen to produce a picture of the developing baby and surrounding structures.

Sperm. The male sex cell produced in the testes, which is needed to fertilize the ovum.

Spermatogenesis. The process of the production and ripening of sperm in the testes.

Sphincter. A circular muscle surrounding an orifice or opening, which, when contracted, closes the orifice.

Spina Bifida. A congenital defect in which the contents of the spinal canal are exposed to the surface of the back, usually in the lower back region. There may or may not be neurological defects as a result.

Spinal Cord. The cord of nerve tissue of the central nervous system, which runs from the medulla through the spinal canal. It contains the nerves to the trunk and limbs and is the center of reflex action.

State. Definite and discrete patterns of activity of the autonomic and central nervous system, which occur in fairly regular sequences resulting in the cyclic variation in sleep, wakefulness, and activity.

Stereopsis. The same as binocular disparity.

Steroids. A group of naturally occurring chemicals derived from or allied to cholesterol. They include the sex hormones, bile acids, and hormones produced by the cortex of the adrenal glands.

Stillbirth. A fetus that is born dead.

Stimulus Generalization. The process whereby a response learned to a particular stimulus is extended, or generalized, to a similar one.

Structure. What an entity is made of. Psychologically, structure refers to hypothetical constructs inferred to exist in the mind, such as intelligence, memory, or emotions.

Subcortical. Referring to regions of the brain below the cortex.

Subcutaneous. Below the skin.

Sudden Infant Death Syndrome; SIDS. The sudden death of an apparently healthy infant from respiratory arrest.

Superego. The part of the personality, according to Freud, that governs morality by incorporating parental and societal standards. Can be roughly equated to conscience.

Symbol; Symboling. A symbol is an arbitrary representation of an event, object, quality, action, or concept by something else such as a picture, a word, a number, or a schematic representation that stands for it.

Symbolic Stage. Bruner's third stage of cognitive development, beginning late in the second year, in which the child can begin to think and express itself through the use of symbols such as language and use of tools.

Symmetrical Reflex. A reflex that involves both sides of the body in the same manner.

Syndrome. A group of symptoms and/or signs that, when occurring together, produce a pattern typical of a particular disease.

Syntax; Syntactical. Rule-bound way of putting words together into meaningful phrases or sentences. Synonymous with grammar.

Tarsal Age. The maturational age of a child based on bone development of the foot.

Taurine. A compound that is part of taurocholic acid found in animal bile. It is also found in plentiful supply in human breast milk.

Tay-Sachs Disease. An inherited disease transmitted by an autosomal recessive gene, which results in neurological degeneration and death. It is found mainly among Jews of East European origin.

Temperament. A cluster of relatively permanent intellectual, emotional, and behavioral characteristics which affect environmental interactions and relationships with others.

Term. The normal gestational period for humans: nine months or 266 days.

Tertiary Circular Reactions. The fifth substage of Piaget's sensorimotor stage, lasting from about 12 to about 18 months. The child actively experiments to discover new means of doing certain activities and produces variations upon these actions.

Testis; Testes. The male reproductive glands, which are responsible for the production of sperm and male hormones and which are located in the scrotal sac.

Testosterone. One of the androgens, or male hormones.

Thalassemia. A genetically transmitted condition in which the hemoglobin of the red blood cells is structurally abnormal. It generally occurs in individuals of Mediterranean origin and produces minimal to severe symptoms of anemia.

Thalidomide. A sedative and sleeping pill used in Europe in the early 1960s that was found to cause severe malformations of the limbs of babies whose mothers had used the drug early in pregnancy.

Theoretical. Relating to theory, which is a set of principles used to explain phenomena, or the hypothetical formulation of principles based on the analysis of certain groups of facts.

Toddlerhood. The period of human development from the end of infancy at about one year to about the age of two.

Tranquilizers. Drugs used to reduce tension and anxiety.

Transition Phase. Part of the first stage of labor in which the cervix becomes fully dilated.

Translocation. The process whereby the correct number of chromosomes become arranged in an unusual manner because one chromosome or a portion of one becomes attached to another one.

Transverse. The presentation of a baby in a crosswise manner during birth.

Trauma. A physically or psychologically stressful event.

Trimester. A three-month period of pregnancy.

Trophoblast. The outermost layer of the developing mammalian blastocyst, which will form the structures outside the embryo.

Turner's Syndrome. A chromosomal abnormality in which a female has an *XO* rather than *XX* sex chromosome pattern, resulting in the failure of the ovaries to respond to pituitary hormone stimulation and the lack of development of secondary sexual characteristics.

Tyrosine. An amino acid found in many proteins, particularly casein.

Tyrosinemia. Hereditary tyrosinemia involves the increase of tyrosine in the blood and can be controlled through the restriction of tyrosine and phenylalanine in the diet. Neonatal tyrosinemia is a transient condition treated by the administration of vitamin C.

Umbilical Cord. The flexible cord that connects the fetus to the placenta, containing the blood vessels carrying nourishment to the fetus and waste products away from it.

Unsaturated Fats. Fats that contain less than the full amount of hydrogen atoms in their structure. They are usually of vegetable origin, are liquid at room temperature, and are less likely to lead to atherosclerosis than are saturated fats.

Uterus. The pear-shaped muscular organ in the female in which the embryo/fetus develops.

Vagina. The passage from the uterus to the external opening of the female genital canal or the vulva.

Variable. An occurrence or event. Independent variables are those that can be manipulated experimentally, while dependent variables change as a result of these manipulations and can thus be studied to determine the effects of the changes in the independent variables.

Venereal Disease. Infections such as gonorrhea, syphilis, and herpes that are transmitted through sexual contact.

Vernix Caseosa. The whitish oily deposit that is secreted by skin glands and covers the fetus to protect the skin from the amniotic fluid.

Vestibular. Referring to a small space or cavity at the beginning of a canal, usually of the semicircular canals of the inner ear that govern balance.

Villi. The short hairlike tufts found on various body surfaces. Chorionic villi are projections on the surface of the chorion, which help to form the placenta.

Visual Tracking. The process of following a moving object with the eyes.

Vitamins. Organic materials necessary in the diet for normal physiological health that are not classified as proteins, carbohydrates, or fats.

Weaning. The replacement of breast-feeding by other forms such as bottle-feeding, cup-feeding or the use of solid foods. Often also refers to the replacement of either breast-feeding or bottle-feeding by the cup.

Wet Nurse. A nursing mother who was hired to breast-feed another child as well.

Wolffian Ducts; Wolffian System. The ducts in the male embryo that will become the sperm ducts and that arise after the Mullerian Inhibiting Substance inhibits the growth of the female forms.

Yolk Stalk. The narrow connection between the yolk sac and the embryo, which becomes incorporated into the developing umbilical cord.

Zygote. The fertilized egg from conception to the completion of implantation two weeks later.

References

Chapter 1: Studying Infants

Aries, P. (1962). *Centuries of childhood.* New York: Alfred A. Knopf.

Bandura, A. (1969). *Principles of behavior modification.* New York: Holt, Rinehart and Winston.

Bandura, A., & Walters, R. (1963). *Social learning and personality development.* New York: Holt, Rinehart and Winston.

Darwin, C. (1877). A biographical sketch of an infant. *Mind, 2,* 285–294.

de Mause, L. (1974). The evolution of childhood. In L. de Mause (Ed.), *The history of childhood* (pp. 1–73). New York: Psychohistory Press.

Dollard, J., & Miller, N. E. (1950). *Personality and psychotherapy.* New York: McGraw-Hill.

Erikson, E. H. (1963). *Childhood and society* (2nd ed.). New York: W. W. Norton.

Freud, A. (1937). *The ego and the mechanisms of defence.* London: Hogarth.

Freud, S. (1938). *The basic writings of Sigmund Freud,* A. A. Brill, (Ed.) New York: Modern Library.

Gesell, A. T. (1928). *Infancy and human growth.* New York: Macmillan.

Gesell, A. T. (1934). *An atlas of infant behavior.* New Haven, CT: Yale University Press.

Gesell, A. T., & Amatruda, C. S. (1947). *Developmental diagnosis.* New York: Hoeber.

Gesell, A. T., Ilg, F., & Ames, L. B. (1974). *Infant and child in the culture of today* (rev. ed.). New York: Harper & Row.

Illick, J. E. (1974). Child-rearing in seventeenth-century England and America. In L. de Mause, (Ed.), *The history of childhood* (pp. 303–350). New York: Psychohistory Press.

Kagan, J., & Klein, R. I. (1973). Cross-cultural perspectives on early development. *American Psychologist, 28,* 947–961.

Lorenz, K. (1955). *Evolution and modification of behavior.* Chicago: University of Chicago Press.

Piaget, J. (1926a). *The language and thought of the child.* London: Routledge & Kegan Paul.

Piaget, J. (1926b). *Judgment and reasoning in the child.* New York: Harcourt, Brace.

Piaget, J. (1951). *Play, dreams and imitation in childhood.* New York: W. W. Norton.

Piaget, J. (1952). *The origins of intelligence in children.* New York: W. W. Norton.

Piaget, J. (1954). *The construction of reality in the child.* New York: Basic Books.

Preyer, W. (1882). *Die Seele des Kindes.* Leipzig: Greiben.

Sears, R. R. (1975). Your ancients revisited: A history of child development. In E. M. Hetherington, (Ed.), *Review of child development research* (vol. 5). Chicago: University of Chicago Press.

Senn, M. J. E. (1975). Insights on the child development movement in the United States. *Monographs of the Society for Research in Child Development, 40* (3–4, Serial No. 161).

Spock, B. M. (1976). *Baby and child care* (4th ed.). New York: Hawthorne Books. (Original work published in 1946 as *The commonsense book of baby and child care*)

Thomas, A., & Chess, S. (1977). *Temperament and development.* New York: Brunner-Mazel.

Tucker, M. J. (1974). The child as beginning and end: Fifteenth- and sixteenth-century English childhood. In L. de Mause (Ed.), *The history of childhood* (pp. 229–257). New York: Psychohistory Press.

Watson, J. B. (1924). *Psychology from the standpoint of a behaviorist* (2nd ed.). Philadelphia: Lippincott.

Watson, J. B., & Rayner, R. (1920). Conditioned emotional reactions. *Journal of Experimental Psychology, 3,* 1–14.

Watson, J. B., & Watson, R. R. (1928). *Psychological care of infant and child.* New York: W. W. Norton.

Wilson, R. S. (1974). Twins: Mental development in the preschool years. *Developmental Psychology, 10*, 580–588.

Chapter 2: Egg and Sperm Formation, Genetic Determination, Fertilization, and Related Topics

Altman, L. K. (1979, April 15). Discovery may simplify prenatal test. *The Courier-Journal* (Louisville, KY).

Baker, M. L., & Dalrymple, G. V. (1978). Biological effects of diagnostic ultrasound: A review. *Radiology, 126*, 479.

Behrman, R. E. (1979). Noninfectious disorders: Disturbances of the blood. In V. C. Vaughan, R. J. McKay, & R. E. Behrman (Eds.), *Nelson textbook of pediatrics* (11th ed.) pp. 449–457). Philadelphia: W. B. Saunders.

Brown, R. L. (1944). Rate of transport of sperma in human uterus and tubes. *American Journal of Obstetrics and Gynecology, 47*, 407–411.

Carr, D. H. (1963). Chromosome studies in abortuses and stillborn infants. *Lancet, 2*, 603–606.

Carr, D. H. (1971). Chromosome studies in selected spontaneous abortions: Polyploidy in man. *Journal of Medical Genetics, 8*, 164–174.

Erickson, J. D. (1978). Down's syndrome, paternal age, maternal age and birth order. *Annals of Human Genetics, 41*, 289–298.

Falace, P., to the author, 19 October 1982.

Fanaroff, A. A. (1983). Ultrasound studies during pregnancy. *Journal of Pediatrics, 103*, 406.

Gemzell, C. A., Roos, P., & Loeffler, F. E. (1968). Follicle stimulating hormone extracted from human pituitary. In S. Behrman & R. W. Kistner (Eds.), *Progress in infertility* (pp. 375–392). Boston: Little, Brown.

Gluck, L., Kulovich. M. V., Borer, R. C., Brenner, P. H., Anderson, G. C., & Spellacy, W. N. (1971). Diagnosis of the respiratory distress syndrome by amniocentesis. *American Journal of Obstetrics and Gynecology, 109*, 440–445.

Hancock, J. L. (1970). The sperm cell. *Social Science Journal* (London), *6*, 31–36.

Hook, E. B., & Lindsjo, A. (1978). Down syndrome in live births by single year maternal age interval in a Swedish study: Comparison with results from a New York study. *American Journal of Human Genetics, 30*, 19–27.

Katz, M. (1978). Procedure update: Amniocentesis. *Perinatal Care, 2*, 33–34.

Mikkelsen, M., Hallberg, A., & Poulsen, M. (1976). Maternal and paternal origin of extra chromosomes in trisomy 21. *Human Genetics, 32*, 17–21.

Moore, K. M. (1977). *The developing human* (2nd. ed.). Philadelphia: W. B. Saunders.

Niswander, K. R. (1981). *Obstetrics.* Boston: Little, Brown.

Nylander, P. P. S. (1969). The frequency of twinning in a rural community in Western Nigeria. *Annals of Human Genetics, 33*, 41–44.

Page, E. W., Villee, C. A., & Villee, D. B. (1976). Human reproduction: The core content of obstetrics. *Gynecology and Perinatal Medicine.* Philadelphia: W. B. Saunders.

Pettersson, F., Smedby, B., & Lindmark, G. (1976). Outcome of twin birth: Review of 1636 children born in twin birth. *Acta Paediatrica Scandinavica, 65*, 473–479.

Pritchard, J. A., & MacDonald, P. C. (1980). *Williams Obstetrics* (16th ed.). New York: Appleton-Century-Crofts.

Raeburn, P. (1982), May 10. Simpler, safer prenatal test developed for discovering dread sickle-cell anemia. *The Courier-Journal* (Louisville, KY).

Rhodes, P. (1965). Sex of fetus in antepartum hemorrhage. *Lancet, 2*, 718–719.

Rorvik, D. M., & Shettles, L. D. (1976). *Choose your baby's sex.* New York: Dodd, Mead.

Rothman, K. J. (1977). Fetal loss, twinning, and birth weight after oral contraceptive use. *New England Journal of Medicine, 297*, 468.

Sigler, A. T., Lilienfeld, A. M., Cohen, B. H., & Westlake, J. E. (1965). Parental age in Down's syndrome (mongolism). *Journal of Pediatrics, 67*, 631–642.

Smith, D. W. (1977). Malformation. In D. W. Smith (Ed.), *Introduction to clinical pediatrics* (2nd ed.). Philadelphia: W. B. Saunders.

Stene, J., Fischer, G., Stene, E., Mikkelsen, M., & Petersen, E. (1977). Paternal age effect in Down's syndrome. *Annals of Human Genetics, 40,* 299–306.

Uchida, I. A., & Summitt, R. A. (1979). Chromosomes and their abnormalities. In V. C. Vaughan, R. J. McKay, & R. E. Behrman (Eds.), *Nelson textbook of pediatrics* (11th ed.). Philadelphia: W. B. Saunders.

Van, J. (1983, August 1). Test for ectopic pregancy may lower maternal death rate. *Lexington (KY) Herald-Leader.*

Waterhouse, J. A. H. (1950). Twinning in twin pedigrees. *British Journal of Social Medicine, 4,* 197–216.

World's first baby from transfer of an embryo born in California. (1984, February 4). *Lexington (KY) Herald-Leader.*

Chapter 3: Prenatal Development and Environmental Effects

Abel, E. L. (1980). Smoking during pregnancy: A review of effects on growth and development of offspring. *Human Biology, 52,* 593–625.

Acker, D., Sachs, B. P., Tracey, K. J., & Wise, W. E. (1983). Abruptio placentae associated with cocaine use. *American Journal of Obstetrics and Gynecology, 146,* 220–221.

American College of Obstetrics and Gynecology (1974). *Nutrition in maternal health care.* Chicago: Author.

Andrews, J., & McGarry, J. M. (1972). A community study of smoking in pregnancy. *Journal of Obstetrics and Gynecology of the British Commonwealth, 79,* 1057–1073.

Annis, L. F. (1978). *The child before birth.* Ithaca, NY: Cornell University Press.

Antonov, A. N. (1947). Children born during the siege of Leningrad in 1942. *Journal of Pediatrics, 30,* 250–259.

Baker, S. W. (1980). Biological influences on human sex and gender. *Signs, 6,* 80–96.

Bergman, A. B., & Wiesner, L. A. (1976). Relationship of passive cigarette smoking to sudden infant death syndrome. *Pediatrics, 58,* 665–668.

Bosley, A. R. J., Sibert, J. R., & Newcombe, R. G. (1981). Effects of maternal smoking on fetal growth and nutrition. *Archives of Disease in Childhood, 56,* 727–729.

Bottoms, S. F., Kuhnert, B. R., Kuhnert, P. M., & Reese, A. L. (1982). Maternal passive smoking and fetal serum thiocyanate level. *American Journal of Obstetrics and Gynecology, 144,* 787–791.

Brien, J. F., Loomis, C. W., Tranmer, J., & McGrath, M. (1983). Disposition of ethanol in human maternal venous blood and amniotic fluid. *American Journal of Obstetrics and Gynecology, 146,* 181–186.

Bureau, M. A., Shapcott, D., Berthiaumes, Y., Monette, J., Blouin, D., Blanchard, P., & Begin, R. (1983). Maternal cigarette smoking and fetal oxygen transport: A study of P50,2,3-diphosphoglycerate, total hemoglobin, hematocrit, and type F hemoglobin in fetal blood. *Pediatrics, 72,* 22–26.

Burke, B. S., Beal, V. A., Kirkwood, S. B., & Stuart, H. C. (1943). Nutrition studies during pregnancy: 1. Problems, methods of study, and group studied. 2. Relation of prenatal nutrition to condition of infant at birth and during the first two weeks of life. 3. The relation of prenatal nutrition to pregnancy, labor and the postpartum period. *American Journal of Obstetrics and Gynecology, 46,* 38–52.

Burke, B. S., Harding, V. V., & Stuart, H. C. (1949). Nutrition studies during pregnancy: 4. Relation of protein content of mother's diet during pregnancy to birth length, birth weight, and condition of the infant at birth: Study of siblings. *Journal of Nutrition, 38,* 453–467.

Caffeine and pregnancy (1980). *FDA Drug Bulletin, 10,* 19–20.

Churchill, J., & Berendes, H. (1969). Intelligence of children whose mothers had acetonuria during pregnancy. In World Health Organization, Pan American Health Organization, *Perinatal factors affecting human development* (pp. 30–35). Washington, DC: Author.

Crosby, W. M., Metcoff, J., Costiloe, J. P., Mameesh, M., Sanstead, H. H., Jacob, R. A., McClain, P. E., Jacobson, G., Reid, W., & Burns, G. (1977). Fetal malnutrition: An appraisal of correlated factors. *American Journal of Obstetrics and Gynecology, 128,* 22–31.

Dunn, P. M. (1977). Congenital postural deformities. In D. W. Smith (Ed.), *Introduction to clinical pediatrics* (2nd ed.) (196–204). Philadelphia: W. B. Saunders.

Experts assess nutritional disorders of American women (1976). *Contemporary Obstetrics/Gynecology, 8,* 35–48.

Fogelman, K. (1980). Smoking in pregnancy and subsequent development of the child. *Child Care Health Development, 6,* 233–249.

Gadd, R. L. (1970). The liquor amnii. In E. E. Philipp, J. Barnes, & J. Newton (Eds.), *Scientific foundations of obstetrics and gynecology* (pp. 129–144). London: Wm. Heinemann.

Goldstein, H. (1977). Smoking in pregnancy: Some notes on the statistical controversy. *British Journal of Preventive and Social Medicine, 31,* 13–17.

Gregg, N. M. (1942). Congenital cataract following German measles in the mother. *Transactions of the Opthalmological Society of Australia, 3,* 35–46.

Hanson, J. W., Jones, K. L., & Smith, D. W. (1976). Fetal alcohol syndrome: Experience with 31 patients. *Journal of the American Medical Association, 235,* 1458–1460.

Haworth, J. C., Ellestad-Sayed, J. J., King. J., & Dilling, L. A. (1980). Fetal growth retardation in cigarette-smoking mothers is not due to decreased maternal food intake. *American Journal of Obstetrics and Gynecology, 137,* 719–723.

Householder, J., Hatcher, R., Burns, W., & Chasnoff, I. (1982). Infants born to narcotic-addicted mothers. *Psychological Bulletin, 92,* 453–468.

Jeans, P. C., Smith, M. B., & Stearns, G. (1955). Incidence of prematurity in relation to maternal nutrition. *Journal of the American Dietetic Association, 31,* 576–581.

Jensen, K. (1932). Differential reactions to taste and temperature in newborn infants. *Genetic Psychology Monographs, 12,* 363–479.

Johnston, C. (1981). Cigarette smoking and the outcome of human pregnancies: A status report on the consequences. *Clinical Toxicology, 18,* 189–209.

Jones, K. L., & Smith, D. W. (1973). Recognition of the fetal alcohol syndrome in early infancy. *Lancet, 2,* 999–1001.

Karim, S. M. M. (1972). *The prostoglandins.* New York: Wiley-Interscience.

Kline, J., Stein, Z. A., Susser, M., & Warburton, D. (1977). Smoking: A risk factor for spontaneous abortion. *New England Journal of Medicine, 297,* 793–796.

Kron, R. E., Kaplan, S. L., Finnegan, L. P., Litt, M., & Phoenix, M. D. (1975). The assessment of behavioral change in infants undergoing narcotic withdrawal: Comparative data from clinical and objective methods. *Addictive Diseases: An International Journal, 2,* 257–275.

Lefkowitz, M. M. (1981). Smoking during pregnancy: Long-term effects on offspring. *Developmental Psychology, 17,* 192–194.

Lenz, W., & Knapp, K. (1962). Foetal malformations due to thalidomide. *German Medical Monthly, 7,* 253–258.

Liggins, G. C. (1973). Fetal influences on myometrial contractility. *Clinical Obstetrics and Gynecology, 16,* 148–165.

Livingston, R. B. (1976). Two million children risk underfed brains. *CNI, 11,* 4–5.

Mau, G. (1980). Smoking in pregnancy—effects on embryo and fetus. *Trends in Pharmacological Sciences, 1,* 345–346.

Miller, R. W. (1979). Radiation injury. In V. C. Vaughan, R. J. McKay, & R. E. Behrman (Eds.), *Nelson textbook of pediatrics* (11th ed.) (pp. 2003–2005). Philadelphia: W. B. Saunders.

Money, J., & Ehrhardt, A. A. (1972). *Man and woman, boy and girl: Differentiation and dimorphism of gender identity.* Baltimore: Johns Hopkins University Press.

Moore, L. K. (1977). *The developing human* (2nd ed.). Philadelphia: W. B. Saunders.

Naeye, R. L. (1979, January 13). Address to a symposium on smoking sponsored by the American Heart Association. Hilton Head. SC (Reported in Study contradicts, supports pregnancy-smoking findings. (1979, January 13). *The Herald* (Lexington, KY).

Naeye, R. L. (1981). Influence of maternal cigarette smoking during pregnancy on fetal and childhood growth. *Obstetrics and Gynecology, 57,* 18–21.

Naeye, R. L., Ladis, B., & Drage, J. S. (1976). Sudden infant death syndrome. *American Journal of Diseases of Children, 180,* 1207–1210.

National Academy of Sciences, National Research Council, Food and Nutrition Board, Committee on Maternal Nutrition (1970). *Maternal nutrition and the course of pregnancy: Summary report.* Washington, DC: National Academy of Sciences.

Niswander, K. R. (1981). *Obstetrics: essentials of clinical practice* (2nd ed.). Boston: Little, Brown.

Osofsky, H. J. (1975). Relationships between nutrition during pregnancy and subsequent infant and child development. *Obstetrical and Gynecological Survey, 30,* 227–241.

Pelosi, M. A., Frattarola, M., Apuzzio, J., Langer, A., Hung, C. T., Oleske, J. M., Bai, J., & Harrigan, J. T. (1975). Pregnancy complicated by heroin addiction. *Obstetrics and Gynecology, 45,* 512–515.

Peterson, D. R. (1981). The sudden infant death syndrome—reassessment of growth retardation in relation to maternal smoking and the hypoxia hypothesis. *American Journal of Epidemiology, 113,* 583–589.

Pritchard, J. A., & MacDonald, P. C. (1980). *Williams Obstetrics* (16th ed.). New York: Appleton-Century-Crofts.

Reid, D. E. (1972). Fetal growth and physiology. In D. E. Reid, K. J. Ryan, & K. Benirschke. *Principles and management of human reproduction* (pp. 783–809). Philadelphia: W. B. Saunders.

Seeds, A. E., Jr. (1968). Amniotic fluid and fetal water metabolism. In A. C. Barnes, (Ed.), *Intra-uterine development* (pp. 129–144). Philadelphia: Lea & Fabinger.

Shepard, T. H., & Smith, D. W. (1977). Prenatal life. In D. W. Smith (Ed.), *Introduction to clinical pediatrics* (2nd ed.) (pp. 44–51). Philadelphia: W. B. Saunders.

Singer, J. E., Westphal, M., & Niswander, K. (1968). Relationship of weight gain during pregnancy to birthweight and infant growth and development in the first year of life. *Obstetrics and Gynecology, 31,* 417–423.

Sisenwein, F. E., Tejani, N. A., Boxer, H. S., & Di Giuseppe, R. (1983). Effects of maternal ethanol infusion during pregnancy on the growth and development of children at four to seven years of age. *American Journal of Obstetrics and Gynecology, 147,* 52–56.

Smith, C. (1947). Effects of maternal undernutrition upon the newborn infant in Holland. *Journal of Pediatrics, 30,* 229–243.

Stearns, G. (1958). Nutritional state of the mother prior to conception. *Journal of the American Medical Association, 168,* 1655–1659.

Steigman, A. J. (1979). Treponematoses. In V. C. Vaughan, J. R. McKay, & R. E. Behrman (Eds.), *Nelson textbook of pediatrics* (11th ed.), Ch. 10, Infectious diseases (pp. 842–851). Philadelphia: W. B. Saunders.

Stuart, M. J., Gross, S. J., Elrad, H., & Graeber, J. E. (1982). Effects of acetylsalicylic-acid ingestion on maternal and neonatal hemostasis. *New England Journal of Medicine, 307,* 909–912.

Taussig, H. B. (1962). A study of the German outbreak of phocomelia. *Journal of the American Medical Association, 180,* 1106–1114.

Visintine, A. M., Nahmias, A. J., & Josey, W. E. (1978). Genital herpes. *Perinatal Care, 2,* 32–41.

Warkany, J. (1944). Congenital malformations induced by maternal nutritional deficiency. *Journal of Pediatrics, 25,* 476–480.

White, L. R., & Sever, J. Y. (1967). Etiological agents. I. Infectious agents. In A. Rubin (Ed.), *Handbook of congenital malformations* (pp. 353–364). Philadelphia: W. B. Saunders.

White, P. (1965). Pregnancy and diabetes—medical aspects. *Medical Clinics North America, 49,* 1015.

Witter, F., & King, T. M. (1980). Cigarettes and pregnancy. *Progress in Clinical and Biological Research, 36,* 83–92.

Chapter 4: Birth and the Neonatal Period

Adler, A. (1927). *The practice and theory of individual psychology* (P. Radin, Trans.). New York: Harcourt, Brace.

Altus, D. W. 1967. Birth order and its sequelae. *International Journal of Psychiatry, 3*, 23–39.

Apgar, V. A. (1953). A proposal for a new method of evaluation of the newborn infant. *Current Researches in Anesthesia and Analgesia, 32*, 260–267.

Babson, S. G., & Clarke, N. G. (1983). Relationship between infant death and maternal age. *Journal of Pediatrics, 103*, 391–393.

Bane, M. J. (1976). *Here to stay: American families in the twentieth century.* New York: Basic Books.

Barden, T. P. (1977). Management of premature labor. In R. E. Behrman (Ed.), *Neonatal-perinatal medicine* (pp. 49–56). St. Louis: C. V. Mosby.

Barnard, K. (1972). *A Program of stimulation for infants born prematurely.* Unpublished manuscript. University of Washington, Seattle.

Barnard, K. (1975). *State of the art, nursing: High risk infants.* Unpublished manuscript. University of Washington, Seattle.

Barnett, C. R., Leiderman, P. H., Srobstein, R., & Klaus, M. H. (1970). Neonatal separation: The maternal side of interactional deprivation. *Pediatrics, 45*, 197–205.

Behrman, R. E. (1979). The fetus and the neonatal infant. In V. C. Vaughan, R. J. McKay, & R. E. Behrman (Eds.). *Nelson textbook of pediatrics* (11th ed.) (pp. 379–468). Philadelphia: W. B. Saunders.

Belmont, L., & Marolla, F. A. 1973. Birth order, family sizes, and intelligence. *Science, 182*, 1096–1101.

Bohen, H., & Viveros-Long, A. (1981). *Balancing jobs and family life.* Philadelphia: Temple University Press.

Bottoms, S. F., Rosen, M. G., & Sokol, R. J. (1980). The increase in the cesarean birth rate. *New England Journal of Medicine, 302*, 559–563.

Brackbill, Y. (1971). Cumulative effects of continuous stimulation on arousal level in infants. *Child Development, 42*, 17–26.

Brackbill, Y. (1978, April 17). Lasting behaviorial effects of obstetric medication on children: Research findings and public health implications. *Hearings.* Senate Committee on Human Resources, Subcommittee on Health and Scientific Research. 95th Cong. 2nd sess.

Bradley, R. W. (1982). Using birth order and sibling dynamics in career counseling. *Personnel and Guidance Journal, 61*, 25–31.

Brazelton, T. B. (1973). *Neonatal behavioral assessment scale: Clinics on developmental medicine* No. 50. London: Spastics International Medical Publications.

Butcher, R. E. (1979). *Behavioral effects from prenatal exposure to psychotropic drugs.* Paper presented at the biennial meeting of the Society for Research in Child Development, San Francisco.

Campbell, D. P. (1971). Admissions policies: Side effects and their implications. *American Psychologist, 26*, 636–647.

Clarke-Stewart, K. A. 1977. *Child care in the family: A review of research and some propositions for policy.* New York: Academic Press.

Condon, W. S., & Sander, L. W. (1974). Neonate movement is synchronized with adult speech: Interactional participation and language acquisition. *Science, 183*, 99–101.

Crook, C. K. (1976). Neonatal sucking: Effects of quantity of the response-contingent fluid upon sucking rhythm and heart rate. *Journal of Experimental Child Psychology, 21*, 539–548.

Crook, C. K., & Lipsitt, L. P. (1976). Neonatal nutritive sucking: Effects of taste stimulation upon sucking rhythm and heart rate. *Child Development, 47*, 518–522.

Drillien, C. M. (1961). Longitudinal study of growth and development of prematurely and maturely born children: VII. Mental development 2-5 years. *Archives of Diseases of Childhood, 36*, 233–240.

Drillien, C. M., Thomson, A. J. M., & Bargoyne, K. (1980). Low birth weight children at early school-age: A longitudinal study. *Developmental Medicine and Child Neurology, 22*, 26–47.

Dubowitz, L. M. S., Dubowitz, V., & Goldberg, C. (1970). Clinical assessment of gestational age in the newborn infant. *Journal of Pediatrics, 77*, 1–10.

Dye, N. S. (1980). History of childbirth in America. *Signs, 6*, 97–108.

Eisner, V., Brazie, J. V., Pratt, M. W., & Hexter, A. C. (1979). The risk of low birth weight. *American Journal of Public Health, 69,* 887–893.

Engen, T., Lipsitt, L. P., & Kaye, H. (1963). Olfactory responses and adaptation in the human neonate. *Journal of Comparative Physiology and Psychology, 56,* 73–77.

Ewy, D., & Ewy, R. (1976). *Preparation for childbirth: A Lamaze guide.* Boulder, CO: Pruett.

Fantz, R. L. (1958). Pattern vision of young infants. *Psychological Record, 8,* 43–47.

Fantz, R. L. (1961). The origins of form perception. *Scientific American, 204,* 66–72.

Fantz, R. L. (1963). Pattern vision in newborn infants. *Science, 140,* 296–297.

Finster, M. (1974). The placental transfer of drugs. In S. M. Shnider, & F. Moya (Eds.), *The anesthesiologist, mother and newborn.* Baltimore: Williams & Wilkins.

Friedman, E. (1978). *Labor: Clinical evaluation and management* (2nd ed.). New York: Appleton-Century-Crofts.

Glasgow, L. A., & Overall, J. C., Jr. (1979). The fetus and neonatal infant: Infections. In V. C. Vaughan, R. J. McKay, & R. E. Behrman (Eds.), *Nelson textbook of pediatrics* (11th ed.) (pp. 468–496). Philadelphia: W. B. Saunders.

Haith, M. M. (1979). Visual competence in early infancy. In R. Held, H. Leibowitz, & H. L. Teuber (Eds.), *Handbook of sensory physiology* (Vol. 8). Berlin: Springer.

Illingworth, R. S. (1975). *The Development of the infant and young child: Normal and abnormal.* New York: Churchill Livingstone.

Jeffcoate, J. A., Humphrey, M. E., & Lloyd, J. K. (1979). Role perception and response to stress in fathers and mothers following preterm delivery. *Social Science and Medicine, 13A,* 139–145.

Jensen, K. (1932). Differential reactions to taste and temperature stimuli in newborn infants. *Genetic Psychology Monographs, 12,* 363–479.

Kaplan, S. (1979). The cardiovascular system. In V. C. Vaughan, R. J. McKay, & R. E. Behrman (Eds.), *Nelson textbook of pediatrics* (11th ed.) (pp. 1249–1352). Philadelphia: W. B. Saunders.

Klein, M., & Stern, L. (1971). Low birth weight and the battered child syndrome. *American Journal of Diseases of Children, 122,* 15–18.

Koch, H. 1956. Some emotional attitudes of the young child in relation to characteristics of his siblings. *Child Development, 27,* 393–426.

Korner, A., Kraemer, H. C., Haffner, M. C., & Cosper, L. (1975). Effects of waterbed gestation on premature infants: A pilot study. *Pediatrics, 56,* 361–367.

Landis, C. (1982), August 31. Home birth controversy didn't scare this couple. *The Lexington (KY) Leader.*

Leavitt, J. W. (1980). Birthing and anesthesia: The debate over twilight sleep. *Signs, 6,* 147–164.

Leboyer, F. (1975). *Birth without violence.* New York: Knopf.

Leonard, C. H., Irvin, N., Ballard, R. A., et al. (1979). Preliminary observations on the behavior of children present at the birth of a sibling. *Pediatrics, 64,* 949–951.

Levitan, S. A., & Belous, R. S. (1981). *What's happening to the American family?* Baltimore: Johns Hopkins University Press.

Liggins, G. C., & Howie, R. N. (1972). A controlled trial of antepartum glucocorticoid treatment for prevention of the respiratory distress syndrome in premature infants. *Pediatrics, 50,* 515–525.

Liggins, G. C., & Howie, R. (1974). The prevention of RDS by maternal steroid therapy. In L. Gluck (Ed.), *Modern perinatal medicine.* Chicago: Year Book Medical Publishers.

Lozoff, B. (1982). Birth in non-industrial societies. In M. H. Klaus, & M. O. Robertson (Eds.), *Birth, interaction and attachment* (Johnson & Johnson Pediatric Round Table No. 6) (pp. 1–6). New Brunswick, NJ: Johnson & Johnson.

MacDonald, A. P., Jr. (1969). Birth order and religious affiliation. *Developmental Psychology, 1,* 628.

MacFarlane, A. (1977). *The psychology of childbirth.* Cambridge, MA: Harvard University Press.

Main, D. M., Main, E. K., & Maurer, M. M. (1983). Cesarean section versus vaginal delivery for the breech fetus weighing less than 1,500 grams. *American Journal of Obstetrics and Gynecology, 145,* 580–584.

Martin, J. N., Harris, B. A., Jr., Huddleston, J. F., Morrison, J. C., Probst, M. G., Wiser, W. L., Perlis, H. W., & Davidson, J. T. (1983). Vaginal delivery following previous cesarean birth. *American Journal of Obstetrics and Gynecology, 146,* 255–262.

Muir, D., & Field, J. (1979). Newborn infants orient to sounds. *Child Development, 50,* 431–436.

Nelson, K. B., & Broman, S. H. (1977). Perinatal risk factors in children with serious motor and mental handicaps. *Annals of Neurology, 2,* 371–377.

Newman, L. F. (1981). Social and sensory environment of low birth weight infants in a special care nursery: An anthropological investigation. *Journal of Nervous and Mental Disease, 168,* 448–455.

Otten, A. L., (1984, Jan. 19). Special surgery: Controversy surrounds the increasing number of caesarean deliveries. *Wall Street Journal, LXIV,* p. 1 & p. 12.

Pakter, J. (1980, Feb. 15). Address to the annual meeting of the American Public Health Association. Reported in Mortality lower in LBW, beech infants delivered by cesarean. *Family Practice News,* 10.

Poole, A. & Kuhn, A. 1973 Family size and ordinal positions: Correlates of academic success. *Journal of Biosocial Science, 5,* 51–59.

Prechtl, H., & Beintema, O. (1964). *The neurological examination of the newborn infant.* London: Heinemann.

Rank, O. (1929). *The trauma of birth.* New York: Harcourt, Brace.

Reid, D. E. (1972). Fetal growth and physiology. In D. E. Reid, R. J. Ryan, & K. Benirschke, *Principles and management of human reproduction* (pp. 783–809). Philadelphia: W. B. Saunders.

Rodier, P. M. (1979). *The morphology of brain damage.* Paper presented at the biennial meeting of the Society for Research in Child Development, San Francisco.

Schaefer, M., Hatcher, R. P., & Barglow, P. D. (1980). Prematurity and infant stimulation:

A review of research. *Child psychiatry and human development, 10,* 199–212.

Schmitt, B., & Kempe, C. H. (1979). Abuse and neglect of children. In V. C. Vaughan, R. J. McKay, & R. E. Behrman (Eds.), *Nelson textbook of pediatrics* (11th ed.) (pp. 120–126). Philadelphia: W. B. Saunders.

Shearer, M. H. (1979). FDA action on the Brackbill-Broman report on long-term effects of obstetric medication. *Birth and the Family Journal, 6* 199–124.

Sherrod, L. R. (1979). Social cognition in infants: Attention to the human face. *Infant Behavior and Development, 2,* 279–294.

Trause, M. A., & Kramer, L. I. (1983). The effects of premature birth on parents and their relationship. *Developmental Medicine and Child Neurology, 25,* 459–465.

Wazach, S. (1980, February 15). Address to District VII meeting, American College of Obstetricians and Gynecologists. Reported in C-section for breech position is justified. *Family Practice News,* 10.

Wertheimer, M. (1961). Psycho-motor coordination of auditory-visual space at birth. *Science,* 134, 1692.

Wertz, R. W., & Wertz, D. C. (1977). *Lying-in.* New York: Free Press.

Wolff, P. H. (1963). Observations on the early development of smiling. In B. M. Foss (Ed.), *Determinants of infant behaviour* (Vol. 2). London: Methuen.

Young, D. (1979). Cesarean in the United States: A sobering situation. *ICEA News, 18,* 6–7.

Young, D. (1982). Policy reversal for vaginal delivery after cesarean. *ICEA News, 21,* 1.

Chapter 5: Growth of Basic Functions

Ainsworth, M. D. S., & Bell, S. M. (1977). Infant crying and maternal responsiveness: A rejoinder to Gewirtz and Boyd. *Child Development, 48,* 1208–1219.

André-Thomas, C. Y., & Ste. Anne-Dargassies, S. (1952). *Études neurologiques sur le nouveauné et le jeune nourrisson* Paris: Masson.

Babson, S. G., & Clarke, N. G. (1983). Relationship

between infant death and maternal age. *Journal of Pediatrics, 103*, 391–393.

Bell, S., & Ainsworth, M. D. S. (1972). Infant crying and maternal responsiveness. *Child Development, 43*, 1171–1190.

Berg, W. K., & Berg, K. M. (1979). Psychophysiological development in infancy: State, sensory functions and attention. In J. D. Osofsky (Ed.), *Handbook of infant development*, (pp. 283–343). New York: John Wiley & Sons.

Booth, C. L., Leonard, H. L, & Thoman, E. B. (1980). Sleep states and behavior patterns in preterm and fullterm infants. *Neuropediatrics, 11*, 354–364.

Brazelton, T. B. (1969). *Infants and mothers.* New York: Dell.

Buss, A. H., & Plomin, R. A. (1975). *A temperament theory of personality development.* New York: John Wiley & Sons.

Cohen, M. M., Jr., & Hooley, J. R. (1977). Oral disorders. In D. W. Smith (Ed.), *Introduction to clinical pediatrics* (2nd ed.) (pp. 340–347). Philadelphia: W. B. Saunders.

Davis, N. E. (1977). Sudden infant death syndrome. In D. W. Smith (Ed.), Introduction to clinical pediatrics (2nd ed.) (pp. 413–415). Philadelphia: W. B. Saunders.

Dennis, W. (1941). Infant development under conditions of restricted practice and of minimal social stimulation. *Genetic Psychology Monographs, 23*, 143–191.

di Leo, J. H. (1967). Developmental evaluation of very young infants. In J. Hellmuth (Ed.), *Exceptional infant* (Vol. 1). New York: Brunner/Mazel.

Dreyfus-Brisac, C. (1970). Ontogenesis of human sleep in human prematures after 32 weeks of conceptual age. *Developmental Psychobiology, 3*, 91–121.

Eichorn, D. H. (1979). Physical development: Current foci of research. In J. D. Osofsky (Ed.), *Handbook of infant development* (pp. 253–282). New York: John Wiley & Sons.

Emde, R. N., Gaensbauer, T. J., & Harmon, R. J. (1976). Emotional expression in infancy: A biobehavioral study. *Psychological Issues* (Vol. X, No. 1) (Monograph 37). New York: International Universities Press.

Etzel, B. C., & Gewirtz, J. L. (1967). Experimental modification of caretaker-maintained high-rate operant crying in a 6- and a 20-week-old infant (Infans tyrannotearus): Extinction of crying with reinforcement of eye contact and smiling. *Journal of Experimental Child Psychology, 5*, 303–317.

Gesell, A. T. (1928). *Infancy and human growth.* New York: Macmillan.

Gesell, A. T. (1934). *An atlas of infant behavior.* New Haven, CT: Yale University Press.

Gewirtz, J. L., & Boyd, E. F. (1977). Does maternal responding imply reduced infant crying? A critique of the 1972 Bell and Ainsworth report. *Child Development, 48*, 1200–1207.

Goren, C. C., Sarty, M., & Wu, P. Y. K. (1975). Visual following and pattern discrimination of face-like stimuli by newborn infants. *Pediatrics 56*, 544–549.

Gotts, E. E. (1972). Newborn walking. *Science, 177*, 1057–1058.

Gregg, C. L., Haffner, M. E., & Korner, A. F. (1976). The relative efficacy of vestibular-proprioceptive stimulation and the upright position in enhancing visual pursuit in neonates. *Child Development, 47*, 309–314.

Guthrie, R. D., Prueitt, J. L., Murphy, J. H., Hodson, W. A., Wennberg, R. P., & Woodrum, D. E. The newborn. In D. W. Smith (Ed.), Introduction to clinical pediatrics (2nd ed.) (pp. 52–65). Philadelphia: W. B. Saunders.

Hales, D. H., Lozoff, B., Sousa, R., & Kennell, J. H. (1977). Defining the limits of the maternal sensitive period. *Developmental Medicine and Child Neurology, 19*, 454–461.

Harper, R. M., Leake, B., Hoffman, H., Walter, D. O., Hoppenbrouwers, T., Hodgman, J., & Sterman, M. B. (1981). Periodicity of sleep states is altered in infants at risk for the sudden infant death syndrome. *Science, 213*, 1030–1032.

Hoppenbrouwers, T., & Hodgman, J. E. (1982). Sudden infant death syndrome (SIDS): An integration of ontogenetic, pathologic, physiologic and epidemiologic factors. *Neuropediatrics,* 13 (Supplement), 36–41.

Illingworth, R. S. (1975). *The development of the infant and young child: Normal and abnormal.* New York: Churchill Livingstone.

Klaus, M. H., & Kennell, J. H. (1976). Maternal-infant bonding: The impact of early separation or loss on family development. St. Louis: Mosby.

Korner, A. F., & Thoman, E. B. (1970). Visual alertness in neonates as evoked by maternal care. *Journal of Experimental Child Psychology, 10,* 67–78.

Lipsitt, L. P., & Jacklin, C. N. (1971). Cardiac deceleration and its stability in human newborns. *Developmental Psychology, 5,* 535.

Lounsbury, M. L., & Bates, J. E. (1982). The cries of infants of differing levels of perceived temperamental difficultness: Acoustical properties and effects on listeners. *Child Development, 53,* 677–686.

Matheny A. P., Wilson, R. S., Dolan, A. B., & Kranz, J. Z. (1981). Behavioral contrasts in twinship: Stability and patterns of differences in childhood. *Child Development, 52,* 579–588.

McCall, R. B. (1971). Behavioural and other measurements in the neonate. *Proceedings of the Royal Society of Medicine, 64,* 465.

McGraw, M. (1940). Neural maturation as exemplified by the achievement of bladder control. *Journal of Pediatrics, 16,* 580–590.

McGraw, M. (1943). Influence of cortical development upon early behavior patterns. In M. McGraw, *Neuromuscular maturation of the human infant.* New York: Columbia University Press.

Naeye, R. L. (1973). Hypoxemia and sudden infant death syndrome. *New England Journal of Medicine, 289,* 1167–1170.

Naeye, R. L. (1980). Sudden infant death. *Scientific American, 242,* 56–62.

Niswander, K. P. (1981). Obstetrics: Essentials of clinical practice (2nd ed.). Boston: Little, Brown.

Owen, G. M., Kram, K. M., Garry, P. J., Lower, J. E., & Lubin, A. H. (1974). *A study of nutritional status of preschool children in the United States, 53* (Pt. 2, Suppl.), 597–646.

Packer, M., & Rosenblatt, D. (1979). Issues in the study of social behaviour in the first week of life. In D. Shaffer, & J. Dunn (Eds.), *The first year of life* (pp. 7–35). New York: John Wiley & Sons.

Parmelee, A. H., Wenner, W. H., & Schulz, H. R. (1964). Infant sleep patterns from birth to 16 weeks of age. *Journal of Pediatrics, 65,* 576–582.

Parmelee, A. H., Wenner, W. H., Akiyama, Y., Schultz, M., & Stern, E. (1967). Sleep states in premature infants. *Developmental Medicine and Child Neurology, 9,* 70–77.

Piaget, J. (1952). *The origins of intelligence in children.* New York: International Universities Press.

Prechtl, H. F. R. (1965). Problems of behavioral studies in the newborn infant. In D. S. Lehrman, R. A. Hinde, & E. Shaw (Eds.), *Advances in the study of behavior.* New York: Academic Press.

Prechtl, H. F. R., Akiyama, Y., Zinkin, P., & Grant, D. K. (1968). Polygraphic studies in the full-term newborn. I. Technical aspects and qualitative analysis. In M. C. Bax & R. C. McKeith (Eds.), *Studies in infancy.* London: Heinemann.

Roffwarg, H. P., Dement, W. C., & Fisher, C. (1964). Preliminary observations of the sleep-dream patterns in neonates, children, and adults. In E. Harms (Ed.), *Problems of sleep and dreams in children.* New York: Macmillan.

Roffwarg, H. P., Muzio, J. N., & Dement, W. C. (1966). Ontogenetic development of the human sleep-dream cycle. *Science, 152,* 604–619.

Rothbart, M. J. (1981). Measurement of temperament in infancy. *Child Development, 52,* 569–578.

Sander, L. (1977). The regulation of exchange in the early infant-caretaker system and some aspects of the context-content relationship. In M. Lewis & L. Rosenblum (Eds.), *Interaction, conversation and the development of language.* New York: John Wiley & Sons.

Schaffer, H. R., & Emerson, P. E. (1964). The development of social attachment in infancy. *Monographs of the Society for Research in Child Development, 29* (3, Serial No. 94).

Schour, I., & Massler, M. (1940). Studies in tooth development: the growth pattern of human teeth, Part II. *Journal of the American Dental Association, 27,* 1918–1931.

Shirley, M. (1933). *The first two years: A study of twenty-five babies. Vol. 1, Postural and loco-*

motor development. Minneapolis: University of Minnesota Press.

Smith, D. W., & Owens, J. W. M. (1977). Infancy and childhood. In D. W. Smith (Ed.), *Introduction to clinical pediatrics* (2nd ed.) (pp. 66–73). Philadelphia: W. B. Saunders.

Sostek, A. M., & Anders, T. F. (1977). Relationships among the Brazelton Neonatal Scale, Bayley Infant Scales and early temperament. *Child Development, 48*, 320–323.

Southall, D. P. (1983). Home monitoring and its role in the sudden infant death syndrome. *Pediatrics, 72*, 133–137.

Sroufe, A. L. (1979). Socioemotional development. In J. D. Osofsky (Ed.), *Handbook of infant development* (pp. 462–516). New York: John Wiley & Sons.

Stern, E., Parmelee, A. H., & Harris, M. Sleep state periodicity in prematures and young infants. *Developmental Psychobiology, 6*, 357–365.

Thelen, E., Fisher, D. M., Ridley-Johnson, R., & Griffin, N. J. (1982). Effects of body build and arousal on newborn infant stepping. *Developmental Psychology, 15*, 447–453.

Thomas, A., & Chess, S. (1977). *Temperament and development*. New York: Brunner-Mazel.

Torgerson, A. M., & Kringlen, C. (1978). Genetic aspects of temperamental differences in twins. *Journal of the American Academy of Child Psychiatry, 17*, 433–444.

Valdes-Dapena, M. (1979). Sudden unexpected death in infancy. In V. C. Vaughan, R. J. McKay, & R. E. Behrman (Eds.) *Nelson textbook of pediatrics* (11th ed.) (pp. 1980–1981). Philadelphia: W. B. Saunders.

Vaughan, V. C. (1979). Developmental pediatrics: growth and development. In V. C. Vaughan, R. J. McKay, & R. E. Behrman (Eds.), *Nelson textbook of pediatrics* (11th ed.) (pp. 10–46). Philadelphia: W. B. Saunders.

Walk, R. D. (1981). *Perceptual development*. Monterey, CA: Brooks-Cole.

Watson, J. (1972). Smiling, cooing and "the game." *Merrill-Palmer Quarterly, 4*, 323–339.

Wolff, P. H. (1959). Observations on newborn infants. *Psychosomatic Medicine, 21*, 110–118.

Zelazo, P. R. (1976). From reflexive to instrumental behavior. In L. P. Lipsitt, (Ed.), *Developmental Psychobiology* (pp. 87–104). Hillsdale, NJ: Lawrence Erlbaum Associates.

Zelazo, P. R., Zelazo, N., & Kolb, S. (1972). "Walking" in the newborn. *Science, 177*, 1058–1059.

Chapter 6: Infant Nutrition, Infant Feeding and Other Routines

Ament, M. (1979). Intestinal malabsorption. In V. C. Vaughan, R. J. McKay, & R. E. Behrman (Eds.), *Nelson textbook of pediatrics* (11th ed.) (pp 1075–1090). Philadelphia: W. B. Saunders.

American Academy of Pediatrics, Committee on Drugs (1983). The transfer of drugs and other chemicals into human breast milk. *Pediatrics, 72*, 375–383.

American Academy of Pediatrics, Committee on Nutrition (1983). The use of whole cow's milk in infancy. *Pediatrics, 72*, 253–255.

Barness, L. A. (1979). Nutrition and nutritional disorders. In V. C. Vaughan, R. J. McKay, & R. E. Behrman (Eds.), *Nelson textbook of pediatrics* (11th ed.) (pp. 173–236). Philadelphia: W. B. Saunders.

Brams, M., & J. Maloney (1983). "Nursing bottle caries" in breast-fed children. *Journal of Pediatrics, 103*, 415–416.

Brook, C. G., Lloyd, J. K., & Wolff, O. H. (1972). Relation between age of onset of obesity and size and number of adipose cells. *British Medical Journal, 2*, 25–27.

Butterfield, F. (1982). *China*. New York: Times Books.

Chisolm, J. J., Jr. (1979). Chemical and drug poisoning: Lead. In V. C. Vaughan, R. J. McKay, & R. E. Behrman (Eds.), *Nelson textbook of pediatrics* (11th ed.) (pp. 2025–2029). Philadelphia: W. B. Saunders.

Cohen, S. N., & Strebel, L. (1979). Drug therapy: Special problems of drug toxicity. In V. C. Vaughan, R. J. McKay, & R. E. Behrman (Eds.), *Nelson textbook of pediatrics* (11th ed.) (pp. 334–336). Philadelphia: W. B. Saunders.

Eichorn, D. H. (1979). Physical development: Current foci of research. In J. D. Osofsky (Ed.), *Handbook of infant development* (pp. 253–282). New York: John Wiley & Sons.

Gartner, L. M. (1978). *Medical value of breastfeed-*

ing. Paper presented at the annual meeting of the American Orthopsychiatric Association.

Goodhart, R. S., & Shils, M. E. (1973). *Modern nutrition in health and disease* (5th ed.). Philadelphia: Lea & Febinger.

Guthrie, R. D., Prueitt, J. L., Murphy, J. H., Hodson, W. A., Wennberg, R. P., & Woodrum, D. E. (1977). The newborn. In D. W. Smith (Ed.), *Introduction to clinical pediatrics* (2nd ed.) (pp. 52–65). Philadelphia: W. B. Saunders.

Hall, C. S., & Lindzey, G. (1957). *Theories of personality.* New York: John Wiley & Sons.

Heinstein, M. (1966). *Child rearing in California.* Berkeley, CA: Department of Public Health, *Bureau of Maternal and Child Health.*

Jakobsson, I., & Lindberg, T. (1983). Cow's milk proteins cause infantile colic in breast-fed infants: A double-blind crossover study. *Pediatrics, 71,* 268–271.

Jelliffe, D. B., & Jelliffe, E. F. P. (1977). Current concepts in nutrition. Breast is best: Modern meanings. *New England Journal of Medicine, 297,* 912–915.

Latham, M. C., McGandy, R. B., McCann, M. B., & Stare, F. J. (1970). *Scope manual on nutrition.* Kalamazoo, MI: Upjohn.

Lozoff, B. (1979). Ordinary care of the newborn infant: Breast feeding. In V. C. Vaughan, R. J. McKay & R. E. Behrman (Eds.), *Nelson textbook of pediatrics* (11th ed.) (pp. 396–398). Philadelphia: W. B. Saunders.

Lyon, M. L., Chilver, G., White, D. G., & Wollett, A. (1981). Current maternal attitudes to infant feeding methods. *Child: Care, Health and Development, 7,* 145–151.

Martinez, G. A., & Dodd, D. A. (1983). 1981 milk feeding patterns in the United States during the first 12 months of life. *Pediatrics, 71,* 166–170.

Owen, G. M., Kram, K. M., Garry, P. J., Lowe, J. E., & Lubin, A. H. (1974). A study of nutritional status of preschool children in the United States, 1968–70. *Pediatrics, 53* (Pt. 2, Suppl.), 597–646.

Popkin, B. M., Bilsborrow, R. E., & Akin, J. S. (1982). Breast-feeding patterns in low-income countries. *Science, 218,* 1088–1093.

Pritchard, J. A., & MacDonald, P. C. (1980). *Wil-liams obstetrics* (16th ed.). New York: Appleton-Century-Crofts.

Schoen, E. J., Cunningham, G. C., & Koch, R. (1983). More on newborn screening for phenylketonuria: Recommendations of the Committee on Genetics. *Pediatrics, 72,* 139–140.

Scott, C. R. (1977). Inborn enzymatic errors. In D. W. Smith (Ed.), *Introduction to clinical pediatrics* (2nd ed.) (pp. 386–393). Philadelphia: W. B. Saunders.

Sears, R. R., Maccoby, E. E., & Levin, H. (1957). *Patterns of child rearing.* Evanston, IL: Row-Peterson.

Shelton, P. G., Berkowitz, R. J., & Forrester, D. J. (1977). Nursing bottle caries. *Pediatrics, 59,* 7776.

Smith, D. W., & Owens, J. W. M. (1977). Infancy and childhood. In D. W. Smith (Ed.), *Introduction to clinical pediatrics* (2nd ed.) (pp. 66–73). Philadelphia: W. B. Saunders.

Smith, N. J. (1977). Nutrition in infancy and early childhood, including obesity. In D. W. Smith (Ed.), *Introduction to clinical pediatrics* (2nd ed.) (pp. 88–102). Philadelphia: W. B. Saunders.

Update (1981–1982). *Childbirth Educator, 1,* 51.

Wolf, M. (1972). *Women and the family in rural Taiwan.* Stanford, CA: Stanford University Press.

Woodruff, C. W. (1976). Milk intolerance. *Nutrition Review, 34,* 33.

Chapter 7: Perceptual Development in Infancy

Abramson, A. S., & Lisker, L. (1970). Discriminability along the voicing continuum: Cross-language tests. *Proceedings of the Sixth International Congress of Phonetic Sciences* (pp. 569–573). Prague: Academia.

Alegria, J., & Noirot, E. (1978). Neonate orientation behaviour towards human voice. *International Journal of Behavioral Development, 1,* 291–312.

Allen, T. W., Walker, K., Symonds, L., & Marcell, M. (1977). Intrasensory and intersensory perception of temporal sequences during infancy. *Developmental Psychology, 13,* 225–229.

André-Thomas, C.Y., & Autgaerden, S. (1961). Au-dibilité spontané de la voix maternelle au-dibilité conditioné à toute autre voix. *Presse médicale, 71,* 64–76.

Barten, S., Birns, B., & Ronch, J. (1971). Individual differences in the visual pursuit behavior of neonates. *Child Development, 42,* 313–319.

Bell, R. Q., & Costello, N. S. (1964). Three tests for sex differences in tactile sensitivity in the newborn. *Biologia Neonatorum, 7,* 335–347.

Birch, H. G., & Lefford, A. (1963). Intersensory development in children. *Monographs of the Society for Research in Child Development, 28* (5, Serial No. 89).

Birch, H. G., & Lefford, A. (1967). Visual differentiation, intersensory integration, and voluntary motor control. *Monographs of the Society for Research in Child Development, 32* (2, Serial No. 110).

Bornstein, M. H., Kessen, W., & Weiskopf, S. (1976). The categories of hue in infancy. *Science, 193,* 201–202.

Bower, T. G. R. (1965a). Stimulus variables determining space perception in infants. *Science, 149,* 88–89.

Bower, T. G. R. (1965b). The determinants of perceptual unity in infancy. *Psychonomic Science, 3.,* 323–324.

Bower, T. G. R. (1972). Object perception in infants. *Perception, 1,* 15–30.

Bower, T. G. R. (1975). Infant perception of the third dimension and object concept development. In L. B. Cohen, & P. Salapatek (Eds.), *Infant perception: From sensation to cognition* (Vol. 2, pp. 33–50). New York: Academic Press.

Bower, T. G. R., (1982). *Development in infancy* (2nd ed.). San Francisco: W. H. Freeman.

Bower, T. G. R., Broughton, J. M., & Moore, M. K. (1970a). Infant responses to approaching objects: An indicator of response to distal variables. *Perception and Psychophysics, 9,* 193–196.

Bower, T. G. R., Broughton, J. M., & Moore, M. K. (1970b). Demonstration of intention in the reaching behavior of neonate humans. *Nature, 228,* 5272.

Bowlby, J. (1958). The nature of the child's tie to his mother. *International Journal of Psychoanalysis, 39,* 350–373.

Brazelton, T. B. (1973). *Neonatal behavioral assessment scale. Clinics in developmental medicine* No. 50 (Spastics International Medical Publications). Philadelphia: Lippincott.

Bronson, G. (1974). The postnatal growth of visual capacity. *Child Development, 45,* 873–890.

Butterfield, E. C., & Cairns, G. F., Jr. (1974). Whether infants perceive linguistically is uncertain, and if they did, its practical importance would be equivocal. In R. L. Schiefelbusch, & L. L. Lloyd (Eds.), *Language perspectives: Acquisition, retardation, and intervention* (pp. 75–102). Baltimore. University Park Press.

Butterfield, E. C., & Siperstein, G. N. (1972). Influence of contingent auditory stimulation upon non-nutritive suckle. In J. Bosma (Ed.), *Third Symposium on oral sensation and perception: The mouth of the infant.* Springfield, IL: Charles C Thomas.

Campos, J. J. Langer, A., & Krowitz, A. (1970). Cardiac responses on the visual cliff in pre-locomotor human infants. *Science, 170,* 169–197.

Campos, J. J., Hiatt, S., Ramsey, D., Henderson, C., & Svejda, M. (1978). The emergence of fear on the visual cliff. In M. Lewis & L. A. Rosenblum (Eds.), *The development of affect* (Vol. 2). New York: Plenum.

Campos, J. J., Svejda, M., Bertenthal, B., Benson, N., & Schmid, D. (1981). *Self-produced locomotion and wariness of heights: New evidence from training studies.* Paper presented at the biennial meeting of the Society for Research in Child Development, Boston.

Caron, A. J., Caron, R. F., Caldwell, R. C., & Weiss, S. J. (1973). Infant perception of the structural properties of the face. *Developmental Psychology, 9,* 385–399.

Cohen, L. B., De Loach, J. S., & Strauss, M. S. (1979). Infant visual perception. In J. D. Osofsky, (Ed.), *Handbook of infant development* (pp. 393–438). New York: John Wiley & Sons.

Conel, J. L. (1952). Histologic development of the cerebral cortex. In *The biology of mental health and disease* (27th Annual Conference of the Milbank Memorial Fund) (pp. 1–8). New York: Hoeber.

Cornell, E. H. (1975). Infants' visual attention to

pattern arrangement and orientation. *Child Development, 46,* 229–232.

De Caspar, A. J., & Fifer, W. P. (1980). Of human bonding: Newborns prefer their mothers' voices. *Science, 208,* 1174–1176.

Dobson, V., & Teller, D. Y. (1978). Assessment of visual acuity in human infants. In J. Armington, J. Krauskopf, & B. Wooten (Eds.), *Visual psychophysics and physiology: A volume dedicated to Lorrin Riggs.* New York: Academic Press.

Dodwell, P. C., Muir, D., & Di Franco, D. (1976). Responses of infants to visually presented objects. *Science, 194,* 209–211.

Duke-Elder, S., & Cook, C. (1963). *System of opthalmology: Vol. 3, Normal and abnormal development.* Pt. 1, Embryology. London: Henry Kimpton.

Dunkeld, J., & Bower, T. G. R. (1977). *Infant responses to impending collision.* Unpublished study, 1976. Cited in T. G. R. Bower, *A primer of infant development.* San Francisco: W. H. Freeman.

Eimas, P. D. (1974). Linguistic processing of speech by young infants. In R. L. Schiefelbusch, & L. L. Lloyd (Eds.), *Language perspectives: Acquisition, retardation, and intervention* (pp. 55–73). Baltimore: University Park Press.

Eimas, P. D. (1975a). Speech perception in early infancy. In B. L. Cohen, & P. Salapatek, (Eds.), *Infant perception: From sensation to cognition* (Vol. 2, pp. 193–231). New York: Academic Press.

Eimas, P. D. (1975b) Auditory and phonetic coding of the cues for speech: Discrimination of the r-1 distinction by young infants. *Perception and Psychophysics, 18,* 341–347.

Eimas, P. D., Siqueland, E. R., Jusczyk, P. W., & Vigorito, J. (1971). Speech perception in infants. *Science, 171,* 303–306.

Eisenberg, R. B. (1965). Auditory behavior in the human neonate: I. Methodological problems and the logical design of research procedures. *Journal of Auditory Research, 815,* 159–177.

Fagan J. F. (1974). Infant color perception. *Science, 183,* 973–975.

Fagan, J. F. (1977). An attention model of infant recognition. *Child Development, 47,* 627–638.

Fantz, R. L. (1961a). A method for studying depth perception in infants under six months of age. *Psychological Record, 11,* 27–32.

Fantz, R. L. (1961b). The origins of form perception. *Scientific American, 204,* 66–72.

Fantz, R. L. (1963). Pattern vision in newborn infants. *Science, 140,* 296–297.

Fantz, R. L. (1965). Visual perception from birth as shown by pattern selectivity. *Annals of the New York Academy of Science, 118,* 793–814.

Fantz, R. L. (1966). Pattern discrimination and selective attention as determinants of perceptual development from birth. In A. H. Kidd, & J. F. Rivoire (Eds.), *Perceptual development in children* (pp. 143–177). New York: International Universities Press.

Fantz, R. L., Fagan, J. F., & Miranda, S. B. (1975). Early visual selectivity. In L. B. Cohen, & P. Salapatek (Eds.), *Infant perception: From sensation to cognition* (Vol. 1, pp. 249–345). New York: Academic Press.

Fantz, R. L., & Nevis, S. (1967a). Pattern preference and perceptual-cognitive development in early infancy. *Merrill-Palmer Quarterly, 13,* 77–108.

Fantz, R. L., & Nevis, S. (1967b). The predictive value of changes in visual preferences in early infancy. In J. Hellmuth (Ed.), *Exceptional infant* (Vol. 1, pp. 349–414). New York: Brunner-Mazel.

Fox, R., Aslin, R. N., Shea, S. L., & Dumais, S. T. (1980). Stereopsis in human infants. *Science, 207,* 323–324.

Fraiberg, S. (1970). Smiling and stranger reactions in blind infants. In J. Hellmuth (Ed.), *Exceptional infant* (Vol. 2, pp. 110–127). New York: Brunner-Mazel.

Fraiberg, S. (1975). Intervention in infancy: A program for blind infants. In B. Z. Friedlander, G. M. Sterritt, & S. E. Kirk (Eds.), *Exceptional infant* (Vol. 3, pp. 40–62). New York: Brunner-Mazel.

Friedman, S. (1972). Habituation and recovery of visual response in the alert human newborn. *Journal of Experimental Child Psychology, 13,* 339–349.

Gibson, E. J. (1969). *Principles of perceptual learn-*

ing and development. New York: Appleton-Century-Crofts.

Gibson, E. J., & Walk, R. D. (1960). The "visual cliff." *Scientific American, 202,* 64–71.

Gordon, F. R., & Yonas, A. (1976). Sensitivity to binocular depth information in infants. *Journal of Experimental Child Psychology, 22,* 413–422.

Goren, C. C. (1975). *Form perception, innate form preferences and visually mediated head turning in human newborns.* Paper presented at the biennial meeting of the Society for Research in Child Development, Denver.

Goren, C. C., Sarty, M., & Wu, P. Y. K. (1975). Visual following and pattern discrimination of face-like stimuli by newborn infants. *Pediatrics, 56,* 544–549.

Greenberg, D. J., & Blue, S. Z. (1975). Visual complexity in infancy: Contour or numerosity? *Child Development, 46,* 357–363.

Gregg, C., Haffner, M. E., & Korner, A. (1976). The relative efficacy of vestibular-proprioceptive stimulation and the upright position in enhancing visual pursuit in neonates. *Child Development, 47,* 309–314.

Haaf, R. A., & Brown, C. J. (1976). Infants' responses to facelike patterns: Development changes between 10 and 15 weeks of age. *Journal of Experimental Child Psychology, 22,* 155–160.

Hainline, L. (1978). Developmental changes in visual scanning of face and nonface patterns in infants. *Journal of Experimental Child Psychology, 25,* 90–115.

Haith, M. M. (1968). *Visual scanning in infants.* Paper presented at the regional meeting of the Society for Research in Child Development, Worcester, MA.

Haith, M. M. (1979). Visual competence in early infancy. In R. Held, H. Leibowitz, & H. L. Teuber (Eds.), *Handbook of sensory physiology* (Vol. 8). Berlin: Springer.

Haith, M. M. (1980). *Rules that babies look by.* Hillsdale, NJ: Lawrence Erlbaum Associates.

Haynes, H., White, B. L., & Held, R. (1965). Visual accommodation in human infants. *Science, 148,* 528–530.

Hebb, D. O. (1949). *The organization of behavior.* New York: John Wiley & Sons.

Hebb, D. O. (1958). *A textbook of psychology.* Philadelphia: W. B. Saunders.

Hecox, K. (1975). Electrophysiological correlates of human auditory development. In L. B. Cohen, & P. Salapatek (Eds.), *Infant perception: From sensation to cognition* (Vol. 2, pp. 151–191). New York: Academic Press.

Held, R., & Hein, A. (1963). Movement-produced stimulation in the development of visually guided behavior. *Journal of Comparative and Physiological Psychology, 56,* 872–876.

Hittelman, J. H., & Dickes, R. (1979). Sex differences in neonatal eye contact time. *Merrill-Palmer Quarterly, 25,* 171–184.

James, W. (1960). *The principles of psychology.* New York: Dover. (Originally published 1890).

Jensen, K. (1932). Differential reactions to taste and temperature stimuli in newborn infants. *Genetic Psychology Monographs, 12,* 361–479.

Kagan, J. (1970). Attention and psychological change in the young child. *Science, 170,* 826–832.

Karmel, B. Z., & Maisel, E. B. (1975). A neuronal activity model for infant visual attention. In L. B. Cohen & P. Salapatek (Eds.), *Infant preception: From sensation to cognition* (Vol. 1, pp. 78–131). New York: Academic Press.

Kessen, W., Salapatek, P., & Haith, M. (1972). The visual response of the human newborn to linear contour. *Journal of Experimental Child Psychology, 13,* 9–20.

Koehler, W. (1959). *Gestalt psychology.* New York: Mentor Books.

Koffka, K. (1955). *Principles of gestalt psychology.* London: Routledge & Kegan Paul.

Langworthy, O. R. (1933). Development of behavior and myelinization of the nervous system in the human fetus and infant. *Contributions to Embryology by the Carnegie Institute of Washington, 24* (Serial No. 139), 1–57.

Last, P. (1968). *Eugene Wolff's anatomy of the eye and orbit.* London: H. K. Lewis.

Lawson, K. R., & Turkewitz, G. (1980). Intersensory functioning in newborns: Effect of sound on visual performance. *Child Development, 51,* 1295–1298.

Lewis, M. (1969). Infants' responses to facial stimuli in the first year of life. *Developmental Psychology, 1,* 75–86.

Lewis, T. L., Maurer, D., & Kay, D. (1978). New-borns' central vision: Whole or hole? *Journal of Experimental Child Psychology, 26,* 193–203.

Lewkowicz, D. J., & Turkewitz, G. (1981). Inter-sensory interaction in newborns: Modification of visual preferences following exposure to sound. *Child Development, 52,* 827–832.

Lipsitt, L. P., Engen, T., & Kaye, H. (1963). Devel-opmental changes in olfactory threshold of neonates. *Child Development, 34,* 371–376.

Lipsitt, L. P., & Levy, N. (1959). Electrotactual threshold in the human neonate. *Child Devel-opment, 30,* 547–554.

Lozoff, B. (1982). Birth in non-industrial societies. In M. H. Klaus, & M. O. Robertson (Eds.), *Birth, interaction and attachment* (Pediatric Roundtable No. 6, pp. 1–6). New Brunswick, NJ: Johnson & Johnson.

Mann, I. (1964). *The development of the human eye.* London: British Medical Association.

Mavilya, M. P., & Mignone, B. R. (1977). *Educa-tional strategies for the youngest hearing-im-paired children.* New York: Lexington School for the Deaf.

Mayer, J. (1976, June 20). The bitter truth about sugar. *New York Times Magazine.*

McArthur, S. A. (1982). *Raising your hearing-im-paired child: A guide for parents.* Washington, DC: Alexander Graham Bell Association for the Deaf.

McCall, R. B., Kennedy, C. B., & Appelbaum, M. I. (1977). Magnitude of discrepancy and the distribution of attention in infants. *Child De-velopment, 48,* 772–775.

McKenzie, B. E., & Day, R. H. (1972). Object dis-tance as a determinant of visual fixation in early infancy. *Science, 198,* 75–78.

Mills, M., & Melhuish, E. (1974). Recognition of mother's voice in early infancy. *Nature, 252,* 123–124.

Morse, P. A. (1972). The discrimination of speech and nonspeech stimuli in early infancy. *Jour-nal of Experimental Child Psychology, 14,* 477–492.

Muir, D., Field, J., & Sinclair, M. (1979). *Infants' orientation to sound from birth to three months of age.* Paper presented at the biennial meet-ing of the Society for Research in Child De-velopment, San Francisco.

Nakayama, F. (1968). Studies in the myelinization of the human optic nerve. *Japanese Journal of Opthalmology, 11,* 132–140.

Northern, J. L., & Downs, M. P. (1978). *Hearing in children* (2nd ed.). Baltimore. Williams & Wilkins.

Notermans, S. L. H., & Tophoff, M. M. W. A. (1967). Sex differences in pain tolerance and pain apperception. *Psychiatria, Neurologia, Neurochirurgia, 70,* 23–29.

Peiper, A. (1925). Sinnesempfindungen des Kindes vor seiner Geburt. *Monatsschrift für Kinder-heilkunde, 29,* 236–241.

Piaget, J. (1951). *Play, dreams, and imitation in childhood.* New York: W. W. Norton.

Piaget, J. (1952). *The origins of intelligence in chil-dren.* New York: International Universities Press.

Piaget, J. (1954). *The construction of reality in the child.* New York: Basic Books.

Piaget, J. (1960). *The psychology of intelligence.* Pa-terson, NJ: Littlefield Adams.

Preyer, W. (1882). *Die Seele des Kindes.* Leipzig: Greiben.

Rader, N., & Stern, J. D. (1982). Visually elicited reaching in neonates. *Child Development, 53,* 1004–1007.

Salapatek, P. (1968). Visual scanning of geometric figures by the human newborn. *Journal of Comparative Physiology and Psychology, 66,* 247–258.

Salapatek, P. (1975). Pattern perception in early infancy. In L. B. Cohen, & P. Salapatek (Eds.), *Infant perception: From sensation to cognition* (Vol. 1, pp. 133–248). New York: Academic Press.

Salapatek, P., & Kessen, W. (1973). Prolonged in-vestigation of a plane geometric triangle by the human newborn. *Journal of Experimental Child Psychology, 15,* 22–29.

Schaller, M. J. (1975). Chromatic vision in human infants: Conditioned operant fixation to "hues" of varying intensity. *Bulletin of the Psychonomic Society, 6,* 39–42.

Schwartz, A., Campos, J. J., & Baiscl, E. (1973). The visual cliff: Cardiac and behavioral correlates on the deep and shallow sides at five and nine months of age. *Journal of Experimental Child Psychology, 15,* 86–99.

Sontag, L. (1966). Implications of fetal behavior and environment for adult personality. *Annals of the New York Academy of Sciences, 134,* 782–786.

Stern, D. N. (1975). *Infant regulation of maternal play behavior and/or maternal regulation of infant play behavior.* Paper presented at the biennial meeting of the Society for Research in Child Development, Denver.

Stern, W. (1924). *Psychology of Early Childhood.* New York: Henry Holt.

Teller, D. Y., Peeples, D. R., & Sekel, M. (1978). Discrimination of chromatic from white light by two-month-old human infants. *Vision Research, 18,* 41–48.

Trehub, S. E. (1973). Infants' sensitivity to vowel and tonal contrasts. *Developmental Psychology, 9,* 91–96.

Trehub, S. E., & Rabinovitch, M. S. (1972). Auditory-linguistic sensitivity. *Developmental Psychology, 6,* 74–77.

von Hofsten, Claes. (1982). Eye-hand coordination in the newborn. *Developmental Psychology, 18,* 450–461.

Walk, R. D. (1966). The development of depth perception in animals and human infants. In H. W. Stevenson (Ed.), *Concept of development. Monographs of the Society for Research in Child Development, 31* (5, Serial No. 107), 82–108.

Walton, D. (1970). The visual system. In U. Stave (Ed.), *Physiology of the perinatal period* (Vol. 2, pp. 875–888). New York: Appleton-Century-Crofts.

Wertheimer, M. Psychomotor coordination of auditory and visual space at birth. *Science, 134,* 1692.

White, B. L. (1963). *The development of perception during the first six months.* Paper presented at the annual meeting of the American Academy for the Advancement of Science, Cleveland.

White, B. L. (1971). *Human infants: Experience and psychological development.* Englewood Cliffs, NJ: Prentice-Hall.

White, B. L., Castle, P., & Held, R. (1964). Obser-

vations of the development of visually-directed reaching. *Child Development, 35,* 349–364.

Wickelgren, L. W. (1967). Convergence in the human newborn. *Journal of Experimental Child Psychology, 5,* 74–85.

Wickelgren, L. W. (1969). The ocular response of human newborns to intermittent visual movement. *Journal of Experimental Child Psychology, 8,* 469–482.

Yonas, A., Bechtold, A. G., Frankel, D., Gordon, F. R., McRoberts, G., Norcia, A., & Sternfels, S. (1977). Development of sensitivity to information for impending collision. *Perception and Psychophysics, 21,* 97–104.

Yonas, A., Oberg, C., & Norcia, A. (1978). Development of sensitivity to binocular information for the approach of an object. *Developmental Psychology, 14,* 147–152.

Yonas, A., & Pick, H. L., Jr. (1975). An approach to the study of infant space perception. In L. B. Cohen, & P. Salapatek (Eds.), *Infant perception: From sensation to cognition* (Vol. 2, pp. 3–31). New York: Academic Press.

Chapter 8: Infant Intelligence I: Definitions, Theoretical Positions, Learning, and Memory

Abrahamson, D., Brackbill, Y., Carpenter, R., & Fitzgerald, H. E. (1970). Interaction of stimulus and response in infant conditioning. *Psychosomatic Medicine, 32,* 319–325.

Bandura, A. Vicarious and self-reinforcement processes. In R. Glaser (Ed.), *The nature of reinforcement* (pp. 228–278). New York: Academic Press.

Bandura, A. (1972). Modeling theory: Some traditions, trends and disputes. In R. D. Parke (Ed.), *Recent trends in social learning theory* (pp. 35–61). New York: Academic Press.

Bandura, A. (1977). *Social learning theory.* Englewood Cliffs, NJ: Prentice-Hall.

Bandura, A. (1978). The self system in reciprocal determinism. *American Psychologist, 33,* 344–358.

Bosack, T. N. (1973). Effects of fluid delivery on the sucking response of the human newborn. *Journal of Experimental Child Psychology, 15,* 77–85.

Bower, T. G. R. (1982). *Development in infancy* (2nd ed.). San Francisco: W. H. Freeman.

Bruner, J. S. (1972). Nature and uses of immaturity. *American Psychologist, 27*, 687–708.

Cattell, R. B. (1971). *Abilities: Their structure, growth and action.* Boston: Houghton-Mifflin.

Cohen, L. B. (1977). *Concept acquisition in the human infant.* Paper presented at the biennial meeting of the Society for Research in Child Development, New Orleans.

Cohen, L. B., & Strauss, M. S. (1979). Concept acquisition in the human infant. *Child Development, 50*:2, 419–424.

Cohen, L. B., DeLoache, J. S., & Strauss, M. S. (1979). Infant visual perception. In J. D. Osofsky (Ed.), *Handbook of infant development* (pp. 393–438). New York: John Wiley & Sons.

Cohen, L. B., & Gelber, E. R. (1975). Infant visual memory. In L. B. Cohen & P. Salapatek (Eds.), *Infant perception: From sensation to cognition* (Vol. 1, pp. 347–403). New York: Academic Press.

DeCaspar, A., & Fifer, W. (1980). Of human bonding: Newborns prefer their mothers' voices. *Science, 208*, 1174–1176.

Fagan, J. F. (1970). Memory in the infant. *Journal of Experimental Child Psychology, 9*, 217–226.

Fagan, J. F. (1971). Infants' recognition memory for a series of visual stimuli. *Journal of Experimental Child Psychology, 11*, 244–250.

Fagan, J. F. (1972). Infants' recognition memory for faces. *Journal of Experimental Child Psychology, 14*, 453–476.

Fagan, J. F. (1973). Infants' delayed recognition memory and forgetting. *Journal of Experimental Child Psychology, 16*, 424–450.

Fagan, J. F. (1976). Infants' recognition of invariant features of faces. *Child Development, 47*, 627–638.

Fagan, J. F. (1977). An attention model of infant recognition. *Child Development, 48*, 345–359.

Fagan, J. F. (1978). Facilitation of infants' recognition memory. *Child Development, 49*, 1066–1075.

Fagen, J. W., Yengo, L. A., Rovee-Collier, C. K., & Enright, M. K. (1981). Reactivation of a vis-

ual discrimination in early infancy. *Developmental Psychology, 17*, 266–274.

Fantz, R. L. (1964). Visual experience in infants: Decreased attention to familiar patterns relative to new ones. *Science, 146*, 668–670.

Fenson, L., & Ramsay, D. S. (1981). Effects of modeling action sequences on the play of twelve-, fifteen- and nineteen-month-old children. *Child Development, 52*, 1028–1036.

Field, T. M., Woodson, R., Greenberg, R., & Cohen, D. (1982). Discrimination and imitation of facial expressions by neonates. *Science, 218*, 179–181.

Fitzgerald, H. E., & Brackbill, Y. (1976). Classical conditioning in infancy: Development and constraints. *Psychological Bulletin, 83*, 353–376.

Flavell, J. H. (1976). Described in Scarr-Salapatek, S. An evolutionary perspective on infant intelligence: Species patterns and individual variations. In M. Lewis (Ed.), *Origins of intelligence* (pp. 165–197). New York: Plenum Press.

Flavell, J. H. (1977). *Cognitive development.* Englewood Cliffs, NJ: Prentice-Hall.

Friedman, S. (1972a) Habituation and recovery of visual response in the alert human newborn. *Journal of Experimental Child Psychology, 13*, 339–349.

Friedman, S. (1972b) Newborn visual attention to repeated exposure of redundant versus "novel" targets. *Perception and Psychophysics, 12*, 291–294.

Friedman, S., Carpenter, G. C., & Nagy, A. N. (1970). Decrement and recovery of response to visual stimuli in the newborn infant. *Proceedings of the 78th Annual Convention, American Psychological Association, 5*, 273–274.

Friedman, S., & Carpenter, G. C. (1971). Visual response decrement as a function of age in human newborns. *Child Development, 42*, 1967–1973.

Guilford, J. P. (1967). *The nature of human intelligence.* New York: McGraw-Hill.

Hirschman, R., Melamed, L. E., & Oliver, C. M. (1982). The psychophysiology of infancy. In B. B. Wolman (Ed.), *Handbook of develop-*

mental psychology (pp. 230–243). Englewood Cliffs, NJ: Prentice-Hall.

Ingram, E., & Fitzgerald, H. E. (1974). Individual differences in infant orienting and autonomic conditioning. *Developmental Psychobiology, 7*, 359–367.

Jones, M. C. (1924). A laboratory study of fear: The case of Peter. *Journal of Genetic Psychology, 31*, 308–315.

Kagan, J. (1972). *The plasticity of early intellectual development.* Paper presented at the annual meeting of the American Academy for the Advancement of Science, Washington, DC.

Kobre, K. R., & Lipsitt, L. P. (1972). A negative contrast effect in newborns. *Journal of Experimental Child Psychology, 14*, 81–91.

Koch, J. (1968). Conditioned orienting reactions to persons and things in two to five month old infants. *Human Development, 11*, 81–91.

Lipsitt, L. P., & Kaye, H. (1964). Conditioned sucking in the human newborn. *Psychonomic Science, 1*, 29–30.

Lipsitt, L. P., & Kaye, H. (1965). Change in neonatal response to optimizing and non-optimizing sucking stimulation. *Psychonomic Science, 2*, 221–222.

Lipsitt, L. P., Kaye, H., & Bosack, T. N. (1966). Enhancement of neonatal sucking through reinforcement. *Journal of Experimental Child Psychology, 4*, 163–168.

Lipsitt, L. P., Pederson, L. J., & DeLucia, C. A. (1966). Conjugate reinforcement of operant responding in infants. *Psychonomic Science, 4*, 67–68.

Marquis, D. P. (1931). Can conditioned responses be established in the newborn infant? *Journal of Genetic Psychology, 39*, 479–492.

Marquis, D. P. (1941). Learning in the neonate: The modification of behavior under three feeding schedules. *Journal of Experimental Psychology, 29*, 263–282.

McClearn, G. E. (1970). Genetic influences on behavior and development. In P. Mussen (Ed.), *Carmichael's manual of child psychology* (3rd ed.) (Vol. 1, pp. 39–76). New York: John Wiley & Sons.

McClearn, G. E. (1971). Behavioral genetics. *Behavioral Science, 16*, 64–81.

Meltzoff, A. N., & Moore, M. K. (1977). Imitation of facial and manual gestures by human neonates. *Science, 198*, 75–78.

Millar, W. S. (1972). A study of operant conditioning under delayed reinforcement in early infancy. *Monographs of the Society for Research in Child Development, 37* (Serial No. 147).

Millar, W. S. (1974). Conditioning and learning in early infancy. In B. Foss, (Ed.), *New perspectives in child development.* Hammondsworth, England: Penguin.

Millar, W. S., & Schaffer, H. R. (1972). The influence of spatially displaced feedback on infant operant conditioning. *Journal of Experimental Child Psychology, 14*, 442–453.

Papoušek, H. (1967). Experimental studies of appetitional behavior in human newborns and infants. In H. W. Stevenson, E. H. Hess, & H. C. Rheingold (Eds.), *Early behavior, comparative and developmental approaches.* New York: John Wiley & Sons.

Papoušek, H., & Bernstein, P. (1969). The functions of conditioning stimulation in human neonates and infants. In A. Ambrose (Ed.), *Stimulation in early infancy.* New York: Academic Press.

Pavlov, I. (1927). *Conditional reflexes.* London: Oxford University Press.

Piaget, J. (1952). *The origins of intelligence in children.* New York: International Universities Press.

Piaget, J. (1954). *The construction of reality in the child.* New York: Basic Books.

Piaget, J. (1970). Piaget's theory. In P. Mussen (Ed.), *Carmichael's manual of child psychology* (3rd ed.) (Vol.1, pp. 703–732). New York: John Wiley & Sons.

Piaget, J., & Inhelder, B. (1973). *Memory and intelligence.* New York: Basic Books.

Rovee, C. K., & Rovee, D. T. (1969). Conjugate reinforcement of infant exploratory behavior. *Journal of Experimental Child Psychology, 8*, 33–39.

Rovee-Collier, C. K. (1979). *Reactivation of infant memory.* Paper presented at the biennial meeting of the Society for Research in Child Development, San Francisco.

Rovee-Collier, C. K., Sullivan, M. W., Enright, M., Lucas, D., & Fagen, J. W. (1980). Reactivation of infant memory. *Science, 208,* 1159–1161.

Rovee-Collier, C. K., & Lipsitt, L. P. (1981). Learning, adaptation and memory. In P. M. Stratton (Ed.), *Psychobiology of the human newborn.* New York: John Wiley & Sons.

Sameroff, A. J. (1971). Can conditioned responses be established in the newborn infant? *Developmental Psychology, 5,* 1–12.

Sameroff, A. J. (1972). Learning and adaptation in infancy: A comparison of models. In H. W. Reese (Ed.), *Advances in child development and behavior* (Vol. 7, pp. 169–214). New York: Academic Press.

Sameroff, A. J., & Cavanaugh, P. J. (1979). Learning in infancy: A developmental perspective. In J. D. Osofsky (Ed.), *Handbook of infant development* (pp. 344–392). New York: John Wiley & Sons.

Scarr-Salapatek, S. (1976). An evoolutionary perspective on infant intelligence: Species patterns and individual variations. In M. Lewis (Ed.), *Origins of intelligence* (pp. 165–197). New York: Plenum Press.

Sigel, I. E. (1981). Child development research in learning and cognition in the 1980s: Continuities and discontinuities from the 1970s. *Merrill-Palmer Quarterly, 27,* 347–371.

Siqueland, E. R., & Lipsitt, L. P. (1966). Conditioned head turning in human newborns. *Journal of Experimental Child Psychology, 3,* 356–376.

Siqueland, E. R., & DeLucia, C. A. (1969). Visual reinforcement of nonnutritive sucking in human infants. *Science, 165,* 1144–1146.

Skinner, B. F. (1938). *The behavior of organisms.* New York: Appleton-Century-Crofts.

Thorndike, E. L. (1933). A theory of the actions of the after-effects of a connection upon it. *Psychological Review, 40,* 434–439.

Waddington, C. H. (1962). *New patterns in genetics and development.* New York: Columbia University Press.

Watson, J. B. (1918). *Psychology from the standpoint of a behaviorist.* Philadelphia: J. B. Lippincott.

Watson, J. B., & Rayner, R. (1920). Conditioned emotional reactions. *Journal of Experimental Psychology, 3,* 1–14.

Watson, J. S. (1971). Cognitive-perceptual development in infancy: Setting for the seventies. *Merrill-Palmer Quarterly, 17,* 139–152.

Watson, J. S. (1979). Memory in infancy. In J. Piaget, J. P. Bronkart, & P. Mounoud (Eds.), *Encyclopédie de la pleiade: La psychologie.* Paris: Gallimard.

Watson, J. S., & Ramey, E. T. (1972). Reactions to response-contingent stimulation in early infancy. *Merrill-Palmer Quarterly, 18,* 219–227.

Wechsler, D. P. (1978). Described in J. D. Matarazzo, *Wechsler's measurement and appraisal of adult intelligence.* New York: Oxford University Press.

White, B. L. (1975). *The first three years of life.* Englewood Cliffs, NJ: Prentice-Hall.

White, B. L., & Watts, J. C. (1973). *Experience and environment* (Vol. 1). Englewood Cliffs, NJ: Prentice-Hall.

Werner, J. S., & Perlmutter, M. (1979). Development of visual memory in infants. In *Advances in child development* (Vol. 14, pp. 1–56). New York: Academic Press.

Werner, J. S., & Siqueland, E. R. (1978). Visual recognition memory in the preterm infant. *Infant Behavior and Development, 1,* 79–94.

Wickens, D. D., & Wickens, C. A. (1940). A study of conditioning in the neonate. *Journal of Experimental Psychology, 26,* 94–102.

Yarrow, L., Rubenstein, J. L., & Pederson, F. A. (1975). *Infant and environment: Early cognitive and motivational development.* New York: John Wiley & Sons.

Chapter 9: Infant Intelligence II: Cognition and the Assessment of Intelligence

Bayley, N. (1969). Consistency and variability in the growth of intelligence from birth to eighteen years. *Journal of Genetic Psychology, 75,* 165–196.

Bayley, N. (1969). *Bayley scales of infant development.* New York: Psychological Corporation.

Bower, T. G. R. (1982). *Object permanence and short-term memory in the human infant.* Unpublished manuscript, 1966. Described in T. G. R. Bower, *Development in infancy* (2nd ed.). San Francisco: W. H. Freeman.

Bower, T. G. R. (1971). The object in the world of the infant. *Scientific American, 225,* 30–38.

Bower, T. G. R. (1982). *Development in infancy* (2nd ed.). San Francisco: W. H. Freeman.

Bower, T. G. R., Broughton, J. M., & Moore, M. K. (1970a). Infant responses to approaching objects: An indicator of response to distal variables. *Perception and Psychophysics, 9,* 193–196.

Bower, T. G. R., Broughton, J. M., & Moore, M. K. (1970b). Demonstration of intention in the reaching behavior of neonate humans. *Nature, 228,* 5272.

Bower, T. G. R., Broughton, J. M., & Moore, M. K. (1971). The development of the object concept as manifested in the tracking behavior of infants between 7 and 20 weeks of age. *Journal of Experimental Child Psychology, 11,* 182–193.

Bruner, J. S. (1968). *Processes of cognitive growth: Infancy.* Worcester, MA: Clark University Press.

Bruner, J. S. (1973). Organization of early skilled action. *Child Development, 44,* 1–11.

Bruner, J. S., Olver, R. R., Greenfield, M. P., et al. (1967). *Studies in cognitive growth.* New York: John Wiley & Sons.

Cattell, P. (1966). *The measurement of intelligence of infants and young children* (rev. ed.). New York: Psychological Corporation. (Originally published 1940)

Cohen, L. B. (1977). *Concept acquisition in the human infant.* Paper presented at the biennial meeting of the Society for Research in Child Development, New Orleans.

Cornell, E. H. (1981). The effects of cue distinctiveness on infants' manual search. *Journal of Experimental Child Psychology, 32,* 330–342.

Dennis, W. (1960). Causes of retardation among institutionalized children: Iran. *Journal of Genetic Psychology, 96,* 47–59.

Dennis, W., & Najarian, P. (1957). Infant development under environmental handicap. *Psychological Monographs, 71* No. 436, whole.

Dunkeld, J., & Bower, T. G. R. (1977). *Infant responses to impending collision.* Unpublished study, 1976. Described in T. G. R. Bower, *A primer of infant development.* San Francisco: W. H. Freeman.

Flavell, J. H. (1977). *Cognitive development.* Englewood Cliffs, NJ: Prentice-Hall.

Gesell, A., & Amatruda, C. S. (1947). *Developmental diagnosis.* New York: Hoeber.

Gibson, E. (1969). *Principles of perceptual learning and development.* New York: Appleton-Century-Crofts.

Goldfield, E. C., & Dickerson, D. J. (1981). Keeping track of locations during movement in 8- to 10-month-old infants. *Journal of Experimental Child Psychology, 32,* 48–64.

Gouin-Décarie, T. (1969). A study of the mental and emotional development of the thalidomide child. In B. M. Foss (Ed.), *Determinants of infant behaviour* (Vol. 4). London: Methuen.

Gratch, G. (1982). Responses to hidden persons and things by 5-, 9-, and 16-month-old infants in a visual tracking situation. *Developmental Psychology, 18,* 232–237.

Hamm, M., Russell, M., & Koepke, J. (1979). *Neonatal imitation?* Paper presented at the biennial meeting of the Society for Research in Child Development, San Francisco.

Harnick, F. S. (1978). *Games babies play.* Dubuque, IA: Kendall-Hunt.

Hayes, L. A., & Watson, J. S. (1979). *Neonatal imitation: Fact or artifact?* Paper presented at the biennial meeting of the Society for Research in Child Development, San Francisco.

Hunt, J. McV. (1961). *Intelligence and experience.* New York: Ronald Press.

Kagan J. (1972). *The plasticity of early intellectual development.* Paper presented at the annual meeting of the American Academy for the Advancement of Science, Washington, DC.

Lehane, S. (1976). *Help your baby learn.* Englewood Cliffs, NJ: Prentice-Hall.

Lewis, M. (1976). What do we mean when we say "infant intelligence scores"? In M. Lewis (Ed.), *Origins of intelligence* (pp. 1–17). New York: Plenum Press.

McCall, R. B., Eichorn, D. H., & Hogarty, P. S. (1977). Transitions in early mental development. *Monographs of the Society for Research in Child Development, 42* (3, Serial No. 171).

Meltzoff, A. N., & Moore, M. K. (1977). Imitation of facial and manual gestures by human neonates. *Science, 198,* 75–78.

Piaget, J. (1951). *Play, dreams, and imitation in childhood*. New York: W. W. Norton.

Piaget, J. (1952). *The origins of intelligence in children*. New York: International Universities Press.

Piaget, J. (1954). *The construction of reality in the child*. New York: Basic Books.

Uzgiris, I. C., & Hunt, J. McV. (1975). *Assessment in infancy*. Urbana, IL: University of Illinois Press.

Wertheimer, M. (1961). Psychomotor coordination of auditory and visual space at birth. *Science, 134*, 1692.

White, B. L. (1975). *The first three years of life*. Englewood Cliffs, NJ: Prentice-Hall.

White, B. L. (1978). *Experience and environment*, Vol. 2. Englewood Cliffs, NJ: Prentice-Hall.

White, B. L. & Watts, J. C. (1973). *Experience and environment*, Vol. 1. Englewood Cliffs, NJ: Prentice-Hall.

Chapter 10: Language Development

Bates, E. (1976). *Language and context: The acquisition of pragmatics*. New York: Academic Press.

Bates, E. (1979). *The emergence of symbols*. New York: Academic Press.

Bates, E., Benigni, L., Bretherton, I., Camaioni, L., & Volterra, V. (1977). *Cognition and communication from 9–13 months: A correlational study program on cognitive and perceptual factors in human development*. (Report No. 12). Boulder, CO: University of Colorado, Institute for the Study of Intellectual Behavior.

Bellugi, U. (1964). *The emergence of inflections and negation systems in the speech of two children*. Paper presented at the annual meeting of the New England Psychological Association, Boston.

Berko, J. (1958). The child's learning of English morphology. *Word, 14*, 150–177.

Bever, T. G. (1964). *Pre-linguistic behavior*. Unpublished honors thesis, Harvard University, Cambridge, MA.

Bloom, L. (1970). *Language development: Form and function in emerging grammars*. Cambridge, MA: MIT Press.

Bloom, L. (1973). *One word at a time*. The Hague: Mouton.

Bloom, L., & Lahey, M. A. (1978). *Language development and language disorders*. New York: John Wiley & Sons.

Bloom, L., Lightbown, P., & Hood, L. (1975). Structure and variation in child language. *Monographs of the Society for Research in Child Development, 40* (2, Serial No. 160).

Bloomfield, L. (1933). *Language*. New York: Holt.

Bowerman, M. F. (1973). *Early syntactical development*. New York: Cambridge University Press.

Bowerman, M. F. (1976). Semantic factors in the acquisition of rules for word use and sentence construction. In D. M. Morehead & A. H. Morehead (Eds.), *Normal and deficient child language*. Baltimore: University Park Press.

Braine, M. D. S. (1963). The ontogeny of English phrase structure: The first phrase. *Language, 39*, 1–13.

Braine, M. D. S. (1971). On two types of models of the internalization of grammars. In D. I. Slobin (Ed.), *The ontogenesis of grammar*. New York: Academic Press.

Braine, M. D. S. (1976). Children's first word combinations. *Monographs of the Society for Research in Child Development, 41* (1, Serial No. 164).

Brazelton, T. B., Koslowski, B., & Main, M. (1974). The origins of reciprocity. In M. Lewis & L. Rosenblum (Eds.), *The effect of the infant on its caregiver*. New York: John Wiley & Sons.

Brown, R. A. (1973). *First language: The early stages*. Cambridge, MA: Harvard University Press.

Brown, R. A., & Bellugi, U. (1964). Three processes in the child's acquisition of syntax. *Harvard Educational Review, 34*, 133–151.

Brown, R. A., & Hanlon, C. (1970). Derivational complexity and order of acquisition in child speech. In J. R. Hayes (Ed.), *Cognition and the development of language*. New York: John Wiley & Sons.

Butterfield, E., & Siperstein, G. N. (1972). In J. F. Bosma (Ed.) Influence of contingent auditory stimulation upon non-nutritive suckle. *Third symposium on oral sensation and perception:*

The mouth of the infant. Springfield, IL: Charles C Thomas.

Capute, A. J., Palmer, F. P., Shapiro, B. K., Wachtel, R. C., & Accardo, P. Q. (1981). Early language development: Clinical application of the language and auditory milestone scale. In R. E. Stark (Ed.), *Language behavior in infancy and early childhood* (pp. 429–436). New York: Elsevier/North Holland.

Chapman, R. S. (1978). Comprehension strategies in children. In J. F. Kavanaugh & W. Strange (Eds.), *Speech and language in the laboratory, school and clinic.* Cambridge, MA: MIT Press.

Chapman, R. S. (1981). Cognitive development and language comprehension in 10- to 21-month-olds. In R. E. Stark (Ed.), *Language behavior in infancy and early childhood* (pp. 359–394). New York: Elsevier/North Holland.

Chomsky, N. (1957). *Syntactical structures.* The Hague: Mouton.

Chomsky, N. (1959). A review of *Verbal behavior* by B. F. Skinner. *Language, 35,* 26–58.

Chomsky, N. (1965). *Aspects of the theory of syntax.* Cambridge, MA: MIT Press.

Clark, H. H., & Clark, E. V. (1977). *Psychology and language.* New York: Harcourt Brace Jovanovich.

Condon, W. S. (1975). Speech makes babies move. In R. Lewin (Ed.), *Child alive.* London: Temple-Smith.

Condon, W. S., & Sander, N. (1974). Neonate movement is synchronized with adult speech; Interactional participation and language acquisition. *Science, 183,* 99–101.

Corrigan, R. (1978). Language development as related to Stage 6 object permanence development. *Journal of Child Language, 5,* 173–190.

Curtiss, S. (1977). *Genie: A psycholinguistic study of a modern-day "wild child."* New York: Academic Press.

Dale, P. (1972). *Language development.* Hinsdale, IL: Dryden Press.

Escalona, S. K. (1973). Basic modes of social interaction: Their emergence and patterning during the first two years of life. *Merrill-Palmer Quarterly, 19,* 205–232.

Fillmore, C. J. (1968). The case for case. In E. Bach, & R. T. Harms (Eds.), *Universals in linguistic theory.* New York: Holt, Rinehart and Winston.

Fillmore, C. J. (1971). Some problems for case grammars. In R. J. O'Brien (Ed.), *Linguistic developments of the sixties: Viewpoints for the seventies. Monograph Series on Languages and Linguistics, 24,* 35–56.

Fischer, K. W., & Corrigan, R. (1981). A skill approach to language development. In R. E. Stark (Ed.), *Language behavior in infancy and early childhood* (pp. 245–273). New York: Elsevier/North Holland.

Fry, D. B. (1966). The development of the phonological in the normal and deaf child. In F. Smith, & G. Miller (Eds.), *The genesis of language.* Cambridge, MA: MIT Press.

Greenberg, J. H. (Ed.) (1963). *Universals of language.* Cambridge, MA: MIT Press.

Greenfield, P. M., & J. H. Smith (1976). *The structure of communication in early language development.* New York: Academic Press.

Jones, M. C. (1965). *An investigation of certain acoustic parameters of the crying vocalization of young deaf children.* Unpublished doctoral dissertation. Northwestern University, Evanston, IL.

Kaye, K. (1977). Toward the origin of dialogue. In H. R. Schaffer, *Studies in mother-infant interaction* (pp. 89–117). London: Academic Press.

Kaye, K., & Brazelton, T. B. (1971). *Mother-infant interaction in the organization of sucking.* Paper presented at the biennial meeting of the Society for Research in Child Development, Minneapolis.

Lenneberg, E. H. (1969). On explaining language. *Science, 164,* 635–643.

Lenneberg, E. H., Rebelsky, F. G., & Nichols, I. A. (1965). The vocalizations of infants born to deaf and hearing parents. *Human Development, 8,* 23–37.

Leopold, W. F. (1939). *Speech development of a bilingual child: A linguist's record.* Evanston, IL: Northwestern University Press.

McNeill, D. (1966). Developmental psycholinguistics. In F. Smith & G. A. Miller (Eds.), *The genesis of language.* Cambridge, MA: MIT Press.

McNeill, D. (1970a). *The acquisition of language.* New York: Harper & Row.

McNeill, D. (1970b). The development of language. In P. H. Mussen (Ed.), *Carmichael's manual of child psychology* 3rd ed. (Vol. 1, pp. 1061–1161). New York: John Wiley & Sons.

Nelson, K. (1973). Structure and strategy in learning to talk. *Monographs of the Society for Research in Child Development, 38* (1–2, Serial No. 149).

Netsell, R. (1981). The acquisition of speech motor control: A perspective with directions for research. In R. E. Stark (Ed.), *Language behavior in infancy and early childhood* (pp. 127–156). New York: Elsevier/North Holland.

Northcott, W. H. (Ed.) (1977). *Curriculum guide: Hearing impaired children and their parents.* Washington, DC: Alexander Graham Bell Association for the Deaf.

Oller, D. K. (1981). Infant vocalizations: Exploration and reflexivity. In R. E. Stark (Ed.), *Language behavior in infancy and early childhood* (pp. 85–103). New York: Elsevier/North Holland.

Phillips, J. (1973). Syntax and vocabulary of mother's speech to young children. *Child Development, 44,* 182–185.

Pollack, D. (1970). *Educational audiology for the limited hearing infant.* Springfield, IL: Charles C Thomas.

Schlesinger, I. M. (1971). Production of utterances and language acquisition. In D. Slobin (Ed.), *The ontogenesis of grammar.* New York: Academic Press.

Shirley, M. (1959). *The first two years: Vol. 1, Postural and locomotor developments.* Minneapolis: University of Minnesota Press.

Sinclair, H. (1970). The transition from sensorimotor behavior to symbolic activity. *Interchange, 1,* 119–129.

Skinner, B. F. (1957). *Verbal behavior.* New York: Appleton/Century/Crofts.

Slobin, D. I., & Welch, C. A. (1967). *Elicited imitation as a research tool in developmental psycholinguistics.* Unpublished manuscript. University of California at Berkeley.

Staats, A. (1968). *Learning, language and cognition.* New York: Holt, Rinehart and Winston.

Stark, R. E. (1980a). Prespeech sequential feature development. In P. Fletcher & M. Carman (Eds.), *Language acquisition.* New York: Cambridge University Press.

Stark, R. E. (1980b). Foreword. In A. P. Reilly (Ed.), *The communication game.* (Pediatric Roundtable No. 4, pp. xv–xxiv). New Brunswick, NJ: Johnson & Johnson.

Stark, R. E. (Ed.) (1981). *Language behavior in infancy and early childhood* (Preface and Section Introductions). New York: Elsevier/North Holland.

Stern, D. N. (1971). A micro-analysis of mother-infant interaction. *Journal of the American Academy of Child Psychiatry, 10,* 501–517.

Stern, D. N. (1974a). The goal and structure of mother-infant play. *Journal of the American Academy of Child Psychiatry, 13,* 402–422.

Stern, D. N. (1974b). Mother and infant at play: The dyadic interaction involving facial, vocal and gaze behaviors. In M. Lewis & L. Rosenblum (Eds.), *The effect of the infant on its caregiver.* New York: John Wiley & Sons.

Wolff, P. H. (1969). The natural history of crying and other vocalizations in early infancy. In B. M. Foss (Ed.), *Determinants of infant behaviour* (Vol. 4). London: Methuen.

Zazzo, R. (1982). The person: Objective approaches. In W. W. Hartup (Ed.), *Review of child development research* (Vol. 6, pp. 247–290). Chicago: University of Chicago Press.

Chapter 11: Socioemotional Development

Ainsworth, M. D. (1973). The development of infant-mother attachment. In B. M. Caldwell & H. N. Ricciuti (Eds.), *Review of Child Development Research* (Vol. 3). Chicago: University of Chicago Press.

Bates, J. E. (1980). The concept of difficult temperament. *Merrill-Palmer Quarterly, 26,* 299–319.

Bell, R. Q. (1968). A reinterpretation of the direction of effects in studies of socialization. *Psychological Review, 75,* 81–95.

Bell, S. M., & Ainsworth, M. D. (1972). Infant crying and maternal responsiveness. *Child Development, 43,* 1171–1190.

Bem, S. L. (1977). Psychological androgyny. In A. G. Sargent (Ed.), *Beyond sex roles.* St. Paul, MN: West Publishing Company.

Bowlby, J. (1951). *Maternal care and mental health* (2nd ed.) (Monograph series No. 2). Geneva: World Health Organization.

Bowlby, J. (1969). *Attachment and loss: Vol. 1, Attachment.* New York: Basic Books.

Bronson, G. (1972). Infants' reactions to unfamiliar persons and novel objects. *Monographs of the Society for Research in Child Development, 32* (4, Serial No. 112).

Carey, W. B. (1970). A simplified method for measuring infant temperament. *Journal of Pediatrics, 77*, 188–194.

Carey, W. B., & McDevitt, S. C. (1978). Revision of the infant temperament questionnaire. *Pediatrics, 61*, 735–739.

Clarke-Stewart, K. A. (1977). *The father's impact on mother and child.* Paper presented at the biennial meeting of the Society for Research in Child Development, New Orleans.

Clarke-Stewart, K. A. (1978). And Daddy makes three: The father's impact on mother and young child. *Child Development, 49*, 466–478.

Cohen, L. J., & Campos, J. J. (1974). Father, mother and stranger as elicitors of attachment behaviors in infancy. *Developmental Psychology, 10*, 146–154.

Condon, W. S. (1977). A primary phase in the organization of infant responding. In H. R. Schaffer (Ed.), *Studies in mother-infant interaction* (pp. 153–176). London: Academic Press.

Condon, W. S., & Sander, L. W. (1974). Neonate movement is synchronized with adult speech: Interactional participation and language acquisition. *Science, 183*, 99–101.

Cowan, C., Cowan, P. A., Cole, L., & Cole, J. D. (1978). Becoming a family: The impact of a first child's birth on the couple's relationship. In L. Newman & W. Miller (Eds.), *The first child and family formation.* Chapel Hill, NC: University of North Carolina at Chapel Hill, Carolina Population Center.

Eibl-Eibesfeldt, I. (1971). *Love and hate.* New York: Holt, Rinehart and Winston.

Emde, R. N., Gaensbauer, T. J., & Harmon, R. J. (1976). Emotional expression in infancy: a biobehavioral study. *Psychological Issues, 10*, No. 1.

Etaugh, C. (1974). Effects of maternal employment on children: A review of the research. *Merrill-Palmer Quarterly, 20*, 71–98.

Fein, G. G. (1975). Children's sensitivity to social contexts at eighteen months of age. *Developmental Psychology, 11*, 853–854.

Fogel, A. (1977). Temporal organization in mother-infant face-to-face interaction. In H. R. Schaffer (Ed.), *Studies in mother-infant interaction* (pp. 119–151). London: Academic Press.

Fraiberg, S. (1974). Blind infants and their mothers: An examination of the sign system. In M. Lewis & L. A. Rosenblum (Eds.), *The effects of the infant on its caregiver.* New York: John Wiley & Sons.

Greenberg, M., & Morris, N. (1974). Engrossment: The newborn's impact upon the father. *American Journal of Orthopsychiatry, 44*, 520–531.

Hales, D., Trause, M. A., & Kennell, J. H. (1976). How early is early contact? Defining the limits of the sensitive period. *Pediatric research, 10*, 488.

Harlow, H., & Harlow, M. K. (1966). Learning to love. *American Scientist, 54*, 244–272.

Harlow, H., & Harlow, M. K. (1969). Effects of various mother-infant relationships on rhesus monkey behavior. In B. M. Foss (Ed.), *Determinants of infant behavior* (Vol. 4). London: Methuen.

Hoffman, L. W., & Nye, F. I. (1974). *Working mothers.* San Francisco: Jossey-Bass.

Jones, M. C. (1924). The elimination of children's fears. *Journal of Experimental Psychology, 7*, 382–390.

Jordan, A. D. (1973). Evaluation of a family-centered maternity care hospital program, Part I: Introduction, design and testing. *Journal of Obstetrical and Gynecological Nursing, 2*, 25.

Kagan, J. (1979). Overview: Perspectives on human infancy. In J. D. Osofsky (Ed.), *Handbook of infant development* (pp. 1–25). New York: John Wiley & Sons.

Kaye, K. (1975). *Gaze direction as the infant's way of controlling his mother's teaching behavior.* Paper presented at the biennial meeting of the Society for Research in Child Development, Denver.

Kaye, K. (1977). Toward the origin of dialogue. In H. R. Schaffer (Ed.), *Studies in mother-infant interaction* (pp. 89–117). London: Academic Press.

Kaye, K., & Brazelton, T. B. (1971). *Mother-infant interaction in the organization of sucking.* Paper presented at the biennial meeting of the Society for Research in Child Development, Minneapolis.

Kennell, J. H., Jerauld, R., Wolfe, H., Chesler, D., Kreger, N. C., McAlpine, W., Steffa, N., & Klaus, M. H. (1974). Maternal behavior one year after early and extended post-partum contact. *Developmental Medicine and Child Neurology, 16,* 172–179.

Kennell, J. H., Slyter, H., & Klaus, M. H. (1970). The mourning response of parents to the death of a newborn infant. *New England Journal of Medicine, 283,* 344–349.

Kennell, J. H., Voos, D. K., & Klaus, M. H. (1979). Parent-infant bonding. In J. D. Osofsky (Ed.), *Handbook of infant development* (pp. 786–798). New York: John Wiley & Sons.

Klaus, M. H., Jerauld, R., Kreger, N., McAlpine, W., Steffa, M., & Kennell, J. H. (1972). Maternal attachment—importance of the first postpartum days. *New England Journal of Medicine, 286,* 460–463.

Klaus, M. H., & Kennell, J. H. (1982). *Maternal-infant bonding* (2nd ed.). St. Louis: Mosby.

Kotelchuk, M. (1972). *The nature of the child's tie to his father.* Unpublished doctoral dissertation. Harvard University, Cambridge, MA.

Kotelchuk, M. (1976). The infant's relationship to his father: Experimental evidence. In M. E. Lamb (Ed.), *The role of the father in child development* (pp. 329–344). New York: John Wiley & Sons.

Lamb, M. E. (1976a). Effects of stress and cohort on mother and father-infant interaction. *Developmental Psychology, 12,* 435–443.

Lamb, M. E. (1976b). Parent-infant interactions in eight month olds. *Child Psychiatry and Human Development, 7,* 56–63.

Lamb, M. E. (1976c). Twelve month olds and their parents: Interaction in a laboratory playroom. *Developmental Psychology, 12,* 237–244.

Lamb, M. E. (1977a). Father-infant and mother-infant interaction in the first year of life. *Child Development, 48,* 167–181.

Lamb, M. E. (1977b). The development of mother-infant and father-infant attachments in the second year of life. *Developmental Psychology, 13,* 639–649.

Lamb, M. E., & Lamb, J. E. (1976). The nature and importance of the father-infant relationship. *Family Coordinator, 25,* 379–385.

Leiderman, P. H. (1969). *Effects of early separation on maternal and infant behavior.* Symposium presented at the biennial meeting of the Society for Research in Child Development, Santa Monica, CA.

Leifer, A. D., Leiderman, P. H., Barnett, C. R., & Williams, J. A. (1972). Effects of mother-infant separation on maternal attachment behavior. *Child Development, 43,* 1203–1218.

Lorenz, K. (1943). Die angeborene Formen möglicher Erfahrung. *Zeitschrift der Tierpsychologie, 5,* 235–409.

Lozoff, B. (1977). *The sensitive period: An anthropological view.* Paper presented at the biennial meeting of the Society for Research in Child Development, New Orleans.

Lozoff, B. (1982). Birth in non-industrial societies. In M. H. Klaus & M. O. Robertson (Eds.), *Birth, interaction and attachment* (Pediatric Roundtable No. 6). New Brunswick NJ: Johnson & Johnson.

Lynn, D. B., & Sawrey, W. L. (1959). The effects of father absence on Norwegian boys and girls. *Journal of Abnormal and Social Psychology, 59,* 258–262.

Marquis, D. P. (1941). Learning in the neonate: The modification of behavior under three feeding schedules. *Journal of Experimental Psychology, 29,* 263–282.

McDonald, D. L. (1978). Paternal behavior at first contact with the newborn in a birth environment without intrusion. *Birth and the Family Journal, 5,* 123–132.

Miller, B. C., & Bowen, S. L. (1982). Father-to-newborn attachment behavior in relation to prenatal classes and presence at delivery. *Family Relations, 31,* 71–78.

Moss, H. A. (1967). Sex, age, and state as determinants of mother-infant interaction. *Merrill-Palmer Quarterly, 31,* 19–36.

Newson, J. (1977). An intersubjective approach to the systematic description of mother-infant interaction. In H. R. Schaffer (Ed.), *Studies in mother-infant interaction* (pp. 47–61). London: Academic Press.

O'Connor, S. M. (1977). *Postpartum extended maternal-infant contact and subsequent mothering and child health.* Paper presented at the biennial meeting of the Society for Research in Child Development, New Orleans.

O'Connor, S. M., Sherrod, K. B., Sandler, H. M., et al. (1978). The effect of extended postpartum contact on problems with parenting: A controlled study of 301 families. *Birth and the Family Journal, 5,* 231.

O'Connor, S. M., Vietze, P. M., Sherrod, K. B., et al. (1980). Reduced incidence of parenting inadequacy following rooming-in. *Pediatrics, 66,* 176.

Papoušek, H., & Papoušek, M. (1974). Mirror image and self-recognition in young human infants: I. A new method of experimental analysis. *Developmental Psychobiology, 7,* 149–157.

Papoušek, H., & Papoušek, M. (1977). Mothering and the cognitive head start. In H. R. Schaffer (Ed.), *Studies in mother-infant interaction* (pp. 63–85). London: Academic Press.

Parke, R. D. (1979). Perspectives on father-infant interaction. In J. D. Osofsky (Ed.), *Handbook of infant development* (pp. 549–590). New York: John Wiley & Sons.

Parke, R. D., O'Leary, S. E., & West, S. (1972) Mother-father-newborn interaction: Effects of maternal medication, labor, and sex of infant. *Proceedings of the annual meeting of the American Psychological Association.* (pp.85–86).

Parke, R. D., & O'Leary, S. E. (1976). Father-mother-infant interaction in the newborn period: Some findings, some observations, and some unresolved issues. In K. F. Riegel & J. Meacham (Eds.), *The developing individual in a changing world: Vol. 2, Social and environmental issues.* The Hague: Mouton.

Parke, R. D., & Sawin, D. B. (1975). *Infant characteristics and behaviors as elicitors of maternal and paternal responsivity in the newborn period.* Paper presented at the biennial meeting of the Society for Research in Child Development, Denver.

Parke, R. D., & Sawin, D. B. (1977). *The family in early infancy: Social interactional and attitudinal analyses.* Paper presented at the biennial meeting of the Society for Research in Child Development, New Orleans.

Parsons, T. (1955). The American family: Its relations to personality and to the social structure. In T. Parsons & W. F. Bales (Eds.), *Family socialization and interaction process.* New York: The Free Press.

Pedersen, E. A., & Robson, K. S. (1969). Father participation in infancy. *American Journal of Orthopsychiatry, 39,* 466–472.

Rajecki, D. W., Lamb, M. E., & Obmascher, P. (1978). Toward a general theory of infantile attachment: A comparative review of aspects of the social bond. *Behavioral and Brain Sciences, 1,* 417–464.

Rebelsky, F., & Hanks, C. (1971). Fathers' verbal interaction with infants in the first three months of life. *Child Development, 42,* 63–68.

Rendina, I., & Dickerscheid, J. (1976). Father involvement with first-born infants. *Family Coordinator, 25,* 373–378.

Rheingold, H., & Eckerman, C. (1973). Fear of the stranger: A critical examination. In H. Reese (Ed.), *Advances in child development and behavior* (Vol. 8). New York: Academic Press.

Ringler, N. M., Kennell, J. H., Jarvelle, R., Navojosky, B. J., & Klaus, M. H. (1975). Mother to child speech at two years—effect of early postnatal contact. *Journal of Pediatrics, 86,* 141–144.

Robson, K. S. (1967). The role of eye-to-eye contact in maternal-infant attachment. *Journal of Child Psychology and Psychiatry, 8,* 13–25.

Roedholm, M., & Larsson, K. (1979). Father-infant interaction at the first contact after delivery. *Early Human Development, 3,* 1–27.

Ross, J. B., & McLaughlin, M. M. (Eds.) (1949). *A portable medieval reader.* New York: Viking Press.

Rutter, M. (1979). Maternal deprivation, 1972–1978: New findings, new concepts, new approaches. *Child Development, 50,* 283–305.

Schaffer, H. R. (1966). The onset of fear of strangers and the incongruity hypothesis. *Journal of Child Psychology and Psychiatry, 7,* 95–106.

Schaffer, H. R. (1977). Early interactive development. In H. R. Schaffer (Ed.), *Studies in mother-infant interaction* (pp. 3–16). London: Academic Press.

Schaffer, H. R., & Emerson, P. E. (1964). The development of social attachment in infancy. *Monographs of the Society for Research in Child Development, 29* (3, Serial No. 94).

Spelke, E., Zelazo, P., Kagan, J., & Kotelchuk, M. (1973). Father interaction and separation protest. *Developmental Psychology, 9,* 83–90.

Sroufe, L. A. (1979). Socioemotional development. In J. D. Osofsky (Ed.), *Handbook of infant development* (pp. 462–516). New York: John Wiley & Sons.

Sroufe, L. A., & Waters, E. (1977). Attachment as an organizational construct. *Child Development, 48,* 1184–1199.

Stayton, D. J., & Ainsworth, M. D. (1973). Individual differences in infants' attachment behaviors. *Developmental Psychology, 9,* 226–235.

Stayton, D. J., Ainsworth, M. D., & Main, M. B. (1973). Development of separation behavior in the first year of life: Protest, following and greeting. *Developmental Psychology, 9,* 213–225.

Stern, D. (1974). Mothers and infants at play: The dyadic interaction involving facial, vocal and gaze behaviors. In M. Lewis & L. Rosenblum (Eds.), *The effects of the infant on its caregiver.* New York: John Wiley & Sons.

Stern, D. (1982). Mothers and infants: The early transmission of affect. In M. H. Klaus, & M. O. Robertson (Eds.), *Birth, interaction and attachment* (Pediatric Round Table No. 6, pp. 43–50). New Brunswick, NJ: Johnson & Johnson.

Svejda, M., Campos, J., & Emde, R. (1980). Mother-infant "bonding": Failure to generalize. *Child Development, 51,* 775–779.

Thomas, A., & Chess, S. (1977). *Temperament and development.* New York: Brunner-Mazel.

Thomas, A., Chess, S., & Birch, C. H. (1968). *Temperament and behavior disorders in children.* New York: New York University Press.

Thomas, A., Chess, S., & Korn, S. J. (1982). The reality of difficult temperament. *Merrill-Palmer Quarterly, 28,* 1–20.

Wachs, D., & Cucinotta, P. (1972). The effect of enriched neonatal experiences upon later cognitive functioning. In T. Williams (Ed.), *Infant care: Abstracts of the literature.* Washington, DC: Consortium on Early Childbearing and Childrearing.

Wapner, J. (1976). The attitudes, feelings and behaviors of expectant fathers attending Lamaze classes. *Birth and the Family Journal, 3,* 3–13.

Watson, J. B., & Rayner, R. (1920). Conditioned emotional reactions. *Journal of Experimental Psychology, 3,* 1–14.

Watson, J. S. (1978). Perception of contingency as a determinant of social responsiveness. In E. B. Thoman & S. Trotter (Eds.), *Social responsiveness of infants* (Pediatric Round Table No. 2, pp. 6–10). New Brunswick, NJ: Johnson & Johnson.

Winberg, J., & De Chateau, P. (1982). Early social development: Studies of infant-mother interaction and relationships. In W. W. Hartup (Ed.), *Review of child development research* (Vol. 6, pp. 1–44). Chicago: University of Chicago Press.

Yarrow, L. (1967). The development of focused relationships during infancy. In J. Hellmuth (Ed.), *Exceptional infant* (Vol. 1). New York: Brunner-Mazel.

Yarrow, L. J., & Pedersen, F. A. (1972). Attachment: Its origins and course. In W. W. Hartup (Ed.), *The young child: Reviews of research* (Vol. 2). Washington, DC: National Association for the Education of Young Children.

Yogman, M. W. (1981). Games fathers and mothers play with their infants. *Infant Mental Health Journal, 2,* 241–248.

Yogman, M. W., Dixon, S., Tronick, E., Als, H., Adamson, L., Lester, B., & Brazelton, T. B. (1977). *The goals and structure of face-to-face interaction between infants and fathers.* Paper presented at the biennial meeting of the Society for Research in Child Development, New Orleans.

Chapter 12: The Infant in the Social Context of Family and Society

Abramovitch, R., Corter, C., & Lando, B. (1979). Sibling interaction in the home. *Child Development, 50,* 997–1003.

Ainsworth, M. D. (1963). Development of mother-

infant interaction among the Ganda. In
B. M. Foss (Ed.), *Determinants of infant be-
havior* (Vol. 2). New York, John Wiley &
Sons.

Auerbach, S., & Freedman, L. (1976). *Choosing
child care: A guide for parents.* San Francisco:
Parents and Child Care Resources.

Bane, M. J. (1976). *Here to stay: American families
in the twentieth century.* New York: Basic
Books.

Barnard, K. (1977). *The nursing child assessment
satellite training project: A study guide.* Seattle: University of Washington.

Baxandall, R. (1975). Who shall care for our children? The history and development of day
care in the United States. In J. Freeman
(Ed.), *Women: A feminist perspective.* Palo
Alto, CA: Mayfield Publishing.

Becker, J. (1977). A learning analysis of the development of peer oriented behavior in nine-
month-old infants. *Developmental Psychology, 13*, 481–491.

Belsky, J., & Steinberg, L. D. (1978). The effects of
day care: A critical review. *Child Development, 49*, 929–949.

Blumberg, M. L. (1974). Psychopathology of the
abusing parent. *American Journal of Psychotherapy, 28*, 21–29.

Bowlby, J. (1951). *Maternal care and mental health*
(2nd ed.). Geneva: World Health Organization.

Bronson, W. (1975). Developments in behavior
with age mates during the second year of
life. In M. Lewis & L. Rosenblum (Eds.),
Friendship and peer relations. New York:
John Wiley & Sons.

Buehler, C. (1933). The social behavior of children.
In C. Murchison (Ed.), *Handbook of child psychology.* Worcester, MA: Clark University.

Caldwell, B. M., & Smith, L. E. (1970). Day care
for the very young: Prime opportunity for
primary prevention. *American Journal of
Public Health, 60*, 690–697.

Caldwell, B. M., Wright, C. M., Honig, A. S., &
Tennenbaum, J. (1970). Infant day care and
attachment. *American Journal of Orthopsychiatry, 40*, 397–412.

Casler, L. (1961). Maternal deprivation: A critical
review of the literature. *Monographs of the
Society for Research in Child Development, 26*
(2, Serial No. 80).

Cochran, M. A. (1973). *Comparison of nursery and
non-nursery childrearing patterns in Sweden.*
Unpublished doctoral dissertation, University of Michigan, Ann Arbor.

Cohen, M. D. (Ed.) (1977). *Developing programs for
infants and toddlers.* Washington, DC: Association for Childhood Education International.

Cowan, C., Cowan, P. A., Cole, L., & Cole, J. D.
(1978). Becoming a family: The impact of a
first child's birth on the couple's relationship. In L. Newman & W. Miller (Eds.), *The
first child and family formation.* Chapel Hill,
NC: University of North Carolina at Chapel
Hill, Carolina Population Center.

David, H. P., & Baldwin, W. H. (1979). Childbearing and child development: Demographic
and psychosocial trends. *American Psychologist, 34*, 866–871.

De Mause, L. (Ed.) (1974). *The history of childhood.*
New York: Psychohistory Press.

Dennis, W., & Najarian, P. (1957). Infant development under environmental handicap. *Psychological Monographs, 71*, No. 7.

Dittman, L. (Ed.) (1973). *The infants we care for.*
Washington, DC: National Association for
the Education of Young Children.

Eckerman, C., Whatley, J., & Kutz, S. (1975).
Growth of social play with peers during the
second year of life. *Developmental psychology, 11*, 142–149.

Etaugh, C. (1974). Effects of maternal employment
on children: A review of the research. *Merrill-Palmer Quarterly, 20*, 71–98.

Etaugh, C. (1980). Effects of nonmaternal care on
children. *American Psychologist, 35*, 309–319.

Farran, D. C., & Ramey, C. T. (1977). Infant day
care and attachment behaviors toward
mothers and teachers. *Child Development, 48*,
1112–1116.

Finkelstein, N. W., Dent, C., Gallacher, K., & Ramey, C. T. (1978). Social behavior in infants
and toddlers in a day-care environment. *Developmental Psychology, 14*, 257–262.

Fontana, V. J., & Bernard, M. L. (1971). *The mal-
treated child.* Springfield, IL: Charles C
Thomas.

Fowler, W. (1975). How adult/child ratios influence infant development. *Interchange, 5,* 17–31.

Fox, N. (1977). Attachment of kibbutz infants to mother and metapelet. *Child Development, 48,* 1228–1239.

Freud, A., & Dann, S. (1951). An experiment in group upbringing. In R. Eissler, A. Freud, H. Hartman, & E. Kris (Eds.), *The psychoanalytic study of the child* (Vol. 6). New York: International Universities Press.

Galdston, R. (1971). Dysfunctions of parenting: The battered child, the neglected child, the emotional child. In J. G. Howells (Ed.), *Modern Perspectives in International Child Psychiatry.* New York: Brunner/Mazel.

Gelles, R. J. (1973). Child abuse as psychopathology: A sociological critique and reformulation. *American Journal of Orthopsychiatry, 43,* 611–621.

Golden, M., & Birns, B. (1976). Social class and infant intelligence. In M. Lewis (Ed.), *Origins of intelligence.* New York: Plenum.

Golden, M., Rosenbluth, L., Grossi, M., Policare, H., Freeman, H., & Brownlee, E. (1978). *The New York City infant day care study.* New York: Medical and Health Research Association of New York City.

Goldson, E., Fitch, M. J., Wendell, T. A., & Knapp, G. (1978). Child abuse: Its relationship to birthweight, Apgar score, and developmental testing. *American Journal of Diseases of Children, 132,* 790–793.

Gordon, I. J. (1975). *The infant experience.* Columbus, OH: Charles E. Merrill.

Gordon, I. J., Guinagh, B., & Jester, R. E. (1977). The Florida parent education infant and toddler programs. In M. C. Day & R. K. Parker (Eds.), *The preschool in action.* Boston: Allyn & Bacon.

Green, A. H., Gains, R. W., & Sandgrund, A. (1974). Child abuse: Pathological syndrome of family interaction. *American Journal of Psychiatry, 131,* 882–886.

Harlow, H. F., & Harlow, M. K. (1962). Social deprivation in monkeys. *Scientific American, 207,* 136–146.

Heber, R., & Garber, H. G. (1975). The Milwaukee project: A study of the use of family intervention to prevent cultural-familial mental retardation. In B. Z. Friedlander, G. M. Steritt, & G. E. Kirk (Eds.), *Exceptional infant* (Vol. 3). New York: Brunner/Mazel.

Herbert-Jackson, E., O'Brien, M., Porterfield, J., & Risley, T. R. (1977). *The infant center.* Baltimore: University Park Press.

Hill, R. (1968). Social stresses in the family. In M. Sussman (Ed.), *Sourcebook in marriage and the family* (3rd ed.). Boston: Houghton-Mifflin.

Honig, A. S., & Lally, J. R. (1972). *Infant caregiving: A design for training.* New York: Media Projects.

Huntington, D. S. (1979). Supportive programs for infants and parents. In J. D. Osofsky (ed.), *Handbook of infant development* (pp. 837–894). New York: John Wiley & Sons.

Jacobson, A. L. (1978). Infant day care: Toward a more human environment. *Young Children, 33,* 14–21.

Johnson, B., & Morse, H. A. (1968). Injured children and their parents. *Children, 15,* 147–152.

Kagan, J., Kearsley, R. B., & Zelazo, P. R. (1978). *Infancy: Its place in human development.* Cambridge, MA: Harvard University Press.

Kanner, L. (1943). Autistic disturbances of affective contact. *The Nervous Child, 3,* 217–250.

Karnes, M. B., Studley, W. M., Wright, W. R., & Hodgins, A. S. (1968). An approach for working with mothers of disadvantaged preschool children. *Merrill-Palmer Quarterly, 14,* 1174–184.

Karnes, M. B., Teska, J. A., Hodgins, A. S., & Badger, E. D. (1970). Educational intervention at home by mothers of disadvantaged infants. *Child Development, 41,* 925–935.

Karnes, M. B., Zehrbach, R. R., & Teska, J. A. (1971). A new professional role in early childhood education. *Interchange, 2,* 89–105.

Lally, J. R., & Honig, A. S. (1975). Education of infants and toddlers from low-income and low-education backgrounds: Support for the family's role and identity. In B. Z. Friedlander, G. M. Starrett, & G. E. Kirk (Eds.), *Exceptional infant* (Vol. 3). New York: Brunner/Mazel.

Lamb, M. E. (1978a). The development of sibling relationships in infancy: A short-term longitudinal study. *Child Development, 49,* 1189–1196.

Lamb, M. E. (1978b). Interactions between 10-month-olds and their preschool-aged siblings. *Child Development, 49,* 51–59.

Lambie, D. Z., Bond, J. T., & Weikart, D. P. (1974). *Home teaching with mothers and infants.* Ypsilanti, MI: High/Scope Educational Research Foundation.

Lambie, D. Z., Bond, J. T., & Weikart, D. P. Framework for infant education. In B. Z. Friedlander, G. M. Sterritt, & G. E. Kirk (Eds.) (1975). *Exceptional infant* (Vol. 3). New York: Brunner/Mazel.

Lewis, M., Young, G., Brooks, J., & Michalson, L. (1975). The beginnings of friendship. In M. Lewis & L. Rosenblum (Eds.). *Friendship and peer relations.* New York: John Wiley & Sons.

Low, S., & Spindler, P. (1968). *Child care arrangements of working mothers in the United States* (Children's Bureau Publication No. 161). Washington, DC.

Maccoby, E. E., & Feldman, S. S. (1972). Mother-attachment and stranger-reactions in the third year of life. *Monographs of the Society for Research in Child Development, 37.* (1, serial no. 146).

Macrae, J., & Herbert-Jackson, E. (1976). Are behavioral effects of infant day care specific? *Developmental Psychology, 12,* 269–270.

Mills, P. (1975). *The effects of day care intervention during the first year of life on maternal attitudes and mother-infant interaction patterns of developmentally high-risk infants.* Unpublished doctoral dissertation. University of North Carolina at Chapel Hill.

Mueller, E., & Brenner, J. (1977). The growth of social interaction in a toddler playgroup: The role of peer experience. *Child Development, 48,* 854–861.

Mueller, E., & Vandell, D. (1979). Infant-infant interaction. In J. D. Osofsky (Ed.), *Handbook of infant development* (pp. 591–622). New York: John Wiley & Sons.

Novak, M. A., & Harlow, H. F. (1975). Social recovery of monkeys isolated for the first year of life: I. Rehabilitation and therapy. *Developmental Psychology, 11,* 453–465.

Orthner, D. K., Brown, T., & Ferguson, D. (1976). Single-parent fatherhood: An emerging family life style. *Family Coordinator, 25,* 429–444.

Pelton, L. H. (1978). Child abuse and neglect: The myth of classlessness. *American Journal of Orthopsychiatry, 43,* 608–617.

Ragozin, A. S. (1980). Attachment behavior of day-care children: Naturalistic and laboratory observations. *Child Development, 51,* 409–415.

Ramey, C., & Campbell, F. (1977). The prevention of developmental retardation in high-risk children. In P. Mittler (Ed.), *Research to practice in mental retardation:* Vol. 1, *Care and intervention.* Baltimore: University Park Press.

Ramey, C., & Smith, F. (1976). Assessing the intellectual consequences of early intervention with high-risk infants. *American Journal of Mental Deficiency, 81,* 318–324.

Ribble, M. (1944). Infantile experience in relation to personality development. In J. McV. Hunt (Ed.), *Personality and the behavior disorders.* New York: Ronald Press.

Ricciuti, H. N. (1974). Fear and the development of social attachments in the first year of life. In M. Lewis & M. Rosenblum (Eds.), *The origins of fear.* New York: John Wiley & Sons.

Rich, S. (1983, October 11). Women today marry, have children later than last generation. *The Courier-Journal* (Louisville, KY).

Ruderman, F. A. (1968). *Child care and working mothers: A study of arrangements made for the day time care of children.* New York: Child Welfare League of America.

Ruopp, R. (1979). Untitled remarks at a symposium, Infant day care: Pros and cons. Presented at the biennial meeting of the Society for Research in Child Development, San Francisco.

Rutter, M. (1978). Diagnosis and definition of childhood autism. *Journal of Autism and Childhood Schizophrenia, 8,* 139–161.

Rutter, M. (1979). Maternal deprivation, 1972–1978: New findings, new concepts, new approaches. *Child Development, 50,* 283–305.

Rutter, M. (1981). *Maternal deprivation reassessed* (2nd ed.) Harmondsworth, Middlesex: Penguin Books.

Sameroff, A. J., & Chandler, M. J. (1975). Reproductive risk and the continuum of caretaking casualty. In F. D. Horowitz (Ed.), *Review of child development research* (Vol. 4, pp. 187–244). Chicago: University of Chicago Press.

Schaefer, E. R., & Aaronson, M. (1977). Infant education research project: Implementation and implications of a home tutoring program. In M. O. Day & R. K. Parker (Eds.), *The preschool in action.* Boston: Allyn & Bacon.

Schaffer, H. R., & Emerson, P. E. (1964). The development of social attachment in infancy. *Monographs of the Society for Research in Child Development, 29* (3, serial No. 94).

Schmid, R. E. (1980, June 22). Median age in U.S. hits 30 for first time since 1950 Census. *Sunday Herald-Leader* (Lexington, KY).

Schmid, R. E. (1984, May 9). Childbearing on increase among women in 30s, report says. *Lexington Herald-Leader* (Lexington, KY).

Schreibman, L., Charlop, M. H., & Britten, K. R. (1983). Childhood autism. In R. J. Morris & T. R. Kratochwill (Eds.). *The practice of child therapy* (pp. 221–251). New York: Pergamon Press.

Schwartz, J. C., Strickland, R. G., & Krolik, G. (1974). Infant day care: Behavioral effects at preschool age. *Developmental Psychology, 10,* 502–506.

Silverman, P. (1979). Choosing child care: The parents' responsibility. *Human Ecology Forum, 10,* 15–17.

Smith, S. M., & Hanson, R. (1975). Interpersonal relationships and child-rearing practices in 214 parents of battered children. *British Journal of Psychiatry, 125,* 513–525.

Spinetta, J. J., & Rigler, D. (1980). The child-abusing parent: A psychological review. In J. V. Cook, & R. T. Bowles (Eds.), *Child abuse.* Toronto: Butterworths.

Spitz, R. (1945). Hospitalism: An inquiry into the genesis of psychiatric conditions in early childhood. In R. Eissler, A. Freud, H. Hartman, & E. Kris (Eds.). *The psychoanalytic study of the child* (Vol. 1, pp. 53–74). New York: International Universities Press.

Spitz, R. (1946). Hospitalism: A follow-up report on investigation described in Vol. 1, 1945. In R. Eissler, A. Freud, H. Hartmann, & E. Kris (Eds.). *The psychoanalytic study of the child* (Vol. 2, pp. 113–117). New York: International Universities Press.

Spitz, R., & Wolf, K. (1946). Anaclitic depression: An inquiry into the genesis of psychiatric conditions in early childhood. In R. Eissler, A. Freud, H. Hartmann, & E. Kris (Eds.), *The psychoanalytic study of the child* (Vol. 2, pp. 312–342). New York: International Universities Press.

Stoltz, L. M. (1960). Effects of maternal employment on children: Evidence from research. *Child Development, 31,* 749–782.

Straus, M. A., Gelles, R. J., & Steinmetz, S. R. (1979). *Behilnd closed doors: Violence in the American family.* Garden City, NY: Doubleday.

Thomas, A., & Chess, S. (1977). *Temperament and development.* New York: Brunner/Mazel.

Trotter, R. J. (1976, September). The Milwaukee project. *APA Monitor.*

U.S. Department of Commerce (1982, March 5). *Commerce News.* Washington, DC.

U.S. Department of Commerce, Bureau of the Census (1979). *Statistical abstract of the United States 1978* (99th annual ed.). Washington, DC.

U.S. Department of Health and Human Services (1981). *National analysis of official child neglect and abuse reporting* (rev. ed.). Washington, DC.

U.S. Department of Health, Education, & Welfare, Administration for Children, Youth, and Families, Day Care Division (1979). *Children at the center: National day care study.* Washington, DC.

U.S. Department of Labor, Bureau of Labor Statistics (1983). *Women at work: A chartbook* (Bulletin 2168). Washington, DC.

U.S. life expectancy hits record; Infant mortality, divorce decline. (1983, October 6). *The Courier-Journal* (Louisville, KY).

Weikart, D. P. (1975). *Parent involvement: Process and results of the High/Scope Foundations' projects.* Paper presented at the biennial meeting of the Society for Research in Child Development, Denver.

White, B. L. (1969). *The Harvard Preschool Project.* Paper presented at the biennial meeting of the Society for Research in Child Development, Santa Monica, CA.

White, B. L. (1978). *Experience and environment* (Vol. 2). Englewood Cliffs, NJ: Prentice-Hall.

White, B. L., & Watts, J. C. (1973). *Experience and environment* (Vol. 1). Englewood Cliffs, NJ: Prentice-Hall.

White, B. L., Kaban, B., & Attanucci, J. (1979). *The origins of human competence.* Lexington, MA: Lexington Books.

Williams, B. A. (1982, June 3). More wait until 30s to have child. *The Courier-Journal* (Louisville, KY).

Yarrow, L. (1961). Maternal deprivation: Toward an empirical and conceptual re-evaluation. *Psychological Bulletin, 58,* 459–496.

Name Index

Subject Index